Introduction to Biopsychology

Visit the *Introduction to Biopsychology, Third Edition* Companion Website at www.pearsoned.co.uk/wickens to find valuable **student** learning material including:

- Interactive Flash exercises with diagrams and questions to enhance and test your knowledge
- Flash animations with explanatory accompanying audio narration
- Multiple Choice questions for student self-study
- Essay writing guide with answers
- Mind Maps to help you learn the parts of the brain and sensory systems

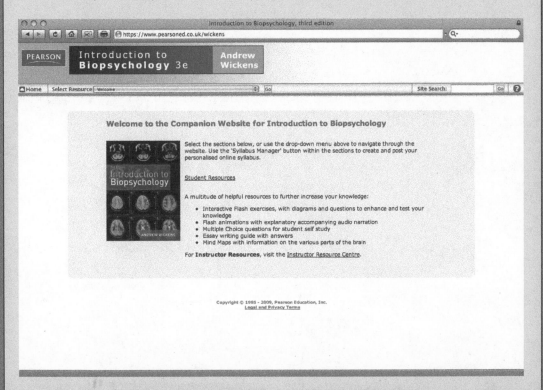

We work with leading authors to develop the strongest
educational materials in **biology**, bringing cutting-edge
thinking and best learning practice to a global market.

Under a range of well-known imprints, including
Prentice Hall, we craft high quality print and
electronic publications which help readers to understand
and apply their content, whether studying or at work.

To find out more about the complete range of our
publishing, please visit us on the World Wide Web at:
www.pearsoned.co.uk

Introduction to Biopsychology

Third Edition

Andrew Wickens

PEARSON

Prentice
Hall

Harlow, England • London • New York • Boston • San Francisco • Toronto
Sydney • Tokyo • Singapore • Hong Kong • Seoul • Taipei • New Delhi
Cape Town • Madrid • Mexico City • Amsterdam • Munich • Paris • Milan

Pearson Education Limited
Edinburgh Gate
Harlow
Essex CM20 2JE
England

and Associated Companies throughout the world

Visit us on the World Wide Web at:
www.pearsoned.co.uk

First published 2000
Second edition published 2005
Third edition published 2009

ISBN 978-0-13-205296-2

British Library Cataloguing-in-Publication Data
A catalogue record for this book is available from the British Library

Library of Congress Cataloging-in-Publication Data
Wickens, Andrew P.
  Introduction to biopsychology / Andrew Wickens. —3rd ed.
     p. cm.
  Rev. ed. of: Foundations of biopsychology. 2nd ed. 2004.
  Includes bibliographical references and index.
  ISBN 978-0-13-205296-2 (pbk.)
  1. Psychobiology. I. Wickens, Andrew P. Foundations of biopsychology. II. Title.
  QP360.W525 2009
  612.8—dc22

                                                                    2008048730

ARP Impression 98

Typeset in 10/13 Sabon by 73
Printed and Bound in Great Britain by Ashford Colour Press Ltd

The publisher's policy is to use paper manufactured from sustainable forests.

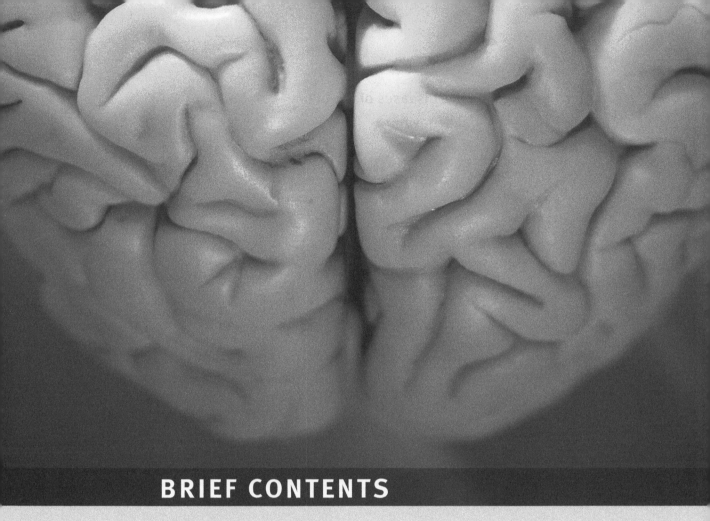

BRIEF CONTENTS

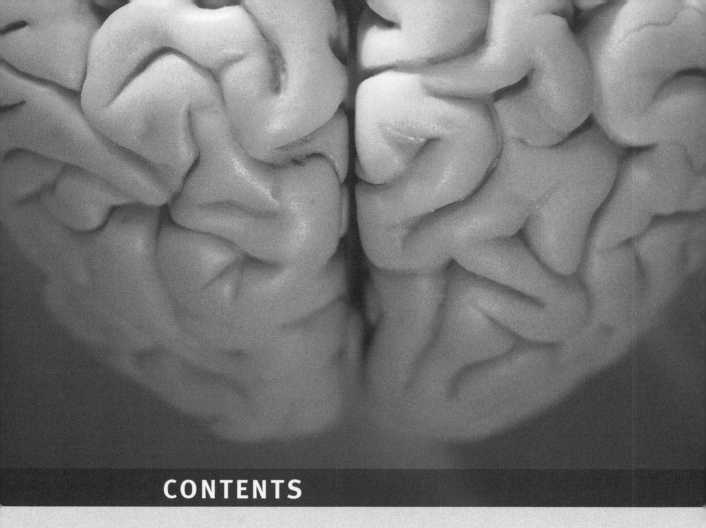

CONTENTS

CHAPTER 1 | **An introduction to neurons, brains and biological psychology**   **1**

CHAPTER 6 **Emotional states**   **209**

CHAPTER 11   **The biological basis of mental illness**   **403**

CHAPTER 14   Genes and behaviour   519

Supporting resources

Visit www.pearsoned.co.uk/wickens to find valuable online resources

Companion Website for students
- Interactive Flash exercises, with diagrams and questions to enhance and test your knowledge
- Flash animations with explanatory accompanying audio narration
- Multiple Choice questions for student self-study
- Essay writing guide with answers
- Mind Maps to help you learn the parts of the brain and sensory systems

For instructors
- Seminar ideas that provide suggestions for questions and areas of discussion
- Testbank of questions

Also: The Companion Website provides the following features:
- Search tool to help locate specific items of content
- Online help and support to assist with website usage and troubleshooting

For more information please contact your local Pearson Education sales representative or visit www.pearsoned.co.uk/wickens

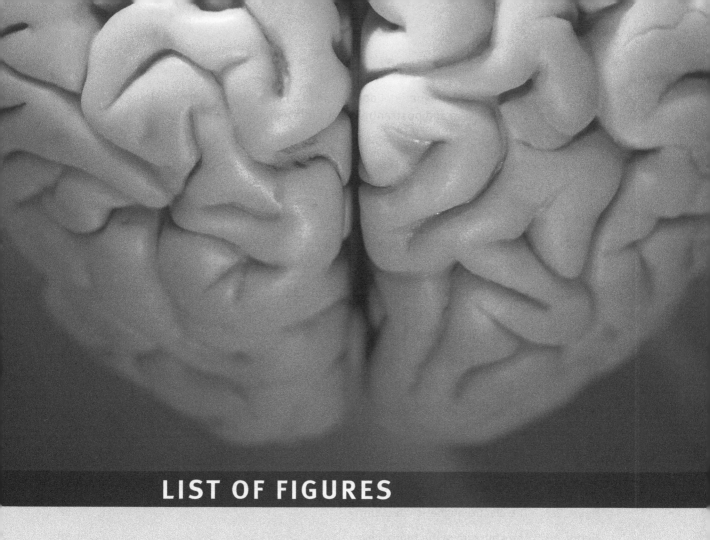

LIST OF FIGURES

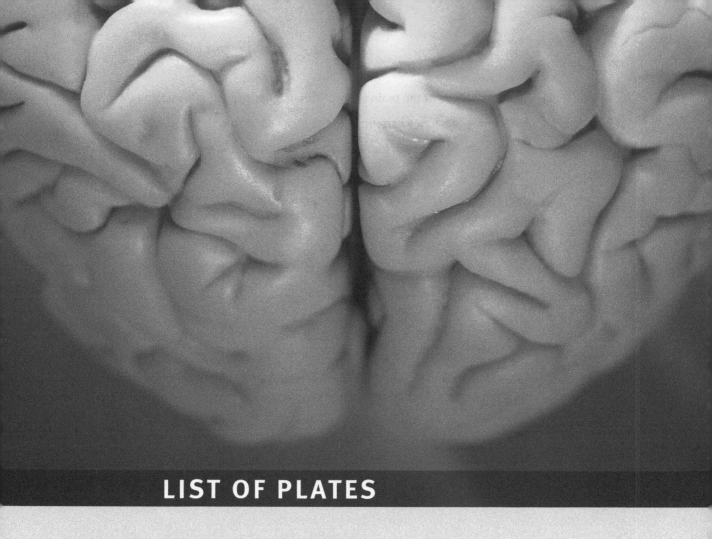

LIST OF PLATES

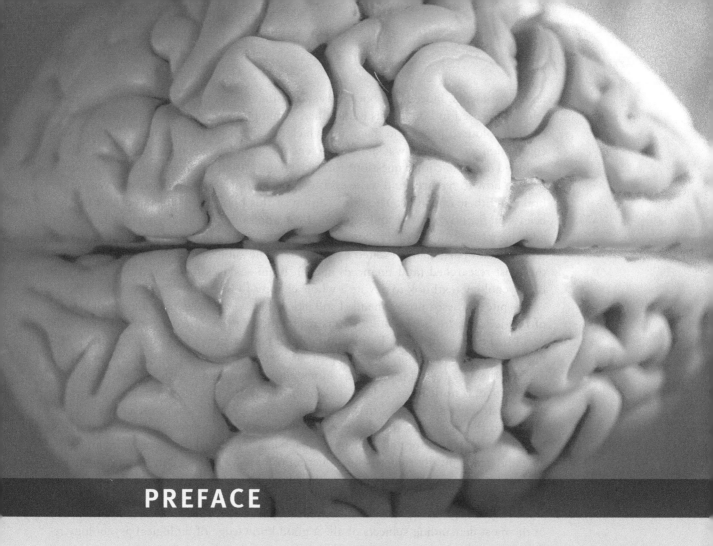

PREFACE

The human brain is the most complex living object known in the universe. Although an average adult brain weighs only about a kilogram and a half, it contains in the region of 1 billion nerve cells (1,000,000,000,000), and thousands of times more connections between them called synapses – tiny gaps constantly awash with neurotransmitters and chemicals. It is at these sites that the main information processing of the brain takes place. Somehow, the electrical and chemical melee of this activity gives rise to the human mind with its remarkable capacity for behaviour, thought and consciousness. How it achieves this remarkable feat is still largely a mystery, and the conundrum taxes the ingenuity of psychologists, neuroscientists and philosophers alike. Nonetheless, the number of ground-breaking scientific discoveries about the brain increases with every year. The aim of this book is to make this ever growing knowledge both accessible and entertaining to the person who may not have any previous knowledge of biological psychology. It is also hoped that the book will take you on a journey that will fascinate, surprise and give you greater insight into your behaviour and that of others. If you are a student, it will even help you to pass your exams!

This is the third edition of a book originally entitled *Foundations of Biopsychology*, which is now entitled *Introduction to Biopsychology* to reflect its broader scope. When writing the first edition I was very conscious of the need to stamp my own personality on the book. There were a number of highly respected textbooks already available (two of the best are also published by Prentice Hall, namely Carlson's *Physiology of Behavior* and Pinel's *Biopsychology*) and it was not always easy to avoid imitation. But, I think, I succeeded in writing my own book and, in doing so, provide a valuable text for students. Indeed, the book was successful enough to warrant a second edition, which appeared in 2005. This edition had a number of new pedagogical features, including coloured pages and diagrams which enhanced its visual appeal. It also had a companion website that was designed to encourage independent learning. This website included multiple-choice questions for each chapter, useful website addresses, information on how to research and write essays, and a section describing various areas of the brain and their functions. The third edition of this book keeps these features but has been significantly revised and expanded. In addition, two new chapters have been added: sensory systems other than vision (Chapter 3) and degenerative diseases (Chapter 13). I am particularly excited by the latter. The subject of degenerative diseases is the most researched (and financed) area in brain sciences today, and this is the first biopsychology textbook to devote a whole chapter to the topic.

Despite all these improvements, I still like to believe that the most important feature of *Introduction to Biopsychology* is its readability. At the time of writing the first edition I had been lecturing in Biopsychology and Neuroscience for over a decade. Nothing is worse that lecturing to a group of disinterested students. And, this soon taught me that the art of good teaching lay in my enthusiasm, along with making the subject informative, historical (or at least making it follow some sort of narrative), entertaining and structured in a way that made the overall picture easy to understand. These were also the principles that I attempted to incorporate in my writing style for this book. Fortunately, tutor and student feedback has confirmed that it provides an enjoyable and academically rigorous introduction to biopsychology. But, I also hope it will be of interest to any reader, whatever their background, who wants to find out more about the brain.

Biological psychology is the study of how the brain produces behaviour, and is one of the most demanding subjects of all. A good knowledge of biological psychology requires more than a passing understanding of many other disciplines, including anatomy, physiology, biochemistry, pharmacology and genetics. Thus, one might be excused for finding a simpler subject to study. But, by doing this, one would miss out on a subject that has no equal when it comes to providing powerful and insightful explanations of human nature. The Nobel laureate Gerald Edelman called the subject 'the most important one imaginable' because, in his view, 'at its end, we shall know how the mind works, what governs our nature and how we know the world'. And, this is only one of the benefits, because as knowledge progresses, better treatments for a wide range of medical, behavioural and psychological problems will arise. Thus, the student who reads this book should never lose sight of the fact that the scope and potential of biopsychology are enormous.

Indeed, the past decade or so has seen many exciting advances in biopsychology. For example, the widespread the use of functional scanning techniques, such as fMRI, has allowed the cognitive processes of the mind to be visualised for the first time. This has led to a new discipline called cognitive neuroscience, which may one day have the power to expose even your own individual thoughts and emotions to scientific scrutiny. At the other end of the spectrum are advances in genetics, allowing the creation of transgenic animals, so that scientists can work out the function of individual genes and their impact on behaviour and disease. These examples not only help illustrate the broad canvas of biopsychology but also show that we are standing on the threshold of a new age in understanding the brain. This is a very exciting time to study biological psychology.

Inevitably, writing a book of this size will reflect the author's interests and biases. But, I have particularly tried to include topics that are likely to be important in the future. This is one reason why the final chapter is on genetics, which introduces some of the new developments taking place in molecular biology and brain science. Some may argue that the gap between molecular biology and behaviour is too great for it to be relevant to psychologists – but, I disagree. If you are to be student of the brain, then you must be prepared to expand your academic horizons in many new ways. After all, biopsychology is a multidisciplinary subject, and this is one of the reasons why it is such a fascinating one. I hope this book can provide you with a thorough grounding in biopsychology and more. But, most of all, I hope it gets across some of the excitement and wonder I feel when contemplating the brain. If this book helps you to pass an exam in biopsychology that is great. But, if it has stimulated you to explore beyond its pages, and develop an ongoing fascination with the brain, then this book will have been a greater success. I like to think that, for some of its readers, *Introduction to Biopsychology* will do just that.

Andrew Wickens
January 2009

GUIDED TOUR OF THE BOOK

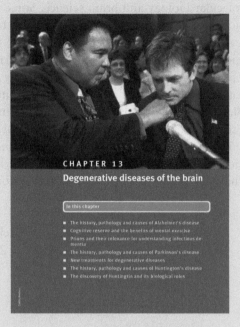

Each chapter opens with a **list of the main themes and issues** that it will explore.

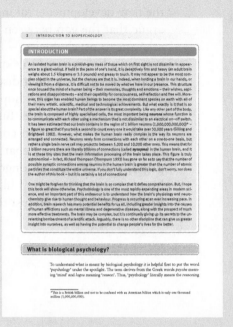

An **Introduction** clearly outlines the scope of the chapter and introduces these for discussion in more detail.

Special interest boxes throughout the text bring biological psychology to life; these include discussions of phenomena such as phantom limb pain and the role of pheromones in human attraction.

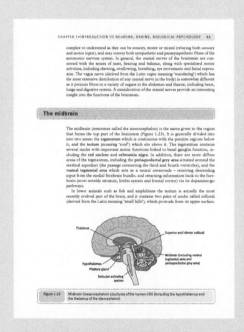

Numerous coloured **Figures and Photographs** illustrate key topics and processed visually, to reinforce learning.

A **Summary** at the end of each chapter helps you to review the main topics discussed. As a re-cap, it's also a useful revision tool.

Essay Questions at the end of each chapter enable you to test your understanding and help track your progress. Each question is accompanied by a list of helpful internet Search Terms, to help negotiate the maze of information available on the web whilst researching for your answer.

Suggested **Further Reading** directs the reader to a variety of useful further information sources.

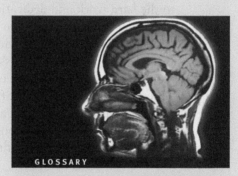

A comprehensive **Glossary** at the end of the book defines the key terms related to biological psychology.

AUTHOR'S ACKNOWLEDGEMENTS

Although writing a book is a solitary endeavour, its ultimate success is in large part due to the hard work and dedication of a large number of people behind the scenes which the reader rarely considers. In this regard I would like to thank my editor Janey Webb who is the main instigator behind this new edition. I also owe much gratitude to Sarah Busby and Catherine Morrissey for their assistance, and to Debra Weatherley who managed to track down some of the great new pictures that adorn the pages of this book. Three other people worthy of mention for their contribution to these pages are Tim Parker, Ruth Freestone King and David Hemsley. But, most of all, I want to thank my girlfriend Lisa Nelson. Without her continual support and love, I doubt if I could have accomplished the task of writing this book.

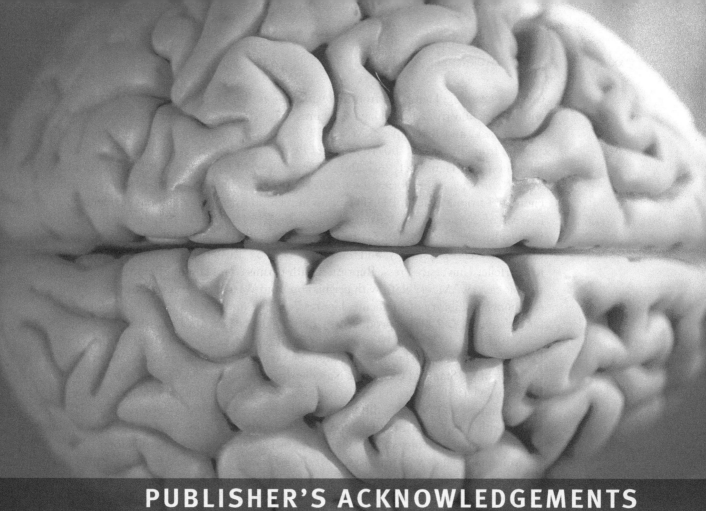

PUBLISHER'S ACKNOWLEDGEMENTS

We are grateful to the following for permission to reproduce copyright material:

Plates 1.1, 1.2 and 1.3 from Toates, F. (2001) *Biological Psychology*, p. 111, photographer Ralph Hutchings, Pearson Education/Ralph Hutchings; Figures 1.10, 1.23, 9.20, 10.5, 10.6, 11.14 and 13.6 from Breedlove, S.M., Rosenzweig, M.R. and Watson, N.V. (2007) *Biological Psychology*, 5th ed; Plate 2.1 from *The Journal of Neuroscience*, August 1991, Vol. 11(8), p. 2392, Figure 7 (Corbetta *et al.* 1991). Copyright © 1991 by the Society for Neuroscience; Figures 1.11, 3.4, 3.8, 3.9, 3.13, 3.14, 4.16, 5.4, 5.5, 7.13, 12.13, 13.2 and Plate 5.2 from Pinel, J.P. (2003) *Biopsychology* © 2003 Reproduced by Permission of Pearson Education, Inc.; Figures 1.18 and 3.10 from *Human Anatomy And Physiology* by Elaine N. Marieb. Copyright © 1989 by The Benjamin Cummings Publishing Company, Inc. Reprinted by permission of Pearson Education, Inc.; Figures 1.25 and 1.26 from Carlson, *Physiology Of Behavior*, © 2001 Reproduced by permission of Pearson Education, Inc.; Figures 2.3, 2.8, 4.13, 5.3, 9.3, 9.6 and 9.19 from Pinel, *Biopsychology*, © 1997 Reproduced by permission of Pearson Education, Inc.; Figure 2.4 from Dowling, J.E. and Boycott, B.B. (1966) *Proceedings of the Royal Society of London*, 166: 80–111, by permission from The Royal Society of London; Figures 2.10, 4.8a & b, and 4.12 from Schneider, A.M. and Tarshis, B. (1995) *Elements of Physiological Psychology*, The McGraw-Hill Companies, Inc.; Figures 2.17, 3.5, 3.6, 3.11, 4.10, 5.8 and Plate 13.3 from Carlson, *Physiology Of Behaviour*, © 2004 Reproduced by permission of Pearson Education, Inc.; Figure 2.21 from Banich, M.T. (2004) *Cognitive Neuroscience and Neuropsychology*, 2nd ed, p. 244, with permission of

Cengage Learning; Figure 3.2 from *Human Anatomy and Physiology* (Carola *et al.* 1990) with permission from John Hagan; Figures 3.7, 3.16 and 4.7 from Rosenzweig, M.R. Leiman, A.L. and Breedlove, S.M. (1999) *Biological Psychology*, 2nd ed; Figures 3.15 and 4.6 from Toates, F. (2007) *Biological Psychology*, 2nd ed, by permission of Pearson Education Ltd, Figure 6.1, 6.7 and 9.9 from Bear, M.F., Connors, B.W. and Paradiso, M.A. *Neuroscience: Exploring the Brain*, 1996, by permission of Wolters Kluwer Health; Figure 6.8 from Maclean, P.D. The brain in relation to empathy and medical education. *Journal of Nervous and Mental Disease*, 1967; 144(5): 374–382, by permission of Wolters Kluwer Health; Plate 6.1 from Flynn, John P. "The Neural Basis of Aggression in Cats." In Neurophysiology and Emotion. © 1967 Russell Sage Foundation and the Rockerfeller University Press. Reprinted with permission; Plate 6.3 Phineas Gage's skull and life cast [WAM 949-950] with permission from Warren Anatomical Museum, Francis A. Countway Library of Medicine; Figures 7.5, 7.11 and 8.10 from Carlson, *Physiology Of Behaviour*, © 2007 Reproduced by permission of Pearson Education, Inc.; Figures 7.10, 10.10, 12.10 and 13.10 from Feldman, R.S., Meyer, J.S. and Quenzer, L.F. (1997) *Principles of Neuropsychopharmacology*, by permission of Sinauer Associates; Plate 7.1 Courtesy of the Stanford Center for Narcolepsy; Figure 8.1 from Carlson, *Physiology Of Behavior*, © 1998, Reproduced by permission of Pearson Education, Inc.; Figure 8.7 from Kimura D. (1992) Sex differences in the brain, *Scientific American*, Sept. 81–87, p. 83, with permission of JSD Infographics; Figure 8.9 from Evolution and Human Behaviour, vol. 22 (Professor J.T. Manning 2001). Reproduced by permission of Professor Manning; Figure 9.2 from *Brain Mechanisms and Intelligence* (Lashley, K.S. 1963) with permission from Dover Publications Inc.; Figure 9.4 from Rosenzweig, Mark & Edward Bennett (eds.), *Neural Mechanisms of Learning and Memory*, Figure 16.1, page 265, © 1976 Massachusetts Institute of Technology, by permission of The MIT Press; Figure 9.11 from 'Navigation-related structural changes in the hippocampus of taxi drivers' from *Proceedings of the National Academy of Sciences* (Maguire, E.A. *et al.* 2000). Copyright © 2000 National Academy of Sciences; Figure 9.15 from *Cognitive Neuroscience: The Biology Of The Mind, Second Edition* by Michael S. Gazzaniga, Rivhard B. Ivy and George R. Mangun. Copyright © 2002 by W.W. Norton & Company, Inc. Used by permission of W.W. Norton & Company, Inc.; Figure 9.18 from *Nature*, 297 (Morris, R.G.M. *et al.* 1982) reprinted with permission from Macmillan Magazines Limited; Plate 10.2, photograph of the Beatles © Betmann/CORBIS, photograph of the MRI brain scanner from the British Neuroscience Association; Plate 10.3 Coronal sections of the brain viewed with magnetic functional imaging (MFI), Science Photo Library; Figures 12.6, 13.7, 13.8 and Plate 5.1 from *Physiological Psychology* (Graham, R.B. 1990), with permission from the author; Figure 12.13 from Neslter, E.J., Hyman, S.E. and Malenka, R.C. (2001) *Molecular Neuropharmacology*, p. 360. The McGraw-Hill Companies, Inc.; Plate 12.1a, an example of a funny cartoon, and the same cartoon with the funny cues omitted from King Features Syndicate, Allsortsmedia; Plate 12.1b from *Neuron*, (Mobbs *et al.* 2003) Copyright 2003, with permission from Elsevier; Plate 13.1 from Thomas, N., Isaac, M. (1987) Alois Alzheimer: a memoir. *Trends in Neuroscience* 10: 306–307, Elsevier; Plate 13.2 (a) and (b), with thanks to Daniel P. Perl, MD, Mount Sinai School of Medicine; Plate 13.2 (c) with thanks to Alfred Pasieka/Science Photo Library; Plates 14.1 and 14.2 Science Photo Library; Plate 14.3 © Bettmann/Corbis; Figure 14.4 from Biological Science 23rd edition (R. Soper, N.P.O. Green, G.W. Stout, D.J. Taylor 1997). Used by permission of Cambridge University Press;

In some instances we have been unable to trace the owners of copyright material, and we would appreciate any information that would enable us to do so.

The publisher would also like to thank the following for their kind permission to reproduce their photographs:

1 Corbis: Visuals Unlimited. 6 Alamy Images. 55 Science Photo Library Ltd: GIPhotostock. 91 Corbis: Image 100. 133 Getty Images: Royalty Free Collection. 173 Rex Features: Jon Angerson. 209 Getty Images: Michael Crabtree. 249 Getty Images: Marina Jefferson. 287 Science Photo Library: Christian Darkin. 323 Getty Images: Chris Windsor. 365 Science Photo Library Ltd: Stephen & Donna O'Meara. 403 Photos 12 collections cinema. 443 Photofusion: S. de Trey-White. 481 Corbis: Reuters. 519 Science Photo Library Ltd: Pasieka

All other images © Pearson Education

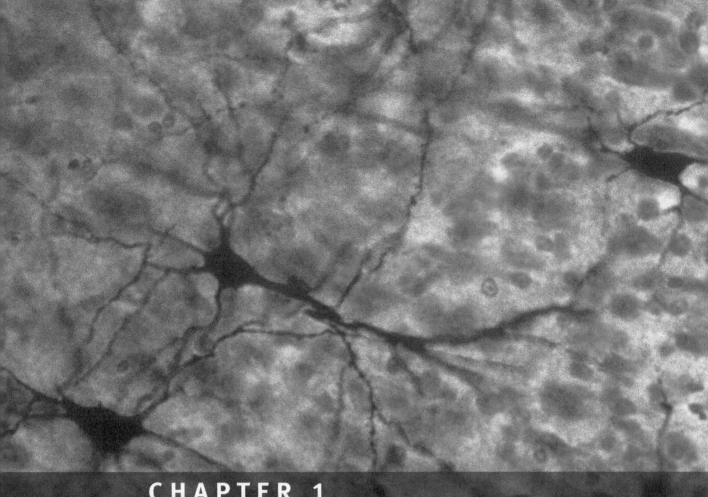

CHAPTER 1

An introduction to neurons, brains and biological psychology

In this chapter

- Historical views concerning brain and behaviour

- The contributions of Descartes, Galvani, Golgi and Ramón y Cajal

- The key breakthroughs in neuroscience that have taken place in the twentieth century

- The formation of the nervous impulse (action potential)

- Neurotransmitters and chemical communication between neurons

- Ion channels and second messengers

- The autonomic and somatic nervous systems

- An introduction to the central nervous system (spinal cord and brain)

INTRODUCTION

An isolated human brain is a pinkish-grey mass of tissue which on first sight is not dissimilar in appearance to a giant walnut. If held in the palm of one's hand, it is deceptively firm and heavy (an adult brain weighs about 1.5 kilograms or 3.5 pounds) and greasy to touch. It may not appear to be the most complex object in the universe, but the chances are that it is. Indeed, when holding a brain in our hands, or viewing it from a distance, it is difficult not to be moved by what we have in our presence. This structure once housed the mind of a human being – their memories, thoughts and emotions – their wishes, aspirations and disappointments – and their capability for consciousness, self-reflection and free will. Moreover, this organ has enabled human beings to become the most dominant species on earth with all of their many artistic, scientific, medical and technological achievements. But what exactly is it that is so special about the human brain? Part of the answer is its great complexity. Like any other part of the body, the brain is composed of highly specialised cells, the most important being **neurons** whose function is to communicate with each other using a mechanism that is not dissimilar to an electrical on–off switch. It has been estimated that our brain contains in the region of 1 billion neurons (1,000,000,000,000)* – a figure so great that if you took a second to count every one it would take over 30,000 years (Gilling and Brightwell 1982). However, what makes the human brain really complex is the way its neurons are arranged and connected. Neurons rarely form connections with each other on a one-to-one basis, but rather a single brain nerve cell may project to between 5,000 and 10,000 other ones. This means that for 1 billion neurons there are literally trillions of connections (called **synapses**) in the human brain, and it is at these tiny sites that the main information processing of the brain takes place. This figure is truly astronomical – in fact, Richard Thompson (Thompson 1993) has gone so far as to say that the number of possible synaptic connections among neurons in the human brain is greater than the number of atomic particles that constitute the entire universe. If you don't fully understand this logic, don't worry, nor does the author of this book – but it is certainly a lot of connections!

One might be forgiven for thinking that the brain is so complex that it defies comprehension. But, I hope this book will show otherwise. Psychobiology is one of the most rapidly expanding areas in modern science, and an important part of this endeavour is to understand how the brain's physiology and neurochemistry give rise to human thought and behaviour. Progress is occurring at an ever increasing pace. In addition, brain research has many potential benefits for us all, including greater insights into the causes of human afflictions such as mental illness and degenerative diseases, along with the prospect of much more effective treatments. The brain may be complex, but it is continually giving up its secrets to the unrelenting bombardment of scientific attack. Arguably, there is no other discipline that can give us greater insight into ourselves, as well as having the potential to change people's lives for the better.

What is biological psychology?

To understand what is meant by biological psychology it is helpful first to put the word 'psychology' under the spotlight. The term derives from the Greek words *psyche* meaning 'mind' and *logos* meaning 'reason'. Thus, 'psychology' literally means the reasoning

---

*This is a British billion and not to be confused with an American billion which is only one thousand million (1,000,000,000).

(or study) of the mind. However, few psychologists would unreservedly accept this definition today. The study of psychology first emerged in the eighteenth century as a branch of philosophy concerned with explaining the processes of thought by using the technique of introspection (i.e. self-reflection). The problem with this method, however, is that no matter how skilled the practitioner, it is subjective and its findings cannot be verified by others. Because of this, a more experimental approach to psychology began to emerge in the late nineteenth century that focused on mental phenomena and, more importantly, overt behaviour, which could be observed and measured (James 1890; Watson 1913). The emphasis on experimentation and measurement has continued to the present day and thus many psychologists would now describe psychology as *the scientific or experimental study of behaviour and mental processes*.

Psychology has now developed into a wide-ranging discipline and is concerned with understanding behaviour and mental processes from a variety of perspectives. As the name suggests, biological psychology is the branch of science that attempts to explain behaviour in terms of biology, and since the most important structure controlling behaviour is the brain, biopsychology is *the study of the brain and how it produces behaviour and mental processes*. Implicit in this definition is the assumption that every mental process, feeling and action must have a physical or neural basis in the brain. This is much the same as saying that the mind is the product of the brain's electrical and neurochemical activity. Although there are philosophical grounds for questioning this viewpoint (Gold and Stoljar 1999; Bennett and Hacker 2003), even the most hardened cynic of **materialism** (the view that the mind is the result of physical processes) would find it hard to disagree that mind and brain are inextricably linked. Indeed, this assumption provides the main foundation on which biological psychology is built.

To link the brain with behaviour, however, is a daunting task. Indeed, any attempt to do so requires a very good understanding of the brain's biology. Traditionally, the two disciplines most relevant to the biological psychologist have been **neuroanatomy** (the study of neural architecture of various brain regions along with the mapping of the pathways that connect them) and **neurophysiology** (the study of how neurons produce action potentials and neural information). However, in the past few decades the study of brain function has expanded greatly and attracted the interest of specialists from many other disciplines, including those from **biochemistry, molecular biology, genetics, pharmacology** and **computer technology**. Not all scientists working in these fields are necessarily interested in behaviour, although their discoveries can sometimes be of great interest to those working in biological psychology. Consequently, in recent years, psychologists interested in the brain have become acquainted with many other areas of biological science that lie outside the traditional domains of anatomy, physiology and psychology.

A number of different names have been used to describe the study of brain and behaviour, and for students these terms can be confusing. For most of the twentieth century, the study of brain and behaviour was called **physiological psychology** because its investigators typically used 'physiological' techniques such as **lesioning** (the removal of various parts of the brain) and **stimulation**, both electrical and chemical, as their main experimental tools. This approach was often complemented by examining human subjects who had suffered brain damage from accidents, stroke, etc. – an area known as **clinical neuropsychology**. Although these terms are still used, there is a growing acceptance that they do not adequately cover many of the newer disciplines and the techniques currently being used to examine the brain. Because of this, some have argued for broader terms such as 'biological psychology' or 'behavioural neuroscience' to describe modern-day research (Davis *et al.* 1988; Dewsbury 1991). Whatever the arguments for and against these terms, they mean roughly the same thing: they are trying to give an appropriate name to the scientific discipline that tries to relate the biology of the brain with behaviour.

Ancient historical beginnings

Among the first people to realise that the brain was the organ of the mind and behaviour were the ancient Greeks. For instance, Plato (429–348 BC) proposed that the brain was the organ of reasoning – although others disagreed, including his pupil Aristotle, who believed that the heart served this function and that the brain merely served to cool blood. Throughout most of the ancient world the human body was considered sacred and autopsies were prohibited. In fact, the first drawings of the human brain were not undertaken until the late fifteenth century AD, by Leonardo da Vinci. Nonetheless, the ancient Greeks were aware of the basic shape of the brain mainly through animal dissection, and of its ventricles – a series of connected fluid-filled cavities that could be seen when the brain was sliced open (see Figure 1.1). Because the ventricles stood out visually as one of the main features of the brain, it is perhaps not surprising that they were used to formulate early theories about how the brain worked.

One of the first writers to propose a theory of brain function based on the ventricles was Galen (AD 130–200) who was the most important physician of the Roman imperial period. He also made many important anatomical discoveries, including the cranial nerves that pass between the brain and the body (see later). Galen believed that the heart was the crucial organ of the body because it contained the *vital spirit* that gave the spark of life to the person. This vital spirit was also thought to provide the 'substance' of the mind, and was transported to a large group of blood vessels at the base of the brain called the *rete mirabile* ('wonderful net'). Here the vital spirit was mixed with air that had been inhaled through the nose, and transformed into *animated spirit* that was stored in the ventricles. When needed for action, the animated spirit was then

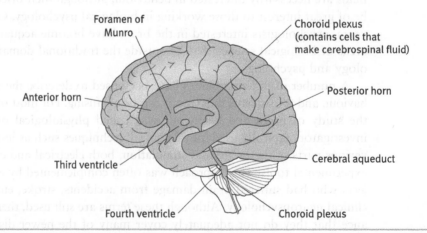

Foramen of Munro

Choroid plexus (contains cells that make cerebrospinal fluid)

Anterior horn

Posterior horn

Third ventricle

Cerebral aqueduct

Fourth ventricle

Choroid plexus

| Figure 1.1 | Lateral view showing the ventricular system of the brain |

believed to enter nerves resembling hollow tubes, that passed into the body where it pneumatically moved muscles to produce behaviour. Galen knew that the brain had four main ventricles (the first two are now called the **lateral ventricles** and they form a symmetrical pair inside the cerebral cortex, which then feed into the **third ventricle** located in the mid-part of the brain, that joins with the **fourth ventricle** in the brain stem).

Others who followed Galen extended his ideas and gave the ventricles different functions. For example, in the fourth century AD, Nemesius, Bishop of Emesa, hypothesised that the lateral ventricles were the site of sensory and mental impressions; the third ventricle the site of reason; and the fourth ventricle the site of memory. This theory was also adopted by Augustine of Hippo (354–430) who was one of the founding fathers of the Christian religion. With respected spiritual authority behind it, the ventricular concept of brain function became the most popular theory in the brain's written history and was accepted as the truth for nearly 1,500 years. In fact, it began to be doubted only in the Renaissance when Vesalius in his great anatomical work *De humani corporis fabrica* (1543) showed that the human brain does not contain a *rete mirabile*. It seems that Galen, who had not been allowed to perform human dissection in Rome, had inferred its human existence by observing it in cattle and oxon.

René Descartes

René Descartes (1596–1650) was a French philosopher and mathematician who more than any other person was responsible for the demise of the intellectual assumptions that characterised the Middle Ages. Indeed, his scepticism of all knowledge expressed in his famous quote *Cogito; ergo sum* ('I think, therefore I am'), which refers to Descartes's doubt of all things except his own existance, is often seen as heralding a new age of reason. The importance of Descartes in the development of psychology lies largely with his attempt to resolve the mind–body problem. Descartes believed, as did Plato, that mind and body are two entirely different things (a theory known as **dualism**), with the body composed of physical matter, and the mind or soul being non-physical and independent of the material world. A problem with this position, however, lies in trying to explain how the non-material mind can control the physical or mechanical workings of the body. In his attempt to provide an answer, Descartes proposed that mind and body interacted in the **pineal gland**. Descartes chose the pineal gland as it was a singular structure (most other brain areas are bilateral, or 'paired') and because he believed that the soul had to be a unified indivisible entity. It also helped that the pineal gland was located close to the third ventricle and bathed by cerebrospinal fluid. This provided the pineal gland with a means by which its minute movements could influence the animated spirits of the brain. In other words, the pineal gland provided an ideal site where the soul could act upon the body (Mazzolini 1991).

Despite this, Descartes also realised that a great deal of behaviour was mechanical and did not require mental intervention. In fact, it was during a visit to the Royal Gardens in Paris as a young man that he began to develop this idea. The gardens exhibited mechanical statues that moved and danced whenever they were approached, which was caused by hydraulic pressure-sensitive plates hidden under the ground. This led Descartes to speculate that the human body might work according to similar principles.

Figure 1.2   The reflex as hypothesised by Descartes

Source: Alamy Images

From this premise, he developed the concept of the automatic **reflex** which occurs, for example, when a limb is quickly moved away from a hot source such as a fire (see Figure 1.2). To explain this response, Descartes hypothesised that a sensory nerve composed of a hollow tube containing *vital spirit* conveyed the message of heat to the ventricles of the brain; these in turn directed animal spirit to flow out through the nerves from the brain, back to the muscles of the affected limb thereby causing its withdrawal. The important point was that this behaviour was reflexive: the mind was not involved (although it felt pain and was aware of what had happened) and therefore not a *cause* of behaviour.

Prior to Descartes, it had generally been accepted that the soul controlled all the actions of the human body. But Descartes showed that the human body worked according to mechanical principles – not unlike the internal workings of a watch – and did not need a soul to make it operate once it had been put into motion. Descartes proposed that not only were functions such as digestion and respiration reflexive, but so too were a number of mental functions, including sensory impressions, emotions and memory. He based this idea partly on his observation that animals, which he believed had no soul, were capable of sensory processing along with emotion and memory. Thus, if these processes did not need the involvement of a soul (or mind) in animals, why not the same in humans? That is, they could be seen as reflexive responses that belonged to the world of physical or mechanical phenomena. The one exception, however, was reasoning and pure thought, which Descartes believed was the exclusive property of the soul and unique to humans. This was a position that allowed his theory to be in accordance with the religious teachings of the time.

Descartes's theory helped lay the foundations for the modern development of physiology and psychology. Although his theory was based on a dualist view of the mind, it helped shift attention towards the practical problem of how reflexes might underlie behaviour without fear of contradicting religious dogma. In addition, it encouraged others to think more deeply about how the brain worked. But, perhaps most importantly, Descartes provided a great impetus for experimental research – not least because some of his ideas could be tested. As we have seen, Descartes believed that the nervous system controlling reflexes was a hydraulic system consisting of hollow tubes through which animal spirits flowed from the ventricles to the muscles. If this idea was correct then it followed that muscles should increase in volume as they 'swelled' with spirit during contraction. When investigators tested this theory by flexing a person's arm in a container of water, however, no increase in the water level occurred. Nonetheless, Descartes had paved a way for a scientific and non-secular approach to understanding human physiology that included the brain.

The discovery of 'animal' electricity

In 1791, the idea of animal spirit as the cause of nervous activity was challenged by the Italian Luigi Galvani who undertook a series of experiments on amputated frog legs which included the exposed ends of their severed nerves. Galvani found that he could induce a leg to twitch in a number of ways – as indeed shown in one famous case where, during a thunderstorm, he connected a nerve stump to a long metallic wire that pointed to the sky and obtained strong muscular contractions in the detached leg (Galvani was obviously unaware of the great dangers of such a demonstration!). But, perhaps more importantly, he also found that similar movements were produced when he suspended a frog's leg between two different metals. Although he did not know it at the time, Galvani had shown that when dissimilar metals make contact, through a salt solution, an electrical current is produced. This was, in fact, the first demonstration of the battery later formally invented by Volta in 1800. These discoveries led Galvani to conclude that nerves are capable of conducting electricity and that their 'invisible spirit' must be electrical in nature. This was finally proved beyond reasonable doubt in 1820 when the German Johann Schweigger invented the galvanometer (named in honour of Galvani) which measured the strength and direction of an electrical current. Indeed, this invention soon showed that nervous tissue contained intrinsic electrical energy. Thus, the twitching frogs' legs marked the end to hydraulic theories of nervous action and the start of a new chapter in understanding how nerve cells work (Piccolino 1997).

One question that fascinated neurophysiologists during this time was the speed of the nervous impulse that flowed down the fibre (axon). Although the galvanometer could detect electrical acitivity, the nerve impulse appeared to be instantaneous and too fast to be measured. In fact, the famous physiologist Johannes Müller wrote somewhat despairingly in 1833 that the speed of the nerve impulse was comparable to the speed of light and would never be accurately estimated. However, Müller was soon proved wrong by the work of Hermann von Helmholtz who managed, in 1850, to extract long motor nerves (some 50–60 mm in length) that were still attached to muscles taken from frogs' legs. Helmholtz recorded the delay between the onset of electrical stimulation and the resulting muscle twitch, and calculated the speed of the impulse to be about 90 feet per second, which translates to around 98 kilometres per hour. We now know that Helmholtz was fairly accurate in his estimation. Moreover, while the nerve impulse was fast, it was not comparable with the speed of light. In fact, neurophysiologists have now established that speed of nerve conduction varies depending on the type of axon, with the impulse being quicker in large-diamter myelinated axons. For example, the fastest neurons can conduct action potentials at up to 120 metres per second (432 kilometres per hour) while small-diameter unmyelinated axons are much slower (about 35 metres per second).

The Nobel Prize in Physiology or Medicine

As a student of biopsychology, the most coveted and important award you can ever aspire to achieving is the Nobel Prize in Physiology and Medicine. As a recipient of this award, you will have been judged to have made 'discoveries' conferring 'the greatest benefit on mankind', and enjoy instant recognition, lifelong celebrity and unrivalled authority. At the time of writing, some 189 persons have been given this accolade in physiology and medicine, with about 50 of these individuals making contributions that can be considered relevant to neuroscience. Put simply, if you win the prize, you will belong to a very select band of scientists whose fame will last for ever in the pages of medical history.

Alfred Bernhard Nobel was born in 1833 in Stockholm, Sweden. The son of an engineer, he moved in his childhood to Russia, where his father made a fortune manufacturing explosives and military equipment. At the age of 17, Nobel went to Paris to study chemistry, and he worked for a time in the United States before returning to Sweden in 1859. In 1864, he started to manufacture nitroglycerine. Unfortunately, an explosion at his factory was to kill Nobel's younger brother Emil and four other workers soon after. In an attempt to make a safer explosive he invented dynamite in 1867. This was to establish Nobel's fame worldwide as it was widely used to blast tunnels, cut canals, and in the building of railways and roads. By the time Alfred Nobel died in 1896 he had made a massive fortune, and in his will he left instructions that most of his money (amounting to SK 31 million) should be used to give prizes that honoured people from all over the world for outstanding achievements in physics, chemistry, physiology or medicine, literature and for peace-making. Although the will was strongly contested, the first awards were made in 1901 on the fifth anniversary of Nobel's death.

The first Nobel Prize in Physiology or Medicine was awarded in 1901 to Emil Adolf von Behring, for his work on developing a vaccine against diphtheria. The first person of interest to psychologists to be awarded the prize was Ivan Pavlov in 1904 (see Table 1.1). However, this was in recognition of research on the physiology of digestion, and not for his experiments on conditioned reflexes. Thus, the first 'neuroscientists' to obtain the award were Camillo Golgi and Santiago Ramón y Cajal, in 1906, for their work on describing the structure of the central nervous system. The award ceremony, however, was not without some degree of acrimony, as during their acceptance speeches Golgi and Cajal gave opposing views on whether neurons were joined together or separated by synapses. Although Golgi accused his rival of not having any 'firm evidence' to support the synapse theory, it was Cajal who was correct. There have also been other controversies. For example, in 1949, Egas Moniz won the prize for introducing the frontal lobotomy to treat mental illness – a procedure that often resulted in many harmful side effects. Protests from over 250 scientists were also raised to the 2000 Nobel Prize (awarded to the neuroscientists Avrid Carlsson, Paul Greengard and Eric Kandel) for the non-inclusion of Oleh Hornkiewicz who is noted for his work on Parkinson's disease. But, perhaps the biggest controversy of all is the omission of Rosalind Franklin in the 1962 award for the discovery of DNA. Although she was the first to take an X-ray picture of DNA, which was seen by Crick and Watson without her permission, and vital in their deductions, Franklin is often forgotten for her work.

Table 1.1	Nobel laureates in neuroscience, 1904–2004		
Date	**Nobel Laureate**	**Nationality**	**Area of Work**
1904	Ivan Pavlov	Russian	Digestion
1906	Camillo Golgi	Italian	Structure of the nervous system
	Santiago Ramón y Cajal	Spanish	
1914	Robert Barany	Austrian	Vestibular apparatus of the ear
1932	Charles Sherrington	British	Function of neurons
	Edgar Adrian	British	
1936	Henry Dale	British	Chemical nature of the nerve impulse
	Otto Loewi	German	
1944	Joseph Erlanger	American	Research on single nerve fibres
	Herbert Gasser	American	
1949	Egas Moniz	Portuguese	Lobotomy
	Walter Hess	Swiss	Functions of hypothalamus
1961	Georg von Beksey	Hungarian	Functions of the cochlea
1963	Alan Hodgkin	British	Ionic basis of neural transmission
	Andrew Huxley	British	
	John Eccles	Australian	
1967	Ragnor Granit	Finnish	Visual processes of the eye
	Haldan Hartline	American	
	George Wald	American	
1970	Jules Axelrod	American	Release of neurotransmitters in the synapse
	Bernard Katz	German/British	
	Ulf von Euler	Swedish	
1973	Konrad Lorenz	Austrian	Ethology and animal behaviour
	Nikolaas Tinbergen	Dutch	
	Karl von Frisch	Austrian	
1977	Roger Guillmin	French	Discovery of neuropeptides
	Andrew Schally	Polish	
1979	Herbert Simon	American	Cognitive psychology
1979	Godfrey Hounsfield	British	Invention of CAT scanning
	Allan MacLeod	South African	
1981	David Hubel	Canadian	Visual cortex
	Torsten Wiesel	Swedish	
	Roger Sperry	American	Functions of the cerebral hemispheres
1986	Rita Levi-Montalcini	Italian	Discovery of neural growth factors
	Stanley Cohen	American	
1991	Erwin Neher	German	Ion channels in nerve cells
	Bert Sakmann	German	
1994	Alfred Gilman	American	G proteins and their role in signal transduction
	Martin Rodbell	American	
1997	Stanley Prusiner	American	Discovery of prions
2000	Arvid Carlsson	Swedish	Discoveries related to synaptic neurotransmission
	Paul Greengard	American	
	Eric Kandel	American	
2003	Roderick MacKinnon	American	Structural properties of ion channels
2004	Linda Buck	American	Discovery of odorant receptors
	Richard Axel	American	

The discovery of the nerve cell

Although Galvani had shown that nervous energy was electrical, there was still much to learn about how nerves worked. For example, until the early nineteenth century there was no real idea of what a nerve looked like, other than it had long thin projections, and many believed that nerves were joined together in much the same way as blood vessels are interconnected (that is, through a system of connecting tubes). These beliefs persisted despite the invention of the microscope in 1665, by Robert Hooke, and the subsequent work of Anton Von Leeuwenhoek who used it to examine biological tissues and was the first to coin the word 'cell'. Unfortunately, the early microscopes did not reveal neural structure in great detail, and it was not until around 1830 when better kinds of lenses were developed that microscopes provided stronger and clearer magnification. Even so, there was the problem of how to prepare the tissue for microscopic work so that nerve cells could be distinguished from other types of material. Although by the 1800s histologists had found new ways to stain nerve tissue, their methods stained all neurons indiscriminately. This meant that the only way to visualise a neuron was to remove it from the mass of tangled cells in which it was embedded. Since neurons were far too small to be seen with the naked eye, this proved extremely difficult and rarely successful.

In 1875, however, a major breakthrough occurred when the Italian anatomist Camillo Golgi (1843–1926) discovered a new stain that allowed individual nerve cells to be observed. By serendipity, he found that when nervous tissue was exposed to silver nitrate, the nerve cells would turn black. This caused them to stand out in bold relief so they could clearly be seen under a microscope. But, more importantly, Golgi's technique only stained around 2 per cent of the cells in any given slice of nervous tissue. This was a great advance as it made individual neurons, and all their various components such as **dendrites** and **axons**, much more clearly observable (see Figure 1.3). This method soon proved indispensable for examining the wide variety of cells in the brain. Indeed, much of the basic terminology which we now use to describe nerve cells was introduced by anatomists at around this time (*c*.1880).

The person, who put the Golgi stain to its greatest use, however, was the Spaniard Santiago Ramón y Cajal (1852–1934) who meticulously described the neural anatomy of the brain using this technique. He showed, for example, that the brain contains a great variety of cells with many different characteristics. Although some cells had short

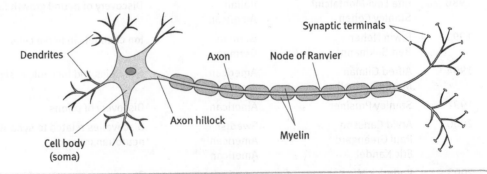

| Figure 1.3 | The main components of a typical brain neuron |

axons that projected to cells within the same structure (**interneurons**), others had long axons that formed pathways that projected to distant brain regions. Ramón y Cajal further showed that the brain was not a random morass of nerve cells as had been widely assumed, but a highly organised structure with clearly defined regions and nuclei (groups of cell bodies). Ramón y Cajal even helped to explain how neurons worked. For example, his observations led him to realise that neurons received much of their input via their **dendrites** (from the Greek *dendron* meaning 'tree') and that they sent information along their cable-like pathways called **axons**. Thus he was one of the first to see how information travels through the nerve cell and pathways of the brain.

But, perhaps, Ramón y Cajal's most important contribution to neuroanatomy was his discovery that nerve cells were separate and individual units. Previously, it had been believed that nerve cells were joined together in a network of tubes which allowed the direct passage of information from cell to cell. In fact, Golgi was a vociferous supporter of the 'reticular' theory. However, Ramón y Cajal showed that nerve cells do not join in this manner. Rather, the axon terminals end very close to the neurons (or dendrites) that they are projecting to, but do not touch. In other words, each neuron is an individual unit separated from its neighbour by a very small gap. These gaps were called **synapses** (meaning 'clasps') in 1897 by the British neurophysiologist Charles Sherrington. This discovery raised many new questions, not least how nerve cells sent information across the synapse, and how synaptic transmission was able to generate a new electrical signal in the postsynaptic neuron.

Following Golgi's discovery, many other staining techniques were developed that enabled investigators to examine nerve cells in more detail. For example, some techniques were able to selectively stain cell bodies (the **soma**), whereas others stained the axons (or rather their **myelin** covering) allowing neural pathways in the brain to be traced. In other instances, staining techniques were combined with lesioning methods to provide useful information (for example, neural pathways can be traced by staining degenerating axons that arise from a structure after it has been experimentally destroyed). By the turn of the twentieth century the study of neuroanatomy had become an established discipline. It also provided one of the foundation stones on which physiological psychology was based, for without knowledge of brain structure and organisation, very little can be said about how the brain produces behaviour (Shepherd 1991).

The discovery of chemical neurotransmission

One of the most important questions that followed from Ramón y Cajal's work concerned the nature of the message that crossed the synapse from the **presynaptic neuron** (the neuron before the synapse) to the **postsynaptic neuron** (recipient neuron). From the time of Galvani it was known that neurons contained electrical energy; but how did this principle extend to synapses? For example, did an electrical current jump across the tiny synaptic gap, or was there another form of communication? As early as 1877 it had been suggested by the German physiologist Emil du Bois-Reymond that chemical transmission might be the answer. And, in 1904, the Cambridge student Thomas Eliott lent support to this idea by showing that adrenaline stimulated the activity of bodily organs that were innervated by the sympathetic nervous system. Indeed, Eliott made what is now regarded as the first clear statement about the feasibility of neurotransmission: '*Adrenaline might then be the chemical stimulant liberated on each occasion when the impulse arrives at the periphery.*' But, arguably, the single most important experiment that proved chemical transmission was performed by Otto Loewi in 1921. According to Loewi's memoirs, on the night of Easter Saturday 1921, he awoke from a sleep and wrote down the details of an experiment that had come to him in a dream. Unfortunately, Loewi went back to sleep, and on waking again, was unable to decipher his notes. The next night he awoke at 3 A.M. with the idea back in his mind, and this time he cycled to his laboratory to perform the experiment. Two hours later, the chemical nature of synaptic transmission had in essence been proved (Finger 1994).

In his experiment, Loewi used frog hearts, which are similar to our own in that they are supplied by two different peripheral nerves: the sympathetic branch that excites the heart and makes it beat more rapidly, and the parasympathetic branch (also called the vagus nerve) which slows it down. Loewi used two hearts: one with the sympathetic and vagus nerve intact, and the other with nerves removed (see Figure 1.4). He then placed the intact heart in a fluid bath and stimulated its vagus nerve causing its beat to slow down. Loewi collected the fluid surrounding this heart and applied it to the second one – and found that its intrinsic beat also began to decrease. The results indicated that the fluid must contain a substance that had been secreted by the previously stimulated vagus nerve projecting to the heart. Later analysis by Sir Henry Dale and

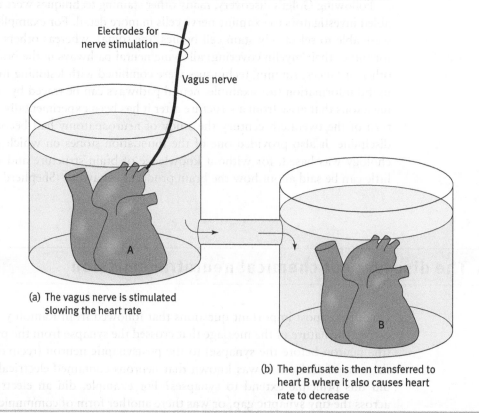

(a) The vagus nerve is stimulated
    slowing the heart rate

(b) The perfusate is then transferred to
    heart B where it also causes heart
    rate to decrease

Figure 1.4   Loewi's experimental set up showing that nerves send messages by releasing chemical substances

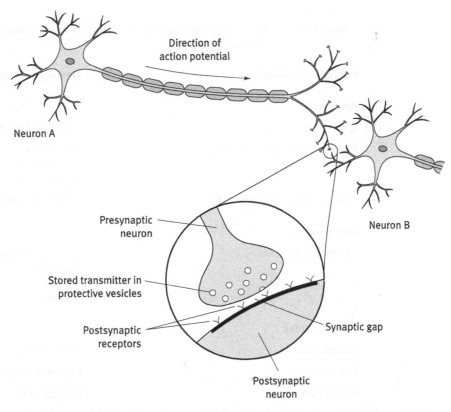

An action potential passes down the axon of neuron A and when reaching the axon terminals it causes the synaptic vesicles to fuse with the membrane thereby spilling transmitter into the synaptic gap. This then crosses the short space where it can bind to postsynaptic receptors.

Figure 1.5	Chemical transmission at the synapse

his colleagues showed this chemical to be acetylcholine, which is an important neuro-transmitter in the peripheral and central nervous systems.

It is now known that most nerve cells in the body communicate with each other by secreting **neurotransmitters** into synapses (see Figure 1.5). The series of events that produce this transmission can be described simply as follows. (1) The axon terminals of the presynaptic neuron receive an electrical impulse called an **action potential,** and in response they secrete a **neurotransmitter.** (2) This chemical diffuses into and across the synapse and binds to specialised sites on the postsynaptic neuron called **receptors.** (3) Activation of receptors leads to the opening of ion channels, allowing positively or negatively charged ions to enter the neuron, which then act to increase or decrease its internal resting electrical voltage. (4) If the neuron is excited past a certain level (by about −15 mV) at its axon hillock, it generates an action potential (nervous impulse) that flows down the axon to its terminals, leading to neurotransmitter release. Much of the rest of this chapter discusses these steps in greater detail.

The brain contains dozens of different neurotransmitters (see Table 1.2). The first to be discovered was **acetylcholine** (Loewi was awarded a Nobel Prize for his dis-covery along with Sir Henry Dale in 1936). This was followed by **noradrenaline** in the 1940s, **dopamine** and **serotonin** in the 1950s, and **gamma-aminobutyric acid** (**GABA**), **glutamate** and **glycine** in the 1960s. In the 1970s, a new group of transmitter

Table 1.2	Some of the neurotransmitters most commonly found in the central nervous system

Family and Subfamily	Neurotransmitter
Amines	
Quaternary amines	Acetylcholine (ACH)
Monoamines (catecholamines)	Adrenaline
	Dopamine (DA)
	Noradrenaline (NA)
Monoamines (indolamines)	Serotonin (5-HT)
Amino acids	
'Small' amino acids	Gamma-aminobutyric acid (GABA)
	Glutamate
	Glycine
	Histamine
Neuropeptides	
Enkephalins	Met-enkephalin, leu-enkephalin
Endorphins	Beta-endorphin
Dynorphins	Dynorphin A
Peptides	
Short chains of amino acids	Cholecystokinin (CCK)
	Neuropeptide Y
	Oxytocin
	Somatostatin
	Substance P
	Vasopressin
Gases	
	Nitric oxide
	Carbon monoxide

substances called neuropeptides were discovered which included opiate-like substances (**endorphins**). More recently, it has been found that certain gases such as **nitric oxide** also have a neurotransmitter function. To make matters more complex, most neurons do not release a single neurotransmitter as was once thought (originally known as **Dale's Law**), but secrete two or more substances together. Many of these 'secondary' chemicals act primarily as **neuromodulators** whose function is to 'modulate' the effect of neurotransmitters.

The discovery of chemical transmission by Loewi is a pivotal point in the history of psychopharmacology because it raised the possibility of modifying brain function and behaviour by the use of drugs that could selectively affect the action of neurotransmitters. This possibility was realised in the latter part of the twentieth century with the development of drugs to treat brain disorders such as Parkinson's disease and various types of mental illness such as depression or schizophrenia. Indeed, many of the drugs that work on the brain do so either by mimicking the action of a neurotransmitter

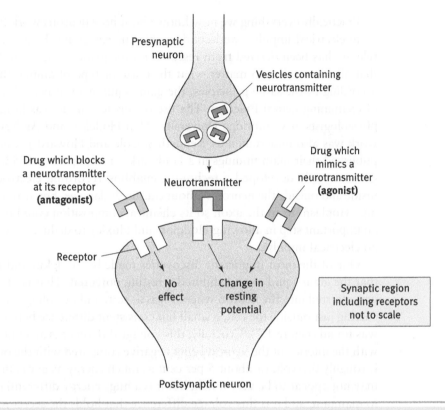

Figure 1.6   Agonist and antagonist effects on receptors

at its receptor site (such drugs are known as **agonists**) or by blocking its receptor (these are known as **antagonists**) (see Figure 1.6). In addition, histochemical advances have enabled neurotransmitters in nerve endings to be visualised, enabling chemical pathways in the brain to be traced and mapped out.

Neural conduction

By the early part of the twentieth century, biologists knew that neurons were capable of generating electrical currents but did not know the finer details of how this energy was being created or conducted along the axon. The main difficulty lay in trying to record from the neuron during these events. Although biologists had at their disposal recording electrodes with very fine tips, along with oscilloscopes and amplifiers that could greatly magnify tiny electrical charges, neurons were too small to enable this type of work to take place. That was until 1936 when the Oxford biologist John Z. Young discovered a neuron located in the body of the squid (*Loligo pealii*) that had an axon nearly 1 mm in diameter (up to 1,000 times larger than a typical mammalian axon). Not only was this axon large enough to allow the insertion of a stimulating or recording electrode, but it could also be removed from the animal and kept alive for several hours. This allowed both the electrical and chemical properties of the neuron to be examined in great detail.

Practically everything we now know about how neurons work (that is, how they generate electrical impulses and conduct this current along the axon to cause transmitter release) has been derived from research on the giant squid axon. Because it is believed that all nerve cells, no matter what their size or type of animal they come from, work according to the same principles, the giant squid neuron provides an invaluable means of examining neural function. The use of this technique was largely pioneered by two physiologists at Cambridge University, Alan Hodgkin and Andrew Huxley (important work was also undertaken by Kenneth S. Cole and Howard J. Curtis in America), who published their main findings in a landmark set of papers in 1952. These two physiologists not only developed a technique enabling recording electrodes to be positioned inside and outside the neuron without causing it damage, but also found a way of removing cytoplasm from the axon so its chemical composition could be examined. This was an important step in allowing Hodgkin and Huxley to deduce how the neuron produced an electrical impulse.

One of the most important discoveries made by Hodgkin and Huxley (*c*.1939) was that the giant squid axon exhibited a **resting potential**. That is, if a recording electrode was inserted into the neuron when it was at rest, and its voltage compared with that occurring just outside the cell, a small but consistent difference between the two electrodes was found (Figure 1.7). Crucially, this voltage difference is around −70 millivolts (mV), with the interior of the neuron being negative compared with the outside, The difference is roughly 0.1 volt, or about 5 per cent as much energy as exists in a torch battery. This may not appear to be very much, but it is a huge energy differential for a tiny nerve cell to maintain, and it is this voltage difference that holds the secret to understanding how the neuron generates electrical current in the form of action potentials.

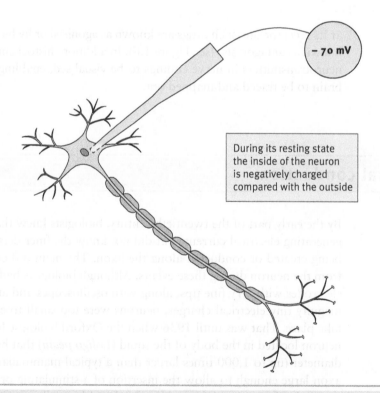

− 70 mV

During its resting state the inside of the neuron is negatively charged compared with the outside

| Figure 1.7 | Measurement of the resting potential of the nerve fibre using a microelectrode |

To explain why the voltage difference of −70 mV occurs, it is important to understand that the intracellular and extracellular environments of the neuron, when it is at rest, are different in their concentrations of ions. An ion is simply an electrically charged atom, or particle, that has lost or gained an electron, which gives it a positive or negative charge, respectively. As any school pupil should know, an atom is composed of a nucleus containing positively charged (+) protons and neutrons, and is surrounded by tiny negatively charged (−) electrons that orbit around it. In the atom's normal state, the opposite charges of protons and electrons cancel themselves out, making the atom neutral. However, if the atom loses an electron, then it will have one less negative charge, and as a result it becomes a positively charged (+) ion. Alternatively, if the atom gains an extra electron it becomes a negatively charged (−) ion. Although only a few types of ion exist in the body, they play a crucial role in the production of the nervous impulse. These ions include **sodium (Na^+)** and **potassium (K^+)** that have lost an electron and are positively charged; and **chloride (Cl^-)** and organic **anions (A^-)** that have gained an electron and are negatively charged (Figure 1.8).

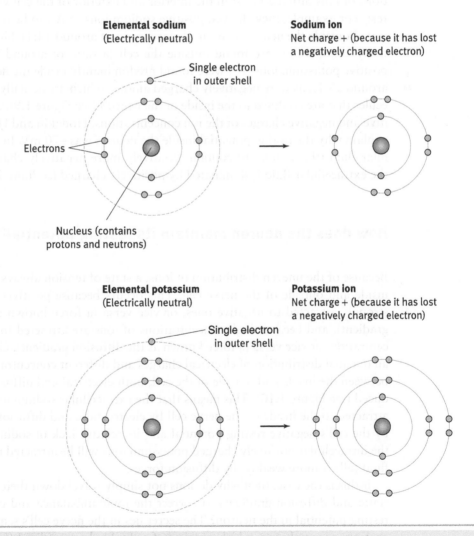

Elemental sodium
(Electrically neutral)

Sodium ion
Net charge + (because it has lost a negatively charged electron)

Single electron in outer shell

Electrons

Nucleus (contains protons and neutrons)

Elemental potassium
(Electrically neutral)

Potassium ion
Net charge + (because it has lost a negatively charged electron)

Single electron in outer shell

Figure 1.8   How sodium and potassium ions are formed

	Concentration of ions in axoplasm (mM)	Concentration of ions outside the cell (mM)
Potassium (K⁺)	400	10
Sodium (Na⁺)	50	450
Chloride (Cl⁻)	40	560
Organic anions (A⁻)	345	0

Figure 1.9   The concentration of the four important ions inside and outside the axon expressed in millimoles (mM)

One of Hodgkin and Huxley's most important discoveries was that the concentrations of ions differed between the interior and exterior of the cell when the cell was at rest. For example, they showed positive sodium ions (NA^+) to be more highly concentrated outside the neuron than inside (at a ratio of around 14:1). Similarly, more negatively charged ions are found outside the cell (a ratio of around 25:1). In contrast, positive potassium ions (K^+) were found predominantly inside the neuron (at a ratio of around 28:1), as were negatively charged anions, which are actually large protein molecules that are confined to the inside of the neuron (see Figure 1.9). Adding up the positive and negative charges of the ion concentrations, Hodgkin and Huxley were able to explain why the resting potential inside the neuron was –70 mV. In short, the intracellular fluid (the axoplasm) contains relatively more negatively charged ions, whereas the extracellular fluid is dominated by positively charged (sodium) ions.

How does the neuron maintain its resting potential?

Because of the uneven distribution of ions, a state of tension always exists between the inside and outside of the nerve cell. This occurs because positively charged ions are strongly attracted to negative ones, or vice versa (a force known as the **electrostatic gradient**), and because high concentrations of ions are attracted to areas of low concentration, or vice versa (a force known as the **diffusion gradient**). Consequently, when an unequal distribution of electrical charges and different concentrations of ions occur between the inside and outside of the cell, both electrical and diffusion forces are produced (see Figure 1.10). This means that the extracellular sodium ions will be strongly attracted to the inside of the nerve cell by electrostatic and diffusion forces (produced by the cell's negative resting potential and its relative lack of sodium ions). Similarly, the intracellular positively charged potassium ions will be attracted to the extracellular fluid (albeit more weakly) by diffusion forces.

If this is the case, then why do ions not simply travel down their respective electrostatic and diffusion gradients to correct the ionic imbalance and cancel the negative resting potential in the neuron? The secret lies in the nerve cell's semi-permeable outer coating, or membrane, which consists of a double layer of lipid (fat) molecules. This acts as a barrier to ion flow. However, embedded in the membrane are a number of

(a) Diffusion

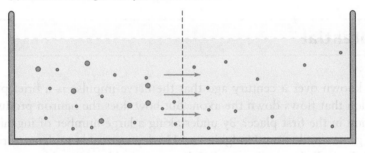

Particles move from areas of high concentration to areas of low concentration. That is, they move down their concentration gradient

(b) Diffusion through semi-permeable membranes

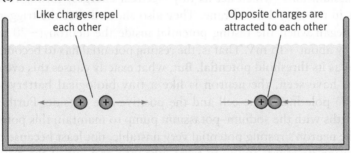

Cell membranes permit some substances to pass through, but not others

(c) Electrostatic forces

Like charges repel each other

Opposite charges are attracted to each other

| Figure 1.10 | Electrostatic and diffusion forces |

Source: S.M. Breedlove *et al.*, *Biological Psychology*, 5th edition, p. 61. Copyright © 2007 by Sinauer Associates, Inc.

specialised protein molecules that act as **ion channels**. These are tiny pores that can open in order to permit certain ions to flow in, or out, of the neuron. There are two main types of ion channel which we will discuss in more detail later: **ligand-gated ion channels** that are opened by ligands (i.e. chemicals) attaching themselves to receptors, and **voltage-gated ion channels** which are opened by voltage changes occurring inside the neuron. Ion channels are also 'leaky'. In fact, when the neuron is in its resting state, the membrane is about 100 times more permeable to potassium ions than sodium – largely because potassium is more able to leak through its own channels. Thus, potassium can move into and out of the cell much more freely than can sodium.

This brings us to another important question: if ions are in constant motion (particularly potassium) how can it be that the resting potential of -70 mV is maintained? Clearly, if physical forces are simply left to operate, the flow of potassium to the extracellular fluid will quickly cause the resting potential inside the neuron to become neutral – and the flow of sodium towards the cell's interior, even at a slower rate of infiltration, will help to do the same. The answer is that the neuron maintains the intra- and extracellular balance of ions by a complex protein molecule located in its membrane called a **sodium–potassium pump**. In fact, this pump forces out of the cell around three sodium ions for every two potassium ions it takes in. This requires considerable energy and it has been estimated that up to 20 per cent of the cell's energy is spent on this pumping process (Dudel 1978). Such is the importance of maintaining the negative resting potential. Without it, the neuron would be unable to generate action potentials.

The action potential

It was known over a century ago that the nerve impulse is a brief pulse of electrical excitation that flows down the axon. But how does the neuron produce this electrical excitation in the first place? By undertaking a large number of ingenious experiments on the giant squid axon, Hodgkin and Huxley were able to demonstrate that the electrical pulse (called an **action potential**) was caused by the sudden movement of sodium and potassium ions (which act as tiny electrcal charges) through their respective ion channels in the neural membrane. They also showed that the triggering event for this process began when the resting potential inside the neuron (-70 mV) became more positive by about $+15$ mV. That is, the resting potential has to become -55 mV, or what is known as its **threshold potential**. But, what exactly causes this event to happen?

As we have seen, the neuron is like a tiny biological battery with the negative (-70 mV) pole inside the cell and the positive one outside. Furthermore, it goes to great lengths with the sodium–potassium pump to maintain this polarity. But, this also makes the neuron's resting potential very unstable, not least because of the electrostatic and diffusion pressures trying to force ions into and out of the cell. In fact, the cell's resting potential is rarely stable at -70 mV, even with the full operation of the sodium–potassium pump. One reason for this lies with neurotransmitters that are constantly bombarding the receptors of the neuron. The main effect of a neurotransmitter binding to its receptor is to briefly open certain **ligand-gated ion channels**. This allows small amounts of ions into the cell, which then causes small changes to the resting potential. Some neurotransmitters, such as glutamate, make the resting potential more positive by increasing the membrane's permeability to positive ions, whereas others, such as GABA, make the resting potential more negative by increasing the influx of negative ions.

Although a few molecules of neurotransmitter binding to a single receptor will probably have a negliable effect on the cell's resting potential, it must be remembered that a neuron may have thousands of receptors (and ion channels) spread over its dendrites

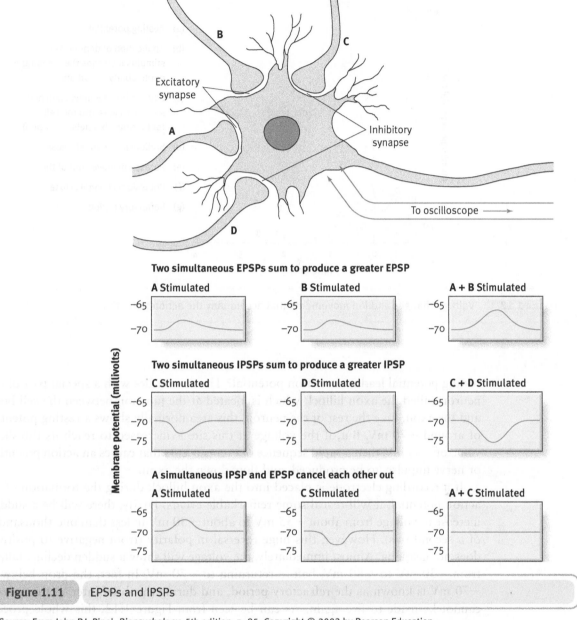

Figure 1.11   EPSPs and IPSPs

and soma, and have a great variety of excitatory and inhibitory neurotransmitters impinging upon it at any moment. Consequently, the **summation** of all this stimulation at a given point in time may produce a significant change in the cell's resting potential. Indeed, if the stimulation causes the voltage inside the cell to become more positive, this is called an **excitatory postsynaptic potential (EPSP)**, and if the cell becomes more negative it is called an **inhibitory postsynaptic potential (IPSP)** (see Figure 1.11).

The change in resting potential produced by the flow of ions into the cell following neurotransmitter stimulation normally begins in the dendrites, and the voltage change (i.e. an EPSP or an IPSP) spreads down into the cell body. But how does a change in

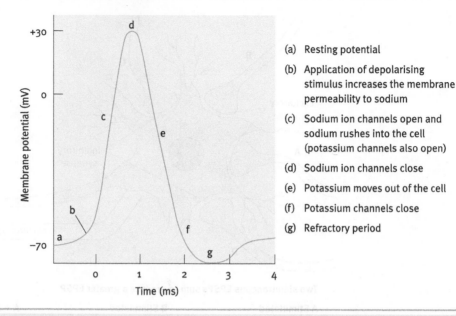

(a) Resting potential

(b) Application of depolarising stimulus increases the membrane permeability to sodium

(c) Sodium ion channels open and sodium rushes into the cell (potassium channels also open)

(d) Sodium ion channels close

(e) Potassium moves out of the cell

(f) Potassium channels close

(g) Refractory period

Figure 1.12   Voltage changes and ion movements that accompany the action potential

resting potential lead to an action potential? The answer lies with a special part of the neuron called the **axon hillock** which is located at the junction between the cell body and the axon. Like the rest of the neuron, this area normally shows a resting potential of around −70 mV. But, if the voltage at this site is increased to reach its threshold value of −55 mV, then a rapid sequence of events occurs that causes an action potential, or nerve impulse, to be produced, and flow down the axon.

If a recording electrode is placed into the axon hillock during the formation of an action potential, it will reveal some remarkable events. Firstly, there will be a sudden increase in voltage from about −55 mV to about +30 mV in less than one-thousandth of a second (ms). However, this huge reversal in polarity (from negative to positive) does not last long. Almost immediately, the voltage will show a sudden decline, falling from +30 mV to −80 mV, before returning to −70 mV. In fact, the drop below is −70 mV is known as the **refractory period**, and during this brief interval the neuron cannot be made to fire again. As can be seen from Figure 1.12, this whole process takes place in just 4 or 5 ms, which is another way of saying that it is possible for a neuron to fire over 100 times a second. This event is the beginning of the nervous impulse that will begin its journey down the axon.

Thus, the axon hillock is the region of the neuron where the integration of excitatory and inhibitory postsynaptic potentials has to take place before an action potential can be generated. This response is **all-or-nothing** as the neuron either fires or doesn't (there is no graded response). However, once the action potential is formed, it has to pass down the axon to reach the axonal endings where the neurotransmitter is stored ready to be released into the synapse. But, here lies a problem: axons are long spindly projections, and if the action potential passively moved down the fibre, its energy would decay before getting very far. Thus, the axon must have some way of actively moving the action potential down its length. The secret of how it does this lies with a fatty sheath called **myelin** which covers the axon and is not dissimilar to the rubber coating that surrounds an electrical cable. Unlike an electrical cable, however, the myelin contains short gaps called **nodes of Ranvier**, and it is at these points that the renewal of the action potential takes place. At each node, the action potential is amplified back to its original intensity. This means the impulse literally 'jumps' down the axon. This process is called **saltatory conduction** (from the Latin *saltare* meaning 'to dance') and explains how the action potential can travel long distances without weakening. Indeed, if you imagine a neural impulse going from a giraffe's brain to its back legs, you will realise the necessity of such a 'renewal' process.

The ionic basis of the action potential

How does the neuron bring about the sudden change in depolarisation (for example, from −55 mV to around +30 mV) to generate an action potential? The answer lies with the sodium and potassium ions – or rather, their respective **voltage-gated ion channels** that lie embedded in the neural membrane. As we have seen, large numbers of sodium ions are found in the extracellular fluid, and these are attracted to the inside of the cell by strong electrical and concentration forces (see Figure 1.10). Yet, the cell's membrane acts as a barrier to sodium and, if any of its ions infiltrate the neuron, they are removed by the sodium–potassium pump. This fine balance is changed, however, when the threshold potential (−55 mV) reached. When this occurs, the voltage-gated sodium channels in the membrane are opened and, as if a door is thrown open, sodium ions flood into the cell propelled by electrostatic and concentration forces. It has been estimated that up to 100,000,000 ions can pass through a channel per second (although the channel remains open for only a fraction of this time) and it is this large influx of sodium current into the cell that transforms its negative resting potential into a positive depolarisation.

At the peak of this sodium flow (1–2 ms after the ion channels have opened) the permeability of the membrane changes again. Now, the neuron closes the sodium channels and fully opens its potassium ones (these actually began to open just after the onset of the sodium influx). Because the inside of the cell at this point is now positively charged (+30 mV) due to the high concentration of sodium, the positively charged potassium ions are propelled out of the neuron by diffusion and electrostatic forces. Not only does this cause the cell's resting potential to become −70 mV again (at which point the potassium channels close), but the flow of potassium ions to the outside of the neuron is so strong that its internal voltage drops further to about −80 mV (the refractory period). It is only after the refractory period has occurred, that the cell's resting potential returns to normal (−70 mV) with the sodium–potassium pump restoring the ionic balance.

A similar pattern of ion movements in and out of the cell also occurs along the axon's length during saltatory conduction. As the electrical energy generated by the action potential passively moves down the axon, it causes the opening of voltage-gated sodium channels in the nodes of Ranvier. This causes a sudden influx of sodium ions into the axon and the formation of a new action potential. As this energy passes to the next node, there is an outflow of potassium ions at the node left behind which restores the resting potential of the axon. As this cycle is repeated, the electrical signal is conducted down the full length of the axon without any loss of strength (Stevens 1979).

Neurotransmitter release

When the action potential reaches the end of the axon, it passes through a large number of smaller axon branches ending in slightly swollen boutons called synaptic terminals. Stored within these terminals are large numbers of **synaptic vesicles** each containing a few hundred molecules of neurotransmitter. As the action potential arrives at the terminal, it causes voltage-gated **calcium channels** to open (not sodium) which allows positively charged calcium ions (Ca^{2+}) to enter the bouton. This produces **exocytosis**, in which the synaptic vesicles fuse with the presynaptic membrane, spilling their contents into the synaptic gap. In fact, vesicles are continually fusing with the axon terminal membrane which results in the ongoing secretion of small amounts of neurotransmitter, although the action potential greatly speeds up the process, causing more to be released. Indeed, the higher the frequency of action potentials, the greater the influx of calcium ions into the synaptic terminals, and the greater release of neurotransmitter.

The synaptic gap is a tiny fluid-filled space that measures about 0.00002 mm across. On one side of this gap is the presynaptic neuron where the axon endings terminate, and on the opposite side is the recipient postsynaptic neuron. When a neurotransmitter is released, it diffuses across the synapse and binds to receptors on the postsynaptic neuron (see next section). However, during this process, the neurotransmitter must also be quickly deactivated and broken down, otherwise it will continue to exert an effect and block the receptor from receiving further input. A number of synaptic mechanisms have evolved to fulfil this requirement. One such mechanism involves the physical removal of the neurotransmitter from the synapse by means of a **reuptake pump** which directs the chemical back into the presynaptic axon terminal for recycling. This process is particularly important for the monoamine neurotransmitters such as noradrenaline, dopamine and serotonin. Moreover, it has important clinical implications since drugs that block the reuptake process for either noradrenaline (for example, imipramine) or serotonin (for example, fluoxetine/prozac) are useful in the treatment of depression (Snyder 1986). Another process involves **enzymatic degradation**. For example, acetylcholine is rapidly broken down into inert choline and acetate by the enzyme **acetylcholinesterase (AChE)** found predominantly in the synapse. Inhibitors of this enzyme have also been used to increase brain levels of acetylcholine in Alzheimer's disease. Another enzyme, this time present in axon terminals and glial cells, is **monoamine oxidase** which breaks down excess levels of monoamines. Indeed, some antidepressant drugs such as iproniazid (Marsilid) work by inhibiting this enzyme.

Receptors

In 1905, the Cambridge physiologist John Langley first used the term **receptor** to refer to hypothetical enitities that he believed must exist on muscle and neurons that were sensitive to chemicals released by the nervous system. We now know that Langley was correct and that neurotransmitters produce their effects by interacting with receptor molecules, most of which are located in the postsynaptic cell's membrane. The receptor and its neurotransmitter have sometimes been likened to a lock and

Table 1.3	Some of the main receptor subtypes found in the central nervous system
Neurotransmitter	**Types of Receptor**
Acetylcholine (ACh)	Muscarinic and nicotinic
Dopamine (DA)	D-1, D-2, D-3, D-4 and D-5
Gamma-aminobutyric acid (GABA)	GABA-A and GABA-B
Glutamate	NMDA, APPA and kainate
Histamine	H-1, H-2 and H-3
Noradrenaline	Alpha (α) and beta (β)
Opioid	Mu (μ), delta (δ) and kappa (κ)
Serotonin (5-HT)	5-HT_1, 5-HT_2, 5-HT_3, 5-HT_4, 5-HT_5, 5-HT_6 and 5-HT_7

Note: This list is not definitive. A large number of neurotransmittesrs are not mentioned. Furthermore, in some cases there are subclasses of receptors within the groups described here. For example, there are known to be five types of cholinergic muscarinic receptor, two types of noradrenergic alpha receptor, three types of noradrenergic beta receptor, five types of serotonergic 5-HT_1 receptors, and three types of 5-HT_2 receptors.

key. In the same way as it takes a specific key to turn a lock, a given neurotransmitter will bind only to its own type of receptor. Once this binding occurs, changes in the conformation of the receptor protein will initiate a series of events leading to the opening of certain ion channels, with the subsequent ion flow then contributing to a change in the cell's internal voltage (i.e. an EPSP or an IPSP). Interestingly, there are often several types of receptor for each neurotransmitter (see Table 1.3). For example, there are two different types of receptor for acetylcholine (called **muscarinic** and **nicotinic**); two for noradrenaline (called **alpha** and **beta**); five for dopamine (designated **D-1** to **D-5**), and seven different classes (with various subtypes) for serotonin (designated $\mathbf{5HT_1}$ to $\mathbf{5HT_7}$). In effect, this means that a neurotransmitter can exert a very different cellular response depending on the receptor it interacts with. This subject is of particular interest to neuropharmacologists who attempt to develop drugs with highly specific effects on certain receptors for the improved treatment of various conditions.

Although the highest concentration of receptors are found on dendrites, and to a lesser extent the cell body (soma) of the postsynaptic neuron, receptors can also occur in other places on the neuron where they serve different functions. In particular, some receptors are found in the vicinity of the axonal endings where they modulate neurotransmitter release by **presynaptic inhibition**. In this instance, stimulation of the axonal receptor causes less neurotransmitter to be released by the presynaptic neuron (see Figure 1.13). GABA-A receptors are important in producing presynaptic inhibition, and when stimulated they reduce the inflow of calcium ions into the axon terminal, thereby slowing exocytosis. Other types of receptors found in the presynaptic axon terminals are responsive to neurotransmitters released into the synapse by its own neuron. These are called **autoreceptors** and they act to turn off neurotransmitter release. It is now known that a number of neurotransmitters have presynaptic autoreceptors that serve this function, including noradrenaline, dopamine, serotonin and GABA.

(a)

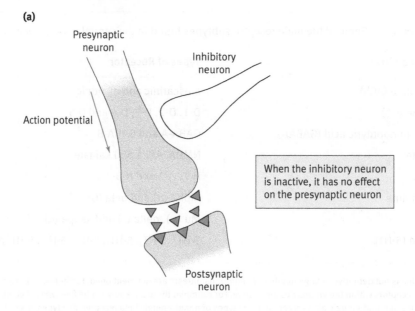

Presynaptic
neuron

Inhibitory
neuron

Action potential

When the inhibitory neuron
is inactive, it has no effect
on the presynaptic neuron

Postsynaptic
neuron

(b)

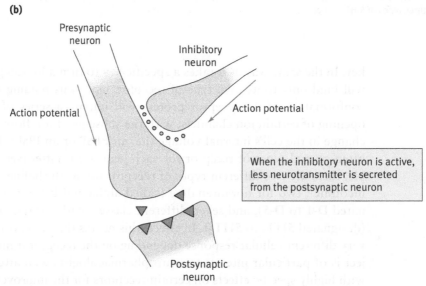

Presynaptic
neuron

Inhibitory
neuron

Action potential

Action potential

When the inhibitory neuron is active,
less neurotransmitter is secreted
from the postsynaptic neuron

Postsynaptic
neuron

Figure 1.13   Presynaptic inhibition

Chemical events in the postsynaptic neuron

Although many types of neurotransmitter receptor exist in the central nervous system, they are all asociated with ion channels in one of two ways: (1) the receptor and ion channel form part of the same molecular unit (these are called **ionotropic receptors**), or (2) the receptor and ion channels are separate entities (these are called **metabotropic receptors**). In the case of iontropic receptors, the binding of the neurotransmitter to its receptor directly brings about a conformational change in the protein molecules making up the ion channel thereby causing it to open for a brief period. However, metabotropic

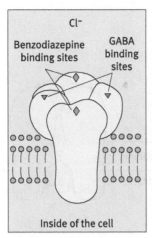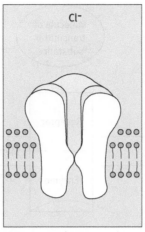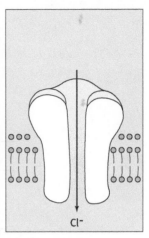

(a) Structure of GABA receptor showing binding sites for GABA. (note also the benzodiazepine binding sites – these will be discussed further in Chapter 6)

(b) Cross-section of the GABA receptor showing the closed chloride channel

(c) Cross-section of the GABA receptor showing the open chloride channel

Figure 1.14   The GABA receptor

receptors are very different. Here, the receptor activates another protein inside the cell called a **G-protein,** which instigates a number of intracellular chemical processes involving various enzymes and **second messengers**. In effect, these chemical events are able to open many ion channels from 'inside' the neuron.

An example of a ionotropic receptor (sometimes called a **ligand-activated channel**) is the GABA-A receptor (Figure 1.14). This consists of a long polypeptide chain which is shaped in such a way that it forms five elongated units, arranged in the shape of a cylinder and which pass through the membrane. These units are tightly held together. But, if GABA binds to a receptor site on the surface of this complex, they briefly change their shape, which creates a channel that allows the influx of negative chloride ions (Cl^-) into the cell. The GABA-A receptor is also notable for having separate binding sites for barbiturates such as pentobarbital, and benzodiazepines such as diazepam (Valium), which increases the chloride current. Thus, both pentobarbital and diazepam enhance inhibitory activity in neurons with GABAergic receptors. Another example of a ligand-activated channel is the cholinergic nicotinic receptor found at the neuromuscular junction. This receptor also contains five units in the shape of a cylinder that pass through the membrane. When opened by the neurotransmitter acetylcholine, an influx of positively charged sodium ions (NA^+) passes into the cell. A distinguishing feature of ligand-gated channels is the rapidity by which they open, and for this reason they are involved in the fastest forms of synaptic transmission which takes only a few milliseconds to occur.

Despite this, the majority of receptors in the brain (including the muscarinic acetylcholine receptor, the GABA-B receptor, and noradrenergic, dopaminergic and sertonergic receptors) are of the metabotropic variety. In this case, the binding of a neurotransmitter at its receptor provides a much slower response by changing the shape of a protein located just inside the cell called a **G-protein**. There are a large number of different G-proteins and they have a wide variety of possible intracellular actions. One of their effects occurs when certain G-proteins increase the activity of an enzyme called **adenylate cyclase** that converts adenosine triphospate (ATP), a substance

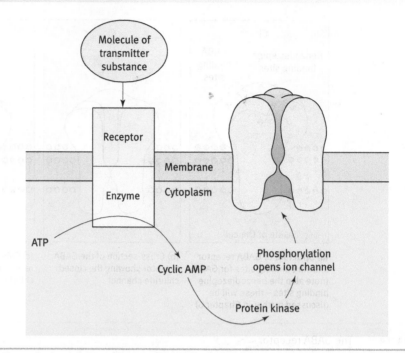

| Figure 1.15 | The main steps in the cAMP second messenger system |

that the cell uses to provide energy, into **cyclic adenosine monophosphate (cAMP)**. This chemical (Figure 1.15) acts as **second messenger** (the first messenger is the neurotransmitter) by diffusing through the cytoplasm of the cell, where it produces a biological response (in this case, the opening of certain ion channels by the process of protein phosphorylation). This mechanism is believed to underlie the action of noradrenergic beta receptors and dopaminergic D-1 receptors. It should be noted, however, that cAMP can affect many different cellular processes depending on the type of cell, and not just those associated with ion channels.

In recent years, a great deal of attention has focussed on another second messenger system which involves G-protein stimulation of an enzyme called **phospholipase C**. This enzyme actually generates two second messengers called diacylglycerol (DAG) and inositol triphosphate (IP_3). DAG is known to be able to activate the enzyme protein kinase C, which can phosphorylate ion channel proteins, whereas IP_3 is able to release stores of calcium ions within the cell which can modify the excitability of the neuron. Certain serotonergic receptors and the histamine H-1 receptor are known to involve these messenger systems. In addition to opening ion channels, certain second messegers are known to enter the cell's nucleus where they influence expression of genes. Such a mechanism may, for example, allow changes in the physical alteration of dendritic synapses that underlie long-term memory.

Second messengers may at first sight appear to be a complex way of going about opening ion channels, but this process actually gives the cell far greater adaptability. For example, activation of ionotropic receptors (such as GABA-A) typically results in the rapid depolarisation of the cell in as little as 2–10 milliseconds. This may be ideally suited for a rapid response such as a muscle contraction or encoding of a pain response, but it shows little variation. In contrast, the slower action of second messenger systems can take from 20 milliseconds to over 10 seconds, and involve many different types of ion channel. However, this may allow the cell to alter its response in many diffferent ways. For example, second messengers may be involved in changing the sensitivity of receptors to neurotransmission, or the adaptability of the neuron to the long-term administration of certain drugs. In addition, such processes are likely to be involved in learning and neural plasticity.

Glial cells

It may come as a surprise to find that neurons are not the most common type of cell in the brain. In fact, this accolade goes to the **glial cells** which are around ten times more numerous than neurons, although they are about one-tenth of their size, which means that they take up roughly the same volume. The first person to discover glial cells in the brain was the German pathologist Rudolf Virchow in 1846 who called them 'nevroglie' (nerve glue) because they appeared to stick the neurons together. We now know that the brain and spinal cord contain several types of glial cell with a wide range of functions that are vital to neural functioning.

The largest and most abundant type of glia cell in the brain, accounting for nearly half of all glial tissue volume, is the **astrocyte**. These are so called because of their star shape with many spindly extensions. Astrocytes provide structural support with their interweaving extensions acting as scaffolding to anchor neurons in place (this is especially helpful to make sure they get a regular blood supply). But, astrocytes also have many other vital functions. For example, they control the ionic composition of the extracellular fluid, help break down neurotransmitters in the synaptic cleft (some contain monoamine oxidase, for instance) and release growth factors, which are chemicals involved in the growth and repair of nerve cells. They are also involved in transporting nutrients into neurons and removing their waste products. Further, astrocytes can increase the brain's activity by dilating blood vessels thus enabling greater amounts of oxygen and glucose to reach the neurons. They also contribute to the healing of brain tissue by forming scar material – although they can give rise to tumours (gliomas) if they proliferate abnormally. There is even evidence that they may be able to release chemicals that act as neurotransmitters.

Another function of astrocytes is to provide a covering to the blood vessels of the brain which forms the so-called **blood–brain barrier**. In the body, capillaries are 'leaky' because the endothelial cells that make up their walls contain gaps which allow a wide range of substances into and out of the blood. However, in the brain, the end feet of the astrocytic extensions cling to the outer surface of capillaries which help push the endothelial cells together. Thus, the walls of the capillaries in the brain are tightly compacted and their outer surface covered by astrocyte extensions. Although this tight binding allows small molecules such as oxygen and carbon dioxide into the brain, along with lipid- or fat-soluble substances (these include nicotine, heroin and alcohol), it bars the entry of most larger molecules and toxins. This feature has to be taken into consideration when developing drugs to treat brain disorders. For example, the neurotransmitter dopamine which would be expected to have a beneficial effect in treating Parkinson's disease does not cross the blood–brain barrier. Thus, doctors prescribe L-dopa which enters into the brain where it is converted into dopamine.

Another type of glial cell is the **oligodendrocyte** which is much smaller than the astrocyte and has fewer extensions (the Greek *oligos* means 'few'). This type of glial cell has a very specific function: it provides the myelin that covers the axons of most nerve fibres in the brain and spinal cord. Myelination occurs because extensions of the oligodendrocytes wrap themselves around the axon, thereby producing an insulating cover. As we saw earlier, this allows the axon to propagate electrical impulses much more efficiently along its length. An autoimmune disorder that causes demyelination by attacking and destroying oligodendrocytes, resulting in the impaired flow of neural transmission throughout the central nervous system, is **multiple sclerosis**. In the peripheral nervous system, however, myelin is produced by the **Schwann cell**, which is not attacked by the immune system.

A third type of glial cell are the **microglial**, which, as the name suggests, are very small. Microglial make up about 15 per cent of all glial cells and are found scattered throughout the brain where they provide its main immune defence. In response to injury or infection, microglial multiply and migrate in large numbers to the sites of injury where they engulf invading micro-organisms or infected neurons. They also help in the removal of debris from injured or dead cells. A fourth type of glial cells is **ependymal cells**, which line the ventricles and the central canal of the spine.

What happened to Einstein's brain?

Albert Einstein was one of the greatest intellectual figures of the twentieth century. In one year alone (1905), at the age of 26, while working in the Swiss Patent Office in Bern, he published five papers that were to profoundly alter the development of physics and change for ever the way we understand the universe. Einstein died in 1955 at the age of 76 from a ruptured aorta, and within seven hours of his death, his brain had been perfused with a 10 per cent formalin solution by injection into the internal carotid artery (to enable its fixation) and removed by pathologist Thomas Harvey. After being stored in formalin for several months, the brain was carefully photographed and measurements were taken of its cerebral structures. The cerebral hemispheres were then cut into around 240 blocks of about 10 cm³, embedded in celloidin (similar to wax) and stored in alcohol. However, close examination of the brain by Harvey revealed nothing unusual about its shape or structure.

Einstein's brain was soon forgotten and stored in two large jars that remained in Dr Harvey's office for the next twenty years or so. In 1978, the brain was 'rediscovered' by journalist Steven Levy who brought it to the attention of the media. The discovery was of interest to Marian Diamond and her colleagues at the University of California. Back in the 1960s, Diamond had shown that rats living in enriched environments had more glial cells per neuron in their cerebral cortices than those raised in impoverished environments. This finding indicated that active neurons required greater metabolic assistance from the supporting glial cells. Later work by Diamond also showed that the prefrontal cortex of humans has more glial cells per neuron compared with the parietal lobe – a finding that implied that the prefrontal area was more active and highly evolved in humans than were other brain regions. But what about Einstein's brain? When Diamond examined it, she actually found significantly more glial cells in the left parietal cortex than in the frontal regions (Diamond *et al.* 1985).

Further examination of Einstein's brain by Sandra Witelson revealed other unique features. Most striking was an absence of a region called the parietal operculum – a ridge (or gyrus) in the parietal cortex located between the Sylvian fissure and the postcentral sulcus (Figure 1.16). Consequently, the Sylvian fissure and postcentral gyrus were partially joined in Einstein's brain – a feature that Witelson was unable to find in over 90 control brains. This resulted in the areas on either side of these sulci becoming enlarged – presumably to compensate for the operculum's loss. In fact, Witelson found that the

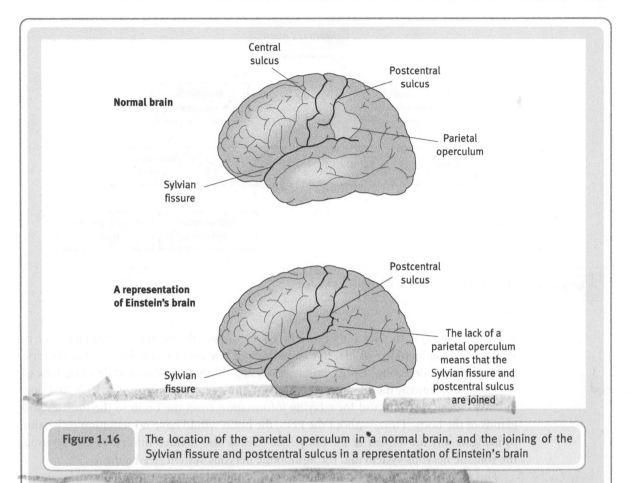

Normal brain

Central
sulcus

Postcentral
sulcus

Parietal
operculum

Sylvian
fissure

A representation
of Einstein's brain

Postcentral
sulcus

The lack of a
parietal operculum
means that the
Sylvian fissure and
postcentral sulcus
are joined

Sylvian
fissure

Figure 1.16 The location of the parietal operculum in a normal brain, and the joining of the Sylvian fissure and postcentral sulcus in a representation of Einstein's brain

parietal lobes were 1 cm wider (an increase in size of 15 per cent) in Einstein's brain compared with the brains of controls, and this enlargement was symmetrical in both right and left hemispheres. Because most people have a relatively large right parietal cortex compared with the left, this meant that Einstein's left parietal lobe was significantly larger than normal (Witelson *et al.* 1999).

One can only speculate the extent to which Einstein's unique brain anatomy contributed to his ideas and, in particular, to the theory of relativity. However, the parietal lobes are known to be involved in visuospatial cognition (particularly the generation and manipulation of three-dimensional spatial images), mathematical ability and visualisation of movement – and these were highly characteristic of Einstein's thought. Indeed, Einstein once said that written and spoken words did not play a major role in his thinking; rather the essential features were 'a combinatory play of certain signs and more or less clear images' (Einstein 1954). Interestingly, enlarged parietal cortices have also been reported for other famous thinkers, including the mathematician Gauss and the physicist Siljestrom.

Introduction to the structure of the nervous system

The complete network of all nerve cells in the human body is divided into two systems: the **central nervous system (CNS)** and the **peripheral nervous system (PNS)**. The CNS is composed of the brain and spinal cord and provides the command and integrating centre

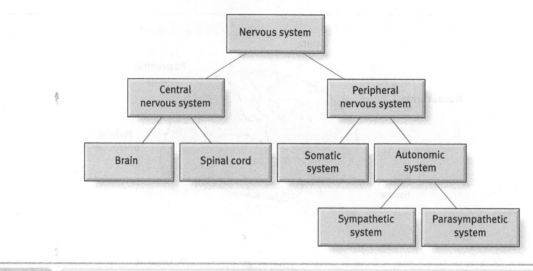

Figure 1.17　Overall organisation of the nervous system

of the nervous system. Not only does the CNS contain all the major command centres vital for the maintenance of life, but its higher regions are crucially involved in decision making (that is, detecting sensory events, analysing this information and deciding how to respond). In contrast, the PNS is responsible for conveying input from the body and outside world to the brain, and for relaying information from the brain to the muscles and glands of the body. Thus, without the PNS, the brain would have no sensation or be able to instigate any movement of the body. The PNS is also divided into two main systems: the **somatic nervous system** and the **autonomic nervous system** (see Figure 1.17).

The somatic nervous system consists of peripheral nerve fibres that send sensory information to the spinal cord and brain, and motor nerve fibres that project to the skeletal muscles of the body. The sensory input conveyed by the somatic system includes information from the skin, muscles, bones and joints (for example, touch, pressure, temperature, pain), along with that from the main senses (for example, vision, audition, olfaction and gustation). In addition, the somatic nervous system is composed of motor nerve fibres that move the bones of the skeleton by its action on skeletal muscles. This is sometimes referred to as the voluntary nervous system as it allows us to purposefully produce movement and behaviour. The cell bodies of the somatic fibres controlling movement are mainly located in the spinal cord, although some are found in the brain that reach the periphery by the cranial nerves. They all secrete the neurotransmitter acetylcholine. We shall discuss the role of this system in more detail when we examine motor behaviour in Chapter 4.

The autonomic nervous system is the part of the peripheral nervous system that controls the activity of involuntary muscle that regulates bodily functions essential for life such as breathing, heart rate, blood pressure, kidney function, and digestion. To provide this function, the autonomic nervous system is composed of two divisions: the **sympathetic nervous system (SNS)** and the **parasympathetic nervous system** (PNS). In general, the sympathetic and parasympathetic divisions act in opposition to each other – although it is more accurate to describe them as complementing each other rather than as being antagonistic. The SNS increases the activity of autonomic structures in the body to prepare it for physical exertion, stressful anticipation or emergencies. Thus, the SNS will increase heart rate, blood pressure and respiration while inhibiting digestion and diverting blood away from the skin to the skeletal muscles (this is why the skin may go white after a sudden fright). It will also stimulate the adrenal glands to secrete adrenaline and noradrenaline. This pattern of physiological activity is sometimes called the **fight or flight response.**

In contrast, the PNS reverses, or normalises, the effects of sympathetic activity and acts to conserve energy or maintain resting body function. Thus, the parasympathetic division generally responds with actions that do not require immediate reactions. For example, it is involved in digestion and body states that occur during sleep. The one part of the body that shows an exception to the relaxation rule is the penis whose 'excitation' (i.e. erections) are under the control of the PNS and not the SNS.

The output fibres of the sympathetic nervous system are more complex than the corresponding ones of the somatic nervous system. This is because they consist of a chain of two motor neurons called **preganglionic nerve fibres** and **postganglionic nerve fibres.** The preganglionic fibres have their cell bodies located in the brain or spinal cord, and their axons extend to cell bodies forming a bundle of fibres (for example, a ganglion) consisting of postganglionic fibres outside the CNS. The neurotransmitter used at this junction is acetylcholine. In turn, the postganglionic fibres project to the effect organs where they secrete the neurotransmitter **noradrenaline.** (The term 'postganglionic' fibres are somewhat misnamed as their cell bodies are located in the ganglion and not beyond it.) The motor neurons of the parasympathetic division are more straightforward as they contain only preganglionic nerve fibres that release acetylcholine which normally inhibits the activity of their effector organs. The somatic and autonomic nervous systems are compared in Figure 1.18.

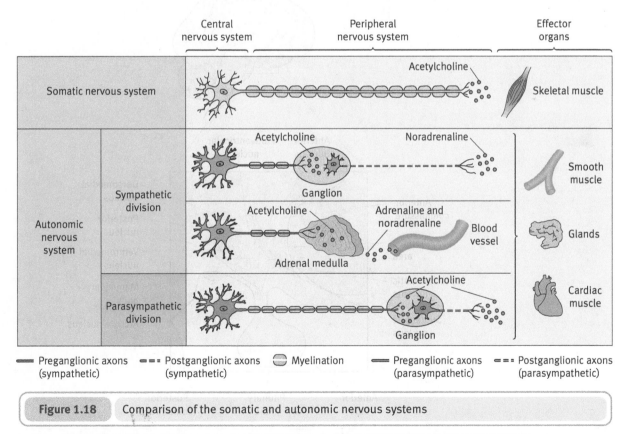

Figure 1.18   Comparison of the somatic and autonomic nervous systems

Source: Adopted from E.N. Marieb, *Human Anatomy and Physiology*, p. 449. Copyright © 1989 by Benjamin Cummings

The endocrine system

The endocrine system consists of a number of ductless glands scattered throughout the body that secrete chemicals into the bloodstream called **hormones** (from the Greek *hormon* meaning 'to excite'). More than fifty different hormones may be circulating through the body at any one time, and these are secreted from a number of organs, including the thyroid, thymus, adrenal glands and the gonads, which include the testes and ovaries. All of these organs are under the chemical control of a pea-sized gland located on the underside of the brain called the **pituitary gland** (Figure 1.19). Although it weighs only about 0.5 g, the pituitary is often regarded as the master gland of the body as it secretes at least nine different hormones that have far-reaching effects on a wide range of bodily activities. The pituitary gland is itself under the control of the **hypothalamus** to which it is attached by a thin stalk of tissue. In fact, the pituitary consists of two glands: the **anterior pituitary** (or adenohypophysis), which is connected to the hypothalamus via a complex series of blood vessels, and the **posterior pituitary** (neurohypophysis), which receives neural connections from the hypothalamus.

The release of hormones from the anterior pituitary is stimulated, or inhibited, by the secretion of releasing factors from the **hypothalamus,** such as adrenocorticotropin-releasing factor (CRF) and growth hormone releasing factor (GHRF). In response to releasing factors, the glandular cells of the anterior pituitary secrete a number of **tropic**

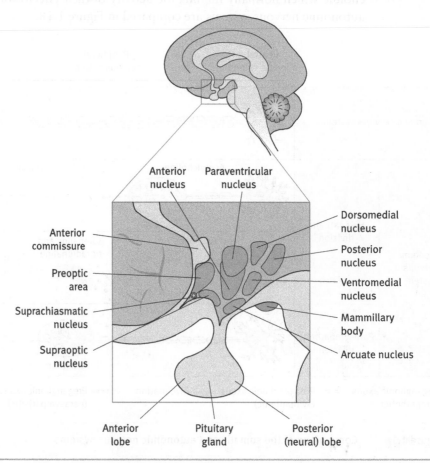

Figure 1.19   The hypothalamus and pituitary gland

hormones into the bloodstream (a tropic hormone is one which stimulates other endocrine glands to release their hormones). These include: **adrenocorticotropic hormone (ACTH)** which acts on the adrenal glands; **thyroid-stimulating hormone** which affects the thyroid gland; **prolactin** which acts on the mammary glands; and **follicle-stimulating hormone** and **luteinising hormone** which work on the ovaries and testes. Another substance secreted by the anterior pituitary is **growth hormone** which acts on most tisures throughout the body. In contrast, the posterior pituitary gland stores and releases just two hormones: **antidiuretic hormone** (or vasopressin) involved in conserving body water, and **oxytocin** (involved in pregnancy).

The control of hormonal release by the pituitary gland works predominantly on the basis of **negative feedback**. That is, when blood levels of a given hormone (say cortisol) begin to rise, the pituitary gland will detect this change and act to decrease the output of its controlling tropic hormone (ACTH). In practice things are generally more complex than this as the hypothalamus (and in some instances other brain regions) will also receive feedback about hormone levels and their effects on the body. Thus, the hypothalamus will also inhibit secretion of its releasing factors thereby helping to regulate the pituitary gland's response to increasing hormone levels. Indeed, the combination of the hypothalamus and the pituitary gland working together means that the control exerted over hormone secretion is complex and finely tuned.

The endocrine and nervous systems provide an important means of communication in the body, and both work together to provide integrated functioning in many types of physiological activity. In general, the nervous system sends messages that require rapid and immediate action, whereas the endocrine system is involved in slower responses. Indeed, certain hormones may take minutes or even hours to reach their target, athough they have a much longer duration of action. Despite this, hormones are very potent regulators of the body's activity and are effective in minute concentrations. Moreover, a slight change in a hormone's concentration can have a significant impact on behavioural functioning. Table 1.4 summarises the main hormone systems in humans.

Table 1.4	Summary of the main hormone systems in the human body	
Endocrine Gland	**Hormone(s)**	**Main Actions**
Adrenal cortex	Glucocorticoids (including cortisol and cortisone)	Adapts the body to long-term stress
Adrenal medulla	Adrenaline (Epinephrine)	Increases sympathetic arousal and stimulates the breakdown of glycogen
Ovaries	Oestrogen and progesterone	Female sexual development and control of the menstrual cycle
Pancreas gland	Insulin and glucagon	Involved in regulation of blood sugar
Pineal gland	Melatonin	Control of circadian rhythms
Pituitary gland (anterior part)	Vasopressin and oxytocin	Control of water balance and female sexual behaviour
Pituitary gland (posterior part)	Master control of other endocrine glands. Also produces growth hormone and prolactin	Wide range of functions. Growth and protein synthesis. Milk production
Testes	Testosterone	Male sexual development and behaviour
Thyroid gland	Thyroxine and triiodothyronine	Increases metabolic rate

Introduction to the central nervous system

The central nervous system (CNS), consisting of brain and spinal cord, is the integrative control centre of the body. In particular, the brain exerts executive control over the peripheral nervous system and endocrine glands, and is the organ of movement, emotion, thought and consciousness. An important prerequisite for understanding how the brain produces behaviour is having a good understanding of its anatomy. This includes knowing where the main brain regions are sited and the ways in which they are connected. This can be a daunting challenge for students. One problem is the terminology. Many Greek and Latin terms are used to describe parts of the CNS (although some areas are named after people such as Broca and Wernicke) and unfamiliar terms can initially be difficult to remember. An added problem lies in trying to visualise the shape of brain structures and their pathways. But, perhaps most disconcerting is that brain structures can rarely be tied down to single behavioural functions. The brain is simply too complex. Trying to pin functions to given brain areas will provide a challenge for most students of psychobiology.

To make matters more complex, because the CNS is a three-dimensional structure, anatomists often use technical terms to help them refer to the exact direction or location of a certain region. This is not too dissimilar to an explorer who uses compass bearings to find his or her way around the environment. One simple way to remember the main anatomical terms used to convey direction in the brain is to imagine a fish. Its front end, or head, is **anterior** (sometimes called **rostral**), and its tail-fin is **posterior** (sometimes called **caudal**). The fish also has a **dorsal** fin on its upper surface – and one on its underside called the **ventral** fin. In addition, the fish has **lateral** fins on its sides – while the term **medial** would be used to describe parts of the body towards the midline. As one becomes more familiar with the brain, the student will see that many of its regions are described using the same terminology. Two other terms that are useful to know, particularly in regards to neural pathways, are **ipsilateral** (referring to structures on the same side of the body), and **contralateral** (referring to structures on the opposite side of the body).

If we take the emergence of primates as the starting point, then the evolution of the human brain has taken place over a period of at least 70 million years. This is a long time, especially as human civilisation has existed only for around 3,000 years. The gradual process of evolution has resulted in new structures emerging and taking over the roles of older ones. However, this does not mean that the older regions of the brain have become redundant. Rather, they remain incorporated into the neural circuits of the brain and still have vital roles to play. In short, the brain always functions as a collective entity, although it also exhibits a **hierarchy of function** where newer structures are more likely to be involved in complex behaviours. Another feature of evolutionary development is **cephalisation**, that is, the massive increase in size of the brain in relation to the body. This trend is most noticeable in the cerebral cortex, which has become so large and complex in humans that it has developed ridges and fissures in order to increase its surface area. In fact, the cerebral cortex is not dissimilar to a screwed-up sheet of newspaper, and it is this adaption that gives the external surface of the forebrain its distinctive wrinkly appearance.

To complete this chapter we will describe the various anatomical structures and pathways of the spinal cord and brain. Although it is important to become familiar with this anatomy, much of it will be covered again in the remaining chapters of this book when we discuss its involvement in behaviour and mental functioning.

The spinal cord

The spinal cord is about the size of a large pencil that forms a cylinder of nervous tissue that runs down the back, and is enclosed and protected in a bony column of thirty-one flexible segments (vertebrae). From top to bottom, these segments comprise eight cervical vertebrae, twelve thoracic, five lumbar, five saccral and one coccygeal. The spinal cord serves many functions, but by far its most important is to distribute motor neurons to the their targets (for examples, muscles and glands), and to convey internal and external sensory information to the brain. Moreover, the nervous tissue of the spinal cord is also capable of producing certain types of behaviour by itself, including simple reflexes such as the knee jerk response, or more complex patterns of automated rhythmical activity, including the postural components of walking.

The most striking visual feature of the spinal cord is its **grey matter** (comprising cell bodies) and **white matter** (comprising myelinated axons). Forming a butterfly shape in the centre of the spinal cord is the grey matter, and this is packed tightly with the cell bodies of various neurons. These include the motor neurons that send their fibres out to innervate the muscles of the body, and a large number of **interneurons** that are confined to the grey matter. Interneurons are important because they are located in pathways between sensory fibres going into the spinal cord, and motor fibres going out, which allow complex reflexes to take place. Furthermore, interneurons allow communication to take place between different segments or regions of the spinal cord. In contrast, the white matter which surrounds the grey material is composed mainly of long myelinated axons that form the ascending and descending pathways of the spinal cord. More precisley, the ascending pathways arise from cell bodies that receive sensory input in the grey matter, and descending axons derive from the brain and pass into the grey matter where they form synapses with motor neurons. Two important tracts here are the **posterior columns** which conveys touch and pressure information to the thalamus, and the **corticospinal tract** which passes information all the way from the motor regions of the cerebral cortex.

Axons enter or leave the grey matter of spinal cord in spaces between the vertebrae, via **spinal nerves** which are ganglia containing large numbers of nerve fibres. There are 31 pairs of spinal nerves along the entire length of the spinal cord, and each one serves either the right or left side of the body. Closer examination of these nerves shows that they comprise two branches as they enter or leave the spinal cord. The **dorsal root** of each spinal nerve provides the pathway that relays sensory information into the spinal cord (the cell bodies of these neurons are actualy located in the root itself), whereas the **ventral root** provides the motor pathway that controls the muscles of the body. The spinal cord also contains cerebrospinal fluid which is connected with the brain's ventricles. Samples of this spinal fluid can be a very useful diagnostic tool in determining various brain disorders.

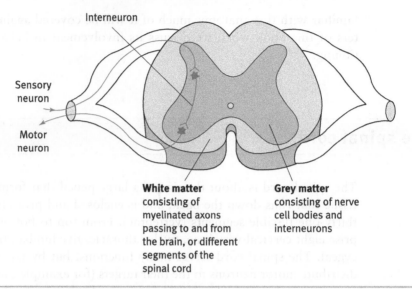

Interneuron

Sensory
neuron

Motor
neuron

White matter
consisting of
myelinated axons
passing to and from
the brain, or different
segments of the
spinal cord

Grey matter
consisting of nerve
cell bodies and
interneurons

Figure 1.20   Cross-section of spinal cord

The brainstem

As the spinal cord enters the brain it enlarges and forms the **brainstem** (Figure 1.21; see also Plate 1.1). The oldest part of the brainstem is the **medulla oblongata** ('long marrow') and this directly controls many functions essential for life, including breathing, heart rate, salivation and vomiting. It also contains a profusion of ascending and descending nerve pathways that connect the spinal cord with the rest of the brain. If the brain is cut above the medulla, basic heart rate and breathing can be maintained, but damage to the medulla itself is inevitably fatal. The next region is the **pons** (from the

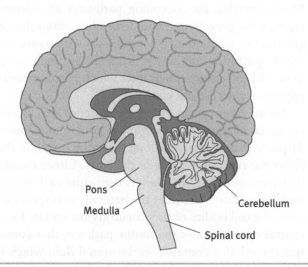

Pons

Cerebellum

Medulla

Spinal cord

Figure 1.21   The main brainstem regions of the human brain

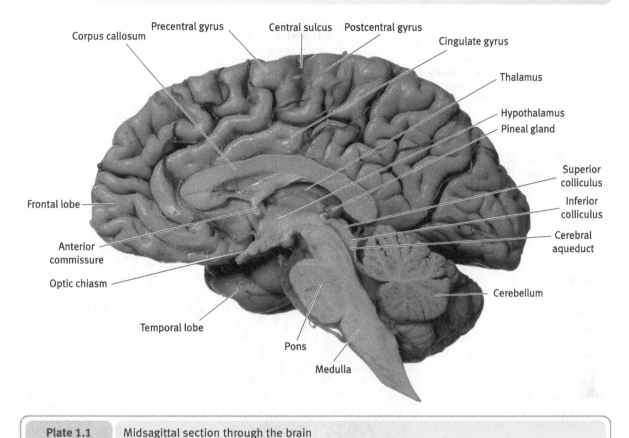

| Plate 1.1 | Midsagittal section through the brain |

Source: F. Toates (2001) *Biological Psychology*, p. 111, Prentice Hall; photographer, R.T. Hutchings

Latin for 'bridge') which appears as a significant enlargement of the medulla. This area also contains many nuclei (sometimes called the **pontine nuclei**) although its increased size is largely due to the many ascending and descending fibre tracts that cross from one side of the brain to the other at this point, including the pyramidal tracts. Two important structures often regarded as pontine nuclei (although they also extend into the midbrain) are the **locus coeruleus** and **dorsal raphe**. These are, respectively, the origin of noradrenergic- and serotonergic-containing fibres in the forebrain.

The pons also includes an area known as the tegmentum, which includes many motor nuclei and secondary sensory cell groups, as well as the beginning of the **reticular formation,** a tubular net-like mass of grey tissue which is involved in arousal. The pons further serves as the main junction between the **cerebellum** ('little brain') and the rest of the brain. The cerebellum, which is discussed more fully in Chapter 4, is located on the posterior part of the brainstem and has a very distinctive wrinkled appearance consisting of small folds called **folia**. It is primarily involved in the co-ordination of muscular activity required for smooth automated movement.

The brainstem (medulla and pons) is also the most important part of the brain, giving rise to the **cranial nerves**, which were first discovered by Galen in the first century AD. There are twelve pairs of cranial nerves directly connecting the brain with bodily structures, and eight of these originate or terminate in the brainstem: four from the medulla (hypoglossal, spinal accessory, vagus and glossopharyngeal), and four from the pons (auditory, facial, abducens and trigeminal) (see Figure 1.22). Cranial nerves are

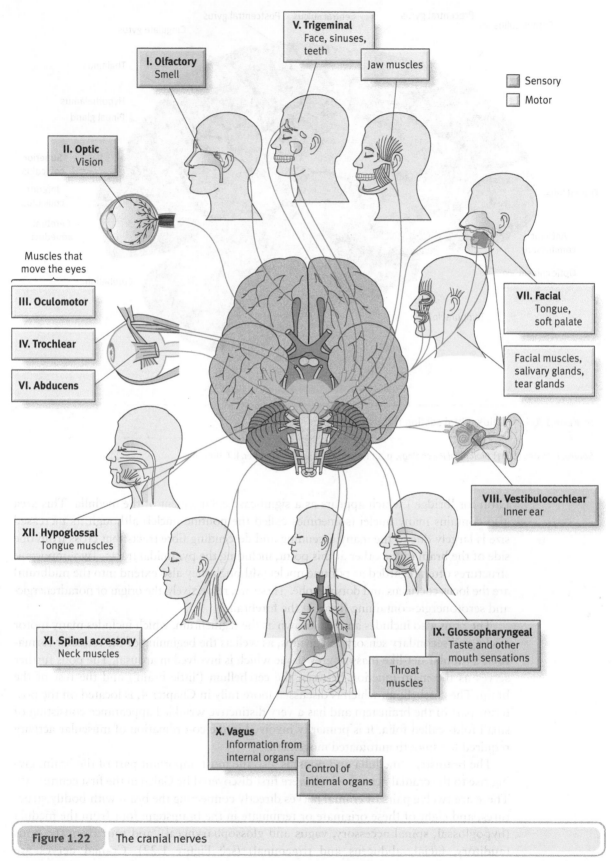

I. Olfactory
Smell

II. Optic
Vision

V. Trigeminal
Face, sinuses, teeth

Jaw muscles

Sensory

Motor

Muscles that move the eyes

III. Oculomotor

IV. Trochlear

VI. Abducens

VII. Facial
Tongue, soft palate

Facial muscles, salivary glands, tear glands

VIII. Vestibulocochlear
Inner ear

XII. Hypoglossal
Tongue muscles

XI. Spinal accessory
Neck muscles

IX. Glossopharyngeal
Taste and other mouth sensations

Throat muscles

X. Vagus
Information from internal organs

Control of internal organs

Figure 1.22   The cranial nerves

complex to understand as they can be sensory, motor or mixed (relaying both sensory and motor input), and may convey both sympathetic and parasympathetic fibres of the autonomic nervous system. In general, the cranial nerves of the brainstem are concerned with the senses of taste, hearing and balance, along with specialised motor activities, including chewing, swallowing, breathing, eye movements and facial expression. The vagus nerve (derived from the Latin *vagus* meaning 'wandering') which has the most extensive distribution of any cranial nerve in the body) is somewhat different as it projects fibres to a variety of organs in the abdomen and thorax, including heart, lungs and digestive system. A consideration of the cranial nerves provide an interesting insight into the functions of the brainstem.

The midbrain

The midbrain (sometmes called the mesencephalon) is the name given to the region that forms the top part of the brainstem (Figure 1.23). It is generally divided into into two areas: the **tegmentum** which is continuous with the pontine regions below it, and the **tectum** (meaning 'roof') which sits above it. The tegmentum contains several nuclei with important motor functions linked to basal ganglia function, including the **red nucleus** and **substantia nigra**. In addition, there are more diffuse areas of the tegmentum, including the **periaqueductal grey area** situated around the cerebral aqueduct (the passage connecting the third and fourth ventricles), and the **ventral tegmental area** which acts as a neural crossroads – receiving descending input from the medial forebrain bundle, and returning information back to the forebrain (most notably striatum, limbic system and frontal cortex) via its dopaminergic pathways.

In lower animals such as fish and amphibians the tectum is actually the most recently evolved part of the brain, and it contains two pairs of nuclei called colliculi (derived from the Latin meaning 'small hills'), which protrude from its upper surface.

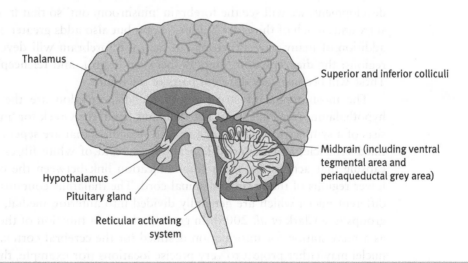

Thalamus

Superior and inferior colliculi

Midbrain (including ventral tegmental area and periaqueductal grey area)

Hypothalamus

Pituitary gland

Reticular activating system

Figure 1.23   Midbrain (mesencephalon) structures of the human CNS (including the hypothalamus and the thalamus of the diencephalon)

These are the **superior colliculi** which are involved in visual processing and reflexes such as blinking and orientation (see Chapter 2), and **inferior colliculi** that serves a similar function for auditory processing (Chapter 3). This part of the brain also gives rise to two cranial nerves: the oculomotor controlling the muscles of the eyeball, and the trochlear involved in eye movement.

Also coursing through the centre of the brainstem and into the midbrain is the **reticular activating system (RAS)**. This contains the ascending projections of the reticular formation, along with other areas of the brainstem, which passes to many areas of the forebrain, including the thalamus. The RAS serves many essential functions, including the various stages of wakefulness and sleep. It also controls the level of electrical activity that governs states of arousal in the cerebral cortex (via its effect on the thalamus) which can be measured by using an electroencephalograph (EEG). The fibres making up the RAS are particularly complex and use a number of neurotransmitters, including noradrenaline, serotonin and acetylcholine.

The forebrain

Thalamus and hypothalamus

Up to this point, the brain can be likened to a neural tube that has evolved and enlarged from the spinal cord. In fact, this is basically what happens during embryonic development. At first, the brain and spinal cord of every vertebrate animal appears as a tube which is only one cell thick. As it develops it begins to show three bulbous swellings called the **primary brain vesicles**. These can actually be observed in the human embryo by the fifth week of gestation. From bottom to top these are called the hindbrain (technically called the rhombencephalon) which becomes the brainstem; the mesencephalon which becomes the midbrain, and the forebrain. If we observe further development, we will see the forebrain 'mushroom out' so that it not only covers and surrounds much of the older 'tubular' brain but also adds greater complexity with the addition of many new structures. In fact, the forebrain will develop into two main regions: the **diencephalon** (literally 'between-brain'), and **telencephalon** ('endbrain'). These will become very different parts of the brain.

The most important structures of the diencephalon are the **thalamus** and the **hypothalamus** (see Plate 1.2). The thalamus (from the Greek for 'inner chamber') consists of a symmetrical pair of egg-shaped structures that are seperated medially by the third ventricle, and bounded laterally by a band of white fibres called the **internal capsule** that acts as the main communication link between the cerebral cortex and lower regions of the brain and spinal cord. The thalamus contains a large number of different nuclei which are generally divided into anterior, medial, lateral and ventral groups (see Clark *et al.* 2005). In general, the main function of the thalamus is to act as a relay station for information destined for the cerebral cortex. In this respect, its nuclei may either project to very precise locations (for example, the **lateral geniculate bodies** which project to the visual cortex), or have very diffuse ones that go to widespread areas of the cerebral cortex (for example, the intralaminar nuclei). The former

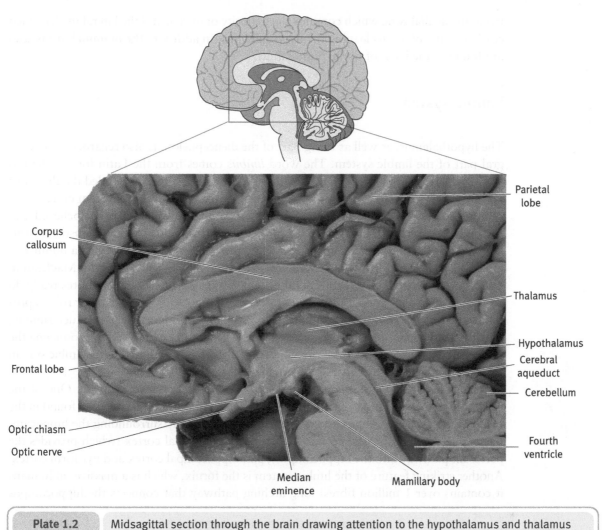

Corpus
callosum

Parietal
lobe

Frontal lobe

Thalamus

Hypothalamus

Cerebral
aqueduct

Cerebellum

Optic chiasm

Optic nerve

Fourth
ventricle

Median
eminence

Mamillary body

Plate 1.2   Midsagittal section through the brain drawing attention to the hypothalamus and thalamus

Source: F. Toates (2001) *Biological Psychology*, p. 108, Prentice Hall; photographer, R.T. Hutchings

are normally associated with a single sensory modality or motor system, whereas the latter appear to be involved in arousal.

Located just underneath the thalamus is a small structure making up only 0.15 per cent of the human brain called the hypothalamus (*hypo* meaning 'below') (see Plate 1.2). Despite its small size (it is roughly the size of a small grape), it plays a critical role in the maintanance of life as it controls both the autonomic and endocrine systems. Indeed, destruction of the hypothalamus will produce death in humans as in other animals (Nauta and Feirtag 1986). One of the most important functions of the hypothalamus is the coordination of **homeostasis**, that is, the ability of the body to maintain a constant internal environment despite continual exposure to various changes and external fluctuations. In addition, the hypothalamus has been described as the interface between our conscious brain, with its emotions and feeling, and the autonomic 'vegetative' processes of the body (Stein and Stoodley 2006). Anatomically, the hypothalamus is very complex, with many different groups of nuclei, although it can be simplified by viewing it as having three zones (Clark *et al.* 2005). These are the **preoptic area** at the front, the **medial zone** which contains the majority of nuclei, and the **lateral nuclei** which contain many of axons leaving the hypothalamus. In addition, the **mammallary bodies** are found at the back of the hypothalamus.

Limbic system

The hypothalamus, as well as being part of the diencephelon, is also regarded as an integral part of the **limbic system**. The word *limbus* comes from the Latin for 'border'; in 1878 Paul Broca applied the name to an area of the brain that surrounded the thalamus and striatum (see below) and appeared to separate the older brainstem from more recent cerebral cortex. Because of its relatively large size in lower animals, Broca believed that the limbic lobe had a mainly olfactory function. But this does a great injustice to this large part of the brain. Later, it was shown that this brain region contained a number of interconnected structures which were designated the limbic system by Paul MacLean in 1952. Although there is still considerable debate over whether these structures really do constitute a 'system', there is little doubt that this brain region plays a major role in producing drives, motivation and emotions. It also plays an important part in determining human behaviour – not least because it has been shown to be involved in producung the feelings of pleasure, anxiety and fear. Consequently, it has been said that the limbic system tends to control us, rather than we it (Stein and Stoodley 2006).

The anatomy of the limbic system is complex and difficult to visualise. One of the most conspicous structures of the limbic system is the **hippocampus**, which is found in the medial aspects of the temporal lobe (see Figure 1.24). Partly surrounding the hippocampus is phylogenetically 'old' cortex, including the entorhinal cortex (which provides the **perforant pathway** into the hippocampus), parahippocampal cortex and pyriform cortex. Another striking feature of the limbic system is the **fornix**, which is a massive (in humans it contains over 1 million fibres) long arching pathway that connects the hippocampus

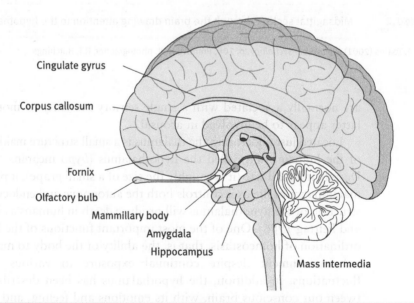

Cingulate gyrus

Corpus callosum

Fornix

Olfactory bulb

Mammillary body

Amygdala

Hippocampus

Mass intermedia

| Figure 1.24 | Location of the limbic system |

with the **mammillary bodies** and hypothalamus. In turn, pathways are known to ascend from this part of the diencephalon via the anterior thalamus to the **cingulate cortex,** which wraps itself around the upper part of the corpus callosum, and contains a large bundle of fibres called the **cingulum,** which projects back to the hippocampus. Another important structure found in the limbic system is the **amygdala,** which lies anterior to the hippocampus. This structure also has two descending pathways to the hypothalamus (the ventral amydalofugal pathway and stria terminalis) and a pathway that projects to the prefrontal cortex via the mediodorsal nuclei of the thalamus.

Basal ganglia

If we move sideways from the thalamus we come to a set of structures that comprise the **basal ganglia** (literally meaning 'basal nuclei') (see Figure 1.25). The three main structures of the basal ganglia are the **caudate nucleus** (which also has a tail that curls over the top of the thalamus); the **putamen** which is separated from the caudate by the fibres of the internal capsule; and the **globus pallidus** (pale globe) which lies medial to the putamen. The caudate nucleus and putamen are also referred to as the **corpus striatum** – a term invented by Thomas Willis in 1664 who noted that this structure had a very distinct striated appearance of white and grey bands. Two other structures generally regarded as important components of the basal ganglia are the **substantia nigra** which innervates the corpus striatum with dopaminergic neurons, and the **subthalamic nucleus** which has reciprocal connections with the globus pallidus.

Traditionally, the basal ganglia have been considered as important structures of the **extrapyramidal motor system** (that is, the motor system of the brain whose output fibres do not cross in the pyramidal regions of the medulla). Indeed, one can discern some of the most important functions of the basal ganglia by examining the main symptoms of Parkinson's disease (rigidity, tremor and 'slow' movement) that are known to result from degeneration of the substantia nigra. Thus, the basal ganglia

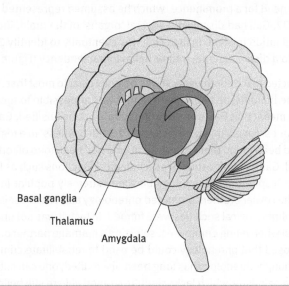

Basal ganglia

Thalamus

Amygdala

| **Figure 1.25** | Location of the basal ganglia |

would appear to be involved in the co-ordination of motor activity, allowing it be automated (i.e. undertaken without 'thinking'), smooth and fluent. Although the substantia nigra provides a significant projection to the corpus striatum, the largest projection derives from motor areas of the cerebral cortex which innervate the corpus striatum with fibres using the neurotransmitter gluatmate. In turn, the output fibres of both caudate and putamen project to, or pass through, the globus pallidus. From here, a major pathway travels back to the cerebral cortex via the **ventral nuclei of the thalamus,** with a smaller projection also going to the substantia nigra.

To make matters more complex the caudate nucleus, putamen and globus palidus also have ventromedial extensions which extend deeper into the brain. In doing this, they appear to take on a more important role in emotional functions. In fact, the ventral striatum is sometimes called the **limbic striatum** for this reason. Other structures associated with the ventral striatum include the **nucleus accumbens, olfactory tubercle, substantia innominata** and **basal nucleus of Meynert** (which provides the forebrain with most of its cholinergic fibres). Much more needs to be learned about this mysterious part of the brain.

The rise and fall of phrenology

One of the most enduring questions in biopsychology is the extent to which functions of the brain, such as language, thought and movement, can be localised to specific areas of the brain. A famous proponent of the localisation theory was the German Franz Joseph Gall (1758–1828), the founder of phrenology, which attempted to measure people's character by examining the shape and surface of the skull. Gall first became interested in this subject as a 9 year old, when he noted a classmate with bulging eyes who was gifted in citing long passages of prose. This led Gall to reason that the ability for verbal memory lay in the frontal region of the brain behind the eyes. Later, Gall examined the cranial features of others, including the insane, criminals, peasants, great writers, artists and statesman. His technique involved feeling the contours of the head for a prominence, which he assumed represented a well developed area of the brain below it. By 1792, Gall had discovered several 'organs' of the brain, including those responsible for murder and the inclination to steal. In fact, Gall was eventually to identify 27 cranial regions that he believed corresponded to a distinct mental trait or behavioural tendency (Figure 1.26).

Gall's work attracted much controversy. It was patently clear to most that the shape of the skull was unrelated to the size of the brain tissue underneath, and it was impossible to measure accurately the bumps of the cranium, which meant that Gall's observations could not be falsified. Gall also used highly suspect data to support his theories. For example, he localised 'destructiveness' to a region above the ear, partly because a prominence had been found there in a student who had been fond of torturing animals. Even had the methods been sound, Gall's classification of psychological functions such as faith, self-love and veneration were highly suspect. Despite this, phrenology became extremely popular in the nineteenth century. Entrepreneurs such as the Fowler brothers promoted phrenology as a tool for self-improvement, and a large number of respectable phrenological societies were formed. In fact, it was not unusual for people to seek the advice of a phrenologist when hiring employees, selecting a marriage partner or diagnosing an illness, while social reformers proposed that phrenology could be used to rehabilitate criminals, or select better members of parliament. Although phrenology has long been discredited, one can still see parallels today with fads such as astrology and palmistry, which lack scientific support yet are still believed by many to be true.

Although phrenology was eventually discredited, some of Gall's contributions to brain research were positive ones. For example, Gall believed that the brain was the physical organ of mind, which governed

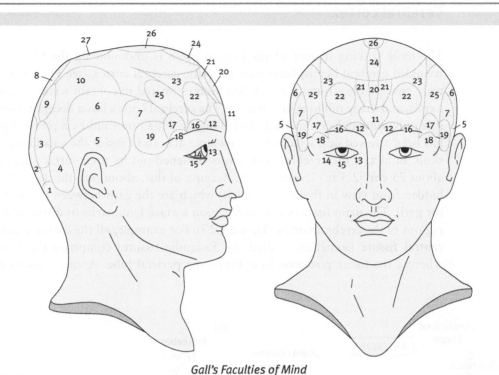

Gall's Faculties of Mind

Faculties shared by humans and animals

1. Reproductive instinct
2. Love of one's offspring
3. Affection or friendship
4. Instinct of self-defence, or courage
5. Destructiveness, carnivorous instinct, or tendency to murder
6. Cunning
7. Desire to possess things
8. Pride
9. Vanity or ambition
10. Circumspection or forethought
11. Memory for facts and things
12. Sense of place
13. Memory for people
14. Memory for words
15. Sense of language
16. Sense of colour
17. Sense of sounds, gift of music
18. Sense of numbers
19. Mechanical or architectural sense

Distinctly human faculties

20. Wisdom
21. Sense of metaphysics
22. Satire and wit
23. Poetic talent
24. Kindness and benevolence
25. Mimicry
26. Religious sentiment
27. Firmness of purpose

Figure 1.26 Gall's system of phrenology as seen from right and frontal views

Source: E.H. Ackerknecht and H.V. Vallois (1956) *Franz Joseph Gall, Inventor of Phrenology and his Collection*

all mental faculties and feelings. This was a modern view for the times, and it encouraged others to explore the brain. One such person was the Frenchman Pierre Flourens (1794–1867) who was the first to use lesioning (the removal of tissue) as a means of experimentally studying the brain's different regions. Gall's idea that the cerebral cortex contains areas with localised functions was another step forward. In fact, he was not entirely wrong, as regions of the cerebrum were later discovered that were specifically involved in language (Broca's area) and movement (the motor cortex). And, as this book will show, many other behavioural functions have also been localised to select areas of the brain.

Cerebral cortex

The most striking feature of the human brain is undoubtedly the two symmetrical wrinkled cerebral hemispheres that form the **cerebral cortex** (see Plate 1.3). This is a truly remarkable structure which has been estimated to contain some 100,000 km of axons, and many millions of synapses. The cerebral cortex has a deceptive appearance: it is only around 2–3 mm thick, but is highly folded (not unlike a piece of paper that has been screwed up), which allows its large area to fit inside the small confines of the skull. In fact, if the cerebral cortex was flattened out its total surface area would be about 75 cm² (2.5 ft²) (Nolte 1999). Because of this, about two-thirds of the cortex is hidden from view in fissures (or sulci), which are the gaps between the surface ridges (or gyri). The main fissures also make good surface landmarks to distinguish different regions of the cerebral cortex (Figure 1.27). For example, all the cortex anterior to the **central fissure** (sometimes called the Rolandic fissure) comprises the **frontal lobe**, whereas the tissue posterior to it forms the **parietal lobe**. Another sulcus called the

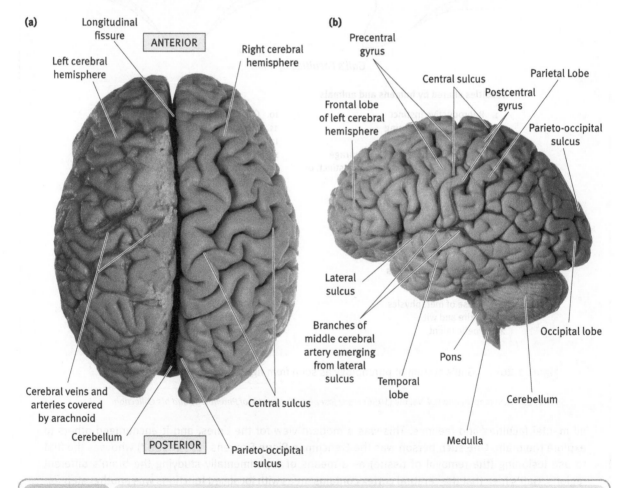

| | Plate 1.3 | The brain, highlighting some sulci and gyri: (a) superior view, (b) lateral view |

Source: F. Toates (2001) *Biological Psychology*, p. 110, Prentice Hall; photographer for (a), R.T. Hutchings; source of photograph (b), Omikron/Photo Researchers, Inc.

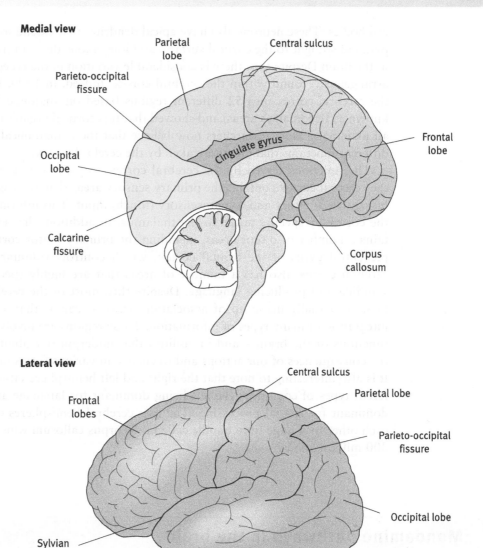

Figure 1.27   The main lobes of the cerebral cortex

parietal–occipital fissure separates the parietal lobe from the **occipital lobe** which is located at the back of the cerebral cortex. The other main region of the cerebral cortex is the **temporal lobe,** which is separated from the frontal and parietal lobes by the **lateral fissure** (sometimes called the Sylvian fissure).

When examined under a high-powered microscope it can be seen that about 90 per cent of the cerebral cortex is made up of six layers (this is sometimes called **neocortex**) which is anatomically more complex than the more primitive three-layered cortex (**archicortex**) found mainly in parts of the limbic system. About two-thirds of neurons in the cerebral cortex are **pyramidal cells,** so called because of their pyramidal shaped cell bodies. These neurons also have **apical dendrites** that extend from the apex of the pyramid straight to the cortical surface, and long axons that can travel some distance in the brain Despite this, there is considerable variation in the types of cells, and their arrangement, found within the cerebral cortex. Indeed, in 1909, Brodmann divided the cerebral cortex into 52 different regions based on anatomical differences (now known as **Brodmann's areas**) and showed that this cortical organisation was similar in all mammals. Most researchers now believe that these anatomical differences reflect different functions that are undertaken by the cerebral cortex.

The functions served by the cerebral cortex are extremely varied. For example, the cerebral cortex contains the **primary sensory areas** that are specialised for receiving visual, auditory and somatosensory (touch) input. This information is relayed to the cortex by specific nuclei in the thalamus. In addition, the cerebral cortex contains a number of motor areas, including the **primary motor cortex**, located in the precentral gyrus of the frontal cortex, which controls voluntary movement. The cerebral cortex also has a number of areas that are highly specialised for understanding and producing **language**. Despite this, most of the cerebral cortex in humans is actually made up of **association areas** – regions that are involved in the integration of many types of information. These regions are involved in many higher functions of the brain – and in abilities that underpin our ability to plan and see the consequences of our actions and to engage in various forms of abstract thought. It is also interesting to note that the right and left hemispheres also tend to show different types of cognition: the left being dominant for language and the right being dominant for spatial processing. The two cerebral hemispheres communicate with each other by a huge fibre bundle called the **corpus callosum** which contains around 300 million axons.

Monoamine pathways in the brain

Examining the main regions of the brain provides one way of understanding its anatomy, but there are also other ways of gaining important insights into its underlying structure. In particular, the brain has a number of neurotransmitter systems that are crucial to its function. The ability to trace chemical pathways in the brain was first developed in the early 1950s when it was found that cells of the adrenal gland would fluoresce if treated with formalin and exposed to ultraviolet light. This occurred because the cells contained monoamines (primarily adrenaline) that reacted with the formalin to produce fluorescent chemicals. This simple discovery was to be a crucial one, because some of the most important neurotransmitter systems in the brain contain monoamines, and this technique provided a way to identify their location. The first use of this method to map neurotransmitter pathways in the brain was undertaken by Dahlstrom and Fuxe in 1964 who were able to distinguish between noradrenaline (NA) and dopamine (DA) – which both fluoresced as green – and serotonin (5-HT), which fluoresced as yellow. This research also showed that neurons containing either NA, DA and 5-HT all arose from fairly small areas of the upper brainstem or midbrain, and that their axons formed large diffuse pathways that projected to many regions of the forebrain.

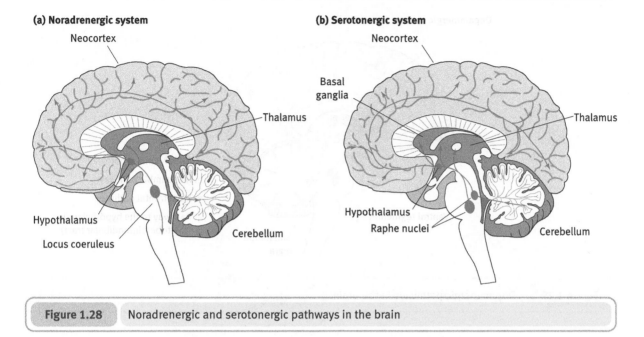

(a) Noradrenergic system

Neocortex

Thalamus

Hypothalamus

Locus coeruleus

Cerebellum

(b) Serotonergic system

Neocortex

Basal ganglia

Thalamus

Hypothalamus

Raphe nuclei

Cerebellum

Figure 1.28   Noradrenergic and serotonergic pathways in the brain

The origin of most NA neurons in the brain is a small nucleus in the pontine region of the upper brainstem called the **locus coeruleus** (see Figure 1.28). Remarkably, in humans, this structure contains only around 24,000 neurons, yet they project with their multiple axon branches to millions of cells throughout the brain, including the cerebral cortex, limbic system and thalamus. In fact, no other brain nucleus has such widespread projections (Foote 1987). The function of this system is not fully understood although it is probably linked to attention and arousal. The **raphe nuclei** (also situated in the pontine region) is a 5-HT counterpart to the locus coeruleus. There are two main raphe nuclei – the dorsal and the median – and they account for about 80 per cent of forebrain 5-HT. Similar to the locus coeruleus, the raphe contains relatively few neurons, but they give rise to many bifurcating axons with widespread projections. Although the destination of the 5-HT axons typically overlap with the NA one, particularly in the limbic system, there are some places (notably the basal ganglia) where the 5-HT input predominates. It is difficult to describe precisely the function of the 5-HT system, although it has been shown to be involved in sleep, arousal, mood and emotion.

The DA pathways (Figure 1.29) show some important differences to the NA and 5-HT systems. Not only are there more DA-containing neurons in the brain than there are NA and 5-HT axons (there are about 40,000 DA cells in total), but also they give rise to four distinct pathways that have different projections. The pathway that has attracted most attention (largely because of its involvement in Parkinson's disease) is the nigral–striatal pathway that projects from the **substantia nigra** to the **striatum** (see Chapter 4). The substantia nigra is embedded in a region of the midbrain called the **ventral tegmental area** which is also the origin of the three remaining DA pathways. Two of these – the mesocortical and mesolimbic pathways – have long axons that project to the frontal cortex and limbic system, respectively (these have been implicated in schizophrenia and reward). The fourth pathway projects to the hypothalamus and controls the release of the hormone prolactin.

Dopaminergic system

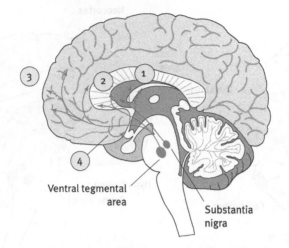

1. Nigral–striatal pathway
2. Mesolimbic pathway
3. Mesofrontal pathway
4. Pathway to the hypothalamus (the tuberoinfundibular tract)

Ventral tegmental area

Substantia nigra

Figure 1.29   Dopaminergic pathways in the brain

Summary

The study of the brain has a long history which stretches back well over two thousand years. One of the earliest theories of brain function was formulate by the Roman physician **Galen** (AD 130–200) who believed that 'animated spirit' (analogous to the soul) resided in the ventricles and that each ventricle had a different mental function. This theory was to remain highly influential for over 1,500 years, partly because it was compatible with Christian beliefs about the immortality and non-material nature of the soul. The first break with this tradition can be said to have began with the French philosopher **René Descartes** (1596–1650) who argued that much of our behaviour is not 'self-willed' by the soul, but is 'mechanical' and reflexive. The gradual acceptance of this view enabled the neural reflex to become a legitimate subject for scientific study that was largely free from religious interference. Approximately 150 years later, in 1791, the Italian **Luigi Galvani** discovered that the 'force' in nervous tissue was not animated spirit but electricity – thereby refuting Galen's doctrine. Although the microscope had been invented in 1665 by **Robert Hooke,** it was not until the late nineteenth century, with the development of more powerful instruments and of biological staining, that the nerve cell and its various components were clearly identified. The first stain to allow individual neurons to be visualised was discovered by **Camillo Golgi** in 1875, and this soon allowed others such as **Santiago Ramón y Cajal** to meticulously draw the structure of different brain regions and their interconnections. It was also realised that nerve cells are not physically joined, but are separated by small gaps – and these were termed synapses by **Charles Sherrington** in 1897. At first the nature of the message that crossed the synapse was not known. However, on Easter Sunday in 1921, an experiment undertaken in the early hours of the morning by **Otto Loewi** showed that synaptic transmission was chemical in nature. Despite this, how neurons generated electrical impulses was still not known. In 1936, **John Z. Young** discovered a giant neuron in the body of the squid which was about 1 mm in diameter and which could be implanted with a recording electrode. It was this preparation which was to allow **Alan Hodgkin** and **Andrew Huxley** to describe the formation and propagation of the action potential (nerve impulse) in 1952.

To understand how an action potential is generated, it is important to realise that the voltage inside a nerve cell, when it is at rest, is negative compared with the outside. In fact, it is about −70 mV, and this is called the **resting potential**. The reason for the voltage difference lies with the distribution of **ions** (atoms that have lost or gained an electron that makes them positively or negatively charged) which are found inside and outside the neuron. More specifically, the inside of the neuron contains a large amount of negatively charged anions, along with positive **potassium ions (K$^+$)**, and the extracellular fluid contains a high solution of positive **sodium (Na$^+$) ions**. This also creates a state of tension with Na$^+$ ions being strongly attracted to the inside of the cell by chemical and electrostatic forces. However, the **neural membrane** forms a partial barrier that stops the flow of ions into and out of the cell, and a **sodium–potassium pump** further helps to maintain this uneven distribution of ions. The neuron is also being bombarded by neural inputs reaching its dendrites and soma, and if these are sufficient to increase the resting potential at the axon hillock by about +15 mV, the membrane opens its **sodium channels**, enabling sodium ions to rush into the cell. This, in turn, increases the voltage in the neuron to about +30 mV in less than one-thousandth of a second. This is the start of the **action potential** which then passes down the axon by the process of **saltatory conduction** until it reaches the axon ending. Here where the fusing of synaptic vesicles with the membrane takes place (**exocytosis**), and **neurotransmitter** is spilled into the synaptic cleft.

The adult brain is believed to contain around 12 billion neurons, and about ten times more glial cells. It begins as an extension of the spinal cord called the **brainstem**. This is composed of the **medulla**, which then enlarges to become the **pons**. Running through much of the brainstem is the **reticular system** (known to govern arousal and sleep), while at the back of the pons lies the **cerebellum** (involved in movement). Sitting above the pons, at the end of the brainstem, is the **midbrain** consisting of the **tectum, tegmentum** and **periaqueductal grey area**. The midbrain has an array of functions, including sensory processing, movement and emotion. The rest of the brain is known as the **forebrain**. This includes the **thalamus** which is situated centrally and acts as a relay station for information going to the cerebral cortex, and the **hypothalamus** which controls the **pituitary gland** (the master gland of the hormone system) and autonomic nervous system. The rest of the forebrain is made up of a number of complex structures and pathways that include the **basal ganglia** which partially surrounds the thalamus and contains the **caudate nucleus, putamen, globus pallidus** and **substantia nigra** (the latter is actually located in the tegmentum). Traditionally, the basal ganglia have been associated with movement. Another important forebrain region is the **limbic system** which is closely associated with old parts of the cerebral cortex, and includes the **cingulate gyrus, hippocampus, fornix, amygdala** and **hypothalamus**. Traditionally, these structures have been implicated in emotion. Finally, the most striking feature of the human brain is the phylogenically recent **cerebral cortex** with its distinctive array of ridges (gyri) and fissures (sulci). The cerebral cortex has four main lobes – **occipital, parietal, temporal** and **frontal** – and is involved in a wide range of higher cognitive functions including thought, language, memory, vision and movement. The two cerebral hemispheres are also joined by a huge fibre bundle called the **corpus callosum**.

Essay questions

1. Trace the history of ideas from antiquity to the present day about the workings of nerve cells. How has animated spirit been replaced by action potentials and chemical messengers?

   Search terms: History of the brain. History of neuroscience. History of neurobiology. Pioneers of brain research. Ancient ideas about the brain.

2. Explain the formation of the action potential, its propagation down the axon, and its contribution to producing exocytosis of neurotransmitter release.

   Search terms: How do neurons work? Action potential. Neurons. Ions and the resting potential. Propagation of the action potential. Exocytosis.

3. What happens when neurotransmitters are released into the synapse? With reference to both ionotropic and metabotropic receptors, explain how neurotransmitters produce excitatory or inhibitory potentials in the postsynaptic neuron.

   Search terms: Neurotransmitter release. Neurotransmitter receptors. Ionotropic receptors. Second messengers. Ion channels. Excitatory and inhibitory postsynaptic potentials.

4. Describe the main structures of the brainstem, midbrain and forebrain, including basal ganglia, limbic system and cerebral cortex. What functions and behaviours are these regions known to control?

   Search terms: Human brain. Functions of the basal ganglia. Neuroanatomy of the brain. Limbic system and behaviour. Cerebral cortex.

Further reading

Afifi, A.K. and Bergman, R.A. (1998) *Functional Neuroanatomy*. New York: McGraw-Hill. A well-illustrated textbook that covers the neuroanatomy of the brain along with discussion of the clinical and functional relevance of the key neuroanatomical structures.

Blumenfeld, H. (2002) *Neuroanatomy through Clinical Cases*. Sunderland, Mass.: Sinauer. A comprehensive and interesting textbook which uses clinical examples to help the student learn more about the neuroanatomy and behavioural functions of the brain.

Breedlove, S.M., Rosenzweig, M.R. and Watson, N.V. (2007) *Biological Psychology*. Sunderland, Mass.: Sinauer. A very good and broad-ranging textbook which is nicely illustrated. Now in its fifth edition.

Carlson, N.R. (2007) *Physiology of Behavior*. Boston: Allyn and Bacon. First published in 1977 and now in its ninth edition. A classic textbook that provides an excellent introduction to biological psychology.

Clark, D.L., Boutros, N.N. and Mendez, M.F. (2005) *The Brain and Behavior: An Introduction to Behavioral Neuroanatomy*. Cambridge: Cambridge University Press. A good introduction to neuroanatomy for first-time students, which also attempts to relate brain structure to behaviour.

Diamond, M.C., Scheibel, A.B. and Elson, L.M. (1986) *The Human Brain Colouring Book*. London: HarperCollins. This book contains detailed diagrams designed to be 'coloured in' to help illustrate the structure and function of the brain. Lots of fun and a godsend for students who find the various parts of the brain and their interrelationships difficult to visualise.

Finger, S. (2000) *Minds Behind the Brain*. Oxford: Oxford University Press. A captivating history of brain research from ancient times, with individual chapters on its greatest pioneers.

Freberg, L.A. (2006) *Discovering Biological Psychology*. Boston: Houghton Mifflin. A textbook that is aimed primarily at undergraduates who are new to biological psychology. It fulfils its aims admirably.

Klein, S.B. and Thorne, B.M. (2006) *Biological Psychology*. New York: Worth. An interesting and well written new textbook which deserves to become a permanent fixture on students' reading lists.

Kolb, B. and Whishaw, I.Q. (2001) *An Introduction to Brain and Behavior*. New York: Worth. Another excellent textbook covering brain and behaviour with a greater emphasis on clinical neuropsychology than Carlson or Pinel.

Nicholls, J.G., Martin, A.R., Wallace, B.G. and Fuchs, P.A. (2001) *From Neuron to Brain*, 4th edition. Sunderland, Mass.: Sinauer. A book which focuses on the biological workings of the nervous system. Although it contains relatively little on behaviour, sensory and motor systems are discussed in detail.

Pinel, J.P. (2003) *Biopsychology*. Boston: Allyn and Bacon. Another classic textbook on biopsychology which is well illustrated. Now in its fifth edition.

Stein, J.F. and Stoodley, C.J. (2006) *Neuroscience: An Introduction*. Chichester: John Wiley. An accessible introduction to neuroscience which is also very informative.

Toates, F. (2007) *Biological Psychology*. Harlow: Prentice Hall. A comprehensive and engaging introduction to biological psychology with an emphasis on comparative and evolutionary aspects of behavior.

Zigmond, M.J., Bloom, F.E., Landis, S.C., Roberts, J.L. and Squire, L.R. (eds) (1999) *Fundamental Neuroscience*. San Diego, Calif.: Academic Press. A massive textbook of 1,600 pages, written by experts in the field, which contains much of interest for the advanced student of biological psychology.

 For self test questions, animations, interactive exercises and many more resources to help you consolidate your understanding, and expand your knowledge of the field, please go to the website accompanying this book at **www.pearsoned.co.uk/wickens**

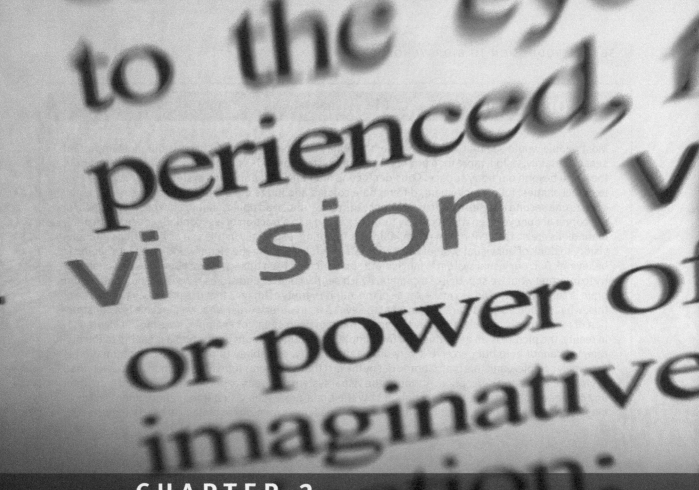

CHAPTER 2

The visual system

In this chapter

- The structure of the eye and retina

- Visual pathways from the retina to visual cortex

- The concept of receptive fields

- How the visual cortex processes orientation, form and depth

- Theories of colour vision

- The dorsal ('where is it?') and ventral ('what is it?') pathways of higher vision

- Visual disorders, including agnosia and Balint's syndrome

- Subcortical structures involved in vision

INTRODUCTION

Most people would say that vision, or rather the ability to detect changes in light, is our most important sense. Certainly, vision, more than any other sensory system, provides us with detailed information about the world beyond our body surface. Consider for one moment what our visual system can do: we are able to detect shapes, follow movement, differentiate colours and judge distances – we can focus on nearby objects one second and see far into the distance the next – and, if an object should unexpectedly appear in the corner of our eye, then we reflexively turn our gaze to it in a fraction of a second. Because these automatic skills are so fast, effortless and reliable, it is tempting, especially in this age of video films and television, to think of our visual system as providing a faithful recording the visual world. After all, 'seeing is believing'. But, our visual system is much more sophisticated than this – not least because we constantly try to interpret what we see. Unlike a camera, which simply collects and stores raw visual information, our brain is continuously trying to make sense of the infinite variety of images that it is processing. Because of this, what we *perceive* is different from what the eyes *see*. In other words, what we perceive is a construction of reality that is manufactured by the brain. This can been seen, for example, if we look at Figure 2.1. In reality, the picture is an assortment of five simple lines. But, once our brains find a meaning to the picture, we cannot help but perceive it very differently. Clearly, our ability to process visual information is extremely complex, and this is also borne out by the fact that about one-third of the human brain is devoted to visual analysis and perception. Although the visual system has been experimentally studied more than any other sensory system, the question of how the brain processes visual information, and constructs meaningful images from it, remains one of the great challenges for modern biological psychology.

Figure 2.1   A jumble of lines – until you realise that there is a picture there! (see answer at the foot of the page)

What is light?

The stimulus for activating the visual system is light, which is a form of electromagnetic radiation generated by the oscillation of electrically charged particles called photons. There are many forms of electromagnetic radiation, including gamma rays, ultraviolet light and radio waves, and all move at the same speed: 300,000 kilometres per second, or 186,000 miles per second. Indeed, one might wonder why something travelling this fast does not hurt us! But what distinguishes each form of electromagnetic radiation is its wavelength (see Figure 2.2) and light is no exception. In fact, light is simply a narrow band of the electromagnetic spectrum that has a wavelength ranging from about 380 to 760 nanometres (nm) (a nanometre is one-billionth of a metre). Put another way, our visual system detects only a very small portion of the electromagnetic spectrum surrounding us.

The two most important qualities that we *perceive* from light are its colour and brightness. The length of the light's wavelength produces colour. For example, the shortest wavelength detectable by the human eye is around 380 nm and this produces the sensation of violet. As the length of the light waves increases, the sensation of colour

Answer: back view of a washer-woman kneeling down with her bucket!

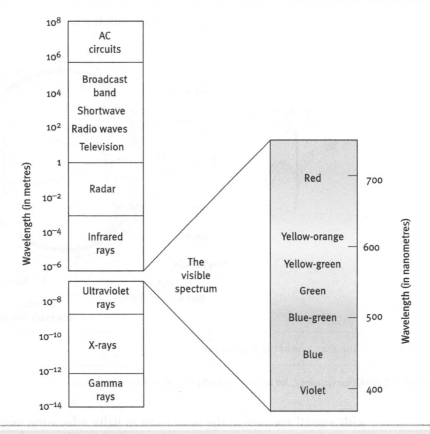

| Figure 2.2 | The electromagnetic spectrum |

changes (for example, approximating to violet, blue, green, yellow and red). Other animals, however, may be sensitive to different parts of the visual spectrum. For example, some animals can respond to much shorter violet wavelengths, whereas others can detect the longer infrared wavelengths. The brightness of a colour, however, is related not to its wavelength but to the amplitude, or height, of its oscillation, which is directly proportional to the density of photons in the wave. Thus, the more photons in the wave, the brighter the light (or colour) will appear to be.

Of course, we rarely see just pure shades of light since most of our visual world is made up of objects that are reflecting a wide range of different wavelengths. In fact, we see an object only if light striking its surface is partially absorbed, so that some of it is reflected back to us. If an object was to absorb all light hitting its surface it would appear to be black, and if the same object reflected all light, it would appear as a mirror surface of the light source. Therefore, it is the patterns of reflection and absorption, along with the many wavelengths they create, that allow us to see the shapes and surfaces of objects.

The structure of the eye

The eye is the organ for sight and its main function is to detect changes in light wavelength and intensity, and transmit this information via the optic nerves to the brain. The human eye can be likened to a camera since both are basically darkened chambers

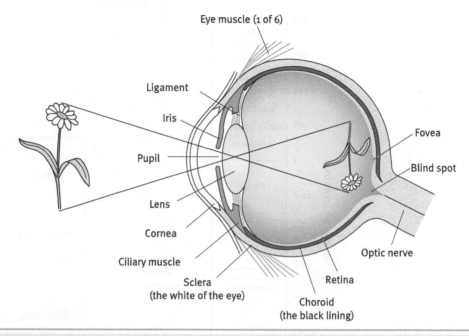

| Figure 2.3 | The structure of the human eye |

Source: John P.J. Pinel, *Biopsychology*, 3rd edition. Copyright © 1997 by Pearson Education

with a small aperture at the front to let in light; a focusing mechanism; and a plate to receive the projected image at the back (Figure 2.3). In the case of a camera it is the photographic film which records the image; with the eye it is the photoreceptors located on the back of the retina that have the same function. Unlike the camera, however, the eye's photoreceptors have to transduce light into neural information so it can be conveyed by the optic nerves to the brain.

If an eye was removed from its socket you would find that it has a spherical shape, and for most part is covered in a tough white tissue called the **sclera**, which we often see as the 'whites of the eye'. The sclera does not completely cover the surface, however: it has a small round window called the **cornea** that enables light to enter the eye. The cornea acts as a simple fixed lens that begins to gather light and gives the eye most of its focusing power. Once light has passed through this transparent layer, it travels through the **aqueous humour** (aqueous means 'watery') to reach the **pupil**. The pupil is an aperture, or gap, that controls the amount of light entering the next chamber of the eye, and its size is controlled by a ring of muscles called the **iris**, which also gives the eye its colour (blue, green or brown). The iris, which is controlled by the autonomic nervous system, acts to enlarge (dilate) the pupil not only if one moves from bright light into the dark (its diameter can change from 2 to 8 mm in this situation), but also if one experiences an arousing or threatening stimulus. Behind the pupil is the **lens**, whose function is to bring visual images into sharp focus by acting as a fine adjustment to the cornea. This process, known as accommodation, is controlled by the **ciliary muscles**, which act to change the curvature of the lens, either by 'bending' it more, enabling vision of nearby objects, or by making it 'flatter', allowing vision of distant objects. After the lens, light passes through a clear gelatinous substance called the **vitreous humour** (vitreous means 'glassy'), which helps to maintain the shape of the eye, before it reaches the **retina**.

The structure of the retina

The neural processing of visual information begins with **photoreceptors** located at the back of the retina called the **rods** and **cones**. There are approximately 120 million rods and 6 million cones in each human retina, with rods located mainly in the periphery and cones in the centre or **fovea** (meaning 'pit'). The rods and cones are also specialised to deal with different types of light. The rods are sensitive to dim light and are mainly used for vision in dark conditions, whereas the cones function best in bright light and provide us with vision of high acuity (i.e. they allow us to see fine detail) and colour. This is why, for example, to see the dimmest lights such as faint stars in the sky, we often turn our heads slightly to one side so the light rays fall on the part of the retina containing the rods. For most of our vision, however, provided there are good lighting conditions, the eye focuses light onto our fovea where the cones are concentrated.

Although the retina is only about 250 micrometres (µm) thick (about the size of a razor blade edge), it contains several layers of cells. The rods and cones are located at the back of the retina and light has to pass through the overlying cell layers to reach them. This arrangement appears to be somewhat odd as one might expect the overlying cells to interfere with the projection of the light's rays, but it seems that no visual disturbance occurs. Both rods and cones contain special chemicals called **photopigments** which absorb light and transduce it into neural information. This activity is conveyed to the next layer of cells, called **bipolar cells**. There are two types of bipolar cell: 'on bipolars' which become depolarised (i.e. they increase activity) to visual information, and 'off bipolars' which are hyperpolarised (i.e. they decrease activity) in response to visual input. In turn, these cells project to the **ganglion cells,** whose cell bodies are found in the outer layer of the retina and whose axons travel on its surface, to form the optic nerve that goes to the brain. The retina also contains **horizontal cells** that project laterally (i.e. sideways) and interconnect the photoreceptors; and many different types of **amacrine cell** that link the bipolar and ganglion cells in much the same way. Although the function of these two types of cell are not fully understood, it is known they are involved in modifying or inhibiting visual information reaching the ganglion cells, and this is important in the formation of their receptive fields (see later). Thus, a considerable amount of neural processing takes place at the retina before it reaches the optic nerve (Figure 2.4).

There are approximately 800,000 axons in each optic nerve and, as we have seen, over 120 million photoreceptors (rods and cones) in the retina. This means that a **convergence** of neural input must take place between the photoreceptors and each ganglion cell (Figure 2.5). In fact, the degree of convergence depends largely upon the location of the photoreceptor in the retina. In the periphery, several hundred photoreceptors may converge onto a single ganglion cell, but this figure gets less towards the centre of the retina. In fact, in the fovea, a ganglion cell may receive input from just one or two cones. This relationship helps to explain the better acuity of foveal vision compared with peripheral rod vision. In contrast, because large numbers of rods send information to a single ganglion cell, this 'extra' stimulation means that the cell is more likely to fire. This helps explain why rods are better at detecting changes in dim light – but at the expense of seeing details.

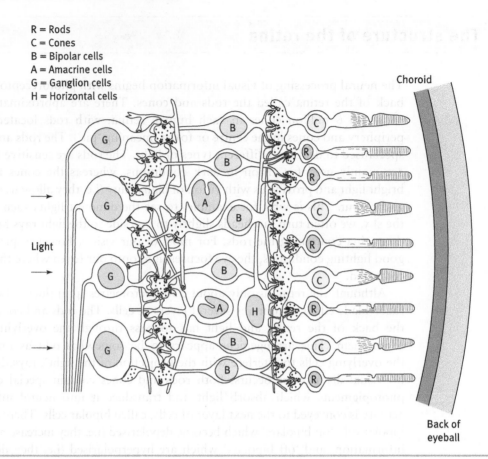

R = Rods
C = Cones
B = Bipolar cells
A = Amacrine cells
G = Ganglion cells
H = Horizontal cells

Choroid

Light

Back of
eyeball

Figure 2.4   The neural structure of the human retina

Source: Adapted from J.E. Dowling and B.B. Boycott (1996) *Proceedings of the Royal Society of London*, 166, 80–111

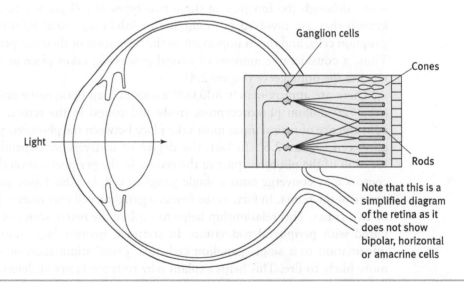

Ganglion cells

Cones

Light

Rods

Note that this is a
simplified diagram
of the retina as it
does not show
bipolar, horizontal
or amacrine cells

Figure 2.5   The convergence of input from cones and rods onto retinal ganglion cells

The visual pathways to the brain

The axons of the ganglion cells come together to form a bundle called the optic nerve which leaves the retina at the **blind spot**, which is approximately 16 mm to the side of the fovea. As the name suggests, an object focused in this area of the retina is not visible – although we are never aware of this, as our eyes are continuously moving and objects are focused on other parts of the retina. The optic nerve forms a clearly observable white fibre tract that travels along the lower surface of the brain until it reaches the front of the pituitary stalk. At this point, the two optic nerves converge and form the **optic chiasm** where some (but not all) of the axons pass to the opposite of side of the brain. More precisely, the pattern of crossing is as follows: the axons arising from the nasal or nose side of the retina, which includes most of fovea, cross to the opposite (contralateral) side of the brain, while the fibres from the rest of the retina continue on the same (ipsilateral) side. Although no synapses occur in the optic chiasm (axons pass straight through), the fibres that leave the chiasm are referred to as the **optic tract**. Each tract then enters the brain, where about 80 per cent of axons terminate in the **lateral geniculate nucleus,** two peanut-sized clusters of neurons located in the thalamus. This is the main part of the thalamus which is responsible for relaying information to the **primary visual cortex**, sometimes called the **striate cortex** because of its striped appearance, located in the **occipital lobes** (the most posterior part of the cerebral cortex). The remainder of the optic tract branches away to various structures before reaching the thalamus. This includes pathways to the **suprachiamatic nucleus** (involved in circadian rhythms), the **pretectum** (pupillary reflexes) and the **superior colliculus** (saccadic eye movements).

Each of the two lateral geniculate nuclei (the word *geniculate* means 'bent like a knee') contains six layers of cells and receives information from both eyes consisting of crossed (contralateral) and uncrossed (ipsilateral) input. At this stage, however, the visual information is segregated, with each cell layer receiving input from a single eye. To make matters more complex, the top four layers of the lateral geniculate nucleus are composed of small neurons known as **parvocellular cells**, which originate mainly from the fovea, and the last two layers are composed of bigger neurons known as **magnocellular cells**, which originate mainly from the periphery of the retina (these cells will be discussed in more detail later).

The axons arising from the geniculate layers then form a pathway called the **optic radiations** that projects to the primary visual cortex on the same side. This is the largest area of the brain devoted to the initial stages of visual processing, and it is here that information from both eyes is combined for the first time. Thus, the primary visual cortex provides the first preliminary analysis of the complete visual image conveyed by both eyes. In the human brain, the primary visual cortex is about 1.5 mm in thickness and similar to the rest of the cerebral cortex as it is composed of six main layers. In fact, the axons from the lateral geniculate nucleus terminate in its fourth layer, which is divided into sub-lamina (4A, 4B, 4Cα and 4Cβ). Layer 4B contains numerous myelinated axon collaterals and is called the **stria of Gennari**, which gives the visual cortex its striped or striated appearance (Figure 2.6). Neurons in layer 4 then project to other layers directly above, or below, in the same column of the visual cortex.

The primary visual cortex is organised topographically, that is, if two adjacent points are stimulated on the retina, causing different ganglion cells to fire, then adjacent areas in the visual cortex will also be activated. In effect, this means that the layout of

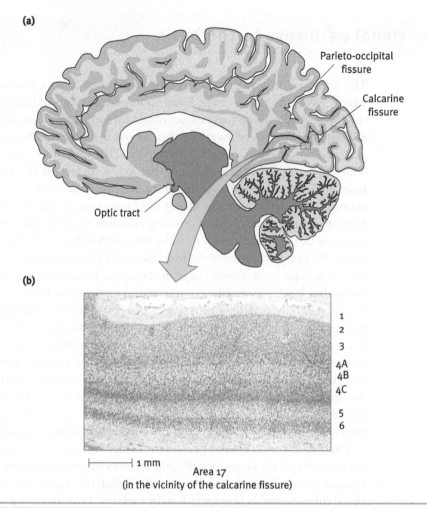

(a)

Parieto-occipital
fissure

Calcarine
fissure

Optic tract

(b)

1
2
3
4A
4B
4C
5
6

⊢———⊣ 1 mm

Area 17
(in the vicinity of the calcarine fissure)

Figure 2.6   Primary visual cortex. (a) Myelin-stained section of the brain showing the visual cortex (seen below the parieto-occipital fissure); (b) inset showing cresyl violet staining of the primary visual cortex, showing different layers, which gives rise to the name 'striate cortex'

the photoreceptors in the retina is mapped out in the visual cortex. Despite this, the organisation of the visual cortex is heavily biased to processing foveal information. Although the fovea forms only a small part of the retina, and is less than 0.5 mm in diameter, about 25 per cent of the visual cortex is devoted to analysing its input. It can also be seen from Figure 2.7 that because axons from the nasal halves of each retina cross to the other side of the brain, each hemisphere receives information from the opposite side of the visual scene. In other words, if a person looks straight ahead, the left visual cortex receives information from the **right visual field** of each eye: and the right visual cortex obtains input from the **left visual field** of each eye. Thus, although each visual cortex receives input from *both* eyes, the left visual cortex processes information only from the right side of its world; and the right visual cortex processes information only from the left side of its world. To fully appreciate this arrangement, you will need to carefully study Figure 2.7.

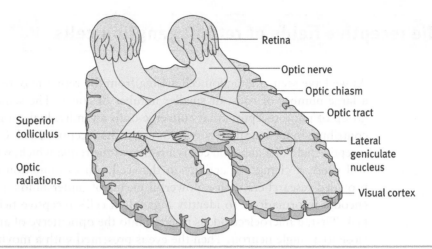

| **Figure 2.7** | The primary visual pathways from retina to cortex |

Source: The Open University, Course SD286, Module C7

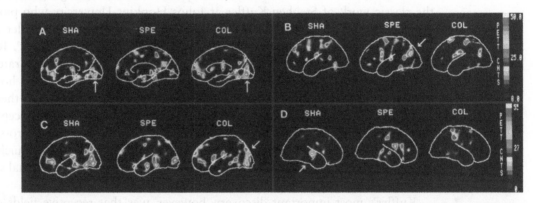

| **Plate 2.1** | Computer-generated drawings of PET scan from an experiment that involved discriminating the shape, colour and speed of a visual stimulus under conditions of selective and divided attention. The subject's task was to compare the first stimulus with a second presented 1500 ms later, and to report if they were the same or different. Frames A shows attention to shape and colour; B shows attention to speed; C shows attention to colour; and D shows attention to shape. Abbreviations: SHA, shape; SPE, speed of movement; COL, colour. |

Source: Corbetta *et al*. Selective and divided attention during visual discriminations of shape, color, and speed, figure 7, in *The Journal of Neuroscience*, August 1991, Vol 11(8), p. 2392. Copyright 1991 by the Society for Neuroscience

Once the visual cortex has encoded information it is then passed to secondary areas of the visual cortex, which are sometimes referred to as extrastriate areas. In fact, there are at least thirty other areas of the cortex, scattered throughout the brain, known to have at least some involvement in higher visual processing (Plate 2.1). These include separate cortical regions for colour and movement, plus other areas involved in reading, object recognition and spatial awareness. Although visual information can take a number of routes through the brain, researchers are now beginning to realise that there are two main routes, one involving a ventral route through the temporal lobe and one involving a dorsal route through the parietal lobes. We will return to these pathways towards the end of the chapter.

The receptive fields of retinal ganglion cells

As we have seen, a ganglion cell arising from the retina may receive information from a large number of rods, or smaller number of cones. The sensory area detected by a group of photoreceptors that converge onto an individual ganglion cell and therefore contribute to its neural activity is known as its **receptive field**. Or, put another way, the receptive field of a ganglion cell is a region of the retina which, when visually stimulated, will cause a change of activity in that cell. An examination of receptive fields has provided researchers with a powerful means of understanding how the visual system encodes information. To identify a ganglion cell's receptive field, however, is no easy task. First, a microelectrode is inserted into the optic nerve of an anaesthetised animal, close to a single neuron. Then the eye is presented with a moving visual stimulus projected either directly into the retina or onto a screen facing the animal, until the electrode picks up the neural activity of the visual input. This search may take hours, but, once identified, the characteristics of the receptive field can be mapped in fine detail.

Much of what we know about the receptive fields of retinal ganglion cells is due to the classic work of Stephen Kuffler at Johns Hopkins University who pioneered this type of research in the 1950s working with cats (see, for example, Kuffler 1953). One of Kuffler's first discoveries was that ganglion cells were never 'silent'. Rather, they were continually generating action potentials with a background firing rate of around 5 impulses per second. But Kuffler was more interested in discovering how ganglion cells respond to different types of stimuli, and to do this he explored their receptive fields with a fine spot of light. Using this technique, he found that the receptive field of each ganglion cell was circular in shape, and the fields varied in size across the retina, with those in the foveal being small and those in the periphery being much larger. He also found that ganglion cells either increased activity in response to visual stimulation, or were inhibited by it.

Kuffler's most important discovery, however, was that receptive fields of ganglion cells actually contained both excitatory and inhibitory areas. In fact, these were arranged in a **centre–surround** fashion. That is, the receptive field of ganglion cells consisted of a circular central area and an outer region that surrounded it – and these areas showed different types of neural activity in response to visual stimulation (see Figure 2.8). For example, in some ganglion cells, a spot of light shone directly into the central region of its visual field greatly increased the background firing rate (an 'on' response), whereas light projected into its surround reduced it (an 'off' response). This was called a **centre-on, surround-off ganglion cell**. However, in other cells, the effect was reversed with illumination of the centre producing an 'off' response and stimulation of the surround an 'on' response. This was called a **centre-off, surround on ganglion cell**.

When a light was shone over the whole receptive field, Kuffler found that the 'on' and 'off' responses tended to cancel each other out. Moreover, the extent of this antagonistic effect depended on the relative proportions of the on–off regions that were stimulated. For example, if a spot of light was progressively made larger in the centre of an on-centre receptive field, the firing rate of the cell increased until the centre was completely filled, at which point the response began to decline as the light encroached into the off-surround. As the surround became increasingly illuminated, however, it cancelled out the cell's 'on' response, returning it to its baseline level of firing. In other words, the ganglion cell showed a graded response to a light stimulus projecting on its receptive field.

Responses of an on-centre cell

There is an 'on' response when a spot of light is shone anywhere in the centre of the field

There is an 'off' response when a spot of light is shone anywhere in the periphery of the field

Responses of an off-centre cell

There is an 'off' response when a spot of light is shone anywhere in the centre of the field

There is an 'on' response when a spot of light is shone anywhere in the periphery of the field

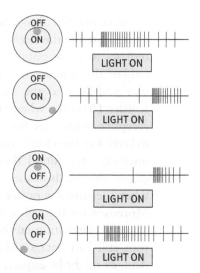

LIGHT ON

LIGHT ON

LIGHT ON

LIGHT ON

| **Figure 2.8** | The receptive fields of an on-centre and off-centre ganglion cell |

Source: John P.J. Pinel, *Biopsychology*, 3rd edition. Copyright © 1997 by Pearson Education

Later studies also showed retinal ganglion cells could be divided into two further categories: **X ganglion cells** and **Y ganglion cells** (although more have been discovered subsequently). Y ganglion cells were found to have receptive fields that were, on average, three times larger than their X counterparts. In addition, Y ganglion cells were responsive to movement whereas X ganglion cells were sensitive to colour (Enroth-Cugell and Robson 1966). And, as might be expected, Y ganglion cells were innervated mainly by rods, and X ganglion cells by cones.

The receptive fields in the visual cortex

In the late 1950s and early 1960s, David Hubel and Tortsten Wiesel began to examine the receptive fields of neurons located in the lateral geniculate nucleus and primary visual cortex (see Hubel and Wiesel 2005). They adopted a similar experimental approach to Kuffler: they presented anaesthetised cats, who wore special contact lenses to keep their eyes open, with small spots of light, and then attempted to detect changes in activity from single neurons in the brain. Their initial expectation was that the receptive fields of cortical cells would be similar to the circular on- and off-centre fields of retinal ganglion cells identified by Kuffler. Although this proved to be true for the lateral geniculate nucleus, the small spots of light used by Kuffler were ineffective at stimulating activity in cortical cells. In fact, it was only by accident when they were removing slides from their projection ophthalmoscope, that Hubel and Wiesel discovered that a line passing over a particular location on the retina caused certain cells in the visual cortex to start firing. This chance discovery led Hubel and Wiesel to realise that most cells in the visual cortex actually have elongated receptive fields and were particularly sensitive to the movement of edges. This discovery was to provide crucial new insights into the cortical processing of vision, and lead to their being awarded the Nobel Prize for Physiology and Medicine in 1981 (see Barlow 1982).

As mentioned above, when Hubel and Wiesel examined the receptive fields of neurons located in the lateral geniculate nucleus, they found that they had similar characteristics to those obtained from retinal ganglion cells. In other words, the receptive field of all the neurons in the visual pathway from retina to visual cortex were monocular and showed the same basic type of concentric on–off response as found by Kuffler. However, when Hubel and Wiesel recorded from cells in the visual cortex, the receptive fields were found to be very different. Indeed, starting with neurons located in layer 4 of the visual cortex (the layer which receives input from the lateral geniculate nucleus), they found that maximal responses were produced by elongated bars or edges. Thus, cells in this layer of the visual cortex showed an increase of activity only when the stimulus presented to their receptive field was in the form of a straight line. Moreover, for the cell to fire maximally, the stimulus had to be in a very precise location and orientation on the retina. This was because the receptive fields of cortical neurons still had antagonistic on–off regions like the receptive fields of ganglion cells. And, as might be expected, these brain cells fired maximally only when the line presented to the retina was orientated in such a way that it fell within the 'on' region of the receptive field. In fact, if the orientation of the line was changed, then the response of the cell was drastically reduced. Hubel and Wiesel called these **simple cells** (see Figure 2.9).

Why do simple cells have oblong shaped receptive fields? The answer lies with the way simple cells receive input from the lateral geniculate nucleus. In short, it appears that each simple cell receives input from an array of lateral geniculate neurons that are 'wired' in such a way as to receive converging input from oblong groups of retinal ganglion cells. The result (in theory at least) is that a line falling on the retina may stimulate many photoreceptors but exert an effect only on a single cell in the cortex. Thus, there is convergence of input from arrays of cells feeding into 'higher' individual neurons (see Figure 2.10).

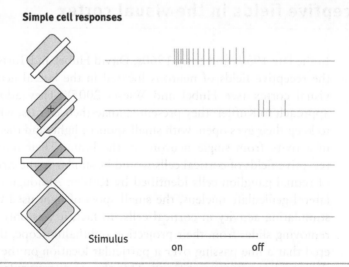

| Figure 2.9 | The response of simple cortical cells to different orientations of stimuli (lines) placed in their visual fields |

Source: D.H. Hubel (1995) *Eye, Brain and Vision*, p. 73

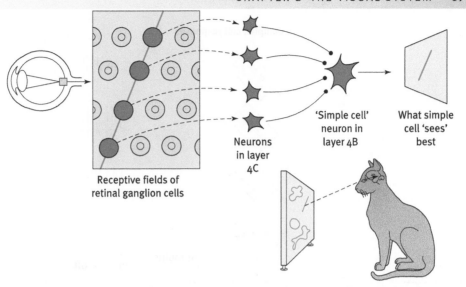

Receptive fields of
retinal ganglion cells

Neurons
in layer
4C

'Simple cell'
neuron in
layer 4B

What simple
cell 'sees'
best

Figure 2.10   An illustration of how simple cells may be 'wired' from geniculate neurons

Source: Schneider, A.M. and Tarshis, B. (1995) *Elements of Physiological Psychology*. The McGraw-Hill Companies, Inc.

Complex and hypercomplex cells

Simple cells are not the only types of cell in the visual cortex. When Hubel and Wiesel moved their recording electrodes to other layers of the visual cortex, they found two other types of cell which they called **complex** and **hypercomplex**. Complex cells are actually the most common type of cell in the visual cortex, and are predominantly found in layers 2 and 3 (which receives input from layer 4), and in layer 5 (which receives most of its input from layers two, three and six). Complex cells are distinct from simple ones since they typically respond maximally when a line falls anywhere in their receptive field provided it is in the correct orientation (see Figure 2.11). Indeed, because the receptive fields of complex cells are larger than those of simple cells, the line stimulus can appear in several different locations and still activate the cell. In addition, complex cells are particularly sensitive to movement. Some complex cells fire when a line stimulus is moved into the receptive field from a particular direction, whereas others respond to line movement of any direction. Hubel and Wiesel also suggested that complex cells are hierarchically organised from arrays of simple cells.

Hypercomplex cells are similar to complex cells, except they have an extra inhibitory area at the ends of their receptive field. This means that they respond best when the line is of a specific orientation *and* of a certain length. In fact, if the line is too long and extends into the inhibitory part of the receptive field, then the firing rate of the cell declines (for this reason they are sometimes called 'end-stopped'). Some hypercomplex cells also respond maximally to two line segments meeting at a particular point, suggesting that they may also act as angle detectors. More recently, the term 'hypercomplex' has fallen out of vogue, as it is known that some simple and complex cells are also end-stopped.

Complex cell responses

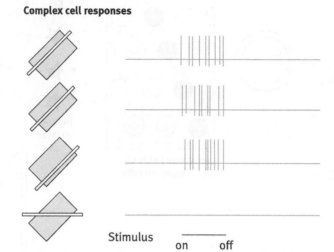

Stimulus

on   off

Figure 2.11	The response of complex cortical cells to different orientations of stimuli (lines) placed in their visual fields

Source: D.H. Hubel (1995) *Eye, Brain and Vision*, p. 75

The arrangement of cells in the primary visual cortex

Another important discovery made by Hubel and Wiesel was that the visual cortex comprises columns in which all the cells share similar properties. The idea that the cerebral cortex processed information in cortical columns in which connections 'up and down' were more important that those going from 'side to side', had first been made by Vernon Mountcastle in the mid-1950s. However, Hubel and Wiesel's work was to give the idea much greater support. For example, if a recording electrode is lowered into the cortex, perpendicular to its surface, not only will one find simple, complex and hypercomplex cells, but the centres of their respective receptive fields will also be approximately the same. In other words, all neurons in a particular column respond maximally to the same line orientation. Thus, if a simple cell is found to respond best to a vertical line, the complex and hypercomplex cells in the same column will also respond to vertical lines (see Figure 2.12). These units were termed **orientation columns**.

As the recording electrode is moved sideways from one column to the next, another interesting feature of the visual cortex is observed. In short, the preferred axis of orientation of the lines rotates in a clockwise or anticlockwise manner, with each 0.05 mm of sideways movement producing a rotation of 10°. In other words, if the cells in one column are all 'tuned' to vertical stimuli, the cells in the next column will respond best to lines 10° from vertical, and so on (although occasionally there are discontinuous jumps). In fact, a transverse of a 1 mm length of cortex is sufficient to detect every possible line orientation across 180°. And, although the cells in each 180° unit respond to many different receptor field orientations, all derive from the same part of the retina, showing that each block of orientation cells is involved with processing visual information from the same part of the world (Hubel 1988).

The columns of the visual cortex are also organised on the basis of **ocular dominance**. Although we have two eyes, we have only one visual world, indicating that convergence

(a) The main cell layers of the visual cortex

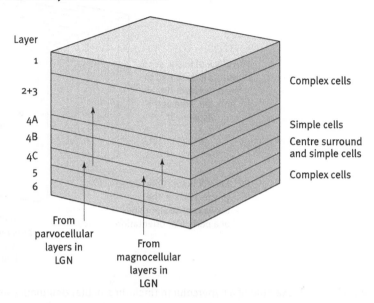

(b) The orientation sensitivity of neurons in the visual cortex

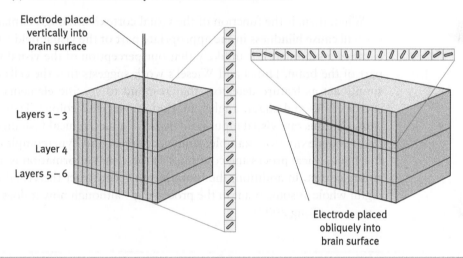

Figure 2.12   The main cell layers, and orientation sensitivity of neurons in the visual cortex

of visual input takes place somewhere in the visual system. The first place where this occurs is the visual cortex. Indeed, it has been found that many cells in the visual cortex have binocular receptive fields (i.e. they respond to information from both eyes), although most show a preference for one of the eyes, that is, they will fire more strongly when the 'favoured' eye is stimulated. The organisation of ocular dominance in the visual cortex follows a pattern similar to that found for orientation. That is, if an electrode is lowered into a cortical column, all of its cells will respond best to input from the same eye. And, as the electrode is moved laterally, the right-eye and left-eye preference alternates, with each band alternating every millimetre or so. As can be seen in Figure 2.13, orientation and ocular columns are arranged in functional units in the visual cortex called **hypercolumns** (Mecacci 1991).

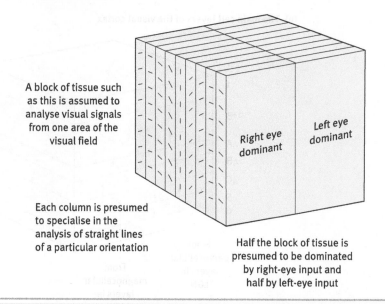

A block of tissue such as this is assumed to analyse visual signals from one area of the visual field

Right eye dominant

Left eye dominant

Each column is presumed to specialise in the analysis of straight lines of a particular orientation

Half the block of tissue is presumed to be dominated by right-eye input and half by left-eye input

Figure 2.13   An example of a hypercolumn (including ocular dominance and orientation columns)

What, then, is the function of the visual cortex? Although damage to the visual cortex will cause blindness in the appropriate part of the visual field (the area of blindness is called a **scotoma**) it is unlikely that our perception of the visual world occurs in this part of the brain. Hubel and Wiesel's work suggests that the cells of the visual cortex simply act as feature detectors that respond to specific elements of the visual scene such as lines and edges, angles, motion, angles and colour. Their research also indicates that this raw visual input is analysed in a hierarchical fashion with increasing levels of complexity (for example, simple, complex and hypercomplex cells). Presumably, this hierarchical processing continues as the visual information is analysed beyond the striate cortex. In addition, the brain has to reconstruct the visual image into a meaningful whole at some point in the processing – although how it does this remains largely a mystery (Tong 2003).

What happens if a blind person is able to see again?

Although it is rare, there are cases where people blind from birth have regained their sight as adults. But, can such a person see and make sense of their world? In 1690, the English philosopher John Locke considered the question of whether a blind person taught to discriminate between a cube and a sphere by touch alone, would be able to recognise the objects visually if sight was returned. Locke reasoned that it would not be possible. However, we now know that Locke was wrong. In 2004, Richard Gregory reported the case of a man known as SB who lost his sight at 10 months old, and regained it fifty years later after receiving a corneal transplant. Gregory found that SB could recognise some objects without having seen them. He could identify cars and trucks, and tell the time from looking at a clock. In both cases, however, SB had tactile knowledge to assist his recognition: he had repeatedly washed his friend's car, and used a watch without a front glass to tell the time. Thus, SB showed cross-modal transfer from touch to vision. But, his vision was abnormal in many other ways. Although SB could judge distances and sizes of objects that were already familiar from touch, such as chairs scattered around in a room, he was hopelessly inaccurate when judging landmarks in the distance. This also affected the way SB perceived pictures. A countryside landscape was seen as a meaningless collage of colours, and drawings as flat and two-dimensional. Like many other blind people who regain their vision, SB never adapted to his new sense. His visual world was dull and uninteresting, and he lacked motivation to learn more. Indeed, we now know that learning to see for an adult is very difficult, and there is a strong temptation for many to revert back to blindness, where they are better adapted to cope.

One reason why learning to see is so difficult for blind people, is because our visual system crucially depends on experience early in life for it to become fully functional. This fact has been known since the nineteenth century when the surgical removal of cataracts became commonplace. For example, when cataracts are removed from individuals who have developed them in later life, the procedure generally reinstates full vision. However, when congenital cataracts are removed from children, full vision is often not restored – even when an artificial lens is used to produce a good image on the retina. This provides evidence to show that a sensitive period must occur in the first few years of life when experience is necessary for the proper development of the visual system. Once this period has passed then vision becomes permanently impaired.

The importance of early experience for the proper development of the visual system was also shown by Hubel and Wiesel in the 1960s who reared young animals (cats and monkeys) with one eye closed. When they reopened the eye and recorded from the visual cortex, they found that nearly all the cells were dominated by the eye that had remained open. Moreover, very few cells ever became activated by stimuli that were presented to the eye that had been closed. In a further set of experiments, it was shown that young animals with restricted visual experience also developed cells with abnormal properties. For example, when a kitten is reared in an environment that contains only horizontal lines, almost all of its simple and complex cells will develop a preference for horizontal lines – so much so, that when the cat is later exposed to a normal environment, it virtually ignores vertical lines and objects.

Introduction to colour vision

The ability to perceive colour is a remarkable ability. It is said that we can perceive some 250 different hues, and these appear to correspond to all the different wavelengths of light that we can detect reflected from objects around us. Indeed, human beings are able to detect light wavelengths from around 400 nm, which produces the sensation of blue, through to about 550 nm, causing the sensation of green-yellow, and finally to around 650 nm, which enables the detection of red. Despite this, the perception of colour is ultimately produced by the visual system since all these frequencies of light are simply patterns of energy and not inherently 'colourful'. Thus, as you look at the colours on this page you might like to contemplate that the brain is actually inventing them.

The first step in colour perception begins with the cones in the retina. In fact, there are three different types of cone: the first absorbs light maximally in short wavelengths of around 445 nm (blue), the second absorbs light at medium wavelengths at around 535 nm (green), and the third absorbs light at long wavelengths of around 570 nm (red) (see Figure 2.14). Despite this, cones show considerable overlap in their detection of wavelengths. For example, light in wavelengths of 600 nm will induce the greatest

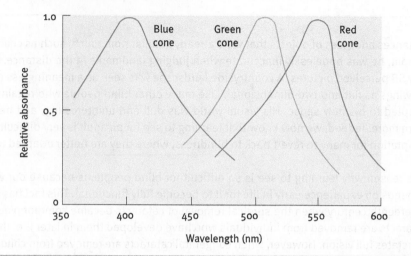

| Figure 2.14 | The absorbance of light by the three types of cone ('blue', 'green' and 'red') in the human retina |

response from the red cones, but it will also produce a weaker response in the green cones. Thus, red-sensitive cones do not respond exclusively to long wavelengths of light, they just respond better – and the same principle holds for the other two cones (Baylor 1987).

Clearly, we detect all these different wavelengths because the light energy reaching our eyes is transduced by the cones into neural impulses. The cones do this by using **photopigments**, which are special molecules embedded in their membrane consisting of **opsin** (a protein) and **retinal** (a lipid). Remarkably, each photoreceptor has as many as 10 million photopigment molecules. When exposed to light, the opsin and retinal molecules split, causing a series of chemical reactions, leading to a change in the cell's rate of firing. There are three forms of opsin found in cones, with each one maximally sensitive to a different wavelength of light (colour). The rods also have their own specialised photopigment known as **rhodopsin** that is made of rod opsin and retinal.

Theories of colour vision

The idea that our eyes contain different receptors for wavelengths of light was first made by the British physicist Thomas Young in 1802 – long before cones were discovered. He made his claim on the basis that any colour can be produced, including white, if three different types of light are mixed in the right proportion – provided the wavelengths are far enough apart from each other. Thus, Young proposed that the retina must also contain three different receptors for colour with their probable sensitivities being for blue, green and red (the so-called 'primaries'). This theory was supported by Hermann von Helmholtz in the 1850s, and it became known as the Young–Helmholtz or **trichromatic theory** of colour vision.

However, one problem with the trichromatic theory was that it could not explain the effect of negative after-images. For example, if one stares at a red square against a white background for a few minutes, and then suddenly looks at a blank card, you will see a green after-image of the square. Alternatively, staring at a blue square produces a yellow after-image, and staring at a black one produces a white effect. A similar type of relationship also exists for colour blindness. For example, the most common form of colour blindness is for red–green, followed by the rarer blue–yellow form (there is no such thing as red–blue or green–yellow colour blindness). Thus, the colours red–green, and blue–yellow, are linked in a way that cannot be explained by the trichromatic theory.

In 1870, the German physiologist Ewald Hering proposed an alternative explanation of colour vision. Although agreeing with Young and Helmholtz that the colour spectrum could be created by mixing three primary colours, Hering did not accept that yellow was derived from a mixture of red and green (as the trichromatic theory held), but rather that it was a primary colour along with red, green and blue. With four primary colours instead of three, Hering saw that the visual system now required only two types of colour detector: one responding to red or green, and the other to blue or yellow. Because each type of detector was hypothesised to produce two different colour sensations which also acted to oppose each other (red–green, yellow–blue and black–white), the theory was called the **opponent theory** of colour vision.

Which theory is correct?

On first sight, there is convincing evidence to support the trichromatic theory. Not only is it supported by colour-mixing experiments but, more importantly, we now know that there are three types of cones in the retina that respond to different wavelengths of light corresponding to blue, green and red. These are, of course, the three primary colours that the trichromatic theory predicted could be used to make all colours.

But, things have turned out not to be so simple. One difficulty with the trichromatic theory is the discovery of ganglion cells in the retina that respond in a way that is consistent with Hering's theory. That is, they increase their activity to one colour and decrease it to another. These are called **dual-opponent colour neurons** and there are two basic types: those that produce opposite responses to red and green, and those responding similarly to blue and yellow. For example, one type of cell is excited by the colour of red and inhibited by green (R^+, G^-) or vice versa (R^-, G^+). And the other type of cell is excited by the colour of blue and inhibited by yellow (B^+, Y^-) or vice versa (B^-, Y^+). These are, of course, exactly the type of responses predicted by the opponent-process theory (DeValois and DeValois 1988).

Interestingly, these opponent cells also have concentric receptive fields as first described by Kuffler – except in this case the centres and surrounds are sensitive to different colours. But the principle remains the same. For example, a ganglion cell might be excited by green and inhibited by red in the centre of its receptive field, while showing the opposite response in the surrounding ring. Similarly, a ganglion cell may show the same response to blue and yellow. There is also a third type of ganglion cell, deriving from cones, which does not respond to colour in this way but instead reacts to differences in brightness. These cells are sometimes called black and white detectors.

Thus, both the trichromatic and opponent-process theories appear to be correct. If this is the case then the fundamental problem is, how do the three types of cone located in the retina (red, green and blue) combine to form the two types of opponent cell

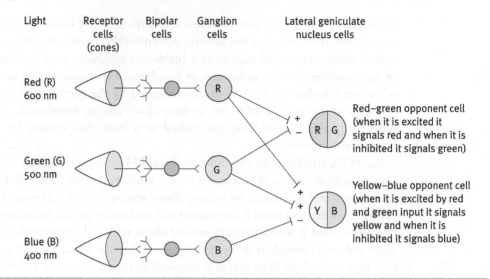

Figure 2.15   Colour coding in the retina as predicted by the opponent-process theory of colour vision

(corresponding to red–green and blue–yellow) in the optic ganglia? Or, put simply, where does yellow come from? The answer to this problem must lie with the neural 'wiring' that occurs between the cones and the ganglion cells. Indeed, assuming this is the case, then the red–green opponent cell is easy to explain as it must receive input from both the red and the green cones. Thus, if the input from the red cones were excitatory, and input from the green cones inhibitory, then this would explain the R^+, G^- opponent cell. Similarly, a reversed system could account for the R^-, G^+ opponent cell. But, using the same logic, how can the blue–yellow opponent cell be explained when there is no cone for yellow?

The best explanation is that the blue–yellow opponent cell receives input from three sources: the blue, green and red receptors. In this scheme, the input to the blue part of the opponent cell is simple as there is a corresponding cone for blue. In contrast, the yellow part of the opponent cell is derived from both red and green receptor input (see Figure 2.15). That is, we see yellow not because we have a specific photoreceptor for yellow, but because it is 'made up' from inputs arriving from the red and green cones. Thus, when we detect the light wavelength corresponding to yellow (which falls between the red and green bands), this stimulates both red and green cones equally, and it this dual activation that causes the yellow part of the yellow–blue ganglion cell to produce its excitation or inhibition.

In order for ganglion cells to show opponent red–green and blue–yellow responses, the 'wiring' of the neural pathways linking the cones with opponent ganglion neurons must take place in the retina. It is believed that this function is served by the horizontal cells which link the cones with the bipolar cells, or by the multi-branched connections of the bipolar cells that synapse with the ganglion cells. Nonetheless, despite this somewhat complex explanation, the trichromatic and opponent theories, even when combined in this way, still cannot account for all the phenomena of colour perception. One serious problem for both these theories is **colour constancy** – the fact that the perceived colour of an object remains very much the same under very different lighting conditions (for example, we are able to see a white cat as white even when we are wearing sunglasses). This indicates that the colours we perceive are not necessarily determined by the exact wavelengths reaching our eyes after all. For a more thorough discussion of this problem see Land (1977).

John Dalton and colour blindness

John Dalton (1766–1844), the British chemist, is one of the fathers of modern science who is famous for developing the atomic theory – in essence the idea that matter is composed of atoms with different weights, and that the combination and rearrangement of atoms forms the basis of all chemical reactions. Dalton, however, made contributions to many other subjects, and gave the first detailed account of colour blindness in 1794. It is said that Dalton first realised he had a colour defect when he wore a scarlet robe to receive his PhD degree, thinking it was dark blue. When Dalton examined his own visual capabilities further by viewing light being passed through a prism, he discovered that while most people could distinguish six colours, he could see just two: blue/violet and yellow. Dalton's brother also had the same affliction, and he was to find a similar defect in 28 other people who were all male. Dalton believed that his colour blindness was due to a blue colouring in the vitreous humour of his eyes, and he instructed that after his death his eye should be dissected and examined to prove the hypothesis. However, when this was done, no blue colouring was found.

We now know that most types of colour blindness are inherited and caused by a faulty gene that makes the photopigments (or opsins) in the cones. The most common type of colour blindness – which occurs in about 8 per cent of males and 0.6 per cent of females – is where the person cannot distinguish between red and green. In fact, there are two forms of this deficit: **deuteranopia,** where the person lacks the photopigment for green, and **protanopia,** where the red pigment is missing. In both cases, the person tends to see their world painted in shades of blue, yellow and grey. The reason why red–green colour blindness predominantly affects males is because both the protan and deuta genes are located on the X chromosome, of which men have one and women two. Thus, women are rarely red–green blind because if one of their X chromosomes is defective, the other will compensate. This also means that red–green colour blindness is handed down from a colour blind male through his daughters (who are normally unaffected) to his male grandchildren. Indeed, his sons will be unaffected as they always receive his Y chromosome and not his defective X chromosome. About 8 per cent of women are carriers of these faulty genes.

There are other types of colour blindness although they are much rarer and include **tritanopia,** where the retina lacks blue cones (here the person is unable to distinguish between blue and yellow), and **achromatopsia** which causes total colour blindness (here the person's view of the world is much the same as a black and white television picture). Tritanopia is not sex-linked as the defective gene occurs on chromosome 7 and thus it occurs equally in male and females. Tritanopia is found in about 1 in every 1,000 people, and achromatopia in 1 in every 100,000.

Returning to John Dalton, we know he suffered from a red–green colour defect, but was it deuteranopia or protanopia? Remarkably, in 1995, investigators from London and Oxford (Hunt *et al.* 1995) extracted DNA from small samples of Dalton's eyes, which had been kept in the possession of the Manchester Literary and Philosophical Society, and discovered that they lacked the pigment for green processing. Thus, Dalton was a deuteranope. Dalton would not only have been gratified that the answer to his visual defect had finally been solved some 150 years after his death, but it is also a quirk of fate that his atomic theory provides the methodological basis that made its analysis possible.

A closer look at the lateral geniculate nucleus

In the human, the lateral geniculate nucleus consists of six layers of cells that are distinguished by their neural input and shape. For example, each layer receives input from one eye only, with layers 1, 4 and 6 receiving axons from the nasal part of the contralateral eye, and layers 2, 3 and 5 getting projections from the outer part of the ipsilateral eye. Although it is hard to picture (see Figure 2.7 on page 63), this means that each lateral geniculate nucleus receives information from the opposite side of the visual world. In addition, the upper four layers of the lateral geniculate nucleus contain small neurons called **parvocellular cells**, while the lower two layers have neurons called **magnocellular cells**.

The parvocellular cells are the ones sensitive to colour and they have concentric receptive fields showing the same opponent red–green and blue–yellow responses as found with ganglion cells. In fact, about 80 per cent of parvocellular cells show this type of response, with the remainder showing no colour preference. In contrast, the magnocellular cells are colour blind and have receptive fields that respond to a wide range of wavelengths. These appear to be encoding luminance contrast. It is also interesting to note that parvocellular cells tend to give a sustained response to an unchanging stimulus, whereas magnocellular neurons respond rapidly but briefly to a constant stimulus. These findings suggest that parvocellular cells are better suited to analysing stationary objects, whereas magnocellular neurons respond best to movement.

These ideas have been largely confirmed by examining the visual capabilities of monkeys after selective lesioning of the lateral geniculate nucleus. For example, damage to the magnocellular layers has little effect on visual acuity or colour vision, but impairs the monkey's ability to see quickly moving stimuli. In contrast, damage to the parvocellular layers has little effect on motion perception but reduces fine pattern vision and abolishes colour perception. These findings show that parvocellular cells are essential for high-resolution vision, which enables the detailed analysis of shape size and colour of objects to take place, whereas the magnocellular cells process information that is vital for analysing the movement of objects (Livingstone and Hubel 1988). Moreover, as we will see in the next section, the parvocellular and magnocellular cells project to different systems in the visual cortex – and remain largely segregated in secondary cortical areas.

Surprisingly, the retina provides only about 20 per cent of the total input to the lateral geniculate nucleus; the rest derives mainly from the visual cortex and, to a lesser extent, from the brainstem, including pons, medulla and tectum. Presumably, the inputs from the cortex represent a feedback mechanism that sharpens the visual image in some way. Alternatively, it has been suggested that the brainstem inputs may 'turn off' the visual signal during eye movements, so one does not see the world jump when the eyes are moved (Noda 1975). Thus, there is still much to learn about the role of this structure in visual processing.

Colour processing in the cortex

It is only within the past few decades that scientists have begun to understand how cells in the visual cortex process colour. Before then, colour-sensitive cells in the upper layers of the visual cortex had been detected, but they were quite rare, and made up about

10 per cent of all cells. Moreover, their location also seemed to occur at random, making it difficult to study them in a systematic way. But, in the late 1970s, a way of identifying colour-processing cells was unexpectedly made possible when researchers stained the visual cortex with a mitochondrial enzyme called cytochrome oxidase (Wong-Riley 1979). Mitochondria are tiny organelles inside the cells that produce energy, and it was found that when they were stained, darkened clusters of cells called **cytochrome blobs** appeared in the visual cortex. In fact, these emerged as peg-like dark columns that gave the visual cortex a polka-dot appearance. A closer inspection showed that they were about 0.2 mm in diameter and passed through all layers of the visual cortex except layer 4. Perhaps more importantly, it was soon found that the cells in these blobs were sensitive to colour. Indeed, their responses were similar to those obtained from the parvocellular cells of the lateral geniculate nucleus, that is, they had concentric receptive fields which responded to either red–green or blue–yellow.

The discovery of cytochrome blobs has led to much research and some degree of controversy. It might be predicted from what we already know about the visual pathways that the colour-processing parvocellular cells will project to the blobs, whereas the magnocellular cells will project to the areas between (known as **interblob** regions). But, this is not entirely the case. Although most of the parvocellular axons from the lateral geniculate nucleus pass into the blob regions, about 30 per cent of them also project to interblob areas. Thus, a significant number of cells in the interblob regions are sensitive to colours, although it appears this occurs only when they define edges or borders (Leventhal *et al.* 1995). To make matters even more confusing, the colour-blind magnocellular cells also send their axons into the blob regions. This is perhaps to provide information about brightness or contrast.

The modular structure of the visual cortex

The discovery of cytochrome blobs led to a revision of ideas concerning the structure of the visual cortex. As we have seen, the visual cortex is organised into columns, with blocks of orientation columns made up of simple, complex and hypercomplex cells, accompanied by ocular dominance columns comprising neurons with a preference for input from one of the eyes. Into this columnar unit the colour processing blobs can now be placed. One term that has been used to describe this complex is the **cortical module** (Figure 2.16). This unit consists of two ocular dominance units, each receiving input from each eye, along with two colour-processing blobs. In addition, each module contains the full range (in fact twice over) of orientation columns that cover every orientation across 180°. Thus, each cortical module has several important functions, including the analysis of pattern, colour, luminance, movement and depth.

It is estimated that the primary visual cortex contains some 2,500 cortical modules with each one containing in the region of 150,000 neurons. They measure roughly between 0.5 and 1 mm square and 2 mm deep. Each module is also responsible for analysing information from the same small part of the visual field, as shown by the fact that removal of a cortical module will cause a scotoma (blind spot) on the retina. Although each individual module receives around 10,000 neural inputs (predominantly from the lateral geniculate nucleus), it sends out around 50,000 axonal projections to

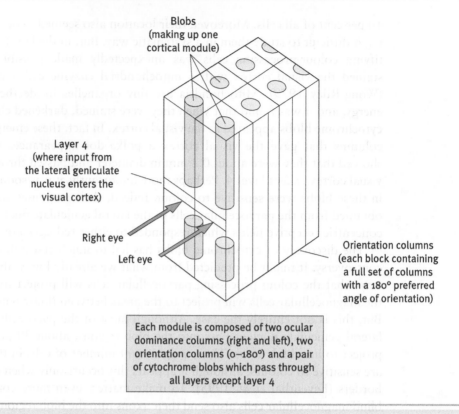

Blobs (making up one cortical module)

Layer 4 (where input from the lateral geniculate nucleus enters the visual cortex)

Right eye

Left eye

Orientation columns (each block containing a full set of columns with a 180° preferred angle of orientation)

Each module is composed of two ocular dominance columns (right and left), two orientation columns (0–180°) and a pair of cytochrome blobs which pass through all layers except layer 4

Figure 2.16 Hubel and Livingstone's model of the modular structure of the visual cortex

other areas involved in visual processing. This includes inputs to secondary areas of the visual cortex (deriving from layers 2 and 3), to the superior colliculus (layer 5), and lateral geniculate nucleus (layer 6). There are also short collateral fibres to adjacent cortical modules. This rich profusion of output fibres is a sure indication that visual processing gets even more complex as we go further away from the striate cortex.

Visual processing in extrastriate areas

Some of the earliest studies that examined the anatomical organisation of the cerebral cortex were performed by Karl Brodmann in the early 1900s, who divided the visual cortex into three areas based on their differences in cell morphology. These regions were labelled as area 17, which we now recognise as the primary visual cortex, and areas 18 and 19, which make up the visual association cortex. Because area 17 is the first region to receive input from the lateral geniculate nucleus, it later became more commonly called **visual area 1 (V1)**, while areas 18 and 19 became known as **V2** and **V3**, respectively. Although relatively little work had been performed on these areas by the late 1960s, it was generally believed that V1 projected to V2, and this area projected to V3. Thus each visual area was thought to provide some sort of elaboration on the processing of the preceding area. Indeed, cells at successive stages were thought to have even larger receptive fields and they re-analysed the same features at progressively more complex levels. In other words, vision was seen as a serial and hierarchical process.

This view began to change dramatically in the 1970s when researchers such as Semir Zeki, and others, began tracing the degeneration of fibres made by discrete lesions to the striate cortex (V1). This work revealed not only that areas 18 and 19 were much more complex than previously thought, but also that there were other important visual areas beyond their boundaries. For example, in addition to projections from V1 to V2 to V3, Zeki found a pathway that branched from V2 to a postage-stamp-size part of the visual cortex (roughly corresponding to the border with the temporal cortex) which he labelled **V4**. In addition, Zeki found yet another pathway, also appearing to derive from V2 (and V4), which terminated in the **inferior temporal lobes** and which he called **V5** (Zeki 1978). Further discoveries soon revealed that the anatomical connections between each of these different areas were highly intricate, with a combination of serial (hierarchical) and parallel pathways mediating different aspects of vision. We do not need to describe all these pathways in detail here, but they can be seen, albeit greatly simplified, in Figure 2.17.

As Figure 2.17 shows, an important stage of visual processing takes place in the prestriate region (V2), which is a band of tissue some 6 to 8 mm wide surrounding the V1 cortex. When V2 is stained with cytochrome oxidase it reveals regions of high and low activity arranged in parallel thin and thick stripes, and which are interrupted by unstained inter-stripe regions (Livingstone and Hubel 1988). As might be expected from their cytological differences, the striped regions of V2 contain cells that receive different types of input from V1. In brief: (1) the thick stripes receive information from layer 4B of the visual cortex, which includes input from the magnocellular cells of the lateral geniculate nucleus, and are primarily involved in processing movement; (2) the thin stripes get information from the blobs and are involved in processing colour; (3) the pale stripes obtain input from the extrablob areas involved in orientation and form. Thus, the prestriate area maintains the segregation of visual input that first takes place in the cortical modules of V1.

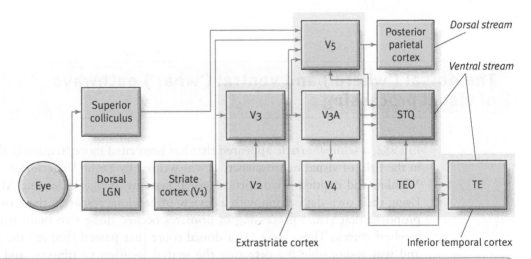

Figure 2.17 Simplified schema of the interconnection of areas of the visual cortex in the rhesus monkey brain

At this point the three streams of visual information diverge and travel into different areas of the brain, although the extrastriate cortex is composed of more than 30 different areas, which makes it difficult to follow the pathways with precision (Van Essen *et al.* 1992). Nonetheless, it appears that one route passes from the thick stripes of V2 (along with direct magnocellular input from V1) to V3, with cells in this latter region being highly sensitive to detecting edges of particular orientations that are important for pattern vision. A second pathway goes from the thin stripes of V2 (along with considerable other input) to V4, which contains a large number of cells sensitive to colour. Indeed, it has been found that patients with damage to V4 suffer from a form of colour blindness known as **cerebral achromatopsia** in which they can see only shades of grey. In fact, if damage is bilateral, then such patients cannot even imagine colours or remember the colours of objects they saw before their brain insult occurred. However, if damage is unilateral, then patients only lose colour vision in half of the visual field. Both V3 and V4 send fibres into the inferotemporal cortex, which is essential for pattern vision and recognition.

A third pathway can be seen to go from the thick stripes of V2 (and V3) to V5, which appears to be important for motion vision. Indeed, researchers have found not only that over 90 per cent of neurons in V5 are highly sensitive to movement of shapes and objects, but also that they have very large receptive fields indicating that they integrate information over a large retinal area (Zeki and Shipp 1988). Although it is very rare, it is known that damage to V5 can produce a condition known as **cerebral akinetopsia**, which impairs the ability of a person to perceive motion. For example, one patient reported that when she attempted to pour coffee, the fluid appeared to be frozen (Zihl *et al.* 1983). Moreover, her inability to see movement in a speaker's mouth made it difficult for her to follow a conversation. Although these people can see objects perfectly at rest, when the objects move they often appear to vanish. This makes certain everyday tasks, such as crossing the street, highly dangerous. Area V5 is also known to send important projections into the parietal lobe (and to a lesser extent the temporal lobe), which contributes to the dorsal stream of visual processing.

The dorsal ('where') and ventral ('what') pathways of visual processing

In 1982, a seminal article appeared that has been cited more frequently than any other in the field of visual neuroscience. It was written by Leslie Ungerleider and Mortimer Mishkin and entitled 'Two cortical visual systems' (Ungerleider and Mishkin 1982). Using their own data along with a review of previous research, these two researchers proposed that visual processing in primates occurs along two main pathways in the cerebral cortex. These were (1) a dorsal route that passed through the parietal lobes and was responsible for detecting the spatial location of objects, and (2) a ventral stream that passed through the temporal lobes and was responsible for the visual recognition of objects. In effect, Ungerleider and Mishkin had proposed an anatomical and functional distinction for two very different visual pathways in the brain that were specialised for 'where is it?' and 'what is it?' processing.

The main evidence for Ungerleider and Mishkin's position was derived from behavioural experiments in which the visual discrimination ability of monkeys was examined by the use of lesions or by single-cell recording. For example, it had been known since the work of Kluver and Bucy in the 1930s that monkeys with lesions to the temporal lobes (particularly the inferotemporal cortex) were greatly impaired in their ability to recognise familiar objects by vision. Yet, the same monkeys had no visual deficits as they could pick up even small objects in order to investigate them. Indeed, it was once noted by the neuroscientist Karl Pribram (cited by Goodale and Milner 2004) that monkeys with temporal lobe lesions, that had been trained for months to no avail to learn a pattern discrimination task, could nevertheless snatch flies out of the air with great dexterity. In contrast, monkeys with parietal lesions have an opposite problem. These animals have little difficulty recognising objects, but are unable to reach or grasp for them accurately. Thus, these monkeys cannot use vision to guide movements with any degree of precision. These animals also show impairments when they have to remember the location of an object in order to obtain a reward, indicating their learning about spatial configurations is impaired.

Although Ungerleider and Mishkin's theory has attracted widespread support, there are other possible interpretations. For example, Goodale and Milner (1992) have proposed that the main function of the dorsal pathway is not to encode the spatial configuration of an object and its relations, but to visually guide motor actions. For example, if someone throws you a ball, you are likely to try to catch it. But, you don't plan the catch, or think about it. You just do it. This action, Goodale and Milner would claim, is a function of the dorsal visual pathway. Moreover, because we perform many of our actions without 'thinking', Goodale and Milner also suggest, somewhat more controversially, that the dorsal pathway is largely automatic and unconscious. In contrast, they propose that the ventral pathways are involved in choosing a goal, and in recognising visual objects. These are believed to be essentially cognitive processes that are available to conscious decision making and interpretation (see Figure 2.18).

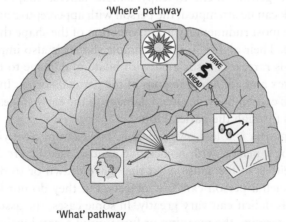

'Where' pathway

'What' pathway

The 'what' and 'where' pathways in the visual system include areas specialised for processing depth perception (symbolised by a pair of spectacles), form (an angle), colour, and direction (the curve ahead sign). The result is object recognition (the 'what' pathway) or object location (the 'where' pathway)

Figure 2.18   The spatial-visual (dorsal route) and object recognition (ventral route) pathways in the brain

Source: M.I. Posner and M.E. Raichle (1997) *Images of Mind*, p. 15

Visual agnosia: seeing without recognising

One clinical condition that lends support to the 'where' (spatial understanding) and 'what' (object recognition) dichotomy of visual processing is **visual agnosia**. This is a rare condition characterised by an inability to recognise familiar objects by vision, although if the person went to an optician they would be found to have 'normal' sight. Consequently, a person with agnosia may be unable to name a given object when it is shown to them visually but able to recognise it when presented in another sensory mode (by touch, say). The term 'agnosia' (derived from the Greek meaning 'lack of knowledge') was coined by Sigmund Freud in 1891, but, a more important contribution to its understanding was made in 1890 by Lissauer, who proposed that this deficit could be divided into two types: **apperceptive** and **associative**. This distinction was partly made on his belief that visual recognition must involve two processes: (1) perceptual integration (apperception) in which sensory data are organised into a meaningful 'whole', and (2) association, where the percept is linked with stored knowledge so its meaning can be established.

An example of apperceptive agnosia is the case of Dr P, the character for whom Oliver Sacks named his book *The Man who Mistook his Wife for a Hat*. Dr P was a well-educated music teacher who was unable to recognise the faces of his students by sight, although he could identify them when they spoke. His ability to recognise a wide range of objects was also impaired. For example, when Sacks gave Dr P a glove, the latter recognised that it had five appendages and guessed it was a cloth container such as a purse. Nonetheless, despite prompting, he was unable to recognise it as a glove. Similarly, when Sacks presented him with a red rose, Dr P described its basic shape as 'a convoluted red form with linear green attachment', but was unable to recognise it until he was asked to smell it. But perhaps the most striking example of his deficit came at the end of his examination when Dr P looking for his hat, tried to pick up the head of his wife!

In apperceptive agnosia, basic vision is intact but the person cannot combine the visual elements into a meaningful percept. Thus, although they can see lines, edges, colour, motion etc., the apperceptive agnostic has trouble 'seeing objects'. This can be demonstrated by getting them to copy simple letters, shapes and line drawings. Although the task can be attempted, the person with apperceptive agnosia is often unable to make even the most rudimentary approximation of the shape they are asked to draw (see Figure 2.19). Their ability to match simple shapes is also impaired. Although this form of agnosia is rare, it is associated with bilateral damage to the extrastriate areas of the visual cortex and adjoining regions of the parietal cortex. In other words, apperceptive agnosia is caused by widespread damage to the early stages of the 'where' pathway that courses through the parietal lobes.

Associative agnosia is a less severe deficit. For example, copying a line drawing is relatively easy for a person with associative agnosia (see Figure 2.20), although they may be unable either to recognise what they have drawn or to draw the object from memory. Thus, such a person can 'see' objects, but they do not know what they are. The extent of this deficit can vary greatly. In some cases, the associative agnostic will not be able to determine the meaning or function of a previously known stimulus. In other instances they may be able to extract enough information to recognise its main category (such as mammal, insect or bird), but be unable to assess its other attributes (for example, whether it is tame or dangerous). The brain sites responsible for associative agnosia extend from the occipital–temporal lobe border, especially the

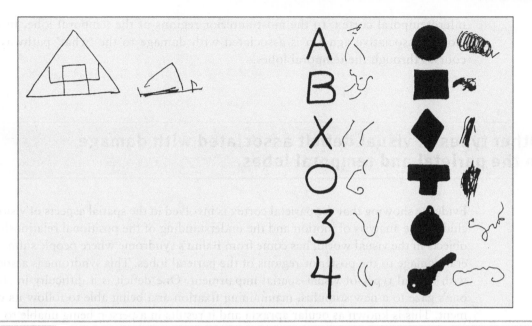

Figure 2.19   Examples of drawings made by patients with apperceptive agnosia

Source: M.T. Banich (2004) *Cognitive Neuroscience and Neuropsychology*, 2nd edition, p. 195

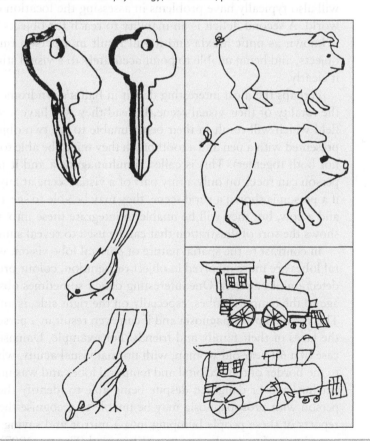

Figure 2.20   Examples of drawings made by patients with associative agnosia

Source: A.B. Rubens and D.F. Benson (1971) Associative visual agnosia, *Archives of Neurology*, 24, 305–316

inferotemporal cortex, to the most anterior regions of the temporal lobe. In other words, associative agnosia is associated with damage to the 'what' pathway that courses through the temporal lobes.

Other types of visual deficit associated with damage to the parietal and temporal lobes

Evidence showing that the parietal cortex is involved in the spatial aspects of vision, including the analysis of motion and the understanding of the positional relationships of objects in the visual world, has come from **Balint's syndrome** where people suffer bilateral damage to the posterior regions of the parietal lobes. This syndrome is associated with several types of visual–spatial impairment. One deficit is a difficulty in shifting one's gaze to a new stimulus, maintaining fixation and being able to follow its movement. This is known as **ocular apraxia** and it results in a person being unable to make a systematic scan of their visual scene or focus on a particular object. Instead, their eyes tend to 'wander' around so that objects come into view for a while and are then replaced by others. Although such a person will recognise what they are observing, they will also typically have problems in assessing the location of that object in their visual world. A second deficit is an inability to reach for objects under visual guidance. This is known as **optic ataxia** and it will result in a person fumbling and misreaching for objects, and being unable to point accurately to a visual stimulus although they can see it clearly.

Perhaps the most interesting deficit in Balint's syndrome is a person's inability to see the totality of their visual scene. Instead they will have a very narrow visual attention field which will result in their being unable to see two objects at once (for example, if presented with a pen and a toothbrush they might be able to see one object at a time, but not both together). This is called **simultanagnosia** and it means, in effect, that such a person can focus on only a tiny part of a visual scene at any one moment. For example, if a person is shown a rural scene, they may be able to see a tree, a river, a house, a field and a cow, but they will be unable to integrate these into a unified whole. Figure 2.21 shows the sort of illustration that can be used to reveal simultanagnosia.

In contrast to the spatial nature of parietal lobe vision, we have seen that the temporal lobes are more involved in object recognition, colour processing and high-resolution detection of patterns. One interesting deficit sometimes observed in patients with damage to the temporal lobes, especially on the right side, is an inability to recognise faces. This is called **prosopagnosia** and it can even result in a person being unable to recognise the faces of their family and friends. For example, Damasio *et al.* (1990) reported the case of a 60-year-old woman, with normal visual acuity, who suffered a bilateral stroke to the border of the occipital and temporal lobes and was unable to recognise the face of her husband or daughter, despite being able to identify them by their voice. Indeed, a person with prosopagnosia may be unable to recognise their own face – and there are reports of these people bumping into a mirror and saying 'excuse me' mistaking their own image for another person (Klein and Thorne 2007). Despite this, people with prosopagnosia are often able to recognise the age and gender of faces, and even their emotional expression.

When asked to describe this picture, an individual with this syndrome could describe the handlebars, the car and the helmet but could not perceive why the girl was trying to flag down the car.

| Figure 2.21 | An illustration of simultanagnosia |

Source: M.T. Banich (2004) *Cognitive Neuroscience and Neuropsychology,* 2nd edition, p. 244

Interestingly, the development of functional bran scanning techniques over recent years has identified an area at the base of the inferotemporal lobe called the **fusiform face gyrus** (see Figure 2.22) that is specially activated by faces but not by other types of visual stimuli (Kanwisher *et al.* 1997). The fact that there is an area of the brain devoted to the processing of faces shows just how special faces are in our visual world. Nor are we alone in the animal kingdom, since a number of mammals have also been shown to have brain regions involved in face recognition. For example, in sheep, cells have been found in the temporal cortex that respond selectively to the faces of horned sheep, unhorned sheep, sheepdogs, wolves and even their own shepherd! (Kendrick and Baldwin 1987).

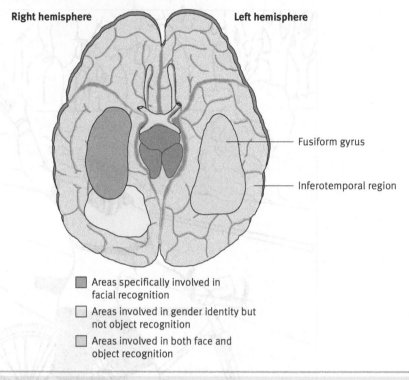

Right hemisphere   Left hemisphere

Fusiform gyrus

Inferotemporal region

☐ Areas specifically involved in
  facial recognition

☐ Areas involved in gender identity but
  not object recognition

☐ Areas involved in both face and
  object recognition

Figure 2.22   The location of the fusiform face gyrus

Subcortical visual systems

The pathway from the retina to the occipital cortex, and beyond, is not the only visual system in the brain. In fact, about 10 per cent of the ganglion cells branch away from the optic nerve before reaching the lateral geniculate nucleus and pass to subcortical regions, including the midbrain tectum located at the top of the brainstem. In many lower species such as fish, reptiles and birds, the tectum provides the highest site for visual analysis, and in primates this region, which is dominated by the **superior colliculus**, remains functionally important. The superior colliculus is involved in the control of automatic reflexes and orientating movements of the head and eyes, especially when new stimuli appear in the visual field. In addition, the superior colliculus helps to co-ordinate **saccadic eye movements** – sudden automatic and rapid movements of the eyes that allow us to explore changing visual scenes and to continually bring new images onto the fovea.

The superior colliculus also sends many of its axons to the secondary visual areas of the occipital lobe. Evidence that this pathway may make an important contribution to human vision has come from the phenomenon of **blindsight** which was first shown in patient DB (Weiskrantz *et al.* 1974). DB was a patient who had much of his right primary visual cortex surgically removed following a tumour. It had long been known that damage to the visual pathways from retina to visual cortex produces blindness in the visual field opposite to the side of the brain where the lesion has occurred – and DB was no exception as the surgery appeared to leave him blind in his left visual field. Despite this, DB was remarkably accurate at pointing to the position of markers on a wall, deciding whether a stick was horizontal or vertical, and distinguishing between the letters X and O. Yet, DB protested that he was guessing and could not see what he was doing! In fact, this type of residual vision has since been found in around 20 per cent of subjects with visual cortex damage.

Blindsight is controversial because not all investigators believe that it is produced by the projections of the superior colliculus innervating the extrastriate regions of the visual cortex. Indeed, another possibility is that blindsight is caused by stray light passing from the blind visual field into the sighted one thereby giving a clue to the target's location (Campion *et al.* 1983). But, even if blindsight has another cause, it remains that the two visual systems (the geniculate striate and superior collicular) have evolved to serve different functions. This was shown in an early study by Schneider (1967), who found that lesions of the striate cortex in hamsters impaired performance on a simple visual discrimination task, but that such animals could take a sunflower seed from the experimenter's fingers. These deficits were reversed, however, in hamsters with lesions of the superior colliculus. In fact, the superior lesioned animals could only orientate towards the seed if it touched their whiskers.

Another important subcortical area for vision is the nearby pretectum, which is involved in producing pupil reflexes. For example, if bright light is suddenly shone into the eye, the pupil will automatically constrict. This reflex occurs because a few of the retinal ganglion cells directly pass to the pretectum, which contains the **Edinger–Westphal nucleus**, a group of cells that, in turn, send axons into the third (oculomotor) cranial nerve which innervates many muscles of the eye, including the pupillary constrictor muscles of the iris. Thus, when the eye is exposed to bright light, it activates the Edinger–Westphal nucleus, and it will cause pupil constriction. Another subcortical structure that receives visual input is the **suprachiasmatic nucleus** located in the anterior hypothalamus. In fact, this tiny structure has its own visual pathway which leaves the optic nerve close to the optic chiasm and is involved in sleep and circadian rhythms.

Summary

Vision, or our ability to detect different wavelengths and intensities of light, is our most important sense, and it has been estimated that around one-third of the human brain is devoted to its analysis and perception. Our visual processing begins with the eyes. Light passes through the transparent **cornea**, into the **aqueous humour**, and then to the **pupil**, which is the aperture (controlled by the **iris**, which gives the eyes their colour) that regulates the amount of light entering the eye. Just behind the pupil lies the **lens**, whose function is to bring visual images into clear focus onto the **retina** and whose shape is controlled by the **ciliary muscles**. Light then passes through the main chamber of the eye containing **vitreous humour** and is projected onto the retina containing the photoreceptors of the eye. There are two types of photoreceptor: the **rods**, which are found predominantly in its periphery and are involved in the detection of light intensity, and the **cones**, which are found in the fovea and are involved in detailed (acute) vision and colour detection. There are three main types of cone, roughly sensitive to blue, green and red wavelengths of light. It is estimated that each retina has in the region of 120 million rods and 6 million cones. From the retina, information from the rods and cones passes to the **bipolar cells** and then to the **ganglion cells**, which make up the optic nerve. There are approximately 800,000 axons in each optic nerve, which pass underneath of the brain before appearing to join in the **optic chiasm**. In fact, the optic chiasm is a crossing-over point where about two-thirds of axons from each eye (or more accurately the nasal side of the retina) cross to the opposite side of the brain. The axons continue into the brain where most (about 80 per cent) terminate in the **dorsal lateral geniculate nucleus** of the thalamus. From here, neurons project via the optic radiations to the **primary visual cortex** (sometimes called striate cortex) situated in the occipital lobe. From the visual cortex there appears to be two main routes involved in visual processing: the **dorsal pathway** extending into the **parietal lobe** concerned with determining *where* in space visual information is located, and the **ventral pathway** which passes down into the **temporal lobe,** and is primarily concerned with **object recognition** (*what*).

The nature of the information processed by the visual system was examined by **Stephen Kuffler** in the 1950s, who recorded the electrical activity of **ganglion cells** in the cat optic nerve by passing a small spot of light across their **receptive fields.** He found that the receptive fields were concentric consisting of a circular central area surrounded by a ring. These zones also produced different types of neural activity in response to visual stimulation. For example, in some cells, light shone in the central region increased its rate of firing (an 'on' response) whereas light falling in the surround inhibited firing (an 'off' response). In other cells, the situation was reversed, with stimulation of the centre producing an 'off' response, and stimulation of the surround producing an 'on' response. This work was extended by **Hubel and Wiesel,** who examined cells in the **primary visual cortex.** This research showed that the visual cortex contained three types of cell – called **simple, complex** and **hypercomplex** – which had elongated receptive fields and were more sensitive to lines than to spots of light. Hubel and Wiesel also showed that the visual cortex contained **columns,** with each one containing six layers and having simple, complex and hypercomplex cells that fired to lines of the same orientation. Moreover, the axis of the lines in adjacent columns rotated in a clockwise manner by about 10° so that approximately each 2 mm of visual cortex contained enough columns to detect every line orientation over 360°. Further research also showed that the visual cortex is made up of **modules** which contain a block of **orientation columns** that cover all line angles over 360°, two blocks of **ocular dominance columns** that have a preference for input from each of the eyes, and a pair of **cytochome blobs,** which are involved in colour processing. It is believed that the human primary visual cortex may contain around 2,500 of these modules, with each one processing a small part of the visual world at the retinal level. From the primary visual cortex (sometimes called **region V1**), information is passed to a number of secondary visual areas (including regions **V2, V3, V4** and **V5**). Although the pathways are anatomically complex, it appears that processing for **colour, motion** and **orientation** is largely independent at this stage. Visual information is then either channelled through the **parietal lobes** (the 'where' pathway) or the **temporal lobes** (the 'what' pathway).

Essay questions

1. Trace the anatomical structure of the visual system from retina to the brain, including its striate cortex and subcortical projections.

   Search terms: Visual system. Retina. Optic chiasm. Lateral geniculate nucleus. Visual cortex. Superior colliculus.

2. Electrical recording of single-cells in the optic nerve and striate cortex have provided scientists with a powerful means of understanding their role in visual processing. Discuss.

   Search terms: Receptive fields. Single-cell recording in visual system. Kuffler and the optic nerve. Hubel and Wiesel. Simple, complex and hypercomplex cells.

3. How is the brain capable of 'seeing' a spectrum of fine colour when the eye contains only three different types of colour detector?

   Search terms: Cones in the retina. Colour blindness. Trichromatic theory. Opponent theory of colour vision. Colour and the visual cortex.

4. What evidence supports the existence of dorsal ('*where is it*?') and ventral ('*what is it*?') visual systems in the cerebral cortex?

   Search terms: Two cortical visual pathways. Ventral visual pathway. Dorsal visual pathway. Visual processing in temporal lobes. Visual and spatial processing in parietal lobes.

Further reading

Bruce, V., Green, P.R. and Georgeson, M.A. (1996) *Visual Perception: Physiology, Psychology and Ecology*, 3rd edition. Hove: Psychology Press. A comprehensive textbook that covers the physiology of the visual system and its involvement in visual processing and perception.

Farah, M.J. (1999) *Visual Agnosia*. London: MIT Press. Describes how brain damage can result in disorders of object recognition, and the implications of this for understanding visual processing.

Gegenfurthner, K.R. and Sharpe, L.T. (eds) (2001) *Colour Vision: From Genes to Perception*. Cambridge: Cambridge University Press. An informative book written by various experts in the field and which brings together in one volume the many facets of colour vision.

Gregory, R.L. (1998) *Eye and Brain*. Oxford: Oxford University Press. A classic book first published in 1966, and now greatly extended, which provides an essential introduction to what visual illusions can tell us about human perception.

Gross, C.G. (1999) *Brain, Vision, Memory: Tales in the History of Neuroscience*. Cambridge, Mass.: MIT Press. Although not exclusively about vision, this book will be of interest to students who want to know more about the history of visual research.

Hubel, D.H. (1988) *Eye, Brain and Vision*. New York: Scientific American Library. A beautifully illustrated text, written by a Nobel laureate, which provides a readable account of how we have come to understand the organisation and function of the visual system.

Hubel, D.H. and Wiesel, T.N. (2005) *Brain and Visual Perception: The Story of a 25-Year Collaboration*. Oxford: Oxford University Press. A book which includes all of Hubels and Wiesel's major academic publications. However, each chapter contains a foreword written by the authors that provides interesting background information.

Mather, G. (2006) *Foundations of Perception*. Hove: Psychology Press. A colourful and well written new textbook on perception, with several excellent chapters on vision.

Milner, A.D. and Goodale, M.A. (1995) *The Visual Brain in Action*. Oxford: Oxford University Press. A book that examines the two main pathways that process vision beyond the striate cortex (i.e. the dorsal and ventral streams) and their relevance for human perception and behaviour.

Palmer, S.E. (1999) *Vision Science: Photons to Phenomenology*. Cambridge, Mass.: MIT Press. A textbook devoted to the science of vision that covers all the major topics from early neural processing in the eye to high-level functions such as memory, imagery and awareness.

Schwartz, S.H. (2004) *Visual Perception: A Clinical Orientation*. New York: McGraw-Hill. Despite its title, this is a student-friendly book that covers a lot of material discussed in this chapter.

Zeki, S. (1993) *A Vision of the Brain*. London: Blackwell. An intriguing and readable book which not only covers a lot of history but also attempts to explain how the visual system produces perception, and its implications for understanding cortical function.

  For self test questions, animations, interactive exercises and many more resources to help you consolidate your understanding, and expand your knowledge of the field, please go to the website accompanying this book at **www.pearsoned.co.uk/wickens**

CHAPTER 3
Sensory systems other than vision

INTRODUCTION

Although vision is generally regarded as our most important sense, it is not the only one that plays a vital role in our lives. To give a simple example: cast your mind back to when you woke this morning. Maybe, you were disturbed by the sound of an alarm clock, which was a signal to pull the covers back to get out of bed. Later, in the kitchen, you made a cup of coffee and some toast. Most of us will be familiar with this scenario, and it shows that from the first moment of our day, different senses provide us with a constant flow of information about the world. The alarm clock elicits sound (the sense of audition), our movements are guided by tactile sensations (touch), the coffee has a nice smell (olfaction) and the toast provides a pleasant taste (gustation). These different senses give such a veritable richness to our lives that it is easy to forget that they evolved in the first place to help us survive. Without audition we would not be able to hear the hissing of a kettle, and the loss of olfaction and gustation would make us unable to smell a gas leak or detect rancid food. Losing our sense of bodily feedback and touch would lead to slow and laboured movement. And, even pain is essential as it alerts us to danger and injury. Although it is often said that humans have five senses, we actually have more. For example, the skin, in addition to touch, senses heat and cold (thermoception), and detects itching and tickling. The ear contains organs that provide us with a sense of balance (the vestibular sense), while the skeletal muscles and joints of the body contain receptors for pressure and movement (proprioception). Other animals may have different senses, or superior ones. For example, bats detect objects by reflected sound, and a bloodhound's ability to smell is 10 million times more sensitive than our own. Because much of our behaviour is dependent on our senses, this area is an important one in biopsychology for it allows the researcher to understand how the brain both makes sense of the external world and processes feedback from the internal workings of the body.

Sound and the sense of audition (hearing)

Unlike light, which can move through a vacuum, the transmission of sound depends on a medium such as air or water which gives rise to vibrations. When an object such as a tuning fork is struck, it vibrates and sets up movements in the surrounding air molecules that cause them to condense and expand. This, produces increases and decreases in air pressure, and a wave that moves away from the source of vibration. Although such waves are extremely tiny, we are able to detect them as sound. The speed of sound is relatively slow: about 0.34 kilometres per second (0.2 miles per second) in air, which is significantly slower than light at 300,000 kilometres per second. This is why a clap of thunder often occurs several seconds behind a flash of lightning. The velocity of sound also differs according to the medium in which it travels: it moves faster in solids and slower in gases such as air.

We can depict a 'perfect' sound wave graphically as a sine wave, in which the compressed pressure is represented by the crest, and the decompression by the trough (see Figure 3.1). This type of wave is the simplest pattern of pressure that is generated by a pure tone. And, a closer examination of this wave reveals two characteristics that are essential to the way we hear the sound: namely the wavelength's frequency and its amplitude. The wavelength is the distance between two consecutive crests (or troughs)

(a) The wavelength of sound is perceived as pitch

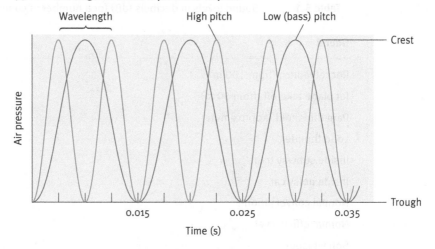

(b) The amplitude of sound is perceived as loudness

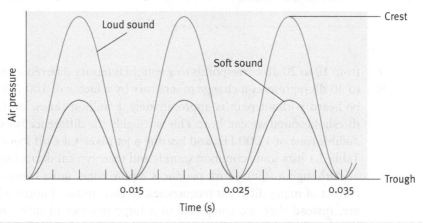

| Figure 3.1 | The wavelength (pitch) and amplitude (loudness) of sound waves |

and is always a constant length for a particular tone. But, since the wave also moves, it has a frequency, that is, the number of waves that pass at a given point in a given time. This is normally expressed as **hertz (Hz)**, or cycles per second. We use this property to help us determine the pitch of a sound, with shorter wavelengths providing tones of higher frequency. Thus, the highest note on a piano (C) produces a wave that 'moves' at about 4,186 Hz, while the lowest note (A) has a frequency of around 27 Hz. Humans with good hearing can detect sounds in the range 20–20,000 Hz, although we are most sensitive to 1,000–4,000 Hz frequencies.

The amplitude of the wavelength is the change from maximum to minimum pressure, or the height of the wave. This is the feature of the wave we use to determine the intensity of the sound (i.e. loudness). In general, if the amplitude of a wavelength increases, we hear this change as an increase in volume. The range of intensities that humans can detect is very large, and because of this, sound intensities are normally reported in logarithmic units called **decibels (dB)** (the basic unit is actually the Bel, invented by Alexander Graham Bell). In the decibel scale, a difference of 10 dB corresponds to a 1 log unit (or factor of 10) change in sound intensity. Therefore an increase in intensity of a sound

Table 3.1	Sound levels in decibels (dB) for a number of common sounds

Sound	Decibels
Rocket launch (from 100 m)	200
Jet plane take-off (from 50 m)	140
Pain threshold (approximate)	140
Loud thunder	120
Inside subway train	100
Inside noisy car	75
Normal conversation	60
Normal office level	50
Soft whisper	20
Threshold of hearing	0

from 10 to 20 dB corresponds to a tenfold intensity difference, while an increase from 10 to 30 dB represents a change in intensity by a factor of 100. The loudest sound that can be heard without pain is approximately 1 million times, or 120 dB, greater than the threshold sound we can hear. This is roughly the difference between listening to a barely audible tone of 1,000 Hz, and hearing a jet plane take off from a distance of 30 metres. Table 3.1 lists some common sounds and their typical decibel level.

Although a tuning fork produces a pure tone, most sounds in our everyday world consist of many different frequencies. In fact, musical notes which sound 'pure' rarely are. Instead they are composed of a large number of different harmonic frequencies that are present in varying amounts. It is these extra frequencies that give musical instruments their own distinct qualities. In fact, if we were to remove all the harmonics, leaving only the fundamental sound wave, any two instruments playing the same note (say a trombone and a piano) would sound identical. To make matters more complex, one can also play different notes to form chords. In this case, to understand the type of sound wave produced, one must take the sine functions for all the notes and add them together. For example, if you play the notes A, C-sharp and E (the chord of A) you will produce a sound wave resembling the one in Figure 3.2. Although it is no longer a sine wave, there is still a repeating pattern to it. This highlights the extremely complex nature of sound waves reaching your ears when you listen to music.

The physiology of the ear

The ear is divided into three components: the outer, middle and inner, and all have a different function. In short: the outer ear 'collects' the sound; the middle ear acts as a mechanical transformer; and the inner ear transduces this into neural energy. The process begins with the external ear, composed of the fleshy **pinna**, whose distinct

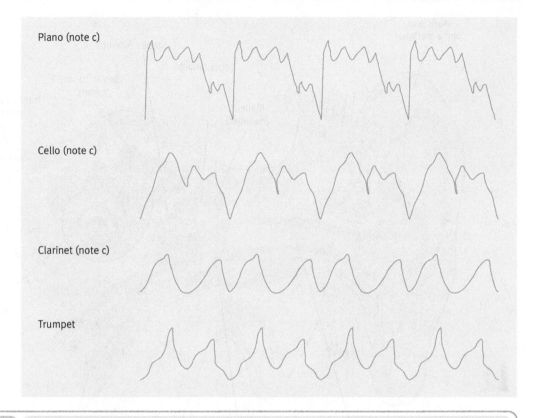

Piano (note c)

Cello (note c)

Clarinet (note c)

Trumpet

Figure 3.2   Complex sound waves for a number of musical instruments

shape helps to direct sound waves into the auditory canal (see Figure 3.3). In many animals the pinna is able to move and acts as a sound-gathering device. In humans, the pinna is immobile (although a few people can wiggle their ears slightly) but still serves an important function in locating the source of sound. A depression in the pinna leads to the **auditory canal,** roughly 3 cm long and 0.6 cm wide, through which sound waves travel to the **tympanic membrane** (ear drum). Because of its tapering shape, the auditory canal enhances the detection of sounds in the range of 3,500 Hz, which is close to the midpoint of human hearing. The tympanic membrane is the boundary between the inner and middle ears and is shaped like a cone with its apex pointing inwards. It is set into vibratory motion when struck by sound waves, and this transfers the energy to the bones of the middle ear.

The small air-filled cavity behind the tympanic membrane is the middle ear and contains the three smallest bones found in the body, known collectively as the **ossicles.** Individually, these are the **malleus** (Latin for hammer), **incus** (anvil) and **stapes** (stirrup). These bones are set into motion by the vibrations of the tympanic membrane, which causes the stapes to hit the **oval window** of the cochlea. The use of three small bones to transmit sound may appear to be a complicated arrangement, but they exist because the middle ear cavity is filled with air (it gets its air from the Eustachian tubes connected to the mouth), while the inner ear contains fluid. Air is not suitable for transmitting mechanical information in the middle ear as it offers less resistance to movement (in fact, if sound waves were to strike the oval window through the medium

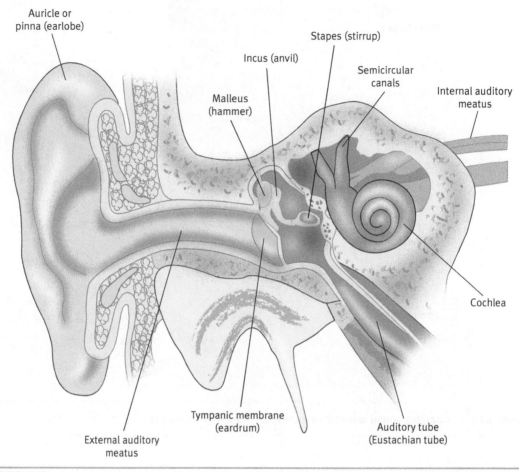

Auricle or
pinna (earlobe)

Stapes (stirrup)

Incus (anvil)

Semicircular
canals

Internal auditory
meatus

Malleus
(hammer)

Cochlea

Tympanic membrane
(eardrum)

Auditory tube
(Eustachian tube)

External auditory
meatus

Figure 3.3   The structure of the ear

Source: P. Abrahams (ed.) *How the Body Works*, p. 122. Copyright © 2007 by Amber Books

of air, 99.9 per cent of the energy would be reflected back). Because the ossicles are made of bone, they amplify the vibrations, thereby providing a mechanism to overcome the resistance difference between the air and fluid-filled inner ear.

On the other side of the oval window lies the inner ear, which is also called the labyrinth because of its intricate structure of interconnecting chambers and passages (Figure 3.4). This complex part of the ear is composed of three cavities: the **vestibule** (or entrance), **cochlea** and **semicircular canals**. The cochlea, which derives from the Greek word for snail, is the crucial structure for hearing. It is a spiral bony chamber that extends from the vestibule and coils for about two and half turns. In fact, it measures only about 4 mm in diameter in humans, but if uncoiled would extend to about 40 mm in length. In cross-section, the tube of the cochlea can be seen to contain three fluid-filled canals. These are called the **scala vestibuli** (vestibular stairway), **scala media** (middle stairway) and **scala tympani** (tympanic stairway) (see Figure 3.5).

The scala vestibuli is the first part of the cochlea to obtain acoustic input. That is, the scala vestibuli receives mechanical vibrations from the stapes hitting the oval

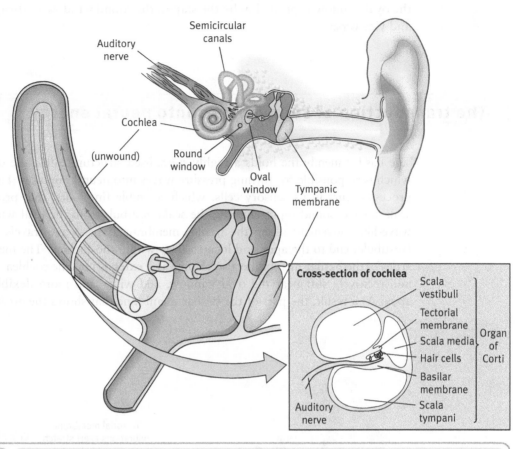

Semicircular
canals

Auditory
nerve

Cochlea

(unwound)

Round
window

Oval
window

Tympanic
membrane

Cross-section of cochlea

Scala
vestibuli

Tectorial
membrane

Scala media

Hair cells

Basilar
membrane

Scala
tympani

Organ
of
Corti

Auditory
nerve

| **Figure 3.4** | The anatomy of the inner ear including the cochlea |

Source: John P.J. Pinel, *Biopsychology*, 5th edition, p. 174. Copyright © 2003 by Pearson Education

window. Lying close to the scala vestibuli is the scala tympani, which also joins the vestibule. This passage has a flexible membrane wall with the middle ear, which contains something called the **round window**. Although the scala vestibuli and scala tympani appear in cross-section to be separate 'canals', they are actually connected deep in the apex of the cochlea by a small opening called the helicotrema. This makes them continuous and they share the same fluid. The middle tube or **scala media**, however, is physically sealed off from both the scala vestibuli and scala tympani.

When sound vibrations 'tap' on the membrane of the oval window, it causes a pressure wave to move through the scala vestibuli towards the tympanic canal. However, because the fluid in this canal is virtually incompressible, the waves also act to deform the **basilar membrane**, which separates the scala vestibuli from the scala media. The basilar membrane, as we will see below, is important for hearing as it contains specialised 'hairs' (projecting into the scala media) that turn acoustic energy into nerve impulses. In fact, the wave not only sends a 'ripple' along the basilar membrane but also causes the only relief point in the inner ear, namely the round window of the tympanic canal, to bulge outwards. In effect, this means that when the oval window is pushed in by the stapes, the round window is always pushed out, and vice versa.

The transduction of sound waves into neural energy

The basilar membrane holds a highly specialised structure called the **organ of Corti**, which is responsible for turning pressure waves into neural impulses (Figure 3.5). This process occurs in its sensory cells, which resemble fine hairs, that protrude into the scala media. Sound input entering the scala vestibuli from the oval window causes a wave-like movement along the basilar membrane. This wave travels from its basal (vestibule) end to the apex end located deep within the cochlea. The mechanical properties of the basilar membrane also change as it extends into the cochlea – being narrow and relatively stiff near the oval window, and wider and more flexible towards the apex. As a result, the part of the basilar membrane that shows the greatest movement

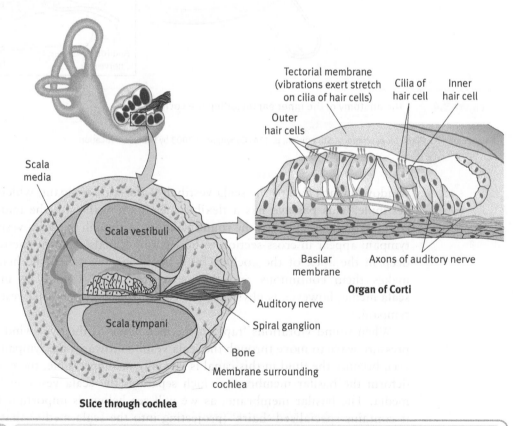

Slice through cochlea

Figure 3.5   A section through the cochlea showing the organ of Corti

Source: N.R. Carlson, *Physiology of Behavior*, 8th edition, p. 206. Copyright © 2004 by Pearson Education

will depend on the frequency of the vibration: low sounds producing more displacement near the apex, and high sounds producing greater displacement towards the vestibule.

The organ of Corti has two different sets of sensory hair cells. There is a single row of about 3,500 inner hair cells that run along its medial surface, and around 12,000 outer hair cells which form three rows more laterally. Closer inspection of these cells shows that on their upper surface there are lots of very fine finger-like protrusions, called **cilia**, which extend upwards towards a thin covering called the **tectorial membrane**. As sound waves enter the cochlea, the pressure causes both the basilar membrane and tectorial membranes to flex, and this forces fluid to flow past the cilia causing them to bend laterally (right and left). This movement is necessary for the transduction of sound pressure into neural energy. Under resting conditions the cilia are connected with their neighbours by very fine filaments known as **tip links**. Normally these tip links are slightly stretched and taut, but when displaced by the flexing of the basilar and tectorial membranes, the movement causes ion channels for potassium to be opened in the cilia. The flow of potassium into the hair cell leads to the cell's depolarisation, which, in turn, acts to open excitatory calcium channels. The result is an action potential that causes the release of neurotransmitter (thought to be glutamate) into the synapse, between the hair cells and those of the auditory nerve.

The ascending auditory pathways

The brain receives auditory information by means of the **cochlear nerve**, which is a branch of cranial nerve VIII. This nerve pathway arises out of the cochlea as the **spiral ganglion**, which contains the cell bodies of **bipolar cells** – neurons that have axons which protrude from both ends of the soma (i.e. two axons). Thus, these neurons have the special property of being able to send action potentials to the brain, or back to the hair fibres. There are around 50,000 nerve cells in each human spiral ganglion, and the vast majority (95 per cent) project to and from the inner hair cells (which actually comprise less than one-third of all hair cells within the organ of Corti). Thus, in terms of numbers, these appear to be the most important in the transmission of auditory information to the brain. The other 5 per cent of neurons in the spiral ganglion receive projections from the more numerous outer hairs.

The ascending projections of the auditory system are complex. From the ear, all fibres of the auditory nerve enter the brainstem, where they project to the **cochlear nuclei** located in the upper part of the medulla (see Figure 3.6). This projection is ipsilateral (fibres from the right ear go to the right cochlear nucleus and from the left ear to the left cochlear nucleus) although the auditory nerve branches at this point, with one arm going to the dorsal (upper) part of the cochlear nucleus and the other going to its ventral (lower) part. This branching is important for segregating auditory input: fibres to the dorsal cochlear nucleus conveying sounds of high frequency, and those to the ventral region low frequency. After the cochlear nucleus, most fibres pass to the opposite (contralateral) side of the brain. Two pathways here are particularly important. The first is the **ventral acoustic stria** and this passes through the **trapezoid body** to the **superior**

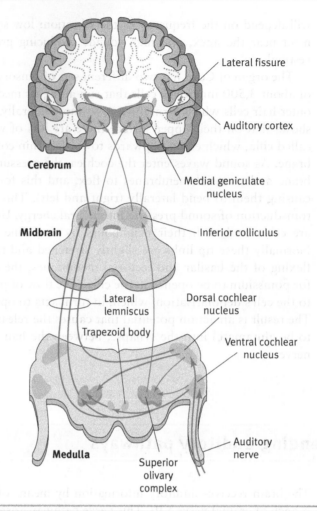

Cerebrum

Lateral fissure

Auditory cortex

Medial geniculate
nucleus

Midbrain

Inferior colliculus

Lateral
lemniscus

Dorsal cochlear
nucleus

Trapezoid body

Ventral cochlear
nucleus

Medulla

Superior
olivary
complex

Auditory
nerve

Figure 3.6	The pathways of the auditory system

Source: N.R. Carlson, *Physiology of Behavior*, 8th edition, p. 210. Copyright © 2004 by Pearson Education

olivary complex located in the pons. The second is the **dorsal acoustic stria**, which ascends in a tract called the **lateral lemniscus** and terminates in the **inferior colliculi**. For many lower animals, such as amphibians, this represents the highest stage of auditory processing. But, in higher animals, such as ourselves, a further pathway passes from the inferior colliculi to the **medial geniculate nucleus** located in the thalamus, and then onwards to the **primary auditory cortex** of the temporal lobes.

The auditory nuclei of the brain and their ascending projections form a complex anatomical system for the processing of sound information. But there is also a descending auditory pathway that carries information in the opposite direction. This pathway originates in the auditory cortex, and projects via the medial geniculate nucleus and inferior colliculi, to the superior olivary complex in the brainstem. This area is the origin of the **olivocochlear bundle**, whose fibres pass to the ear and synapse onto the hair cells of the cochlea. This pathway has an inhibitory effect on the hair cells and may function to reduce the responses of these cells to non-essential information. It is believed that this inhibition sharpens the perception of pitch, and suppresses background noise when attention is being focused on a particular sound.

The perception of pitch

The ability to hear pitch – the 'high' and 'low' quality of a sound – is a vital auditory function. Without this ability we would not be able to hear different sounds or make sense of music and language. But, how are we able to distinguish one type of sound wave from another? Traditionally, there have been two main theories: the **place theory** and the **frequency theory**. The place theory was proposed by Hermann von Helmholtz in 1863, who argued that we hear differences in sound (he believed that we could distinguish around 5,000 different pitches) because particular points on the basilar membrane vibrate maximally to sound waves of a particular frequency. In fact, Helmholtz compared the membrane to a piano and its hair cells to piano strings, each tuned to vibrate to a particular note. Extending this concept, he argued that each frequency must result in a different set of neurons firing in the nervous system. Not all investigators agreed with this idea, however. In 1886, shortly after the telephone was invented, William Rutherford proposed a different theory. Rutherford's work led him to believe that sound waves cause every hair cell to be stimulated to some degree. Thus, pitch was more likely to be encoded by the overall pattern of neural activity in the auditory nerve (and not by selective subsets of neurons). To give a hypothetical example: the neurons of the auditory nerve could be imagined to fire at the same frequency as vibrations of the basilar membrane. Thus, if the ear was presented with a tone of 1,000 Hz, all neurons in the auditory nerve neurons might respond by firing at the same rate (in this example, 1,000 times a second).

Early evidence tended to support Rutherford's theory. For example, Weaver and Bray (1930) recorded from the cat's auditory nerve and found that neural responses were similar in frequency and amplitude to the sounds received by the ear. The main problem with the frequency theory however, was that there is a limit to how many times a neuron can fire. The highest rate of firing that a neuron can achieve is around 1,000 impulses per second – yet, humans can detect tones up to 20,000 Hz. To resolve this problem, Wever and Bray devised an explanation which became known as the volley principle. In short, they proposed that, at higher frequencies, the fibres of the auditory nerve do not fire in synchronisation but send impulses in quick succession. The idea is similar to the way in which a group of soldiers can achieve constant fire with single-shot rifles. That is, they can maintain a constant volley only if one group is shooting while another is reloading. However, even with this explanation, the volley principle could not explain neural frequency rates beyond 4,000 Hz.

In the 1950s, evidence began to support the place theory, largely through the work of Georg von Békésy, a Hungarian scientist, who was awarded the Nobel Prize in 1961. Using cochleas taken from humans at post-mortem, Békésy stimulated the oval window with an electronically powered piston and observed the movement of the basilar membrane by using a microscope. Békésy found that sound caused the basilar membrane to bulge in a wave-like manner, beginning at the base of the cochlea and moving along its length towards the apex. Békésy also discovered that the frequency of the sound determined where along the membrane the wave would produce its greatest peak: a high-frequency sound producing the highest bulge at the base, and lower frequencies causing the peak to be closer to the apex. However, very low frequencies did not produce the same effect. Instead, they caused a broad bulge that covered the entire basilar membrane and made it vibrate at the frequency of the incoming sound.

Békésy's research shows that both the frequency and place theories are correct to some extent. Low-frequency sounds are coded by rate of firing in the auditory neurons as Rutherford thought, although this occurs only for a limited part of the auditory spectrum. For most of the sounds we hear, pitch is coded by the place at which the basilar membrane is vibrated to its maximal degree. This, presumably, is then encoded by a specific set of neurons. Exactly where the transition from frequency to place processing occurs is not known, but it is likely that the frequency principle works below 400 Hz, the place principle operates above 4,000 Hz, and that both mechanisms work together to code the frequencies in between.

Because the cilia of the hair cells at the base of the cochlea are displaced by high-frequency sounds, and those at the apex by low-frequency sounds, the basilar membrane has a **tonotopic representation**. That is, the basilar membrane shows an orderly arrangement of sensitivity to sounds (see Figure 3.7). This tonotopic representation is maintained throughout the auditory system, including the cochlear nucleus, inferior colliculus, medial geniculate nucleus and auditory cortex. The discovery of the basilar membrane's tonotopic map has also enabled the development of cochlear implants – electronic devices implanted in the inner ear to allow deaf people to hear. In essence, a miniature microphone is attached to the outside of the ear and detects the frequencies of incoming sounds. It then relays the information to the appropriate place on the basilar membrane through tiny wires, allowing the person to perceive sound with different pitches. Although cochlear implants do not restore normal hearing, and their effectiveness varies among individuals, they provide a sense of sound to help users understand speech.

The perception of loudness

Loudness is caused by changes in the amplitude of a sound wave. In his classic work on the cochlea, Békésy found that although pitch determined the distance the bulge in the basilar membrane travelled, loudness was produced by the height and expanse of the bulge. In other words, by increasing the loudness of a sound, the basilar membrane was displaced over a much larger area and with increasing vigour. This indicated that loudness might be encoded by the auditory system in two ways. Firstly, as the sound gets more intense, the basilar membrane vibrates with greater amplitude, and this might be expected to produce higher rates of depolarisation in the hair cells. This, of course, would increase the number of action potentials in the auditory nerve. Secondly, the greater expansive movement of the basilar membrane would be expected to recruit a larger number of neurons to fire. Although there is still some disagreement (see, for example, Relkin and Doucet 1997), most research supports the idea of these two mechanisms working together to provide the neural code for loudness.

The localisation of sounds

A vital requirement for survival is being able to locate the source of a sound. If you close your eyes, it is likely you will be able to determine exactly where the sounds of your world are originating from – whether they are coming from right or left, front or back, above or below. This ability is largely dependent on our having two ears. If

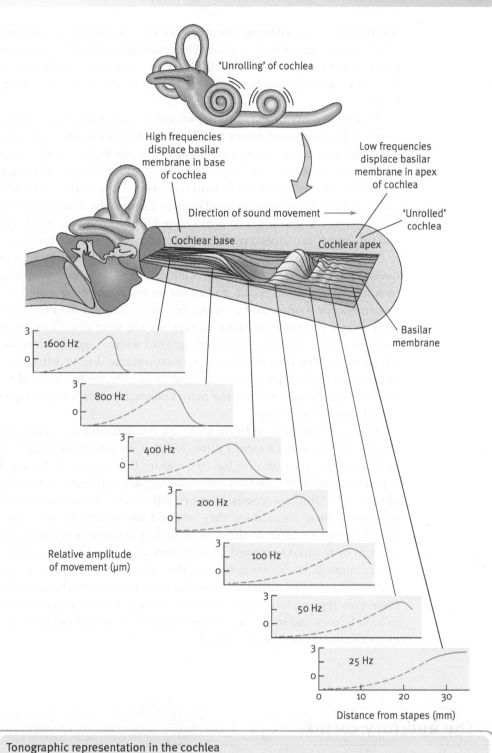

Figure 3.7   Tonographic representation in the cochlea

someone strikes a tuning fork to your right, it is easy to picture the sound waves reaching the right ear before the left. Moreover, the head will also create a barrier to make the distance to the left ear even greater. Thus, the sound waves reaching the right ear will be out of phase with those to the left. This is called the **interaural time difference**.

Although the time difference between the two sound waves reaching the ears is generally less than one-tenth of a second (it is maximal when the sound source is at right angles to your gaze, and minimal if directly in front of or behind you), it still provides enough time for the auditory system to accurately work out where sound is coming from.

Another feature of the auditory stimulus that can be used to locate the source of sound is the **interaural intensity difference**. Because sound waves get weaker as they travel through air, a tuning fork sounded to our right will also result in less intense sound waves reaching our left ear compared with the right. This, again, will be accentuated by the head, which will tend to restrict the sound waves hitting the left ear. In fact, for many locations, the head creates a sound shadow for the opposing ear. Thus, the only way for the far ear to detect sound is to have it reflected back from some other surface, which produces a further weakening of the sound's intensity.

Since the ears can use interaural differences in both time and frequency, an obvious question to ask is, which is the most important of these in determining the localisation of sound? The answer is that it depends on the pitch of the sound wave. For example, low-frequency sounds tend to wrap themselves around the head and reach the far ear with almost the same intensity as they do the near ear. Consequently, at lower frequencies sound waves travel around the head without significant reductions in intensity, which means that the ears have to rely on interaural time differences to locate sound. In contrast, high-frequency sounds tend to be reflected by the head before reaching the opposite ear. Because of this, the main cue used to locate high frequencies is the interaural intensity difference.

Although a number of brain areas are involved in the coding of binaural cues, the most important is the superior olive, which is the first brain area to receive input from both ears. The superior olive has two regions that respond to binaural cues: the **medial superior olive** (MSO), which processes latency differences, and the **lateral superior olive** (LSO), which processes intensity differences. Recordings taken from individual neurons in these areas show they respond best when the two ears receive the same sound at slightly different times or at slightly different intensities. For example, some neurons in the MSO respond at high rates when the left ear receives sound first, and others respond in the same way to the right ear. A similar type of neural response occurs for intensity differences reaching the neurons in the LSO. In fact, neurons in these two regions have been shown to detect a wide range of binaural differences in both latency and intensity, and these responses are believed to be crucial in allowing us to localise the source of a sound.

The auditory cortex

The most advanced level of sound processing takes place in the auditory cortex, which, in humans, lies on the upper (or superior) part of posterior temporal lobe, buried just inside the lateral fissure in a region known as **Heschl's gyrus** (Figure 3.8). It contains two main areas: (1) the **primary auditory cortex** (area A1), which receives input from the **medial geniculate nucleus**, and (2) the surrounding **secondary auditory cortex** (area A2), sometimes known as association cortex, which lies towards the outer

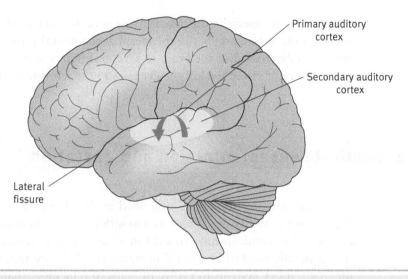

Primary auditory
cortex

Secondary auditory
cortex

Lateral
fissure

Figure 3.8	The auditory cortex

Source: John P.J. Pinel, *Biopsychology*, 5th edition, p. 176. Copyright © 2003 by Pearson Education

surface of the temporal lobe. An interesting feature of the primary auditory cortex is its tonotopic map for pitch. That is, cells with similar pitch preferences lie close to each other, with an orderly progression of frequency bands as one moves across the cortex. Closer examination of the map reveals that the anterior end of the primary auditory cortex contains cells that encode sound information derived from the apex of the cochlea, whereas the posterior regions process high-frequency sounds from the base of the cochlea. This tonotopic representation is also maintained in the auditory brainstem nuclei, inferior colliculi and medial geniculate nucleus.

On first sight, the neuroanatomical structure of the primary auditory cortex appears to have some similarities with the corresponding area of the visual cortex. Indeed, both areas have six layers of cells arranged in columns that have specificity for either sound frequency or visual line orientation. But this is where the similarity ends. For example, only a certain proportion of neurons in the primary auditory cortex (perhaps 60–70 per cent) are sensitive to sound. Moreover, these show a great variety of responses, with some neurons showing sustained responses to sound and others exhibiting brief or transient responses. To make matters more confusing, within the same cortical column, some cells will respond to many different types of sound, including clicks, noise and tone bursts, whereas others will fire only to a specific type of auditory stimulus. Further, a significant number of neurons in the auditory cortex are selectively activated by sounds such as species specific vocalisations (Wolberg and Newman 1971). From this, one has to conclude that the auditory cortex is probably concerned with a wide-ranging analysis of sound signals, both simple and complex.

Differences between the visual and auditory cortex are also seen after their damage. For example, a unilateral lesion to the primary visual cortex will result in blindness in the corresponding part of the eye's visual field. However, deafness does not occur following damage to the primary auditory cortex. In fact, a person with a lesion to this area of the brain will normally show a remarkable level of auditory function. The main deficit of damage to the primary auditory cortex is an inability to localise precisely the source of a sound, accompanied by a difficulty in following and comprehending fast speech. This is especially the case if damage occurs to the left side. The reason for this preservation of function lies in the fact that the neural projections of the auditory system are fully crossed in the brain at several different levels – unlike the visual system where the right visual field of the eye goes to the left side of the brain (and vice versa).

The chemical senses: olfaction and gustation

Smell and taste are sometimes described as the chemical senses. This is because they depend on the ability of the nose and mouth to detect chemical compounds. In the case of smell, the chemicals have to exist in an airborne or vapour state, whereas for taste they generally need to be soluble in water. It is believed that the chemical senses were the first sensory systems to evolve (it helps to remember that life first evolved in a sea of chemicals) and they occur in the most primitive of organisms. Despite this, they still provide crucially important functions for higher organisms, including primates. Apart from its obvious pleasurable qualities, taste provides a means of evaluating the safety of food. In contrast, for many animals smell serves a large number of vital functions, including obtaining a mate, marking territory, identifying others of the same species and finding food. Although smell and taste are often said to be poorly developed in humans, they are still important determinants of behaviour, and may be more significant than we realise. For example, mothers can recognise their babies by smell (Porter *et al.* 1983), women living together often synchronise their menstrual cycles on the basis of olfactory cues (McClintock 1971), and the body odours of men significantly affect women's mate choices (Wedekind *et al.* 1995).

The olfactory pathways from nose to brain

In humans, the receptors for smell are found in a small patch of mucus membrane roughly the size of a postage stamp known as the **olfactory epithelium**. This small region is located in the roof of each nasal cavity. Curiously, because this site lies at the top of the nasal cavities, where they make a sharp turn into the respiratory passageways, the olfactory receptors are not located in the most effective position to be stimulated by air currents. This is why we often have to sniff the air to increase its flow across the olfactory epithelium. Each olfactory epithelium contains about 5 million receptors, which are actually specialised nerve endings of the first cranial nerve. More specifically, these are bipolar neurons that project to the surface of the epithelium and whose axons bear specialised endings that contain around 10–20 long hairs or cilia. Not only do these 'hairs' significantly increase the sensory surface area of the olfactory epithelium, but they are also covered by a thin coat of mucus which flows constantly (it is replaced about every 10 minutes) to act as a solvent for the odour molecules. Interestingly, the bipolar cells are constantly being replaced every 60 days or so. No other type of neuron in the nervous system is known to be renewed so quickly.

The size of the olfactory epithelium is an indicator of an animal's olfactory sensitivity. For example, the surface area of the human olfactory epithelium is around 10 cm², whereas in certain dogs it can be as large as 170 cm². The effectiveness of a larger olfactory epithelium is largely due to its containing a far greater number of receptors. For instance, not only does the German Shepherd dog have some 100–150 cilia per bipolar cell that project into the mucus layer of the olfactory epithelium, but this greater area is able to provide some 224 million receptors compared with just 10 million for humans (Wenzel 1973).

Each bipolar olfactory neuron also has an axon arising from the soma that passes from the olfactory epithelium and through the **olfactory foramina,** which are a series of tiny holes in the cribriform plate (the floor of the cranium). Immediately above the cribriform plate is the **olfactory bulb** lying at the base of each cerebral hemisphere. This olfactory pathway is unique among cranial nerves as it does not directly project to the brainstem or thalamus. Instead, it passes directly to higher areas of the forebrain. The olfactory bulb is anatomically complex. When reaching the olfactory bulb, the bipolar fibres project to a **mitral cell,** which has a triangular body and is named for its resemblance to a bishop's mitre. In the human brain, there are around 50,000 mitral cells and each receives input from around 250 axons. The mitral cells are also bundled together in clumps (in essence a dense accumulation of synapses and dendrites) known as **olfactory glomeruli.** There are around 1,000 glomeruli in each olfactory bulb, and each one appears to receive information from a particular type of olfactory receptor responsible for encoding a certain smell. Hence, different odorants will activate different groupings of glomeruli.

The olfactory bulb also contains a number of other neuron types, including **tufted cells,** which arise from the glomeruli and send their axons into the olfactory tract, and **granule cells,** which appear to inhibit mitral cells so that only highly excited olfactory impulses can be transmitted. This inhibition is believed to be important in olfactory adaptation where we quickly become habituated to a new smell (this is often noticeable when entering a new house). The granule cells also receive input from other brain areas, and it is believed that these descending projections may modify the reaction to smell under certain conditions. For example, the aroma of certain foods are perceived differently depending on whether we are hungry or have just finished eating.

From the olfactory bulb, the axons of mitral and tufted cells pass into the **olfactory tract,** which runs under the frontal cortex (see Figure 3.9), before dividing into the **lateral olfactory stria** and **medial olfactory stria.** The first of these pathways projects to the **primary olfactory cortex,** which is located deep in the medial aspects of the temporal lobe. This region is not only phylogenetically much older than the primary visual and auditory cortex (for example it contains only three layers of cells rather than six), but has a number of regions, including the **piriform cortex** and the amygdala. From here, olfactory information is dispersed to other areas of the limbic system, including the entorhinal cortex (sometimes called association olfactory cortex) and the orbitofrontal cortex via the thalmus. In contrast, the medial olfactory stria (which is not well developed in humans) projects to structures lying close to the hypothalamus, of which the most important is the **septal nuclei.** This pathway is believed to be involved in producing motivational emotional responses (mating behaviour, aggression and so on) that are elicited by olfactory stimuli.

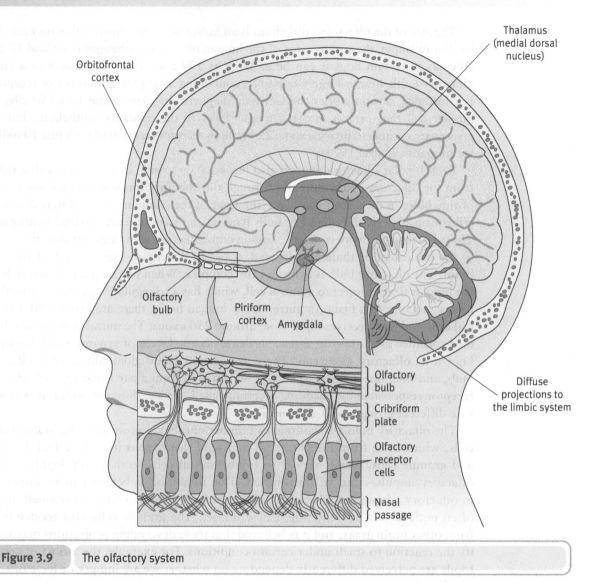

Orbitofrontal cortex

Thalamus (medial dorsal nucleus)

Olfactory bulb

Piriform cortex   Amygdala

Olfactory bulb

Cribriform plate

Olfactory receptor cells

Nasal passage

Diffuse projections to the limbic system

Figure 3.9 The olfactory system

Source: John P.J. Pinel, *Biopsychology*, 5th edition, p. 187. Copyright © 2003 by Pearson Education

The discovery of olfactory receptors

It is estimated that human beings are able to recognise up to ten thousand different types of smell, and other types of animal can detect many more (Shepherd 1994). The fact that we are sensitive to such a large number of odours has long interested researchers, who have sought ways of categorising them into a simpler classification. One of the first attempts to do this was undertaken by the Swedish botanist Linnaeus in 1752 who grouped odours into seven classes: (1) aromatic, (2) fragrant, (3) musky, (4) garlicky, (5) goaty, (6) repulsive, and (7) nauseous. This classification was expanded by the Dutch physiologist Hendrik Zwaardemaker in 1895 who added two more classes (tobacco-like and perfume-like) along with various subclasses for each primary smell.

However, this classification never gained widespread support – partly because it did not explain the underlying physical nature of the odour, or the reason for the differences between them.

By the early part of the twentieth century, researchers had established that odours were likely to be chemical in nature, but were puzzled by findings showing that similar substances often produced different smells. The opposite was also known: that some chemicals with different structures evoked similar smells. In 1949, the Scottish scientist Robert Moncrieff proposed that it was the size and shape of the chemical molecule, and not its chemical composition, that were the important determinants of an odorant. This also implied that, to be odorous, airborne chemicals had to have a molecular configuration that fitted into its own specialised receptor, which was presumably located in the olfactory epithelium.

During the 1960s, John Amoore studied the molecular structure of over 600 odorant compounds, and came to the conclusion that the three-dimensional shape of a molecule was indeed the most important cause of its smell. That is, molecules with similar sizes and shapes produced the same type of smell. In fact, by noting the shape and size of a given molecule (say, a spherical molecule with a diameter of 6 angstroms) Amoore was able to predict its smell (in this case musk). On the basis of his work, Amoore categorised odorous molecules into seven groups, with each one being responsible for a 'primary' odour.* This suggested that the olfactory system was likely to have seven basic types of receptor, with each odorant molecule fitting into one type of site. This idea was called the **stereochemical theory of olfaction**.

The theory, however, was soon shown to have problems – not least because there were many molecules that did not conform to Amoore's predictions. Despite this, there was some evidence that indicated the general principles of the stereochemical theory might still hold true. This came from studies of **anosmia** in which people have lost the ability to detect certain smells. In fact, several dozen different types of anosmias are now known and some are surprisingly common (for example, one person in ten is insensitive to the smell of cyanide, and one in one thousand cannot detect butyl mercaptan). The simplest explanation for anosmia is that the person lacks the receptor for the smell they cannot detect. But, of course, if this is true, then the olfactory system must contain specialised receptors for every individual type of smell. In other words, it must contain huge numbers of different receptors.

Recent research has shown that the olfactory epithelium does indeed have hundreds of different receptors. The breakthrough came when Jones and Reed (1989) discovered a **G-protein** that was specifically located in the sensory neurons of the olfactory epithelium. G-proteins are important components of receptor molecules, and responsible for stimulating the synthesis of second messengers inside the cell, such as cAMP. In this way, the occupation of a receptor by its neurotransmitter or ligand is able to open ion channels and perform other intracellular functions (see Chapter 1). But, how could the discovery of a new G-protein cast new light on olfactory receptors? The answer came from the ingenious work of Linda Buck and Richard Axel at Columbia University (Buck and Axel 1991). These researchers decided to hunt for the genes that were responsible for producing odorant receptors. To do this, Buck and Axel took types of amino acid sequences known to occur only in G-protein-coupled receptors and matched them with DNA taken from olfactory epithelia. Using this technique Buck and Axel found

---

*Amoore's groups were camphoraceous, musky, floral, pepperminty, etheral, pungent and putrid.

that there were literally hundreds of matches – or, put another way, there were hundreds of genes encoding for receptors in the olfactory epithelium. To confirm that this was the case, Buck and Axel also showed that these genes were expressed only in olfactory epithelium neurons, and not in other tissues of the body.

Remarkably, this work has now shown that the human genome contains around 950 odorant receptor genes, and in the mouse this figure is approximately 1,500. Despite this, around 60 per cent of these genes in the human, and 20 per cent in the mouse, appear to be redundant and not transcribed into receptors. Thus, the numbers of functional odorant receptors is estimated to be around 400 in humans and 1,200 in mice. If this figure is accurate, and assuming that each receptor protein can bind only to a specific type of odour molecule, we have hundreds of individual smell detectors in our nose. In fact, odorant receptors form the largest known gene family in the human genome and they comprise some 3–5 per cent of all our genes. Buck and Axel have also shown that axons from neurons expressing each type of odorant receptor project to the same segment of the olfactory bulb. Thus, the encoding of different smells appears to be segregated at the first stage of olfactory processing. The pioneering research of Buck and Axel has sparked a new chapter in the exploration of olfaction, and they were jointly awarded the Nobel Prize in 2004.

Synesthesia: the merging of the senses

Synesthesia (from the Greek *syn* meaning 'together' and *aisthesis* meaning 'perception') is a condition in which sensation in one modality simultaneously causes a 'real' sensation in another. Although there are many forms of synesthesia, it most commonly occurs when letters or numbers are seen as certain colours (for example, the number 8 may be seen as purple), or when certain tones are perceived with a given hue (G-sharp may be green). These perceptions are also unique to each individual. Synesthesia was first described by Sir Francis Galton in 1883, but, while many cases have been documented since (including one by the renowned Russian psychologist A.R. Luria in his book *The Mind of a Mnemonist* (1968)), many researchers have remained sceptical about whether it really existed. Indeed, synesthesia seemed just too far-fetched and subjective for it to be taken seriously. However, one person who helped to change this view was the neurologist Richard Cytowic, who, in 1993, published *The Man Who Tasted Shapes*, a book that described the case of his friend Michael Watson. The first time that Cytowic became aware that Watson was a synesthete occurred when the two men were having dinner together. When making the sauce for the meal, Watson suddenly said, 'There aern't enough points on the chicken.' When he was questioned about this strange remark, Watson replied that tastes always produced shape sensations that swept down his arms to his fingertips. He also felt the shapes of the taste in the grasp of his hand – although some taste shapes (such as points) were felt all over his body. For the meal, Watson had wanted the taste of the chicken to have 'a pointed shape', but instead it had come out 'all round'. Apologetically, he added, 'I can't serve this if it doesn't have points.'

How common is synesthesia? According to some estimates, synesthesia occurs only in 1 in 20,000 people (Cytowic 1997), whereas others put the figure as high as 1 in 200 (Ramachandran and Hubbard 2001). Perhaps a more realistic figure is 1 in 2,000. What is more certain is that synesthesia occurs more frequently in females (there is a 6:1 female/male ratio) and there is a positive family history of the condition in around one-third of cases (Baron-Cohen *et al.* 1996). This has raised speculation that, at least in some instances, synesthesia is genetic with an autosomal or X-linked transmission. It has also been claimed that there is a tendency for people with synesthesia to be left-handed and have superior memory skills (Cytowic 1995). A number of gifted people are also believed to have been synesthetic, including the poet Arthur Rimbaud, physicist Richard Feynman, and painter Wassily Kandinsky – whose work was sometimes intended to evoke sounds in those who viewed it. Another synesthete is the British pop artist David Hockney.

The most popular theory of synesthesia is that, during development, the brain of a synesthete becomes wired in such a way, that extra neural links are formed between areas serving different senses. If this is true then one might expect to find more brain areas at work in the brain of a synesthete. This question was examined by Paulesu *et al.* (1996), who undertook a PET study that measured cerebral blood flow in six female synesthetes who were asked to indicate what colours they sensed when hearing words and tones. The results showed that both synesthetes and controls exhibited increased activity in the main language areas that border the Sylvian fissure. However, the synesthetes showed far greater and more extensive activation of the visual association areas, including posterior temporal cortex and the junction between parietal and occipital cortices. Surprisingly, there was little activation of the primary visual cortex (V1) and adjacent areas (V2 and V4), showing that synesthesia involves higher levels of brain processing.

Gustation (taste)

The word 'taste' come from the Latin *taxare* meaning 'to touch or estimate'. The receptors for taste are located primarily on the top and sides of the tongue, although a few can also be found on the soft palate, inner surface of the cheeks, and even the epiglottis of the larynx. The tongue's receptors are located within taste buds, which contain around 50–150 receptor cells, and these occur in raised bumps called **papillae** which give the tongue its slightly abrasive feel. Each taste bud is a globular structure consisting of three types of cell: supporting cells, taste cells and basal cells (Figure 3.10). **Supporting cells** form the bulk of the taste bud and surround the **taste cells**, which contain **microvilli** (sometimes called gustatory hairs) which protrude through a taste pore to the surface of the taste bud where they are bathed by saliva. It is here, within the microvilli that the transduction of taste information into neural input takes place. The taste cells do not have their own axons to carry gustatory information to the brain. Instead, they make synapses with nerve fibres lying at the bottom of the taste bud. Taste cells have a short lifespan and are constantly replaced by new sensory cells derived from the division of the basal cells.

Taste sensations can be divided into four categories: sour, salty, bitter and sweet. Each of these sensations is produced by a different group of chemicals. The taste of sour is produced by acids, or, more specifically, their hydrogen ions; salty tastes are produced by metal ions (inorganic salts); and bitter ones are produced by alkaloid compounds. In contrast, the taste of sweetness is elicited by many organic substances, including sugars and some amino acids. The sensitivity to these four basic tastes varies over the tongue. In general, sweet tastes are detected most easily at the tip, sour at the sides, and bitter at the back. The ability to taste salt is more evenly distributed, although increased sensitivity occurs at the front and around the sides of the tongue.

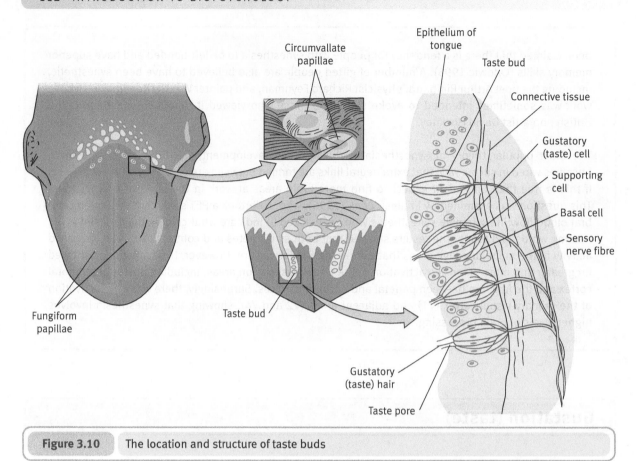

Figure 3.10 The location and structure of taste buds

Source: E.N. Marieb, *Human Anatomy and Physiology*, p. 488. Copyright © 1989 by Benjamin Cummings

Despite this, taste sensation is not as simple as at first appears. For example, most taste buds can respond, at least to some degree, to two, three or even four taste qualities (Nowlis and Frank 1977). To make matters more complex, many substances also produce a mixture of taste sensations (for example, lemonade can be broken down into sweet, sour and bitter sensations (Mather 2006)). In fact, some substances even change flavour as they flow through the mouth. Saccharin, for example, is tasted as sweet initially, but leaves a bitter aftertaste at the back of the tongue.

For a chemical to be tasted it must be dissolved in saliva and diffuse into the taste bud, where it stimulates the gustatory hairs that contain the taste receptors. These hair cells do not form action potentials themselves, but generate excitatory potentials that summate in unison to trigger action potentials in the sensory neurons lying at the base of the taste bud. These sensory neurons form components of three cranial nerves that project to the brain. The **facial nerve** (cranial nerve VII) transmits impulses from taste receptors in the anterior two-thirds of the tongue, whereas the **glossopharyngeal nerve** (cranial nerve IX) relays information from the posterior part of the tongue. Taste impulses from the few taste buds in the epiglottis and pharynx are conducted by the **vagus nerve** (cranial nerve X). Consequently, damage to the glossopharyngeal nerve impairs the ability to detect bitter substances, and injury to the facial nerve reduces sensitivity to sweet, sour and salt tastes.

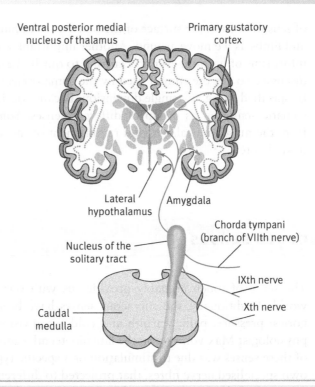

Ventral posterior medial nucleus of thalamus

Primary gustatory cortex

Lateral hypothalamus

Amygdala

Nucleus of the solitary tract

Chorda tympani (branch of VIIth nerve)

IXth nerve

Xth nerve

Caudal medulla

Figure 3.11   The neural pathways of the gustatory system

Source: N.R. Carlson, *Physiology of Behavior*, 8th edition, p. 236. Copyright © 2004 by Pearson Education

All three cranial nerves enter the brainstem and project to the **solitary nucleus** located in the upper part of the medulla (see Figure 3.11). From here, the taste fibres diverge and take one of two routes into higher areas of the brain. The main pathway ascends to the **ventral posterior medial thalamus,** which is also the main relay for somatosensory information that carries touch, pain and temperature from the face and mouth (see next section). This region of the thalamus also projects to several other areas of the cortex, the most conspicuous being the **primary gustatory cortex** located deep in the lateral fissure, in a part of the brain called the **insula,** close to the part of the somatosensory cortex, an area that receives sensory afferents from the tongue and pharynx. The second route from the solitary nucleus avoids the thalamus and goes instead to the **amygdala** and **hypothalamus** located in the 'emotional' limbic system.

The somatosensory system

The somatosensory system (derived from the Greek word *soma,* meaning 'body') provides us with a surprisingly wide range of sensation from the skin, via the **cutaneous senses,** which include touch, pressure, pain and temperature, and with feedback about joint and muscle position from within the body itself, via the **proprioceptive senses.** Thus, without the somatosensory senses we would not be able to experience any form of sensation from the surface of the body, or to monitor the location of our body parts and limbs as we move around. Another important somatosensory sense is pain, which informs us of harmful events occurring to our bodies. Unlike the other senses we have discussed so far, the stimuli used by the somatosensory system are diverse and cannot be specified along any single dimension. Because of this, it is more accurate to think of somatic sensation as group of different senses. Somatosensory feedback, especially from the muscles, is also a vital requirement of movement and will be covered in the next chapter.

The cutaneous senses

The sense of touch arguably provides us with our most intimate contact with the world. Traditionally, the cutaneous senses have been grouped into four broad categories: pressure, pain, warmth and cold – a division first proposed by the German physiologist Max von Frey in the late nineteenth century. Frey also proposed that each of these senses was due to stimulation of a specific type of receptor, connected with its own specialised nerve fibres, that projected to different sites in the central nervous system. Although we now know that the skin does indeed contain specialised receptors (discussed below), the processing of somatosensory information by nerve fibres is much more complex than Frey could have imagined.

The most common type of cutaneous receptor found in the skin are **free nerve endings** (or naked endings), although they also occur in other tissues, including muscle, bone, blood vessels and heart. These are fine (small diameter), multi-branching, unmyelinated (bare) nerve endings that appear to be the specialised extensions of dendrites. Ever since the work of Frey, these nerve endings have been known to be sensitive to noxious stimuli and act as pain receptors or **nociceptors** (from the Latin *nocere* meaning 'to hurt'). However, free nerve endings also respond to many other types of stimuli, including touch, heat and cold. For example, some free nerve endings preferentially respond to stimuli that come into prolonged contact with the skin, whereas others act specifically as heat or cold detectors. Another type of free nerve ending is known to signal temperature changes at low levels of activity (i.e. it acts as a **thermoreceptor**) and pain at higher intensities.

In addition, the skin also contains a variety of other sensory receptors where the nerve ending is encased in a specialised capsule. These are commonly described as **mechanoreceptors** because their primary function is to detect changes in the movement of the skin. These receptors include **Merkel discs**, which are found in the deeper layers of skin, and **Meissner corpuscles**, which are abundant in the skin's surface (see Figure 3.12). The latter are found in particularly high numbers in sensitive skin areas, including the eyelids, lips, nipples, clitoris and penis. Another type of receptor sensitive to movement is the **Pacinian corpuscle**, some of which are over 2 mm long and visible to the naked eye. These are believed to be sensitive to changes in pressure and to stretching. Two types of somatosensory receptor, however, whose function are less well understood are **Krause's endbulbs** and **Ruffini's corpuscles**. Although these receptors probably encode pressure or sustained touch, there is some evidence that they may also act as temperature detectors, with the former sensitive to cold stimuli and the latter more sensitive to hot ones.

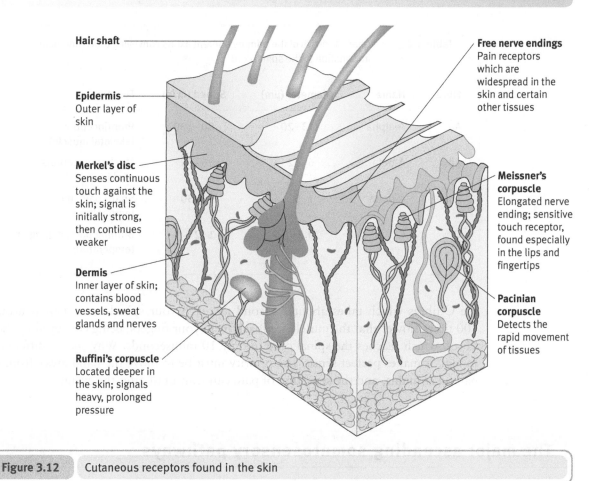

Hair shaft

Epidermis
Outer layer of
skin

Merkel's disc
Senses continuous
touch against the
skin; signal is
initially strong,
then continues
weaker

Dermis
Inner layer of skin;
contains blood
vessels, sweat
glands and nerves

Ruffini's corpuscle
Located deeper in
the skin; signals
heavy, prolonged
pressure

Free nerve endings
Pain receptors
which are
widespread in the
skin and certain
other tissues

Meissner's
corpuscle
Elongated nerve
ending; sensitive
touch receptor,
found especially
in the lips and
fingertips

Pacinian
corpuscle
Detects the
rapid movement
of tissues

| Figure 3.12 | Cutaneous receptors found in the skin |

Source: P. Abrahams (ed.) *How the Body Works*, p. 430. Copyright © 2007 by Amber Books

The different types of cutaneous receptor are attached to fibres (axons) that pass to the dorsal roots of the spinal cord. In fact, four different types of fibre have been found and these are distinguished by the diameter of their axons. This is significant because axon diameter determines the conduction velocity of the nervous impulse, with larger axons providing faster transmission. The smallest fibres are named **C fibres**. These are around 1 μm in diameter, unmyelinated, and conduct action potentials at around 1 metre per second (1 m/s). The next smallest are the **A-delta fibres (Aδ)**. These are 2–4 μm in diameter, myelinated, and have a speed of about 5–30 m/s. The remaining two types of fibre are **A-beta (Aβ)** and **A-alpha (Aα)**. Both these fibres are myelinated and have large diameters of approximately 10 and 15 μm, respectively. This allows them to conduct action potentials at speeds of 35–55 m/s and 80–120 m/s, respectively. It appears that most types of pain and temperature information are conveyed by nerve fibres with small diameters, whereas light touch and pressure information is conveyed by larger-diameter nerve fibres (Table 3.2). The largest nerve fibres also convey information from the muscles regarding stretch. It is important to note that there is no exact correspondence between type of receptor and type of fibre as postulated by Frey.

The differences in fibre diameter also means that the various types of cutaneous information arrives at the spinal cord (and brain) at different times. For example, if you accidentally hit your fingers with a hammer, the information will be carried along

Table 3.2	Characteristics of the primary afferent axons conveying touch and pain information to the spinal cord			
Fibre	**Name**	**Diameter (µm)**	**Speed (m/s)**	**Function**
Aα	A-alpha	13–20	80–120	Proprioception (skeletal muscle)
Aβ	A-beta	6–12	35–75	Mechanoreceptors of skin
Aδ	A-delta	1–5	15–30	Sharp pain and temperature
C	C	0.2–1.5	1–2	Burning pain, itching and temperature

the C fibres which takes about 1 second to reach your spinal cord. This is around 100 times slower that the muscle feedback from your fingers, being conveyed by the A fibres, which reaches the spinal cord in only 10 milliseconds. Why such a difference? In fact, it makes perfect sense. The priority must be to move the hand away from the painful stimulus, and the sensation of pain can wait until after the event.

The major ascending somatosensory pathways

All the neural fibres carrying sensory information from the cutaneous receptors join together in the peripheral nerves (which also contain the motor fibres *going* to the skeletal muscles) and enter the spinal cord via bundles known as the **dorsal roots**. The spinal cord is divided into 30 segments, and each one receives sensory information from a pair of sensory roots. The region of skin innervating each spinal root is called a **dermatome**, and if they are mapped out on the body's surface they appear as a set of stripes wrapping around a limb or part of the trunk. There are 30 dermatomes on each side of the body (60 in total) and they are labelled according to the regions of the spinal cord they enter (for example, cervical, thoracic, lumbar and sacral). Although a section of each dermatome is also innervated by a neighbouring spinal nerve, a touch examination of these skin areas can provide a neurologist with important information concerning the location and extent of a spinal cord injury.

From the dorsal roots, cutaneous input passes through the spinal cord and brain via two routes: the **dorsal-column medial-lemniscus pathway**, which carries cutaneous information about touch (along with pressure and vibration), and the **anterolateral pathway**, which is concerned with pain and temperature (see Figures 3.13 and 3.14). These two pathways begin to separate as they enter the dorsal roots, with the large-diameter (touch) fibres entering the ganglia medially, and small-diameter ones (pain and temperature) laterally. As the large-diameter 'touch' axons pass into the spinal cord, where they branch and then take one of three routes: (1) they make synapses with the grey matter in the same segment, (2) they descend into other spinal segments, or (3) they project to the brain. If the fibre takes the latter route, it forms part of the spinal cord's

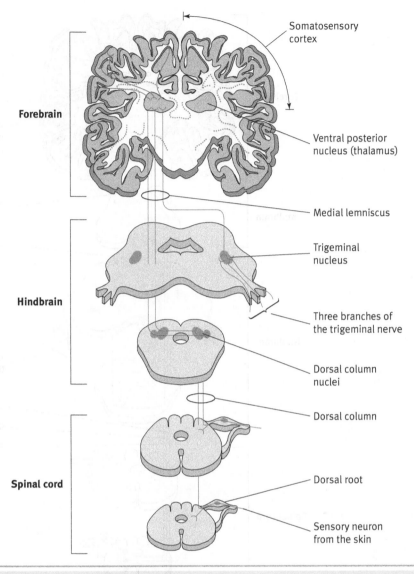

| Figure 3.13 | The dorsal-column medial-lemniscus system |

Source: John P.J. Pinel, *Biopsychology*, 5th edition, p. 180. Copyright © 2003 by Pearson Education

white matter, called the **dorsal columns**. These tracts can be seen on both sides of the spinal cord and provide a fast, direct highway to the **dorsal column nuclei** (comprising the **nucleus gracilis** and **nucleus cuneatus**) in the medulla of the brainstem. At this point, the axons synapse onto neurons that cross over to the other side of the brain. They then ascend in another white tract known as the **medial lemniscus** which goes to the **ventral posterior nucleus of the thalamus**. From here, axons project to the primary (SI) and secondary (SII) regions of the **somatosensory cortex**, located in the postcentral gyrus of the parietal lobe.

The small-diameter 'pain' axons arising from the skin and which form the antereo-lateral pathway take a different route to the brain. Although these neurons again enter the dorsal roots, they synapse with spinal cord cell bodies located in the **substantia gelatinosa**. At this point, the neurons cross to the opposite side of the spinal cord,

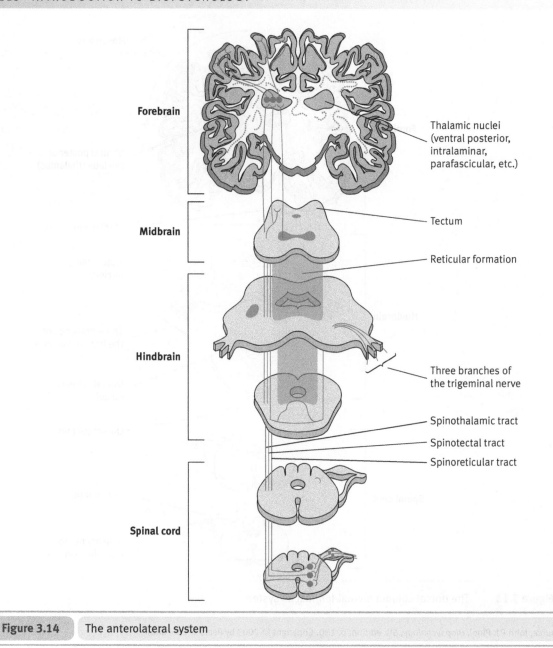

Forebrain

Thalamic nuclei
(ventral posterior,
intralaminar,
parafascicular, etc.)

Midbrain

Tectum

Reticular formation

Hindbrain

Three branches of
the trigeminal nerve

Spinothalamic tract

Spinotectal tract

Spinoreticular tract

Spinal cord

Figure 3.14 The anterolateral system

Source: John P.J. Pinel, *Biopsychology*, 5th edition, p. 181. Copyright © 2003 by Pearson Education

where they form a major white ascending tract of fibres known as the anterolateral system. This pathway comprises three tracts. In humans, the largest is the **spinothalamic tract**. This receives input from the Aδ fibres, and it passes directly to the brain where it reaches the ventral posterior nuclei of the thalamus (the same thalamic region as receives input from the lemniscus system). In turn, this gives rise to a major pathway to the somatosensory cortex. The two other pathways forming the anterolateral system are made mainly from C fibres and comprise the **spinoreticular tract**, which projects to widespread areas of the reticular formation (known to be important in arousal), and the **spinotectal tract,** which passes to the midbrain.

The somatosensory cortex

The primary somatosensory cortex lies in the postcentral gyrus of the cerebral cortex, located just posterior to the central sulcus (the part of the brain that separates the frontal and parietal lobes). It exists as a long strip of cortex that runs from ear to ear across the head (see Figure 3.15). This area was first mapped in humans by the Canadian neurosurgeon Wilder Penfield in the 1930s who pioneered the use of brain surgery to treat patients with severe epilepsy. The problem facing Penfield was not so much to identify the tissue where epileptic seizures originated, as to remove tissue without causing speech loss or paralysis. To do this, Penfield stimulated the brain with an electric current in conscious patients (a technique that caused no distress as the brain does not contain pain receptors). By observing sudden movements and outbursts of speech in his patients, or recording their experiences, Penfield was able to locate language and motor areas (the sites of these can vary considerably between individuals) which then

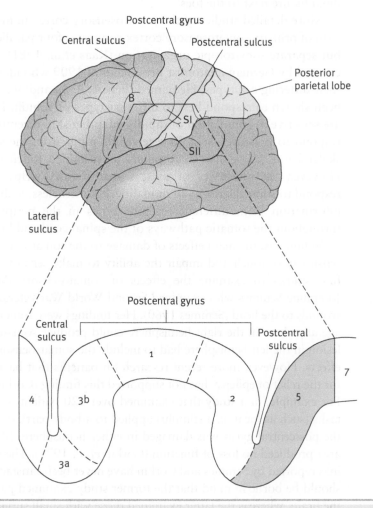

| **Figure 3.15** | Strips of the somatosensory cortex |

Source: F. Toates, *Biological Psychology*, 2nd edition, p. 234. Copyright © 2007 by Pearson Education

were avoided during surgery. Penfield found that when he applied the stimulation to the postcentral gyrus, the patients reported touch sensations from various parts of the body, such as a tingling sensation in the arm.

When Penfield compared the site of stimulation and the parts of the body in which the sensation was felt, he found that the somatosensory cortex was topographically organised. That is, the point-to-point relationship of the body was represented in a highly organised map. The motor cortex next to the somatosensory cortex has a similar organisation (see Figure 4.13). More precisely, the areas receiving sensory information from the legs and trunk were found in the superior (upper) part of the somatosensory cortex, and the areas receiving input from the hands and face were found in the inferior (lower) part of the cortex. In addition, Penfield found that the somatosensory cortex is somewhat distorted, with the greatest proportion of its brain tissue devoted to processing information from areas of the body that are capable of making the finest tactile discriminations such as the hands and face. In contrast, areas such as the thighs and trunk had relatively little cortex devoted to them. The one body region that is an exception to the topographic rule is the genitals, which are located deep in the longitudinal fissure next to the toes.

More detailed studies of the somatosensory cortex in monkeys have found that the strip of primary somatosensory cortex comprises four parallel strips, each with a similar but separate somatotopic organisation (Kaas *et al.* 1981). These strips were first discovered by German anatomist Brodmann in 1909 who identified them on the basis of their differing cell types. He named them 1, 2, 3a and 3b. These four strips have now been shown to respond best to different types of stimuli. For example, cells in area 1 are sensitive to stimulation of rapidly adapting skin receptors, whereas those in area 2 respond to pressure. Area 3a receives its input from the stretch receptors located in skeletal muscles, while 3b responds to sustained touch stimulation from the skin. However, the selectivity of these somatosensory strips is not absolute, and they respond to some degree to all modalities. Nonetheless, it shows that the segregation of information from different receptor types in the periphery is largely maintained throughout the somatic pathways of the spinal cord and brain (see Figure 3.15).

In humans, the main effects of damage to the somatosensory cortex are to reduce the sensitivity of touch and impair the ability to make sensory discriminations. One of the first studies to examine the effects of somatosensory damage was undertaken by Josephine Semmes who examined Second World War veterans who had received missile wounds to the head (Semmes 1960). Her findings were somewhat surprising in that damage anywhere in the right hemisphere could produce somatosensory deficits, whereas a lesion in the left hemisphere had to include the somatosensory cortex to produce similar effects. However, more recent research on patients that have received cortical excisions for the relief of epilepsy has not supported this finding (Corkin 1964; Corkin *et al.* 1971). For example, in a study that examined over 120 patients on a range of somatosensory tasks (such as locating a stimulus applied to a body part), deficits were found only when the postcentral gyrus was damaged in either hemisphere. Moreover, lesions outside this area produced no loss of function (Corkin *et al.* 1971). The difference between the findings reported by Semmes and Corkin have never been satisfactorily explained, although it should be borne in mind that the former study examined patients with large wounds to the brain, whereas the latter examined those with small surgical excisions.

Damage to the somatosensory cortex can also result in two types of tactile agnosia. The first is **astereognosis** (from the Greek *stereo* meaning 'solid') in which the person is unable to recognise an object by touch, although they have no cutaneous impairment.

The other type of tactile agnosia is **asomatognosia**, which refers to the loss of knowledge about one's own body or bodily condition. Sufferers of this condition may not only be unaware of their own body parts, but in some cases may even deny the existence of certain illnesses. This condition is extremely rare and is associated with damage to the right parietal lobe, which presumably also includes secondary areas of the somatosensory cortex (Kolb and Whishaw 2003).

The phenomenon of pain

The cutaneous senses provide us with another important form of sensation known as pain. As we all know, this provides an unpleasant experience, typically resulting from noxious stimulation, which is often an indicator of harm occurring to our body. Thus, pain serves as an important signal of danger, and attempting to avoid it is one of our best defences against injury. Despite this, the relationship of pain with injury is not straightforward. For example, some fatal diseases do not produce obvious pain, and there are conditions that cause excruciating discomfort yet have relatively little risk for the person (for example, toothache). The amount of pain experienced by a person is further strongly influenced by their psychological state. Indeed, pain can be ignored in times of battle, sporting endeavour and passion, or enhanced by anticipation, fear and anxiety. But one thing is certain, though the experience of pain, especially if prolonged, is always highly distressing to the individual, often sapping their body and mind of vigour, and causing health to deteriorate. It is estimated that 11 per cent of the UK population have some form of chronic pain disorder. One only needs to walk into a chemist and view the great variety of pain remedies to realise that pain is big business, reflecting the suffering of many millions of people.

Avoiding pain is essential to our well-being, and this can be seen in a rare condition where individuals are born without the ability to sense pain, called **congenital analgesia**. These individuals often badly injure themselves by sustaining extensive burns, bruises and lacerations. Moreover, they often move in a heavy and awkward way as their movement is not governed by normal sensory feedback. Consequently, people with congenital analgesia typically have worn and inflamed joints, along with damaged muscle tissue. A case of congenital analgesia is that of Miss C, who was a young student at McGill University in Montreal (Melzack and Wall 1988). This woman felt no pain when parts of her body was subjected to strong electric shock, scalding hot water, or prolonged exposure to ice. A variety of other procedures, including inserting a stick up her nose, pinching tendons, or injecting histamine under the skin, also failed to elicit responses. And, she exhibited no changes in blood pressure, heart rate or respiration when subjected to these ordeals.

Her insensitivity to pain caused Miss C to experience many medical problems. As a young girl she had bitten off the end of her tongue while eating, and later she developed damage to her knees, hip and spine which required orthopaedic operations. She also developed a condition known as 'Charcot joint' where her ankles, knees, wrists and elbows became deformed and swollen. This problem arose because of her inability to shift weight properly when standing, walking, sitting and even sleeping, and was exacerbated by a further inability to protect herself after injury. One consequence of this condition is the occurrence of secondary infections in the dying tissue of the damaged joints. Sadly, this was to occur with Miss C, whose infections became so severe that they spread into the bone marrow where they could not be controlled by antibiotics. Miss C died at the age of 29 years from massive infection.

The receptor basis of pain

The receptors responsible for producing pain are the free nerve endings found throughout the skin and other organs of the body. Free nerve endings detect both temperature and touch, although some appear to be specialised for encoding pain, especially when they are stimulated at high intensities. In fact, these are believed to contain receptors for pain (or **nociceptors**) which can be divided into three different types: (1) mechanical nociceptors that respond to potentially damaging pressure or touch, (2) temperature nociceptors that respond to extremes of heat and cold, and (3) chemical nociceptors that respond to noxious chemicals. The last type of nociceptor may react not only to externally applied chemicals but also to substances released from the skin itself following injury (for example, potassium ions and histamine), from cells in the blood (for example, serotonin), and from nerve endings (for example, substance P). In addition, some of these chemicals contribute to the process of inflammation that further increases the sensitivity of nociceptors to pain.

A further subdivision of nociceptors can be made on the basis of whether they are **unimodal** (responding to only one type of pain sensation) or **polymodal** (responding to a variety of stimuli). In general, unimodal nociceptors have a much lower threshold for stimulation (so they provide a rapid response to noxious stimuli), but produce only a transient or short-lasting neural signal. In contrast, polymodal nociceptors require a higher threshold to be activated, but they produce a much more sustained neural response.

Information arising from the nociceptors travel to the spinal cord via two types of axon: unimodal Aδ fibres, which conduct pressure and touch information at speeds of 15–30 m/s, and polymodal C fibres, which conduct action potentials at slower rates of 1–2 m/s. These two type of fibres are also associated with different sensations of pain, with the Aδ fibres producing short-duration 'pricking' pain and the C fibres generating longer-lasting 'burning' pain sensations. The difference in the conduction times of these two fibre types also helps to explain why pain often seems to occur in two different phases: a painful stimulus will typically cause a sharp, localised pain (sometimes called **fast pain**), followed by a more dull and diffuse pain (called **slow pain**).

Recently, researchers have started to identify specialised nociceptors on the free nerve endings of Aδ and C fibres. A chemical used to discover these pain receptors is **capsaicin**, a natural ingredient of 'hot' chilli peppers which produces pain if applied to free nerve endings. This discovery of capsaicin's pain-producing properties led to the realisation that the chemical must bind specifically to nociceptors, and it enabled those nociceptors to be isolated and cloned. One receptor that has been identified in this way has been called vanilloid 1. It has been shown that transgenic mice lacking the vanilloid receptor are unable to sense the pain of mild heat, although they still respond to mechanical pain (Caterina *et al.* 2000). Thus, the vanilloid receptor may act as a heat detector that enables us to sense changes in temperature. It is expected that many more types of nociceptor will discovered in the future.

Brain regions involved in pain

To identify the brain regions involved in pain, it is necessary to be familiar with the projections of the anterolateral system, which conveys noxious information from the periphery through the spinal cord, to the brain (Figure 3.16). This system is a complex grouping of neural pathways that has three main sites of termination in the brain: the somatosensory cortex, the reticular formation and the midbrain. To understand the role of these regions better, researchers have divided the anterolateral pathways into **lateral** and **medial** systems. The lateral system passes to the ventral posterior thalamus and provides the main route by which pain information reaches the somatosensory cortex. In contrast, the medial system includes the reticular and midbrain projections. Not only is this second pathway much older in evolutionary terms (it is present in all vertebrates,

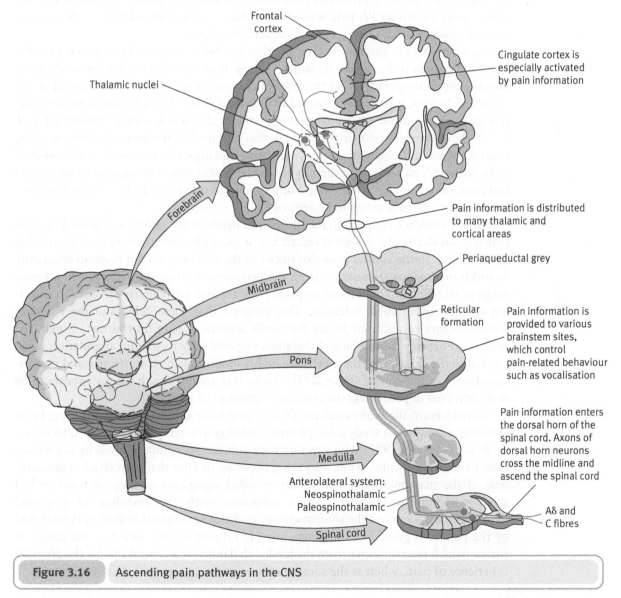

Frontal cortex

Cingulate cortex is especially activated by pain information

Thalamic nuclei

Forebrain

Midbrain

Pons

Medulla

Spinal cord

Pain information is distributed to many thalamic and cortical areas

Periaqueductal grey

Reticular formation

Pain information is provided to various brainstem sites, which control pain-related behaviour such as vocalisation

Pain information enters the dorsal horn of the spinal cord. Axons of dorsal horn neurons cross the midline and ascend the spinal cord

Anterolateral system:
Neospinothalamic
Paleospinothalamic

Aδ and C fibres

Figure 3.16   Ascending pain pathways in the CNS

Source: M.R. Rosenweig *et al.*, *Biological Psychology*, 2nd edition, p. 212. Copyright © 1999 by Sinauer Associates, Inc.

including fish and amphibians that have no lateral pathways), but the reticular formation and midbrain, in turn, have projections to the thalamus. These in fact pass to the medial nuclei of the thalamus which has a much more diffuse set of projections than the ventral posterior nuclei, including frontal cortex, cingulate cortex and limbic system. Thus, whereas the lateral system has a fairly precise site of termination in the somatosensory cortex, the medial system has a more diffuse set of target sites.

These two systems have been shown to have different roles in the processing of pain-related information. More specifically, the lateral pathways are more involved in detecting the location of pain in the body, whereas the medial pathways are concerned with its affective–motivational (or aversive) aspects (Melzack and Casey 1968). Several lines of evidence support this distinction. For example, it has long been known that damage to the somatosensory cortex in humans does not reduce the sensitivity to pain, although it impairs the ability to localise it correctly. In other words, the unpleasant feeling of pain must be produced elsewhere, and this conclusion is supported by the classic work of Wilder Penfield who showed that electrical stimulation of the primary somatosensory cortex rarely produced sensations of pain.

So, where is pain produced? One site that has been found to be important for the sensation of pain is the medial thalamus. This is shown by the fact that one of the most effective surgical operations for the relief of chronic pain is the surgical removal of this structure. Indeed, it has been reported that around two-thirds of patients report effective pain relief without any somatosensory deficits after it is lesioned (Jeanmoned et al. 1993). Furthermore, two of the regions that the medial thalamus projects to – the frontal cortex and cingulate cortex – can also be surgically removed for the relief of pain. Although patients with these types of lesion still report being able to locate and feel pain, the pain does not seem to bother them. In other words, the aversive or emotional quality of pain seems to be removed.

Further evidence supporting the distinction between the lateral and medial systems comes from electrophysiological research. For example, investigators have found that most neurons in the ventral posterior nuclei of the thalamus do not respond differently to touch or noxious stimulation from the periphery. Rather, they respond to a broad range of stimuli from mild touch to pain. They are also particularly sensitive to detecting changes in stimulus intensity. This suggests that these cells, and the recipient somatosensory cortex, may locate the tactile sources of pain. In contrast, a high percentage of neurons in the medial thalamus respond only to painful stimulation when applied to the skin – and, these cells are highly modifiable by the affective and motivational state of the animal (Price 2002). Thus, this area of the thalamus appears to be more involved in processing the emotional qualities of pain.

More recently, the brain areas involved in pain have also been examined using brain scanning techniques. A study using positron emission tomography (PET) was undertaken by Rainville et al. (1997) who exposed their subjects to painful stimuli by immersing their hands in hot water, while also using hypnosis to alter their perceived unpleasantness of the manipulations. The results revealed significant changes in pain-evoked activity within the cingulate cortex consistent with the encoding of perceived unpleasantness – but not the somatosensory cortex where neural activity was unaltered by the perceived pain. These findings provide support for the idea that the cingulate cortex (which receives input from the medial thalamus) is a crucial site for the affective experience of pain, whereas the somatosensory cortex has an entirely different role.

Phantom limb pain

In 1866, after treating soldiers injured in the American Civil War, the eminent neurologist S. Weir Mitchell first coined the term 'phantom limb' to refer to a state where a person still experiences the sensations from a bodily organ after it has been amputated following injury. Despite this, he was not the first to describe such a phenomenon. For example, in 1797, at the battle of Santa Cruz, Lord Nelson had his right arm shattered by gunfire and it had to be amputated. Afterwards, he reported phantom limb pain (most notably from his fingers digging into his palm) which he reasoned was also proof of his eternal soul. Despite such evidence, instead of publishing his work in a medical journal for fear of ridicule, S. Weir Mitchell wrote his article as a short story under a pseudonym. Despite his reputation, he was still not confident that his colleagues would accept the idea that sensation could arise from a limb that no longer existed (Melzack 1992).

Investigators now know that around nine out of ten amputees actually have phantom experiences that can last for years or even decades. To the amputee, the phantom limb is very real. For example, they may feel a lost arm swinging in co-ordination with the other when walking, or a lost hand gesticulating as they talk. Alternatively, a phantom leg may bend when its owner gets into bed, or become upright again during standing. Such a limb may also become hot or cold, feel sweaty or have an irritating itch. And, phantoms are not confined to the main limbs as there are cases of phantom eyes, breasts, and even penises that have erections. Unfortunately, in the majority of cases (70–80 per cent), phantom limbs are accompanied by pain. Often described as cramping, burning, crushing or shooting, the pain may also sometimes be caused by a distortion of an appendage such as a badly twisted foot, or finger-nails pushing into the flesh of the palm. This type of pain is often excruciating and may be more debilitating than the loss of the limb itself. It can persist for years and, despite a wide range of attempted remedies, is notoriously difficult to treat (Sherman 1980).

What causes phantom limb pain? The traditional explanation is that it arises from exposed nerve endings (called **neuromas**) of the amputated limb, which continue to send nerve impulses to the brain. Indeed, the work of Penfield showed that direct stimulation of the somatosensory cortex was able to evoke tactile sensations that gave the impression of being felt in the body. However, we now know the peripheral theory is wrong for the simple reason that paraplegic patients who have absolutely no sensation below a spinal cord break can still experience phantom limb pain. An alternative theory is that the defunct parts of the somatosensory cortex caused by the amputation, start to respond to stimuli from other parts of the body. The somatosensory cortex, similar to the motor cortex (see Figure 4.13 on page 161), contains a distorted but topographic map of the body in which the face is represented next to the hand and the feet lie next to the trunk. Thus, if redundant parts of the somatosensory cortex are beginning to process new sensation from other body regions, we might predict that stimulation of the face will produce phantom limb sensations of the hand – or that stimulation of the trunk will cause sensations in the foot. In fact, this is exactly what was found by Dr Vilayanur Ramachandran who used cotton wool buds to probe the body surface of amputees (see Ramachandran and Blakeslee 1998). Thus, it would appear that the phantom limb pain is at least partly due to the reorganisation of the somatosensory cortex. It is also interesting to note that Ramachandran found a patient who felt orgasms in his phantom foot during sexual activity. A closer examination of the somatosensory map indeed shows the area of the penis to lie adjacent to the feet.

The gate theory of pain

It has long been known that pain can be modified by a large number of factors. For example, everyone knows from experience that rubbing a knock or injury will help diminish its painfulness. In addition, there are many recorded cases where the excitement of a sporting event or being in a dangerous situation has suppressed the pain of a serious injury. This type of effect was also observed by army surgeon Henry Beecher during the Second World War (Beecher 1959). He found that upon reaching hospital, only one in three injured soldiers complained of enough pain to require an analgesic. Despite this, the men were not in a state of shock and were able to feel pain, as shown by their protests when given an inept injection. Even the wounded themselves were often surprised at their own lack of discomfort. To explain their indifference, Beecher argued that psychological factors were reducing the impact of the pain. Indeed, any pain experienced by a wounded soldier on the battlefield was being compensated by the relief of being removed from the combat. A similar type of injury occurring in civilian life would be likely to have very different psychological consequences.

A highly influential theory that explains how cutaneous stimulation and emotional activation can affect the sensitivity pain was proposed by Canadian psychologist Ronald Melzack and British physiologist Patrick Wall in 1965. Their idea, which became known as the **gate control theory of pain** (Figure 3.17), did not regard pain simply as noxious sensation that flows unaltered from the peripheral nerve endings to the brain. Rather, they saw it as information that is modified by the shutting or opening of a gate-like mechanism in an area of the spinal cord called the **substantia gelatinosa**. This is a region of the spinal cord that contains a large number of enkephalin (opiate) interneurons (small neurons that are confined to the substantia gelatinosa), that receive input from *both* the small Aδ and C fibres that convey pain information, and the larger fibres that transmit touch (or non-pain) information.

But, why should these interneurons receive these two different types of neural information? The answer according to Melzack and Wall is that it allows the activity in one set of fibres to affect neural transmission in the other. For example, they argued that when the small pain fibres are stimulated, they excite the interneurons of the substantia gelatinosa, whereas input from the larger touch fibres inhibit the same cells. This means that if the large touch fibres are activated at the same time as the Aδ and C fibres, then the neural activity in the interneurons will be inhibited. In effect, this will 'close the gate' to pain impulses travelling into the spinal cord. This gating mechanism also explains why rubbing an injured area provides an effective way of diminishing the sensation of pain.

In addition, Melzack and Wall used a similar type of argument to explain how the emotional or psychological state of the person can act to reduce pain. In short, they proposed that there is second pathway which descends from the brain to the interneurons of the substantia gelatinosa – where it exerts a similar type of effect to the neurons conveying touch information from the periphery. In this way, activity in the brain can also affect the gating mechanism of the spinal cord to increase or lessen the flow of painful stimuli into the central nervous system.

If this theory is correct, then there should be areas in the brain where electrical stimulation can be applied to suppress pain. One region that produces this type of analgesia is the **periaqueductal grey area** (**PAG**), a region that surrounds the cerebral aqueduct in the brainstem. In fact, the pain relief from this type of stimulation is so effective that it enables surgical procedures to take place without anaesthesia. This phenomenon, called **stimulation-produced analgesia,** has been demonstrated in a wide range of species, including humans, and it suppresses pain without affecting the sensitivity of touch. The PAG produces this effect by means of a pathway that passes to the **nucleus raphe magnus** (one of several raphe nuclei located in brainstem) and regions of the adjacent medulla. From here, fibres travel down in the dorsolateral columns of the spinal cord to laminae V of the dorsal horns (lying adjacent to the substantia gelatinosa). Studies have indeed confirmed that stimulation of the PAG inhibits the responses of these dorsal horn cells to noxious skin stimuli while leaving their responses to gentle tactile stimulation unaffected (Meyer 1979).

Although the gate control theory has been modified in some minor ways since it was first proposed in 1965, it has nevertheless stood the test of time. Indeed, the theory has been characterised as 'an excellent first approximation of the neural mechanisms underlying the transmission of nociceptive information' (Price 1977). But perhaps the most important contribution of the gate theory has been to provide a theoretical framework for over four decades of pain research – and to show that pain has many dimensions, both physiological and psychological.

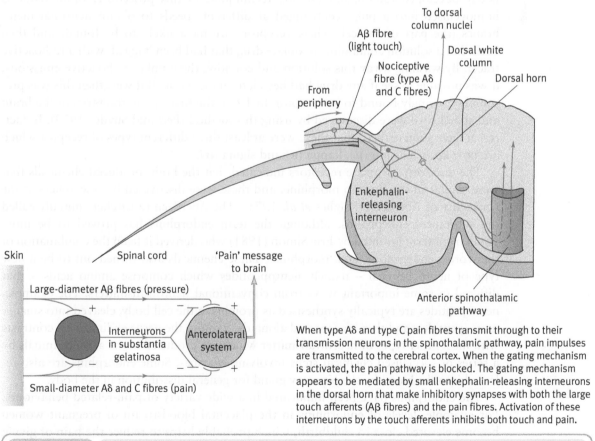

When type Aδ and type C pain fibres transmit through to their transmission neurons in the spinothalamic pathway, pain impulses are transmitted to the cerebral cortex. When the gating mechanism is activated, the pain pathway is blocked. The gating mechanism appears to be mediated by small enkephalin-releasing interneurons in the dorsal horn that make inhibitory synapses with both the large touch afferents (Aβ fibres) and the pain fibres. Activation of these interneurons by the touch afferents inhibits both touch and pain.

Figure 3.17   The gate theory of pain

Source: Based on A.M. Schneider and B. Tarshis, *Elements of Biological Psychology*, p. 308. Copyright © 1995 by McGraw-Hill, Inc.

The endorphins

For thousands of years, drugs derived from the opium poppy have been used to treat pain. The most useful of these for doctors is morphine (the main psychoactive ingredient in opium), which has the ability to produce analgesia without significantly affecting basic sensations such as touch or consciousness. For a long time, though, morphine and other types of opiate drugs provided a puzzle for researchers. One reason was their high potency. For example, a number of the opiate drugs can produce analgesia in humans at doses that are a small fraction of a milligram (Snyder 1986). This type of potency could not be explained unless such drugs were able to fit into a specialised receptor site in the brain. Another factor supporting the existence of opiate receptors was the discovery of antagonists, that is, drugs that could reverse the effects of opiates. For example, the intravenous injection of a small quantity of the opiate antagonist **naloxone** can reverse, within 30 seconds, the effects of a potentially fatal heroin overdose, rendering the patient alert and apparently normal.

But, researchers asked, why should the brain be equipped with receptors for a substance that was derived from the opium poppy? The likely answer was that similar drugs must also occur naturally in the brain. In the early 1970s, researchers set about trying to discover whether this was the case by first identifying opiate receptors using newly developed radioligand binding techniques. In this procedure, brain tissue is homogenised into a pulp, centrifuged at different speeds to obtain neuronal membranes (the part of the cell where receptors are most likely to be found) and then bathed in a solution containing an opiate drug that had been 'tagged' with a radioactive tracer. By washing away this solution and counting the number radioactive emissions, it was possible to see if any drug had been left on the tissue. If it was, then this was presumably strongly bound to its receptor. In 1973, the first opiate receptors in the brain and spinal cord were discovered by using this method (Pert and Snyder 1973). In fact, researchers soon realised that there were at least three different types of receptor which are now known as **mu (μ)**, **kappa (κ)** and **sigma (σ)**.

The discovery of opiate receptors indicated that the brain produced chemicals that were similar in structure to morphine, and these were discovered by researchers at the University of Aberdeen (Hughes *et al*. 1975). The Aberdeen researchers initially called the substances enkephalins, although the term **endorphins** has proved to be more popular – a term invented by Eric Simon (1981) who derived it from the combination of the words 'endogenous' and 'morphine'. These chemicals also turned out to be a new type of neurochemical – namely **neuropeptides** which comprise amino acids – that differed in some important ways from conventional neurotransmitters. For example, neuropeptides are typically synthesised as proteins in the cell body, cleaved into smaller units (peptides) and then transported along the axon to the nerve ending. This contrasts with most other types of neurotransmitter which are produced in the axon terminals by a series of specialised chemical steps involving enzymes. Some endorphins are also released into the blood by the pituitary gland for general distribution in the body.

The endorphins have been implicated in a wide variety of pain-related behaviours. For example, levels of endorphins in the placental bloodstream of pregnant women become elevated close to childbirth, which probably helps to reduce the pain of giving birth. Some studies have also shown increased levels of endorphins in long distance runners and other athletes. This might explain how some athletes can resist discomfort and pain during strenuous exercise, and account for the sense of euphoria they sometimes

report. High endorphin levels have also been found in anorexic women, which then show decline when body weight returns to normal. This may help explain why some anorexic women report feeling 'high' after starvation, and have a tendency to engage compulsively in physical exercise. On a more curious note, it has been shown that laboratory rats like eating chocolate, but will eat less if given injections of naloxone. This has raised speculation that the pleasure of eating chocolate may in part be linked to the release of endorphins (see Levinthal 1988).

Summary

The **auditory system** provides us with our sense of hearing. Sound in transduced into neural impulses after it passes through the outer and middle parts of the ear (the latter contains the three smallest bones in the body called the **malleus, incus** and **stapes**), and stimulates hair cells located on the **organ of Corti** inside the **cochlear** (inner ear). Information then passes to the **cochlear nuclei** located in the medulla via the **cranial nerve VIII**. The auditory pathways in the brain are complex and bilaterally crossed at all levels. Two pathways from the cochlear nucleus are important. One passes through the trapezoid body to the **superior olivary complex** in the tegmental area of the pons. The second ascends in the **lateral lemniscus** to the **inferior colliculi**. From here, a pathway extends to the **medial geniculate nucleus** in the thalamus, and then to the **primary auditory cortex** in the temporal lobes. This pathway is important for higher auditory processing.

Smell (olfaction) and **taste (gustation)** are known as chemical senses because both the nose and tongue contains receptors that respond to chemical stimuli. Neurons from the **olfactory epithelium** of the nose pass into the **olfactory bulb,** which lies just below the frontal cortex. From here, the majority of neurons travel to the **primary olfactory cortex** lying deep in the medial aspects of the temporal lobe and which contains the **piriform cortex** and **periamygdaloid cortex**. In humans, a smaller pathway also goes to the septum near to the hypothalamus. In contrast, taste information from the tongue passes to the **solitary nucleus** in the upper medulla, and then ascends to the **ventral posterior medial thalamus** before reaching the **primary gustatory cortex**. This is located close to the part of the somatosensory cortex that receives sensory afferents from the tongue and pharynx.

The **somatosensory system** provides us with information regarding a wide range of sensation from the skin, including touch, pressure, pain and temperature (known collectively as the **cutaneous senses**), and feedback from joint and muscle position (the **proprioceptive senses**). Somatosensory information is processed by two main pathways: the **dorsal-column medial-lemniscus pathway**, which carries information about touch, and the **anterolateral pathway**, which is concerned mainly with pain and temperature. The first passes through the dorsal columns of the spinal cord to the **dorsal column nuclei,** where the pathway crosses to the other side of the brain and forms the **medial lemniscus** which goes to the **ventral posterior nucleus of the thalamus**. This, in turn, is the main relay for the **somatosensory cortex** located in the postcentral gyrus of the parietal lobe. In contrast, the antereolateral pathway crosses to the other side of the body in the spinal cord, and forms three tracts whose main destinations are (1) the **ventral posterior nuclei of the thalamus** and somatosensory cortex, (2) the **reticular formation**, and (3) the **midbrain**. This system is important in the processing of pain, although this sensation is modified by the existence of 'gates' in the spinal cord that are influenced by other types of touch fibre, and by descending pathways arising from the **periaqueductal grey area** and **nucleus raphe magnus** located in the brainstem. Both these latter inputs can inhibit pain reaching the higher areas of the brain.

Essay questions

1. Describe the physiology of the ear, the ascending auditory pathways, and the main regions of the brain involved in audition. How are pitch, sound localisation and loudness accomplished by the auditory system?

    Search terms: Cochlea. Organ of Corti. Auditory nerve (eighth cranial nerve). Superior olivary complex. Medial geniculate nucleus. Auditory cortex. Pitch. Sound localisation. Loudness.

2. What is meant by the chemical senses? Describe how receptors transduce chemical information into neural input and how this is processed by brain areas involved in smell and taste.

    Search terms: Olfaction. Gustation. Olfactory epithelium. Buck and Axel. Olfactory bulb. Primary olfactory cortex. Taste buds. Solitary nucleus. Ventral posterior medial thalamus. Primary gustatory cortex.

3. Describe how cutaneous information reaches the spinal cord and brain. What is the function of the somatosensory cortex, midbrain and reticular formation in processing cutaneous information?

    Search terms: Cutaneous senses. Dorsal-column medial-lemniscus pathway. Anterolateral pathway. Dorsal column nuclei. Ventral posterior nucleus of the thalamus. Somatosensory cortex. Midbrain. Reticular formation.

4. With detailed reference to the gate theory of pain explain how peripheral stimulation (for example, rubbing a 'painful knock'), and psychological factors (i.e. brain activity) can alter the sensitivity of pain at the spinal cord level.

    Search terms: Pain. Substantia gelatinosa. Aδ and C fibres. Melzack and Wall. Stimulation-produced analgesia. Periaqueductal grey area. Nucleus raphe magnus. Dorsolateral columns of the spinal cord. Endogenous opiates.

Further reading

Abrahams, P. (ed.) (2007) *How the Body Works*. London: Amber Books. A comprehensive and beautifully illustrated encyclopaedia of anatomy with a large section on sensory processes.

Bartoshuk, L.M. and Beauchamp, G.K. (1997) *Tasting and Smelling*. New York: Academic Press. A good introduction to the human aspects of taste and smell, including coverage of broader issues such as perception and cognition.

Blakeslee, S. and Ramachandran, V.S. (1998) *Phantoms in the Brain*. London: Fourth Estate. An engaging and well-written foray for the general reader into how the brain copes with neurological traumas, including loss of touch and phantom limbs.

Bromm, B. and Desmedt, J.E. (1995) *Pain and the Brain: From Nociception to Cognition*. New York:

Raven Press. A very comprehensive academic guide which contains just about everything the clinician needs to know about the neural and psychological basis of pain.

Coren, S., Ward, L.M. and Enns, J. (1999) *Sensation and Perception*. Fort Worth, Texas: Harcourt College Publishers. Now in its sixth edition, this is one of the best textbooks to cover all aspects of sensory processing including its neurobiological basis.

Doty, R.L. (2003) *Handbook of Gustation and Olfaction*. New York: Dekker. A detailed and thorough guide to the sensory processes involved in taste and smell.

Fields, H.L. (1987) *Pain*. New York: McGraw-Hill. Although this book is now rather dated, and is not aimed at undergraduates, it may nevertheless provide a useful source of information for the student.

Finger, T.E., Silver, W.L. and Restrepo, D. (eds) (2000) *The Neurobiology of Taste and Smell.* New York: John Wiley. Written by a series of experts, and not an easy read. Nonetheless it includes everything a student of biopsychology would want to know about gustation and olfaction.

Levine, M.W. (2000) *Fundamentals of Sensation and Perception.* Oxford: Oxford University Press. An excellent introductory textbook aimed at undergraduate students, with well-written chapters on all the main senses.

Mather, G. (2006) *Foundations of Perception.* Hove: Psychology Press. A colourful and nicely illustrated textbook for the undergraduate psychology student which is also interesting and easy to read.

Melzack, R. and Wall, P. (1988) *The Challenge of Pain.* London: Penguin. An engaging and excellent introduction to pain that can be understood by the general reader and which covers many topics, including the gate theory.

Pickles, J.O. (1988) *An Introduction to the Physiology of Hearing.* London: Academic Press. A book that focuses exclusively on how the acoustic system, including the brain, processes acoustic signals.

Stern, P. and Marx, J. (1999) Making sense of scents. *Science*, 286, 703–728. This special issue on olfaction includes a number of papers highlighting some of the exciting advances taking place in olfactory research.

Yost, W.A. (2000) *Fundamentals of Hearing: An Introduction.* London: Academic Press. An excellent introduction to how the ear encodes auditory information and how this is processed by the brain.

For self test questions, animations, interactive exercises and many more resources to help you consolidate your understanding, and expand your knowledge of the field, please go to the website accompanying this book at **www.pearsoned.co.uk/wickens**

duction to pain that can be understood by the general reader and which covers many topics, including the gate theory.

Pickles, J.O. (1988) An Introduction to the Physiology of Hearing. London: Academic Press. A book that focuses exclusively on how the acoustic system, including the brain, processes acoustic signals.

Sereno, R. and Maya, J. (1999) Making sense of scents. Science, 286, 703–725. This special issue on olfaction includes a number of papers highlighting some of the exciting advances taking place in olfactory research.

Yost, W.A. (2000) Fundamentals of Hearing: An Introduction. London: Academic Press. An excellent introduction to how the ear encodes auditory information and how this is processed by the brain.

Finger, T.E., Silver, W.L. and Restrepo, D. (eds) (2000) The Neurobiology of Taste and Smell. New York: John Wiley. Written by a series of experts, and not an easy read. Nonetheless it includes everything a student of these subjects would want to know about gustation and olfaction.

Levine, M.W. (2000) Fundamentals of Sensation and Perception. Oxford: Oxford University Press. An excellent introductory textbook aimed at undergraduate students, with well-written chapters on all the main senses.

Mather, G. (2006) Foundations of Perception. Hove: Psychology Press. A colourful and nicely illustrated textbook for the undergraduate psychology student which is also interesting and easy to read.

Melzack, R. and Wall, P. (1985) The Challenge of Pain. London: Penguin. An engaging and excellent intro...

CHAPTER 4

The control of movement

INTRODUCTION

The human brain processes an enormous amount of sensory information, gathering and analysing input from the external environment and receiving feedback from the internal state of its own body. But, no matter how much information is analysed, it is of little use unless it can be acted upon. Indeed, one characteristic of all animals, from the simplest to the most complex, is the ability to generate movement – whether it is to control and maintain the automated functions of the body (such as respiration, heart rate, digestion), or to move the skeletal bones in order to produce reflexive or purposeful behaviour. Attempting to understand how the brain and spinal cord control the action of muscles in the body presents a considerable and unique challenge. For example, imagine a simple behaviour such as walking. How does the central nervous system decide which joints need to be moved, exactly where they should bend, and by how much? And then how does it manage to co-ordinate all the various body parts while sending out the correct series of impulses along its output nerves to activate the appropriate combination of muscles? The capacity for movement appears to be almost miraculous. Indeed, one only has to observe the movements made by the most technologically sophisticated robots built today, to gain an insight into the great dexterity of even the simplest creatures who are able to propel themselves, swim, fly or run. For movement to evolve in mammals, an intricate form of neural organisation has had to develop in the central nervous system, with increasing levels of complexity – from simple reflexes in the spinal cord, to more complex patterns of behaviour controlled by the brain. This also includes an important role for the cerebral cortex which is intimately involved in thought and cognition. Although movement presents a complex puzzle, by attempting to understand to this remarkable phenomenon, the psychologist will be getting to the heart of what causes human behaviour.

Muscles

There would be no movement without muscles. (Incidentally, the word 'muscle' is based on the Latin *musculus* meaning 'little mouse' – so called because of the imagined resemblance of some muscles under the skin, such as the biceps, to mice.) The body contains three different types of muscle: **skeletal**, which is attached to the bones; **smooth**, which is found in the walls of organs such as blood vessels, gut and bladder; and **cardiac**, which forms the bulk of the heart. In this chapter we will be most concerned with the action of skeletal muscles, sometimes called striated muscle (because of its striped appearance), which are mainly under the control of the somatic nervous system. The human body contains over 600 different types of skeletal muscle, making up about 50 per cent of its weight, and these are responsible for posture, locomotion and voluntary movement. In contrast, the smooth and cardiac muscles, controlled by the autonomic nervous system and certain hormones, govern the involuntary functioning of the body's organs. Although smooth and cardiac muscle can function in the absence of neural input (for example, the heart has its own pacemaker cells that produce contractions), skeletal muscle requires neural innervation for it to contract. Skeletal muscle also contracts quickly and fatigues easily.

One of the most important functions of skeletal muscle is to bend the joints that allows the limbs to move, and to do this it has to be attached to a pair of bones. In fact, regardless of how complex a movement may be, these muscles work only one way: by

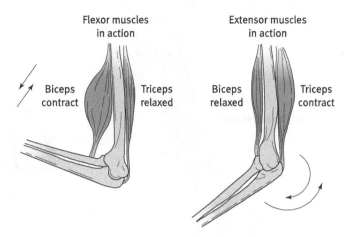

Flexor muscles in action

Extensor muscles in action

Biceps contract

Triceps relaxed

Biceps relaxed

Triceps contract

Figure 4.1   The flexion and extension muscles of the upper arm

contraction, or pulling on a joint. It follows, therefore, that at least two muscles, or sets of muscles, must be used to move a bone into one position and back again. In other words, joints are controlled by two sets of muscles whose effects oppose, or antagonise, each other. For example, the arm consists of the upper bone (the **humerus**) and the lower bones (the **ulna** and **radius**), which are connected at the elbow joint. The biceps (the flexion muscles) connect the upper and lower bones at the *front* of the joint, and when they contract the elbow is made to bend (Figure 4.1). In contrast, the triceps (the extensor muscles) run along the *back* of the upper and lower arm bones, and their contraction causes the limb to be straightened out. In practice, the flexor and extensor muscles are finely co-ordinated, with the contraction of one muscle being counterbalanced by relaxation of the other. However, it is unusual for a movement to involve a single pair of antagonistic muscles. Even the simple movement of the elbow requires the integrated action of many different muscles, and this principle holds true for all other types of joint and movement.

The fine structure of muscle

If a skeletal muscle is examined closely with a microscope it is found to consist of a large mass of long, thin **muscle fibres**, each of which is a living cell containing several nuclei (this arrangement is not found in other muscle types) and enclosed by an outer membrane called the **sarcolemma**. The length of muscle cells can vary enormously, with the longest being found in the sartorius muscle of the thigh and reaching over 30 cm in length, and the smallest occurring in the stapedius muscle of the inner ear and being less than 1 mm. But, no matter the muscle's size, packed tightly *within* each individual muscle fibre are hundreds, sometime thousands, of long cylindrical structures called **myofibrils** that run the entire length of the cell. These make up about 80 per cent of the muscle cell's volume and are the components that allow it to contract in response to a neural impulse. When examined closely, the myofibrils can be seen to be

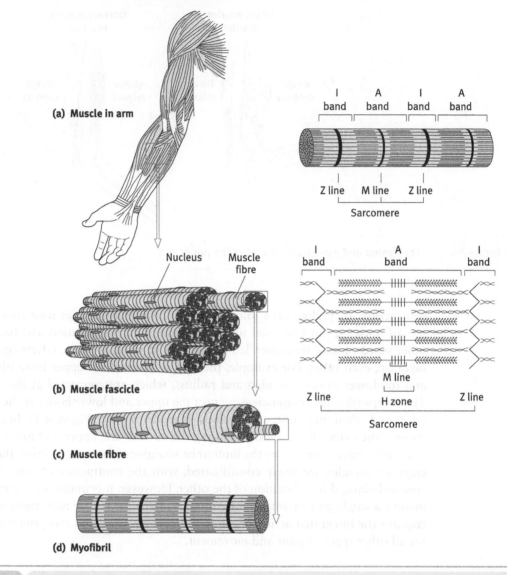

(a) Muscle in arm

Nucleus   Muscle fibre

(b) Muscle fascicle

(c) Muscle fibre

(d) Myofibril

I band A band I band A band

Z line M line Z line

Sarcomere

I band A band I band

M line

Z line H zone Z line

Sarcomere

| Figure 4.2 | The anatomy of a skeletal muscle |

Source: R. Carola *et al.*, (1990) *Human Anatomy and Physiology*

made up of thousands of short segments called **sarcomeres** that contain filaments made from **actin** (thin filaments) and **myosin** (thick filaments) that partially overlap like interlocking fingers. The sarcomere has two darkened ends (called Z lines) to which the actin filaments are attached, and a lighter middle (H zone) that contains only myosin filaments which are anchored to a fine M line. It is the Z lines and M lines that give the muscle its striated appearance (see Figure 4.2), and the movement of the filaments that gives it the ability to contract. The sarcomere is the functional unit of muscle and by explaining how it contracts, we can explain how the whole myofibril contracts.

How, then, do the actin and myosin filaments produce muscle contraction? The simple answer is that they are made to slide over each other, and by doing this the myosin filaments that are attached to the Z lines pull the two ends of the sarcomere towards each other. This occurs because the myosin and actin lie sandwiched between each other and have different shapes: the myosin filaments are thick with protruding hooks, whereas the actin filaments are thinner and have a more twisted, knobbly appearance. In effect, the myosin filaments hook themselves to the actin filaments, forming cross-bridges. When an action potential arrives at the muscle fibre, it causes a rotation in the shape of the myosin's hook, and this catches the actin filaments forcing the cross-bridges to slide along its surface (not unlike a straight finger bending). To be more precise, the cross-bridges detach and reattach at a new position in a sort of rowing motion. In fact, these cross-bridges can form and reform between 50 and 100 times per second. The result is that the sarcomeres contract, and this causes the myofibrils to shorten (in some cases by as much as 60 per cent of their length), resulting in muscle fibre contraction. The combined activity of large numbers of muscle fibres will ultimately cause the contraction of the much larger skeletal muscle.

The innervation of muscle

Skeletal muscles are stimulated by motor neurons that project from the ventral horn of the spinal cord, or in some cases the brain via its cranial nerves. Each individual muscle is served by at least one motor neuron, known as an **alpha motor neuron,** which typically gives rise to hundreds of multi-branching axonal endings that innervate a large number of its muscle fibres. Consequently, when the motor neuron fires, it causes all of its target muscle fibres to contract at the same time. Alpha motor neurons are among the largest neurons in the body and their axons conduct information very rapidly – often at speeds of more than 220 m/s. The number of fibres innervated by a single axon varies depending on the type of muscle. For example, the ocular muscles of the eye receive about one motor axon for every 10 muscle fibres; some muscles of the hand may have a motor neuron for every 100 muscle cells; and this figure may rise to 2,000 for the large muscles of the trunk and leg. In general, muscles with low ratios are involved in fine and dextrous movement, and those with high ratios are involved in less flexible responses.

The synapse that lies between the axon endings of the motor neuron and the muscle fibre is called the **neuromuscular junction.** Closer examination of this site shows that as the motor neuron axon reaches the muscle, it divides many times into fine unmyelinated branches, with each branch containing swollen protrusions called synaptic knobs. In turn, these knobs fit into 'pits' located on a specialised part of the muscle fibre known as the **motor endplate.** When stimulated by action potentials, the synaptic knobs release the neurotransmitter **acetlycholine.** This neurotransmitter crosses the synapse and binds to **nicotinic acetylcholine receptors** which increases the permeability of the muscle fibre membrane to sodium and potassium ions. The result is a small depolarisation known as an **endplate potential.** This form of synaptic transmission is fast and reliable as the endplate potential nearly always produces an action potential in the muscle fibre (this is in contrast to neurons, which often require the summation of many inputs before a nervous impulse is produced). The reliability of the muscle fibre to respond to acetylcholine is due to the large and highly folded surface area of the motor endplate, which contains thousands of synaptic knobs and is packed full of receptors.

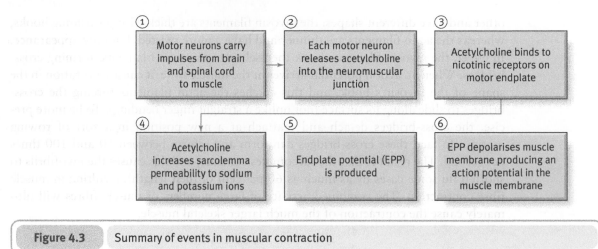

①
Motor neurons carry impulses from brain and spinal cord to muscle

②
Each motor neuron releases acetylcholine into the neuromuscular junction

③
Acetylcholine binds to nicotinic receptors on motor endplate

④
Acetylcholine increases sarcolemma permeability to sodium and potassium ions

⑤
Endplate potential (EPP) is produced

⑥
EPP depolarises muscle membrane producing an action potential in the muscle membrane

Figure 4.3 Summary of events in muscular contraction

How, then, does the action potential trigger muscle contraction? The answer lies with an organelle called the **sarcoplasmic reticulum**, which is a highly intricate network of tubes and sacs found in the cytoplasm of each muscle fibre. As the action potential moves through the muscle fibre, it causes large numbers of **calcium ions** (Ca^{2+}) to be released from the sarcoplasmic reticulum. In turn, these ions bind to the filaments, and it is this molecular reaction that causes changes in the shape of the cross-bridges that bond together the actin and myosin. The result is that filaments start to slide over each other, setting into motion muscle contraction.

Disorders that affect the neuromuscular junction

An understanding of the neuromuscular junction also has a broader significance for understanding certain diseases. One condition which affects this site is **myasthenia gravis**. This is an illness where the body's own immune system attacks and destroys the nicotinic cholinergic receptors located at the neuromuscular junction. Although new nicotinic receptors are made to replace the loss, they cannot fully correct the damage, and the cholinergic message is less efficiently translated into a muscle contraction. The main result is muscle weakness and fatigue. The course of the illness is highly variable, and fatal in about 10 per cent of cases. It normally begins in the facial muscles, which produces drooping of the eyelids, along with those of the throat and tongue, where it leads to chewing and swallowing difficulties. As the disorder progresses, it may affect the limbs, making it impossible for the person to engage in muscular exertion. Thus, muscle wasting may occur in the later stages of the disease. One of the main types of treatment for this disorder is the anticholinesterase drugs, such as physostigmine and neostigmine, which inhibit the action of the enzyme **acetylcholinesterase** (AChE) which acts to break down acetylcholine after it has been released into the synapse. Consequently, AChE drugs extend the lifetime of acetylcholine at the neuromuscular junction by preventing its destruction. In turn, this increases cholinergic stimulation at the remaining receptors. Unfortunately, these drugs have no effect on the progression of the underlying disease, and treatment may have to be supplemented by immunosupressive agents such as corticosteroids. The prevalence of myasthenia gravis is about 1 in 25,000 and it is twice as common in females as in males. One of the most famous victims of the disease was the Greek shipping tycoon Aristotle Onassis who married Jacqueline Kennedy, the widow of the assassinated American president John F. Kennedy.

It should come as no surprise that a large number of poisons also interfere with transmission at the neuromuscular junction. One of the best known is **curare**, which is a mixture of toxins derived from plant species *Chondodendron tomentosum* found in the Amazon region of South America. This has long been used by the indigenous Indians as a lethal substance to tip their darts for hunting and warfare. The main active ingredient in curare is the alkaloid δ-tubocurarine, which is a potent antagonist at nicotinic cholinergic receptors. Consequently, if nicotinic receptors are blocked by δ-tubocurarine, skeletal muscles can no longer be activated by motor neurons and the result is paralysis. Another highly toxic poison that acts on the neuromuscular junction is α-bungarotoxin. This toxin is one of many peptides found in the deadly venom of the banded krait *Bungarus multicinctus* found in south-eastern Asia. Indeed, because of its high affinity for nicotinic receptors this toxin has become a very useful experimental substance for visualising the molecular structure of the receptor. Other animals that use venom with agents that block nicotinic receptors include cobras and several types of sea-snake.

It may be of interest to note that nicotine, which is derived from the dried leaves of the tobacco plant *Nicotinia tabacum*, not only acts as an agonist (stimulant) at cholinergic nicotinic receptors, both at the neuromuscular junction and in the brain, but is also highly poisonous. In fact, a dose of 60 mg is often cited as the lethal dose (Koob and Le Moal 2006). Smokers avoid posioning by ingesting tiny doses, since a cigarette typically contains 10–20 mg of nicotine. Nonetheless, even at small doses, nicotine taken into the body by smoking may act on the neuromuscular junction to produce fine tremor, decreased muscle tone and a reduction in the strength of skeletal reflexes.

Proprioception

It is often said that we have five senses: sight, hearing, taste, touch and smell. Perhaps it is because we all tend to be consciously aware of these senses that we attach so much importance to them. However, one often overlooked sense, which is also vitally important, is **proprioception** (from the Latin *proprius* meaning 'oneself'). Proprioception, sometimes known as our kinaesthetic sense, deals with the position of the body and its relationship with the external world. That is, proprioception provides us with detailed and continuous information about the position of our limbs and other body parts in space, along with the speed and force of their movements. It is therefore the part of the nervous system that keeps track of, and controls, the different parts of the moving body. Because proprioception is involved with movements of the joints and limbs, it is generally considered to be a crucial component of the motor system.

It may be tempting to think that movement simply results from a series of commands that arises in the brain, or spinal cord, that informs the muscles of the body how to act. But, things are not so straightforward. In fact, most movements also depend on sensory information feeding back from the peripheral sense organs to the central nervous system. For example, the motor control areas of the spinal cord and brain require proprioceptive feedback to determine whether the intended movement is being executed as planned, or whether adjustments are necessary to finely tune the tension, contraction or co-ordination of the muscles. Indeed, without proprioception the brain cannot 'feel' what the body is doing, and the process of movement has to be carried out using a more conscious and considered approach. An account of a young lady without proprioception is given in 'The disembodied lady' which is to be found in Oliver Sack's book *The Man who Mistook his Wife for a Hat* (1985). Although the lady was able to move, she could only do so by using vision as a guide, and even then her actions were cumbersome and awkward.

Proprioception depends on many receptors in the body. These include, for example, muscle spindles, Golgi tendon organs, and joint receptors, which monitor stretching, tension, pressure and velocity. In addition, the visual system provides important sensory feedback to increase the accuracy of movement, and tactile receptors provide information regarding weights and pressure applied to the skin. Another crucial factor involved in movement is the position and motion of the head. Feedback about these is obtained via specialised proprioceptors which include the **vestibular system** – a fluid-filled set of chambers in the inner ear that helps the body feel the force of gravity and keeps it properly orientated and balanced. It is a remarkable feat of the brain, and to a lesser extent the spinal cord, that all of these senses are continuously being monitored and processed in an unconscious and automated fashion, in order to provide us with posture, balance and movement.

Feedback from muscles (muscle spindles)

Embedded within the layers of most skeletal muscles, lying parallel and squashed within their fibres, are specialised proprioceptors called **muscle spindles**. In fact, our most detailed knowledge of proprioception has come from studying these structures. The muscle spindle consists of a cluster of slender fibres called **intrafusal fibres**, which are contained within a fluid-filled capsule. Wrapped around the middle section of the spindle are very large and fast axons (known as **Ia sensory fibres**) that project into the spinal cord. The muscle spindle also receives input from a **gamma motor neuron** originating from the spinal cord that can cause it to contract – although this has no effect on the main contraction of the muscle in which it is embedded (see later). The muscle spindle has two main functions: (1) provide information to the central nervous system on the state and position of the muscles, and (2) initiate reflex contraction of the muscle when it is stretched by a load. Because the main role of the muscle spindle is to provide sensory information about the stretch of the muscle, muscle spindles are sometimes referred to as stretch receptors.

The importance of stretch receptors can be seen when a heavy weight is placed in a person's hand. At first the arm will begin to drop from the elbow, and the bicep muscles of the upper arm will be forced to stretch. As this movement occurs the muscle spindles in the biceps will become extended, and this causes them to relay information about the stretching to the spinal cord. This input then causes the **alpha motor neurons** (see page 137) projecting to the biceps to fire, producing their contraction

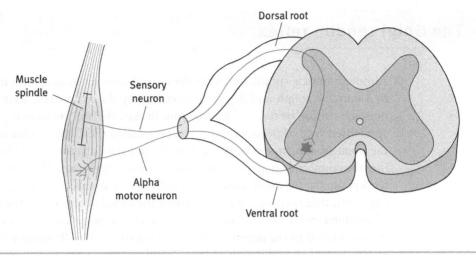

Dorsal root

Muscle
spindle

Sensory
neuron

Alpha
motor neuron

Ventral root

| **Figure 4.4** | The spinal monosynaptic reflex |

and helping them to resist the stretch. In this way, the biceps make a reflexive movement to the force of the weight. In fact, a basic prerequisite for smooth movement throughout the body is the ability to adjust muscle tone very quickly in response to such sudden shifts in muscle length. The stretch reflex is vital in this respect and essential for maintaining muscle tone and posture. It also has to take place very rapidly, which explains why the stretch reflex is controlled by the spinal cord and not by the brain.

The best-known example of the stretch reflex is the **patellar tendon reflex** (knee jerk), which is used by doctors to assess the condition of the nervous system. When the doctor strikes the tendon of the patient's knee, the impact causes the extensor muscle running along the thigh (the quadriceps) to be stretched. The sudden stretching of the quadriceps causes the muscle spindles to pass this information to motor neurons in the spinal cord, which then react by sending action potentials down their axons back to the stretched muscle. The result is a compensatory muscle contraction and sudden leg extension. This type of reflex is also called a **monosynaptic stretch reflex** (Figure 4.4) because only one synapse, located in the spinal cord, is encountered along the route from receptor (muscle spindle) to effector (leg muscle). Thus, the sensory neuron from the muscle spindle directly synapses with the motor neuron controlling the movement.

We have mentioned above that muscle spindles are innervated by a gamma motor neuron. But why should this be necessary when the muscle spindle does not directly contribute to the contraction of the muscle? The answer is that the muscle spindles have to contract with the muscle fibres surrounding it, otherwise they would become 'limp', causing their Ia sensory fibres to stop signalling to the spinal cord. If this happened, then the central nervous system would have no way of knowing how long the muscle was, or the weight acting on it. To solve this problem, alpha motor neurons which directly cause the contraction of muscle fibres, and gamma motor neurons are activated simultaneously by input from spinal cord and brain. In this way, the gamma motor neuron causes a small contraction of the muscle spindle at the same time as the muscle fibres are contracting. Thus, the spindle matches the length of the muscle, and the Ia sensory fibres can provide continuous feedback to the spinal cord.

The Golgi tendon reflex

Although muscle spindles provide the central nervous system with information relating to a muscle's length and degree of stretch, they do not provide feedback relating to the muscle's tension or force of contraction. In fact, this information is provided by another specialised type of proprioceptive receptor called the **Golgi tendon organs**, which lie at the point of attachment between muscles and the collagen fibres that form the tendons (i.e. the connective material that attaches muscle to bone). There are hundreds of Golgi tendon organs for every muscle, and each one is attached to 10–15 muscle fibres. Consequently, these organs are excited when the muscle contracts actively from stimulation of an alpha motor neuron, or when it is stretched passively by a load. This information is then relayed to the interneurons of the spinal cord by **Ib sensory fibres**. In turn, these interneurons form inhibitory synapses to alpha motor neurons.

The way the Golgi tendon organ feedback works to compensate for muscle tension is not too different from the way that muscle spindles help adjust for stretching. For example, if a weight is placed in your hand, the Golgi tendon organs respond to the resulting increase in muscle tension by sending excitatory input to the spinal cord's interneurons by the Ib sensory fibres. In response to this information, the interneurons inhibit the alpha motor neurons projecting back to the muscles. This then reduces the amount of contraction being applied to the muscle, thereby causing it to relax and lengthen. Things are not quite so simple, as the reduced muscle tone will also result in less Golgi tendon activity, resulting in muscle contraction again. Consequently, a step-by-step process helps to maintain the appropriate level of muscle tension. In this way, the muscle avoids damage or, in the worst case, being ripped away from the bone. But, just as importantly, this mechanism also helps to maintain the steady control over muscle tension that we need for a wide range of movements.

In addition to receiving feedback about muscle length and tension, the brain and spinal cord also receive sensory input about position and movement from mechanoreceptors in the ligaments and tissues surrounding the joints. These types of mechanoreceptor, which include **panician corpuscles**, appear to fire when the joint is moved and become quiet when it is at rest. However, the encoding of joint position is not well understood, and much of this information may well be provided by muscle spindles and Golgi tendon organs.

Polysynaptic reflexes

So far, we have examined two types of reflex: the patellar tendon reflex, which involves only one synapse (i.e. a **monosynaptic reflex**), and the Golgi tendon reflex, which requires neural input to be processed in the spinal cord by interneurons and therefore involves more than one synapse (i.e. a **polysynaptic reflex**) (Figure 4.5). In fact, the second type of reflex is by far the more common type of reflex produced by the central nervous system, and underlies just about every kind of movement. A further example of a polysynaptic reflex is where a person pulls away their hand in pain after touching a hot surface. This is also known as a **flexion reflex**. In this situation, pain receptors in

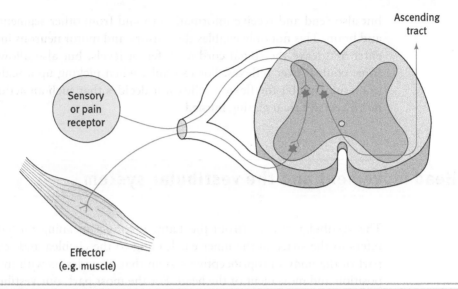

Ascending
tract

Sensory
or pain
receptor

Effector
(e.g. muscle)

Figure 4.5   The spinal polysynaptic reflex

the fingers send input to the spinal cord via a sensory neuron that synapses with several **interneurons** located within the grey matter of the spinal cord. At this point, the neural input takes several routes through the spinal cord, with the end result being a complex and co-ordinated response involving several muscles. Although this reflex is slower than the monosynaptic reflex owing to the involvement of extra interneurons, it is significantly more complex. For example, the interneurons excite the alpha motor neurons serving the flexor muscles of the arm (including the biceps) and those of the hand and fingers, while at the same time inhibiting the alpha motor neurons innervating the extensor muscles such as the triceps. The result is that the hand is successfully pulled away from the heat source.

The above example also illustrates an important function provided by polysynaptic reflexes, namely the phenomenon of **reciprocal inhibition**. As discussed earlier in the chapter, joints require two sets of muscles in order to move. For instance, the biceps cause the arm to bend (flex) whereas the triceps enable it to extend. Consequently, for the arm to move away from a painful stimulus, the biceps (flexor muscles) need to be excited by the alpha motor neurons, while the triceps (extensor muscles) need to be inhibited. In fact, if this did not occur there would be a muscle stand-off with little movement of the arm. Consequently, reciprocal inhibition, controlled by interneurons in the spinal cord, allows the flexor muscles to be excited while simultaneously acting to inhibit the extensors (or vice versa).

Reciprocal inhibition is also involved in the **crossed extensor reflex**. For example, if you step on something sharp, not only will the leg be withdrawn from the painful stimulus, but the opposite leg will support the weight suddenly shifted to it. In other words, flexion of the stimulated limb is accompanied by an opposite reaction in the contralateral limb. This type of reflex importantly allows the movement of several limbs to be co-ordinated all at once. In fact, polysynaptic reflexes involving reciprocal inhibition are involved in just about every type of movement one can imagine. Moreover, the spinal cord interneurons responsible for reciprocal inhibition not only receive input from sensory neurons (such as those from muscle spindles and pain receptors), but also send and receive information to and from other segments of the spinal cord and brain. This not only enables the sensory and motor neurons involved in reflexes to enter and leave the spinal cord at different levels, but also allows the brain to have some control over reflexes. For example, when picking up a scalding cup of tea, the brain may inhibit the flexion reflex if it decides that such an action might actually be more aversive than getting burned.

Head movement and the vestibular system

The vestibular system (from the Latin *vestibule* meaning an 'entrance hall', which refers to the space in the inner ear leading to the cochlea and semicircular canals) is part of the body's proprioceptive system that provides us with information about the position and movement of the head. For the most part, our vestibular system operates in the background, and only comes to the attention of our conscious mind when we become dizzy after being spun around. Yet, the function of this system is crucial to our everyday existence. For example, sensory information encoding the motion and spatial orientation of the head is important for adjusting muscular activity and body position to provide balance and posture. It is also necessary to stabilise the fixation point of the eyes so that a stable image on the retina occurs when the head moves. The knowledge of where our head is relative to our body and environment requires the brain to be able to integrate information from several sensory systems (including the eyes and proprioceptive receptors in the neck) as well as the vestibular structures of the inner ear. Indeed, without this system we would be unable to maintain a correct head position, or adopt an appropriate balance in a limitless variety of body manoeuvres, positions and postures. Even when we are completely motionless, the vestibular system is still at work signalling the relentless pull of gravity on our bodies.

The vestibular system has two main components: the **semicircular canals** and the **otolith organs**, which consist of the saccule and utricle (see below). The semicircular canals consist of three looping D-shaped chambers at approximately right angles to each other (Figure 4.6), and their main function is to relay sensory information about rotational movements of the head to the brain. These canals are essentially perpendicular to each other and provide a mechanism that allows a three-dimensional representation of all angular head movements to be monitored. Thus, the semicircular canals will detect movement when you nod your head up and down, shake it left to right (or vice versa), or tilt it from side to side. Indeed, when any of these actions occurs, the liquid (or **endolymph**) inside the corresponding canal to the plane of motion will, after a short lag period, move in the same direction as the head movement. This fluid motion deforms specialised **vestibular hair cells** that lie at the base of each canal. In turn, these cells respond by producing action potentials in the vestibular neurons that encode the direction of movement and its rate of displacement (speed).

The vestibular apparatus of the inner ear also contains two sac-like structures called the **utricle** and **saccule** which provide information about the passive position of the head relative to the body and gravity, as well as its acceleration during movement. Like the semicircular canals, the utricle and saccule are filled with endolymph and contain specialised hair cells that detect movement. However, the latter are embedded in a gelatinous mass which contains small stones of calcium carbonate. When the head is tilted, or the body's position is changed with respect to gravity, the displacement of the stones

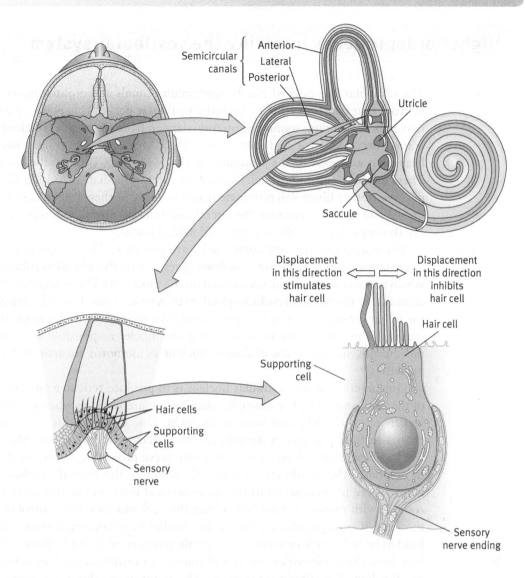

| Figure 4.6 | The vestibular apparatus |

Source: F. Toates, *Biological Psychology*, 2nd edition, p. 227. Copyright © 2007 by Pearson Education

cause the hair cells to bend. For this reason, the utricle and saccule are sometimes called the **otolith organs** (from the Greek *ot* meaning 'ear' and *lithos* meaning 'stone'). The hair cells in the utricle and saccule are orientated differently. In the utricle they are roughly horizontal (that is, parallel to the ground) when the head is upright, whereas those in the saccule are positioned more vertically. Consequently, because of their orientations, the hairs inside the utricles are particularly sensitive to the magnitude and direction of head movements that occur in a horizontal plane (such as those that occur in a car when pulling away at traffic lights), whereas the saccules are more responsive to vertical acceleration of the head (as occurs when ascending in an elevator). The weight of the otoliths caused by the force of gravity will also constantly be acting to bend the hairs in a specific pattern for each position of the head. In this way, the brain receives continuous feedback about the head's location relative to the body.

Higher-order reflexes involving the vestibular system

The vestibular hair cells within the semicircular canals and otolith organs synapse with neurons that come together to form the **vestibular nerve**. This pathway also combines nerve fibres encoding sound information derived from the cochlea nucleus and it forms cranial nerve VIII (or auditory nerve). The fibres of the vestibular nerve enter the brainstem and pass to the **vestibular nuclei**, which lies close to the cochlea nucleus. There are four vestibular nuclei (called the lateral, medial, superior and inferior) and most vestibular fibres will terminate in one or more of these cell groups. In general, the utricle and saccule innervate the lateral and inferior nuclei, whereas the semicircular canals supply input to the superior and medial nuclei.

The outputs of the vestibular nuclei are complex. The lateral vestibular nucleus (sometimes known as **Deiter's nucleus**) gives rise to the **lateral vestibulospinal tract**, which projects down to the spinal cord on the same side. The medial vestibular nucleus gives rise to the **medial vestibulospinal tract**, whose axons descend bilaterally to reach the upper cervical levels of the spinal cord. The medial vestibular nucleus also has ascending fibres that pass to other brainstem nuclei responsible for controlling eye movements, including the abducens nucleus oculomotor nucleus and the trochlear nucleus.

One function of the vestibular nucleus is to produce reflexive postural adjustments of the head and body. For example, imagine you are walking when you slip, with your feet flying to the left, and head to the right. One effect of this movement will be a change in fluid pressure in the semicircular canals of the inner ear. Movement to the right will increase activity in the vestibular nerve projecting to the vestibular nucleus. In response, the vestibular nucleus will stimulate the **medial vestibulospinal tract**, whose nerve fibres descend to the upper cervical levels of the spinal cord, where they connect with motor neurons innervating the neck muscles that control the position of the head. Consequently, activity in the medial vestibulospinal tract will enable the head to be reflexively brought to an upright position as the body moves. Another pathway from the semicircular canals will connect to vestibular nucleus neurons innervating the **lateral vestibulospinal tract**. The input from this tract exerts a powerful excitatory influence on the extensor muscles of the trunk and limbs. Thus, as the body slips, this pathway will increase muscle tension in the right-sided arm and leg to break the fall and to right ourselves after slipping.

Control of movement by the brain and spinal cord

A large number of structures in the central nervous system contribute to movement, and are hierarchically organised so that the lower areas tend to control simple reflexes whereas higher regions govern more complex behaviours. The lowest level of the central nervous system that produces movement is the spinal cord. We have already seen how the spinal cord is responsible for producing simple monosynaptic and polysynaptic reflexes. But, importantly, it also contains neural circuits that govern more complex reflexes. Researchers have shown, for example, that the spinal cord in both

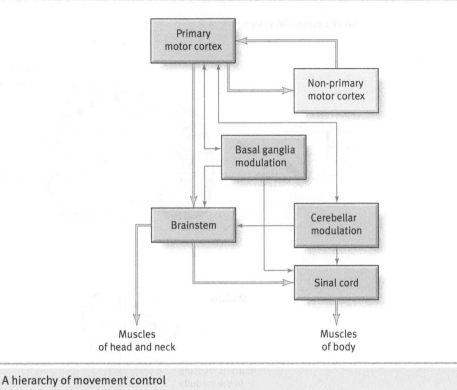

| **Figure 4.7** | A hierarchy of movement control |

animals and humans contains groups of neurons, called central pattern generators, that control rhythmical activities such as walking, running and swimming. Indeed, electrical stimulation of the lumbar region in paraplegic human patients who have a complete upper section of the spinal cord, has been shown to induce gross stepping movements of the legs with rhythmical bending of the knees (Dimitrijevic *et al.* 1998). Similarly, the vigorous scratching movements produced by a dog in response to a flea are believed to be caused by patterns of interneurons in the spinal cord (Grillner 1996).

Although the spinal cord can generate some complex patterns of movement, the most important part of the central nervous system responsible for producing movement is undoubtedly the brain. Four main regions of the brain are recognised as having a particularly vital role in movement and they are: the **brainstem**, the **cerebellum**, the **basal ganglia** and the **motor cortex** (see Figure 4.7). Although the functions of these structures are quite different, when combined they act as an integrated unit. Indeed, most purposeful human behaviour will depend on the simultaneous co-ordination of numerous motor pathways that involve all of these regions, along with their control over neural circuits in the spinal cord. In general, it is fair to say that the highest levels of the motor system are responsible for voluntary action, especially in terms of reaching locations and goals, whereas the lowest levels transform this plan into smooth and properly co-ordinated movement.

All brain regions involved in movement are connected to the motor neurons of the spinal cord via one of two major systems: the **pyramidal system** (Figure 4.8a) and the **extrapyramidal system** (Figure 4.8b). Traditionally, the extrapyramidal system has

(a) The pyramidal system

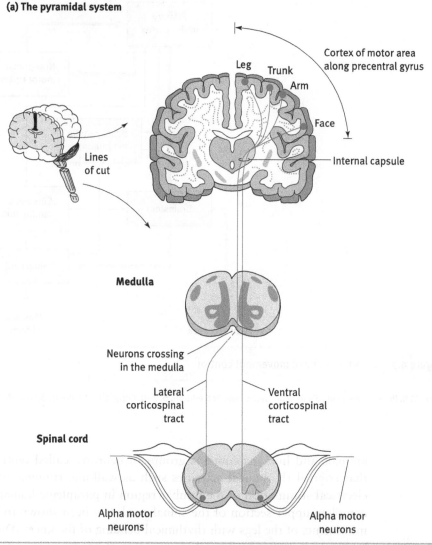

| Figure 4.8(a) | The pyramidal neural system of the brain and spinal cord |

Source: Schneider, A.M. and Tarshis, B. (1995) *Elements of Physiological Psychology*. The McGraw-Hill Companies, Inc.

been associated with postural, reflexive and stereotypical forms of movement, and the pyramidal system with voluntary or purposeful movement that is under the control of higher cognition. Although this division is now recognised as being far too simple, it still serves as a useful generalisation. The cell bodies of the pyramidal system originate in the cerebral cortex (mainly from the motor cortex and its adjacent areas) and form the **corticospinal tract** – a massive bundle of axons that passes down into the spinal cord. Before reaching the spinal cord, about 80 per cent of these axons will cross to the contralateral (opposite) side of the brainstem, in a region of the pons called the **pyramidal decussation**, which is where the pyramidal system gets its name. The remaining uncrossed axons continue down into the spinal cord and pass to the opposite side only when they reach the spinal segment in which they terminate. Thus, the pyramidal system is completely contralateral, with the right motor cortex controlling

(b) The extrapyramidal system

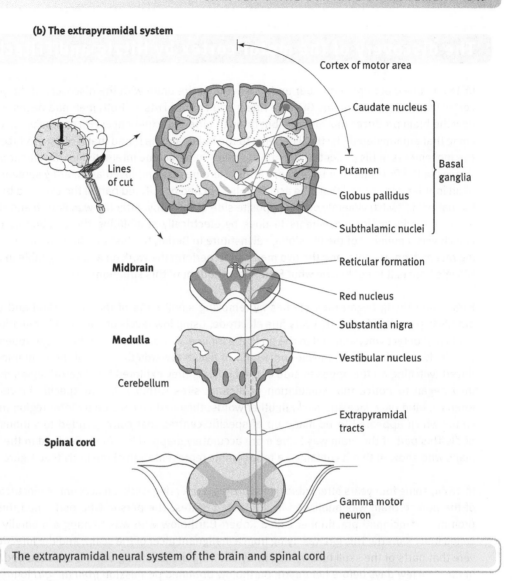

Figure 4.8(b)   The extrapyramidal neural system of the brain and spinal cord

Source: Schneider, A.M. and Tarshis, B. (1995) *Elements of Physiological Psychology*. The McGraw-Hill Companies, Inc.

movement on the left side of the body, and vice versa – although there are two routes by which this occurs.

In contrast, the extrapyramidal system is composed of the motor regions and pathways of the brain whose output does not contribute to the pyramidal system. It is also distinct from the pyramidal system as many of its fibres (although there are exceptions) do not cross over to the opposite side of the spinal cord. Thus, its pathways tend to pass down to the same side of the body. One of the most important sites contributing to the extrapyramidal system is the brainstem, which is the origin of several descending tracts to the spinal cord. However, the two most striking areas of the brain that contribute to the extrapyramidal system are the **basal ganglia** and **cerebellum**. Both these structures give rise to a number of complex and multisynaptic pathways, which, although having no direct link with the spinal cord, are nevertheless integrated with other movement areas that do, including the brainstem motor areas of the cerebral cortex.

The discovery of the motor cortex by Hitzig and Fritsch

In 1870, a new era opened in our understanding of the brain with the discovery of the primary motor cortex by the German doctors Gustave Hitzig and Eduard Fritsch. Both men had become interested in how the brain produces movement – but through different experiences. Hitzig was an inventor of a machine that administered electrical currents to the head, and he found that it often produced involuntary eye movements in his patients. In contrast, Fritsch had become interested in movement after his experiences in the Prussian–Danish war of 1864, where he was employed as an army surgeon who treated head injuries. He noticed that if he accidentally touched or irritated part of the exposed brain, it caused the patient to twitch violently on the opposite side of the body. After the war, Fritsch and Hitzig decided to elicit similar motor movements in dogs by electrically stimulating the cerebral cortex. Although Fritsch was a member of the Physiological Institute in Berlin, the Institute had no facilities for conducting research on animals, and the two men had to perform the work on a dressing table in a bedroom of Hitzig's house. It is not known what Frau Hitzig thought of this situation!

Fritsch and Hitzig began their studies by removing small parts of the dog's skull and exploring the brain's exposed surface with a very fine electrode, using low levels of electrical stimulation which they could just detect when applied to the tip of the tongue. Although most of the cortex appeared to be unresponsive to stimulation, they found a strip of tissue towards the back of the frontal lobes that produced twitching on the opposite side of the body. As they explored this 'motor' region more carefully, they began to notice that stimulation of distinct sites within it led to specific movements of the forepaw, hind paw, face and neck. In other words, they had discovered a motor region in the cerebral cortex which appeared to be made up of specific centres that corresponded to various parts of the body. This part of the brain was to be more accurately mapped by Wilder Penfield in the 1920s in humans who showed that it contained a topographic representation of the body (see Figure 4.13).

In 1874, some four years after Fritsch and Hitzig's pioneering work, an account of electrical stimulation of the human brain was published in the United States. The person who performed this work was a prominent Cincinnati practitioner called Robert Bartholow who was treating a mentally retarded girl called Mary Rafferty. This girl was dying from a malignant ulcer of the scalp, and the infection was so severe that parts of the skull had wasted away allowing the pulsating brain to be observed. Remarkably, in the final few days before her death, Bartholow obtained permission *from the girl* to insert wires into her brain so he could stimulate the motor cortex. Bartholow described one of his observations as follows: 'Distinct muscular contractions occurred in the right arm and leg. The arm was thrown out, the fingers extended, and the leg was projected forward. The muscles of the neck were thrown into action, and the head was strongly deflected to the left'. In another instance, Bartholow stimulated the parietal cortex and produced a generalized seizure that lasted five minutes. Mercifully, the girl died a few days later and her brain removed for post-mortem allowing Bartholow to check the placements of his electrodes. This report was to attract severe criticism in both America and Europe, although it provided further support for Fritsch and Hitzig.

Motor pathways in the spinal cord

We have already mentioned one of the major pathways from the brain to the spinal cord: namely the corticospinal tract that arises from the motor areas of the cerebral cortex. If we follow this pathway down, remembering that most of it crosses in the pyramidal region of the brainstem, then we will see that it runs through the spinal cord in a distinct

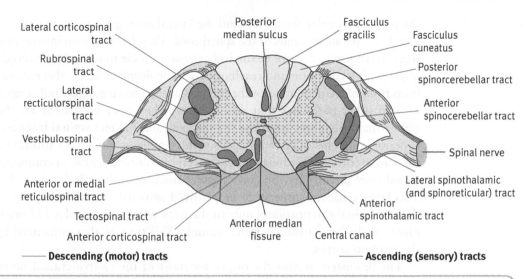

Lateral corticospinal tract
Rubrospinal tract
Lateral recticulorspinal tract
Vestibulospinal tract
Anterior or medial reticulospinal tract
Tectospinal tract
Anterior corticospinal tract
Posterior median sulcus
Fasciculus gracilis
Fasciculus cuneatus
Posterior spinorcerebellar tract
Anterior spinocerebellar tract
Spinal nerve
Lateral spinothalamic (and spinoreticular) tract
Anterior spinothalamic tract
Central canal
Anterior median fissure

——— Descending (motor) tracts   ——— Ascending (sensory) tracts

| Figure 4.9 | The tracts of the spinal cord involved in movement |

Source: Based on G. Tortora and N. Anagnostakos, *Principles of Anatomy and Physiology*, 6th edition, p. 362. Copyright © 1990 by Harper & Row

path, called the **lateral corticospinal tract** (see Figure 4.9). This is the pathway by which the higher areas of the brain controls voluntary fine movement, especially of the hands, arms and legs. However, there are a number of alternative routes by which the brain controls movement and these are generally referred to as the as the **ventromedial pathways** (these are shown as the grey-blue tracts in Figure 4.9). These tracts arise from several areas of the brainstem and midbrain, and are more likely to be involved in reflexes such as maintaining posture and muscle tone, or automated behaviours such as walking. An examination of the descending motor tracts of the spinal cord shows that the production of movement by the central nervous system is highly complex and may involve the simultaneous activation of several pathways.

The brainstem

The brain stem consists of the medulla, pons and midbrain, and contains a central core called the **reticular formation** which is a network of fibres and diffusely connected cell groups (see Plate 1.1 on page 39). In particular, nuclei in the medulla part of the reticular formation, along with those in the lower pons region, are responsible for a wide range of reflexive motor functions, including respiration and cardiovascular function, eye movements and postural adjustment. We have already seen how the vestibular nuclei in the medulla give rise to two tracts that pass through the spinal cord, called the medial and lateral **vestibulospinal tracts**, that are involved in maintaining the balance and stability of the head as the body moves. But, there are also other pathways from the brainstem to spinal cord that contribute to movement. The most conspicuous of these are the **reticulospinal tracts** which arise from a number of reticular nuclei in both the medulla and pontine regions. There are two of these pathways: the medial arising from the pontine reticular formation and the lateral arising from the medulla – and they descend in separate columns of the spinal cord. They terminate on interneurons, where they work in tandem to control flexor and extensor muscle movements involved in the control of posture, locomotion and reaching. The reticulospinal tracts also receive dense projections from movement areas of the cerebral cortex, basal ganglia and cerebellum.

Two other pathways that descend from the upper brainstem are the **rubrospinal tract** which originates from the red nucleus, and the **tectospinal tract** arising from the superior colliculus. The red nucleus is interesting as it receives substantial input from the motor cortex. This means that the cerebral cortex is able to communicate with the spinal cord directly by the corticospinal tract, or indirectly by the rubrospinal tract. This latter pathway appears to be involved primarily in arm movements. In contrast, the tectospinal tract projects only to the neck where it is involved in orientating movements of the head towards visual stimuli. This tract is also influenced by axons from the cerebral cortex.

The brainstem is also the origin for most of the twelve cranial nerves, which are controlled by distinct nuclei or local circuits of neurons (see Figure 1.22). These are involved in a variety of reflexes, including chewing, facial expression, hiccuping, yawning and swallowing – along with other vital functions such as respiration and heart rate. In addition, other areas of the brainstem – especially those in its upper parts – store more complex patterns of reflexes that are responsible for producing many types of **species-typical behaviour** (i.e. behaviour unique to that species), including reflexes involved in aggression, threat displays, sex and mating rituals, and grooming. Thus, the brainstem has a diverse and complex role in producing movement. Despite this, the movement produced by the brainstem is reflexive in nature as it is unable to attach meaning to any given motor act. As Leonard (1998) has pointed out, an animal with a brainstem that has been severed from the rest of the brain will still be able to walk and show no obvious deficit in locomotion. However, they will not notice an obstacle such as a wall in their path, and if they bump into it they will continue to produce stereotypical walking movements. Thus, without the rest of the brain to guide behaviour, the brainstem's walking reflex becomes a purposeless act.

The cerebellum

The cerebellum (Latin for 'little brain') is one of the oldest structures in the vertebrate brain. It is well developed in fish and reptiles, more elaborate in mammals, and has become noticeably large and intricate in humans, where it stands out as a large protrusion at the back of the brainstem. Although by weight it makes up only about 10 per cent of our brain's mass, it contains more than 50 per cent of its neurons. It has also been estimated that the cerebellum receives around 200 million fibres from other areas of the brain, and projects to most other areas of the motor system – although curiously it has no direct connections with the basal ganglia. In terms of appearance, the cerebellum is one of the most striking of brain regions, with its surface containing many small fissures and ridges similar to those found in the cerebral cortex. Indeed, folds provide it with a much larger surface area than would otherwise be the case (an 'unfolded' human cerebellum measures about 120 cm by 17 cm). It is likely that the neural complexity of the cerebellum gives it a capacity for information processing that is comparable to the cerebral cortex.

When examining the outer surface of the cerebellum one can see that it contains a number of banded or folded fissures. Visually, the two most important 'folds' are the **primary fissure** and the **posterolateral fissure** since they divide the cerebellum into three main lobules: the **anterior lobe** (at the top), the **posterior** or **intermediate lobe** (at the back) and the **flocculonodular lobe** (at the bottom). However, these three lobules (which can also be further divided into smaller lobules numbered from 1 to 10) tend only to be used for descriptive purposes as they have no significant clinical relevance. More important functionally are the three longitudinal zones of the cerebellum which cut across the anterior, posterior and flocculonodular lobes. These are called the **vermis**, the **parveramis or intermediate lobe** and the **lateral lobe** (see Figure 4.10b). Confusingly, these parts of the cerebellum are less distinct visually as their boundaries

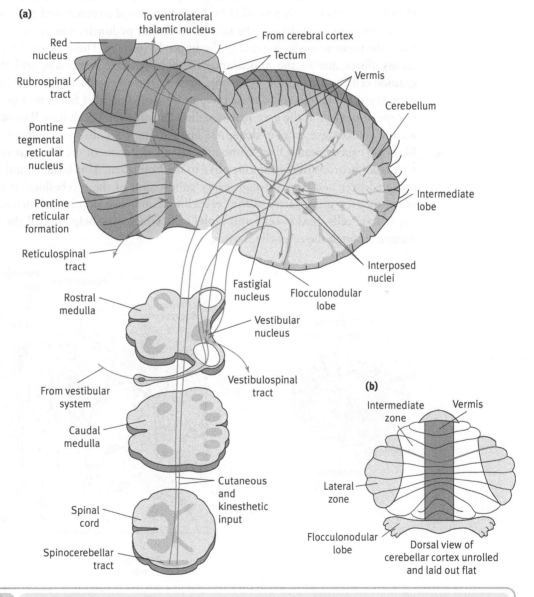

| Figure 4.10 | The cerebellum |

Source: N.R. Carlson, *Physiology of Behavior*, 8th edition, p. 269. Copyright © 2004 by Pearson Education

do not follow any clear fissures – although anatomically these three zones receive different types of neural input and have different projections to the deep cerebellar nuclei (i.e. the output nuclei of the cerebellum). In brief, the vermis receives information from the vestibular system; the intermediate zone receives feedback from the spinal cord; and the lateral zone receives massive input (via the pontine nuclei) from the motor cortex in the cerebral hemispheres. This shows that the three longitudinal regions of the cerebellum are associated with different functions.

The internal neural structure of the cerebellum is complex. If the cerebellum is cut open it will appear as a three-layered cortex which contains deeply folded convolutions called **folia**. The three cellular layers comprise (1) an outer cortex of grey matter made up of tightly packed cell bodies, (2) an inner layer of white matter comprised of myelinated axon fibres, and (3) a central group of deep cerebellar. The neural input to (and from) the cerebellum is provided by large bundles of axons called peduncules, and the most conspicuous of these is the **middle cerebellar peduncle**, which conveys information from the pontine nuclei located in the upper brainstem. These axons are also known as **mossy fibres** due to the appearance of their synaptic terminals, and they project to **granule cells** located in the outer grey layer of the cerebellar cortex (see Figure 4.11). In turn, the granule cells form branching axons called **parallel fibres** that project to another type of neuron in the grey matter called **Purkinje cell** which have flask-shaped cell bodies and an extensive array of dendrites. The Purkinje cells also receive input from **climbing fibres** (so called because they 'climb around' the dendrites of the Purkinje cells) that originate from neurons of the **inferior olive** in the brainstem. This basic neural architecture is repeated over and over through every subdivision of the cerebellum. It should also be noted that the grey matter of the cerebellum contains a number of interneurons including **stellate cells**, **basket cells** and **Golgi cells** which also help control the flow of information through the cerebellar cortex.

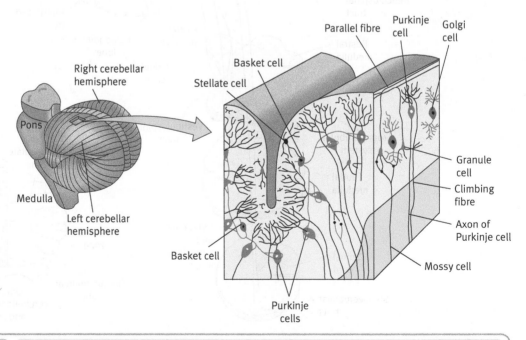

Figure 4.11 The internal structure of the cerebellum

Source: S.B. Klein and B.M. Thorne, *Biological Psychology*, p. 292. Copyright © 2007 by Worth Publishers

In turn, the Purkinje cell sends its axons (forming the white matter) to a group of three output structures enclosed within the cerebellum known as the **deep cerebellar nuclei**. These are called the **dentate, interposed** and **fastigial nuclei**. In general, each pair of deep nuclei (the cerebellum has two hemispheres) is associated with a corresponding region of cerebellar surface anatomy. The dentate nuclei receive input from the lateral hemisphere; the interposed nuclei receive input from the paravermal (intermediate) zone; and the fastigial nuclei receive input from the vermis. As might be predicted from the type of inputs arriving at the cerebellar zones, neurons in the fastigial nuclei send their axons to the vestibular nucleus and other motor nuclei in the reticular formation; the interposed nuclei largely to the red nucleus; and the dentate nucleus to the premotor and prefrontal areas of the cerebral cortex via the ventrolateral thalamus. The cerebellum is therefore at a pivotal point in a number of polysynaptic circuits involved in motor control.

The functions of the cerebellum

One way of understanding what the cerebellum does is to examine the effects of its damage. In humans, cerebellar damage reduces the fluidity of voluntary movement and makes it appear mechanical and robot-like. This is most noticeable in tasks that require a series of rapid movements, as occurs during dancing, playing sports or playing a musical instrument. Although a person with damage to the cerebellum may make accurate individual movements, they are unable to link them together into a continuous smooth sequence. For example, imagine you are to throw a ball with your right hand: if you act out this movement the chances are you will shift your body weight to the right, stretch out your left arm for balance, and move your head towards the throwing arm. A person with cerebellar damage, however, will tend to throw the ball without making these adjustments to the body. This action is also likely to be jerky and the arm may show an 'intentional' tremor that disappears once the movement has ceased. This type of tremor is different from the 'resting tremor' seen in Parkinson's disease which disappears during movement.

The precise type of deficit found after cerebellar lesions will also depend on what parts of this structure are damaged. For example, damage to the vermis will cause disturbances in posture and balance; damage to the intermediate zone will tend to produce limb rigidity; and damage to the lateral lobes will impair the timing of **ballistic movements**, that is, rapid and automated movements of the limbs, especially the arms, which occur so quickly that they are not controlled by sensory feedback. A good example of a ballistic movement is a golf swing. Once a golfer begins her swing, the stroke will be completed – no matter what type of sensory feedback she receives during the action. This shows that the cerebellum is crucial in the execution of rapid coordinated responses or habits that underlies much of our motor behaviour.

The cerebellum, therefore, regulates the fluidity of movement, enabling it to be smooth, quick and free of tremor. But, how it performs this function is still largely unclear. There are several hypotheses (see Bastian *et al.* 1999), although one popular theory is that the cerebellum is involved in assessing the rate of movement required for a particular action and then calculating the time necessary for the limbs to reach their intended position. For example, when we make a rapid or ballistic movement, the cerebellum cannot rely on sensory feedback to guide and stop the movement. Indeed, if it tried to use sensory feedback when throwing a ball, our arms would probably overshoot at the end of the movement and the ball would not reach its intended target. Thus, the cerebellum must be able to anticipate the distance that the arm needs to travel and the point at which the movement has to be terminated. One way it may do this is by timing the duration of the rapid muscle movements that have to be produced, along with help from proprioceptive feedback that helps to keep track of the limbs. This implies that the cerebellum contains an internal 'model' of the intended ballistic movements and is able to correct for small errors during their execution. In this way, the cerebellum may also be responsible for the programming of all voluntary movement.

The cerebellum is also involved in other motor functions. For example, damage to the cerebellum impairs the regulation of saccadic eye movements, leading to attention deficits. It also causes **dysarthria,** which is an inability to make fine articulatory movements of the vocal system, resulting in slurred speech. In addition, there is evidence that the cerebellum is involved in motor learning. For example, lesions of the cerebellum disrupt the acquisition and retention of classical conditioning, as occurs in the case of an eye blink response to a puff of air. If a neutral stimulus such as a tone is sounded just in advance of an air puff to the eyes, subjects soon learn to close the eyes when the tone is sounded. However, this may not occur in someone with damage to the cerebellum. The problem is not one of an impaired motor response, as the subject is still able to blink to the air puff; rather the difficulty lies in learning or predicting that the tone and air puff are co-occurring.

Evidence from studies involving PET and fMRI shows that the cerebellum is also involved in higher cognitive functions. These include linguistic processing, shifts of attention, imagining movements, and even the modulation of emotion. Perhaps the timing or anticipatory function of the cerebellum is just as useful for thinking about and predicting the future as it is for movement and planning action (Stein and Stoodley 2006).

The basal ganglia

The basal ganglia is the name given to a group of extrapyramidal structures and pathways that lie buried underneath the folds of the cerebral hemispheres on each side of the brain (see Figure 4.12). These include the **caudate nucleus** and **putamen** (which are separated from each other by a pathway conveying axons from the cerebral cortex, called the internal capsule) and the **globus pallidus** ('pale globe'), which is divided into internal and external segments. The caudate nucleus and putamen are often referred to as the **corpus striatum** (meaning 'striped body') because of the heavily myelinated axons that run through these structures. They are also phylogenetically newer that the globus pallidus, and for this reason are sometimes called the **neostriatum** (new striatum). A number of other regions also belong to the basal ganglia and these include the **subthalamus** and the highly pigmented **substantia nigra** (black substance). Both these areas are located in the midbrain tegmentum.

One way to understand the anatomy of the basal ganglia is to view it as a circuit that is connected with the cerebral cortex. Indeed, most regions of the cerebral cortex

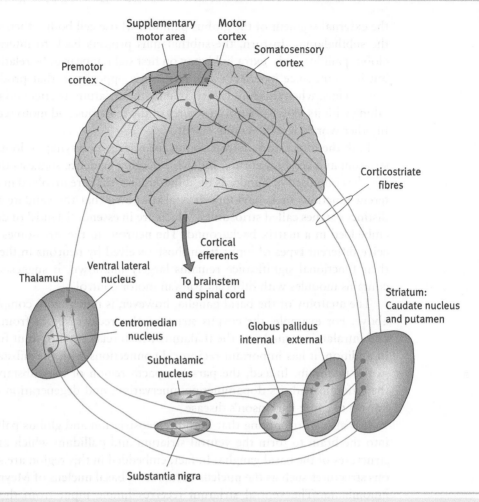

Figure 4.12   The anatomical structures and connectivity of the basal ganglia

Source: Schneider, A.M. and Tarshis, B. (1995) *Elements of Physiological Psychology*. The McGraw-Hill Companies, Inc.

involved in movement, including the primary motor cortex, secondary motor areas and association areas of the parietal lobe, project heavily via glutamate-containing fibres to the corpus striatum. To be more precise, fibres from the motor and somatosensory cortices tend to pass to the putamen, whereas those from association areas, especially those arising from the prefrontal cortex, project to the caudate (Nolte 1999). In turn, the striatum sends a substantial part of its output to the internal segment of the globus pallidus, via GABAergic fibres, which then pass to the **ventral anterior nucleus** and **ventrolateral nucleus** of the thalamus. Both these regions of the thalamus convey input from the basal ganglia to the whole of the frontal cortex, including the premotor cortex, supplementary motor area and primary motor cortex.

The neural circuit described above (striatum, internal segment of the globus pallidus, ventral thalamus and cortex) is often referred to as the direct route. Its main effect on movement is excitatory since activation of the caudate and putamen causes inhibition of the globus pallidus, which then releases it of its inhibitory control over the thalamus and motor cortex. In addition, there is a second pathway called the indirect route. This is similar to the first circuit – except that input from the striatum passes to the external segment of the globus pallidus, whose cell bodies then send projections to the subthalamus. In turn, the subthalamus projects back to internal segment of the globus pallidus. This 'extra link' may on first sight appear to be relatively unimportant – but it is not, since its effect on movement is opposite to that produced by the direct route. Thus, when this link is activated by the striatum its effect on the globus pallidus (along with its 'downstream' structures of the thalamus and motor cortex) is inhibitory. In other words, it inhibits movement.

Both the direct and indirect routes form large polysynaptic loops that connect the striatum and cerebral cortex. Indeed, emerging evidence suggests that these pathways may be composed of hundreds of 'mini-circuits' that are involved in a vast range of different functions or behaviours. It is also known that the caudate and putamen have distinct patches called **striosomes,** which are in essence 'islands' of densely packed cells embedded in a matrix background. The neurons in the striosomes also appear to receive different types of input from those received by neurons in the matrix. Although their functional significance remains largely unknown, it suggests that the striatum contains modules with different roles in motor control.

The anatomy of the basal ganglia, however, is much more complex than described above. For example, the corpus striatum also receives input from the **centromedian** and **intralaminar nuclei** of the thalamus which relay it with input from the brainstem. In addition, it has important reciprocal connections with the substantia nigra located in the midbrain. Indeed, the pars compacta region of the substantia nigra provides the striatum with its dopaminergic innervation, and degeneration of this pathway is known to cause Parkinson's disease.

It is also worth noting that both the neostriatum and globus pallidus extend down into the brain to form the **ventral striatum** and **pallidum** which are not regarded as structures of the basal ganglia. In fact, embedded in this region are somewhat mysterious structures such as the **nucleus accumbens, basal nucleus of Meynert** and **substantia innominata.** The ventral striatum receives limbic input from the cingulate cortex, along with information from the temporal lobe and frontal cortex. In turn, the ventral striatum completes the loop by returning information to the frontal and cingulate cortices by the **mediodorsal nucleus** of the thalamus. This pathway is functionally different from the neural circuit involving the neostriatum, and is involved in emotion, motivation and reward.

The functions of the basal ganglia

The basal ganglia have long been regarded as part of the brain's motor control system, especially as a number of disorders with striking movement abnormalities, including Parkinson's disease and Huntington's disease, are caused by striatal damage. Closer examination of the effects of striatal dysfunction shows that it is characterised by two kinds of motor disturbance, which have been termed positive and negative. Positive symptoms are characterised by exaggerated or 'overactive' motor actions such as **tremor,** which occurs during intentional movement; **dystonia,** where the person exhibits abnormal or distorted positions of the limbs, trunk or face; and **hemiballismus,** where the person has a propensity to suddenly throw limbs out. In contrast, negative symptoms are impoverished or slow movements that include **akinesia,** where movement is absent, and **bradykinesia,** where actions are performed slowly and with great effort. Damage to the striatum can also cause depression and slowness of thought, which is sometimes called subcortical dementia.

The combination of positive and negative symptoms gives interesting clues to the nature of the striatal involvement in movement. For example, the positive symptoms can be regarded as motor programs that are 'fully formed' and properly co-ordinated, but released at the wrong time. That is, they are not timed properly. In contrast, the negative symptoms seems to show that the basal ganglia is importantly involved in the initiation of movement, or perhaps in the selection of the correct motor programs (Stein and Stoodley 2006).

Electrophysiological recording of the striatum during movement, however, presents a different picture of its function. For example, recordings taken from cells in the puta-men and globus pallidus show that they generally do not become active until *after* a movement has been initiated by the motor areas of the cerebral cortex. Indeed, this compares with the 50 per cent or so of cells in the primary motor cortex which discharge prior to the onset of movement (Rothwell 1994). Thus, the striatum does not initiate movement (this is left to the cerebral cortex), but once an action has begun, it backs up the motor plan of the cerebral cortex with automatic adjustments. The precise nature of this control remains unclear. One possibility is that the striatum determines the sequencing of movements. For example, it has been suggested that a person with Parkinson's disease has far greater difficulty in performing sequential movements than individual ones – and that this difficulty is more than one would expect from a simple addition of the deficits of each component of the movement. An alternative theory is that the striatum acts to disinhibit certain areas of the cerebral motor system from producing competing responses, while allowing the appropriate movement to occur. Indeed, evidence indicates that it does this by generating the right amount of force for a particular movement to occur by acting on the direct and indirect pathways to the globus pallidus. This effect is not dissimilar to the way an accelerator and brake pedal work in a car (Mink 1999).

This idea is supported by the fact that people with some types of basal ganglia damage produce movement that contains too much strength (as occurs in Huntington's disease), whereas other types of damage cause a poverty of movement, with insufficient force (for example, Parkinson's disease). There is also experimental evidence to support this theory. For example, Keele and Ivry (1991) gave people with basal ganglia damage a task where they had to exert appropriate amounts of force to maintain the length of a line presented on a television screen, with another one of set length. The results showed that subjects with basal ganglia damage were poor at performing this task as they generated too much, or too little, force, resulting in a line that was too short or too long. Thus, the basal ganglia can be likened to a volume control whose output determines whether a movement will be weak or strong.

Another way in which the basal ganglia may improve the fluency of movement is by making 'large' postural adjustments to the body, thereby leaving the motor regions of the cortex 'free' to produce finer movements. That is, the basal ganglia may be responsible for making gross body movements, whereas the cortex controls actions involving the fingers, hands and face. In support of this idea is the fact that people with basal ganglia damage often show marked postural dysfunction and have difficulty making gross movements of the limbs. It has been suggested that the pathway for postural movement does not involve the striatal input to the cortex, but rather its output to the substantia nigra. In turn, the substantia nigra projects to brainstem areas such as the **pedunculopontine nucleus** known to be involved in locomotion (Rothwell 1994). It is also interesting to note that the basal ganglia appear to have a more important influence over the control of slow movements. For example, when monkeys move their arms slowly, neural activity increases in the putamen, but this does not occur when they move their arms quickly (DeLong 1974).

The motor areas of the cerebral cortex

In 1870, Gustav Fritsch and Eduard Hitzig, working on a table in the bedroom of Hitzig's house in Berlin (see box on page 150) were the first to show that electrical stimulation of a localised region in the cerebral cortex produced a wide range of bodily movements. In particular, it produced muscular contractions of the face and neck along with forepaw extension and flexion. It is said that Fritsch first became interested in exploring the cortex when, as a doctor treating soldiers in the battlefield during the Prussian–Danish war (1864), he noted that if he accidentally touched part of the exposed brain when attempting to dress severe head wounds, it caused violent twitching on the contralateral (opposite) side of the body (Finger 2005). In fact, what Fritsch had accidentally discovered, and later confirmed in his dog experiments, was the existence of the **primary motor cortex** – an area which exists as a strip of tissue located in the precentral gyrus of the posterior frontal cortex.

Later research by the Canadian Wilder Penfield, beginning in the 1930s, mapped this region (also known as Brodmann's area 4) in conscious humans by electrical stimulation that was used to map sites of epileptic tissue in patients prior to surgery. Because the brain contains no pain receptors, electrodes can be placed into its tissues without discomfort, although the dura and scalp need to be anaesthetised. Penfield's work showed that the body's representation in the motor cortex was **topographically organised,** that is, the layout of this cerebral region contained a point-to-point map of the body. This is sometimes called the **motor homunculus** or 'little man'. For example, if the motor cortex is stimulated along its length, from top to bottom, it produces movement of the feet, legs, body, arms and then head (see Figure 4.13). Moreover, the amount of motor cortex given over to each part of the body is related to the precision of its movement. For example, a large proportion of the motor cortex is responsible for controlling the small muscles of the face and hands, but little of its area is devoted to moving the trunk and legs. Another interesting observation made by Penfield was that his subjects did not realise that body movements were being produced by the electrical stimulation, and they had no memory of them afterwards (Penfield and Rasmussen 1950).

Penfield also recognised that the primary motor cortex is surrounded by other areas that have an important bearing on its function. Indeed, stimulation of these 'secondary' areas often produced much more complex types of movement such as body turning or extension of the whole contralateral arm. For example, immediately in front of the motor cortex in the superior (top) part of the frontal lobe is the **supplementary motor cortex.** And inferior to (below) to this region is the **premotor area** (both were grouped together by Brodmann as area 6). Moving further forward we come to the **prefrontal cortex,** whereas just posterior to the primary motor cortex, on the other side of the central sulcus, is the **primary somatosensory cortex,** which receives touch,

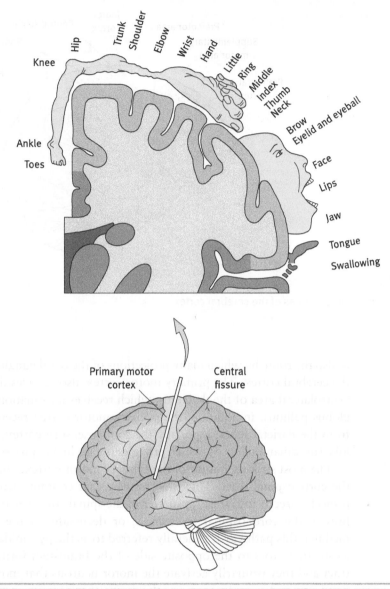

Figure 4.13   Topographic representation of the human motor cortex

Figure 4.13   Topographic representation of the human motor cortex

Source: John P.J. Pinel, *Biopsychology*, 3rd edition. Copyright © 1997 by Pearson Education

temperature and proprioception input from the body. Penfield also explored this latter area of the brain by electrical stimulation, which typically produces tingling sensations, and found that it was arranged in a topographical fashion similar to the motor cortex. The close proximity of the somatosensory cortex to the primary motor cortex shows the importance of continuous sensory feedback from the body for the generation of movement.

As might be expected with so many cortical areas involved in movement (Figure 4.14), the nature of the pathways between these regions is complex. But, put simply, the primary motor cortex receives its main input from the supplementary motor cortex and premotor areas, which in turn receive most of their input from the frontal association cortex. This

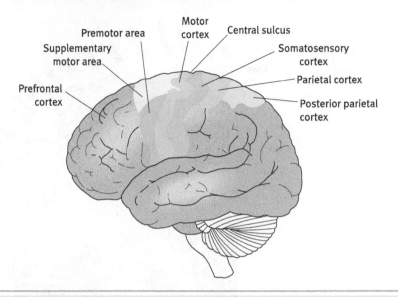

Premotor area
Supplementary
motor area
Prefrontal
cortex
Motor
cortex
Central sulcus
Somatosensory
cortex
Parietal cortex
Posterior parietal
cortex

Figure 4.14	Motor areas of the cerebral cortex

is also the route by which many projections of the basal ganglia reach the motor areas of the cerebral cortex. The primary motor cortex also receives direct projections from the ventrolateral area of the thalamus, which receives information from the cerebellum and globus pallidus. In addition, the primary motor cortex receives important projections from the parietal lobes, especially the somatosensory cortex, and the superior parietal lobe (Brodmann's area 5), which provides it with highly processed visual input.

The most striking output of the primary motor cortex, and its surrounding areas, is the **corticospinal tract.** This is a pathway that contains around 1 million fibres and projects directly into the grey matter of the spinal cord. Because some 85 per cent of fibres in the corticospinal tract cross, or decussate, in the pyramidal region of the medulla, this pathway is generally referred to as the **pyramidal system.** The majority of axons that cross to the opposite side of the brainstem form the **lateral corticospinal tract** and they primarily activate the motor neurons that move the limbs such as arm, hand, leg and foot. In contrast, the axons that remain on the original side form the **ventral corticospinal tract** and they move the trunk of the body. Thus, the neurons of the cortical motor areas in the right hemisphere control the trunk on the right side of the body, but the limbs on the left side – and vice versa for the left hemisphere. The primary motor cortex contributes about 40 per cent of all corticospinal tract fibres, and the remainder arise from the premotor and supplementary motor areas (20 per cent) and areas of the parietal lobes (40 per cent).

Although the cerebral cortex has direct access to the spinal cord via the corticospinal tract, it can also affect movement in a number of other ways. For example, the primary motor cortex is also the origin of the **corticobulbar tract,** which projects to the medulla and synapses on motor neurons of the cranial nerves innervating the face and tongue. In addition, there are many cortical fibres that directly terminate on brainstem nuclei, such as the red nucleus (the origin of the rubrospinal tract), pontine nuclei and vestibular nuclei, which form important components of the extrapyramidal system. In addition, widespread areas of the cerebral cortex send substantial projections to the basal ganglia (especially the striatum) and cerebellum.

Mirror neurons and the motor basis of imitation

The ability to imitate occurs early in human infants. If an adult sticks out their tongue to a baby, even in its first week of life, the baby often imitates the gesture (Anisfeld 1996). This behaviour is not as simple as it first seems. If one considers how imitation occurs, it is apparent that it requires the observer not only to carefully see what the model is doing, but also to be able to recreate the behaviour. This is an exceptional skill for a baby in the first weeks of life. Although imitation is important for social interaction, its role in human development may be more profound. Indeed, many psychologists believe that imitation allows us to develop empathy, that is, our capacity to put ourselves in the place of others and 'read' their minds. Humans are very good at this: if we see somebody cry we are likely to feel sad, and when we observe laughter we are often happy. As long ago as 1903, the German Theodore Lipps noted that the perception of another individual's emotional expression, or gesture, automatically activates the same emotion in the perceiver. Thus, according to Lipps we do not even have to consciously think about empathy, we do it automatically. More recently, this type of imitating response has been shown to occur in the motor system of the brain. For example, Fadiga *et al.* (1995) recorded EEG evoked potentials from the motor cortex in subjects who were observing actions in others, and found that this activated (i.e. primed) the same muscle groups as were needed to perform the same action. Thus, just by watching an action, we are getting ready to perform it too.

Another important discovery has been the identification of specific neurons in the brain that are involved in imitation. These were first discovered in the monkey by Giacomo Rizzolatti and his colleagues at the University of Parma in 1996. Initially, these investigators were examining the role of premotor cortex in planning movements, and they identified neurons that fired when the monkey performed a precise hand action such as pulling, pushing, or picking up a peanut. However, closer examination showed that the same cells also became active when the monkey observed another monkey (or even the experimenter) perform the same action. For example, the neurons did not fire to the sight of an object (for example, a peanut), but to the sight of a whole action (picking up the peanut). These cells were also highly selective in their firing. They might respond, for example, to the experimenter picking a raisin from a tray, but not from a food well. These cells were called 'mirror neurons' (Rizzolatti *et al.* 1996).

Rizzolatti also looked for these neurons in humans by using PET scanning (see Rizzolatti *et al.* 2001). In one study, subjects were asked to imitate an experimenter making a grasping movement, or to imagine the action taking place. In both tasks, increased neural activity was found in the lateral frontal lobe of the left hemisphere, which also included Broca's area. The discovery of mirror neurons in Broca's area raised great interest as it led to speculation that our capacity to communicate with language may have evolved from the mirror neuron system. Indeed, the simple observation of others shows that gesturing is closely related to speech. For example, many of us make gestures when speaking on the telephone, and congenitally blind people are known to gesture – even when speaking to other blind individuals.

The function of the primary motor cortex

The location of the primary motor cortex puts it in an ideal position to be accessed by conscious thought from the frontal and parietal lobes, and therefore to be involved in the production of voluntary movement. Moreover, because the motor cortex is the origin of neurons entering the corticospinal tract, we might expect damage to this region of the brain to cause serious movement deficits and paralysis. However, damage to the primary motor cortex in humans produces less disability than might be expected. For example, injury to this area often occurs as a result of a cerebrovascular accident to the **middle cerebral artery**, which supplies widespread areas of the cerebrum with its oxygenated blood. Although such accidents initially produce paralysis, the majority of patients show considerable recovery at performing voluntary movements, including the ability to walk and reaching for objects. In fact, the most likely long-term deficit involves an inability to make fine dextrous movements of the fingers such as those required for buttoning clothes, writing or typing. Damage to the primary motor cortex may also impair the ability to grip objects, or to move a single muscle or limb (for example, the person cannot flex their elbow without moving their shoulder). This will be likely to reduce the speed, accuracy and force of a person's movement.

Thus, lesions of the primary motor cortex do not abolish voluntary movement. On first sight this may appear to be a somewhat surprising finding. One explanation is that other regions of the cerebral cortex instigate movement, and also store a variety of motor programs for action. Because these areas also send projections into the corticospinal tract, they can presumably bypass the effects of primary motor cortex damage.

Deficits in fine movement also occur in monkeys following lesions of the primary motor cortex and corticospinal tracts. For example, Lawrence and Kuypers (1968) bilaterally lesioned the corticospinal tracts in rhesus monkeys, and found that within a day of the operation, the animals could stand upright, hold the bars of their cage and freely move about. Their recovery progressed so that after six weeks the monkeys could run, climb and reach for food. That is, posture and locomotion were not permanently affected by the lesion. Yet, manual dexterity was very poor. Although the monkeys could reach for objects and grasp them, they were unable to manipulate their fingers when attempting to pick up small pieces of food. And, once they had food held in their hands, they were unable to release it from their grasp, which led them to use their mouth in order to pry their hands open. Curiously, they had no difficulty releasing their grip when climbing the bars of their cage, which suggests that this behaviour is controlled by a different pathway or brain region.

The primary motor cortex, therefore, appears to contribute to the speed, force and agility of movements, especially those requiring the precise or fine actions of 'nonpostural' body parts such as the fingers. Traditionally, it has been thought that the primary motor cortex controls fine movement by its sequential action on individual muscles. However, it is now known that this is not the case. In fact, researchers have now found that if one takes any single cell in the primary motor cortex, with an axon that passes into the corticospinal tract, and follows it down to the spinal cord, it does not control just a single muscle in the body; rather, it is more likely to project to many motor neurons, sometimes at different spinal levels, which innervate a number of muscles (Cheney *et al.* 1985). Thus, each point in the primary motor cortex ultimately connects to many muscles.

It is also becoming increasingly clear that huge numbers of cells in the primary motor cortex are involved in even the simplest movement. For example, in one study the firing rates of cells in the motor cortex were examined as monkeys learned to move their arm to one of eight possible locations (Georgopoulos *et al.* 1993). It was found that individual cells in the motor cortex would fire most vigorously to a 'preferred' location – although the cell was often 'imprecise' and showed activity over a wide spatial area. In fact, the best way to predict the direction of the arm was to pool the information from many neurons as examination of the activity of several hundred neurons provided a much better indication of the direction of the reaching arm. Thus, movement in the primary motor cortex is encoded by populations of neurons rather than by single cells. This means that large numbers of motor cortex cells, rather than a small group, will be active during any type of movement.

The contribution of other cortical areas to movement

The primary motor cortex is not the only area of the cerebral cortex involved in the production of movement. Lying close to the primary motor cortex are two other regions also essential for motor function: the **supplementary motor area**, located on the medial surface of the frontal lobe just anterior to the primary motor cortex, and the **premotor cortex**, lying laterally and inferior to this area. Both these regions are richly interconnected with fibres that allow the integration of information arriving from other cortical areas, especially those from the **prefrontal cortex**. In turn, these areas innervate the primary motor cortex. The supplementary and premotor cortices were first shown to have a motor function in humans by Penfield who found that electrical stimulation of these regions often gave rise to complex postural movements, such as a raised hand before the face with head and eyes turned towards the hand (Penfield and Rasmussen 1950). Stimulation of these areas also elicits an urge to make a movement, or the feeling of anticipating a movement (Bradshaw and Mattingly 1995). Indeed, it is now becoming clear that the supplementary and premotor areas play a crucial role in initiating actions – although how this occurs remains a mystery.

The study of how the brain produces movement has been greatly extended in recent years by the use of functional scanning techniques. This technology has allowed the activity of the brain to be directly observed while the subject is planning or performing an action or particular series of movements. For example, Roland (1993) working in Sweden, used single-photon emission computer tomography (SPECT) to track brain activity in the form of regional blood flow during the performance of various hand movements. When subjects were asked to perform a simple tapping movement of the right index finger, it was found that blood flow was restricted to the opposite (left) primary motor cortex and somatosensory cortex. However, when subjects were asked to perform a complicated set of 16 movements involving the sequencing of several fingers, increased blood flow was also found bilaterally in the supplementary motor area and inferior prefrontal cortex. Thus, larger areas of the brain are needed for more complex actions.

Perhaps the most interesting findings of all were found when subjects were asked to carry out the finger movements from memory. The first brain regions to show increased activity in response to this command were the parietal lobes and prefrontal cortex, followed by the supplementary motor area and premotor area (see Figure 4.15). These findings indicate that the decision to act lies in diffuse areas of the brain (parietal lobes and prefrontal cortex), whereas the execution of the movement involves the motor areas (supplementary motor area and premotor area). Interestingly, when subjects were asked to mentally rehearse (that is, imagine) the movements, increased blood flow was most noticeable in the supplementary cortex.

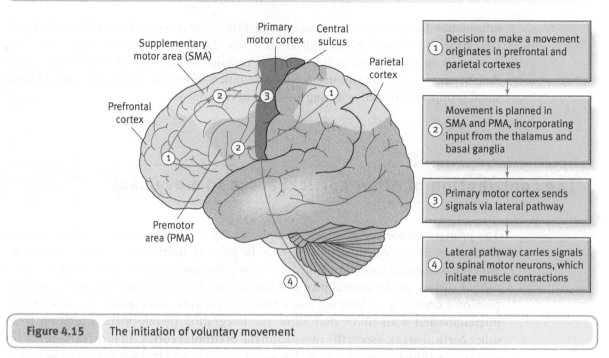

Figure 4.15   The initiation of voluntary movement

Source: L.A. Freberg, *Discovering Biological Psychology*, p. 242. Copyright © 2006 by Houghton Mifflin Company

Another study that has used functional scanning techniques to powerful effect to study the functional anatomy of motor sequence learning was undertaken by Jenkins *et al.* (1994). These researchers used positron emission tomography (PET) to measure regional blood flow in a large number of brain regions using a trial and error task, with auditory feedback, in which subjects had to learn a number of eight-move key press sequences by using just four keys on a computer keyboard. In addition, subjects also had to demonstrate the same sequences after they had been well learned. One of the main findings to emerge from this study was that the prefrontal cortex becomes highly activated during the learning of a new sequence, but not after the sequence has been learned. Thus, the prefrontal cortex appears to be important during the early stages of motor learning, especially when the task is being performed under conscious control.

This study also highlighted different functions for the supplementary and premotor cortices. For example, the opposite (contralateral) premotor cortex was more active during the sequence learning, whereas the supplementary area was more active bilaterally after the sequences had been well learned. This pattern of results is consistent with other findings (see for example, Passingham 1987) and indicates that the premotor cortex has a greater involvement in learning motor actions when performance is being guided by external or sensory cues (for example, juggling). This differs from the supplementary cortex, which shows more activation during well practised motor sequences which can be run off automatically without such feedback.

The study by Jenkins *et al.* (1994) also showed that the primary motor cortex and somatosensory cortex were active under both learning and performance conditions of the experiment (Figure 4.16). This appears to show that the primary motor cortex is putting into 'action' the commands from other brain areas during both learning and automatic performance conditions, and that reafferent feedback from the somatosensory

Sensorimotor areas activated by performing a well practised sequence of finger movements

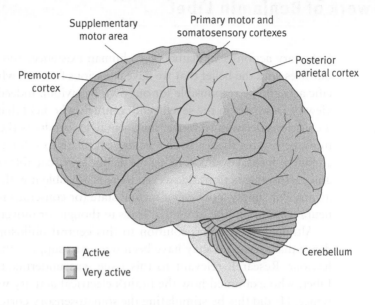

Sensorimotor areas activated by performing a newly learned sequence of finger movements

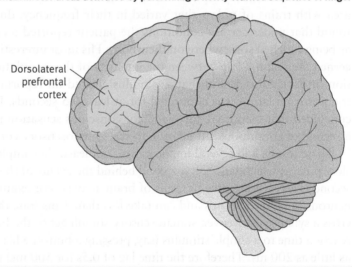

| Figure 4.16 | Brain activity recorded by positron emission tomography during the execution of newly learned and well practiced movements of the fingers |

Source: John P.J. Pinel, *Biopsychology*, 5th edition, p. 218. Copyright © 2003 by Pearson Education

cortex is a vital component for this to occur. Two other brain regions examined in this study were the putamen and cerebellum. The putamen was similar to the primary motor cortex and somatosensory cortex in that it showed contralateral activation during both learning and automatic performance. However, both sides of the cerebellum showed a greater level of activation during the learning condition of the experiment. This supports the idea that the cerebellum is importantly involved in motor learning and the acquisition of new tasks.

The work of Benjamin Libet

Voluntary action is fundamental to human existence, and most of us navigate through our lives with the belief that we have conscious free will which allows us to perform specific acts and be responsible for our own behaviour. Indeed, this was the famous dualist view of Descartes in the seventeenth century, who held that when a person freely makes a conscious decision to move, this mental act produces the neural activity which causes movement. This theory is one we can all relate to – for we do seem to have a private stream of mental events running inside our head, capable of making conscious decisions and performing actions. However, there is a problem with this theory, as Descartes was aware. Put simply, how can a mental state (or conscious intention) *initiate* the physical neural circuitry in the brain that leads to thought or movement?

Although there is no solution to this central philosophical question, there is evidence that Descartes may have been wrong to suppose that consciousness initiates behaviour. Research relevant to this issue was undertaken in the 1950s by Benjamin Libet, who examined how the brain's electrical activity was linked to conscious experience. He did this by stimulating the somatosensory cortex – the area of the brain that receives direct sensory input from all areas of the body and skin. Libet stimulated this area with trains of pulses that varied in their frequency, duration and intensity, and found that under certain conditions the patient reported a conscious experience such as being touched somewhere on their body. His most interesting finding, however, concerned the relationship between the intensity of the stimulation and conscious perception. In fact, Libet found that a stimulus elicited no reportable experience unless the train of stimulation was continued for at least 0.5 seconds. From these findings Libet concluded that 'neuronal adequacy' for conscious sensation is achieved only after half a second of continuous stimulation to the somatosensory cortex.

These results had several implications. Not least, they implied that consciousness is a slow process which lags half a second behind the events of the real world. In fact, half a second is a very long time in terms of brain activity. For example, impulses travel along neurons at about 100 m/s and can take less than 1 ms (one-thousandth of a second) to cross a synapse. Moreover, somatosensory stimuli get to the brain in about 15 ms and a reaction time to a simple stimulus (say, pressing a button when a light comes on) may be as little as 200 ms. Therefore the time lag of 0.5s (or 500 ms) is remarkably slow.

Further work examining the timing of experience was performed by Libet in the 1970s. It was known that a strong stimulus to the somatosensory cortex could interfere with sensations coming from touch on the skin. So, if consciousness took half a second to build up, then it should be possible to touch someone on the skin, and then block that sensation by stimulating the cortex up to half a second later. This is exactly what Libet found. For example, if an electrical shock to the skin was given during the cortical stimulation, only the sensation associated with the cortical stimulation was experienced. But, more importantly, the effect of skin shock was blocked even if it was given 300–500 ms before the beginning of cortical stimulation.

In the 1980s, Libet began to examine the amount of time it took for the conscious mind to produce movement (Libet *et al.* 1983). To do this, subjects were asked to watch a small clock hand that completed each full revolution in 2.56 seconds. While fixated on the clock the subject voluntarily flexed their wrist at a time of their choosing. After the movement the clock had continued to rotate for a random time and then stopped. The subject then reported the position of the clock hand at the time when they first became aware of the will to move. Libet called this subjective judgement 'W' (for will). In other parts of the experiment, subjects had to judge when they actually moved, and Libet called this judgement 'M' (for movement). The timing of the W and M told Libet when a subject 'subjectively' formulated a will to move and actually moved.

Libet also measured two other parameters: the electrical (EEG) activity over the motor areas of the brain, and the electrical activity of the muscles involved in the wrist movement. To examine the motor areas, Libet measured what is known as the readiness potential (RP). This is a ramp-like build-up of electrical activity that precedes voluntary action by nearly one second (800 ms). By also recording the activity of the muscles involved in the wrist movement, Libet precisely determined the onset of muscle activity related to the RP. As expected, Libet found that the W came before the M. But, Libet also found a consistent temporal relationship between the subjective experience and individual neural event. In short, the neural preparation to move always preceded conscious awareness of the intention to move by 300–500 ms. Thus, the brain was preparing movements before the subject had consciously decided to move.

Although these results are controversial, it suggests that unconscious brain events start the process of voluntary action. That is, voluntary acts are initiated by unconscious cerebral processes before conscious intention appears. However, this does not mean we are controlled by the unconscious. This is because, before the movement has time to be carried out, conscious awareness of the act occurs, and makes the final decision of whether to perform the behaviour. In effect, therefore, consciousness has a veto over the final decision to act. If we accept this chain of events, then not only is the conscious control of motor performance explained, but a framework is also provided by which to understand free will, individual liberty and moral responsibility.

Summary

Bodily movement is always the result of muscle contraction. The body contains three types of muscle – **smooth, cardiac** and **striated** – with the latter being responsible for movement of the skeletal bones and posture. There are over 600 striated muscles in the human body and these make up around 50 per cent of the body's weight. Muscles are made from bundles of long, thin **muscle cells** that contain large numbers of smaller cylindrical structures called **myofibrils**. These contain sliding filaments of **actin** or **myosin** which give the myofibril, and ultimately the muscle fibre, its ability to contract. All skeletal muscles are innervated by **alpha motor neurons,** whose cell bodies are located in the ventral horn of the spinal cord. The synapse between the alpha motor neuron and its muscle cell is called the **neuromuscular junction,** which uses the neurotransmitter **acetylcholine** (ACh). When ACh binds to a highly specialised part of the muscle cell called the **motor endplate**, it sets into motion a series of chemical events in the cell that pulls the actin and myosin filaments together, thereby contracting the muscle. The spinal cord provides the first level of movement control and is capable of producing both **monosynaptic** and **polysynaptic** reflexes, which in some cases may underlie quite complex patterns of autonomous behaviour. More importantly, the spinal cord is also under the direct control of the brain. There are a number of motor pathways that descend into the spinal cord from the brain, and that derive either from the **pyramidal system** or **extrapyramidal system.** The pyramidal system originates in the cerebral cortex, especially the primary motor cortex, and its axons enter the **corticospinal tract.** En route, about 80 per cent of these fibres cross to the contralateral (opposite) side of the brain in a region of the brainstem called the **pyramids** before passing into the spinal cord. The remaining fibres also cross to the other side of the spinal cord – but only when they reach the spinal segment in which they terminate. The extrapyramidal system contains all the motor regions and pathways not belonging to the pyramidal system, and its descending pathways include: the **reticulospinal tract,** which originates from a number of reticular nuclei; the **rubrospinal tract,** originating from the red nucleus; and the **vestibulospinal tract,** which arises from the vestibular nuclei. Most, but not all, of these pathways pass down into the spinal cord without crossing over to its contralateral side.

A number of brain areas are responsible for producing and regulating movement. One such structure is the **cerebellum** ('little brain'), which contains many millions of neurons and is highly intricate in terms of its neural circuitry. The cerebellum is important for the co-ordination of movement as it controls the force and timing of muscular contractions and reflexes, especially for rapid and well-learned actions. Thus, the cerebellum regulates the fluidity of movement, enabling it to be smooth, quick, and free of tremor. Another part of the brain involved in movement is the **basal ganglia** – a set of interconnected structures that includes the **striatum** (caudate nucleus and putamen), **globus pallidus** and **substantia nigra**. The striatum has reciprocal connections with movement areas of the cerebral cortex, and appears to be involved in making smooth postural adjustments of the body, particularly in regards to voluntary movement. Indeed, in support of this idea is the fact that people with basal ganglia damage (for example, **Parkinson's disease**) often show gross postural dysfunction and have difficulty initiating voluntary movement. A number of regions in the cerebral cortex are involved in producing movement, and these include the **frontal cortex, premotor cortex, supplementary motor cortex** and **primary motor cortex** (the latter being the main source of fibres projecting into the corticospinal tract). The primary motor cortex also lies adjacent to the **somatosensory cortex,** which receives sensory and proprioceptive information from the muscles. Both are also **topographically organised** containing a point-to-point representation of the body. The motor areas of the cerebral cortex are important for the learning, planning and initiation of purposeful and voluntary movement.

Essay questions

1. From processes operating at the neuromuscular junction, to the movement of actin and myosin in the myofibrils, explain how impulses in alpha motor neurons ultimately cause muscle contraction.

   Search terms: Neuromuscular junction. Muscle contraction. Muscle cells. Alpha motor neurons. Myofibrils. Skeletal muscle.

2. Describe the brain structures and anatomical pathways that make up the extrapyramidal and pyramidal motor systems. What are the main functions of these two systems?

   Search terms: Extrapyramidal system. Pyramidal system. Cerebellum. Basal ganglia. Motor cortex. Corticospinal tract.

3. What are the behavioural functions of the striatum?

   Search terms: Caudate nucleus. Putamen. Positive and negative motor symptoms. Dystonia. Akinesia. Motor cortex. Sequencing. Basal ganglia.

4. What regions in the cerebral cortex are known to be involved in movement? How do these areas contribute to the production of motor behaviour?

   Search terms: Primary motor cortex. Somatosensory cortex. Frontal cortex and voluntary movement. Cortical control of movement. Motor function in cerebral cortex and basal ganglia.

Further reading

Asanuma, H. (1989) *The Motor Cortex*. New York: Raven Press. A summary of research that has attempted to understand the organisation and function of the motor cortex.

Berthoz, A. (2000) *The Brain's Sense of Movement*. Cambridge, Mass.: Harvard University Press. Provides new insights and theories into how the brain is able to maintain balance and co-ordinate movement.

Latash, M.L. (1998) *Neurophysiological Basis of Movement*. Champaign, Ill.: Human Kinetics. A comprehensive textbook that covers all levels of the motor system, from muscle contraction to brain function, and attempts to explain the production of voluntary movement.

Leonard, C.T. (1998) *The Neuroscience of Human Movement*. St Louis, Mo.: Mosby. A very readable account that covers the role of central nervous system and its pathways in the control of movement.

Passingham, R. (1995) *The Frontal Lobes and Voluntary Action*. Oxford: Oxford University Press. A book that focuses on how animal research and human studies have contributed to our understanding of the motor functions of the frontal lobes.

Porter, R. and Lemon, R. (1995) *Corticospinal Function and Voluntary Movement*. Oxford: Oxford University Press. A comprehensive analysis of how the cerebral cortex controls the performance of skilled voluntary movement.

Quinn, N.P. and Jenner, P.G. (eds) (1989) *Disorders of Movement*. San Diego, Calif.: Academic Press. Written by various experts, this covers the clinical, pharmacological and physiological characteristics of a range of movement disorders, and includes a large section on Parkinson's disease.

Rosenbaum, J. (1991) *Human Motor Control*. San Diego, Calif.: Academic Press. A user-friendly introduction to how cognitive processes are involved in the sequencing of movement, with relevance to many areas of interest including dance, physical education and robotics.

Zigmond, M.J., Bloom, F.E., Landis, S.C., Roberts, J.L. and Squire, L.R. (eds) (1999) *Fundamental Neuroscience*. San Diego, Calif.: Academic Press. Although this is a monumental textbook on neuroscience, the eight chapters on motor systems, including separate ones on the basal ganglia and cerebellum, are excellent.

 For self test questions, animations, interactive exercises and many more resources to help you consolidate your understanding, and expand your knowledge of the field, please go to the website accompanying this book at **www.pearsoned.co.uk/wickens**

CHAPTER 5

Hunger, satiety and body weight

INTRODUCTION

Hunger is a compelling motive and the need to eat is one of the most important determinants that shapes our daily routines and activities. Clearly, we share our basic reliance on food for energy and sustenance with other animals as it is essential for life. Yet, for humans, eating behaviour is much more complex than the simple replenishment of nutrients. Indeed, one only has to consider the wide variety of eating-related information in our world, including magazine articles, TV programmes, advertisements for food and restaurants, diets and obesity clinics, to realise the importance of eating to our everyday existence. The complexity of this behaviour is further seen when we examine the brain mechanisms responsible for hunger and eating. It is tempting at first to explain hunger as a simple physiological response to declining levels of nutrients, with important roles for peripheral mechanisms (stomach and liver) that are monitored by areas in the brainstem and hypothalamus. It is now clear, however, that our eating behaviour cannot be adequately explained this way. Instead, eating and hunger are the products of a highly complex biological system with a multitude of interacting of physiological, psychological and social factors which are not determined by any obvious nutrient deficiency. We can demonstrate this by a simple observation: we often eat not in response to direct hunger pangs but in *anticipation* to the pleasure of eating, or predicted hunger. The quest to understand the psychobiological mechanisms of eating has become an important area of research in recent years, not least because of the high prevalence of illnesses such as obesity, diabetes, anorexia and bulimia. This situation has also helped contribute to several recent discoveries, including the hormone leptin in 1994, which has opened up new areas of research. Indeed, this is an unparalleled time for researchers interested in achieving a greater understanding of appetite, satiety and body weight.

Homeostasis

In 1865, in his *Introduction to Experimental Medicine*, the French physiologist Claude Bernard wrote that the 'constancy of the internal milieu was the essential condition to a free life'. In other words, he was noting that the body's internal environment has to remain relatively constant despite large fluctuations in the external environment. This fundamental property of the body was later coined **homeostasis** by the American physiologist Walter Cannon in 1932, who derived the word from the Greek *homos* meaning 'same' and *stasis* meaning 'standing'. To appreciate the importance of homeostasis it is necessary to realise that, in order to survive, living organisms must maintain the physiological and chemical balance of their bodies within very fine limits. For example, human beings are warm-blooded and must keep their body temperature at about 37 °C regardless of whether they live in the Antarctic or the tropics. A change in core body temperature of just a few degrees will alter the rate of chemical reactions taking place in our cells, leading to organ failure and death. Thus, it is essential that the body is able to regulate its temperature within a narrow margin (that is, maintain homeostasis).

Clearly, the body must have a way of detecting alterations in temperature, and then be able to instigate physiological reactions that will correct any change if it deviates too far from 37 °C. Indeed, such adaptive responses include increased perspiration to cool the body and shivering to provide warmth. These responses also point to some important features that are common to all homeostatic systems: (1) there is a set point or optimal level that the system tries to maintain, (2) there are receptors, such as thermoreceptors, in the body that can detect the changes taking place, (3) there is a control centre, presumably in the brain, which is analysing the body state and deciding what action needs to be taken, and (4) there is a way of switching off the compensatory responses when the correct level of the variable (for example, temperature) has been reached. This is sometimes referred to as a **negative feedback response**.

Thus, homeostatic systems are not as simple as they first appear. Moreover, there must be many different types of homeostatic process in the body working to the same principles. These include, for example, those regulating the body's need for water, its oxygen and carbon dioxide levels, and its concentration of various hormones. In addition, many nutrients involved in feeding behaviour are known to be controlled in a similar manner. For example, the concentration of glucose in the blood needs to be between 60 and 90 milligrams per 100 cubic centimetres of blood. If it falls below this range, then hypoglycaemia is likely to result, with coma and death, whereas increased levels of glucose produce hyperglycaemia, with increased excitability.

Traditionally, hunger has often been viewed as homeostatic process, that is, dependent on a feedback mechanism to the brain signalling a deficiency in some nutrient, such as glucose, below a given set point. Similarly, satiety has been viewed as an event that occurs when nutrient levels have reached a certain point that enables hunger to be switched off. In other words, researchers have tended to assume that hunger occurs when the brain detects an energy deficit or decline in the level of a vital nutrient. In turn, eating is the response by which the energy or nutrient source is replenished, that will eventually provide the negative feedback response that terminates the hunger. Such analogies still dominate much biopsychological thinking about eating behaviour (Figure 5.1).

It should be noted, however, that while homeostatic systems governing nutrient levels occur in the body, eating behaviour does not fit easily into this type of nutrient deficit model. One reason might be the fact that there are many types of homeostatic system that govern eating behaviour. Indeed, one has only to consider the various type of feedback signal that may convey nutrient information to the brain, including the concentration of various chemicals and hormones, along with neural information from structures such as the gut and liver, to see how this could hold true. Thus, the complexity of the

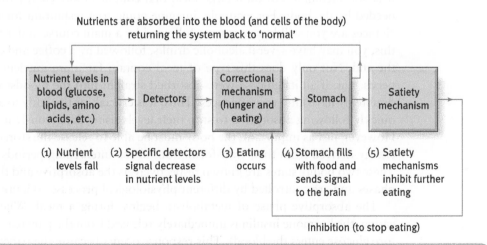

| Figure 5.1 | A hypothetical outline of a homeostatic system that controls eating |

interacting homeostatic systems may mitigate against simple explanations in terms of one nutrient or factor. But, it is also the case that higher cognitive or anticipatory factors may override the homeostatic mechanisms at work in the underlying biology of hunger. Thus, mental factors play a vital role in human eating behaviour.

The process of digestion

Food is a collection of proteins, fats and carbohydrates along with a small amount of essential vitamins and minerals. Digestion is the process by which these foodstuffs are broken down into simple molecules so they can be absorbed into the blood and used by the body. The process of digestion begins in the mouth, where food is broken up and mixed with saliva that turns starch-like substances into sugars. This mixture is then swallowed to reach the stomach, where it is mixed with gastric juices containing hydrochloric acid and pepsin to produce a semifluid mixture called chyme. This is then emptied into the small intestine where absorption takes place. The upper part of the small intestine is called the **duodenum** and contains a duct from the **pancreas gland** which secretes pancreatic juice containing a number of digestive enzymes. In addition, the pancreas gland releases two hormones that play a vital role in the digestive process: **insulin** and **glucagon** (see next section). The remainder of the small intestine, which is about 600 cm in length, absorbs the chyme's nutrients. From here, emulsified fats are absorbed into the lymphatic system where they will eventually reach the blood, and other nutrients (such as glucose) are absorbed into blood vessels that pass to the liver via the hepatic portal system.

Absorption and fasting

It is not uncommon to eat a large meal that contains more energy than is immediately needed by the body. For example, imagine going to a restaurant for a large meal. The chances are you will have a starter, followed by a main course and a dessert. On top of this, you may have several alcoholic drinks, followed by a coffee and chocolate sweet at the end. Not only does this type of meal contain far more nutrients than your body needs, but, if all its glucose were absorbed straight into the bloodstream it would un-doubtedly have fatal consequences. Thus, it is crucial for the body to store the nutrients quickly following absorption to stop their levels rising dangerously in the bloodstream. However, just as important, the body must be able to release the stored nutrients, or the energy derived from their transformation, in the intervening periods between feeding. These two bodily states are known respectively as the **absorptive** and the **post-absorptive phases** and are controlled by different physiological processes (Figure 5.2).

The absorptive phase of metabolism begins during a meal. When a person starts eating, the hormone **insulin** is immediately released from the pancreas gland (that is, be-fore glucose enters the blood). This response occurs because the pancreas gland is stim-ulated by the parasympathetic vagus nerve that conveys gustatory (taste) information from the mouth. The main function of insulin is to lower blood glucose levels. It does this by circulating in the blood where it facilitates glucose transport across the cellular

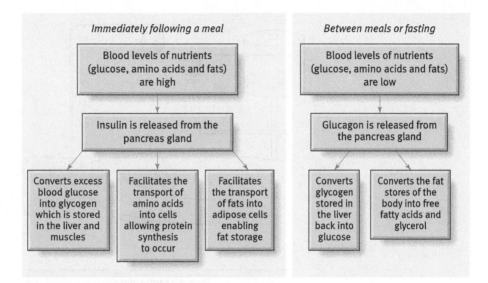

| **Figure 5.2** | Flowchart of metabolic events that take place following absorption (immediately following a meal) and post-absorption (between meals) |

membranes. Thus, insulin allows glucose to escape from the blood and enter the cells of the body, where it can be safely stored and used to produce energy. The only exception to this rule is the brain, whose cells are freely permeable to glucose. Insulin also has three other important ways of controlling the level of blood glucose during absorption: (1) it converts excess blood glucose into glycogen which is stored by the liver and muscles; (2) it facilitates the transport of amino acids into cells allowing protein synthesis to occur, and (3) it facilitates the transport of fats into adipose cells enabling fat storage.

Once nutrients have been absorbed into the blood the post-absorptive phase of metabolism takes over. The main signal for this phase to begin is believed to be a drop in blood glucose which is detected by the brain. The result is an increased sympathetic stimulation of the pancreas gland, which halts insulin secretion. Now, the pancreas gland releases the hormone **glucagon**. In the short term, glucagon has an effect opposite to insulin as it causes the liver to convert its glycogen back into glucose. This process is known as **gluconeogenesis**. However, if the fasting period is prolonged, glucagon will also begin to break down the body's fat stores into fatty acids which are used by body cells for energy. In addition, glycerol, which is also found in fats, will be converted back into glucose by the liver. These processes are particularly important for the brain as it cannot utilise fatty acids or glycerol for energy and has to rely on glucose provided by the liver during the post-absorptive period.

What causes hunger?

What causes hunger is a deceptively simple question. One possible answer is that hunger is caused by empty movements of the stomach. Common sense tells us we feel 'full' when the stomach is distended, and that we often attribute hunger pangs to the contractions produced by an empty stomach. An experimental test of this idea was

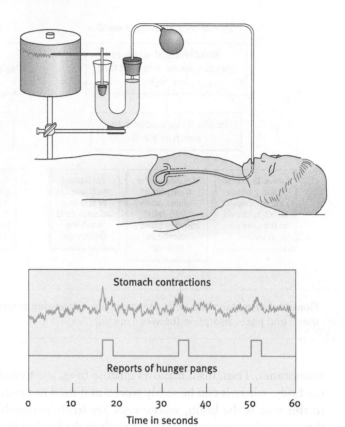

| | Stomach contractions |
| | Reports of hunger pangs |

Time in seconds

Figure 5.3   The type of experimental set-up used by Cannon and Washburn (1912)

undertaken in 1912 by W.B. Cannon who persuaded his research student A.L. Washburn to swallow a balloon that was inflated in his stomach. The balloon was then connected by a tube to a water-filled glass U-tube, and when a stomach contraction occurred, it caused an increase in the water level that resulted in an upward mark on a moving piece of paper (see Figure 5.3). It was found that Washburn's reported hunger pangs were nearly always accompanied by stomach contractions (Cannon and Washburn 1912). Further support linking an empty stomach with hunger was also obtained in a study where a patient had accidentally swallowed acid that caused his oesophagus to fuse shut. This person could only be fed by passing wet food through a tube that had been surgically implanted into the stomach. This tube also enabled researchers to observe the internal activity of the stomach directly, which confirmed that contractions were often associated with feelings of hunger (Carlson 1912).

There is now further evidence to confirm that stomach cues are involved in hunger and satiety. For example, the stomach wall is richly endowed with stretch receptors whose activity increases in proportion to the volume of the stomach. These signals are communicated by way of the vagus nerve to the **nucleus of the solitary tract** and adjacent **area postrema** in the brainstem, From here, pathways pass to a number of other areas, including the hypothalamus. Indeed, stomach distension has been shown to change the rate of firing in cells of the ventromedial hypothalamus (Stunkard 1975), which is a brain area implicated in feeding behaviour (see later). Experiments with laboratory animals also implicate gastric factors in feeding behaviour. For example, preloading the stomach of a rat with food in order to produce stomach distension causes a significant reduction in eating. Alternatively, removing food from a rat's stomach after it has just eaten a large meal will induce hunger. Indeed, such an animal will consume almost exactly the same amount of food, or amount of calories, that has just been taken out (Deutsch and Gonzalez 1980). These findings suggest that animals are able to monitor the volume of food, and its caloric value, in their stomachs, and use this as a feedback signal to govern hunger and satiety.

Despite this, it is also clear that many other factors besides the mechanical signalling of an empty or full stomach must inform the brain of a need to initiate or terminate eating. This is shown, for example, by studies that have lesioned the vagus nerve, which conveys the neural input from the stomach to the brain. In this case, the operation has little effect on hunger, although the vagal-lesioned animals tend to overfill their stomach (Gonzalez and Deutsch 1981). The relatively unaffected regulation of eating in these rats may occur because the stomach also releases chemical factors that govern food intake. This was shown, for example, by Koopmans (1981) who transplanted an extra stomach into rats (the main blood vessels of the implanted organ were connected to the circulatory system of the recipient). Koopmans found that when he injected food into the extra stomach, and kept it there by a noose around the pyloric sphincter, the animal became satiated and stopped eating. Since the transplanted stomach had no neural connections with the brain, and because food absorption does not actually occur from the stomach, this indicated that chemical messengers from the gut were being released in response to the food (see Figure 5.4).

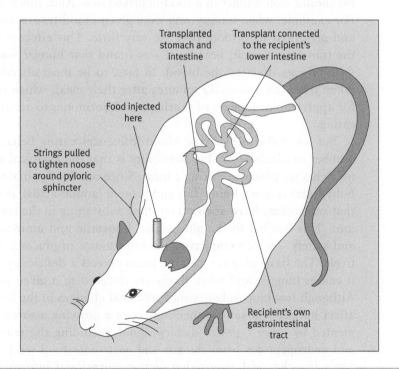

| Figure 5.4 | Transplantation of an extra stomach |

We now know that the stomach does indeed release a number of different substances (mainly neuropeptides) in response to food, which inform the brain of the stomach's nutrient status (see later). But, even allowing for the fact that the stomach sends chemical feedback signals to the brain, there are still many other non-gastric factors signalling hunger. Indeed, some of the strongest evidence to demonstrate this has come from patients who have undergone surgical removal of the stomach. This may occur after removal of a tumour which necessitates their oesophagus to be connected directly to the duodenum. These patients report normal sensations of hunger, and although they tend to eat smaller meals they still show proper regulation of food intake (Wangensteen and Carlson 1931). Thus, a full or empty stomach is not the only regulator of hunger or satiety.

The chemical signals of hunger

Most researchers believe that the most important events signalling hunger and satiety involve chemical substances. Indeed, convincing evidence that post-absorptive blood-borne chemicals play a role in signalling satiety has come from a classic study where hungry and food-deprived rats were given blood transfusions from satiated and well-fed ones (Davis *et al.* 1969). Clearly, if the blood contains a substance that signals whether an animal has eaten, then the transfusion of blood from a well-fed rat should stop hunger in a food-deprived one. And, this is exactly what was found. For example, when hungry rats were given blood transplants from satiated animals and presented with food, they ate very little. This effect could not be explained by the transfusion itself, because it was found that hunger was suppressed only when well-fed rats donated the blood. In fact, to be most effective, the blood had to be taken from the donors 45 minutes after their meal, which is about the time it takes for appreciable amounts of nutrients and hormones to accumulate in the blood after eating.

But what chemical in the blood influences eating behaviour? There are a large number of candidates. One possibility is that the chemical signal is provided by the nutrients we consume during a meal. Since our food is mainly a combination of carbohydrates (sugar), lipids (fat) and protein (amino acids), it is perhaps not surprising that researchers have focused on these substances in the regulation of eating behaviour. This has led to the **glucostatic**, **lipostatic** and **aminostatic** theories of hunger and satiety – which emphasize the importance of glucose, fat and proteins, respectively. The basic idea is when the brain detects a deficiency in one of these nutrients it causes hunger, and when levels are restored to a given point the result is satiety. Although few biopsychologists doubt that changes in the level of these nutrients can affect hunger and satiety, there has been a growing awareness that they are supplemented by other types of dietary signal, including the release of certain hormones and neuropeptides from the gut and gastrointestinal tract (Table 5.1). Thus, there are many chemical agents that convey nutritional information to the brain, along with neural signals from structures such as the stomach, intestine and liver (to name a few).

Table 5.1	Neurotransmitters and peptides that affect hunger and satiety
Factors which Increase Food Intake	**Factors which Inhibit Food Intake**
Noradrenaline	Serotonin
Orexins	Dopamine
Growth hormone releasing hormone	Cholecystokinin
Galanin	Corticotropin-releasing factor
Neuropeptide Y	Neurotensin
Melanin-concentrating hormone	Bombesin
Ghrelin	Gastrin-releasing factor
Agouti-related peptide	α-melanocyte stimulating hormone
	Leptin

The glucostatic theory of hunger

Glucose has long been seen as the obvious contender for providing the most important metabolic signal that governs hunger and satiety. Following a meal, carbohydrates are broken down into smaller sugars, which means that much of our digested food enters the bloodstream as glucose. And, as mentioned earlier, glucose is the main sugar used by our body for immediate energy and longer-term energy storage. It should come as no surprise, therefore, to learn that considerable evidence supports the notion that glucose levels in the blood are involved in hunger. For example, it has long been known that injections of glucose into hungry animals will suppress eating, whereas insulin administration, which significantly lowers blood glucose levels, will cause them to start eating. In experiments where blood glucose has been monitored (Figure 5.5), it has been shown that baseline levels tend to be relatively constant (rarely fluctuating by 2 per cent) until about 10 minutes before a meal, when they drop by about 8 per cent (Campfield and Smith 1990). These researchers also found that an injection of glucose at the point when glucose levels were beginning to drop would postpone eating (although curiously this does not occur some 3–4 minutes prior to eating). Thus, eating does not necessarily occur at the lowest blood glucose level.

In 1953, Jean Mayer proposed the **glucostatic** theory of hunger. The theory proposes that hunger is caused by low levels of blood glucose which is detected by specialised glucoreceptors located in the body or brain. Thus, if there is a drop in blood glucose reaching the cells of the body the animal gets hungry, and if there is an increase in glucose they become satiated. However, the simple version of this theory suffered from a number of difficulties. The most problematical is that people with **diabetes** who are unable to produce insulin, and who have very high levels of blood glucose since it cannot be taken up into their cells, are often ravenously hungry. Thus, if glucose is the signal for eating and satiety there must be a more complex mechanism than its concentration in the blood.

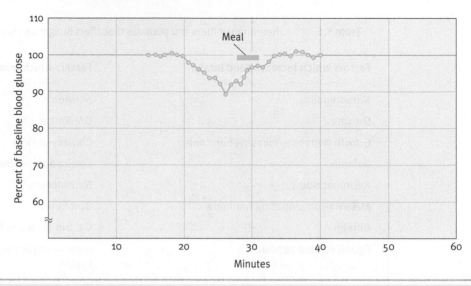

| Figure 5.5 | Glucose and feeding behaviour |

Source: John P.J. Pinel, *Biopsychology*, 5th edition, p. 308. Copyright © 2003 by Pearson Education

To get around this problem, Mayer proposed that the brain contains special cells called **glucostats** that measure the rate at which glucose is being utilised to provide energy. More specifically, he believed the cells provided this function by comparing the difference between levels of arterial blood glucose entering the brain and the 'used' venous blood leaving it. A difference between the two values would show how much sugar was being removed from the blood as it passed through the brain, and if there was a significant discrepancy hunger would occur (Mayer 1953). Soon after Mayer proposed the idea of glucoreceptors in the brain, his theory received support (Mayer and Marshall 1956). Mayer reasoned that if glucoreceptors existed, then they would be identified by injecting animals with a compound called gold thioglucose, a substance that mimics glucose, but which is neurotoxic. This substance would attach itself to the cells containing the glucoreceptors and cause them to die. Indeed, after injecting mice with gold thioglucose, it was found that the animals began to eat huge quantities of food and became obese. When the brains were examined, marked damage to the **ventromedial hypothalamus** was found. In other words, this appeared to be the region that contained the glucostats.

Do hypothalamic glucoreceptors really control feeding?

Further support for the existence of glucostats in the brain came from studies showing that some 25–45 per cent of neurons in the ventromedial hypothalamus are glucoresponsive (that is, are sensitive to increasing levels of glucose). In one study, injections of glucose into this region of the hypothalamus significantly changed the activity of many of its neurons (Anand *et al*. 1964). Similarly, increased radioactivity levels in the ventromedial hypothalamus were found to occur after peripheral injections of radioactively labelled glucose. Despite this, the role of ventromedial hypothalamic glucose-sensitive cells in eating behaviour is not well understood. For example, if these cells are involved in controlling food intake, then infusions of glucose into the ventromedial hypothalamus would be expected to reduce food intake in hungry animals; but this does not occur (Epstein *et al.* 1975). In fact, so-called hypothalamic glucoreceptors appear to be responsive to a range of different chemicals and hormones, and most researchers now believe that these cells are more likely to be involved in energy home-ostasis or body weight regulation (Williams *et al.* 2001).

Although Mayer believed that glucoresponsive cells controlling hunger and satiety existed in the hypothalamus, the main site for glucoreceptors is now known to be the liver. For example, when glucose is injected into the jugular vein that carries blood into the brain, there is little effect on eating behaviour. However, when glucose is injected into the hepatic portal vein, which is the main blood vessel from the intestines to the liver, hungry animals stop eating (Russek 1971). Evidence linking the liver with glucose detection has also been provided by Stricker *et al.* (1977) who injected rats with insulin to lower blood glucose and cause hunger. The animals were then given the sugar fruc-tose. Although this type of sugar is metabolised by the liver, it cannot be detected by the brain as it is too large to cross the blood–brain barrier. In other words, these rats had low glucose levels in the brain but high glucose passing through the liver. If glucorecep-tors in the brain have an important role in hunger, then these animals should have eaten when presented with food. But, this did not happen. Thus, the liver provides the brain with an important satiety signal regarding the availability of glucose.

These findings should perhaps not surprise us: the liver is the first organ of the body to receive nutrients from the small intestine and is in an ideal position to monitor food intake. Moreover, the liver sends information regarding blood glucose levels to the brain via the hepatic branch of the vagus nerve, which ascends to the nucleus of the solitary tract (in the brainstem) and hypothalamus. Indeed, this pathway has been shown to be important as the administration of glucose into the hepatic portal vein in-creases neural activity in the ventromedial hypothalamus and decreases the firing rate of cells in the lateral hypothalamus (Shimizu *et al.* 1983). Thus, the hypothalamus is an important control centre for monitoring glucose levels in the liver. Despite this, if the vagal input to the brain is severed, animals still exhibit relatively normal patterns of eating. This shows that other mechanisms must compensate for the loss of informa-tion from the liver. In other words, the liver is only one component of the peripheral system that provides feedback to the brain regarding the nutrient status of the body.

The role of neuropeptides in producing satiety

It has been increasingly recognised in recent years that chemical substances released by the gut and intestines in response to food intake are particularly important in pro-viding feedback signals to the brain. In fact, over two dozen substances, all composed of small chains of amino acids known as **neuropeptides**, are released by various cells throughout the gastrointestinal system. While most act locally, some are also trans-ported in the blood as hormones to reach the brain. In the main, they act to suppress feeding, although a few also increase food intake. To make matters more complicated, a number of these peptides are also synthesised by neurons in the brain where they act as neurotransmitters or modulators. Neuropeptides are different from classical neurotransmitters in a number of respects (see Figure 5.6). For example, the sequence

Neurotransmitters

Most classic small neurotransmitters are derived from enzymatic modifications of a substance (typically an amino acid) that is transported into the neuron from general circulation. For example, serotonin synthesis begins with tryptophan (obtained from the diet) which is converted into 5-hydroxytryptophan (5-HTP) by the action of the enzyme tryptophan hydroxylase. In turn, 5-HTP is converted into serotonin by the action of 5-HTP decarboxylase. All of these processes take place in the nerve terminal.

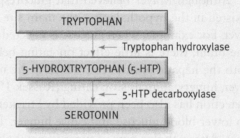

Neuropeptides

In contrast to neurotransmitters, neuropeptides (similar to the formation of proteins) require the translation of DNA sequences in the nucleus, and the formation of amino acid chains at the ribosome in the cytoplasm. These are further processed in the endoplasmic reticulum and Golgi apparatus to make a protein precursor. This can then be cleaved to make a number of small active peptides, which are then packaged into vesicles, and transported down the axon to the nerve terminal (in some cases this processing actually takes place in the vesicle as it travels down the axon). For example, the biosynthesis of cholecystokinin (CCK) is believed to follow this pathway.

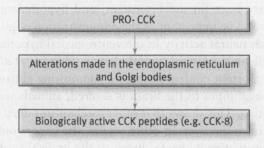

Figure 5.6 Steps in the formation of neuropeptide synthesis

---

of amino acids in a neuropeptide is stored in the genetic material (nucleus) of the neuron, and is synthesised in the cell body. In most instances a large **protein precursor** is made, which is than cleaved into smaller peptides (despite this, these molecules are much larger than conventional neurotransmitters). Following this, the peptides are transported down the axon to be stored in synaptic vesicles. Neuropeptides are also different from classical neurotransmitters in the way they are removed from the synapse. Unlike the rapid deactivation of conventional neurotransmitters, the actions of neuropeptides tend to be prolonged, and exert an effect until they diffuse away from the synapse.

The first gut hormone to be implicated in hunger and feeding was **cholecystokinin (CCK)**, which is released by cells of the duodenum in response to the presence of fat or protein. CCK had first been shown to act on the stomach where it controlled the rate at which it empties its contents into the duodenum thereby ensuring proper digestion.

It had also been found to act on the gall bladder and pancreas gland. However, in the early 1970s, CCK was shown to reduce meal size in rats in a dose-dependent manner (Gibbs *et al.* 1973). This finding was later extended to humans, where administration of CCK was shown to suppress food intake by 19 per cent (Kissileff *et al.* 1981). In fact, later studies showed that this suppressive effect could be as high as 63 per cent depending on dose and other experimental conditions. For example, injection of CCK coupled with mild gastric distension produced the largest decrease in meal size. Thus, CCK acts as a signal that monitors food intake and inhibits eating when a sufficient amount of food has been consumed.

It is likely that CCK relays information regarding satiety to the brain in a number of ways. For example, there are two types of cholecystokinin receptor: **CCKa** and **CCKb**, with the former located primarily in the gastrointestinal tract and the latter in the brain. One possibility is that activation of CCKa receptors in the stomach and intestine stimulates the vagus nerve, which transmits the satiety message to the hypothalamus via the nucleus of the solitary tract (see Figure 5.7). Support for this idea comes from the finding

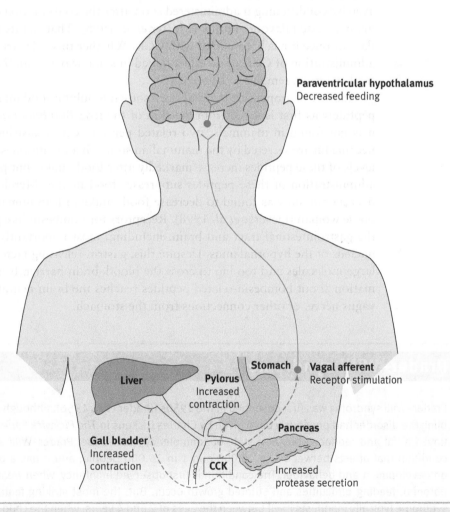

| Figure 5.7 | The roles of CCK in feeding behaviour |

Source: Adapted from J.E. Blundell and J. Halford (1998) Appetite: physiological and neurobiological aspects, in Salder, M. (ed.) *Encyclopaedia of Human Nutrition*, p. 5

that cutting the vagus nerve to the brain significantly reduces or eliminates the satiety-inducing effect of CCK injections (Bray and York 1979). In addition, drugs that block CCKa receptors have been shown to increase feeding in experimental animals. However, an alternative possibility is that CCK directly activates receptors in the brain which are found in high numbers in the ventromedial hypothalamus and paraventricular nucleus. Indeed, CCK can cross the blood–brain barrier to act on **neuropeptide Y** neurons in the brainstem and hypothalamus (Lopez *et al.* 2007). In addition, drugs that block central CCKb receptors are much more effective than CCKa antagonists in stimulating food intake in animals that had previously been satiated.

Despite this, the role of CCK in feeding behaviour is somewhat controversial. The main reason for this is that it causes feelings of nausea in humans, and it has been proposed that this effect might account for its actions on feeding behaviour in animals. One way of examining this issue is to determine whether CCK can cause **learned flavour aversion**. For example, both people and animals will readily learn to avoid food or drink that has contained a toxin which has led to nausea and illness, even if the sickness results some hours or even days after ingesting the toxin. A similar situation can be produced in the laboratory. Indeed, it has been found that CCK will cause taste-aversive conditioning if administered soon after the consumption of a novelty and normally ingested flavoured drink (Moster *et al.* 1998). That is, rats will always avoid the flavour once it has been paired with CCK. Whether this is an artefact of experimental administration of CCK or an effect linked in some way to satiation which discourages further eating, remains to be seen.

Another neuropeptide that has been shown to inhibit food intake is **bombesin**. This peptide was first isolated from the skin of the frog *Bombina bombina*, and although it is not found in mammals, two related peptides called **gastrin-releasing factor** and **neurmedin** are secreted by the mammalian stomach and intestines. Not only do plasma levels of these peptides increase markedly after food intake, but peripheral and central administration of these peptides suppresses food intake (Merali *et al.* 1993). Moreover, bombesin was found to decrease food intake in lean human subjects but not in obese woman (Lieverse *et al.* 1998). Receptors for bombesin-like peptides are found in the gastrointestinal tract and brain, including, most importantly, the paraventricular nucleus of the hypothalamus. Despite this, gastrin-releasing factor and neurmedin are large molecules and too big to cross the blood–brain barrier. It is believed that information about bombesin-related peptides reaches the brain neurally, perhaps from the vagus nerve, or other connections from the stomach.

Prader–Willi syndrome

Prader–Willi syndrome was first described in the 1950s (Prader *et al.* 1956), although an account resembling the disorder had previously been given by Charles Dickens in *The Pickwick Papers* (1836) who portrayed a 'fat and red-faced boy in a state of somnolency', called Joe. Prader–Willi syndrome is a rare condition that affects between 1 in 10,000 and 1 in 25,000 people, and it has a profound influence on development and behaviour. The condition is first observed in infancy, when weak muscle tone (hypotonia), feeding difficulties and stunted growth occur. But, the most striking feature of Prader–Willi syndrome typically manifests itself between the ages of 2 and 4 years, when the child begins to show an insatiable obsession with food. In fact, a lifetime desire and interest in food becomes central in individuals with Prader–Willi syndrome: they enjoy thinking about it, talking about it and most of all eating it. Not surprisingly, weight gain leading to severe obesity is common. To make matters worse, individuals with Prader–Willi syndrome also have a reduced metabolic rate, along with a high fat versus lean body mass, which means they require fewer calories than other people. Other symptoms of Prader– Willi syndrome include distinct facial features (almond shaped eyes, narrow forehead and downturned lips) and poor motor co-ordination. People with Prader–Willi syndrome also tend to exhibit learning disabilities (they have an average IQ of 60), accompanied by behavioural problems, including severe temper outbursts, obsession for collecting things, poor temperature regulation and abnormal sleep patterns.

Most cases of Prader–Willi syndrome (about 70 per cent) are caused by the deletion of active genes from the long arm of chromosome 15 during the early stages of foetal development. These genes are unusual because they do not follow the normal Mendelian pattern of inheritance (see Chapter 14). Although the foetus receives two copies of chromosome 15 in accordance with Mendel (one from each parent), some of the genes on this chromosome are functional only if they come from the father (the paternal chromosome). In fact, Prader–Willi syndrome occurs when the region of the paternal chromosome 15 containing the critical genes is missing. Most other cases of Prader–Willi syndrome (about 25 per cent) occur when the person inherits two copies of chromosome 15 from the mother (maternal copies) instead of one from each parent. Because the critical genes on the maternal chromosome are 'silent', the effect is very similar to the loss of gene function occurring with the paternal deletion. Interestingly, the situation in which two paternal and no maternal chromosomes 15 are inherited is called **Angelman syndrome** – a disorder characterised by epilepsy, tremors and a perpetually smiling facial expression.

Although no gene has yet been identified as the sole cause of Prader–Willi syndrome, five genes have been identified on the long arm of chromosome 15 that show genetic imprinting from the father. It is also believed that many of the symptoms of Prader–Willi syndrome, including slow developmental and sexual maturation, along with its eating abnormalities, are due in some way to dysfunction of the hypothalamic–pituitary axis. In support of this, individuals with Prader–Willi syndrome have a deficiency of growth hormone and show decreased adult levels of sex hormones. Also, importantly, a reduction in the number of oxytocin-containing cells in the paraventricular nucleus of the hypothalamus has been found. Oxytocin is known to be involved in suppressing appetite, and its low hypothalamic levels may help explain the insatiable hunger of people with Prader–Willi syndrome.

Neuropeptides and hunger

One of the most exciting discoveries in appetite research over the past few years has been the peptide hormone **ghrelin**, which is produced cells in of the stomach and other regions of the gastrointestinal tract. Part of the excitement lies with the fact that this is the only peripherally active peptide known to stimulate appetite. Ghrelin is also found in other tissues of the body, including the pituitary gland, where it acts as a releasing factor for growth hormone (GH). In fact, the name 'ghrelin' is derived from GH releasing, which reflects the ability of this peptide to stimulate growth hormone release. However, it is as a peripheral appetite stimulant that ghrelin has attracted most attention. For example, in humans it has been found that ghrelin concentrations increase with fasting and decline rapidly after each meal (Cummings *et al.* 2001). Moreover, increases in ghrelin correlate with feelings of hunger. In fact, ghrelin was found to subjectively enhance the sensation of hunger, and increase energy intake during lunch by

28 per cent when injected into healthy human volunteers (Wren *et al.* 2001). Researchers have further found that the ingestion of glucose-containing carbohydrates has a greater effect on reducing ghrelin levels than meals containing high levels of fat. This contrasts with CCK whose levels are regulated more by fats and proteins passing through the gastrointestinal tract.

It is not yet clear if ghrelin produces its appetitive stimulant effects on the brain by activating vagal afferents from the stomach or via the bloodstream. Nonetheless, it appears that, whatever the signal, the **arcuate nucleus** of the hypothalamus (see Figure 5.8) is important for its effect as it contains high numbers of ghrelin receptors. Not only is this a region of the hypothalamus which lies outside the blood–brain barrier and is therefore sensitive to circulating factors in the blood, but it also contains neurons that synthesise several peptides known to be involved in feeding behaviour, including **neuropeptide Y** and **agouti-related peptide (AGRP)** which are orexigenic (that is, they stimulate appetite), and **alpha-melanocyte stimulating hormone (α-MSH)** which is anorexic (it inhibits appetite). All these peptide-containing neurons are known to project to the **paraventricular nucleus** and **lateral hypothalamus** (see later). The production of both neuropeptide Y and AGRP is stimulated by the administration of ghrelin (Arora 2006).

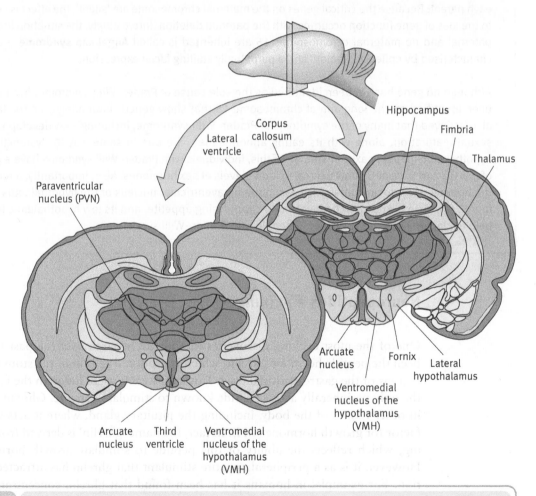

Figure 5.8	The location of the arcuate nucleus

But, perhaps more importantly, it has also been shown that drugs which block neuropeptide Y and AGRP abolish the feeding produced by ghrelin (Nakazato *et al.* 2001). Thus, there is now good evidence to show that the effects of ghrelin on short-term food intake are mediated by these two peptides.

The role of ghrelin in feeding behaviour has also become more complex with the recent discovery that ghrelin can be broken down to produce another biologically active peptide called **obestatin**, from the Latin *obedere* meaning 'to devour' (Zhang *et al.* 2005). As might be expected, obestatin is also found in the stomach, blood and hypothalamus. But, unlike ghrelin which increases food intake, obsestatin decreases food intake and body weight in rodents. It also decelerates gastric emptying and decreases intestinal contractility which is also opposite to the effects of ghrelin. The fact that ghrelin and obestatin have opposing actions indicates that they have important roles to play in the peripheral control of gastrointestinal functions. Table 5.1 on page 181 summarises the neurotransmitters and peptides that influence hunger and satiety.

Brainstem regions involved in feeding behaviour

The most basic level of the central nervous system for governing food intake is the brainstem, which contains a number of structures involved in ingestion, digestion and absorption of food. For example, the medulla contains the nucleus of the solitary tract and adjacent area postrema which receives afferent information from the vagus nerve and which relays input from the stomach, intestines, pancreas and liver. In addition, the same brainstem areas receive sensory information from cranial nerve VII (facial) which derives from gustatory (taste) receptors in the mouth and throat, areas that are likely to be important in assessing the palatability of food. In turn, several regions of the brainstem contribute to the motor parasympathetic nervous system that controls digestive processes. The most important of these is the **dorsal motor nucleus of the vagus (DMN)**, which is the main source of vagal efferents innervating the gut and stomach. The brainstem also contains receptors for several types of blood-borne signal that are involved in feeding behaviour, including leptin, insulin, glucose and several neuropeptides.

Evidence showing that the brainstem exerts a primitive form of control over food intake has come from studies involving rats whose forebrain, including the hypothalamus, has been severed from the brainstem at the level of the superior colliculus (a 'decerebrate rat'). Although this type of animal only has a functioning brainstem, it still has posture, grooms spontaneously, and can walk, run and jump when stimulated. In addition, it shows taste discrimination, consumes food, and terminates eating when satiated. Indeed, it will reflexively swallow liquid food put in its mouth, but is not 'fooled' by non-food such as water or saline. Further, it will not swallow a sucrose solution if it has a full stomach or has received an injection of CCK. This shows that the brainstem contains regions that maintain the basic reflexes of satiety. It is also capable of stopping ingestion if the taste is aversive or when its detectors sense noxious or toxic stimuli. Despite this, the decerebrate rat does not show increased consumption of food in response to food deprivation, indicating that higher areas of the brain, such as the hypothalamus, are necessary for this behaviour. In addition, such an animal does not have the capacity to seek food, nor is it able to modify dietary intake on the basis of learning or experience (Grill and Kaplan 2002).

The hypothalamus and feeding behaviour

The hypothalamus has been recognised for a long time as a pivotal structure in the regulation of feeding behaviour. In fact, it was known in the early nineteenth century that tumours to the hypothalamus in humans were associated with eating dysfunction and obesity. This effect was initially believed to be due to hormonal imbalances resulting from damage to the nearby pituitary gland, and it eventually came to be known as Fröhlich's syndrome. However, in the early part of the twentieth century, with the development of more precise stereotaxic surgery, researchers began to realise that the crucial part of the brain for producing obesity lay in the basomedial hypothalamus. This was shown, for example, in the late 1930s by Hetherington and Ranson, who found that lesions to the ventromedial hypothalamus (VMH) in rats caused excessive eating (**hyperphagia**) and weight gain. This type of effect was not produced by hypophysectomy, that is, removal of the pituitary.

The VMH, however, was not the only area to be linked with feeding behaviour. In 1951, Anand and Brobeck made the dramatic discovery that lesions to the **lateral hypothalamus** (LH) caused profound **aphagia** in which the animal stopped eating and drinking. In fact, these animals would die of starvation even though food and water were freely available. The importance of the hypothalamus in feeding was also confirmed by studies using electrical stimulation. For example, stimulation of the LH produced voracious eating in animals that had been previously satiated, whereas stimulation of the VMH inhibited eating in hungry animals (Smith 1956). These findings along with the lesion data strongly suggested that the hypothalamus was involved in the initiation and termination of feeding. In 1954, a theory based on this notion was proposed by Eliot Stellar, who argued that the VMH acted as the brain's satiety centre, and the LH as its hunger centre (Stellar 1954).

This theory, which became known as the **dual-centre set-point theory**, viewed the VMH and LH as the main control centres that governed hunger and feeding. Indeed, both these structures are in an ideal position to integrate information from other brain regions (see Figure 5.9), and are known to receive feedback from peripheral organs such as the gut and liver. And, as mentioned previously, the VMH had been shown to contain glucostats by Jean Mayer in 1956. The close anatomical proximity of the VMH and LH also encouraged the idea that the two structures directly interacted with each other. Put simply, the theory held that when the VMH was activated by neural or hormonal information signalling food intake, this acted to inhibit the LH feeding centre, and satiation was the result. In contrast, when the LH was activated by signals specifying declining nutrient availability, this acted to inhibit the VMH, thereby causing hunger (see Figure 5.10). This theory also had the benefit of fitting nicely into a homeostatic framework of feeding. The only problem, it seemed at the time, was to identify the signals and receptors that initiated hunger and satiety, and to determine how they were integrated in the hypothalamus.

A closer look at ventromedial hypothalamic lesions

It soon become clear that the dual-centre set-point model was not as convincing as it first appeared. For example, the VMH had been viewed as the satiety centre because its lesioning led experimental animals to become ravenously hungry and seemingly

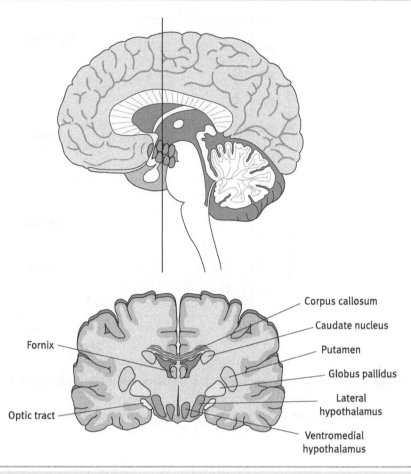

Figure 5.9   The location of the ventromedial and lateral hypothalamus in the human brain

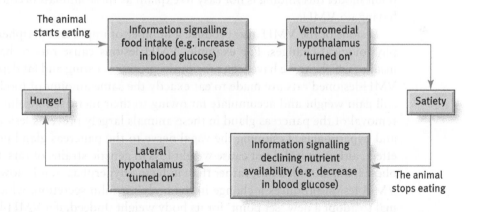

Figure 5.10   The dual-centre set-point model of feeding

unable to stop feeding. On closer inspection, however, it was apparent that things were more complex than this. Although VMH-lesioned rats eat almost continually at first, which may lead to a doubling of body weight within the first few weeks, the period of weight gain does not last, and food intake drops off with the animal returning to

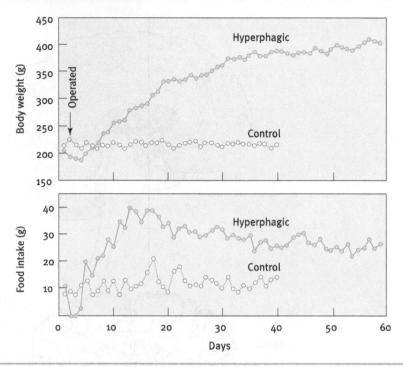

Source: Adapted from P. Teitelbaum (1955) *Journal of Comparative and Physiological Psychology*, 48, 156–163

Figure 5.11   The effects of ventromedial hypothalamic lesions on body weight and food intake

patterns of normal feeding (see Figure 5.11). In other words, the animal undergoes a dynamic phase of weight gain, followed by a static phase where it maintains its new weight and shows a normal satiety response to eating. In terms of the dual-centre set-point model this finding is not easy to explain as these animals become satiated despite having no VMH.

Lesions of the VMH also produce a number of important peripheral metabolic and physiological changes. For example, VMH lesions cause rats to have high levels of insulin, which, as we have seen previously, promotes eating and fat deposition. Indeed, if VMH-lesioned rats are made to eat exactly the same amount of food as controls, they still gain weight and accumulate fat owing to their increased insulin levels. Moreover, removal of the pancreas gland in these animals largely prevents lesion-induced obesity and hyperphagia. Lesioning the vagal nerve to the pancreas gland produced the same effect, although it did not cause weight loss in genetic strains of rats that were already obese (King 2006). Thus, rather than inducing hyperphagia, it is now believed that the VMH lesion produces a change in the body's insulin secretion, which causes the animal to adopt a new 'set point' for its body weight. Indeed, if a VMH-lesioned rat in the static phase is force-fed, its weight will increase even further. But, if this animal is allowed to feed normally again, the weight returns to its initial static phase level. Similarly, if a VMH-lesioned rat loses weight by being starved, and is then allowed free access to food, it will soon regain its static phase weight.

Although rats with VMH lesions have elevated levels of insulin, they also show other digestive abnormalities, including increased gastric secretions and faster stomach emptying time. These effects are believed to occur because VMH damage disrupts the fibres arising from the paraventricular nucleus of the hypothalamus. These fibres are important because they project to brainstem nuclei that regulate the parasympathetic vagus nerve. Because this vagal pathway sends input to and from the pancreas gland, stomach and liver, lesions of the VMH would disrupt functioning in all these structures.

There are also other interesting characteristics of VMH-lesioned animals. For example, once these animals have stabilised their weight, they are very finicky and prefer to eat palatable food (for example, food with extra fat or sugar) rather than their normal 'dry' diet of laboratory food. In fact, if these animals are given food that is slightly stale, or made to taste bitter by the addition of quinine, they eat less than controls. Thus, animals with VMH lesions show exaggerated reactions to palatability. In addition, these animals appear to be 'lazy' and will show a marked decrease in eating if required to perform a task such as pressing a lever in an operant box to obtain food.

Plate 5.1   A hyperphagic rat with a lesion of the ventromedial hypothalamus

Source: R.B. Graham (1990) *Physiological Psychology*, p. 451, Wadsworth

A closer look at lateral hypothalamic lesions

The other main source of evidence for the dual-centre set-point model came from the observation that lesions to the LH causes the animal to stop eating (aphagia) and drinking (adipsia). Since the removal of the LH abolished these functions, it implied that this region of the brain was the critical control centre for the initiation of feeding. But, again, on closer inspection the theory soon ran into problems. Perhaps most difficult was that the aphagia and adipsia produced by LH lesions could be reversed. For example, while rats with LH lesions initially do not consume food, they can be coaxed into eating by first being fed through a tube. After several weeks of this force-feeding, they begin to eat by themselves especially if they are provided with palatable food such as biscuit crushed in milk. Finally, the rat will return to its 'normal' regime of dry rat chow and water (Teitelbaum and Epstein 1962). Thus, LH lesions do not permanently abolish eating and drinking – a finding that indicates that other areas of the brain must take over, or be involved, in this behaviour. Indeed, we now know that eating can be elicited by stimulation of many other areas of the brain, including other hypothalamic nuclei, as well as the amygdala, hippocampus, thalamus and frontal cortex (Rolls 1999).

It also become clear that LH lesions produced a wide range of other behavioural impairments. For example, the LH-lesioned animals did not move around or right themselves when placed on their sides, and they demonstrated **sensory neglect** as shown by their unresponsiveness to touch and visual stimulation. Moreover, these animals appeared grossly under-aroused – an idea that gained further support when it was found that a mild pinch to the tail could induce LH lesioned rats to start eating (Antelman *et al.* 1975). Further suspicion about the role of the LH in eating behaviour arose when it was found that LH lesions caused damage to **fibres of passage,** or axon pathways, that arose from other brain areas which passed through the hypothalamus en route to other destinations. One pathway that goes through the LH is the dopaminergic **nigral–striatal pathway,** which links the substantia nigra with the striatum, and is known to be involved in attention and movement. Indeed, damage to this pathway causes sensorimotor deficits along with aphagia and weight loss that closely resemble the effects of LH damage (Ungerstedt 1971).

During the 1970s it became possible to selectively destroy neurons in the LH without damaging fibres of passage by the use of neurotoxins such as kainic acid and ibotenic acid. These drugs destroy neurons by overstimulating glutamate receptors, which causes excessive neural excitation and an influx of harmful ions into the cell. The result is that the outer membrane ruptures and the cells die. But, since axons do not have glutamate receptors they are spared degeneration. When these types of drugs were injected into the LH, it was found that they caused a decrease in food intake and body weight, but no deficits in motor or sensory function (Winn *et al.* 1984). This supported the idea that the LH is involved in stimulating food intake, whereas the sensorimotor deficits produced by the electrolytic lesion were the result of damage to the nigral striatal pathway.

Electrophysiological evidence also confirms the importance of the LH in feeding behaviour. For example, it has been found that there is a group of neurons in the LH that respond to the taste of food. These neurons fire when substances such as glucose are placed in the mouth, but not to water. The firing rates of the neurons correlate with the concentration of the glucose, and they decline when the animal has been fed to satiety. Other neurons in the LH become active when a hungry monkey has sighted food. Typically, such LH neurons start firing within a very short time (150–200 ms) of a food stimulus being shown, but no response occurs to a neutral stimulus (Rolls *et al.* 1979). Finally, some hypothalamic neurons that fire in response to the sight of food are also activated by **brain stimulation reward** in which the animal will self-administer an electrical current into the brain for its pleasurable effects (see Rolls 1999). In other words, it would appear that some of the pleasurable effects of eating are mediated by activity in the LH (see also Chapter 13).

A new understanding of satiety and appetite: neuropeptide Y

The realisation that peripheral neuropeptides are important in feeding behaviour, along with evidence showing that these substances also exist in the brain where they act as neurotransmitters and neuromodulators, has transformed our knowledge of hunger, satiety and energy homeostasis. One neuropeptide that has attracted attention is **neuropeptide Y (NPY)**. This 36 amino acid is closely related to peptides found in the pancreas gland and gut, and was first identified in the central nervous system during the early 1980s. When injected directly into the ventricles of the brain, close to the hypothalamus, NPY was found to produce a voracious and prolonged increase in food intake (Clark *et al.* 1984). In fact, the feeding response to NPY is unparalleled by any other type of substance. For example, rats injected with NPY not only appear to be ravenously hungry but will press a lever hundreds of times for food reward, consume food made bitter with quinine, and even endure painful electric shocks to their tongue in order to drink milk (Jewitt *et al.* 1992).

Neuropeptide Y is now recognised as the most abundant neuropeptide in the brain, with a wide range of functions. For example, NPY has been found in the cerebral cortex, hippocampus, thalamus and brainstem, and linked with a wide range of behaviours, including memory processing, body temperature, blood pressure and sexual function (see Gehlert 1999). In the hypothalamus, NPY-containing neurons are found primarily in two regions: the **dorsomedial hypothalamus (DMH)** and **arcuate nucleus**. The DMH is a region that also contains high numbers of cholecystokinin receptors and many of these are located on neurons that synthesise NPY. As we have seen, CCK is a powerful appetite suppressant, and accordingly it has been found that CCK injections into the DMH inhibits feeding in hungry rats. This effect is due to CCK acting on the genes that are involved in making NPY (Bi 2006). Thus, reduced levels of NPY in the DMH is clearly important for suppressing appetite.

The role of NPY in the arcuate nucleus of the hypothalamus has also attracted attention, partly because the arcuate nucleus is one of the few areas in the brain where the blood–brain barrier is modified to allow entry of peripheral peptides and insulin. As might be expected, the neurons in the arcuate nucleus contain a large number of different receptor types, including those for leptin (to be discussed later). The arcuate nucleus has neurons that are sensitive to ghrelin, which in turn stimulates the production of NPY. One of the most important destination for the NPY-containing neurons of the arcuate nucleus is the **paraventricular nucleus (PVN)**, which lies in the upper part of the third ventricle. This area is particularly important for stimulating appetite. For example, infusion of NPY into the PVN increases carbohydrate and fat intake, leading to weight gain if administered daily (Stanley *et al.* 1989), and produces a number of metabolic changes in the body, including increased insulin secretion, decreased breakdown of fats in adipose tissue, and a drop in body temperature. Moreover, when animals are deprived of food and lose weight, levels of NPY increase in the PVN (Sahu *et al.* 1988). This appears to show that increased levels of NPY in the PVN are an important signal of hunger.

Other neuropeptides

The arcuate nucleus contains neurons that synthesise a number of other neuropeptides involved in feeding behaviour. For example, the terminals of NPY neurons arising from the arcuate nucleus release a peptide called **agouti-related peptide (AGRP)**. Curiously, this peptide is also found in hair follicles, where it affects pigmentation by inhibiting the binding of **alpha-melanocyte stimulating hormone (α-MSH)** to certain melanocortin receptors. But, in the hypothalamus, AGRP is a potent inhibitor of food intake. Moreover, if a small dose is injected into the ventricles it can cause an increase of food intake that lasts for over a week (Lu *et al.* 1994). Another group of neurons in the arcuate nucleus produce a different set of peptides. These neurons produce a precursor protein called pro-opiomelanocortin (POMC) which is then broken down into α-MSH. In contrast to AGRP, α-MSH significantly suppresses appetite. Moreover, POMC expression in the hypothalamus has been shown to drop during fasting, which presumably increases hunger. The neuropeptide-containing neurons of the arcuate nucleus project to many other areas of the hypothalamus, including the dorsomedial, lateral and paraventricular hypothalamus. As we have seen above, all of these hypothalamic regions are implicated in feeding behaviour.

The NPY-containing neurons of the arcuate nucleus that project to the lateral hypothalamus have attracted particular interest. These neurons have been shown to synapse with lateral hypothalamic neurons that produce peptides called **orexins**. Two types of orexin are found in the hypothalamus – orexin A and orexin B – and these are both strong stimulators of eating. In fact, injections of orexins into the hypothalamus of rats caused a tenfold increase in food intake, with the appetite-stimulation lasting 4 hours. Furthermore, in keeping with the notion of the appetite-promoting activity of the orexins, the precursor mRNA levels of these substances were significantly increased after a 48-hour fast (Meier 1998). Perhaps an even more interesting fact about orexins is that they are found in neurons that project outside the hypothalamus, including the brainstem, where they are involved in arousal, including sleep and waking. It is interesting to note that some orexin neurons also produce the morphine-like neuropeptide **dynorphin**, which has been implicated in reward and even in drug addiction (DiLeone *et al.* 2003). This may be another mechanism by which food produces its pleasurable effects.

The influence of learning on eating behaviour

Do we experience hunger because of a decline in blood glucose, or some other nutrient variable, acting on the hypothalamus? Alternatively, do we become satiated because of a cacophony of chemical and neural signals reaching our brain about the quantity of food we have just consumed? In fact, we do not have to look far to see that eating behaviour is not as homeostatically controlled as it may first appear. For example, one of the most important factors that determines whether we feel hungry is time of day. Indeed, most of us not only eat at fixed times of the day, but also become hungry in anticipation of a meal. And, other animals behave in a similar way. For example, as early as 1927, Richter showed that rats given one meal a day came to anticipate their feeding time with increased running in activity wheels. The importance of learning in feeding behaviour was nicely demonstrated by Weingarten (1983) who presented a light and tone to rats every time they were given a meal of evaporated milk. Animals were fed this way 6 times every day over a period of 11 days. After this conditioning, the rats were given unlimited access to food to produce satiation. Although these animals were well fed, they started to eat when re-presented with the light and tone. Clearly, these rats were not consuming food to restore an energy deficit. Rather, they were eating because they had been conditioned to do so.

This finding should not surprise us. When an animal is exposed to food it exhibits so-called **cephalic reflexes** to stimuli, such as the taste and smell of a meal, that help prepare the body to digest, metabolise and store the food. These reflexes include, for example, the secretion of saliva, gastric juices and insulin. But the secretion of these substances can also be conditioned to external events, such as time of day, smells, or a sight of a food store. This preparation for eating is likely to produce a state known as **conditioned hunger**. It is also possible that satiety may be conditioned in a similar way. For example, it has been proposed by Booth (1990) that the stimuli at the end of a meal may become associated with the bodily changes that occur after eating such as the release of glucagon. In turn, this would help produce a physiological satiety response.

Learning also influences our choice of foods. For example, few of us would find squid cooked in its own ink, fried grasshoppers or sheeps' eyes very appetising. Yet these are delicacies eaten in other parts of the world. The great difference in diet around the world shows that we learn what we like to eat as a result of upbringing, food availability and cultural influences. Some types of learned food preferences may begin at a surprisingly early point in life, since it has been shown that exposure to certain flavours through the amniotic fluid or breast milk is able to influence food choices later on (Mennella *et al.* 2001). Similarly, our dislike of certain foods may be learned. For example, we may avoid a certain food if it has caused illness in the past, and the same is true for other animals. For example, rats will normally consume large amounts of sweetened water, but will not do so if drinking is followed by illness induced by agents such as X-ray irradiation or lithium chloride injections (Garcia *et al.* 1955). This is known as **taste aversion learning** and is a highly specialised type of learning which occurs even if the delay between eating and illness is 24 hours or more.

Although there are undoubtedly many areas of the brain involved in learning about the pleasurable and aversive aspects of food, some areas are more important than others. For example, Holland and Petrovich (2005) trained food-deprived rats to consume food in a conditioning procedure not unlike the one used by Weingarten (see above), in which visual and auditory cues were paired with food. After training, the cues were able to elicit eating when the rat was satiated and not hungry. This cue-potentiated eating, however, was abolished by lesions of the **basolateral amygdala**, which is a region with major projections to the hypothalamus. The researchers also examined the the expression of certain 'early onset genes' which are known to start protein synthesis following neural activation. This showed that neurons in the basolateral amygdala, medial frontal cortex and lateral hypothalamus were selectively activated by the conditioning procedure. Holland and Petrovich conclude that cue-potentiated feeding is mediated by the frontal and amygdala neurons that directly target the lateral hypothalamus.

Sensory-specific satiety

Another important factor in feeding behaviour is the anticipated pleasurable effect of eating. For example, most of us will choose a dessert even after eating a large meal at a restaurant. This shows that it is the **palatability** of the food, and not the amount of prior consumption or its nutrient value, that stimulates eating. The same phenomenon also occur in animals. For example, adding a small amount of sugar to standard laboratory rat food tends to produce a large increase in its consumption and a rise in the animal's body weight. The addition of bitter-tasting quinine has the opposite effect. Moreover, an effective way of increasing food intake in laboratory animals is to feed them a highly varied diet. For example, rats given bread and chocolate along with their normal diet increased their food intake by 60 per cent and showed a 49 per cent increase in weight gain after only 120 days of feeding (Rogers and Blundell 1980).

This effect is caused by **sensory-specific satiety**, or the tendency to get 'bored' with a single type of food if it is consumed over a long period of time. Laboratory rats are highly susceptible to this effect because they are normally given a diet of only dry chow and water. Thus, the introduction of new food into their cages significantly increases the rat's 'pleasure' of eating. The same principle applies to humans. It has been found that if subjects are given a free meal (say, cheese and crackers) and then unexpectedly given a second course of something different (say, bananas), they will eat much more of the new food compared with a second helping of the first (Rolls *et al.* 1981). In other words, the second type of food now becomes much more appetising than the first one. Sensory-specific satiety has certain benefits as it encourages us to have a varied diet. Indeed, a diet composed of different foods will be more likely to contain a greater variety of nutrients, minerals and vitamins. Furthermore, sticking to one type of food is more likley to cause illness if it is contaminated with toxins.

Sensory-specific satiety has also been shown to have a neural basis in the hypothalamus. For example, Rolls found that if a lateral hypothalamus neuron had ceased to respond to a substance on which a monkey had been fed to satiety, the same neuron might nevertheless start firing to a different food. This occurred with responses associated with either the taste (i.e. food placed in the mouth) or to the sight of food. Moreover, these responses could predict the behaviour of the monkey, since the animal would reject the food on which it had been fed to satiety but accept other foods that it had not yet eaten. A similar type of sensory-satiety effect has been found in the primate **orbitofrontal cortex** (a region of the prefrontal cortex) where neurons sensitive to food-related sights, tastes and odours have been discovered (Rolls 1999).

The problem of obesity

For the first time in human history, at the beginning of the twenty-first century, most of the earth's population has access to plentiful food supplies, and accompanying this development is an increasing number of people who are obese or overweight. It is estimated that over 300 million people worldwide are obese as defined by a body mass index (BMI) of over 30 (that is, the person's body weight is 15–20 per cent higher than is ideal for their height), and nearly 1 billion are overweight as defined by a BMI of 25. In England in 2003, 60 per cent of adults were overweight and 23 per cent were obese (Department of Health 2004). To make matters worse, these figures are increasing at an alarming rate. For example, the years 1980 to 1998 saw obesity in England rise from 6 per cent to 17 per cent among men, and from 8 per cent to 21 per cent among women. The figures for childhood obesity are even more worrying, with government figures for 2001 showing that approximately 8.5 per cent of 6-year-olds and 15 per cent of 15-year-olds are obese. As anyone who has attempted to lose weight will know, obesity is not easily reversed, and the great majority of these children will carry their weight problems into adulthood.

The health costs of obesity and being overweight are considerable. Over two thousand years ago, the health risks of obesity were noted by Hippocrates, who wrote that 'persons who are naturally very fat are apt to die earlier than those who are slender', and modern evidence supports his claim. Each year in the UK alone, about 1,000 people die prematurely from obesity or its complications. Being obese doubles the person's chances of getting bowel and breast cancer, and is an important contributor to diabetes, hypertension and lung disease. In addition, excessive eating raises the level of cholesterol, which is a leading cause of strokes and heart attacks. It is perhaps not surprising, therefore, that the National Audit Office has estimated the direct and indirect annual costs of obesity for the National Health Service to be in the region of £3.6 billion. But, obesity also has psychological and social implications. People who are overweight are more likely to be depressed, have a lower than average income, a higher divorce rate and are more likely to commit suicide (Bloom 2003). And, if this was not bad enough, obese people are also often perceived as being gluttonous, lazy, or simply lacking in willpower – whether this is justified or not.

The causes of obesity

Obesity develops when the energy intake of the body exceeds energy expenditure over time (usually many years), leading to the accumulation of excess fat tissue. Considering that a rough guideline for the daily energy intake of calories for young men is generally given as 2,500, and for women 2,000, it can be readily seen how such limits are easily breached in our modern world. But obesity is more complex than the overconsumption of calories. As we have seen, there are a large number of different hormones and neurotransmitters responding to circulating nutritional signals involved in hunger and satiety. There are also many psychological and social factors at work that affect our eating behaviour. Thus, the causes of obesity are likely to be multifactorial. Nonetheless, obesity is likely to arise through an interaction of environmental and genetic influences. In general, it appears that severe obesity developing at a young age is likely to be caused by major genes that control energy balance, whereas obesity occurring later in life is more likely to have a strong environmental component with some influence from minor genes (Wilding 2006).

The rapid increase in obesity over the past few decades, however, can be attributed to adverse environmental influences that have acted to disturb the normal homeostatic mechanisms involved in eating. Central to this problem is our increasing reliance on diets with high calorific and fat content. In westernised countries, marked changes in diet have occurred over the past fifty years, especially with the increased consumption of energy-rich food and drinks. This type of food produces a less power-ful satiety response and a tendency to eat bigger portions. The problem is compounded by food marketing which makes these diets more attractive. Indeed, one study showed that watching food commercials on television increased calorific intake (for example, pizza and macaroni cheese) by up to 71 per cent (Blass *et al.* 2006). This type of information and advertising is not easy to avoid. In 2003, the UK food industry spent £727 million advertising food, soft drinks and chain restaurants, which was more than sixty times the entire annual budget of the NHS Development Agency. It is perhaps not surprising, therefore, that portion sizes for many popular food items have increased dramatically over the past thirty years (Young and Nestle 2002).

Many other factors also encourage overeating. For example, in our modern lifestyles we generally eat not in response to immediate nutritional deficits arising from the body, but as a result of habit, anticipation or circumstance. Because of this, meal size can be difficult to judge, and can be strongly influenced by psychological and so-cial factors. We also live in a time when there is a huge variety of different foods avail-able and this may encourage overeating through the process of sensory-specific satiety. Moreover, because food acts as a reward we can easily become conditioned to food-related stimuli, which leads to strong cravings and increased consumption. In particular, foods that are rich in sugar have been shown to trigger anticipatory insulin secretion which produces both a craving and an increased storage of the meal into fat. These problems are made worse by the fact that there has been a marked decline in physical activity over recent years. In the UK it has been estimated that the average individual now walks about 25 miles (40 km) less per week than they did in 1950. Moreover, the use of labour-saving devices, greater car use, and increased involvement in sedentary leisuretime pursuits such as television and computer games, have also contributed to the decline in physical activity (Wilding 2006).

Genetic factors also have a significant impact on our eating behaviour. Although single gene defects can cause obesity in humans (an example is a mutation in the gene that encodes for the melanocortin-4 receptor), these are extremely rare. Other inherited conditions, such as the **Prader–Willi syndrome** (see box on page 186) are likely to be the result of mutations to several genes. Despite this, family and twin studies show that body weight and the tendency to develop obesity are partly inherited. For example, it has been shown that children with two obese parents have an approximate 70 per cent chance of being overweight compared with 40 per cent for children with one obese parent and 10 per cent when neither parent is obese (Logue 1986). Other studies have shown that identical twins not only are more likely to be similar in weight, and obesity, compared with fraternal twins, but also have very similar weights (often within 4 kg of each other) across the lifespan. An examination of such studies has suggested a concordance, or heritability rate, of about 60–70 per cent for identical twins and 30–40 per cent for fraternal twins (Plomin *et al.* 1997). Although genetic association studies have identified several hundred genes that may influence body weight, few of these have been directly linked with obesity. Thus, the interaction of many genes with environmental factors is likely to be involved.

During each decade of life, the average adult will consume around 10 million calo-ries, yet gain only a few pounds. This type of 'metabolic efficiency' appears to be largely genetic. For example, C. Bouchard *et al.* (1990) took 12 pairs of identical twins who had no history of weight problems, and overfed them daily by 1,000 calo-ries over a period of 100 days. During this time, subjects consumed an extra 84,000 calories above normal which caused them to gain around 8 kg of extra weight.

Although there was a high variability between the different sets of twins (for example, one pair gained 4 kg and another pair gained 12 kg), the differences within each pair were very small. These results show that weight gain is due mainly to the inherited metabolism of the individual.

Want to live longer? Try calorie restriction

The wish to extend lifespan is a strong desire for most human beings. But is it possible? In fact, the answer is yes, and the secret has been known for many years. The method is called calorie restriction – or, more specifically, reduced feeding without malnutrition – and no other form of life extension comes close to being as effective. Calorie restriction was first performed on laboratory animals by the American physiologist Clive McCay during the 1930s. McCay believed that animals could not 'age', that is, show signs of decline, if they were still growing, and this led him to examine the effects of slowing down the growth of laboratory rats. To do this, McCay fed his rats as little as possible, but with enough nutrition to maintain health. To achieve the lowest rates of growth, McCay used a technique where he kept the animal at a constant weight for between one and four months, before allowing a small weight gain of 10 grams by increasing the rat's food. This was very successful since the deprived rats remained small and continued to grow throughout their life. In fact, after 18 months, when normal rats had been fully grown for more than a year, the deprived animals were only about one-quarter size. None ever reached the full adult size. But the most important finding was the difference in the lifespan between the two groups: the calorie-restricted rats lived nearly 70 per cent longer (on average 820 days) compared with the fully fed animals (483 days). Even more striking was the healthy demeanour of the calorie-restricted animals. These rats at the age of 1,000 days (at which time all controls had died) had the appearance of much younger animals. They had sleek, glossy coats, were active and mobile, and exhibited superior levels of intelligence. In other words, the calorie-restricted animals appeared to be more youthful and healthy.

These findings have been supported hundreds of times, in a great variety of species, from protozoa to primates. Although most researchers agree that placing animals on calorie restriction after weaning is the most effective means of extending lifespan, a number of studies have shown that beneficial results can still be obtained if food deprivation is started in adulthood. This suggests that it is not the slowing of growth that is important in dietary restriction, but something to do with the diet itself. Although no comparable long-term experimental studies have been performed on humans, a volunteer study is currently under way at Washington University (begun in 2002) with members of the Calorie Restriction Society. Preliminary results are showing that people following a diet of less than 2,000 calories a day are experiencing a dramatic drop in cholesterol levels and blood pressure.

How does calorie restriction work? There are many theories, but one of the most popular is that it reduces free radical damage. Free radicals are chemicals that contain an unpaired outer electron, and are normally derived from the breakdown of oxygen in cellular energy metabolism. Although they exist for only a few milliseconds, free radicals react with other biological molecules and cause considerable damage to the cell. This is also a popular theory of why we age. Another theory is that calorie restriction works by activating a gene called Sir2 (or 'silent information regulator 2') which suppresses DNA instability. Recent studies are exciting as they show that intermittent fasting may even slow down brain degeneration in both Alzheimer's and Parkinson's disease.

The discovery of leptin

Although there can be large fluctuations in our energy intake, most individuals maintain a relatively constant body weight over time. This indicates that the brain has some 'idea' of its ideal set-point body weight which it attempts to maintain and defend. But, until recently, the means by which the brain accomplished this feat was not known, although it was believed to be largely inherited. Indeed, it has long been known that certain genes have an important influence on controlling body weight in experimental animals. This was shown as early as 1950 when a genetic mutation occurred in a colony of mice being housed in a laboratory at Bar Harbour, USA, which caused them to become extremely obese and weigh up to three times more than normal. Because these animals had to carry two copies of the *ob* (or obese gene) they became known as *ob/ob* mice (Plate 5.2). Not only did these mice eat large amounts of food and have increased levels of insulin, but they also had a lower body temperature, indicating a slower metabolism. They also had a greater susceptibility to diabetes, which is similarly found in many obese people. How, then, could a mutation in *ob* genes set in motion the biological events that caused these changes?

In the early 1970s, it became clear that the *ob/ob* mice were overweight because they lacked a satiety chemical that was being released into the blood. This discovery was made by Coleman (1973), who joined *ob/ob* mice with normal lean ones in a parabiotic preparation. In this technique, two mice are surgically joined along flank incisions running from forelimb to hindlimb, which enables vascular networks to develop between the two animals, although the neural systems never join. The results of this procedure showed that the *ob/ob* mice ate less and lost weight – a finding which implied that something in the blood of the lean mice was acting on their obese counterparts to make them less fat. In other

| Plate 5.2 | An *ob/ob* mouse and a control mouse |

Source: John P.J. Pinel (2003) *Biopsychology*, 5th edition, p. 319, Allyn & Bacon. Reprinted with permission from the Jackson Laboratory and the publisher

words, the blood of the normal mouse was carrying a weight-regulating substance that was presumably encoded by the normal *ob* gene, and absent in the *ob/ob* mice.

But what could this substance be? In order to answer this question it was necessary to locate the *ob* gene in the genome and then to determine its amino acid sequence. The *ob* gene was located on chromosome 6 in *ob/ob* mice by Coleman (1976), and cloned and sequenced by Zhang *et al.* (1994). This work revealed that the *ob* gene produced a 167 amino acid protein, called **leptin** (from the Greek *leptos* meaning 'thin'), which is produced by the adipocytes (fat cells) of the body and secreted into the blood. It was also found that the amount of fat in the body determined the levels of leptin in the blood. That is, high levels of leptin were associated with high amounts of body fat. Thus, for the first time, researchers had identified a chemical signal that the brain could use to monitor body weight. Not only was this substance missing in *ob/ob* mice, but when leptin was injected into these animals it led to a marked decrease in their food intake and body weight. Indeed, a daily injection of leptin over the course of two weeks caused the mice to lose 30 per cent of their body weight (Halaas *et al.* 1995). Therefore, *ob/ob* mice overeat and become obese because they are deficient in the leptin protein.

Leptin has been shown to exert its effects on body weight regulation by acting on receptors located in the hypothalamus (Figure 5.12). For example, when leptin is injected directly into the lateral ventricle of the brain of rats and mice it produces a decrease in food intake. This effect is believed to be produced by leptin acting on the arcuate nucleus of the hypothalamus where it inhibits the secretion of NPY into the paraventricular nucleus (Elmquist *et al.* 2005). As we have seen previously, when NPY is injected into the hypothalamus it produces a prolonged increase in food intake. Thus, by reducing NPY secretion, leptin reduces food intake. Alternatively, animals who are deficient in leptin produce higher levels of NPY, and this may be an important contributor to overeating and weight gain (Schwartz and Seeley 1997). Leptin also enhances the release of other substances in the hypothalamus, including α-melanocyte stimulating hormone and corticotropin-releasing hormone. Thus, it exerts complex effects on the hypothalamus and could well be involved in other behavioural functions as well.

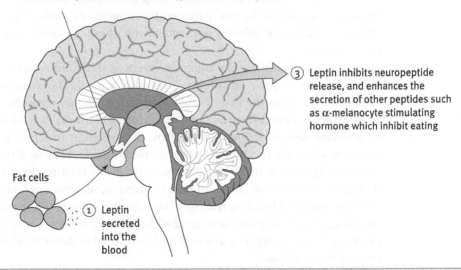

② Leptin binds to receptors in the arcuate hypothalamus.
Its neurons project to the lateral hypothalamus and paraventricular nuclei

③ Leptin inhibits neuropeptide release, and enhances the secretion of other peptides such as α-melanocyte stimulating hormone which inhibit eating

Fat cells

① Leptin secreted into the blood

Figure 5.12   How leptin is believed to influence feeding and body weight

Leptin and obesity

The discovery of leptin in the early 1990s, and evidence showing it was able to significantly reduce the body weight of *ob/ob* mice by reducing their food intake, raised many questions regarding its potential role in human obesity. For example, do obese humans, like *ob/ob* mice, have a mutation in their *ob* gene? The answer to this question turned out to be no, as only a few people worldwide have been found with mutations in their *ob* genes although these make interesting cases. The first report on leptin deficiency was published by Montague *et al.* (1997) who described a boy and a girl from the same family who were presumed to have *ob* mutations. Although the children had a normal weight at birth, they quickly became excessively obese. For example, at the age of 8 years the girl weighed 86 kg and had 57 per cent body fat compared with the normal range of 15–25 per cent, and her 2-year-old male cousin weighed 29 kg with 54 per cent body fat. The treatment of the girl with genetically produced (recombinant) leptin was began when she was 9 years old, and within two weeks she started to lose weight. Remarkably, after just one year of treatment her amount of body fat had decreased by 15.6 kg. Moreover, her eating habits changed and her constant hunger disappeared.

But what about obese individuals who are not leptin deficient or who have mutations in their *ob* genes? As we have seen, these people do not represent the vast majority of people who are overweight. Moreover, because leptin is secreted into the bloodstream in amounts directly proportional to the level of body adipose mass, obese people tend to have higher levels of leptin in contrast to *ob/ob* mice who have lower levels. Thus, if leptin plays a role in human obesity, the most likely mechanism would be a reduced sensitivity to this hormone, rather than decreased secretion. Nonetheless, attempts have also been made to treat obesity with subcutaneous injections of leptin (Heymsfield *et al.* 1999). The results show that there is a great deal of variability between obese subjects in their response to leptin, with only a small percentage of individuals obtaining significant weight loss after 24 weeks of treatment. However, uncomfortable reactions tended to occur at the injection sites, which caused many subjects to drop out of the studies. Thus, leptin does not appear to be the panacea for obesity as some had hoped. It has been suggested that only about 5 per cent of the obese population will benefit from leptin treatment.

In humans, diet-induced weight loss has been shown to result in a decrease in plasma leptin concentrations. Thus leptin may play a particularly important role in stimulating hunger when the body is subjected to low energy reserves, as occurs during periods of starvation. Unfortunately, the same mechanism may also help to explain the high failure rate of dieting. In humans, the secretion of leptin is not driven by meal patterns, although the same is not true for rodents. That is, leptin does not increase significantly after a meal and does not, by itself, lead to the termination of a meal (Friedman and Halaas 1998). In fact, in humans, secretion of leptin is highly regulated over the course of the day, with low basal levels between 0800 and 1200 hours, which rise progressively to peak between 2400 and 0400 hours. These findings indicate that there are as yet unexplained neural and hormonal systems regulated by the brain that control leptin release.

Anorexia nervosa and bulimia

The term 'anorexia' means loss of appetite and was first used by the English physician Sir William Gull in 1873. Although the term has remained, it is not an accurate description of the disorder as people with anorexia still experience hunger. Rather, anorexics are obsessed with being thin and have an extreme fear of becoming fat. This is generally accompanied by a distorted body image and an enhanced concern about physical appearance. Because of this, a person with anorexia is driven to eat tiny amounts of food, especially if the food is perceived as fattening, and this may be accompanied by self-induced vomiting, excessive exercise, the misuse of laxatives, or the drinking of water to suppress appetite. The result is often a dramatic loss of body weight to a level that is 60–70 per cent of what is normal for height and age. Anorexia is a relatively common disorder that affects around one teenager in every 200, and reaches a peak incidence of one in 100 among adolescents between the ages of 16 and 18. Although most common in teenage girls, about one in 10 cases occurs in males. The effects on health are serious and include loss of the menstruation, lowered blood pressure, sleep disturbances and metabolic abnormalities, including excess secretion of cortisol and decreased thyroid function. Remarkably, anorexia nervosa has the highest mortality of any psychiatric disorder in the United States, with an annual mortality rate of 5.6 per cent, which is twelve times higher than the death rate in control women. Sadly, therefore, about 5 per cent of anorexics will die from complications arising from their illness, with a famous case in point being the singer Karen Carpenter who died at the age of 32 in 1983.

Another eating disorder is bulimia. This is characterised by bouts of binge eating where individuals consume large amounts of food in a short space of time. Indeed, it is not unusual for bulimics to gorge themselves with thousands of calories, which is then followed by self-induced vomiting or the use of laxatives to purge themselves of the food they have just eaten. Although about 40 per cent of anorexics show similar binge eating, many people with bulimia do not develop anorexia. Thus bulimia qualifies as an eating disorder in its own right. It is found in 1–2 per cent of females aged 16 to 35 years, and is much less common in males.

The biological causes of anorexia (and bulimia) are poorly understood. Since anorexics are, by definition, underweight, a number of biological abnormalities are bound to exist. It therefore becomes difficult to know whether these abnormalities represent causal factors or are a secondary consequence of excessive dieting. One brain structure suspected of being involved in anorexia nervosa is the hypothalamus. Evidence linking this brain region with anorexia has come from the finding that as many as 25 per cent of anorexic females show loss of menstruation and low levels of reproductive hormones before significant weight loss occurs. In addition, the high cortisol levels often found in anorexic individuals are a result of increased secretion of corticotropin-releasing factor (CRH), which is under the control of the hypothalamic–pituitary axis. Nonetheless, it remains that in most individuals both menstruation and cortisol tend to normalise with clinical recovery, which casts considerable doubt on their aetiological involvement (Kaye 2000).

People with anorexia may show decreased levels of noradrenergic metabolites in their urine and cerebrospinal fluid, which may partly represent the breakdown of noradrenaline in the brain. Moreover, these metabolites tend to remain low after recovery from anorexia (Kaye *et al*. 1985). This is noteworthy since it has been found that injections of noradrenaline into the hypothalamus cause animals to eat, and that low levels have the opposite effect. However, noradrenline is also found throughout the brain and low levels may be linked to mood and depression. In support of this idea is the finding that anorexics tend to exhibit persistent cognitive distortions concerning body shape long after recovery, and they often suffer from dysphoric mood (Ferguson and Pigott 2000). Another neurochemical that may be involved in anorexia is serotonin. Anorexic subjects tend to show elevated levels of the serotonergic metabolite 5-HIAA, which persists into the recovery phase of their illness. It has been suggested that this may help account for the obsessive–compulsive personality traits that are common in the disorder (Kaye *et al*. 1997). It is interesting to note that antidepressants such as fluoxetine (Prozac) which block the reuptake of serotonin have been shown to be of use in the treatment of anorexia and bulimia.

There is also some evidence that anorexia nervosa may lead to brain damage. For example, Katzman *et al*. (1996) compared the MRI scans of 13 low-weight adolescent girls with anorexia nervosa with 8 healthy age-matched controls, and found that the anorexic subjects showed enlarged ventricles (an indicator of cortical atrophy) accompanied by reductions in both white (axon) and grey (cell body) matter. A year later, 6 of the 13 anorexic girls had recovered from their illness and were again subjected to MRI scanning. These scans showed that while the white matter volume had been restored, the grey matter remained significantly reduced (Katzman *et al*. 1997). Thus brain imaging studies show that anorexia nervosa causes permanent changes in the brain that are not always reversed by treatment or recovery.

Summary

Although eating is an essential behaviour vital for the maintenance of life, it is affected by many variables, both biological and psychological. Traditionally, physiological accounts of eating and hunger have viewed eating as a **homeostatic process** in which the body attempts to maintain its various levels of nutrients (glucose, fats, proteins, vitamins, etc.) within fine limits. However, it is also clear that psychological factors play an important role in eating, as shown by the fact that we often feel hungry in anticipation of food, rather than passively reacting to a decline in nutrient levels.

The process of digestion begins in the **mouth** where food is chewed and mixed with saliva, and passed to the **stomach** where it is broken down into **chyme** by gastric juices. The chyme is emptied into the **small intestine** where absorption takes place, with most nutrients entering the general circulation by the **villi** and entering the **hepatic portal vein** (which passes to the **liver**), although emulsified fats are absorbed into the lymphatic vessels. During a meal, the **pancreas gland** releases **insulin,** which allows glucose to enter the cells of the body – although not the brain. However, in the periods between eating (the post-absorptive phase) the pancreas gland secretes **glucagon,** which helps to convert **glycogen** (stored in the liver) into glucose, and stores of fatty acids into glycerol. A large number of peripheral mechanisms are believed to play a role in keeping the brain informed of the nutrient status of the body. Such mechanisms include neural signals from the **vagus nerve,** which conveys stretch information from the stomach and glucoreceptors in the liver, and various hormones secreted into the blood, including **cholecystokinin** and **leptin.**

Many brain areas are involved in eating behaviour, but most attention has focused on the hypothalamus. In particular, lesions of the **lateral hypothalamus** (LH) have been shown to produce **aphagia** (cessation of eating) whereas damage to the **ventromedial hypothalamus** (VMH) causes **hyperphagia** (excessive eating and weight gain). These observations led to the formulation of the **dual-centre set-point theory** in the 1950s, which postulated that stimulation of the LH induced eating, while stimulation of the VMH produced satiety. This theory is now regarded as incorrect. Although the LH appears to have a role in food intake, so do many other regions of the hypothalamus, including the **paraventricular nucleus** (PVN) – as is shown by marked increases in eating following injections of **neuropeptide Y** into this region. Moreover, the severe sensory and motor deficits in aphagia following LH lesioning are now known to be largely due to damage of fibres of passage that belong to the **nigral–striatal pathway,** which passes through this area. The weight of evidence also shows that the VMH is much more important in regulating the body's weight than in acting as a 'satiety centre'.

The discovery of **leptin** in the early 1990s, which is a hormone secreted by fat cells in the body, has provided new insights into the regulation of body weight and eating behaviour. For example, it has been shown that the more fat an individual has stored, the more leptin that is released. Thus, leptin provides the brain with a feedback signal concerning the size of its fat stores. However, leptin may also influence appetite. For example, high numbers of leptin receptors are found in the **arcuate nucleus** of the hypothalamus, which has projections to both the LH and PVN – areas where leptin is known to inhibit the secretion of neuropeptide Y, which is an important regulator of food intake and hunger.

Essay questions

1. What are the main roles of insulin and glycogen? What types of neural and chemical feedback from the body does the brain rely on to govern food intake?

    Search terms: Insulin and glycogen. Feedback signals in hunger. Digestive system. Hunger and eating. Glucostatic hypothesis.

2. Critically evaluate the roles of the lateral hypothalamus and ventromedial hypothalamus in hunger and satiety. What other brain sites are known to be involved in eating behaviour?

    Search terms: Dual-centre set-point model of eating. Hypothalamus and hunger. Neural control of eating. Neuropeptides and food intake. Brainstem and hunger.

3. Can eating be explained in terms of a homeostatic model? What evidence shows that non-homeostatic mechanisms also contribute to feeding?

    Search terms: Homeostasis and hunger. Sensory-specific satiety. Regulation of food intake. Classical conditioning of food intake. Factors influencing eating behaviour.

4. How has the discovery of leptin transformed our understanding of eating behaviour and the maintenance of body weight?

    Search terms: Leptin. Leptin and obesity. Leptin and hunger. Hypothalamus and body weight. Neuropeptide Y and body weight.

Further reading

Bouchard, C. (ed.) (1994) *The Genetics of Obesity*. Boca Raton, Fla.: CRC Press. A technical compilation of evidence, written by experts in their field, regarding the role of genetic factors in the aetiology of obesity.

Bouchard, C. and Bray, G.A. (eds) (1996) *Regulation of Body Weight: Biological and Behavioural Mechanisms*. New York: John Wiley. A comprehensive account that covers animal models, aetiology, physiological mechanisms, and social factors in obesity.

Bray, G.A., Bouchard, C. and James, P.T. (1998) *Handbook of Obesity*. New York: Dekker. A massive tome: 1,012 pages, 49 chapters and 88 authors. A very comprehensive overview of present research into obesity.

Broch, H. (2001) *The Golden Cage: The Enigma of Anorexia Nervosa*. Cambridge, Mass.: Harvard University Press. First published in 1978, and although dated in some respects, this still provides a vivid insight into the mind of an anorexic and her pursuit of thinness.

Bromwell, K.D. and Fairburn, C.G. (eds) (2001) *Eating Disorders and Obesity: A Comprehensive Handbook*. New York: Guilford Press. Contains a wealth of information, including the aetiology of obesity, the role of leptin and the treatment of eating disorders.

Kirkham, T. and Cooper, S.J. (eds) (2006) *Appetite and Body Weight: Integrative Systems and the Development of Anti-obesity Drugs*. Burlington, Mass.: Acadmic Press. Although a specialised text and not ideally suited to the undergraduate, it provides useful information concerning the neural, neurochemical, autonomic and endrocrine underpinnings of appetite and body weight.

Legg, C.R. and Booth, D. (1994) *Appetite: Neural and Behavioral Basis*. Oxford: Oxford University Press. Examines the psychology and neurobiology of appetite in relation to food, drugs, sex and gambling in an attempt to find common denominators.

Logue, A.W. (1991) *The Psychology of Eating and Drinking*. New York: Freeman. Not written for a student of psychobiology, but it contains some relevant background material.

Smith, G.P. (ed.) (1998) *Satiation: From Gut to Brain*. New York: Oxford University Press. A detailed but readable account of the physiological and hormonal mechanisms underlying satiety.

Stricker, E. and Woods, S. (eds) (2004) *Neurobiology of Food and Fluid Intake*. Volume 14 of *Handbook of Behavioral Neurobiology*. New York: Springer. A book of over 600 pages with some relevant chapters for the student interested in the psychobiology of eating behaviour.

For self test questions, animations, interactive exercises and many more resources to help you consolidate your understanding, and expand your knowledge of the field, please go to the website accompanying this book at **www.pearsoned.co.uk/wickens**

CHAPTER 6

Emotional states

In this chapter

INTRODUCTION

The term 'emotion' is derived from the Latin *emovere* meaning 'to move' or 'to disturb'. The word is appropriate, as emotions do indeed prepare or prompt us into action and signal that something significant is happening. They also create a feeling – love, elation, happiness, fear, anger, joy and surprise, to name a few – that colours our perception and adds richness to our personal world. Emotions are a constant and essential part of human life, and it is hard to imagine the dull, grey world that would exist without them. But, for psychologists, emotions are an enigma. As early as the third century BC, Plato wrote that emotions are to be distrusted as they arise from the lower part of the mind and prevent rational thought. As we all know, emotions often seem to arise involuntarily, trigger strong physiological reactions, and produce thoughts and behaviours that can be difficult to control. Thus Plato was possibly near to the truth when viewing emotions as the antithesis of reason. Later, in 1872, Charles Darwin pointed out that many of our emotions can also be recognised in other animals, which suggests that emotions have evolved to serve important functions. His theory is supported by the finding that the expression of many emotions is universal across all cultures.

Although the study of emotional behaviour is plagued with a number of conceptual difficulties, most would agree that an emotion is composed of four components: (1) a cognitive appraisal of an arousing event; (2) physiological changes in the viscera or main organs of the body; (3) an increased readiness to act; and (4) a subjective sense of feeling. Because emotions are such a powerful determinant of human behaviour, they have always been an important subject in biopsychology. But trying to explain how the viscera of the body and neural machinery of the brain give rise to the sensation of emotion presents a unique challenge. Despite this, an understanding of the biological mechanisms of emotion brings many benefits, as emotional disturbances can result in anxiety and stress, and underpin many other behavioural conditions and illnesses. By understanding the biological nature of emotion not only do we gain a far deeper insight into our own human nature but we are also in a stronger position to help those with emotional problems.

The autonomic nervous system and emotion

The most obvious sign of emotional arousal involves changes in the autonomic nervous system (ANS) such as a pounding heart, increased respiration or 'butterflies' in the stomach. The term 'autonomic' means self-governing, and this aptly describes the ANS which for most part operates beyond our voluntary or conscious control. This system uses motor nerves to control the **viscera** or internal organs of the body, along with some endocrine organs, including the **adrenal medulla**, which secretes adrenaline (and noradrenaline) into the bloodstream. The ANS comprises two divisions: the **sympathetic nervous system (SNS)** and **parasympathetic nervous system (PNS)**. The first of these acts to mobilise the body's resources in response to emergency or stressful situations. In the 1920s the famous physiologist Walter Cannon called the pattern of responses produced by the SNS the **fight or flight response** because it prepares the body for danger. For example, activity in the SNS increases respiration, heart rate and blood pressure to ensure that the main organs of the body receive higher levels of oxygen and blood sugar. In addition, it shunts blood away from skin to the muscles where it is better utilised for vigorous exercise (this is the reason why the skin goes pale after a shock). The SNS will also increase perspiration to cool the body, which may lead to sweaty palms in an anxious situation, while inhibiting non-essential functions such as digestion. All of these changes are adaptive reactions that help to prepare the body for a potential or actual threatening situation that requires a sudden energy output.

In contrast, the PNS promotes relaxation and is generally most active during non-stressful conditions. This system operates mainly when the body is at rest, during which time it may be involved in diverting blood away from skeletal muscles to the gut where it assists digestion. In addition, the PNS is also concerned with conserving body energy. But, just as important, the PNS also acts to reduce the neural tone of the SNS. For example, the sympathetic system will increase heart rate whereas activity in the parasympathetic system returns it back to normal. It follows that the PNS will also reduce the physiological arousal associated with a given emotion. To provide this type of autonomic balance, it is necessary for the motor branches of both systems to innervate the same body organs (Figure 6.1). Thus, both the SNS and PNS work closely together to control visceral changes in the body.

Although the ANS has evolved over millions of years to control the vital functions of the body and their possible adaptations to flight or fight situations, it has also become closely linked with the production of emotion. And, curiously, it appears that activity in the ANS is similar for both positive emotions, such as happiness and love, and negative ones, such as anger and fear. For example, both love and fear can be characterised by a rapidly beating heart, increased respiration, enlarged pupils, and stomach sensations. Although investigators do not yet agree whether the autonomic activity occurring during such disparate emotions is identical or different (see later), it is clear that the arousal produced by the ANS is an important component of most, if not all, emotional states. The involvement of the ANS in emotion has perhaps evolved to help us organise our behaviour in a way that motivates us to approach pleasant stimuli (as in the case of positive emotions), and to avoid unpleasant or noxious stimuli (in the case of negative emotions). This indicates, if nothing else, that Darwin was right and that emotions are important for our survival.

The James–Lange theory of emotion

At first sight, identifying the cause of an emotion appears to be straightforward. For instance, if you are walking in the park and suddenly see a snake, the chances are you will feel an emotion (fear), accompanied by physiological changes such as deep gasps for breath and a faster heartbeat. These changes will allow you to more effectively jump out of the way. Thus, there appears to be a clear chain of events: (1) we see the snake, (2) we feel emotion, (3) we experience a physiological reaction, and (4) we flee. However, around the turn of the century the American philosopher William James and Danish physiologist Carl Lange, who published separate papers at around the same time, suggested an alternative theory. Instead of saying that we run because of fear (as the above example suggests), they proposed that we become afraid because we run. That is, they believed that the autonomic changes, and the resulting action, come before the emotion is experienced. Put another way, the conscious sensation of an emotion occurs only after we receive feedback about the changes taking place in our body.

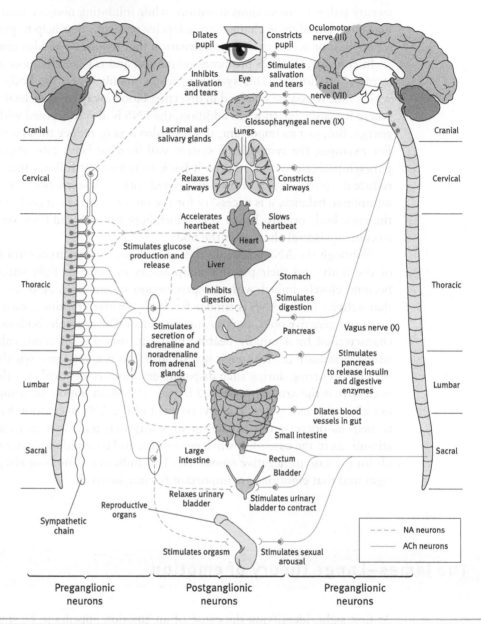

Sympathetic division   **Parasympathetic division**

Dilates pupil — Constricts pupil — Oculomotor nerve (III)

Inhibits salivation and tears — Eye — Stimulates salivation and tears — Facial nerve (VII)

Cranial

Lacrimal and salivary glands — Glossopharyngeal nerve (IX)

Lungs

Cervical — Relaxes airways — Constricts airways — Cervical

Accelerates heartbeat — Slows heartbeat

Heart

Stimulates glucose production and release — Liver

Thoracic — Stomach — Thoracic

Inhibits digestion — Stimulates digestion

Pancreas — Vagus nerve (X)

Stimulates secretion of adrenaline and noradrenaline from adrenal glands — Stimulates pancreas to release insulin and digestive enzymes

Lumbar — Dilates blood vessels in gut — Lumbar

Small intestine

Sacral — Large intestine — Rectum — Sacral

Bladder

Relaxes urinary bladder — Stimulates urinary bladder to contract

Reproductive organs

Sympathetic chain

Stimulates orgasm — Stimulates sexual arousal

- - - - NA neurons
———— ACh neurons

Preganglionic neurons   Postganglionic neurons   Preganglionic neurons

Figure 6.1   Sympathetic and parasympathetic divisions of the autonomic nervous system and the organs they innervate

Source: Adapted from M.F. Bear *et al.*, *Neuroscience: Exploring the Brain*. Copyright © 1996 by Lippincott Williams & Wilkins

This theory is known as the **James–Lange theory of emotion** and it can be briefly summarised as follows. A stimulus is processed by the appropriate part of the brain, such as the visual or auditory cortex, which assesses its relevance. If the stimulus is emotionally significant, information is passed to the ANS, which sets into motion components of the fight–flight response. The bodily arousal is then detected by the conscious part of the brain, which interprets the emotional nature of the physiological state it is experiencing (see Figure 6.2). Clearly, if this theory is correct, then an emotion

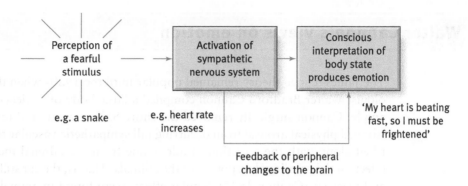

Figure 6.2   The James–Lange theory of emotion

will become conscious only after it has been produced first in the periphery. Running away from a frightening stimulus such as a snake with a pounding heart and gasping breaths will cause you to be afraid.

The main difficulty with this theory is that emotions such as love and hate 'feel' very different. How, then, can we possibly decide what emotion we are experiencing from our bodily reactions? The answer, according to the James–Lange theory, is that each emotion produces a different set of physiological responses. In other words, the theory holds that each emotion has its own unique group of visceral and somatic changes – and, it is this set of reactions that informs the brain of what feeling it is experiencing. In support of this idea, James argued that it was impossible to feel an emotion without experiencing the bodily response that accompanies it. In addition, he also pointed out that people can sometimes feel anxious, angry or depressed without knowing why, indicating that bodily states can be independent from cognitive or conscious analysis. However, the basic proposal that different emotions arise from different patterns of physiological activity has proved surprisingly difficult to confirm scientifically (see later).

One way in which the James–Lange theory has been tested is by examining emotional responding in paraplegic men. For example, if the theory is correct, then reduced sensation from the body reaching the brain should decrease the intensity of emotion. This prediction was tested by George Hohmann (1966), who measured the emotional responses of 25 second World War veterans who had suffered wounds to the spine and lost all sensation below the level of the injury. Some of the men had low-level lumbar damage where most of the spinal cord was intact, whereas others had high-level cervical or thoracic damage where most of the sensation from the body was lost. Hohmann conducted interviews with his subjects that included questions about their emotions, including fear, anger, grief and sentimentality. The results showed that the men with the lumbar damage reported little change in their perceived feelings of emotion. In contrast, the men with higher-level spinal damage with little peripheral sensation reported differences. These subjects often spoke of intense mental emotions with little bodily involvement. For example, one subject described the change that had occurred in his experience of anger: 'It just doesn't have the heat to it that it used to. It's a mental kind of anger.' These findings partly support the James–Lange theory (that visceral feedback is an important component of emotion), although it cannot explain how a mental form of emotional responding can occur without physiological arousal.

Walter Cannon's views on emotion

The James–Lange theory remained popular until the 1920s when the American physiologist Walter Bradford Cannon compiled a large body of evidence against it. For example, Cannon surgically removed the entire SNS in a cat, and found that while this stopped physical arousal from occurring (all sympathetic vascular reactions were abolished along with the secretion of adrenaline from the adrenal medulla), it had little effect on the emotional responses of the animals. That is, the cat still showed anger, fear and pleasure (Cannon 1927). Similar effects were found in animals that had received complete transactions of the spinal cord. Cannon also made an important observation by noting that emotions were 'experienced' by the brain before many parts of the body, such as smooth muscle and endocrine glands, had time to react to autonomic stimulation. According to his research, it took around 0.8 s for the SNS to become aroused by a stimulus, which was roughly the same time as it took a person to feel an emotional reaction. Since the James–Lange theory held that arousal produced by the SNS had to be relayed back to the brain for emotion to be produced, Cannon reasoned that, if this was so, it had to lag behind the beginnings of the mental sensation. He concluded, therefore, that the feeling of emotion was not dependent on physiological changes in the body. And, even if the ANS was involved, Cannon believed that visceral feedback was neither variable nor sensitive enough to provide unique differences for each of the wide range of emotions that animals are able experience (Cannon 1927).

Further evidence against the James–Lange theory came from studies in which human subjects were injected with adrenaline to produce physiological reactions resembling excitement and strong fear, including heart palpitations, trembling, tightness in the throat and drying of the mouth. Despite the elicitation of these bodily changes, the injection procedure did not cause the subjects to experience fear or any other strong emotion. In fact, subjects were able to interpret their bodily reactions coolly and objectively without experiencing them as emotional (Cannon 1927). Thus, a distinction can be made between peripheral changes and the emotion: they do not appear to be inextricably linked.

This evidence led Cannon to formulate a different theory of emotions from that advocated by James and Lange. This is now known as the **Cannon–Bard theory of emotion**. Whereas the James–Lange theory held that emotion resulted from a sequential chain of events leading from physiological response to cognitive feeling, Cannon proposed that physiological and mental responses occur simultaneously and independently. Put another way, he held that external emotional events have two separate effects on the brain: (1) they stimulate the ANS to induce physiological arousal preparing the body for threat, and (2) at the same time, they cause emotion to be perceived in the cerebral cortex. Thus, the initiation of autonomic arousal and the cognitive interpretation of the emotional event occur by separate routes. The pivotal structure in the brain where the two pathways diverged was, according to Cannon, the **thalamus**. This structure was believed to relay sensory information to the cerebral cortex as well as to send descending input to the spinal cord to trigger visceral changes accompanying emotion (see Figure 6.3).

Cannon also believed that emotional events affected the SNS indiscriminately by causing general arousal, that is, he did not accept that each emotion had its own individual pattern of body activity as the James–Lange theory maintained. Rather, the ANS responded in exactly the same way to all types of emotion (Cannon 1927). In fact, as we have just seen, Cannon also believed that the central nervous system had the ability

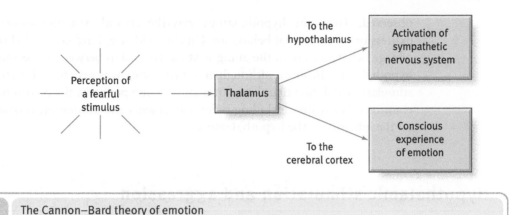

| Figure 6.3 | The Cannon–Bard theory of emotion |

to produce an emotion without requiring feedback from the peripheral nervous system. Thus, according to Cannon, if we see a snake, we run away because we have a mental sensation of fear that will be closely tied to, but independent of, bodily arousal.

The work of Philip Bard

Cannon's theory was developed in the 1930s by a colleague at Harvard University, Philip Bard, who attempted to identify the brain areas responsible for producing emotion. One of Bard's most important findings was that cats deprived of their **cerebral cortex** became highly emotional and aggressive, responding with pronounced responses (arching their backs, hissing, snarling etc.) to the slightest provocation (Bard 1934). This behaviour also showed all the usual autonomic features associated with emotion, such as increased heart rate and blood pressure. However, the emotional response was not entirely normal as it was not directed towards the threatening stimulus and it quickly stopped whenever the threat was removed. Bard called this reaction **sham rage**. These findings suggested that the cerebral cortex did not produce emotional behaviour but acted to direct it to the appropriate situation.

Bard's discovery also indicated that the cerebral cortex was inhibiting emotion and aggression produced by lower, or more primitive, areas of the brain. This was also in accordance with several other observations. For example, surgeons and dentists have long known that some patients show a strong emotional response, such as crying, laughter and aggression, during the early stages of anaesthesia when the neural activity in the cerebral cortex is becoming inhibited. Another interesting behaviour was sometimes observed in **hemiplegia** where there is paralysis on one side of the body due to motor cortex damage. Although these patients exhibit paralysis of the face muscles, there are instances when involuntary responses such as a smile can occur in response to a happy emotional event. These findings indicate that areas below the level of the cerebral cortex are involved in producing some of the signs of emotional behaviour.

Bard showed that sham rage could be elicited by brain lesions all the way down to the level of the **hypothalamus**. However, if the hypothalamus was removed, rage did not occur, although some uncoordinated components of the behaviour were still observed. Thus, the hypothalamus was the critical structure associated with the expression of emotional behaviour. On this evidence, Bard concluded that the control of rage behaviour lay in the antagonistic relationship between the cerebral cortex and hypothalamus. In short, although an intact cortex was necessary for receiving sensory stimulation and directing the emotional response properly, the co-ordinated pattern of emotional behaviour, including reflex movements and autonomic responses, depended on the integrity of the hypothalamus.

Hypothalamic stimulation and aggression

Around the same time as Philip Bard was examining the behavioural effects of decortication, Walter Hess, working in Switzerland, was pioneering the technique of electrically stimulating the brain in freely moving animals. He was to examine the functions of many brain regions using this method and was awarded a Nobel Prize for his work in 1949. Hess obtained some of his most striking results by stimulating the hypothalamus, which caused the ANS to become activated and provide a wide range of visceral responses. Indeed, he found that stimulation of the posterior hypothalamic nuclei caused strong sympathetic activation, whereas stimulation to more anterior regions resulted in parasympathetic activity. But perhaps most interesting of all was the finding that stimulation of the **medial hypothalamus** elicited aggressive behaviour with strong sympathetic arousal, in which the cat arched its back with raised fur, hissed and struck out towards a threatening object with unsheathed claws (Plate 6.1). Thus, unlike the rage

| Plate 6.1 | Stimulation of the medial hypothalamus produces affective aggression |

Source: J.P. Flynn (1967) The neural basis of aggression in cats, in D.C. Glass (ed.) *Neurophysiology and Emotion*, p. 45, Rockefeller University Press

produced by decortication, stimulation of the hypothalamus in a cat with a cerebral cortex elicited an aggressive and threatening attack that was directed specifically *towards* an object such as 'the nearest person participating in the experiment' (Hess and Brügger 1943). Hess called the reaction an 'affective defence reaction' and suggested that the medial hypothalamus was responsible for organising responses necessary for fighting or fleeing.

These findings lent further support to the Cannon–Bard theory of emotion. Despite its small size, the hypothalamus was clearly an important centre for control of the ANS, and the production of bodily states associated with emotion. Moreover, it was also apparent that electrical stimulation of the hypothalamus caused certain types of species-specific emotional behaviour (fighting or fleeing) to be elicited. Thus, in terms of the Cannon–Bard model, it made sense to view the hypothalamus as an 'emotional' centre that received input from the thalamus and sensory areas of the cerebral cortex, which then translated this message into motor reflexes and behaviour. Cannon also believed that the hypothalamus had a pathway back to the cerebral cortex, which informed the conscious part of the brain about the emotion it was experiencing.

The cognitive-arousal theory

An alternative theory of emotion was proposed by Stanley Schachter in 1964. This is called the **cognitive-arousal theory** and its basic premise is that when we become aware of our body's physiological arousal, we seek to understand cognitively what is causing this to happen. By doing this, we generally attribute our emotion to the prevailing environmental conditions. Evidence supporting this theory was provided by Schachter and Singer in 1962. These researchers undertook a study in which they told subjects that they intended to evaluate the effects of vitamin A injections on visual skills. However, unknown to the participants, they received either a placebo injection or one containing adrenaline to induce sympathetic arousal. In addition, some subjects were given accurate details about the physiological effects of the injection whereas others were misinformed or not given information. After the injection, subjects were put into a room that contained a confederate (an actor employed by the experimenters) who asked the participants to complete a questionnaire. Unknown to the subjects, the confederate had been instructed to act in a happy way, or insulting way, while asking the questions. For example, the confederate either started laughing at the questions and folded the sheets into paper aeroplanes, or became annoyed and screwed the paper up into balls which he angrily threw across the room.

When the subjects were later questioned about their own experiences of the experiment, it was found that the group who had been given adrenaline and misinformed about its effects, reported much stronger feelings of euphoria or anger than subjects who had been correctly informed about the drug's effects. In other words, the individuals who had been made physically aroused but who were unaware that their arousal was due to an injection of adrenaline, attributed their bodily state to the environmental conditions. This led to feelings that matched the 'emotion' of the confederate. In contrast, the informed and placebo groups experienced little emotional change in response to the acting of the confederate (see Figure 6.4).

What does this study tell us about emotion? Firstly, it supports the idea that a general state of physiological arousal may underlie different emotions such as happiness

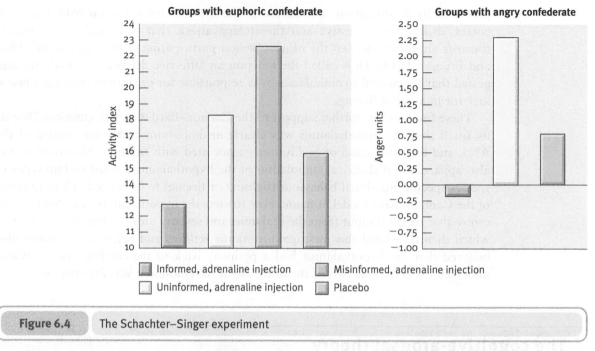

Figure 6.4 The Schachter–Singer experiment

Source: Adapted from S.B. Klein and B.M. Thorne, *Biological Psychology*, p. 428. Copyright © 2007 by Worth Publishers

and anger, as proposed by Cannon and Bard. In addition, it shows that autonomic arousal provides important feedback to enable the individual to interpret what is happening to them. In other words, a bodily sensation such as a rapid heartbeat may serve as a signal to trigger emotion, although it is up to the person to decide (by means of the cognitive analysis provided by the cerebral cortex) what emotion they are experiencing. This lends a degree of support to the James–Lange theory, which views visceral responses as the most important determinant of an emotion. But the theory is only partially supported as Schachter and Singer show that one type of physiological arousal – that produced by an injection of adrenaline – can cause different types of emotion (for example, happiness or anger). In short, the key to understanding different emotions would appear to lie with the cognitive interpretation of the event, including analysis of both internal body state and external situation (Figure 6.5).

Interestingly, there is evidence that our cognitive interpretation of physical states can sometimes be 'fooled' into associating them with the wrong emotion. For example, in one study, young men were asked to walk over a 450 foot long suspension bridge

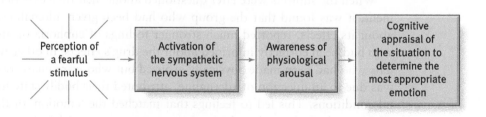

Figure 6.5 The Schachter–Singer theory of emotion

over Capilano Canyon in British Columbia (Dutton and Aron 1974). This experience was terrifying for the subjects as the bridge had low handrails, swayed easily, and was suspended 230 feet above rocks and rapids. After crossing the bridge, each male was interviewed by an attractive female researcher. In one condition, the interview took place immediately after the crossing when the participants were still highly aroused by the experience. In the second condition, the interview took place 10 minutes later when the subjects were more calm. After the interview, the female researcher gave each subject her telephone number, and told them they could phone later to learn more about the study. The researchers predicted that if the men found the woman attractive, they would be more likely to phone if they were physiologically aroused in her presence. And, this is indeed what occurred, with 65 per cent of men in the aroused condition phoning the women compared with just 30 per cent in the second 'calm' condition.

Does the same pattern of arousal underlie all emotions?

One of the main features of the Cannon–Bard theory, and also supported by Schachter and Singer, is that there is one state of physiological arousal which underpins all emotion. But, there is also evidence to contradict this view, Indeed, some researchers believe that different emotions are associated with their own form of physiological arousal. One of the earliest studies to examine this issue was that of Ax (1953) who measured fourteen different physiological responses in subjects made to feel fear and anger (subjects were fooled into believing that they were participating in a study measuring hypertension with an inept laboratory technician). Self-reports from the subjects following the study confirmed that the confederate had been convincing and evoked the appropriate emotions. But, more importantly, seven physiological measures were found to be different between the two emotional states. For example, increases in pulse rate and blood pressure were much greater when invoked by fear than by anger. In a similar type of study, Funkenstein (1955) showed that while the adrenal glands respond to fear by releasing adrenaline, they react to anger by secreting noradrenaline.

More recently, Paul Ekman and his colleagues have shown that distinct patterns of autonomic activity accompany different emotions (Ekman *et al.* 1983). These investigators asked subjects to make a facial expression for each of six emotions (anger, fear, sadness, happiness, surprise and disgust), or to imagine re-enacting a past emotional experience. During both conditions a number of physiological variables were recorded. The results showed that a different pattern of autonomic arousal accompanied each emotion. For example, increased heart rate was found in response to anger and fear, but increased body temperature occurred only in response to anger. A similar pattern of responses was obtained from members of the Minangkabau tribe of Western Sumatra, showing that these physiological changes may be universal (Levenson *et al.* 1992). In another study, the same six basic emotions were induced by showing subjects emotionally loaded pictures while a number of physiological variables such as skin conduction and blood flow were measured. Again, the results showed different patterns of autonomic activity between the emotions (Collet *et al.* 1997).

This area of research, however, is fraught with problems of interpretation – not least because of the difficulty of knowing whether the physiological differences are due to the nature of the emotion itself or to its severity (i.e. anger may produce a more severe emotion than imagined fear). Similarly, there may be considerable variation in an individual's physiological response to an emotional event. For example, if a person has mild hypertension, it might be expected that they will show a greater change in blood pressure than, say, respiration. On balance, it is probably the case that the same type of autonomic arousal does not underpin all emotions as the Cannon–Bard theory maintains, although this does not necessarily mean that each emotion has its own individual pattern of physiological activity as held by the James–Lange theory. Even if autonomic activity helps differentiate some emotions, it is unlikely that it differentiates *all* emotions.

The facial feedback hypothesis

It is also possible that feedback from parts of the body not controlled by the ANS, such as the skeletal muscles, may influence emotion. In particular, facial expressions may contribute to this type of behavioural response. According to Keltner and Ekman (2000) there are seven basic facial expressions for emotion that are innate and occur across all emotions: anger, contempt, disgust, fear, happiness, sadness and surprise. Another emotion often added to this list is embarrassment (Figure 6.6). All of these facial expressions serve important functions. For example, they play an essential role in verbal and social communication by providing clues about the person's feelings. In addition, they may contribute to the emotion itself. One way this has been tested is to ask subjects to perform movements of the face that correspond to a particular emotion, without letting them know what they are mimicking. Thus, subjects can be asked to follow a set of instructions such as 'pull your eyebrows down and together, raise your upper eyelids and tighten your lower eyelids, narrow your lips and press them together' (Ekman and Friesen 1978). This facial expression will resemble anger although it is not apparent to the subject. Alternatively, subjects may be asked to clench a pen between their teeth to mimic a smile, or hold a pen between the lips to simulate a frown.

Experiments using these types of procedure have shown that facial expression influences the subject's emotion. For example, when subjects were asked to judge a series of cartoons, the ones who had been biting a pen between their teeth (i.e. 'smiling') rated them as funnier compared with those who were 'frowning' (Strack *et al.* 1988). Alternatively, when subjects performed either happy, angry or neutral movements of the face while watching neutral or emotionally charged slides, they reported feeling happier when making a happy face, and angrier when making an angry expression (Rutlidge and Hupka 1985). A theory that provides a physiological explanation for this type of effect has been proposed by Zajonc *et al.* (1989) who believe that positive facial expressions, such as smiling, cause blood to drain from the face into the cavernous sinus (a large vein that collects blood at the base of the brain). This, they argue, will cool the brain slightly, which helps to produce a positive sensation of emotion. In contrast, they believe that facial expressions that involve a large number of muscle contractions, such as frowning, will increase blood flow to the face. This, will increase the temperature of the brain, thereby producing a negative emotion.

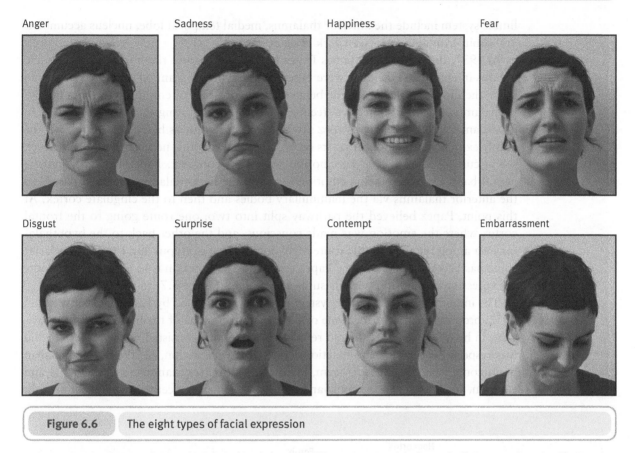

Anger Sadness Happiness Fear

Disgust Surprise Contempt Embarrassment

| Figure 6.6 | The eight types of facial expression |

Source: Based on S.M. Breedlove *et al., Biological Psychology*, 5th edition, p. 455. Copyright © 2007 by Sinauer Associates, Inc. Photographs by Andrea Bannuscher

Introduction to the limbic system

As the work of Philip Bard and Walter Hess has shown, the hypothalamus provides an important collection of nuclei for the behavioural expression of emotion. This structure, however, forms an integral part of a much larger brain region called the **limbic system**. The existence of the so-called limbic lobe was first recognised in 1878 by Paul Broca, who described several structures, including the **hippocampus** and **cingulate gyrus,** that form a ring of tissue separating the cerebral cortex from the rest of the brain. For this reason, Broca called this region of the brain the limbic lobe (from the Latin *limbus* meaning 'border'). Broca hypothesised that this area was important for a wide variety of primitive behaviours, especially those requiring the use of olfaction. In fact, he speculated that in humans it represented the beast within (*le sens brutal*), although this 'brute force' was held in check by the larger expanses of the cerebral cortex, where intelligence and moral behaviour resided. Later anatomical research showed that the limbic lobe was more complex than Broca had envisaged, and contained many other structures and pathways, which included the amygdala, septum and fimbria–fornix. For this reason, the limbic lobe has now become known as the limbic system (MacLean 1949). Other brain structures closely connected with the limbic system include the anterior thalamus, medial temporal lobe, nucleus accumbens and orbitofrontal cortex (see Clark *et al.* 2005).

In 1937, the neurologist James Papez began to recognise the importance of limbic regions in emotion. His ideas were based on the work of Cannon and Bard, who had made the distinction between the behavioural expression of emotion requiring the hypothalamus, and the subjective 'feeling' of emotion requiring the cerebral cortex. In accordance with this theory, Papez saw the hypothalamus as being responsible for the bodily expression of emotion via its control of the autonomic nervous system. However, the circuit for the 'feeling' of emotion was more complex. Papez believed that the neural basis for experiencing emotion began in the hypothalamus but then passed to the anterior thalamus via the mammillary bodies and then to the cingulate cortex. At this point, Papez believed the pathway split into two: one route going to the frontal cortex where the emotion was made conscious, and the other back to the hypothalamus via a polysynaptic limbic route involving the hippocampus and fornix. This latter route has become known as the Papez circuit and its function is to link the behavioural expression of emotion with its subjective feeling (Figure 6.7).

The importance of the limbic system was also emphasised by Paul MacLean who, in 1952, proposed that it formed one of three major divisions of the brain. The three divisions in his view were: (1) the old **reptilian brain**, which consisted of the brainstem and was responsible for vital life functions and stereotyped action, (2) the **old mammalian brain** comprising the limbic system, involved in primitive mammalian behaviours and emotion, and (3) the **new mammalian** brain, or neocortex, concerned with higher thought

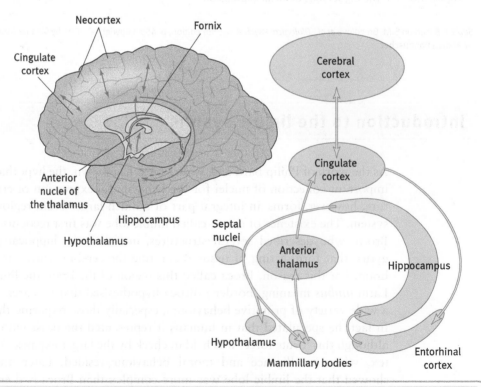

Figure 6.7   The main structures of the Papez circuit

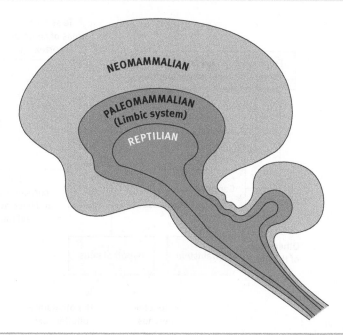

Figure 6.8   MacLean's triune theory of the brain

processes (Figure 6.8). MacLean also saw the limbic system and cerebral cortex interacting together, with the former being responsible for what we 'feel' and the latter for what we 'know'. This view was also consistent with the James–Lange theory of emotion.

The amygdala and the effect of its lesion on emotion

Some of the most striking evidence for the involvement of the limbic system in emotional behaviour came in the late 1930s when Heinrich Kluver and Paul Bucy found that bilateral removal of the temporal lobes, which included the amygdala and parts of the hippocampus, had a dramatic effect on reducing fear in rhesus monkeys. Normally these animals are highly aggressive, but Kluver and Bucy found they became docile and showed no signs of fear or rage following lesioning. These monkeys also exhibited a number of other bizarre behaviours. For example, they were hypersexual as shown by frequent masturbation and indiscriminate attempts to mate with other male and female monkeys. They were also obsessed with touching things, including harmful objects such as broken glass. Further, they did not seem to recognise objects unless they were able to put them in their mouths (Kluver and Bucy 1938). These constellation of symptoms became known as the **Kluver–Bucy syndrome**.

One problem was that Kluver and Bucy's lesions destroyed large areas of the temporal lobes, including parts of the cerebral cortex and limbic system. Thus they set about to more precisely identify the brain area causing the taming effect. This research soon showed that the amygdala was the crucial structure. This area is located in the anterior (frontal) part of the temporal lobe and it contains three main groups of nuclei (see Figure 6.9). The largest (in humans) is the **basolateral nuclear group**, which contains

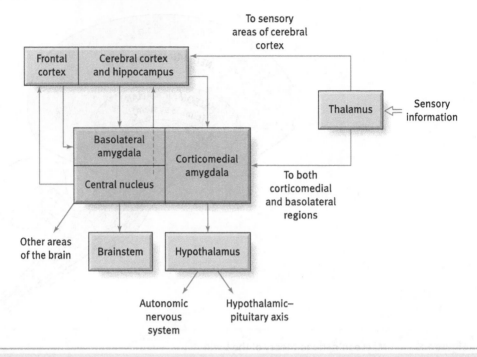

Figure 6.9   The main anatomical connections of the amygdala

the **lateral nucleus**. This receives extensive input from sensory areas (especially visual association regions) of the temporal and frontal cortex. The second region of the amygdala is the phylogeneticaly 'older' **corticomedial nuclei** (sometimes called the **medial nucleus**), which receives projections from the limbic system and olfactory bulb. The third area is the **central nucleus**, which receives input from the lateral and medial nuclei of the amygdala.

These nuclei also have different outputs. For example, the basolateral nuclei have diffuse projections that pass to the central nucleus before they are sent to many other regions of the brain, including the periaqueductal grey area (in the upper brainstem) and diffuse areas of the cerebral cortex. In contrast, the corticomedial nuclei project predominantly to the hypothalamus via the **stria terminalis**. The anatomical connections of the amygdala suggest that it occupies a pivotal link in the circuitry of neural pathways involved in emotion. In fact, it has been called 'the heart and soul of the brain's emotional network' (LeDoux 1998).

It has been shown that several components of the Kluver–Bucy syndrome can be attributed to regions close to the amygdala. For example, hypersexuality results from loss of the piriform cortex, and visual recognition deficits from damage to the inferior aspects of the medial temporal lobes (Nolte 1999). The taming effect, however, result from destruction of the amygdala. Despite this, Kluver and Bucy's findings have not always been replicated. For example, Bard and Mountcastle (1948) found that removal of the amygdala produced animals that exhibited *increased* rage and emotion. Why lesions of the amygdala have produced differing effects is debatable, but one reason may lie with its structural complexity. For example, the amygdala contains 22 separate cell groups (nuclei), and it is possible that researchers have produced different patterns of damage. Indeed, slight variations in the size and location of lesions is likely to produce discrepant results – especially as the amygdala has both excitatory and inhibitory effects on aggression, and these regions lie in close proximity.

Another reason is that the animal's previous learning has a significant bearing on how the amygdala lesion manifests itself. For example, Rosvold *et al.* (1954) lesioned the amygdala in the most dominant and aggressive monkey of a group of eight, and found that this animal quickly dropped to bottom of the dominance hierarchy. However, when a similar lesion was made in the third most dominant monkey, there was no decline in aggressive behaviour or status. A possible explanation is that the effects of amygdala lesions are dependent upon the monkey's previous experience. For example, the aggressive monkey may have learned to become successful at fighting, and the amygdala lesion disrupted this behaviour more than it did in the less experienced animal.

Amygdala stimulation in humans: the case of Julia S

Further evidence linking the amygdala with emotional and aggressive behaviour has come from observations where it has been electrically stimulated in humans. The use of electrodes to stimulate areas of the brain has been used by neurosurgeons in the surgical treatment of epilepsy. Prior to removing areas of epileptic tissue, a surgeon needs to know whether the surgery will have a debilitating effect on language and movement, and to do this they will stimulate the brain areas suspected of giving rise to seizures with a weak electrical current. Since the brain contains no pain receptors, electrodes can be placed in a conscious patient without discomfort (although the scalp is anaesthetised). The surgeon can then stimulate the brain and observe its behavioural consequences. By making sure the stimulation does not cause limb movements or arrest language, the surgeon can avoid producing lesions that will have even worse effects for the patient. The best known use of this technique was undertaken by Wilder Penfield, who used it to map out the human motor cortex in the 1950s (see Chapter 4).

The amygdala has also been examined in this type of procedure, as it is a site where excessive neural activity can cause temporal lobe epilepsy (Gloor 1992). This type of epilepsy (sometimes called a complex partial seizure) does not generally lead to a grand mal seizure, but instead produces a semi-unconscious state or 'absence'. The seizure may also be accompanied by odd automated behaviour such as the person repeatedly buttoning their clothes, or drumming their fingers on a table. Other symptons include visual and olfactory hallucinations, feelings of *déjà vu*, and behavioural episodes of violence. One patient who, exhibited a form of this disorder was Julia S who, at the time of her operation, was a 22-year-old woman with a history of aggressive attacks (Mark and Ervin 1970). Julia had begun to experience seizures with brief lapses of consciousness at the age of 10. In addition, she often exhibited temper tantrums that could result in violent behaviour, the most serious occurring when Julia was 18 years old and at the cinema with her parents. Feeling unwell, Julia visited the washroom where she looked into a mirror and perceived herself as 'shrivelled, disfigured and evil'. At this point, and without provocation, she struck out at another girl with a knife, almost stabbing her in the heart.

Julia was examined by the neurosurgeon Vernon Mark who used electrical stimulation to identify the amygdala as the site of seizure origin. This led to an operation which destroyed Julia's left amygdale, but as this produced little change in behaviour, a second operation was undertaken on the right side. However, prior to this second operation, Mark decided to stimulate the remaining amygdala with implanted electrodes that could generate current from a radio transmitter located some distance away. Mark also decided not to tell Julia when this stimulation was to occur (Julia and her parents had agreed to this procedure beforehand). Although Mark stimulated several electrodes placed in the amygdala, there was only one which elicited rage behaviour. He stimulated this on two occasions. In the first instance, Julia was sitting on her bed. Following stimulation, she showed facial grimacing and lip retraction that resembled a primate threat display. Then, suddenly, she lurched and violently beat the wall with her fists. On the second occasion, Julia's amygdala was stimulated when she was singing and playing a guitar. After 5 seconds of stimulation, she stopped, stared blankly ahead, and was unresponsive to questioning by her psychiatrist. This was followed by a sudden and powerful swing of the guitar which smashed against the wall (Mark and Ervin 1970).

Although these results show that electrical stimulation of the amygdala can produce violent behaviour in humans, these procedures do not cause aggression in most individuals. In fact, a feeling of fear and anxiety is much more likely when the amygdala is stimulated in humans, and in some instances this may be so intense that the patient screams as if they are experiencing the most extreme terror (Gloor 1990). It appears that aggression occurs only if the individual has a violent nature or background. The second operation on Julia proved a great success. Mark destroyed a small amount of tissue that was located at the tip of the electrode that had caused the aggression, and soon after Julia became free of rage attacks and temporal lobe seizures. Julia went to university (she studied psychology) and her improvement has continued up until the present time.

The amygdala and fear

An animal's ability to experience fear, or to sense potential danger before it strikes, is essential for survival. Indeed, one effect of fear is to trigger the 'fight or flight' response which physiologically prepares the organism either to flee from threat or to defend itself against an attack. But fear also produces a highly unpleasant feeling, which in humans comprises anxiety and panic. This emotion may be the evolutionary key to survival in nature, but it can also have negative effects in humans, especially if levels of fearfulness and anxiety become excessive and chronic. Unhappiness, maladaptive behaviour and physical illness are some of the consequences of fear and its associated emotions.

More is known about the brain mechanisms underlying fear than any other emotion. This is because fear is easily recognised in other animals and can be elicited under experimental conditions. For example, fear can be produced through **classical conditioning** in which a rat is presented with a light or tone stimulus paired with an aversive event such as an electric shock. After a few trials, the animal will normally begin to show behavioural signs of fear if the tone is presented by itself. Typically, the rat will freeze when the tone is sounded, startle easily, increase its heart rate and respiration, and show frantic signs of wanting to flee from the situation. When these responses are produced by the neutral stimulus alone, the pattern of behaviour is known as a **conditioned emotional response**. The strength of this reaction can also be quantified using physiological measurements, and this has allowed the neural circuitry of the fear reaction to be understood in some detail.

Studies using the conditioned emotional response procedure have shown that the amygdala plays an important role in the behavioural expression of fear. For example, in one set of experiments by Kapp *et al.* (1979, 1984), rabbits were presented with two tones, one of which was followed by electric shock, and the other with no punishing effect. It was found that, prior to conditioning, neurons in the amygdala did not respond to either of the tones. After the conditioning, however, they fired selectively when the tone signalling shock was sounded. In addition, the rabbits developed a 'fearful' behavioural anticipatory response to this tone. This response, however, was abolished by lesions to the central nucleus of the amygdale, that is, the animal no longer appeared to be afraid of the tone that had signalled shock.

The lack of a conditioned emotional response in these animals is believed to occur because the central nucleus is the main output pathway of the amygdala, which includes a major projection to the hypothalamus. As we have seen above, the hypo-thalamus exerts control over the autonomic nervous system, which is vital for produc-ing the behavioural manifestations of fear (Kapp *et al.* 1992). In contrast, the lateral nuclei of the amygdala appears to play an important role in the acquisition and storage of memory associated with fear conditioning. This region of the amygdala receives sensory input from a number of brain areas, including the cerebral cortex and thala-mus, which puts it in a prime position to associate a wide range of stimuli with threat and danger (Phelps and LeDoux 2005). Evidence linking the lateral amygdala with the acquisition of fear conditioning has come from studies using **long-term potentiation**. For example, if a pathway entering the amygdala, say from the thalamus, is stimulated with a brief tetanus (a short burst of electrical current which triggers thousands of action potentials over a few seconds), neurons in the lateral amygdala will show increased excitatory postsynaptic potentials (EPSPs) for several minutes, or even hours, afterwards. This means that the cells in the lateral amygdala will be more likely to gen-erate action potentials if the stimulation is repeated. It has been shown that long-term potentiation can be produced in amygdala neurons by a tone signalling shock (this is conveyed to the amygdala by a pathway from the thalamus) but not by a neutral tone (Rogen *et al.* 1997). Thus, there has to be a 'fearful' or punishing association. These results show that the lateral amygdala is involved in emotional conditioning and in helping the animal to evaluate the significance of fearful associations with events in its environment.

Fear involves a subcortical route

The most conspicuous route providing auditory input to the brain, and which might be expected to be important for conveying information about a tone signalling an electric shock, are the pathways from the ear that ascend all the way to the primary auditory cortex located in the temporal lobes (see Figure 3.6). In turn, the auditory cortex has direct connections with the amygdala. One might predict that this route is important in learning about fearful events. However, lesion of the primary auditory cortex does not abolish the learning of a fearful conditioned emotional response in-volving tone stimuli (LeDoux and Reis 1983). In fact, the critical structures, as shown

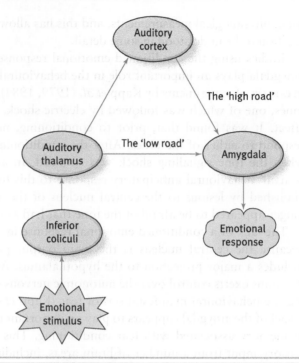

Figure 6.10   The 'low' and 'high' roads to the amygdala

by lesioning studies, are the **inferior colliculi** and **medial geniculate nucleus** (auditory thalamus), which are located deeper in the brain (LeDoux *et al.* 1984). Thus, auditory input does not have to reach the cerebral cortex before reaching the amygdala. Rather, there must be a second pathway. In fact, LeDoux and his colleagues have shown that the medial geniculate nucleus, in addition to its input to the primary auditory cortex, has a smaller but more direct projection to the amygdala. And it is this pathway that is responsible for producing conditioned emotional responses (Figure 6.10). The cortical and the thalamic routes to the amygdala have been called respectively the 'high road' and 'low road' (LeDoux 1998).

This finding makes a great deal of sense. When faced with a dangerous situation, animals require an alarm mechanism which allows them to respond as quickly as possible to the situation. The subcortical input to the amygdala provides this faster response. It has been shown that the medial geniculate nucleus activates the amygdala at around the same time as the primary auditory cortex. This arrangement is one that enables fear processing to begin in the amygdala, before we are completely aware of what is happening to us. Because failing to respond to danger is, for most animals, likely to prove fatal, it is safer to react first by instigating an avoidance fight–flight response, than to spend extra time analysing the situation. Thus, the subcortical route to the amygdala allows this quick 'react first, think later' response to take place (LeDoux 1994).

The cortical route to the amygdala is still important, however, because it enables us to form a more accurate understanding of the fear-provoking stimulus. Cortical analysis allows us to interpret what is happening to us and to make decisions based on previous experience. The amygdala also receives input from the hippocampus, which appears to inform us about the location of dangerous environments. For example,

Phillips and LeDoux (1998) found that lesions to the hippocampus had no effect on a rat's ability to learn a conditioned emotional response. However, when the same animals were placed back in the apparatus where they had been conditioned, they showed no fear responses. This was in marked contrast to normal rats who exhibited signs of fear and anxiety.

LeDoux and his colleagues have also examined the output pathways from the amygdala involved in producing fearful responses (Figure 6.11). They lesioned various structures receiving input from the central nucleus of the amygdala, and then determined to what extent the damage interfered with the behavioural expression of a conditioned emotional response. The results showed that at least two pathways are involved in the behavioural expression of fear. Lesions to the **lateral hypothalamus** abolished conditioned changes in blood pressure, and damage to the **periaqueductal grey matter** disrupted the expression of the freezing response (LeDoux *et al.* 1988). Other pathways from the amygdala are involved in producing startle responses and in controlling the release of hormones from the hypothalamus–pituitary axis (Kim and Gorman 2005).

Perceiving fear in others

In addition to its involvement in the acquisition of fear responses, the human amygdala has also been shown to be important in recognising emotional expressions. For example, Breiter *et al.* (1996) used functional magnetic resonance imaging (fMRI) to measure amygdala activity in volunteers who were presented with pictures of fearful, happy or neutral faces. The results showed that the amygdala was activated in response to the fearful faces, but it was not marked for the other two types of expression (although the left amygdala showed increased activity in response to the happy faces). However, the reaction to the fearful faces declined (i.e. habituated) with repeated presentations. Interestingly, this effect still occurs when the subject is asked to view images that are presented so briefly that they are subliminal. In fact, the reaction to subliminal fearful faces is as strong as the response to faces that are seen consciously (Whalen *et al.* 1998).

In another study, using positron emission tomography (PET), Cahill *et al.* (1996) had subjects watch a set of twelve neutral films, or highly emotionally arousing ones such as scenes of violent crimes. Three weeks later, the experimenters asked the subjects to recall the films. The results showed that increased glucose utilisation in the right amygdala during presentation was strongly correlated with recall. That is, the films which initially caused the most activation in the right amygdala were the ones that were best remembered. These findings support the view that the amygdala is not only involved in the immediate elicitation of fear responses, but also concerned with the formation of long-term memory associated with emotionally arousing events.

Further support for the involvement of the amygdala in emotional memory has come from patients with a very rare genetic condition called **Urbach–Wiethe disease**, which causes bilateral calcification and degeneration of the amygdala and anterior–medial temporal lobes. Subjects with this condition have been shown to have difficulty remembering emotionally arousing stories but no problem recalling neutral ones (Adolphs *et al.* 1997). In another case, a 30-year-old woman known as SM with

(a) The anatomical location of the amygdala

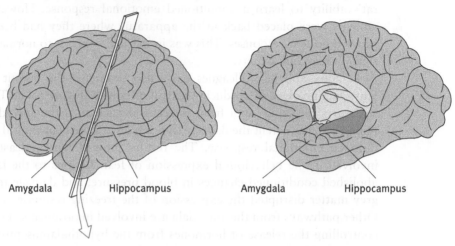

(b) Proposed neural circuits for learned fear

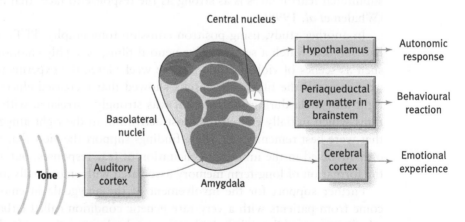

Figure 6.11   The different outputs of the amygdala for the behavioural expression of fear

Source: M.F. Bear *et al.*, *Neuroscience: Exploring the Brain*. Copyright © 1996 by Lippincott Williams & Wilkins

Urbach–Wiethe disease was unable to recognise fearful or angry facial expressions portrayed in pictures but could recognise the emotions of happiness and sadness (Adolphs *et al.* 1994). Another patient with the disease could not recognise vocal expressions of fear, although they were able to detect those of joy, anger and sadness. It is also interesting to note that individuals with autism also have problems identifying the emotions of other people, and they often have abnormalities of the amygdala (see box).

Autism and the amygdala

Autism is a lifelong disorder that manifests itself in early childhood and was first described by Leo Kanner in 1943. One of the main signs of autism is an inability to communicate and relate emotionally to others. Autistic individuals often appear to be in their own world and unaware of others (in fact the word 'autism' is derived from *autos* meaning 'self'). Thus, many autistic people have great difficulty learning to engage in the give-and-take of everyday interaction. This problem can often be observed in the first few months of life when an autistic baby may avoid eye contact with its parents, and resist attention and affection. Although they may passively accept hugs and cuddling, they generally prefer to be alone. This type of unresponsiveness often continues into adulthood and severely affects the person's ability to form relationships. Another characteristic of autism is poor use of language. About half of autistic children never learn to speak and are mute throughout life. Those who do speak often use language in unusual ways, with some being unable to combine words into sentences, and others just using single words. Others repeat the same phrase no matter what the situation. The tone of voice may also be 'flat' and 'robot-like', and be accompanied by inappropriate facial movements and gestures. Despite this, some autistic people have unique skills. Like the character portrayed by Dustin Hoffman in the film *Rainman*, some can memorise entire television shows, pages of the phone book, or the scores of every major league baseball game for the past twenty years.

The prevalence of autism is 30–40 per 100,000 children, and it is about four times more common in boys than in girls. The cause of autism is unknown, although genetic factors are believed to be important as the condition is at least fifty times more frequent in the siblings of affected persons than in the general population. Twin studies also show a concordance rate of around 60 per cent for identical twins, in contrast to fraternal twins where there is no concordance. Despite this, many researchers now believe the disorder could have its origins in early pregnancy. Not only is there an increased frequency of complications in pregnancy and childbirth in mothers who give birth to autistic children, but there is also evidence that foetal exposure to toxins, metabolic disorders or viral infections can also cause autism.

Abnormalities in certain brain structures have been found in autism. Post-mortem studies, for example, have shown that some autistic brains have a smaller brainstem with the near absence of the facial nucleus (which controls facial expression) and superior olive, which is a relay for auditory input (Rodier 2000). In addition, magnetic resonance imaging (MRI) studies have shown that the temporal, parietal and occipital lobes are often bigger in autistic brains, which may reflect immature development (Piven 1997). Despite this, the corpus callosum has been reported to be smaller. But perhaps the most interesting finding concerns the amygdala. This brain region is not only involved in fearful emotion but also in the recognition of faces. Indeed, when 'normal' subjects are given a face recognition task, they show increased activity in the amygdala and adjacent temporal lobes. In autism, however, not only is the amygdala larger in size, but it has little involvement in face recognition as shown by functional MRI (Pierce *et al.* 2001). In autism, this function appears to be taken over by other 'aberrant' brain sites.

Introduction to the frontal lobes

A brain area that is richly connected with the limbic system, including the hypothalamus and amygdala, and which has also been implicated in emotion is the **frontal lobes**. In humans, the frontal lobes are especially well developed and comprise almost one-half of the cerebral cortex (Damasio 1991). Damage to this brain region can produce a bewildering variety of symptoms. We have already seen (Chapter 4) that the posterior part of the frontal lobes, or precentral gyrus, is the site of the motor cortex that is responsible for voluntary movement. But, as we come forward from the precentral gyrus, the functions of the frontal lobes change. In particular, damage to these regions is more likely to affect social interaction, personality and emotional responding. Moreover, many functions that are uniquely human, such as intentionality, self-awareness and abstract thinking, are also impaired (Table 6.1). Despite this, the functions of the frontal lobes are somewhat enigmatic – not least because damage does not have a marked effect on intelligence as measured by standard IQ tasks (Kolb and Whishaw 2003). And, in many cases, people with frontal lobe damage appear, on first sight at least, to be relatively normal.

The frontal lobes consist of several different regions. The motor cortex lies in the postcentral gyrus, and anterior to this region is the **premotor cortex** and **supplementary motor area**. Two other areas with motor functions are the **frontal eye fields**, which control voluntary eye movements, and **Broca's area**, which is involved in the production of language. The rest of the frontal cortex is made up of the **prefrontal cortex** (a name first proposed by Rose and Woosey in 1948), which receives a massive projection from the **dorsomedial nucleus of the thalamus (DMT)**. The prefrontal cortex also increases in size with evolutionary development. According to Brodmann (1912), it constitutes 29 per cent of the total cortex in humans and 17 per cent in chimpanzees. For dogs and cats the respective figures are 7 per cent and 3.5 per cent. Although the use of these sorts of comparisons has pitfalls, the large size of the prefrontal cortex in humans is particularly striking.

In humans, the prefrontal cortex can be divided into three main regions: (1) the **dorsolateral area** lying on the outer surface of the frontal lobes, which receives extensive input from the adjacent motor areas, along with other regions of the cerebral cortex; (2) the **orbitofrontal region** situated at the base of the frontal lobes and which gets its

Table 6.1	Some of the behavioural functions ascribed to the frontal lobes	
Restraint	**Initiation**	**Cognition**
Judgement	Curiosity	Working memory
Concentration	Drive	Sequencing
Foresight	Personality	Insight
Inhibiting socially unacceptable behaviour	Mental flexibility	Seeing the consequences of one's actions
Perseverance	Motivation	Abstract thought

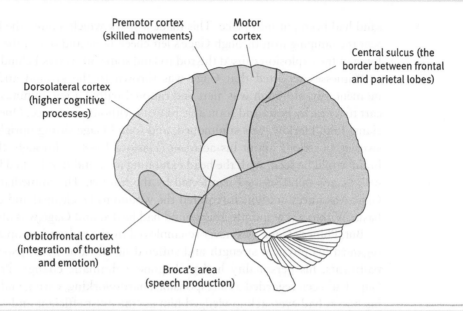

Premotor cortex
(skilled movements)

Motor
cortex

Central sulcus (the
border between frontal
and parietal lobes)

Dorsolateral cortex
(higher cognitive
processes)

Orbitofrontal cortex
(integration of thought
and emotion)

Broca's area
(speech production)

Figure 6.12   The main regions of the frontal cortex

name from the orbits, or bones, of the eye sockets that lie just underneath it; and (3) the **medial frontal cortex**, which lies deep in the frontal lobes and which is sometimes considered part of the **anterior cingulate region** (Figure 6.12). Both the orbitofrontal region and the medial frontal cortex have connections with many regions of the limbic system including the cingulate cortex, hippocampus, lateral hypothalamus and amygdala. These are also the regions most strongly implicated in emotion.

The remarkable case of Phineas Gage

Phineas Gage is perhaps the most famous person to have survived damage to the brain, and although his accident happened in 1848, his case remains a topic of scientific debate today. One reason for the interest in Phineas Gage lies in the fact that not only did he survive a massive wound to the front of his brain which attracted public and medical interest at the time, but also that the injury appeared to specifically affect his emotions, personality and intellect. Prior to the mid-1800s, these types of psychological function were believed to be relatively unaffected by brain damage. However, as Gage's story shows, even the most uniquely human traits are dependent on the brain. His case was also one of the first to spark an interest in the frontal lobes (Macmillan 1996).

Phineas Gage (1823–1860) was a foreman of a railway construction gang who worked in New England. The main task of the gang was to flatten the ground to allow new rail tracks to be laid, and this required rock to be removed from the path using dynamite. Although this was a simple task, it was also dangerous since a hole had to be bored into the rock which was filled with explosive. A fuse was then inserted into the dynamite, and sand poured on top to protect the mixture. Gage's job was to tamp down the sand using a large iron rod which was 1.1 m long and weighed over 6 kg. It was also 30 mm in diameter at one end, tapering to about a 6 mm at the other end. During the morning of 13 September 1848, Gage accidentally dropped his tamping iron onto the rock before the sand had been put into place. This made a spark which ignited the blasting powder and sent the tamping iron through Gage's left cheek bone and out of the top of his head. The force of the explosion caused the rod to land some 30 metres behind him.

Witnesses reported that Gage was thrown to the ground and lost consciousness momentarily, although was alert and rational within a few minutes. He was taken on a cart to a nearby hotel and soon able to walk without assistance. One of the town's physicians, John Harlow, was summoned, and found Gage sitting upright in a chair and answering questions about his accident (Harlow 1848). Although 'the pulsations of the brain' could be seen, with the head exhibiting a wound that looked like an 'inverted funnel', Gage's mind seemed unaffected by the trauma. The immediate danger to Phineas Gage was infection, which required the wound to be cleaned and drained on a regular basis. Within a few months the wound had healed and Gage was able to return home.

But, Phineas Gage was never re-employed by the railroad company. Although he had regained his physical strength and suffered no obvious motor, speech or memory impairments, his personality had undergone a dramatic change. Prior to the accident, Gage had been regarded as a responsible, hard-working, caring and polite worker – and his bosses had even acknowledged him as 'the most efficient and capable man' in their employ. After the accident, though, Gage became childish, selfish, impatient and disrespectful. He did not care for social graces and often became angry or higly emotional. Previously energetic and reliable, he now become erratic and unpredictable. He had trouble forming and executing plans, and lacked concern about his actions. As John Harlow put it: 'The equilibrium or balance, so to speak, between his intellectual faculties and animal propensities, seems to have been destroyed.'

Little is known for certainty about Gage's life after his accident, although he held a number of short-term jobs, including being shown as a freak in the New York Barnum museum. In 1860, some twelve years after his accident, Gage's health began to fail and he suffered from epileptic seizures. Gage died at the age of 38. Although no autopsy was performed on the brain, his body was exhumed in 1867 and the skull sent to Dr John Harlow. He estimated that the tamping iron had passed through the left anterior part of the frontal lobes, including the orbitofrontal cortex. The skull was preserved in a museum at Harvard Medical School (where it is still on show) and re-examined using the technique of magnetic resonance imaging in the 1990s (Damasio *et al.* 1994). This analysis showed that the rod had severely damaged the frontal lobes of both hemispheres with the lesion being especially marked in the left orbitofrontal cortex.

Egas Moniz and the development of psychosurgery

In the years following Gage's accident a number of other clinical cases were reported that linked the frontal cortex with behavioural and personality change. However, not all cases of frontal lobe damage produced these effects. For example, in 1884, the American neurologist Moss Starr showed that damage to the frontal lobe, including bullet wounds, did not always give rise to neurological or psychological symptoms, although he admitted there were cases where victims showed excitability and lack of self-control. This led to considerable uncertainty regarding the role of the frontal cortex in emotion. That was until 1935, when John Fulton and Carlyle Jacobsen described a volatile and highly emotional chimpanzee called Becky that had became docile after bilateral lesions to the frontal lobes. This finding was to have far-reaching consequences.

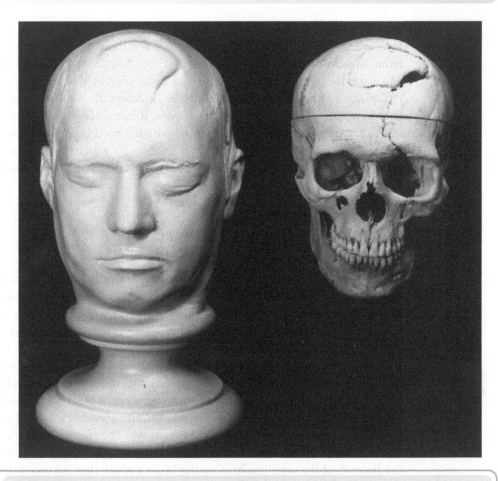

Plate 6.2   Death mask and skull (showing exterior damage) of Phineas Gage

Source: The Warren Anatomical Museum, Francis A. Countway Library of Medicine

On hearing about this work, the Portuguese neurologist Egas Moniz realised that similar lesions could be used to treat emotionally disturbed patients. Within three months, Moniz had persuaded neurosurgeon Almeider Lima to perform a frontal lobotomy on a female patient suffering from severe depression and paranoia. The operation involved holes being drilled into a skull, with pure alcohol injected into the white matter of the prefrontal area to destroy the pathway to the thalamus. According to Moniz, the operation was a great success and considered a 'clinical cure'.

Moniz soon refined his surgical technique by designing a 'leucotome', which was an instrument with a retractable steel wire loop. After inserting it into the brain, the steel loop was opened and then twisted to cut out cores of tissue, a procedure known as leucotomy. In 1936, Moniz reported the results of this procedure in his first group of patients. He stated that the 'psychosurgery' produced full recovery in seven patients, and a favourable outcome in seven more cases. The remaining six patients showed little improvement. But, all patients survived the operation and did not suffer any morbidity. A year later, Moniz reported on more patients using a technique where he cut six cores of tissue from the white matter of each hemisphere. Again, he reported favourable results. His outcomes with mentally ill patients who had been deemed incurable were so remarkable that many other physicians began to adopt his procedures.

After this work, Moniz supervised only a limited number of lobotomies. Nonetheless, the treatment seemed to improve life for patients who had previously suffered from intractable psychiatric illnesses. In 1949, Moniz was awarded the Nobel Prize in Medicine for his work. However, in the same year, at the age of 76, Moniz became a paraplegic when a paranoid patient (who, incidentally, had not received a leucotomy) shot him four times. Despite the accolades, it has since become clear that Moniz was less than thorough in his evaluation of patients, and he provided little verifiable evidence regarding their improvement. Other doctors who examined Moniz's patients described the improvements as slight, and one even called the procedure 'pure cerebral mythology' (Valenstein 1986).

The rise and fall of psychosurgery

In 1936, within a year of Moniz's first operation, the first psychosurgery was performed in the United States by neurologist Walter Freeman and his colleague James Watts. Their first patient was a woman who suffered from agitated depression, and after six 'cores' were cut, she reported herself to be more relaxed and no longer fearful. Encouraged by their success, Freeman and Watts operated on more patients. Freeman was also a pioneer in developing new psychosurgical techniques, and in 1938 introduced a procedure where holes were drilled into the side of the skull, allowing the insertion of a thin knife. The fibrous tracts between frontal cortex and thalamus could then be cut by sweeping the instrument up and down. However, in 1948, Freeman invented a more controversial method. This was the **transorbital lobotomy**, which involved a leucotome being positioned beneath the upper eyelid and then driven through the bottom of the cranium by a mallet (a procedure that became popularly known as **'ice pick'** surgery; see Figure 6.13). Because this method cut fewer fibres than the standard

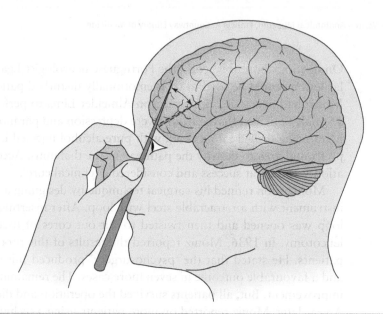

| **Figure 6.13** | 'Ice pick' surgery |

Source: Adapted from W. Freeman (1949) *Proceedings of the Royal Society of Medicine*, 42 (suppl.), 8–12

lobotomy, it was believed to produce fewer side effects. Due to the simplicity of the operation, the transorbital lobotomy was performed on some 50,000 patients in the United States during the 1940s and 1950s (Culliton 1976). In some cases it was even performed in a physician's office. Freeman himself undertook or supervised more than 3,500 operations before he retired in 1970.

The ethical justification of psychosurgery along with its effectiveness has always been a matter of controversy. Indeed, criticism and public debate prompted the formation of national commissions to evaluate the effectiveness of psychosurgical procedures and to encourage legislation. Despite this, the response to psychosurgery was often reported as favourable. For example, a survey in England and Wales showed that 10,365 patients had undergone some form of psychosurgery between 1942 and 1954, and a follow-up study examining 9,284 of these patients showed that 41 per cent had recovered or greatly improved, while 28 per cent were minimally improved. Only 2 per cent had become worse and 4 per cent had died. Patients with severe depression experienced the best outcome, with 63 per cent showing recovery compared with 30 per cent with schizophrenia (Tooth and Newton 1961).

Nonetheless, it was also becoming apparent by the 1960s that psychosurgical operations were having adverse effects on patients that often went unreported. In particular, patients were often listless, apathetic and lacking spontaneity. Emotions tended to be dampened indiscriminately, which led to patients having no social inhibitions, or concern for others. It also became clear that patients had difficulty solving problems, following instructions and making plans. Indeed, many psychiatrists questioned whether the drawbacks of surgery were preferable to the disadvantages. Fortunately, by the early 1960s, the introduction of effective antidepressants and major tranquillisers greatly reduced the need for psychosurgical operations. In fact, psychosurgery is rarely performed today, and in the UK fewer than 100 such operations are normally carried out each year.

The role of the orbitofrontal cortex in emotion

The region of the frontal lobes most implicated in emotional behaviour is the **orbitofrontal cortex**. This area, which sits just above the orbits of the eyes, has important neural connections with the limbic system, including the cingulate gyrus, amygdala and hypothalamus. It also has direct a pathway to brainstem nuclei in control of the autonomic nervous system (Hurley *et al.* 1991). An interesting case study of a person who had extensive bilateral damage to the orbitofrontal cortex, caused by surgery to remove a tumour, has been provided by Eslinger and Damasio (1985). At the time of the operation, the 35-year-old subject, known simply by his initials EVR, was married with two children and employed as a financial officer. In the months after the operation, EVR lost his job, went bankrupt, and was divorced by his wife. He married a prostitute and was divorced again within two years. During this time EVR was tested by Eslinger and Damasio on a number of psychological tests. He had a high IQ of 125, and above-normal comprehension of complex social and political issues. He was also capable of sound social judgement when given hypothetical 'moral dilemma' situations that required him to make a decision about whether a certain behaviour in a given situation was right or wrong. He provided sensible answers to these types of imaginary problems, and justified them with sound logic.

However, EVR's own personal behaviour did not adhere to the same rules when he was confronted with real-life problems. For example, he had great difficulty in making the simplest of decisions, including which toothpaste to buy, which restaurants to visit or what clothes to wear. Previously regarded as a respectable member of his community, EVR was now described by his acquaintances as irresponsible, disorganised, obsessive and lazy. But, he showed little concern about these criticisms. The lack of emotional reactivity was also shown experimentally when EVR failed to exhibit increased autonomic skin conductance in response to arousing visual images. For example, EVR's skin conductance remained 'flat' to pictures of a horribly mutilated car accident victim, whereas normal subjects showed increased arousal and distress. At the end of the testing session, EVR admitted he had not experienced the kind of feeling that he thought he should have (Neafsey 1993).

These results help illustrate how damage to the orbitofrontal cortex causes the individual to be emotionally flat and apathetic. In fact, Damasio has termed EVR's deficit 'acquired sociopathy' because it resembles the behaviour of a psychopath – that is, an individual who is intelligent but has poor self-control, no sense of remorse and responds inappropriately in social situations. Interestingly, psychopaths also show impaired skin conductance responses (Damasio *et al.* 1990). To account for acquired sociopathy, Damasio has proposed a theory which holds that the orbitofrontal cortex is involved in learning about punishing or aversive events that occur in social situations. When the orbitofrontal cortex is damaged, it is unable to provide an emotional response warning signal for behaviours that are likely to have a negative consequences.

This theory is supported by a study of risk-taking in frontal lobe patients by Bechera *et al.* (1997). Here, subjects were given a task where they had to turn over cards from four packs of cards. Turning over certain cards in two of the decks produced a reward of $100, whereas the same cards in the remaining decks had a reward value of $50. However, in the high reward conditions there was also a greater penalty if certain punishment cards were picked (a loss of $1,250) compared with the low reward deck (less than $100). It was found that subjects with frontal lobe damage were more likely to choose cards from the high reward packs despite their very harsh penalties. Damasio has likened these subjects to children who find it hard to resist taking a cake even when they know the theft will lead to punishing consequences. Another important finding was that by the fiftieth card, normal subjects were showing an anticipatory skin conductance response when considering a 'hunch' associated with a 'risky' pack. This was absent in the patients with orbitofrontal damage. In other words, normal subjects had 'feelings' about what was right or wrong that guided their behaviour. This was lacking in individuals with frontal lobe damage. This appeared to explain the behaviour of EVR, who could rationally decide whether something was right or wrong when given a hypothetical problem, but could not implement this knowledge in real life.

Introduction to anxiety and stress

Fear and anxiety are closely related. Anxiety is usually distinguished from fear by the lack of an immediate external threat; in other words, anxiety comes from within us, and fear from the outside (LeDoux 1998). Thus, the sight of a snake in long grass may elicit fear, but anticipation that a snake may be hiding in the grass causes anxiety. Anxiety is therefore fearful anticipation, and this can occur in situations that are not inherently dangerous. Despite this, anxiety is an important necessity of life because it helps to increase apprehension and caution, while acting as a brake against excessive or careless behaviour. Both anxiety and fear share a similar biological basis, with increased activation of the sympathetic nervous system. The physiological arousal produced by fear, however, is more intense (the body is prepared for a fight–flight situation), whereas anxiety tends to produce less arousal, but a response that is more prolonged.

A closely related phenomenon to anxiety is stress. Although stress is difficult to define precisely, most view it as a similar state to anxiety arising from the individual's percep-tion of danger and threat. Another definition was provided by one of the great pioneers of stress research, Hans Selye (1907–1982), who put it more broadly: 'the rate of all the wear and tear caused by life'. Whatever the definition, there is little doubt that stress can have a significant bearing on our mental well-being and health. Moreover, prolonged stress has a predictable effect on the organism. Selye performed hundreds of experi-ments, mainly with rats, that examined the impact of various long-term stresses on the organ systems of the body. No matter what type of stressor he used, Selye observed a consistent physiological reaction. He called this the **general adaptation syndrome.**

The general adaptation syndrome consists of three stages (Figure 6.14). When the animal is first exposed to the stressor the initial response is an **alarm reaction,** which is in essence the fight–flight response produced by the sympathetic nervous system. This primes, or mobilises, the body's resources to cope with a threatening situation. It is also accompanied by increased secretion of **adrenaline** and **noradrenaline** from the **adrenal medulla.** But, this is a short-term response. If the stressor is prolonged, the animal will enter the second stage of the general adaptation syndrome known as the **resistance stage.** Because the animal cannot maintain the high level of physiological arousal produced by the alarm reaction, it will alter its metabolism in order to produce a new homeostatic balance. The most notable change at this stage is that the hypothalamus stimulates the release of **adrenocorticotropic hormone (ACTH)** from the anterior pituitary gland. This is released into the bloodstream where it causes the secretion of **glucocorticoid hormones** from the **adrenal cortex.** There are a number of glucocorticoid hormones, which include hydrocortisone, corticosterone and cortisol, and they have many metabolic effects on the body. For example, they increase the tone of the sympathetic nervous system, and con-vert fats and proteins into sugars to help the body with its increased energy needs. They also reduce the 'non-essential' functioning of the immune system, which slows down anti-body formation and decreases white blood cell formation.

If the stressor is prolonged or frequently repeated, the organism will be unable to maintain this increased level of energy expenditure, and its physiological resources will slowly but surely become depleted. Eventually, the organism will enter the **exhaustion stage,** which is characterised by reduced strength and energy, with increased suscepti-bility to illnesses such as ulcers, cardiovascular disease and depression. Additional stressors, which the organism would previously have coped with, may now result in serious ill health or even death.

Anxiety disorders

A certain amount of anxiety is a necessary part of everyday life. Anxiety stops us being rude to the boss, speeding on motorways, and lying in bed all day. It is also a powerful determinant for making students go to their lectures and study for their exams.

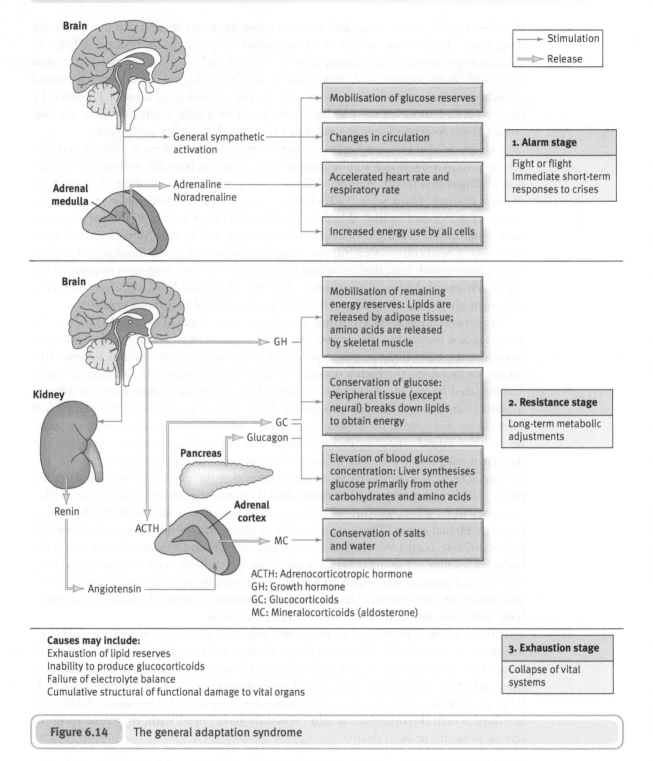

| | Stimulation |
| | Release |

Brain

Adrenal medulla

General sympathetic activation

Adrenaline
Noradrenaline

Mobilisation of glucose reserves

Changes in circulation

Accelerated heart rate and respiratory rate

Increased energy use by all cells

1. Alarm stage

Fight or flight
Immediate short-term responses to crises

Brain

Kidney

Renin

GH

Mobilisation of remaining energy reserves: Lipids are released by adipose tissue; amino acids are released by skeletal muscle

GC

Glucagon

Pancreas

Adrenal cortex

ACTH

MC

Angiotensin

Conservation of glucose: Peripheral tissue (except neural) breaks down lipids to obtain energy

Elevation of blood glucose concentration: Liver synthesises glucose primarily from other carbohydrates and amino acids

Conservation of salts and water

2. Resistance stage

Long-term metabolic adjustments

ACTH: Adrenocorticotropic hormone
GH: Growth hormone
GC: Glucocorticoids
MC: Mineralocorticoids (aldosterone)

Causes may include:
Exhaustion of lipid reserves
Inability to produce glucocorticoids
Failure of electrolyte balance
Cumulative structural of functional damage to vital organs

3. Exhaustion stage

Collapse of vital systems

Figure 6.14   The general adaptation syndrome

Source: Adapted from S.B. Klein and B.M. Thorn, *Biological Psychology*, p. 444. Copyright © 2007 by Worth Publishers

Unfortunately, for some people, anxiety can become so intense that it loses its adaptive function and causes mental problems and ill health. In clinical practice, anxiety disorders are common. It has been estimated that around 15 per cent of the population will suffer from an anxiety disorder at some time in their life. These illnesses can also take many forms. One condition is **generalised anxiety disorder,** which is characterised by such high levels of psychological worry and stress that the individual may not be able to work or leave their house. The prevalence of this disorder in the general population has been estimated at 2.5 per cent (Holmes 1991).

The most common type of anxiety disorder are **simple phobias,** which affect about one person in ten, and are twice as common in women (Barondes 1993). These are called 'simple' not to minimise their importance, but because they involve a clearly defined dreaded object (for example, snakes or spiders) or situation (for example, heights). A more serious type of fear occurs in **social phobia,** where the person is highly anxious about engaging in social interaction. This occurs in men and women equally and may have a prevalence as high as 3 per cent. A similar condition is **panic disorder,** whose symptoms include attacks of intense terror accompanied by choking, palpitations and shortness of breath. These symptoms are sometimes so extreme that the person thinks they are going to die. This can be so frightening that a fear of public places or **agoraphobia** develops. The incidence of panic disorder is around 1 per cent. Another condition which is classified as an anxiety disorder is **obsessive–compulsive disorder** (see box).

Obsessive–compulsive disorder

Obsessive–compulsive disorder (OCD) is a condition characterised by the intrusion of thoughts (obsessions) that lead to patterns of strange and ritualistic behaviour (compulsions). The most common type of compulsion is hand washing, accompanied by obsessive thoughts about dirt and contamination. This may be so severe that the person washes their hands hundreds of times each day, and uses paper towels when they touch objects. A compulsion to check lights, doors, locks or electric switches before leaving the house is another frequent manifestation of OCD. In other cases, OCD may take the form of strange doorway rituals. For example, Rapoport (1989) reports the case of a person who had to take 74 steps in a specific zigzag pattern before he could enter his front door. And there are others who engage in rituals that involve rolling about on the grass and touching various trees before entering doors. Not only is this behaviour embarrassing for the individual, but the obsessive thoughts can be repugnant as well. Yet, the thoughts persist and the person is compelled to perform the actions at whatever cost. OCD is classified as an anxiety disorder because of the severe anxiety that is felt if the intrusive thoughts are not acted upon. The disorder is also surprisingly common. It is estimated that more than 2 per cent of the population suffer from OCD, making it more common than schizophrenia, bipolar disorder or panic disorder.

Clinical trials in recent years have shown that drugs which affect the neurotransmitter serotonin (5-HT) can significantly improve the symptoms of OCD. The first of these to be discovered (in the early 1980s) was the 5-HT uptake blocker clomipramine. This was followed by drugs with a similar action, including flouxetine (Prozac) and fluvoxamine. Large-scale studies have shown that at least 60 per cent of patients show a significant improvement with these drugs, especially if combined with behavioural therapy. The discovery of clomipramine was also important since it indicated that OCD could be due to 5-HT dysfunction. However, the nature of this dysfunction remains unclear. Although some people with OCD have higher levels of the 5-HT metabolite 5-HIAA in their cerebrospinal fluid, indicating overactivity of 5-HT in the brain, this is not always found. The fact that drug treatment often requires several weeks to become effective suggest that changes in the sensitivity of certain 5-HT receptors may be a more important causal factor.

Although much remains to be learned about the role of 5-HT in OCD, there is strong evidence that the anatomical basis of the disorder involves the basal ganglia and frontal cortex. For example, studies using positron emission tomography (PET) have shown that resting blood flow and glucose metabolism are abnormally increased in the orbitofrontal cortex and caudate nucleus. Moreover, when OCD patients are exposed to phobic stimulation (for example, skin contact with dirty objects), blood flow increases even more in the orbitofrontal cortex and caudate nucleus – along with the putamen, thalamus and anterior cingulate cortex (Baxter 1995). As we saw in the previous chapter, the striatum has long been implicated in movement, and the frontal cortex in emotion and planning. Thus, the involvement, and dysfunction of these two brain regions in OCD makes a great deal of sense – especially as they both receive 5-HT innervation from the raphe nuclei.

The above figures indicate that a significant number of people suffer from a serious anxiety disorder of some form. In addition, most of us suffer periods of anxiety from the pressures of modern living. There are large variations in individual responses to anxiety-provoking events, and many people will seek medical help at certain points in their life in response to events such as death or loss of a job. Anxiety is also a prominent symptom in many other psychological disorders, including depression, as well as in many physical illnesses. In fact, about one-third of patients seen in general practice have problems that are primarily due in some way to anxiety or stress (Beaumont 1991). Thus, anxiety is the single most common type of complaint confronting the general practitioner.

Anxiolytic drugs

Human beings have always turned to drugs to help them cope with the stresses of life, and there has long been a need for effective sedatives and hypnotics such as sleeping pills. In the past, alcohol, opium and bromides were some of the substances that served this purpose, and in the early twentieth century these agents were replaced by the barbiturates. Despite their benefits as sedatives and anti-epileptic agents, the barbiturates were potentially dangerous as they could produce fatal overdoses, especially when taken with alcohol. Two film stars who committed suicide with these drugs were Judy Garland and Marilyn Monroe. However, in the late 1950s and early 1960s, a new class of drugs was developed by Roche Drug Company that was much safer than the barbiturates. These were called **benzodiazepines** (BZPs) and they included **chlordiazepoxide (Librium)** first marketed in 1960, and **diazepam (Valium)** which appeared in 1962.

These drugs had a number of advantages over the barbiturates. They rarely caused fatal overdoses, and once the user had become tolerant to their effects they did not produce sedation. It was also claimed that they did not produce addiction or withdrawal symptoms, although this was later found to be untrue. But, most remarkably, they appeared to selectively reduce the symptoms of anxiety. After taking benzodiazepine medication, the patient's fears, restlessness and somatic symptoms of anxiety faded and often disappeared. They were seemingly 'true anxiolytics', and within a decade of their introduction they had become the most prescribed drugs in the world. The extent of their popularity can be seen by annual prescription figures for the UK, which rose from 3 million in the early 1960s, to 18 million in 1972, to over 30 million by 1979 (Beaumont 1991). At the height of their use in the late 1970s, it was estimated that one in five women and one in ten men were regularly taking these drugs (Lader 1983).

During the 1970s, doctors began to realise that benzodiazepines were not as safe as they first appeared, with a large number of people becoming dependent on them. Long-term users of these drugs often experienced physical withdrawal symptoms such as fear, insomnia and muscle tremor when trying to stop their use. Psychological dependence, where the person felt unable to cope with the pressures of life without the regular use of these drugs, was a further problem. Consequently, there has been a significant curtailing in the prescribing of these agents and a sharp decline in their use. Despite this, there are still around 1 million long-term benzodiazepine users in the UK and several million worldwide. Because of their addictive potential, benzodiazepines are now more commonly used as short-term hypnotics (sleeping tablets) than for the relief of anxiety.

Benzodiazepines have also been shown to reduce the symptons of anxiety in animals. This can be demonstrated by use of a **conflict test** (Gellar 1962). In this situation, a rat is trained to press a lever in an operant box for food reward. Following training, the animal is put back into the box and an intermittent tone is introduced. If the lever is pressed during its presentation, the dispensation of food will be accompanied by a mild electric shock. Normal rats soon show signs of 'nervousness' during the tone presentation and stop pressing the lever. However, if animals are injected with a benzo-diazepine, they continue to press the lever for food reward (Figure 6.15). Since benzo-diazepines neither increase hunger nor suppress pain, it appears that they are acting on

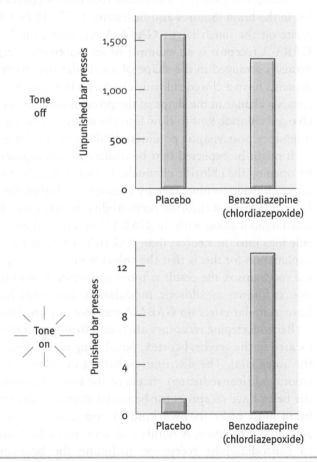

Figure 6.15   The effect of benzodiazepines on punished responding (as recorded by the number of bar presses) in the Gellar conflict test

the conflict itself. That is, the drugs make the animal less 'anxious' about being punished. Similar results are obtained with barbiturates and alcohol – except that these drugs cause sedation, with a depression of responding in both unpunished (tone off) and punished (tone on) conditions. This does not occur with benzodiazepines, except at very high doses, indicating that the drugs exert a genuine anxiolytic effect.

The neurochemical basis of anxiety

The discovery of the benzodiazepines led to attempts to understand how they worked on the brain. It soon become apparent that they had a different pharmacological mechanism of action from many other agents that caused sedation. Experiments in the 1960s showed that benzodiazepines enhanced the inhibition of motor neurons which passed out of the spinal cord to the body's skeletal muscles. It was known that the neurotransmitter released by the spinal fibres projecting onto the motor neurons was **gamma-aminobutyric acid (GABA)**. Thus, benzodiazepines were suspected of potentiating the action of GABA. This was an intriguing finding because, at the time, GABA had not been proved to exist as a neurotransmitter in the brain. In fact, GABA is now recognised as the most common inhibitory neurotransmitter throughout the central nervous system.

During the 1970s, it was found that benzodiazepines have their own specific receptor in the brain (Squires and Braestrup 1977). In fact, the benzodiazepine receptor was a site on the much larger **GABA-A** receptor complex. As we saw in Chapter 1, the GABA-A receptor is an example of an ionotropic receptor consisting of five elongated proteins arranged in the shape of a cylinder that passes through the membrane. These proteins form a closed chloride channel. However, when GABA binds to the receptor, it causes a change in the shape of the proteins forming the ion channel, allowing negatively charged chloride ions to flow into the neuron. This creates a local hyperpolarisation, or inhibitory postsynaptic potential (IPSP), which helps to prevent the neuron firing.

It might be expected that benzodiazepine receptors act in a similar fashion, that is, by opening the chloride channels. In fact, research shows that benzodiazepines do not affect chloride conductance by themselves. Rather, they potentiate, or facilitate, the effects of GABA on chloride permeability. In other words, if the benzodiazepine receptor is stimulated along with the GABA-A receptor, there is a greater flow of negative chloride ions into the neuron than if GABA-A receptor is stimulated by itself. The likeliest explanation for this is that the chloride ion channel remains open for longer. Whatever the mechanism, the result is more pronounced neural inhibition. This facilitatory action is known as **alloseric modulation**. Interestingly, both alcohol and barbiturates have a similar effect on GABA-A receptors by an alloseric mechanism.

Benzodiazepine receptors are found throughout the brain, with the highest numbers located in the cerebral cortex, basal ganglia, cerebellum and limbic system (especially the amygdala). The distribution helps to explain the cognitive, muscle relaxant, and emotional (fear-reducing) effects of the benzodiazepines, respectively. But why should the brain have receptors for benzodiazepines in the first place? The answer is that the brain must make its own kind of endogenous 'benzodiazepine-type substance' that acts on the receptor. A number of substances have been found in the brain that bind to benzodiazepine receptors, including the beta-carbolines, and a peptide called diazepam-binding inhibitor. Interestingly, these substances appear to increase anxiety rather than reduce it. Thus, they may be chemicals that help produce fear.

The function of the benzodiazepine receptor has turned out to be more complex than first thought. While benzodiazepines potentiate the action of GABA, other substances have been found that act on the same receptor to decrease GABA's ability to open chloride channels. A drug which produces an effect on an receptor opposite to the main one is called an **inverse agonist**. In fact, the benzodiazepine receptor was the first to be discovered where this type of bidirectional effect was shown to occur. To make matters more complex, there are other substances (for example, flumazenil) that are antagonists at the benzodiazepine receptor. These can block the effects of both agonists and inverse agonists. Thus, endogenous benzodiazepines may have several roles in the brain, with some having anxiety- or fear-inducing effects, and others possibly acting as anxiolytics.

New developments

Because of the addictive potential and side effects associated with benzodiazepine use, attempts have been made to develop alternative drugs for the treatment of anxiety. One such substance is **buspirone** (BuSpar), first introduced into clinical practice in 1986. This drug has been shown to be as effective as diazepam in the treatment of anxiety, but with fewer side effects. Buspirone does not cause sedation, muscle relaxation, or interact with alcohol. Nor does it cause dependence or withdrawal symptoms. For example, in one study, patients underwent benzodiazepine or buspirone treatment for six months, after which they were switched to placebo. The results showed that 80 per cent of the benzodiazepine group suffered side effects, including the recurrence of original symptoms, which required them to resort to 'reserve' medication, whereas none of the buspirone group reported withdrawal symptoms or a need for extra drug treatment (Rickels *et al.* 1988).

Buspirone is structurally unrelated to the benzodiazepines and does not bind to benzodiazepine or GABA receptors. Although buspirone has a complex pharmacological action that includes an antagonistic effect on both dopamine D-2 and noradrenergic alpha-2 receptors, it appears to produce its main anxiolytic effect by having an agonist effect on serotonergic 5-HT_{1a} receptors. These receptors are found in high concentrations postsynaptically in the hippocampus, amygdala and dorsal raphe, and they act to reduce the neuronal excitability of these structures. Because buspirone inhibits dorsal raphe neurons, this reduces serotonin release in the forebrain, including the striatum and cerebral cortex. The discovery of buspirone has led drug companies to search for new 5-HT_{1a} agonists, which are known collectively as second-generation anxiolytics.

Unfortunately, buspirone has a slower onset of action than the benzodiazepines. It may take up to two weeks before it has an anxiolytic effect, which limits its usefulness for treating sudden or short-term anxiety. Moreover, buspirone is not effective in alleviating anxiety associated with benzodiazepine withdrawal. Despite this, the discovery of buspirone, along with the fact that at least seven different types of serotonin receptor are now known to exist, has led to optimism that more efficient anxiolytic serotonergic drugs can be developed. Indeed, as well as the 5-HT_{1a} agonists, drugs which antagonise 5-HT_{1c}, 5-HT_2 and 5-HT_3 receptors have also been found to have anxiolytic effects and these are currently being tested for this purpose.

Summary

Emotions are an important determinant of behaviour. They create a feeling which signals that something significant is happening to us, and they often propel us into action. When we experience a significant emotion a number of bodily changes take place which resemble the **fight–flight response** that is governed by the **sympathetic division** of the **autonomic nervous system** (ANS). These changes may include a rapid heartbeat, increased respiration, dilated pupils and sweaty palms. The relationship between the physiological response and the subjective experience of the emotional event is still a matter of some conjecture. The **James–Lange theory** holds that each type of emotion is associated with a specific set of physiological changes that are put into motion before they are experienced as an emotion. In contrast, the **Cannon–Bard theory** proposes not only that we are capable of experiencing an emotion before the accompanying bodily changes take place, but also that all emotions produce the same physiological response. **The Schachter–Singer** theory also proposes that there is only one basic physiological response – but we determine the nature of our emotion by combining a cognitive appraisal of both our body state and the environmental situation. None of the above theories is wholly convincing, partly because some emotions appear to differ slightly in terms of physiological response, and partly because emotions also appear to be appraised at an unconscious level before they reach consciousness.

The **hypothalamus** has been shown to be an important brain structure in the regulation of the autonomic nervous system and emotional behaviour. For example, in the 1930s, Philip Bard showed that lesions of the hypothalamus eliminated rage (for example, hissing and snarling) in cats, whereas lesions of the **cerebral cortex** tended to elicit this type of behaviour. These results indicate that the cerebral cortex inhibits the hypothalamus in its expression of emotional behaviour. The hypothalamus is also part of a brain region known as the **limbic system**, which contains a number of other structures that contribute to emotional behaviour. Of particular importance is the **amygdala**. For example, in the late 1930s, **Kluver and Bucy** showed that lesions of the amygdala had a dramatic effect on reducing aggression and fear in rhesus monkeys. Electrical stimulation of this structure has also been shown to induce fear and aggression in humans (for example, the case of Julia S). Both subcortical (unconscious) and cortical (conscious) pathways have been shown to influence neural activity in the amygdale, with the former providing a quick 'alarm' response. The frontal lobes are another region known to affect emotion. This was seen most dramatically in the case of **Phineas Gage**, a railway worker who, in 1848, suffered a horrifying accident when a tamping iron was blown through the front of his brain. Although Gage had been regarded as an exemplary worker, in the years after the accident he was described as 'gross, profane, coarse and vulgar, to such a degree that his society was intolerable to decent people'. Lesions of the frontal lobe and its pathways (**psychosurgery**) have also been used to treat severe forms of mental illness, including depression and obsessions. More recently a number of drugs have been developed to treat emotional problems, including the benzodiazepines for anxiety.

Essay questions

1. Critically evaluate the main theories that have been used to explain emotion. Which do you think is the best theory and why?

   Search terms: Theories of emotion. James–Lange theory. Cannon–Bard theory. Schachter–Singer theory. Cognitive appraisal of emotion.

2. In what ways has the limbic system been shown to be involved in emotional behaviour?

   Search terms: Limbic system and emotion. Hypothalamus and emotion. Amygdala and emotion. Kluver–Bucy syndrome. Emotion and the hippocampus.

3. What are the main functions of the frontal lobes? Using evidence from human data, show how this region of the brain contributes to emotion.

Search terms: Frontal lobes and emotion. Phineas Gage. Frontal lobe damage in humans. Anatomy of frontal lobes. Frontal lobotomy for depression. Orbitofrontal cortex.

4. What is known about the neurobiological basis of anxiety? What types of drug have been used to treat this disorder?

Search terms: Amygdala and fear. Anxiety disorders. Benzodiazepines and anxiety. Drugs for anxiety. Hippocampus and anxiety. Brain and anxiety.

Further reading

Aggleton, J. (ed.) (2000) *The Amygdala: A Functional Analysis*. Oxford: Oxford University Press. Although this is a wide-ranging account of the amygdala and not limited to emotion, it contains much of relevance to this chapter.

Borod, J.C. (2000) *The Neuropsychology of Emotion*. Oxford: Oxford University Press. A comprehensive review of the psychology and neurobiology of emotion with an emphasis on how this knowledge can be used to understand emotional disorders.

Damasio, A.R. (1994) *Descartes Error: Emotion, Reason and the Human Brain*. New York: Putnam. Drawing on his experience with brain-damaged patients, Damasio shows how emotions and feelings contribute to reason and adapative social behaviour.

Davidson, R.J., Scherer, K.R. and Goldsmith H.H. (eds) (2003) *Handbook of Affective States*. Oxford: Oxford University Press. Consisting of 59 chapters written by various experts, and over 1,000 pages in length, this is a comprehensive and surprisingly lucid overview of research into the psychobiology of emotion.

LeDoux, J. (1998) *The Emotional Brain*. London: Weidenfeld & Nicolson. A well-written account, based partly on LeDoux's own research, that explores the brain mechanisms underlying emotion.

Oatley, K. and & Jenkins, J.M. (1996) *Understanding Emotions*. Oxford: Blackwell. A well-written book aimed at general psychology students but containing much of interest to the reader interested in the brain.

Panksepp, J. (1998) *Affective Neuroscience: The Foundation of Human and Animal Emotions*. Oxford: Oxford University Press. An account that shows the similarity between human and animal emotions, and how they can be understood in terms of the neurochemistry and neurobiology of the brain.

Pert, C.B. (1997) *Molecules of Emotion*. London: Simon & Schuster. A very readable account of how opiate receptors were discovered in 1972, and how our emotions are determined by a variety of neurochemicals in the brain.

Plutchik, R. (1994) *The Psychology and Biology of Emotion*. New York: Harper & Row. A wide-ranging textbook which covers topics such as general theories of emotion, neurophysiology of facial expression, evolutionary influences, and brain function.

Rolls, E.T. (1999) *The Brain and Emotion*. Oxford: Oxford University Press. An examination of the brain mechanisms involved in emotion and motivated behaviours such as hunger, thirst, sexual behaviour and addiction.

Sapolsky, R.M. (1994) *Why Zebras Don't Get Ulcers*. New York: Freeman. A beautifully written and engrossing account of the body's stress response and its importance for physical and psychological well-being.

 For self test questions, animations, interactive exercises and many more resources to help you consolidate your understanding, and expand your knowledge of the field, please go to the website accompanying this book at **www.pearsoned.co.uk/wickens**

CHAPTER 7

Sleep and circadian rhythms

INTRODUCTION

The urge to sleep is an extremely powerful one. We spend around one-third of our life asleep – that is, roughly 25 years of an average life in a state of inertia where normal consciousness is suspended. Sleep occurs in all mammals, and probably all vertebrates as well, which indicates that, whatever it does, it serves a very important purpose. And, as we all know, the need for sleep is never far away. We crave sleep if deprived of it, and animal studies have shown that forced sleep deprivation can have fatal consequences. But, why do we sleep? On first sight, sleep appears to be a simple form of rest or recuperation. Yet, on closer inspection, it is clear that there is much more to sleep than this. Sleep is a state of arousal, consisting of at least two distinct stages, called slow-wave sleep and rapid eye movement sleep, produced by multiple neuronal and chemical systems found in the oldest parts of the brain (for example, brainstem and hypothalamus). Moreover, it is clear that sleep is not simply a passive winding down in response to tiredness, but an organised set of brain states whose neural 'activity' can at times be greater than that found during wakefulness. Sleep states are also particularly complex as they affect every level of biological organisation, from genes and intracellular mechanisms, to networks of neurons and physiological systems that control behaviours such as movement, autonomic functions and even cognition. But, why the brain should have evolved to produce this complex state is an enigma. Indeed, one leading sleep researcher has gone so far as to say that after nearly a century of research, all we can conclude about the function of sleep is that it overcomes sleepiness (Horne 1988). Obviously, there is much more to sleep than this, although proving it is not easy. On top of this, we have the tantalising puzzle of dreaming which accompanies certain stages of sleep to add further interest to the mystery.

Hans Berger and the electroencephalogram (EEG)

The modern history of sleep research begins with the invention of the **electroencephalogram (EEG)** by the German psychiatrist Hans Berger in 1929. This machine, which records electrical brain activity by means of electrodes, or small metal discs, placed on the scalp, was developed in his spare time and in complete secrecy during the latter part of the 1920s. (In fact, during its development, Berger gave talks on telepathy as a diversionary tactic to disguise his true research, and only tested it on his son.) The EEG detects very small voltages of neurons firing beneath the skull, and the activity is amplified thousands of times to increase the tiny electrical signals. This is then recorded on a polygraph consisting of a moving strip of paper and marker pens for each electrode placement. In this way, a visual trace of the brain's activity is produced.

It might be expected that this procedure, with each electrode recording from many tens of thousands of neurons, would produce a random and disorganised mess of activity. But, this was not the case. Instead, Berger showed that the electrical activity of the brain, as recorded on the surface of the cerebral cortex, was regular and wave-like. In other words, the electrical activity had a 'beat', indicating that large numbers of neurons were firing together in a synchronised pattern. Berger also identified two different types of activity that occurred during waking, which he called **alpha waves** and **beta waves**. Beta waves were the most common and were characterised by low amplitude and very irregular (desynchronised) waves that varied between 13 and 30 cycles (Hz) or 'beats' per second. This pattern occurred when subjects were aroused, or engaged in some mental activity. During periods of rest and relaxation,

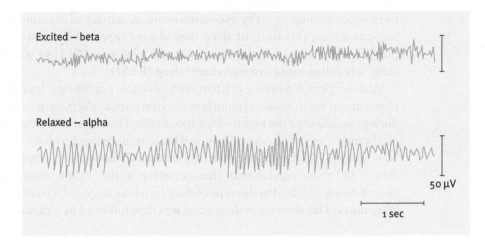

Figure 7.1   Alpha and beta EEG waves

however, the waves slowed down (8–12 Hz), producing a more synchronised 'high amplitude' pattern of alpha waves (Figure 7.1).

The publication of Berger's 'On the electroencephalogram of man' in 1929 opened a new chapter in the understanding of the brain, as it allowed its electrical activity to for the first time be constantly monitored and measured. Sadly, Berger never received the recogntion he deserved for his invention. By the late 1930s, there was interest in the EEG, and plans were made for Berger to visit the United States. However, this was also the time of the Nazis' rise to power in Germany. Because of his Jewish background, Berger was forced to retire from university life in 1938. Suffering from depression, and later institutionalised, Berger hung himself in 1941. Had he managed to survive a few more years, his achievements would have surely led to fame and recognition.

The discovery of REM sleep and slow-wave sleep

Nathaniel Kleitman established the world's first sleep laboratory, in Chicago in 1925, but despite the invention of the EEG, human sleep was not a major research area. This changed in 1950 when a student called Eugene Aserinsky joined the laboratory. At the time, Kleitman had noticed that slow rolling movements of the eyes sometimes occurred in infant sleep, and he gave Aserinsky the task of finding out more. To do this, Aserinsky began recording eye movements and the brain's EEG throughout the night using his 6-year-old son. At the time, no scientist had made a continuous measurement of sleep throughout the night, partly because nobody had suspected that sleep changes significantly after its onset, and partly because a full night's recording would generate more than half a mile of paper. However, Aserinsky soon got a surprise when he found periods in his son's sleep when the eyes darted around under their lids, and the EEG became highly active.

The results were so unexpected that Aserinsky suspected there was a fault with his equipment. In 1952, however, he began a series of studies with a more reliable EEG machine, running more than fifty sleep sessions on two dozen subjects. The results again supported his initial observations: sleeping subjects showed periods in which their EEG more closely resembled the type of brain waves found during waking, which were accompanied by jerky eye movements. Aserinsky also found that when he woke subjects during this form of sleep they always reported dreaming. The findings were published in a short article (Aserinsky and Kleitman 1953) in which the new type of sleep was called **rapid eye movement sleep (REM)**.

Another person working in Kleitman's laboratory at the time was William Dement. His observations led to another important discovery about sleep, namely that it follows a cycle during the course of the night. More specifically, Dement showed that when we fall asleep our brain waves start to slow down and become more synchronised. This was called **slow-wave sleep (SWS)**. In fact, Dement found that SWS not only had an EEG 'beat' which was slower and more regular than that occurring in the waking state, but it progressively slowed down. He divided this type of sleep into four stages which lasted in total for around 90 minutes. This slow wave sleep stage was then followed by a period of REM sleep.

A closer look at slow-wave sleep

The onset of sleep (stage 1) is identified by **theta waves**, which are slightly slower (4–7 Hz) than the alpha waves (8–12 Hz) which occur when we are relaxed and awake. Although the first signs of theta waves signify the transition between waking and sleep, if the person is woken at this point, they will report being drowsy rather than asleep. As sleep progresses, however, stage 2 sleep is reached in which the person is 'properly' asleep. This stage is also characterised by theta activity, although it is also interrupted with 0.5 second bursts of 12–15 Hz activity called sleep spindles. In stage 3, the number of sleep spindles declines and the EEG shows the first signs of very slow (1–4 Hz) high-amplitude waves called **delta waves**. Finally, stage 4 is reached, which is the deepest sleep state and the most difficult to be woken from. This stage is similar to the previous one except that delta waves predominate and make up at least 50 per cent of the brain waves (Figure 7.2).

A number of changes also take place in the brain and body during SWS. For example, the energy consumption of the brain as measured by cerebral blood flow gradually declines, falling to about 25 per cent of its waking value by the fourth stage of sleep. Thus, the brain appears to slow down and become more 'restful'. Similarly, the body shows signs of resting, with reduced muscle tone and inactivity. In fact, during SWS, the person may move only sporadically by changing their body position every ten or twenty minutes. This is accompanied by increased activity in the parasympathetic nervous system which decreases heart rate, blood pressure, respiration and body temperature.

A closer look at REM sleep

After about 90 minutes of SWS, a sudden and dramatic change takes place in the brain's electrical activity. The EEG pattern begins to show a highly desynchronised state in which the brain waves are faster and smaller (i.e. have less amplitude) than before. These waves appear to be similar to the desynchronised beta waves that occur during arousal and waking. Moreover, if oxygen consumption and blood flow are measured in the cerebral cortex at this point, they are found to be similar to when the person is awake. At this point, the person is in REM sleep, and it appears that the brain has decided to leave its slow-wave resting state behind.

When REM sleep occurs, a new set of physiological changes take place in the body. For example, there is a loss of muscle tone with the body showing signs of paralysis, apart from

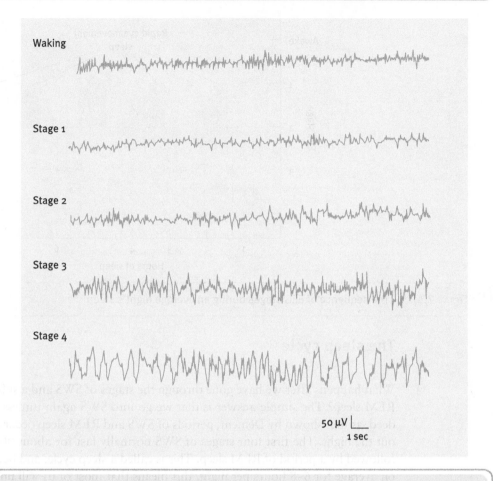

Waking

Stage 1

Stage 2

Stage 3

Stage 4

50 μV |___
1 sec

| Figure 7.2 | The stages of sleep as recorded from the EEG |

periodic (or phasic) 'twitches' of the facial and eye muscles along with those of the fingers and toes. Because the activity of the body and brain are so different at this point (the brain appears to be awake, but the body paralysed) this form of sleep was called 'paradoxical' by Jouvet in 1967. In addition, REM sleep causes increased activation of the sympathetic nervous system, with periods of cardiac acceleration, increased blood pressure and changes in resperation. In males there is also often penile erection, and in females increased vaginal blood flow. It cannot be said that the body is resting during this phase of sleep!

The most intriguing feature of REM sleep, however, is the occurrence of dreaming. For example, Dement and Kleitman (1957) found that when people were woken up during REM sleep, 80 per cent of them reported dreaming, although only 20 per cent did so in SWS. This also helps to explain the lack of muscle tone in REM sleep, as it acts as a brake to stop the dreamer acting out their dreams. The two forms of sleep are also associated with different types of dreaming. REM sleep produces dreams that typically follow a narrative, or story line, with vivid or intense situations that on waking may appear bizarre or illogical, whereas SWS dreams involve repetition of ideas that do not progress (Hobson 1988). Indeed, night terrors in children, or nightmares where the person feels trapped, tend to occur in SWS. However, dreams are quickly forgotten, and subjects who are woken only minutes after the end of a REM episode rarely remember them. It is likely that all people dream, but because dreams are quickly forgotten some individuals claim not to.

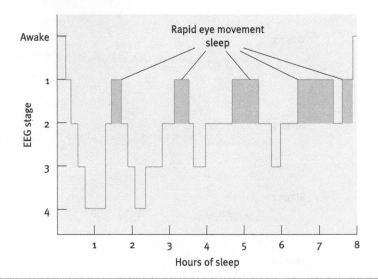

| Figure 7.3 | The sequence of EEG stages during an average night's sleep |

The sleep cycle

What happens after we have gone through the stages of SWS and a subsequent period of REM sleep? The simple answer is that we go into SWS again (unless we wake up). Indeed, as first shown by Dement, periods of SWS and REM sleep occur in cycles throughout the night. The first four stages of SWS normally last for about 90 minutes, and are followed by a period of REM sleep. This is called a **sleep cycle**, and because people sleep on average for 6–8 hours per night, this means that most of us will undergo four of five sleep cycles in this time. It appears that all mammals show this cycle, although its length varies considerably. Moreover, SWS generally takes up a far larger proportion of the cycle than REM sleep. This is also true for humans, who spend around 80 per cent of sleeping time in SWS and the remainder in REM sleep (Figure 7.3).

In humans, the relative proportions of SWS and REM in each cycle change as sleep progresses through the night. Although the REM periods will occur at roughly 90 minute intervals, the actual amount of time spent in REM sleep will tend to increase, from about 20 minutes in the first REM period to around 40 minutes in the last. This means that, as sleep progresses, the time spent in SWS declines. In fact, things are more complex than this because SWS also gets shallower, with stages 3 and 4 eventually dropping out of the cycle. Thus, the last sleep cycle just before waking may consist entirely of stage 2 SWS (stage 1 is a transitional stage that occurs only when the person starts to fall asleep).

Sleep in other animals

As far as we know, all mammals and birds exhibit slow-wave sleeping patterns and REM activity, although the exact characteristics depend on the species. For example, the champion sleeper among mammals is the two-toed sloth, which sleeps on average 20 hours a day (or more than 80 per cent of its life), although its close cousin the three-toed sloth sleeps for only 17 hours a day (Martin 2002). At the other end of the spectrum are cows, elephants, horses and deer which sleep for around 3–4 hours each day (Table 7.1). This appears to be the minimum for mammals. Humans sleep for around 8 hours a day, the chimpanzee 9–10 hours, and the gorilla around 12 hours. Birds are also great sleepers, although they tend to sleep in short periods. For example, pigeons sleep on average just under 10 hours a day, with about 40 minutes in REM sleep. Interestingly, they do not show the pronounced relaxation of muscles which occurs in most mammals during REM sleep, and they enter REM periods for only a few seconds. It is also the case that pigeons repeatedly open their eyes during sleep – presumably to look out for predators. However, when pigeons sleep in groups they open their eyes less, which suggests that the group as a whole may be sharing the task of surveillance (Borbély 1986).

There is also evidence that reptiles sleep, although in the few studies where their brain waves have been recorded, the patterns differ from mammals and birds. For example, high-amplitude spikes have been recorded in the brain of the caiman during apparent sleep or behavioural quiescence (Lavie 1996). Similar electrical activity also occurs in turtles and tortoises. However, whether this is true sleep remains debatable, especially as it is difficult to distinguish this state from the torpor that affects cold-blooded animals at low temperatures (Borbély 1986). In fact, a number of researchers believe that while cold-blooded animals show periods of rest and activity, 'true' patterns of SWS and REM sleep occur only in warm-blooded animals.

Table 7.1	The average number of hours slept per day by other animals
Species	**Hours of Sleep**
Giant Sloth	20
Bat	19
Giant Armadillo	18
Cat	14
Golden Hamster	14
Rat	12
Hedgehog	10
Fox	10
Chimpanzee	10
Baboon	9
Rabbit	9
Human	8
Cow	4
Elephant	4
Goat	4
Sheep	3
Horse	2

It is not just cold-blooded animals that show periods of rest and activity. All forms of life appear to show this characteristic. Moreover, it tends to follow a **circadian rhythm**. In other words, there is always a daily period in which animals are relatively quiet and less responsive to external stimuli. For example, the fruit fly *Drosophila melanogaster* not only remains immobile for periods lasting up to seven hours around the same time each day, but generally rests in a preferred location (Shaw *et al.* 2000). Another example is the giant marine snail *Aplysia californica* (see also Chapter 9). When kept in an aquarium, this simple animal moves around the tank during the day and spends much of its time searching for food. At sunset, however, it withdraws to a corner and remains still, with only sporadic movements of the head and attennae. Even the most primitive multicellular organisms with a simple nervous system, such as jellyfish, have been shown to have regular rest periods that resemble sleep (Kavanau 2006).

Why do we sleep?

It is clear that cycles of rest and activity are a universal feature of animal behaviour, and that sleep is a variation of this basic requirement. But why do animals engage in cycles of rest and activity? Surprisingly, there is no satisfactory answer to this question. From a Darwinian perspective it is certain that sleep has bestowed some advantage to the animals that have indulged in it. Otherwise it would not have evolved. The fact that all animals sleep, or need periods of rest, indicates that sleep is vital for life. This is shown by the observation that nature has found ingenious ways to produce it in the face of formidable obstacles. Perhaps this can best be illustrated by the case of the bottlenose dolphin, which continually has to break the surface of the water to breathe. These animals 'sleep' with one eye open at a time, which allows the two sides of the brain to take turns at sleeping. In this way, there is always one hemisphere awake to guide behaviour. This ability allows dolphins to sleep under water without drowning. Similar forms of sleep are also believed to occur in whales, porpoises and seals.

Most theories that explain the reasons for sleep fall into one of two categories: those that highlight the importance of **body restoration**, and those emphasising **evolutionary adaptation**. The first theory suggests that the body needs regular periods in which to rest and recuperate. The implication is that being awake impairs the functioning of the body in some way, and sleep restores it to an optimal state. This makes sense, not least because the body does appear to be in a more restful state during SWS. But, if sleep is restorative, what is it restoring? Curiously, the theory flounders because nobody has clearly identified a specific physiological process that is restored by sleep. For example, if the function of sleep is to repair the daily effects of wear and tear, then one might predict that strenuous exercise would increase the duration of sleep. However, the support for this idea is not convincing. People who perform strenuous exercise, such as running a marathon, tend to sleep more after the activity, although the increase is modest (about 30 minutes) and does not occur in all individuals (Kubitz *et al.* 1996). In fact, for most people, exercise makes them fall asleep more quickly, but not for longer (Horne 1988). But perhaps we need only to look at the animal world to see a problem with this theory. The two-toed giant sloth sleeps for around 20 hours a day, and is clearly not the most active of animals.

Evidence supporting the restorative hypothesis, however, has come from the finding that, in humans, a huge increase in **growth hormone** release from the pituitary gland occurs during the first few hours of sleep. In fact, the surge of growth hormone is directly linked to the onset of SWS stages 3 and 4. Although the main role of this hormone in children is to promote growth, it has several other important roles in adults, including the uptake of amino acids into cells, along with protein and ribonucleic acid (RNA) synthesis. Several studies have reported that protein synthesis is higher during REM activity, which suggests that this stage of sleep has a cellular growth or restorative function. Further support for this idea comes from the finding that REM sleep predominates *in utero* when brain development is taking place, and that long periods of REM sleep occur in young children when learning is at its most intense. Another relevant finding is that REM sleep tends to increase after learning has taken place, and that REM deprivation interferes with memory storage (Hobson 1999). Increased protein synthesis may underlie this effect by contributing to the formation of new receptors or dendrites – or by replenishing neurotransmitters that have become depleted during the day (Hobson 1995). Despite this, the restorative role of growth hormone in sleep is controversial because the release of this hormone can be suppressed without altering the normal course of sleep (Lavie 1996).

In contrast, adaptive theories of sleep function propose that sleeping has evolved to enhance the survival of the species. For example, it has been suggested that animals such as lions have evolved a rest pattern that allows them to sleep for long, uninterrupted periods because they have little threat from other predators. In contrast, grazing animals such as zebras need to be more vigilant, and they sleep for shorter periods of time. Other types of evolutionary pressure may also influence sleep patterns. Some species may sleep as an adaptive response to conserve energy rather than to avoid danger. In support of this idea, small animals with high metabolic rates tend to sleep for longer than larger animals with slower metabolic rates. Or maybe the pattern of sleep is determined by the amount of time the animal has to spend searching for food and eating. That is, sleep may impose a rest on animals at a time of day when they would not be very efficient at finding food. Although such evolutionary pressures have undoubtedly shaped the patterns of sleeping, it still remains that sleep must provide some essential biological need to justify its universal occurrence in the animal kingdom.

Sleep across the lifespan

Another way to consider the function of sleep is to examine how it changes across the lifespan (Figure 7.4). Although everybody knows that newborn infants sleep a great deal (they generally sleep for 16–17 hours a day), it may come as as surprise to find out that much of this time is spent in REM sleep. In fact, around 50 per cent of a newborn infant's sleep is made up of REM sleep, and this proportion is even greater in premature infants (for example, babies born after only 30 weeks of gestation), who spend about 80 per cent of their sleep in the REM state. While the young baby shows rapid movements of the eyes at this stage, there is no motor paralysis. Instead, there are spasmodic movements of the hands, feet and facial muscles, and occasionally the facial expressions associated with crying, anger and rejection. It has also been reported that first smile made by the infant is likely to occur during REM sleep. As the child develops, however, the percentage of time spent in REM sleep decreases, falling from 50 per cent at 3 months, to 33 per cent at 8 months, and stabilising at about 25 per cent at one year of age (this is roughly the same proportion of REM sleep as occurs in young adults).

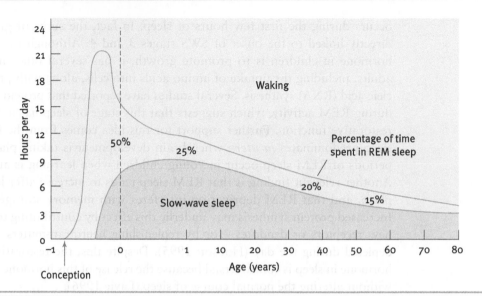

| Figure 7.4 | The duration and pattern of sleep as a function of age |

There are also other differences between a young infant's sleep and that of an adult. For example, an infant's full sleep cycle takes around an hour, compared with 90 minutes for an adult. Moreover, there is a tendency for babies to enter their first REM episode immediately upon falling asleep, unlike adults who enter this stage at about 90 minutes after sleep onset. It is also interesting to note that after the first 8 months of life the child sleeps for only 14–15 hours a day (i.e. they are awake for an extra three hours each day) and that the 'lost' sleep is almost exclusively REM sleep (Hobson 1988).

The fact that a high amount of REM sleep occurs in the first year of life, and during foetal development, indicates that this type of sleep has an important role in neural maturation of the brain. For example, Roffwarg *et al.* (1966) proposed that REM sleep plays a role in the development of the nervous system which is not unlike that of physical exercise in the formation of muscles. Just as muscles require activity to develop properly, so Roffwarg argued that the brain requires exposure to sensory stimulation at critical stages of development. This is seen, for example, in the case of kittens reared in total darkness from birth who show impaired vision and degeneration of cells in the visual cortex. Roffwarg suggested that REM sleep may serve a similar role by ensuring that the cerebral cortex receives 'stimulation' that is crucial to the development of nerve cells during a critical period. In support of this theory, it has been shown that REM deprivation in rats, starting 11 or 12 days after birth, is associated with a reduction in size of the cerebral cortex (Mirmiran 1986). The problem with this theory is that it does not explain why REM sleep continues after the brain has fully developed. An alternative theory is that REM sleep is necessary for the storage of information in the brain to allow learning and memory to take place (see also sleep deprivation studies discussed below). Indeed, it is generally accepted that we learn more during our first year of life than at any other time, and perhaps this is reflected in the time we spend in REM sleep.

The maturation of the sleep cycle normally occurs by early adolescence, at which point the young adult will probably sleep between 6–8 hours each night, with about one-quarter of this time spent in REM sleep. However, as ageing takes place, the nature of the sleep cycle changes. The amount of time spent sleeping falls to approximately 4–6 hours by the age of 50 – and, even more dramatic is the decline in SWS, particularly stages 3 and 4, which by the age of 60 is about half of what is was at 20 years. This decline appears to start in the late twenties, and its gradual loss means that by the age of 90, stages 3 and 4 SWS have virtually disappeared. Nobody knows for sure why this decline occurs, and it could be partly responsible for the deterioration of cognitive abilities that can accompany getting older. Support for this idea comes from the fact that there is often a marked reduction of SWS in people with Alzheimer's disease. In contrast to the decline of SWS in normal ageing, periods of REM sleep are well maintained into extreme old age.

Sleep habits in famous people

'Early to bed, early to rise, makes a man healthy, wealthy and wise' is a saying that many people might agree with. But is it really true? In fact, there are many notable individuals whose sleeping habits do not, or did not, follow this advice. For example, Napoleon needed little sleep. Apparently, he went to bed about midnight and slept for about two hours, after which he would get up and work until 5 A.M., before returning to bed for another two hours. Napoleon is also quoted as saying that five hours' sleep is enough for a man, six for a woman and seven for a fool. Although few would accept Napoleon's views on sleep today, he was not alone in his unusual sleeping habits. For example, Winston Churchill worked until 3 or 4 A.M. and was up again by 8 A.M. (although he generally took a two-hour nap in the afternoon), and it is known that Margaret Thatcher needed only a few hours sleep each night. On the other hand, there are others who needed far longer. For example, Ronald Reagan often slept until 9 A.M., including the morning of his inauguration, and Albert Einstein enjoyed spending ten hours a day in bed where he 'discovered' crucial aspects of his relativity theory. Another long sleeper was French mathematician Abraham de Moivre, who allegedly slept for twenty hours a day in his old age.

What, then, are the norms for patterns of sleeping in human beings? According to Empson (1993), surveys show that adults sleep on average 7½ hours with a standard deviation of about 1 hour. This means that about two-thirds of the population can be expected to sleep between 6½ and 8½ hours per night. In addition, another 16 per cent regularly sleep over 8½ hours and 16 per cent sleep under 6½ hours. However, healthy individuals who regularly sleep less than 5 hours (and in some cases as little as 2 hours each night) represent a sizeable minority. For example, Jones and Oswald (1968) verified in a sleep laboratory the cases of two middle-aged Australian men who claimed that they needed only 2–3 hours sleep per night. Interestingly, not only did their sleep contain more deep SWS (stages 3 and 4) but it exhibited more REM, which occurred soon after the onset of sleep. But, perhaps, the shortest 'healthy' sleeper examined by sleep researchers is the case of Miss M, a 70-year-old retired nurse who slept for only about 1 hour each day (Meddis 1977). Although this lack of sleep is highly unusual, other individuals have been reported with similar patterns.

Nonetheless, all people sleep – although there have been claims to the contrary. For example, Oswald and Adam (1980) report the case of a man who claimed he had not slept for ten years following a car accident (for which he had been awarded £12,000 in compensation). When examined in a sleep laboratory, the man remained awake for the first few nights. However, by the fifth day he became sleepy and fell asleep and snored loudly until his wife woke him two and a half hours later. According to Oswald, this was a clear case of a short sleeper who attempted to make a profit out of his alleged disability. But, the best evidence showing the necessity of sleep comes from the rare genetic condition called **fatal familial insomnia**. This progressive and fatal disease typically strikes in middle age and results in an almost total inability to sleep. It is caused by damage to the thalamus and also causes serious attention and memory deficits. Death typically occurs within 18 months after the onset of the disease.

The effects of sleep deprivation in humans

There have been many attempts to keep humans awake for long periods to determine the behavioural effects of sleep deprivation. One of the first studies to do this was by Patrick and Gilbert (1896) who kept three people awake for 90 hours. The results showed that the subjects were not seriously affected by their sleep loss although there was a deterioration in reaction time, memory and sensory responsiveness along with a decline in body temperature. A more famous example of sleep deprivation is the case of Peter Tripp, a disc jockey who attempted to stay awake for 200 hours as a publicity stunt to raise money for charity. During this time he made radio broadcasts from a glass booth in New York's Times Square and was constantly supervised to prevent sleeping. Three days into the experience, Tripp started to become emotional and abusive, and after five days was slurring his speech and experiencing auditory hallucinations and paranoia. By the end of his ordeal he believed that he was being drugged and refused to co-operate with his helpers. Tripp stopped the stunt after 201 hours of continual wakefulness. At this point, Tripp's EEG brain waves were indistinguishable from that of a sleeping person, and he fell into a deep sleep that lasted 24 hours (Dement 1976; Martin 2002). It is now known that Tripp was using amphetamine to keep him awake during the ordeal which may have contributed to his psychotic episodes.

A few years later, in 1965, a 17-year-old student from San Diego, California, called Randy Gardner challenged the world sleep deprivation record of 260 hours (10 days, 20 hours) that was given in the *Guinness Book of Records*. Gardner was constantly under the scrutiny of two observers and for the last five days observed by William Dement and George Gulevich from Stanford University. During his attempt, Gardner experienced blurred vision, irritability and memory problems. On the fourth day he began to experience mild hallucinations, and after nine days was unable to concentrate or to complete sentences. Also by this time, his EEG no longer showed the normal patterns of alpha waves associated with being awake. But, these symptoms showed considerable fluctuation, and on the last night he went to an amusement arcade for several hours where he played William Dement at a penny basketball game. They played about one hundred games and Gardner won every game! After breaking the record, Gardner gave a coherent and impeccable account of himself at a national press conference. He then slept for 15 hours, followed by another night's sleep of 10½ hours, after which he showed no adverse effects from the ordeal.

The results of these two examples show that the effects of prolonged sleep deprivation can vary significantly and may depend to some extent on personality factors and age. Nonetheless, lapses of concentration, irritability, and episodes of disorientation with hallucinations are all possible consequences of sleep loss. But, most puzzling is that these changes fluctuate greatly over the deprivation period. Indeed, the performance of another sleep-deprived subject was described as being 'like a motor that after much use misfires, runs normally for a while, then falters again' (quoted in Breedlove *et al.* 2007). A different perspective has been given by Horne (1978), who has reviewed over fifty studies where humans have been deprived of sleep for varying lengths of time. His main finding is that sleep deprivation impairs the performance of complex mental or physiological tasks that require a steady or continuous degree of concentration. In contrast, simple tasks are not seriously affected by sleep deprivation. It is difficult to ascribe a function for sleep on the basis of such studies.

Researchers have also examined the effects of selective sleep deprivation by waking subjects every time they enter REM sleep, or in some cases SWS stages 3 and 4. The results from these experiments have been variable, with deficits in some studies but not others (Bonnet and Arand 1996). One interesting finding, however, is that the amount of REM sleep can be increased by mental effort and learning. For example, the REM sleep of college students increases during exam time when they are likely to be spending more time learning new information (Smith and Lapp 1991). It is also well documented that the brain attempts to make up for lost REM sleep after periods of deprivation. For example, a person who is deprived of sleep for 24 hours will usually make up the 'sleep debt' in a day or two, although this is most marked for REM sleep. If a subject is woken every time they enter the REM state, they often show a 50 per cent rebound increase of REM next time they sleep. If subjects are deprived of REM sleep for several days, the recovery may be as high as 90 per cent.

One might be tempted to conclude that REM sleep serves an essential purpose. But, there are contradictory findings. For example, there is a case of a 33-year-old man called YH who, as a young man in the Israeli army, suffered a shrapnel injury to the brain which abolished his capacity for REM sleep (Lavie et al. 1984). When YH was examined in a laboratory, he showed no REM sleep in three of his eigth night sleeps, and for the remaining five nights the average time spent in REM was 6 minutes. This did not seem to produce any ill effects. In fact, after the injury YH completed high school, graduated in law and became a successful lawyer (Lavie 1996). Another example that casts doubt on the importance of REM sleep comes from subjects who take tricyclic antidepressant drugs to treat depression. These drugs significantly reduce the occurrence of REM sleep, but they do not appear to have any any adverse cognitive effects for their users.

The effects of sleep deprivation in animals

Although sleep deprivation in humans does not appear to produce any obvious life-threatening effects, the same is not true for laboratory animals. One of the earliest studies was performed in the late nineteenth century by Russian scientist Marie de Manacéine who deprived puppies of sleep by keeping them constantly active. They all died within 4–5 days (Martin 2002). The puppies also showed a decline in body temperature, which is a consistent finding from similar studies. More recently, sleep deprivation has been produced in laboratory rats by use of a carousel apparatus, which consists of two separate chambers in a Plexiglas cylinder that share a rotating turntable as a floor (Rechtschaffen et al. 1983). A rat is placed in each chamber, with food and water, with both animals attached to electrodes that record EEG and body temperature (Figure 7.5). One of the rats is destined to be sleep deprived and the other its control. When EEG recordings show that the 'to be' deprived rat is beginning to sleep, the floor automatically begins to rotate, forcing the 'dozing' rat to walk backwards or fall into a shallow pool of water. But, during the periods when the deprived rat is awake, and the floor is motionless, the control animal can snatch periods of sleep. In this way the control animal gets exactly the same amount of exercise as the deprived rat but gains more sleep.

This procedure is effective at producing sleep deprivation. In one study it reduced the amount of sleep by 87 per cent in the deprived condition, and by 31 per cent in the control (Rechtscaffen et al. 1989). Most striking, however, are the behavioural

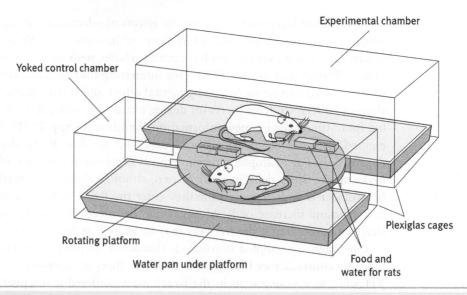

| **Figure 7.5** | The sleep carousel apparatus as used by Rechtschaffen |

Source: N.R. Carlson, *Physiology of Behavior*, 6th edition. Copyright © 1998 by Pearson Education

consequences of this forced deprivation for the animal. Although there are few obvious effects in the first 7–10 days, after this period the deprived rats show marked deterioration. They stop grooming, which gives their fur a debilitated appearance, and they begin to look increasingly ill. The rats start to lose weight although food intake increases. Curiously, their metabolic rate increases while body temperature declines. If sleep deprivation is continued, the animals die within 2–3 weeks of the ordeal (Rechtschaffen *et al.* 1983).

What is the cause of death in these animals? Surprisingly, there is no obvious answer. For example, when various body organs such as brain, liver, spleen, stomach, thyroid and thymus are examined, no difference is found between the two groups of animals. There is, however, an increase in the size of the adrenal glands and release of cortisol in the final few days before death in the deprived rats, which is accompanied by a drop in core body temperature. In fact, Rechtschaffen initially believed that the sleep-deprived animals were dying because they could not maintain their body temperature. But, when these rats were kept warm with increased external heating they still died. Another possible cause is the increase in body metabolism, which might be the reason why the deprived rat eats more. Nonetheless, if the rats are given a high-calorie diet, to compensate for the increased metabolism, it makes no difference. Thus, the cause of death of forced sleep deprivation is not known. Interestingly, if the animals are removed from the apparatus when close to death and allowed to sleep, they quickly recover. They also show a huge increase in REM sleep, which can be ten times greater than normal.

Some scientists have speculated that sleep deprivation is fatal because it produces a decline in the body's immune defences. In support of this, it has been found that rats subjected to severe sleep deprivation have lymph nodes that are heavily infected with dangerous bacteria that have migrated from the intestines (Everson and Toth 2000). There is also evidence that the overall functioning of the immune system is seriously compromised by sleep deprivation. Although the role of infection as cause of death in sleep-deprived animals is controversial, sleep loss has been shown to impair the human immune system. For example, even moderate sleep loss lasting two or three days produces a marked decline in the production of interleukin-2, which in turn affects the ability of lymphocytes and natural killer cells to fight off invading bacteria and viruses (Irwin *et al.* 1996).

Brain mechanisms of sleep

Until the late 1930s it was widely believed that sleep was a passive process that occurred in response to sensory deprivation. In short, the idea was simple: deprive the brain of sensory input and the animal will fall into a resting state (i.e. sleep). In humans, the onset of sleep was therefore attributed to the gradual decay in the level of stimulation reaching the brain that occurs over the course of the day. One of the first to test this idea was the Belgium neurophysiologist Frédéric Bremer (1937) who made a complete cut in the upper brainstem of cats (called a *cerveau isolé* preparation), which eliminated most of the sensory input getting to the higher reaches of the brain (Figure 7.6). If the passive theory was correct then this lesion should produce sleep. Indeed, this appeared to be the case, as the lesioned animals appeared to be continuously asleep, and their EEG exhibited slow, large and synchronised waves that resembled a sleep pattern.

However, Bremer soon discovered a problem with his theory. When he made a cut at the base of the brainstem where it joined the spinal cord (called *encéphale isolé*), he found that the pattern of sleep was not the same as produced by the *cerveau isolé* lesion. Rather, these animals were hypervigilant and showed almost

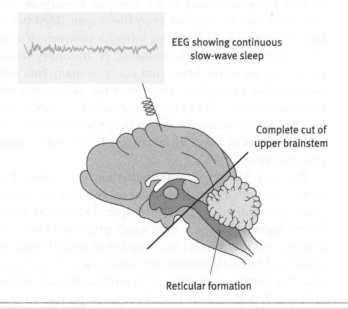

EEG showing continuous slow-wave sleep

Complete cut of upper brainstem

Reticular formation

Figure 7.6   The *cerveau isolé* preparation

uninterrupted wakefulness. This was despite being deprived of almost all sensory input (in fact, the only difference between the *cerveau* and *encéphale isolé* preparations is that the former does not sever input from the trigeminal nerve, which provides tactile information from the head and face). Thus, instead of sleep being a passive 'winding down' process to reduce external stimulation, these findings indicated that sleep was actively produced by the brain, and that the mechanism for producing sleep and wakefulness was located somewhere between the two transections in the brainstem.

Further support for this idea came from Lindsley *et al.* (1949) who made lesions to the upper part of the reticular formation, but unlike those produced by Bremer spared the ascending sensory (visual, auditory etc.) pathways to the cortex. In other words, these lesions selectively severed the connections of the brainstem with the rest of the forebrain but did not stop the sensory input from the body. This lesion was found to produce EEG activity characteristic of deep sleep. Thus, a lack of sensory input to the cortex could not explain sleeping. The importance of the reticular formation for sleep was further shown when researchers began to undertake electrical stimulation of the reticular formation (Figure 7.8). This was found to produce an array of EEG changes, including those found in both sleep and wakefulness (Moruzzi and Magoun 1949). In short, these findings indicated that it was the reticular formation which provided the critical site in the active control of sleep.

The ascending reticular activating system

The brainstem is a tubular structure that enters the brain from the spinal cord, and is composed of the medulla oblongata, pons and midbrain. Running through the inner core of these structures is the **reticular formation,** a complex network of neurons (*reticulum* means net) and axon fibres embedded between a number of functionally important nuclei. In fact, this intricate network of neurons extends from the spinal cord all the way up to thalamus. In evolutionary terms, the reticular formation is a primitive part of the brain that controls many functions essential for survival. This includes, for example, control over the autonomic nervous system, many vital reflexes and some types of species-specific behaviour. But, the reticular formation has another vital function: it controls the level of arousal in other areas of the brain, including that of the cerebral cortex. In this way it regulates sleep, waking and even consciousness.

But, how does the reticular formation affect arousal in other areas of the brain? The answer lies with a type of reticular neuron that has a long axon that allows it to ascend from the brainstem to reach widespread regions of the forebrain. In fact, these axons form a highly complex system which originates from several areas of the reticular formation, and they project to a number of crucial areas involved in sleep, including the thalamus hypothalamus and cerebral cortex. Moreover, depending on their site of origin, they contain a number of neurotransmitters, including noradrenaline, serotonin and acetylcholine. This large brainstem projection is called the **ascending reticular activating system,** and it is responsible for generating states of arousal in the forebrain (as revealed by the EEG) which govern sleep and wakefulness (Figure 7.8).

(a)

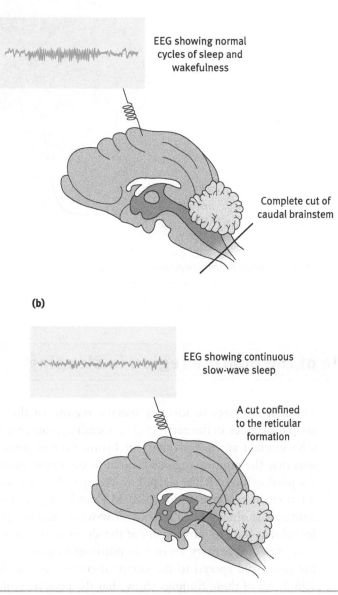

EEG showing normal cycles of sleep and wakefulness

Complete cut of caudal brainstem

(b)

EEG showing continuous slow-wave sleep

A cut confined to the reticular formation

| Figure 7.7 | Two other types of brainstem lesion and their effect on sleep |

By the 1960s, lesion and stimulation experiments had shown that certain areas of the reticular formation were actively involved in producing sleep and that it was affecting levels of arousal in the forebrain by the ascending reticular system. There was even evidence that electrical stimulation of some regions in the reticular formation could put a laboratory animal to asleep (Magnes *et al.* 1961). The evidence was strong, therefore, that the reticular formation contained centres that governed wakefulness and sleep. But, where were these centres located exactly? Investigators set about trying to locate them more precisely.

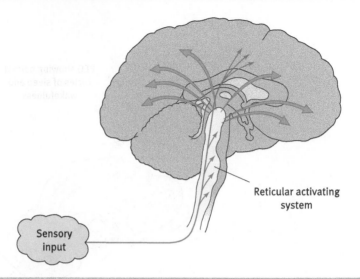

Reticular activating
system

Sensory
input

Figure 7.8 The ascending reticular system

The role of the pontine region in sleeping

The first attempts to identify specific regions of the reticular formation involved in sleep took place in the early 1960s. A leading pioneer was the Frenchman Michel Jouvet who worked at the University of Lyons. One of Jouvet's most important discoveries was that the **pontine region**, located in the upper brainstem, was a crucial region for the production of REM sleep. For example, Jouvet found that electrical stimulation of the pons in cats could induce REM sleep lasting as long as 15 minutes, provided the animal was already well into its slow-wave sleeping phase (Jouvet 1962). Jouvet also found that the eye movements of the sleeping animal occurred when a sequential pattern of neural activity known as **ponto-geniculo-occipital (PGO) waves** first arose in the pons, and spread to the occipital cortex, via the midbrain and thalamus (Jouvet 1967). All of these findings show that the pontine region of the brainstem is involved in the production of REM sleep. This was also confirmed when Jouvet found that bilateral damage to this area produced a marked decrease in the amount of REM sleep that lasted between 5 and 10 days (Jouvet 1967).

The pons (the word is derived from the Latin word for 'bridge' which refers to its position that connects the two sides of the cerebellum) lies above the medulla and below the midbrain. It also contains a great variety of fibre tracts and nuclei associated with a wide range of functions. The next step for Jouvet was to locate more precisely the areas in the pons where REM sleep was produced. At this point, Jouvet's search was assisted by the development of histofluorescent techniques (see also Chapter 1) that allowed certain neurotransmitters in the brain to be visualised, along with their axonal pathways. Two transmitters mapped out in this way were **noradrenaline** and **serotonin**. Although fibres containing these neurochemicals were found to innervate large areas of the brain, including the cerebral cortex, limbic system and basal ganglia, their site of origin was traced to small structures in the pons. The site of noradrenaline-containing fibres was a tiny purple nucleus called the **locus coeruleus** and the site of serotonin fibres was the **raphe nuclei** (see Figure 1.28, p. 51).

The new techniques also allowed the raphe and locus coeruleus to be lesioned with a reasonable degree of precision. When Jouvet destroyed the raphe in cats, he found that it caused marked insomnia that lasted for 3–4 days (Jouvet and Renault 1966). Although there was some partial recovery of sleep after this period, it never exceeded 2½ hours each day (cats normally sleep about 14 hours a day). The raphe was further linked with sleep when it was found that drugs such as p-chlorphenylalanine, which blocked the synthesis of serotonin thereby causing its depletion in the brain, produced a dramatic reduction in SWS sleep. Such animals did not regain normal patterns of sleep for some 10 days after the injection. This effect could be reversed, however, within a few minutes by an injection of the serotonin precursor **5-hydroxytryptophan (5-HPT)**, which restored serotonin levels in the brain. Jouvet noted that the amount of serotonin loss was also highly correlated with the amount of sleep loss. Thus, the evidence pointed to the raphe as an area for the promotion of SWS.

Another area that was implicated in sleep by Jouvet was the locus coeruleus. For example, in the 1960s, Jouvet found that lesions of the dorsolateral pons which included the locus coeruleus abolished REM sleep (Jouvet and Delorme 1965). In addition, electrical stimulation of the locus coeruleus produced an 'aroused' EEG pattern that in some ways resembled the brain waves found in REM sleep. Hence, Jouvet suggested that noradrenaline may play a role in producing REM sleep that is similar to the one that serotonin plays in bringing about SWS. In fact, he went so far as to call the locus coeruleus the 'REM executive' (Jouvet 1972).

Acetylcholine and the generation of REM sleep

Although Jouvet identified the locus coeruleus as having an important role in the generation of REM sleep, and claimed that lesions to this structure prevented REM sleep, this idea was disproved by subsequent research. Importantly, it was found that precise lesions to the locus coeruleus using the neurotoxin 6-hydroxydopamine, which selectively destroys the cell bodies of noradrenergic neurons but spares axons passing through this area, does not abolish REM sleep (Hartmann *et al.* 1971). Despite this, it was clear that several areas lying close to the locus coeruleus were involved in REM sleep. For example, Jouvet (1979) lesioned an area just below the locus coeruleus called the **subcoerulear region** which has axons that travel to the **magnocellular nucleus** located in the medial medulla. As a result of this surgery, the cat entered REM sleep without any loss of muscle tone. In other words, this area appears to be the one that causes muscle paralysis in REM sleep and stops us acting out our dreams. In fact, Jouvet's cats exhibited a set of very complex behaviours in REM sleep which included forms of attack, defence and exploration. Although the cats were sleeping they appeared to be awake.

A number of other studies showed that an important area for the production of REM sleep lay in the **medial pontine reticular formation** (Figure 7.9). Because this region contains some very large neurons it is sometimes referred to as the **gigantocellular tegmental field (GTF)**. Cellular recording studies have found that neurons in this region are 'quiet' during waking and SWS, but start to show increased activity just prior to REM sleep. This is followed by neurons exhibiting a high rate of discharge

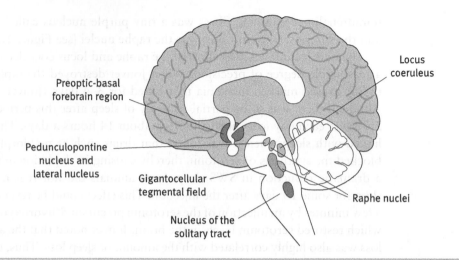

Locus
coeruleus

Preoptic-basal
forebrain region

Pedunculopontine
nucleus and
lateral nucleus

Gigantocellular
tegmental field

Raphe nuclei

Nucleus of the
solitary tract

Figure 7.9   Some of the most important brain regions involved in the regulation of sleep

throughout the REM period. The GTF is also a crucial site for the generation of PGO waves (McCarley *et al.* 1995) and it has been shown that large lesions of this region disrupt REM sleep while leaving SWS intact (Jones 1979). Despite this, kainic acid lesions, which selectively destroy the gigantocellular cells while sparing axons that pass through the region from other areas, do not completely prevent REM sleep.

The axons of neurons in the GTF provide a major component of the ascending reticular formation, and they release the neurotransmitter **acetylcholine** into forebrain regions. In addition, the GTF cells located in the pons are also sensitive to acetylcholine. Indeed, it has long been known that cholinergic drugs can induce sleep states, and an important area for this effect is the pons. For example, injections of the muscarinic cholinergic agonist **carbachol** into the GTF not only initiates REM sleep but dramatically increases its duration (McCarley *et al.* 1995). Conversely, the muscarinic antagonist atropine, which is a poison derived from the deadly nightshade plant *Atropa belladonna*, decreases REM sleep activity when given systemically. But, perhaps more importantly, *in vivo* measurements using microdialysis techniques have shown that levels of acetylcholine increase in the GTF during REM sleep (Kodama *et al.* 1990).

It is now known that the neurons of the GTF receive cholinergic projections from two nearby areas in the pons called the **laterodorsal tegmental nucleus (LTN)** and the **pedunculopontine tegmental nucleus (PTN)** (Figure 7.10). These are sometimes grouped together and referred to as the **peribrachial area**. Both the LTN and PTN exercise important regulatory control over neural activity in the GTF. For example, it has been shown that there are 'REM on' cells in the LTN and PTN that fire only during REM sleep (Steriade *et al.* 1990). Kainic acid lesions of these two areas also significantly reduce the amount of REM sleep (Webster and Jones 1988). The importance of the LTN and PTN in REM sleep is further emphasised by the fact that both receive projections from the raphe and locus coeruleus. In fact, serotonin from the dorsal raphe has a marked suppressant effect on the activity of neurons in the LTN and PTN. Although both the LTN and PTN project to the GTF, they also have independent projections to the forebrain, including those to the thalamus, hypothalamus and basal forebrain. This may explain why kainic acid lesions of the GTF, which spare its fibres of passage, do not abolish REM sleep.

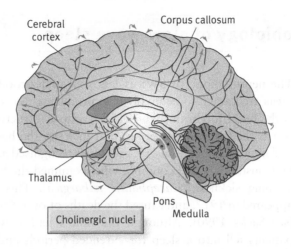

Cerebral cortex

Corpus callosum

Thalamus

Pons

Medulla

Cholinergic nuclei

Figure 7.10	Cholinergic pathways

Source: D. Purves *et al.*, *Neuroscience*, 3rd edition, p. 677. Copyright © 2004 by Sinauer Associates, Inc.

What, then, is the role of the locus coeruleus and raphe in sleep? One way this question has been addressed is to measure the firing rates of their neurons with microelectrodes during sleep and wakefulness. This type of research has shown that neural activity in the raphe and locus coeruleus is actually highest during waking. It declines during SWS, and is non-existent during REM sleep (Hobson *et al.* 1975). In contrast, neural activity in the GTF increases during REM sleep (and the same occurs for the LTN and PTN) (Table 7.2). This has led to the **reciprocal interaction model of REM sleep**, which proposes that the cholinergic LTN and PTN neurons become excited as activity in the raphe and locus coeruleus declines (McCarley and Hobson 1975). Thus, the raphe and locus coeruleus appear to be structures that instigate REM sleep by their facilitatory effect (disinhibition) on cholinergic neurons in the LTN and PTN. When the cholinergic neurons in the LTN and PTN are active, they stimulate the production of REM sleep by 'turning on' neurons in the GTF, while inhibiting those in the raphe and locus coeruleus (see McCarley 1995).

Table 7.2	Response rates of neurons in three brainstem areas importantly involved in sleep		
	Waking	**SWS**	**REM Sleep**
Locus coeruleus	Slow and steady activity (about 3 spikes per second)	Decreased	Nearly zero
Dorsal raphe	Slow and steady activity (about 3 spikes per second)	Decreased	Nearly zero
Gigantocellular tegmental field	Very slow activity (a spike every few seconds)	Increased	Fast (about 10 spikes per second)

The neurobiology of slow-wave sleep

The neurobiology of SWS is less well understood. Nonetheless, a number of brain areas are known to be involved in producing this form of sleep. One important region is the **basal forebrain,** which is a group of structures lying above the brainstem, towards the front of the brain, that includes the **basal nucleus, substantia innominata** and **hypothalamus.** This area was first recognised as having a role in sleep in the 1920s by Constantin von Economo, who examined the brains of people that had died from sleeping sickness (*Encephalitis lethargica*). This was an illness that mysteriously appeared in 1917, and caused the deaths of over 5 million people over a ten-year period (see Sacks 1990). Although the illness had varying effects, in one-third of cases patients fell into a sleep for extended periods and from which they could rarely be woken. Indeed, many slept for 20 hours or more per day, waking only briefly to eat and drink. When Economo examined the brains of these victims he found they had damage to the posterior part of the hypothalamus. In other cases where the person showed hyperactivity and was unable to sleep, he found damage to the anterior portions of the hypothalamus. Subsequent animal work confirmed that large posterior hypothalamic lesions produce a prolonged sleep-like state (Nauta 1946), whereas lesions to the preoptic-anterior hypothalamus cause severe insomnia (McGinty and Sterman 1968). In addition, electrical stimulation of the anterior hypothalamic region is one of the few places in the brain that reliably induces SWS.

These findings show that the hypothalamus is an important sleep centre. This idea makes a great deal of sense when considering that sleep follows a circadian rhythm, and that the hypothalamus contains a 'clock' for the generation of internal circadian rhythms (see below). But, how do lesions of the hypothalamus disrupt arousal and sleep? One possibility is that lesions sever important projections of the ascending reticular activating system. In fact, this pathway has two main branches. The first passes to the thalamus and is important for the relay of information to the cerebral cortex. The main source of input to this pathway are the LTN and PTN, which provide it with cholinergic fibres (Saper *et al.* 2005). However, there is a branch of this pathway that bypasses the thalamus, and projects to the basal forebrain, including the hypothalamus, before reaching to the cerebral cortex. This pathway contains a predominance of monoaminergic neurons, including noradrenergic neurons of the locus coeruleus and serotonergic neurons of the raphe (Saper *et al.* 2005). Thus, lesions to the hypothalamus would disrupt this second pathway and be expected to produce marked disturbances in sleep.

More recently, investigators have discovered other pathways from the basal forebrain that are involved in SWS. For example, neurons have been found in the **ventrolateral preoptic area (VLPA)** of the hypothalamus which increase their activity when the animal begins to sleep (Szymusiak *et al.* 1998). Moreover, this region of the hypothalamus contains GABA-secreting neurons which project throughout the upper reaches of the pons, including the locus coeruleus and raphe (Sherin *et al.* 1998). The same GABA projection also passes to a nearby structure in the posterior hypothalamus called the **tuberomammillary nucleus.** This region is implicated in sleep as it contains neurons that use the neurotransmitter **histamine** which project to the cerebral cortex and are involved in cortical activation and behavioural arousal (Gallopin *et al.* 2000). In fact, this has been exploited by drug companies who market antihistamine drugs as sleeping tablets.

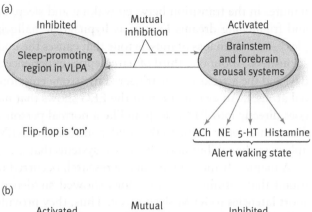

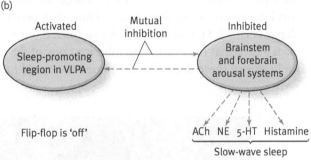

Figure 7.11   The flip-flop switch

Source: N.R. Carlson, *Physiology of Behavior*, 9th edition, p.312. Copyright © 2007 by Pearson Education

Since GABA is an inhibitory neurotransmitter, increased activity of the VLPA of the hypothalamus at the onset of sleep would suppress activity in the pons and tuberomammillary nucleus. In turn, this would decrease cortical arousal, which is a important requisite for sleep. It is also noteworthy that the VLPA receives feedback from the locus coeruleus, raphe and tuberomammillary nucleus, which further highlights its close relationship with these structures. In fact, the VLPA has been likened to a 'flip-flop' switch that turns sleep on and off (Saper *et al.* 2001). In short, when the VLPA becomes active, the brainstem and hypothalamic arousal systems (including those utilising acetylcholine, noradrenaline, serotonin and histamine) are inhibited. This produces decreases in behavioural arousal and the production of SWS. When the VLPA becomes inhibited, the brainstem and hypothalamic arousal systems are 'set free' from their GABAergic inhibition. The result is an increase in behavioural arousal with waking and alertness (Figure 7.11).

Narcolepsy and the discovery of orexins

Narcolepsy is a disorder in which people suffer frequent, intense attacks of sleep that usually last from 5 to 30 minutes, thereby making them prone to falling asleep at dangerous or inappropriate times. Although the narcoleptic will often sleep poorly at night, which exacerbates their daytime sleepiness, the condition is more than this. For example, the narcoleptic may show sleep paralysis where they cannot move or speak for several minutes in the transition between waking and sleep, and this may be followed by vivid and frightening dreams known as hypnagogic hallucinations. Another feature is cataplexy – a sudden loss of muscle tone that causes the body to collapse without loss of consciousness. About one-third of narcoleptics experience at least one cataplexic attack each day, and the attacks can be triggered by strong emotions such as laughter, anger and sexual arousal. An examination of the EEG shows that narcolepsy occurs when the person goes directly into REM sleep, unlike a normal person who enters a period of SWS first. Thus, narcolepsy is due to the sudden intrusion of REM sleep into wakefulness, and cataplexy to the inhibition of the motor systems that is associated with this state.

A major advance in narcolepsy research occurred in the early 1970s when scientists found that certain strains of dogs showed sudden motor inhibition (cataplexy) and short latencies to REM sleep onset. Thus, they provided an ideal animal model of narcolepsy (Plate 7.1). Canine narcolepsy turned out to be a recessive genetic condition, which meant that the dog had to inherit a copy of the mutant gene from both its parents. The brains of these dogs also contained increased numbers of cholinergic receptors in

Plate 7.1   Narcoleptic dogs

Source: Courtesy of the Stanford Center for Narcolepsy

the pons, and noradrenergic alpha-2 receptors in the locus coeruleus. But, human narcolepsy is not a recessive condition, or even strongly genetic. For example, most narcoleptics do not have any first-degree relatives with the disorder, and identical twins are no more likely to share the condition than unrelated strangers.

Nonetheless, scientists set out to identify the gene that caused the canine narcolepsy and, after a ten-year search, they located it on chromosome 12 (Lin *et al.* 1999). Curiously, the only gene known to lie within this region was called *Hcrtr2*, which was responsible for making a receptor for a class of neuropeptides called **orexins** (sometimes called **hypercretins**) that had been associated with eating. But, the lack of this receptor turned out to be crucial for narcolepsy. For example, when knockout mice without the orexin gene were created, they exhibited increased REM sleep and episodes of cataplexy (Chemelli *et al.* 1999). This indicated that orexin dysfunction might also be involved in human narcolepsy. Indeed, this was soon confirmed when it was found that narcoleptics had a marked reduction of orexin neurons in the hypothalamus compared with controls (Thannickal *et al.* 2000).

The orexin neurons are now known to be important in the regulation of sleep. These peptides have been found to be produced exclusively by a cluster of neurons in the posterior half of the **lateral hypothalamus**, and have ascending projections to the cerebral cortex, and descending projections to the cholinergic and monoaminergic cell groups of the pontine brainstem. And, as might be expected, the VLPA also has a direct projection to the orexin neurons in the lateral hypothalamus. It has been shown that orexin neurons are predominately active during wakefulness, and especially during motor activity when animals actively explore their environment (Lee *et al.* 2005). Thus, orexin pathways reinforce the arousal systems of the brain. It has also been suggested that they act as a 'finger' on the 'flip-flop' switch that might prevent unwanted intrusions into sleep (Saper *et al.* 2005). This would explain why narcotic people and animals are more vulnerable to sudden bouts of sleepiness.

An introduction to circadian rhythms

The rotation of the earth causes predictable changes in light and temperature in our environment, and, without exception, all land animals co-ordinate their behaviour with these daily patterns. These daily patterns of behaviour are called **circadian rhythms** from the Latin *circa* meaning 'about' and *dies* meaning 'a day'. The most conspicuous daily rhythm is the sleep–wake cycle, but less obvious is that every physiological and biochemical activity in the body follows a circadian rhythm. For example, body temperature fluctuates by about 3 °F during the 24-hour day, reaching its peak in the late afternoon and dropping to its lowest value in the early hours of the morning. The drop in body temperature which occurs in the evening appears to be an indicator that it is time for sleep. Hormones are also released in regular and orchestrated circadian patterns. Peak levels of **melatonin** are released late in the evening, and **growth hormone** in the early part of the night. In contrast, most **cortisol** and **testosterone** is released in the morning around waking, and **adrenaline** in late afternoon. Even birth and death appear to follow a circadian rhythm, with around one-third of natural births occurring around 3 A.M., whereas death is more likely at 5 A.M. (Groves and Rebec 1992).

At first sight, the existence of circadian rhythms may not appear to be too surprising. After all, it is easy to imagine that they are directly caused in some way by the world around us, that is, by our brain responding to daily and predictable cues, in order to keep the biological processes of the body synchronised with the surrounding environment. But, this is not the case. In fact, humans and other life forms, including insects, bacteria and even plants, are equipped with internal biological clocks that time and control their own circadian rhythms. Thus, they predict the external changes that are about to take place in the world. Circadian clocks must have developed early on in evolutionary history to impart a survival advantage by enabling an organism to anticipate daily environmental changes and to tailor its behaviour and physiology to the appropriate time of the day (Panda *et al.* 2002).

The first recorded experiment to show circadian rhythms was undertaken in 1729 by the French astronomer Jean DeMarian, who noted that a heliotrope plant opened its leaves during the day and closed them at night. DeMarian also found that when the plant was shut away in a dark cupboard, it continued to open and shut its leaves in synchronisation with the light and dark cycles outside. This also occurred when the plant was kept in constant temperature conditions. The plant appeared to have its own innate clock. Later, in 1832, the Swiss botanist Augustin de Candolle performed a similar experiment, except this time he noted something else: when placed in the dark, his plant opened and shut its leaves every 22 hours. Thus, the plant's clock was not very accurate. In fact, this was the first demonstration of a **free-running rhythm**, that is, a rhythm which is not quite in synchronisation with the outside world. It also suggested that the plant was able to keep accurate time only by 'resetting' its clock using external time cues. Indeed, stimuli, including light and temperature, are now recognised as important regulators of circadian rhythms, and are collectively called **zeitgebers** (from the German for 'time-givers').

One of the most fascinating examples of circadian rhythms has been found in microscopic golden brown algae called *Hantzschia virgata*, which live in the tidal sands of Cape Cod, in the north-eastern United States (Figure 7.12). These tiny organisms produce energy by photosynthesis, and every day when the tide goes out, they rise to the surface of the sand to bathe themselves in sunlight. However, moments before the tide returns, they move back down into the safety of the sand. This behaviour is not generated by the tide, but by their own internal clock. For example, when these algae were transferred to a laboratory some 27 miles from the beach, they continued to rise and burrow at times that

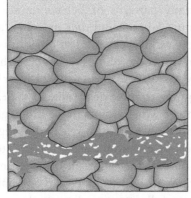 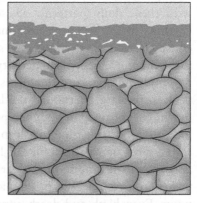

Before the tide comes in the algae burrow under the sand

When the tide goes out the algae return to the surface

Figure 7.12   The algae of Cape Cod

corresponded to the Cape Cod tides. Perhaps even more remarkable is the fact that the tides follow a lunar cycle (a lunar day is 24.8 hours in length) and there are two tides each day. Thus, the algae show what is known as a bimodal lunar-day rhythm (Palmer 1975).

Free-running rhythms in humans

What evidence is there that humans have internal biological clocks with their own time-keeping mechanism? To show that such clocks exist it is necessary to prove that circadian rhythms still operate in the absence of time cues. However, this is not as simple as it first appears. The problem with using humans is that it is extremely difficult to separate them from this type of zeitgeber information. Even in the confines of a laboratory with constant light and temperature, there are many subtle time cues such as the sound of the outside world, or people coming and going, that provide information about the time of day. How, then, does one go about cutting off all time cues from a human subject? One possibility is to keep subjects isolated deep in underground rooms, or even caves, separated from all time variables in the outside world.

The first experiments to attempt this type of isolation were undertaken in 1962 by German physiologist Jürgen Aschoff, who built a specially constructed 'time-free environment' in a basement under a Munich hospital which could house small groups of subjects. This was later replaced by a NASA-funded facility at Andechs in Bavaria. One of Aschoff's most important findings was that the free-running circadian rhythm of sleep and waking is close to 25 hours. That is, subjects kept in conditions without external cues would tend to go to sleep one hour later each day, and wake one hour later too. A similar rhythm appeared also to apply to temperature and to urinary sodium and potassium excretions. But, the sleep–waking rhythm was also variable and could sometimes lengthen to 28 hours or shorten to 22 hours. The consequence of this effect was that the sleeping cycle would 'break free' or uncouple from the other circadian rhythms of the body. Aschoff called this state 'internal desynchronisation' (Aschoff 1967).

Perhaps the most famous isolation experiment was performed by the French geologist Michel Siffre, who, in 1972, lived for six months in a carefully prepared cave 100 feet below the ground in Texas. During his time underground, Siffre was cut off from all forms of time information from the outside world, and the temperature of his cave was maintained at 70 °F. Although linked to the surface by a telephone which was manned at all times, his conversations were kept to a minimum. He had a stockpile of food which was the same type as used on the Apollo 16 space mission, and 780 one-gallon jugs of water. When wanting to sleep, Siffre attached himself to equipment that enabled his sleep cycles to be recorded, along with his heart rate, blood pressure and muscle activity. He then phoned the operators at the surface to instruct them to switch off the lights. Siffre also saved his beard cuttings, recorded his temperature several times a day, and sent his urine samples to the surface for analysis.

The results from this study largely confirmed those obtained by Aschoff and his colleagues. For example, Siffre's sleep–waking cycle tended to free run between 25 and 32 hours, which meant that he went to sleep at a later time each day, and also that his 'days' were much longer than normal. In fact, Siffre was on his 151st sleep–wake cycle by the last (179th) day of the experiment, so that he had psychologically 'lost' 28 days. However, Siffre's temperature rhythm was more stable and ran consistently on a 25-hour cycle with little fluctuation. This meant in effect that his temperature cycle went in and out of synchronisation with the sleep–wake cycle – an unusual situation since we normally go to sleep when our body temperature is beginning to drop. This state of internal desynchronisation had emotional and psychological effects on Siffre who, by the 80th day of his isolation, was experiencing depression, failing memory and poor manual dexterity as shown by an inability to thread beads onto a string. And, at this point the experiment was to continue for another 100 days! In fact, long after the confinement had ended, Siffre complained of weakened eyesight caused by the ordeal and 'psychological wounds' that he did not 'understand' (Siffre 1975).

More recent research, however, has shown that the internal circadian clock may be more accurate than previously thought. For example, Charles Czeisler working at Harvard University has shown that the use of artificial light in isolation experiments, even at low intensities and 'self-timed' by subjects when wanting to sleep, may interact with the circadian clock to lengthen the rhythms. Indeed, when Cziesler forced his subjects to go to bed four hours later each day, thus making them live by a 28 hour clock, he found that the internal pacemaker had a much more regular rhythm. In fact, the daily rhythms of temperature and hormones in his subjects rose and fell on an average cycle of 24 hours and 11 minutes (Czeisler *et al.* 1999).

The discovery of the circadian clock

If the sleep–wake cycle is under the control of a circadian pacemaker then where in the brain does it exist? One of the first scientists to address this question was Carl Richter, who, beginning in the 1950s, focused his attention on the endocrine glands of the body. But, removing the main endocrine glands had little effect on altering the circadian rhythms of laboratory animals, and Richter turned to the brain. He made lesions to many different brain structures and examined their effects on circadian patterns of locomotion, feeding and drinking behaviour. In fact, he undertook over 200 experiments over a period of some 20 years in order to locate the whereabouts of the endogenous pacemaker. Yet, only one structure appeared to disrupt circadian behaviour and this was located in the anterior part of the hypothalamus (Richter 1967). Because this region was small and anatomically complex, he was unable to go further with his investigations.

However, in 1972, two independent groups of researchers found a small cluster of neurons in the front part of the hypothalamus, called the **suprachiasmatic nucleus (SCN)**, where lesions disrupted a variety of circadian rhythms, including the release of corticosterone (Moore and Eichler 1972), along with drinking and locomotion (Stephan and Zucker 1972). It was also found around the same time, that the SCN has its own visual pathway, called the **retinohypothalamic tract**, which branches off from the main optic nerve close to the optic chiasm. Although lesions of this pathway did not affect vision, they nevertheless abolished the ability of the internal circadian clock to be synchronised to external light–dark cycles. This was also an effect of SCN lesions. Although SCN lesions did not change the length of time spent sleeping, or the relative proportions of REM and SWS, they did alter the normal sleep pattern so that it occurred more randomly during the 24-hour day. In other words, lesions of the SCN abolished the circadian rhythmicity of sleep. These experiments demonstrated that the SCN exhibited two important properties required of a circadian clock: (1) lesions of the SCN abolished a range of circadian rhythms, and (2) lesions of the retinohypothalamic tract abolished entrainment of the clock to visual signals.

Why did it take so long to discover the SCN? One reason is that it is extremely small. In humans, each nucleus comprises approximately 10,000 tightly packed neurons that are confined in a space of about 0.3 mm³. Further, the SCN also contains some of the smallest neurons to be found in the human brain, and these can only be identified with specialised staining techniques. Moreover, in rodent brains the size of this nucleus is even smaller. It is not surprising, therefore, that Richter, with his relatively crude lesioning techniques, was unable to narrow his search down to this tiny structure.

A closer look at the suprachiasmatic nucleus

One special characteristic of the SCN is that it generates its own intrinsic circadian pattern of electrical activity. For example, if microelectrodes are implanted into the rat's SCN, its neurons show a pattern of electrical activity that is highest during the day and lowest at night. The neurons continue to show this rhythmical activity when a fine rotating knife cut is made around the SCN to isolate it from the rest of the brain. This operation abolishes circadian rhythmicity in other brain areas but not the SCN (Inouye and Kawamura 1979). This discovery showed that output pathways from the SCN must be providing timing information to other areas of the brain.

It is also possible to keep slices of brain tissue that contain the SCN in a saline bath for a few hours and then to record the electrical activity of its neurons. This work has also shown that the SCN neurons display discharge rates of electrical activity that are synchronised to the light–dark cycle that the animal experienced when alive (Bos and Mirmiran 1990). As with previous research, it was found that the activity of the SCN neurons was higher during the day than during the night. Similar results have been obtained when animals are injected with **2-deoxyglucose**, which is a radioactive form of glucose that is taken up by neurons but cannot be metabolised by them. Because the more active neurons take up greater amounts of 2-deoxyglucose, where it accumulates and gives off radioactivity, this substance provides a way of measuring regional differences in brain activity. This research has shown that the SCN is metabolically more active during a 12-hour light phase of a circadian cycle and that no other brain region exhibits such a dramatic and pronounced rhythm (Schwartz and Gainer 1977) (Plate 7.2).

Some of the best evidence supporting the SCN as the brain's circadian clock has come from transplantation studies. For example, in 1988, Martin Ralph and Mike Menaker, working at the University of Oregon, discovered a strain of hamsters (now called tau mutation hamsters) that had a circadian activity period of around 20 hours. This was far shorter than had been observed before. It also raised an intriguing question: what would happen if the SCN of these hamsters were transplanted into normal animals? Would the recipient show a circadian rhythm of the donor or the recipient? Working with foetal tissue that contained the SCN, Ralph et al. (1990) found that when the SCN from tau hamsters was transplanted into the brains of normal animals, they showed a circadian pattern of around 20.2 hours. However, when the transplantation was performed with the SCN from normal animals transplanted into the mutant hamsters, the 24-hour circadian period was restored.

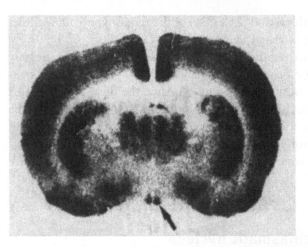 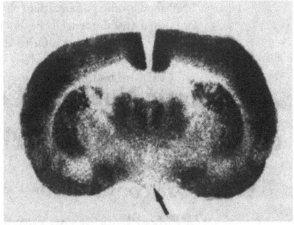

Plate 7.2	Increased metabolic activity of the suprachiasmatic nucleus during the day compared with the night using 2-deoxyglucose

Source: W.J. Schwartz and H. Gainer (1977) *Science*, 197, 1089–1091

Are you a lark or an owl?

Since the earth began there have been around 10^{14} sunrises and sunsets (Sack and Lewy 2001). It is not surprising, therefore, that adaptation to the solar light–dark cycle has shaped the evolution of almost all animals on earth, with a large number of biological processes showing intrinsic circadian rhythms. The most obvious circadian rhythm is sleep. Although this state is vital for health and well-being, sleep problems are surprisingly common. Indeed, it has been estimated that 25 per cent of the UK population suffer some form of sleep disorder that either causes insomnia or excessive sleepiness. And, in some cases, sleep problems appear to arise directly from abnormalities in the underlying circadian clock it-self. One example is delayed sleep phase syndrome (DSPS), first described by Weitzman *et al.* (1981), which occurs in about 10 per cent of the population with sleeping difficulties. Individuals with this dis-order tend to fall asleep in the early hours of the morning and have great difficulty waking at the appro-priate time. However, if they are allowed to sleep freely, then people with DSPS will sleep for a normal length of time, and show no abnormalities in their sleep patterns. Because these people are awake for much of the night they are commonly referred to as owls. Unlike most other individuals, owls feel more alert later in the day, and function better in the evening and early part of the night.

Individuals with DSPS show a number of circadian abnormalities, including a delayed temperature rhythm (the lowest point of core body temperature occurs later in the day) and a delayed melatonin surge. These people also can experience very real difficulties with their daily life, especially if they have to function on a normal 9 A.M. to 5 P.M. schedule. This may not only cause them to become seriously sleep deprived, but also require recuperation at weekends. The problem is made worse by the fact that sleep deprivation does not reset the circadian clock of DSPS patients as it does with normal people. In other words, a lack of sleep will not make them sleep earlier the next day. A further problem is depres-sion. About half of people with DSPS suffer from clinical depression, although it is not known if this is caused by lifestyle stresses or by some intrinsic aspect of the disorder itself.

The discovery of DSPS has also led to the recognition of advanced sleep phase syndrome (ASPS) where sleep is forward in relation to the desired clock time. People with ASPS feel a strong urge to sleep earlier in the evening than is normal, and as a consequence awaken earlier. Such individuals are commonly referred to as larks. ASPS constitutes 1–2 per cent of all sleep disorders, although this small figure may be masked by the likelihood that advanced sleeping is better tolerated than DSPS in the sense that it is easier to keep oneself awake for a few hours after the usual bedtime than it is to force oneself to sleep a few hours before bedtime. As might be expected, people with ASPS tend to show circadian rhythms that are advanced (i.e. occur earlier than usual), including high levels of cortisol just after waking. Both ASPS and DSPS tend to run in families, and molecular studies are beginning to understand this relationship more fully. Around a dozen genes are known to be involved in the production of circadian rhythms, and a polymorphism in a clock gene called *hPer3* has been associated with DSPS, while a small mutation in a gene called *hPer2* has been found in people with ASPS.

The suprachiasmatic nucleus and melatonin

How does neural activity in the SCN cause the circadian rhythms in physiological systems and behaviour? After the discovery of the SCN in the early 1970s, attention focused on a tiny structure called the **pineal gland** (Figure 7.13). This structure had long intrigued researchers, not least because in the seventeenth century Descartes had speculated that it might house the soul. In the early 1960s a more realistic view of the pineal gland developed when it was found to be an endocrine gland that secreted the hormone **melatonin**. It was further found that melatonin release is under the direct control of light, that is, melatonin secretion is inhibited by light and stimulated by darkness. The inhibitory effect of light on the pineal gland was produced by a pathway called the **superior cervical ganglion** which obtained information from the SCN. Curiously, this pathway has a rather unusual route: output fibres from the SCN terminate in the **parventricular nucleus** of the

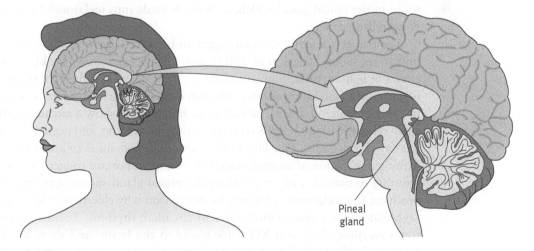

Pineal gland

| Figure 7.13 | The location of the pinal gland in the human brain |

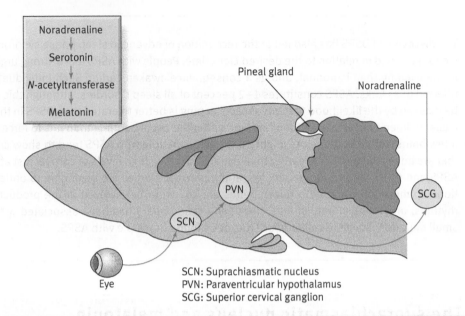

Figure 7.14 The production of melatonin

hypothalamus, which in turn projects to the thoracic part of the spinal cord. From here, fibres form the superior cervical ganglion (a branch of the sympathetic nervous system), which ascends into the brain to innervate the pineal gland (Figure 7.14).

In fish, amphibians and many reptiles, the pineal gland contains photoreceptor cells similar to those in the eye, and is located just under the cranium on the dorsal surface of the brain. However, the pineal gland of birds and mammals contains no photoreceptors and consists of a collection of secretory cells called **pinealocytes**. Interestingly, in humans the pineal gland has moved towards the centre of the brain and forms part of the **epithalamus**. During darkness, the fibres of the superior cervical ganglion (under the control of the SCN) release noradrenaline, which stimulates the formation of serotonin in the pineal gland which, in turn, is made into melatonin by an enzyme called *N*-acetyltransferase.

The pineal is a richly vascular organ and is said to have a rate of blood flow second only to the kidney (Clark *et al.* 2005). Moreover, most animals are highly sensitive to the effects of light on melatonin secretion. In rats, for example, the light from a candle flame is sufficient to inhibit its release, although it takes much higher intensities of light to suppress melatonin in humans. Nonetheless, humans still show a circadian pattern of melatonin release, with high levels secreted during the evening, and negligible amounts during the day (Lewy 1980). One effect of melatonin in humans is to lower body temperature, causing a reduction of arousal, which may be an important trigger for sleep. It is also interesting to note that as we get older the pineal gland shows signs of calcification and produces less melatonin. This may be one reason why elderly people sleep less.

Melatonin is a crucial modulator of circadian rhythms. At least two types of melatonin receptor (MT^1 and MT^2) are found in the brain, and these are found in high numbers in the SCN. Melatonin has been shown to inhibit electrical activity in SCN neurons, and to 'reset' its circadian clock, especially around the time of dusk (Zee and Manthena 2007). This signal is likely to be important in the regulation of the sleep–wake cycle. But, melatonin has many other effects. In particular, it helps to synchronise the activity of other hormones to the sleep–wake cycle. For example, melatonin contributes to the release of growth hormone which occurs early into the sleep cycle. Melatonin also acts on a group of cells in the hypothalamus, which projects to the pituitary gland, which secretes **gonadotropin-releasing hormone**. This substance controls the release of luteinising hormone and follicle-stimulating hormone from the pituitary which is important in the formation of testosterone and oestrogen. High numbers of melatonin receptors are also found in an area of the pituitary gland called the **pars tuberalis** involved in the secretion of prolactin. Although this hormone is best known for milk production in pregnant women, it is also involved in food intake and metabolic rate which show circadian rhymicity.

In addition to its contribution to the superior cervical ganglion, the efferent pathways of the SCN also extend to the **subparaventricular zone of the hypothalamus (SPZ)**. In turn, this region has widespread connections with other hypothalamic regions, including the preoptic areas and dorsomedial nuclei. The SPZ is believed to be particularly important in generating sleep–wake and activity rhythms. Indeed, lesions to the SPZ disrupt a large number of circadian rhythms, including sleep–waking, feeding, locomotor activity, cortisol secretion and neural activity in the locus coeruleus. Lesions of the SPZ, however, spare the circadian rhythms of body temperature and melatonin (Mistelberger 2005). The SPZ also has connections with the orexin neurons that are located in the ventrolateral preoptic area of the hypothalamus. The SPZ is increasingly being recognised as a pivotal structure in the control of circadian rhythms.

Abnormal circadin rhythms: jet lag and shift work

There are many instances in our modern world where the body's circadian rhythms fall out of synchronisation with the external world. One example occurs where people take intercontinental flights across several time zones. A common effect of this travel is **jet lag**. To give an example: imagine flying from London to San Francisco. The flight takes approximately 11 hours and flies across eight time zones. If you set off from London at noon you would arrive in San Francisco at around 5 P.M. (US time), although your wristwatch would be showing 11 P.M. In other words, the circadian rhythms of your body would be 6 hours out of synchronisation with the external world. This is sometimes called a phase delay shift as the flight has in essence lengthened the day for the individual by adding 6 hours. The situation becomes even more confusing when you fly back. For example, if you set off from San Francisco at noon, you would arrive in London at about 5 A.M. *the next day* (British time), yet your wristwatch would indicate that it was only 11 P.M. This is sometimes called a phase advance shift as the flight has now shortened the new day for the traveller.

The effects of jet lag are well known. The person will typically feel fatigued and listless, with increased irritability and a decline in their powers of concentration. Headache, a loss of appetite, anxiety and a general feeling of malaise often add to the suffering. In addition, the jet-lagged individual may have difficulty sleeping at the appropriate time in their new environment. These effects occur because the person's circadian rhythms are out of synchronisation with the new environment. In fact, it may take several days to completely reset the circadian clock. Although jet lag occurs after flights in both directions, the adjustment of body rhythms to time zone shifts is more difficult following eastbound flights. Thus, its easier for your body to lengthen its day after flying west (phase delay), than to shorten it after flying east (phase advance). For example, one study that looked at American servicemen who were transferring to Germany found that it took eight days to completely adjust their circadian clocks to their new environment, whereas it only took three days when returning to the United States (Wright *et al.* 1983). This difference is probably because our natural body clock runs on a daily rhythm of 25 hours and so can better adjust to longer days.

Although the effects of jet lag are relatively harmless for the majority of travellers, the same may not be true for airline crew who regularly undertake long-haul flights. For example, studies have shown that flight attendants who operate on international flights, compared with those on domestic service, show elevated cortisol levels and perform more poorly on tests of memory (Cho *et al.* 2000). In another study, the brains of female flight cabin crew with at least five years' regular flying experience were compared with those who had less severe flying schedules over the same length of time. They were also given brain scans with MRI. The results showed that the women with the most long-haul experience had slower reaction times, poorer memory and shrunken right temporal lobes. In fact, the subjects with the highest levels of cortisol were the ones with the most damage (Cho 2001).

A number of strategies can be used to help the traveller to speed up the adjustment of their internal clock after a long-haul flight. One technique is to expose the person to bright light, which helps to shift the biological clock. However, the light has different effects depending on the time of day it is administered. For example, light exposure during the early part of the night delays the clock, making us sleep at a later time next day. In contrast, light exposure in the early morning, especially if it occurs a couple of hours before the person wakes, advances the clock and makes us sleep earlier. Another important regulator of circadian rhythms is melatonin. As we have seen, a surge of melatonin occurs in the evening, and levels remain high during the night as we sleep. Several studies have shown that if one takes melatonin during the early evening at one's destination, it is possible to quickly shift the body's circadian rhythm into phase with the new conditions (Arendt *et al.* 1987). Melatonin has even been shown to synchronise circadian rhythms and improve sleep in some blind people who cannot use light as a zeitgeber (Skene *et al.* 1999).

Another instance where circadian rhythms go out of phase with the external world is in shift work. This practice is more common than many people imagine. For example, it has been estimated that 20 per cent of American workers rotate shifts, sometimes working at night and at other times working during the day. But, more worryingly, an increasing amount of evidence shows that shift work poses significant health risks for the individual. Working at night not only leads to sleepiness but also significantly increases the risk of accidents. Indeed, one study of hospital nurses found that those on night shift were twice as likely to have a car accident as those on day shift (Gold *et al.* 1992). In addition, shift work increases the risk of a number of stress-related problems such as ulcers, cigarette smoking and poorer pregnancy outcomes (Klein and Thorne 2007). More serious still is the increased risk of heart disease and cancer. For example, another study found that those who had worked night shifts for over ten years were twice as likely to develop heart disease, and another found a 60 per cent increase in breast cancer in women who routinely engaged in long-term shift work over a period of several years (Davis *et al.* 2001). These are disturbing statistics which highlight the importance of finding new ways of minimising the effects of abnormal circadian rhythms caused by night-time working conditions. One approach may be to change the lighting conditions for those who are employed in shift work. It has been suggested that people are likely to adapt better to their working conditions if strong artificial light is used at work, but their bedroom is kept as dark as possible (Eastman *et al.* 1995).

Summary

We spend about one-third of our lives asleep (roughly 25 years of an average life). Yet, remarkably, nobody is absolutely sure why we do it. This is all the more confusing when one considers that all mammals (and probably all vertebrates) show patterns of sleep. Despite the uncertainty, it is likely that sleep either produces some form of tissue restoration that helps to combat the wear and tear of living, or it helps maintain the plasticity of the brain.

The experimental investigation of sleep began with the invention of the **electroencephalograph** (EEG) by Hans Berger in 1929, which allowed the electrical rhythms of the brain to be measured. In 1954, Kleitman and Aserinsky showed that the brain has two sleep states: **slow-wave sleep** (SWS) and **rapid eye movement sleep** (REM). There are four stages of SWS, with EEG waves 'slowing down' from 8 to 1 Hz, and these are accompanied by a physiological relaxation of the body. The SWS cycle takes about 90 minutes to complete and is followed by a period of REM sleep characterised by much faster and desynchronised EEG rhythms (similar to when we are awake), accompanied by muscle twitches, eye movements and general loss of body tone. REM sleep is also the stage of sleep in which we **dream**. The four consecutive stages of SWS followed by REM sleep is called a **sleep cycle**. There are normally 4–5 sleep cycles in an average night's sleep. As sleep progresses through the night, the REM periods tend to get longer, and SWS periods get shorter, with stages 3 and 4 showing the greatest reduction.

Sleep is an active process (and not a passive response to sensory deprivation, as once believed) that is predominantly controlled by various regions in the **brainstem** that influence the electrical activity of the **cerebral cortex** through their action on the ascending **reticular activating system**. In the 1960s, Michael Jouvet appeared to show that the **locus coeruleus** (the main source of **noradrenaline**-containing fibres to the forebrain) was responsible for producing many of the manifestations of REM sleep, and that the **raphe** (the main source of **serotonin**-containing fibres to the forebrain) was involved in producing SWS. This view is no longer accepted although their involvement in sleep cannot be ruled out. A more important region for producing REM sleep is now believed to be the **gigantocellular tegmental field** (GTF), which sends acetylcholine-containing fibres into the forebrain. This site is also the origin of **PGO waves,** which are known to precede REM sleep. In turn, the GTF receives cholinergic projections from two nearby brainstem areas: the **laterodorsal tegmental nucleus** (LTN) and **pedunculopontine tegmental nucleus** (PTN). The neurobiology of SWS is less well understood, although one crucial area is the **anterior preoptic hypothalamus,** where damage causes severe insomnia. This area is also the source of galanin and GABA containing neurons that project to the brainstem. The medial and lateral hypothalamus contain **orexin** neurons that also pass down to the brainstem and are involved in sleep and **narcolepsy**. The hypothalamus also contains the **suprachiasmatic nucleus,** which governs certain **circadian rhythms**, partly through its influence on the **pineal gland,** which releases the hormone **melatonin**.

Essay questions

1. Describe the different types of brain wave and behaviour that occur during a sleep cycle. How does a sleep cycle change during the course of a night?

   Search terms: Sleep cycle. EEG brain waves and sleep. Slow-wave sleep. Rapid eye movement sleep. Behaviour in sleep.

2. What brain regions and neurochemical systems are known to be involved in the regulation of sleep?

   Search terms: Neural basis of sleep. Neurobiology of sleep. Gigantocellular tegmental field. Hypothalamus and sleep. Reticular formation. Neurochemistry of sleep.

3. What are the functions of slow-wave sleep (SWS) and rapid eye movement (REM) sleep?

   Search terms: Functions of sleep. Functions of REM sleep. Functions of slow-wave sleep. Restoration and sleep. Adaptive theories of sleep. Why do we sleep? Sleep deprivation.

4. What is known about the neurobiology and endocrinology of circadian rhythms?

   Search terms: Circadian rhythms. Suprachiasmatic nucleus. Melatonin. Pineal gland. Circadian clocks in the brain. Circadian rhythms in depression. Neurobiology of circadian rhythms.

Further reading

Carkadon, M.A. (ed.) (1993) *Encyclopaedia of Sleep and Dreaming*. New York: Macmillan. Over 700 pages with hundreds of interesting entries (for example, 'Dreams of the blind', 'Short sleepers in history and legend') that summarise the many medical, biological and psychological facets of sleep.

Dement, W.C. (1972) *Some Must Watch While Some Must Sleep*. New York: Norton. Now dated, but nonetheless a useful short introduction to the topic of sleep research written by one of the pioneers in the field.

Dunlap, J.C., Loros, J.J. and DeCoursey, P.J. (2003) *Chronobiology*. Basingstoke: Freeman. A much needed textbook which provides a thorough overview of biological rhythms, from molecular mechanisms to physiological systems in humans and other animals.

Empson, J. (2001) *Sleep and Dreaming*. New York: Harvester Wheatsheaf. A concise and well-written account for undergraduate students which includes information on the electrophysiology and neurophysiology of sleep, along with sleep disorders.

Foster, R. and Kreitzman, L. (2005) *Rhythms of Life*. London: Profile Book. A so-called popular science book likely to be found on the shelves of your local bookshop that provides an ideal introduction for the student. Despite its intended market, the book covers material in a scientific and detailed way, and includes sections on genes and molecular biology.

Hobson, J.A. (1989) *Sleep*. New York: Scientific American Library. A beautifully illustrated book that covers everything from the evolution of sleeping patterns, to the biochemistry of the brain during sleep, and the interpretation of dreams.

Horne, J. (1988) *Why We Sleep: The Functions of Sleep in Humans and Other Mammals*. Oxford: Oxford University Press. A book that attempts to evaluate the biological reasons why humans and other mammals have to sleep.

Jouvet, M. (1999) *The Paradox of Sleep*. Cambridge, Mass.: MIT Press. A short and readable book in which the author takes the reader on a scientific tour of sleep and dream research, concluding with his own ideas on the function of dreaming.

Klein, D.C., Moore, R.Y. and Reppert, S.M. (1991) *The Suprachiasmatic Nucleus: The Mind's Clock*. New York: Oxford University Press. An academic text which covers in rich detail research on the suprachiasmatic nucleus up until the 1990s. Although not written for the student it contains much of interest.

Kryger, M.H., Roth, T. and Dement, W.C. (2005) *Principles and Practice of Sleep Medicine*, 4th edition Philadelphia: Saunders. A standard academic text of over 1,500 pages written by various authors. Despite its title, this contains just about all you need to know about the biopsychology of sleep. Moreover, many chapters are surprisingly lucid and informative for general readers.

Lavie, P. (1996) *The Enchanted World of Sleep*. New Haven, Conn.: Yale University Press. A highly enjoyable and thought-provoking overview of what we know about sleep and dreaming, including an examination of the brain centres involved in sleep regulation.

Martin, P. (2002) *Counting Sheep: The Science and Pleasures of Sleep and Dreams*. London: HarperCollins. A readable, well-written and entertaining introduction to sleep and dreaming. Although written for a lay market, many students will find this book interesting and highly informative.

Moorcroft, W.H. (1993) *Sleep, Dreaming, and Sleep Disorders: An Introduction*. Lanham, Md.: University Press of America. A book that is suitable for psychology undergraduates and provides a broad account of sleep, including its characteristics, functions, physiology and disorders.

Schwartz, W.J. (ed.) (1997) *Sleep Science: Integrating Basic Research and Clinical Practice*. Basle: Karger. A highly technical account aimed at scientists and clinicians interested in linking the neurobiology of sleep with its associated disorders.

For self test questions, animations, interactive exercises and many more resources to help you consolidate your understanding, and expand your knowledge of the field, please go to the website accompanying this book at **www.pearsoned.co.uk/wickens**

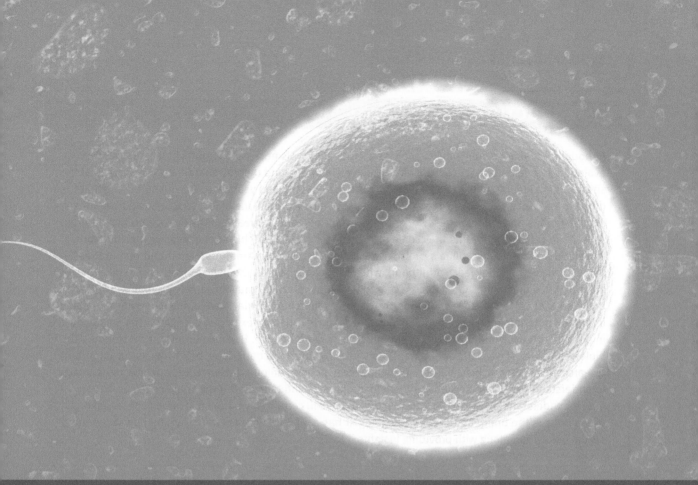

CHAPTER 8

Sexual development and behaviour

In this chapter

- The principles of sexual development

- Hormonal developmental disorders and genetic syndromes

- The organisational effects of testosterone

- The activational effects of sex hormones on adult behaviour

- Brain structure and cognitive differences between males and females

- What digit ratio can tell us about behaviour

- Brain areas and sexual behaviour

- The biological basis of sexual orientation

INTRODUCTION

Although sexual behaviour satisfies no vital tissue need, or is necessary for individual survival, from an evolutionary perspective it is crucial as it produces offspring and thereby guarantees the survival of the species. Considering that life first began on earth over 300 million years ago, it is not surprising that the drive to reproduce and engage in sexual activity is a very powerful one. It is also a behaviour with many manifestations and complexities. Not only has evolution gone to great lengths to develop two different sexes, but it also requires that they come together in an act of courtship to engage in sexual intercourse. In addition, most higher animals provide their offspring with territorial protection and parental assistance to ensure that they reach adulthood, when they can look after themselves. It is easy to take this for granted, but if one thinks about it more carefully, sexual behaviour must be largely programmed into the brain as a direct result of evolutionary pressures. Moreover, sexual development provides a vitally important determinant of human behaviour. Our sexual gender, for example, is arguably the single most important influence on how we think about ourselves and behave. Because of this, understanding the biological basis of sexual development and how it comes to shape later behaviour is an important research area in biopsychology. The subject, however, poses a unique challenge, especially when it comes to understanding human sexuality with all its prejudices and taboos. But the challenge is an important one, for understanding who we are and why we behave in certain ways. The most important sexual organ of the body is the brain, and the biopsychologist has a vital role to play in explaining how it produces sexual behaviour, along with providing insights into its dysfunction.

Why have sex?

The obvious answer to this question, as any undergraduate student will be quick to tell you, is that it is enjoyable! But, as true as this answer is, we must ask why sexual behaviour has evolved in the first place. On first sight the answer appears to be simple: sexual behaviour is necessary for the continuation of the species. But, again, this is not an entirely satisfactory answer because reproduction without sex, or **asexual reproduction**, is also possible. Indeed, many plants produce seeds that are clones of themselves, and most single-celled organisms (for example, bacteria) replicate by dividing into two. Some other creatures also reproduce asexually. For example, female greenfly give birth to 'virgin' young for several generations, and there are some vertebrates that reproduce without sex. These include the whiptail lizard (Plate 8.1) and a type of fish called the Amazon Molly which are all-female. Since these forms of life can reproduce successfully, why go to the bother of inventing sexual reproduction? Sex is all the more puzzling when one considers that it is not without its risks: it can cause harmful genetic mutations, result in sexually transmitted diseases, and prove potentially hazardous during the establishment of territory, courtship and copulation. Indeed, most aggression in the animal kingdom is linked to these behaviours. Yet sexual behaviour is the norm in nature. Why?

The main reason for the evolutionary development of sex lies with the great variety of gene combinations that it produces compared to asexual reproduction. With sexual reproduction, each parent transmits a random and unique set of genes, comprising about half of its genome, to each of its progeny. Because the array of genes in every

| Plate 8.1 | Pseudosex in parthenogenic lizards |

Source: Neil Campbell (1993) *Biology*, 3rd edition, p. 933, Benjamin Cummings

sperm and every egg is different, each offspring will be genetically unique, differing, from its parents and from its brothers and sisters – unless it has an identical twin which develops from the same single egg. Thus, sexual reproduction allows a couple to produce an infinite number of genetically discrete offspring. This constant shuffling of genes, and the large number of different individuals it creates, produces 'variation' in the population that is of great evolutionary advantage to the species. For example, if all of us were genetically identical, or even close to being the same, we would be equally vulnerable to the same viruses, diseases, environmental catastrophes, or other threats to our survival. But, a species with many genetically different individuals is more likely to survive a catastrophe. Variability between individuals also means that some will become better suited to their environments than others, and these will be the ones more likely to survive, mate and pass on their genes. In this way, the survival of the 'fittest' ensures that a species is able to adapt optimally to its own ecological niche. Thus, sexual reproduction not only assists the process of evolution, it underpins it.

Sexual development and differentiation

Nearly every cell in the human body contains 23 pairs of **chromosomes**, which carry the 30,000 or so **genes** that we inherited from our parents at the moment of conception. One exception to this rule are the **gametes**, otherwise known as the **sperm** and **ovum** (egg), which have only 23 single chromosomes. In fact, it is only when the sperm and ovum come together during fertilisation that the chromosomes become paired again, and a new genetic entity is created. Remarkably, we all start life as this single microscopic cell which is smaller than the head of a pin. Even more astonishing is the fact that encoded in the DNA of our first set of chromosomes are the genetic instructions that will turn the egg into an adult human being containing more than 100 million million cells. And, there is another surprising fact: males and females differ only in terms of one single chromosome. Thus, all genetically normal humans, regardless of their sex, share 23 pairs of chromosomes with only one pair being different. These are called the sex chromosomes and they exist in two forms: X and Y. Put simply, if a fertilised egg (known as a **zygote**) inherits two **X chromosomes** (XX) it will normally become female, and if it receives X and **Y chromosomes** (XY) it will usually be male. Because males carry both types of chromosome, it is the father that determines the genetic sex of the fertilised egg.

In the days following conception, the fertilised egg begins to divide, slowly growing until, after 4 days, there are around fifty cells in a tiny ball. After that, the set of cells grow more quickly, becoming a tiny sphere with a tiny heart beginning to beat at around 21 days. However, it is not until the sixth week of foetal development that the first sex differences emerge. Up to this point, males and females are identical and, despite their different XY and XX genes, have the potential to develop into either sex. This is because both types of foetus contain the precursor tissue for making either **testes** or **ovaries** (called collectively **gonads**). The precursor gonadal tissue is connected to two primitive tubular structures: the **Wolffian duct** that has the potential to develop into the internal structures of the male reproductive system (seminal vesicles, prostrate and vas deferens), and the **Müllerian duct** which is capable of developing into female ones (uterus, fallopian tubes and upper portion of the vagina). However, only one of these ducts will develop to determine the internal sex of the foetus. The event that initiates this change occurs in the sixth week of gestation when a gene called *SRY* (an abbreviation for sex-determining region of Y), located in the middle of the short arm of the Y chromosome, produces a chemical called **testis-determining factor** which causes the foetal gonadal tissue to develop into **testes**. There is no female equivalent of this substance and in its absence the differentiation of the ovaries begins around the seventh week of gestation. The foetal ovary is generally considered inactive until late in development although it produces small amounts of oestrogen at about 12 weeks.

Experimental evidence showing the importance of the Y chromosome for male sexual development was provided by Koopman *et al.* (1991). These experimenters took a segment of the Y chromosome containing the sex-determining gene *SRY* from a mouse embryo, and injected it into a fertilised egg containing two X chromosomes (i.e. female). The results showed that at 14 days the embryo started to give rise to normal testis development, and the genetic 'female' mouse developed into a male with testis and a penis. In a similar way, if the *SRY* gene is not present on the Y chromosome, the primitive undifferentiated gonads of the foetus become ovaries, and a female develops.

The differentiation of gonadal tissue into testes or ovaries is the first stage of sexual development where a difference between the sexes can be observed. It also marks the point where the genetic influence on foetal sexual development lessens and hormonal influences take over (see Figure 8.1). The testes and ovaries have a critical role to play at this stage because they produce the male or female hormones that set in motion the changes that ultimately produce the sex of the individual. In the case of a male, the testes produce two hormones called **testosterone** and **Müllerian-duct-inhibiting substance**. The first of these acts to masculinise the sex organs by developing the Wolffian duct system into the internal male sex organs, and the second prevents the (female) Müllerian system from forming. Although the ovaries do not secrete sex

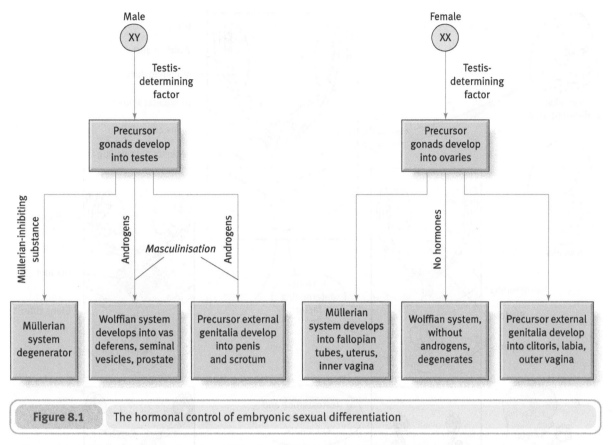

Figure 8.1   The hormonal control of embryonic sexual differentiation

Source: Adapted from N.R. Carlson, *Physiology of Behavior*, 6th edition. Copyright © 1998 by Pearson Education

hormones at this stage, the lack of endocrine stimulation still exerts an important effect on the foetus as it causes the Wolffian system to degenerate and the Müllerian system to develop into the female internal sex organs.

The external genital anatomy, which in the male includes the penis and scrotum, and in the female includes vagina, labia and clitoris, start to appear at 8–12 weeks of gestation, and the same principles of hormonal organisation hold as for internal development. That is, the release of testosterone by the testes acts on epithelial tissue to cause the male sex organs to be formed, and its absence results in the development of the female genitalia. However, at this stage, testosterone is turned into a more potent androgen called **5-alpha-dihydrotestosterone** by an enzyme called **5-alpha-reductase**, which is particularly important for the differentiation of the penis and scrotum. In fact, without dihydrotesterone, the foetus will not develop as a male, and the immature genitalia will form into a female pattern. With the differentiation of the external genitalia the foetus can be visually observed to be either male or female.

The adrenogenital syndrome

The normal sexual development of the foetus, as we have just seen, depends on the differentiation of the gonads into testes or ovaries to provide the necessary hormonal environment for the internal and external sex organs to develop (Figure 8.2). But, what

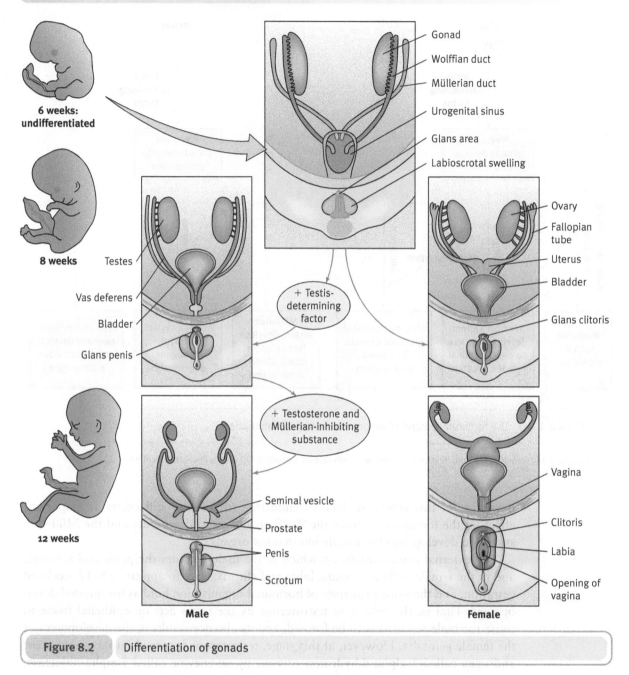

6 weeks: undifferentiated

8 weeks

12 weeks

Gonad
Wolffian duct
Müllerian duct
Urogenital sinus
Glans area
Labioscrotal swelling

Testes
Vas deferens
Bladder
Glans penis

Ovary
Fallopian tube
Uterus
Bladder
Glans clitoris

+ Testis-determining factor

+ Testosterone and Müllerian-inhibiting substance

Seminal vesicle
Prostate
Penis
Scrotum

Male

Vagina
Clitoris
Labia
Opening of vagina

Female

Figure 8.2 Differentiation of gonads

Source: L.A. Freberg, *Discovering Biological Psychology*, p. 289. Copyright © 2006 by Houghton Mifflin Company

if something goes wrong at this stage? What happens, for example, if the female foetus is exposed to high levels of testosterone around the sixth week of gestation when differentiation of the sex organs is taking place? In fact, this type of event occurs in a recessive genetic condition called **congenital adrenal hyperplasia** where the foetal adrenal glands fail to produce an enzyme called 21-hydroxylase which is involved in making cortisol. The result is that the adrenal glands start to secrete relatively high levels of male steroids or **androgens**. A similar situation can also occur when the mother uses androgenic drugs such as **anabolic steroids** during the early stages of pregnancy. In both cases, the consequences of high androgen exposure is the masculinisation of the female genitalia. Consequently, the newborn often have a small penis intermediate in size between a normal phallus and clitoris, surrounded by skin folds that resemble a poorly formed scrotum. Despite this, the internal sexual organs such as the ovaries are normal because the adrenal androgens are released too late in development to stimulate the formation of the Wolffian system. In other words, adrenal hyperplasia produces a female with gonads that match their sex chromosomes, but with a genital appearance of the opposite sex. This type of person is sometimes referred to as a **pseudo-hermaphrodite**.

There is considerable controversy about the best way to treat children with congenital adrenal hyperplasia. In the past, these children were often untreated, and contrary to what might be predicted, happily reared as boys. Unfortunately, problems of sexual development would arise during adolescence when there was a failure of puberty. Today, such individuals are more likely to be raised as girls, and treated with a hormone such as hydrocortisone to restore normal levels of androgens. In severe cases, surgical correction of the genitalia, especially the reconstruction of the vaginal opening, may take place early in life (normally between 3 and 6 months of age). Despite this, girls with adrenal hyperplasia still have a greater tendency to show masculine behavioural characteristics in childhood, and they are often described as 'tomboys' by their parents. In addition, they show enhanced ability on cognitive tests that normally favour males such as spatial puzzles (Berenbaum 2001).

In addition, these females are more likely than other women to be homosexual or lesbian. For example, Money *et al.* (1984) questioned 30 young adult women who had adrenogenital syndrome. When asked to describe their sexual orientation, 37 per cent described themselves as bisexual or homosexual; 40 per cent exclusively heterosexual; and 23 per cent refused to disclose their sexuality. In short, these findings indicate that high prenatal androgen levels in females may bias them towards bisexuality or homosexuality. But, since there appears to be more heterosexual women than bisexual or homosexual ones in the group, this is far from inevitable. There is also evidence to show that the frequency of homosexual activity increases with ageing in adrenogenital woman, indicating that they begin sexual life trying to play the role of the heterosexual female (Dittmann *et al.* 1992).

Androgen insensitivity syndrome

Although increased amounts of androgens in foetal development have little effect on changing the sexual appearance of males, a decrease in the levels of these hormones, or reduced sensitivity to them, can produce feminine effects. One such condition is **androgen insensitivity syndrome** (sometimes called testicular feminisation syndrome), which occurs when testosterone and other androgens have no biological action on body tissues. This is caused when the androgen (testosterone) receptor, whose gene is found on the X chromosome, is dysfunctional and insensitive to the effects of androgens. The result is a failure of androgens to affect sexual development. Although the gonads of these individuals still express the *SRY* gene, and testis develop, the 'male' forms external female genitalia (labia and clitoris) and the infant appears to be a female at birth. However, because the testes continue to produce Müllerian-duct-inhibiting substance, which causes the internal female sexual organs to degenerate, the foetus does not develop a uterus or fallopian tubes. The result is a male pseudo-hermaphrodite.

A newborn baby with androgen insensitivity syndrome looks like a girl, and will often be mistaken for one unless the testes have descended into the labia. Consequently, these children are normally raised as females and their condition not recognised until the lack of menstruation in puberty is noticed. In fact, during adolescence the individual may develop feminine breasts because some of their testosterone is metabolised into oestrogen. Thus, these 'genetic XY males' appear to be girls, and because they have a vagina their sexual behaviour is also typically female, although without ovaries and a uterus they are infertile. In many cases of androgen insensitivity, physicians recommend that the child should be raised as a girl, since neither surgery nor hormonal treatment can create a functioning penis or alter the feminine appearance of the body (Masters *et al.* 1995). This does not generally present a problem as the great majority of these individuals regard themselves as female anyway. They typically dress as women, are sexually attracted to males, and their underlying genetic condition is often unsuspected by others, including close friends.

A similar developmental outcome occurs in individuals who have a defect in the enzyme 5-alpha-reductase. This enzyme, as we have seen above, is involved in turning testosterone into dihydrotestosterone, which is responsible for the masculinisation of the external genitalia in the foetus. Without this enzyme, however, the foetus develops female genitalia, and the individual appears to be a girl at birth. These individuals are also normally raised at girls. However, the development of the male internal sexual organs are not affected in this condition, and at puberty the testes, which tend to be hidden in the vagina, secrete testosterone. The result is a surprising turn of events, with the girl now turning into a boy as a small phallus grows to form a penis and partially fused labia develop into a scrotum complete with testes. In effect, the young female has now become a teenage male.

Sex chromosome abnormalities

Although we normally inherit 23 pairs of chromosomes, including a pair of sex chromosomes (XX or XY), there are occasions when this does not occur. The most common sex chromosome abnormality is **Turner's syndrome**, which is found in about one in 2,500 live births. This condition arises when the egg is fertilised by a sperm that has lost its X chromosome. Thus, the individual only inherits one X chromosome (X0). Because the Y chromosome is missing, the gonads do not differentiate into testes and the male sex organs fail to develop. Although the formation of the ovaries begins normally, their proper development requires both X chromosomes, and at birth they appear as abnormal streaks of connective tissue. Despite this, the infant appears to be female. Indeed, at birth these infants have a vagina which appears to be normal. In fact, it is only at puberty when the effects of their non-functioning ovaries manifest themselves that problems begin, with stunted growth, a lack of menstruation, and non-development of the breasts. There can also be webbing of the neck and heart abnormalities. Many of these abnormalities can be corrected with hormone replacement. Intelligence is usually normal (although spatial aptitude may be impaired) and gender identity is always female (Money and Ehrhardt 1972). The male version of Turner's syndrome (Y0) does not exist because embryos with this combination are aborted.

There are also genetic conditions where females inherit extra copies of the X chromosome including triple (XXX), tetra (XXXX) and even penta (XXXXX) inheritance. Of these, the triple X anomaly is by far the most common and may occur in as many as 1 in 2,500 females. Although sexual development in the triple X female proceeds normally, the adult is normally beset with menstrual cycle irregularities and a premature menopause. Despite this, they are often fertile and give birth to normal offspring. There is also an increased likelihood of intellectual impairment. In cases where tetra and penta inheritance occurs, there are greater problems with sexual development and functioning, accompanied by high risks of mental retardation.

Another sex-related genetic condition is **Klinefelter's syndrome**, where males inherit an extra X chromosome (XXY). This disorder occurs in about 1 in every 700 live births and increases the feminine characteristics of the individual, although this is not usually noticed until adulthood. The main problem with the extra X chromosome is that it causes abnormal development of the testes with low plasma testosterone concentrations, but raised luteinising hormone and follicle-stimulating hormone levels. Consequently, these men have a high oestrogen-to-testosterone ratio. The most striking characteristic of these individuals is their tall stature, along with poor muscular definition and enlarged breasts. In addition, they are often infertile with low sexual desire or impotence, which may be accompanied by mild mental retardation. Testosterone therapy may be successful at treating this condition, although the individual usually remains infertile.

Males can also be born with an extra copy of the Y chromosome (XYY). The only sexual abnormality of this inheritance appears to be an increased risk of infertility, although this is far from inevitable. There is also evidence of increased testosterone levels, which may increase height and muscle mass. This condition is highly controversial, however, since it has been associated with individuals who are mentally retarded or have criminal and violent tendencies. This is supported by evidence showing that whereas XYY inheritance occurs only in about 1 in 1,000 births, these individuals may make up 2–3 per cent of the inmates of mental or penal institutions (Emery and Mueller 1992). However, such statistics may also be misleading. For example, it has been reported that XYY men found in institutions are characterised by offences against property rather than people, which indicates an increased incidence of behavioural problems. And, it must be remembered that the majority of XYY individuals are neither delinquent, aggressive nor mentally retarded, and live their lives without any problem or stigma.

The organisational effects of hormones

In the developing foetus, androgen secretion exerts an effect not only on the internal and external reproductive organs that determine gender, but also on the neural circuits of the brain where it organises the nervous system for later male or female behaviour. One of the first studies to show this was undertaken by Phoenix et al. (1959) which looked at female sexual behaviour in guinea pigs that had been exposed to high testosterone levels during early development. Around the time of ovulation, an adult female guinea pig will often show **lordosis** – a mating position that includes raising the hind quarters and moving the tail to one side – signalling sexual receptivity for a male. Lordosis is under hormonal control and can be induced by giving the female a priming dose of oestrogen for a few days followed by an injection of progesterone. This procedure mimics the hormonal state of ovulation and makes the guinea pig sexually receptive a few hours later. However, when Phoenix *et al.* (1959) attempted to induce lordosis by hormone injections in females that had been given testosterone during the first few days of life, the behaviour did not occur. In other words, the early exposure to testosterone abolished this adult form of female sexual behaviour.

Clearly, the testosterone injection had exerted a masculinising influence on the brain, which was to affect later behaviour as an adult. That is, the early administration of testosterone had altered the structure of the developing brain to make it less sensitive to the lordosis-inducing effects of oestrogen and progesterone. However, this effect occurred only if the testosterone was given during the first ten days of life. Once this period had passed, testosterone injections had no effect on lordosis behaviour. Critical periods of development occur in all types of animals, including humans, although their timing and length depend on the species being examined. For example, guinea pigs must be exposed to androgens soon after birth for adult lordosis behaviour to be affected.

What is the situation regarding males? Male rats do not normally show lordosis behaviour when given injections of oestrogen and progesterone. But, interestingly, if males rats are castrated at birth, they show lordosis behaviour when administered female sex hormones during adulthood (Phoenix *et al.* 1959). Similarly, if male rats are castrated at birth, they do not show male sexual behaviour as adults, even when given injections of testosterone to stimulate this type of activity. It is clear, therefore, that the neural circuits governing sexual responses in rats are organised early in development, although the effects on adult sexual behaviour do not occur until much later.

The important lesson to be learned from these examples is that sex hormones, such as testosterone, exert two types of effect. During development, they have an **organisational effect** on the animal that determines its gender and helps to organise the structure of the brain for later adult behaviour. These events also typically require a critical period in which to occur. However, once development is complete, the sex hormones continue to exert an important effect on behaviour. At this point they produce **activational effects** where they stimulate certain behaviours such as lordosis. These two effects are not entirely separate, for, as we have just seen, whether a hormone is able to exert an activational effect on behaviour is largely dependent on the way the brain has been 'organised' during development. A number of activational effects have been found for testosterone, including aggression, courtship, rough-and-tumble play, and even taste preferences (Breedlove 1994). In females, the activational effects of hormones also include those that control the menstrual cycle.

There have also been attempts to see if early exposure to high levels of sex hormones in humans, or primates, produces similar effects to those found in rats. Although the behaviour of higher animals is much more complex, it does appear that a hormonal influence is at work. For example, Goy *et al.* (1988) examined the behaviour of female monkeys given prenatal androgens, and found they engaged in more rough-and-tumble play than normal. Similar findings have been found with humans. For example, females who have been exposed to high levels of testosterone in early development as a result of adrenogenital syndrome (see above) are often described as masculine and show an increased sexual preference for the same sex. Similarly, 'males' with androgen insensitivity syndrome, where androgen receptors are insensitive to testosterone, are generally regarded as girls.

Adult sexual development

At birth, apart from the differences in sexual anatomy, human males and females are physically quite similar, and they remain so until puberty, when **secondary sex characteristics** begin to develop. This is the final stage of sexual development and it transforms the young person into an adult capable of sexual intercourse and reproduction. One of the most striking changes that takes place during this period is the adolescent growth spurt which results in both sexes growing taller. In males, this is influenced by maturation of the testes, with high testosterone production, that increases skeletal and muscle mass, along with growth of pubic hair, a deepening of the voice and the ability to produce sperm. In females, the release of sex hormones from the ovaries promotes breast growth, a fuller figure, and development of the external genitalia and uterus. Furthermore, some two years or so after the start of puberty, the first signs of menstruation occur. This marks the point at which pregnancy should become possible, although it normally takes another year before the release of mature ova from the ovaries finally occurs.

The most important event causing the onset of puberty is the release of sex hormones from the gonads – namely, testosterone from the testes, and oestrogen and progesterone from the ovaries. The trigger for this final stage of sexual development occurs in the brain, when the testes and ovaries come under the control of the **hypothalamus** and **pituitary gland** (Figure 8.3). At the onset of puberty, the hypothalamus secretes

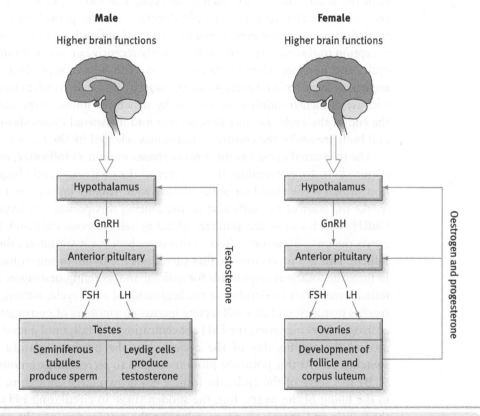

Figure 8.3 Flowchart showing how the hypothalamic–pituitary system influences activity of the testes and ovaries

gonadotropin-releasing hormone (GnRH), which diffuses through the hypophyseal portal blood vessels to the anterior part of the pituitary. This hypothalamic hormone then causes the pituitary gland to release **luteinising hormone (LH)** and **follicle-stimulating hormone (FSH)** into the bloodstream where they are transported to the gonads. Although males and females release the same hormones, the hormones have different effects. In males, the release of LH causes the **Leydig cells** of the testes to manufacture testosterone, whereas in the female the same hormone stimulates the production of oestrogen. In contrast, FSH in males stimulates the formation of sperm, whereas in females it causes the secretion of progesterone.

The activational effects of sex hormones

The menstrual cycle

So far, we have looked at some of the ways in which sex hormones can influence foetal and pubertal development. But, long after these hormones have shaped sexual differentiation and 'organised' the central nervous system, they still continue to exert important effects on behaviour. In females, the most obvious 'activational' effect of sex hormones is in the production of the **menstrual cycle**. For most species, the female is sexually receptive and able to conceive only during a specific period known as **oestrus** when ovulation occurs. However, human females, along with certain other primates, are an exception to this rule as they can be sexually receptive at any point in their reproductive cycle, and not just when ovulation occurs. The human reproductive cycle is called a menstrual cycle (from *mensis* meaning 'month') and it also differs from the oestrus cycle because of menstruation – the process by which the lining of the uterus is discarded at the end of the cycle. Despite this, oestrus and menstrual cycles show some similarities, and both are under the control of hormones released by the pituitary gland.

The menstrual cycle has three main phases known as **follicular**, **ovulatory** and **luteal** (Figure 8.4). By convention, the first day of the menstrual cycle begins with menstruation, which is the shedding of the uterine wall (usually lasting for a few days) and this marks the start of the follicular phase. During this period, the hypothalamus secretes GnRH, which causes the pituitary gland to release both FSH and LH. It is FSH that exerts the most important effect at this stage because it stimulates the development of a **follicle**. This is a protective sac that surrounds the **ovum** or unfertilised egg in the ovary. In turn, the follicle is responsible for making and secreting **oestrogen**. As many as twenty follicles may start to develop at the beginning of each cycle, although only one usually reaches maturity, and this will secrete increasing amounts of oestrogen. Moreover, as the oestrogen level increases, the FSH concentration will fall, until a level is reached, usually around the twelfth day of the cycle, when the pituitary gland's release of FSH is switched off. At this point the pituitary begins to secrete large amounts of LH.

By this stage of the cycle, the follicle has grown large enough to form a large bulge in the lining of the ovary. But, the sudden surge in circulating LH causes the walls of the follicle and ovary to rupture, releasing the mature egg into the upper sections of the fallopian tubes in a process known as **ovulation**. At this point the egg can be fertilised by a male sperm. However, the timeframe for this event is relatively short since the egg

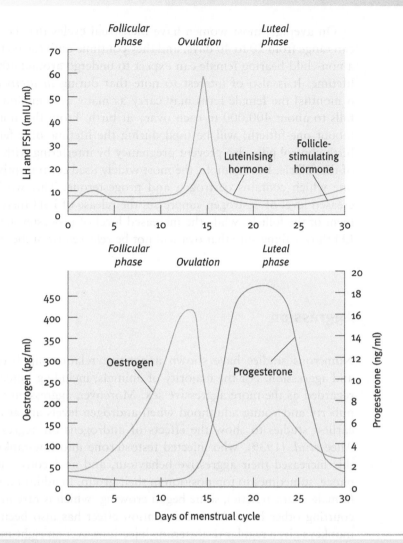

Figure 8.4   The menstrual cycle

is viable only for 12–24 hours, and most sperm exist in the female reproductive tract only for about a day (although some 'super' sperm may survive up to 72 hours). Thus, there is a period of around three days in every menstrual cycle when pregnancy can take place as the egg moves down the fallopian tubes into the uterus.

Following ovulation, the ruptured follicle in the ovary forms a yellow mass of tissue called the **corpus luteum** and begins to secrete large amounts of **progesterone**, and to a lesser extent oestrogen, which initiates the luteal phase of the menstrual cycle. The main function of progesterone ('pro-gestation') is to build up the lining of the uterus with blood and nourishment for the implantation of the egg, should it be fertilised. The increase in progesterone also turns off GnRH secretion from the hypothalamus, producing a rapid decline in LH and FSH. If fertilisation of the egg occurs, the level of progesterone remains high and the womb's lining will continue to develop. However, if fertilisation does not take place, the corpus luteum will shrink and reduce its secretion of hormones. Because the lining of the uterus cannot be maintained without progesterone, it will fall away, causing menstruation. The daily discharge of blood lost is usually around 30 millilitres, or one-twentieth of a pint.

On average, most women have menstrual cycles that last 28 days, although they can range from 20 to 40 days, and they continue until the menopause. This means that a non-child-bearing female can expect to undergo around 400 menstrual cycles in her lifetime. It is also of interest to note that during *in utero* development (at around 6 months) the female fetus may carry as many as 7 million primary follicles, which falls to about 400,000 in each ovary at birth. From this number, relatively few eggs (about one-fiftieth) will be used during the lifetime of a female. Interestingly, most birth-control pills also prevent pregnancy by interfering with the normal development of the follicle. For example, the most widely used contraceptive pill is the combination one which contains oestrogen and progesterone. This works in two ways: the increased level of oestrogen suppresses the release of FSH thereby blocking the development of the follicle, while the increased level of progesterone inhibits the secretion of LH thus making sure that ova will not be released from the ovary.

Aggression

Numerous studies have shown a positive relationship between testosterone levels and aggression. For the majority of animals, including humans, the male is generally regarded as the more aggressive sex. Moreover, aggression is frequently seen around puberty and young adulthood when androgen levels are at their highest. One of the earliest studies to show the effects of androgens on aggression was undertaken by Allee *et al.* (1939), who injected testosterone into low-ranking hens and found that this increased their aggressive behaviour, and as a consequence they rose in dominance, sometimes to top position in their group. In addition, their comb size increased (a male characteristic), some began crowing (which is rare in hens), and a few started courting other hens. A masculinisation effect has also been found in female rhesus monkeys given regular testosterone injections over an eight-month period. These monkeys became so aggressive that they replaced the males in the top position of the social hierarchy (Joslyn 1973). Similarly, a reduction of testosterone can decrease aggressive behaviour. Indeed, for thousands of years, humans have castrated domestic animals to control aggression and make them more manageable, and this has also been shown in numerous experimental studies (Beatty 1992). The effects of castration on aggression can normally be reversed by the administration of testosterone, although this is generally dependent on the earlier organisation of the nervous system. Thus, if the animal is castrated early in life before brain 'organisation' has occurred, and given testosterone as an adult, there is often little enhancement of aggression.

However, the relationship between testosterone and aggression in humans is not a straightforward one. Although males undoubtedly engage in more aggression than females, studies have shown that high levels of testosterone do not necessarily cause or predict this type of behaviour. For example, Archer (1994) reviewed ten studies in which aggressive and non-aggressive groups (for example, prisoners or young offenders with matched control groups) were compared for androgen levels. Although only one of the studies failed to find a difference in circulating androgens, the overall correlation between levels of aggressive behaviour and testosterone was in the region of +0.3. This is far from being a perfect positive relationship, which is represented by the value of +1.0. A similar type of finding was reported by Dabbs and Morris (1990), who measured testosterone levels in 4,462 US military veterans. These researchers found that those with levels in the top 10 per cent were also the ones who had previously shown greater amounts of antisocial behaviour, including assault; but, although this relationship was significant, it was relatively small. In fact, the tendency to produce aggressive behaviour was found to be more pronounced in the men from lower socio-economic groups. This finding shows that the type of environment can be an important factor in the expression of antisocial and aggressive behaviours.

There is also evidence to show that social interaction is an important determinant of testosterone levels. This can be seen, for example, in species that live in social groups with dominance hierarchies. It is well known that the highest-ranked individuals in such groups (alpha males) are the ones with greater levels of testosterone. On first sight, it is reasonable to suppose that they have risen to the top of their group through acts of aggressive behaviour produced by high testosterone levels. But this is not necessarily the case. For example, Rose *et al.* (1975) found that a monkey's testosterone level before the animal was placed into a new social group did not correlate with the rank it would later attain in the group. In fact, once the social groups were established and dominance ranking stabilised, a significant rise in testosterone (as much as tenfold) could often be found in the dominant male. The most important determinant of this rise was found to be success in aggressive encounters. In other words, victory increased levels of androgens whereas defeat reduced them. Indeed, studies have shown that a defeated monkey may show a fall in testosterone of some 10–15 per cent within 24 hours, and this level can remain depressed for several weeks (Monaghan and Glickman 1992).

Similar findings have also been reported for humans. For example, testosterone in athletes rises shortly before their sporting events, and levels remain high in the winner one or two hours after the match. Increases in testosterone have even been found in chess players and laboratory contests of reaction time (Mazur and Booth 1998). It appears that competition is the key variable, since testosterone levels are greater during a judo competition than during an equally energetic session of exercise. Remarkably, even watching a competitive event may affect testosterone levels. For example, after the 1994 World Cup soccer final between Brazil and Italy (which Brazil won 1–0), testosterone levels were taken from a small group of both fans. The results showed that testosterone levels rose in 11 of the 12 Brazilian fans by an average of 27.6 per cent, and decreased by 26.7 per cent in the 9 Italian fans (Fielden *et al.* 1994).

Sexual behaviour

We have mentioned an activational effect of sex hormones in producing sexual behaviour in the case of lordosis, and shown that this behaviour is dependent on the way the nervous system has been organised by androgens, along with the activating level of certain hormones, most notably oestrogen and progesterone, circulating in the body. The same type of principle also holds true in some instances for male reproductive behaviour. For example, if an adult male rat is castrated, it shows a marked decline in sexual activity and little interest in a receptive female. Reproductive interest is restored, however, by testosterone administration, which appears to show that this hormone is necessary for producing sexual motivation and activity (Becker *et al.* 1993).

For humans and primates, the relationship between testosterone and sexual activity is more complex. Male primates are typically able to maintain sexual behaviour for some years after being castrated, although castration does eventually produce a decrease in activity and libido. The situation appears to be similar in humans, with a gradual waning of sexual motivation. However, there is also great variability between individuals. Some castrated men quickly becoming impotent, whereas others show relatively normal sexual function for years or even decades after the operation (Money and Ehrhardt 1996). Indeed, historical accounts of eunuchs who were employed as harem guards, or young men castrated for their opera singing abilities, point to a similar conclusion (Heriot 1955). Furthermore, many reliable reports show that castrated men are capable of both erections and orgasms (Kinsey *et al.* 1948). Thus, it would appear that a loss of testosterone is not crucial for male sexual activity, although, with time, a lack of androgenic stimulation may lead to a decline in this behaviour. Clearly, there is more to human sexual behaviour than just the activational effects of certain hormones.

Despite this, testosterone is still capable of producing activational effects on sexual behaviour in such males. For example, when hypogonadal men with abnormally low levels of testosterone are given hormone replacement therapy, they often report increases in sexual activity along with increased frequencies of sexual thoughts and fantasies (Davidson *et al.* 1979). This effect may not be specific to males since the adrenal glands in women also produce small amounts of testosterone, and females who have injections of this hormone also often report a heightened sexual desire (Michael 1980).

Sexual dimorphism in the central nervous system

Sexual dimorphism is a term first coined by Charles Darwin that refers to the sex differences in physiology and appearance of males and females. Although researchers had known since the late 1950s that sex hormones exerted important organisational effects on development, there was little evidence to show that they changed the structure of the central nervous system. This changed in the early 1970s when Raisman and Field (1973) found that the pattern of synaptic connections in the **medial preoptic area** of the hypothalamus was different between male and female rats. These researchers found that the female preoptic area contained significantly more synapses than the male one. However, when males were castrated soon after birth the number of synapses increased to female levels. Alternatively, testosterone given to young females resulted in a decrease of synapses to male levels. This was the first direct proof that differences existed between male and female brains, and it showed that early androgen exposure could alter the neural structure of brain sites known to be associated with sexual behaviour.

Soon after this discovery, a more striking pattern of changes was reported in zebra finches and canaries by Nottebohm and Arnold (1976), who identified two brain nuclei that control birdsong – called the **robustus archistriatum** and **high vocal centre** – which were five to six times larger in male birds. Although this observation was not too surprising as males of both these species sing much more than females, the structural difference was found to be due to the organisational effects of sex hormones. For example, when researchers exposed a hatchling female zebra finch to testosterone, it caused the birdsong nuclei to become much larger in adulthood, and the female sang more like a male. It was also found that, in the male, the song nuclei grow larger in the spring when the bird sings most, and become smaller in the late summer when singing is less frequent. Again, the growth and shrinkage appear to be due to the changes in male testosterone levels, which are highest in early summer and low in late summer (Nottebohm 1985).

A similar type of discovery was also made in rats when Roger Gorski and his colleagues found a small nucleus embedded in the preoptic area of rats that was 3–5 times larger in males than in females (Gorski *et al.* 1978). In fact, this difference was so prominent that it could be distinguished from brain slices with the naked eye. This nucleus was called the **sexually dimorphic nucleus** (Figure 8.5) and its size was shown to be directly linked with early androgen stimulation. For example, males castrated at birth showed much smaller dimorphic nuclei, whereas females given androgens at birth had a much larger nucleus. In fact, the size of the sexually dimorphic nuclei could only be altered during a critical stage that corresponded to the first 10 days after birth. If male rats were castrated after this period, or females given androgens as adults, this had no effect on the size of the nucleus.

Another sexually dimorphic difference occurs in a group of motor neurons in the lower half of the spinal cord called the **bulbocavernosus nucleus**. These neurons control the bulbocavernosus muscles that surround the base of the penis, and are important in controlling the reflexes of copulation. This structure shows a difference between the sexes, with adult male rats having around 200 neurons in their nucleus and females fewer than 70. The size increase in males is due to early testosterone exposure. For example, females given testosterone during a critical period of development will show an increased number of bulbocavernosus neurons in adulthood, whereas male rats castrated at birth will develop a nucleus that resembles the female one. Bulbocavernous motor neurons are also found in humans, in a spinal structure

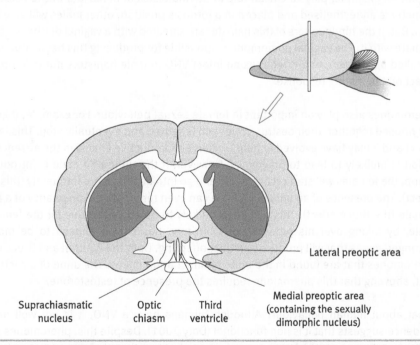

Suprachiasmatic nucleus
Optic chiasm
Third ventricle
Lateral preoptic area
Medial preoptic area (containing the sexually dimorphic nucleus)

Figure 8.5 The location of the sexually dimorphic nucleus in the rat brain

called **Onuf's nucleus**, and they are under voluntary control, with men using them to eject the last drops of urine after urination, and women using them to constrict the opening of the vagina (Breedlove 1993). The difference in the number of bulbocavernosus neurons between males and females in humans is believed to develop in the 26th week of gestation when the male foetus produces high amounts of androgens (Forger and Breedlove 1986).

How, then, does testosterone affect the development of the nervous system? The answer lies in the fact that many neurons in the brain and spinal cord have receptors for testosterone and other steroids. But, unlike the effects of neurotransmitters, whose main function is to affect the electrical excitability of the neuron, activation of sex steroid receptors initiates a cascade of events inside the neuron, which acts on the DNA in the genome to affect the transcription of certain genes. It appears that sex steroids influence cell numbers primarily by altering the incidence of programmed cell death, although in other instances they may act as tropic factors that promote the growth of cell size, dendritic branches and possibly synaptic numbers (Pfaff *et al.* 2002).

Pheromones: do they play a role in human sexual behaviour?

Pheromones are chemicals that act as odour signals which are secreted by animals to convey information – normally for attraction, repulsion, or about sexual condition – to other members of the same species. It is often overlooked by humans, who get much of their information about the world from sight and sound, that many other species rely heavily on this type of information to guide communication and social interaction. In fact, most mammals have a special structure in their nostrils called a vomeronasal organ (VNO) that has evolved to detect a wide range of pheromone signals. This organ, for example, plays a crucial role in the male sexual behaviour of the golden hamster. If a male hamster is anaesthetised and placed in a lordosis position, other males will give it a cursory examination. But, if the hindquarters of this hamster are smeared with a vaginal discharge, then the males will try to mate with it. The vaginal pheromone responsible for producing this behaviour has been isolated and is called *aphrodism*, and it requires an intact VNO in male hamsters if it is to produce its stimulatory effect on the mating response.

Pheromones also play an important in female sexual behaviour. For example, if groups of female mice are housed together, their oestrus cycles will lengthen and eventually stop. This is called the Lee–Boot effect and it may have evolved to help conserve reproductive energy in the absence of males when ovulation is unlikely to lead to pregnancy. However, if the urine of a male is introduced into the female group, the females will start cycling again and go into oestrus more frequently (this is called the Whitten effect). The presence of an unfamiliar male can even terminate the pregnancy of a recently impregnated female (the Bruce effect). This response is likely to be advantageous for the female because the new male, by taking over his predecessor's territory, has shown himself to be more 'fit' and to have 'stronger' genes that will produce healthier offspring. Both the Whitten and Bruce effects are caused by pheromones that are found in the urine of intact adult males. The urine of a castrated male has no effect, showing that this pheromone requires the presence of testosterone.

What about human behaviour? Although humans have a VNO, it is not well developed, and some evidence suggests that it is non-functional (Doty 2001). Despite this, pheromones still influence human behaviour. For example, when groups of women live together, their menstrual cycles will tend to become synchronised. The chemical responsible for this effect may derive from the armpits because when an extract from this region of the body was swabbed on the upper lips of a group of women three times each week, their menstrual cycles began to synchronise with the cycle of the donor (Russell *et al.* 1980). Pheromones may also play a role in human sexual attraction. In one study, males were asked to wear a T-shirt in bed for two consecutive nights, and to give a blood sample that enabled the genes governing their immune system to be determined (Wedekind *et al.* 1995). When these shirts were smelt by woman, it was found that they preferred the ones that had been worn by males with genetically dissimilar immune systems. In fact, this preference would be highly beneficial for the offspring since a greater mix of different immunity genes would give them greater protection to a wider range of diseases. Thus, humans may be more susceptible to the effects of pheromones than is generally recognised.

Sex differences in human brain structure

It has long been known that women tend to have smaller brains than men. For example, the average brain volume for men has been reported to be around 1,260 cc and for women 1,130 cc (Allen *et al.* 2002). It is sometimes argued that this difference reflects the fact that women tend to have smaller bodies. Although there is some truth in this, it may not be the full story. For example, while men's brains are approximately 15 per cent larger than women's, men's bodies are only 8 per cent larger. If such a sex difference in brain size does exist (small as it is), then it is likely that the higher secretion of sex steroids (androgens) during early development is involved in this effect.

When examined visually, male and female brains appear to be very similar, although in recent years the use of scanning techniques (such as MRI) has begun to reveal important differences. For example, the ratio of grey matter (composed of neural cell bodies and glia) to white matter (axons fibres) differs between males and females. More specifically, it has been reported that men have a higher percentage of white matter, and females a higher proportion of grey matter throughout the cerebral cortex (Cosgrove *et al.* 2007). Despite this, there is also evidence that one large region of the cerebral cortex called the **inferior parietal lobe**, including its grey matter, is bilaterally larger in men (Frederiske *et al.* 1999). This area of the brain is known to be involved in spatial and mathematical abilities, and was an area shown to be especially large in Albert Einstein (see Chapter 1). In contrast, females have been shown to have larger areas of the brain associated with language. For example, one MRI study has found 23 per cent more grey matter in Broca's area, and 13 per cent more grey matter in Wernicke's area in females compared with men (Schlaepfer *et al.* 1995). This may help explain why females tend to have superior verbal skills on certain tasks (see below).

Another area that has attracted a great deal of interest in sex difference research is the **corpus callosum,** which is the huge bundle of white matter that connects the two cerebral hemispheres. In 1982 it was reported that the posterior part of the corpus callosum, called the **splenium,** which joins the occipital and parietal regions, was significantly larger in females (Lacoste-Utamsing and Holloway 1982). This finding has been confirmed by several other researchers, although it is highly controversial – especially as one study that undertook a thorough meta-analysis of 49 studies found no significant differences in the size of the corpus callosum (Bishop and Wahlsten 1997). Part of the dispute appears to lie in the fact that while men have slightly bigger brains than women, the size of the corpus callosum remains roughly the same. Some have taken this finding to mean that females have a *relatively* larger corpus callosum than men (LeVay 1993).

If a difference could be reliably found to exist between the sexes in the size of the corpus callosum, it would lend support to the idea that the two cerebral hemispheres are more richly connected in women. This finding may help to explain why there are some significant differences between the sexes in terms of how they perform cognitive tasks. For example, the use of functional scanning techniques has tended to show that the two cerebral hemispheres of the female share more activity on mental tasks (i.e. are less lateralised) than those of the male. This is most noticeable for language tasks. For example, Shaywitz *et al.* (1995) compared 19 males with 19 females on a number of language tasks using fMRI, and found that brain activity in males was predominantly left hemispheric. In contrast, the females showed a more bilateral pattern of activation. Language functioning in a male is therefore more lateralised towards a single hemisphere, whereas it is spread more evenly in a female. This also explains why males who suffer a stroke to the left cortex are more likely to exhibit serious language deficits than are females, who have a greater degree of function across both hemisphere (Levy and Heller 1992) (see Figure 8.6).

It is sometimes said that the size of the right hemisphere compared with the left is greater in males than in females. This finding has generally not been found to hold true, although an increase in right hemispheric size in males occurs in certain conditions such as autism. Nonetheless, it is interesting to note that a larger right hemisphere is found at certain stages in the developing human male foetus, and that some animals, such as rats, show a larger right hemisphere as adults. The asymmetry in rats appears to be caused by testosterone because animals castrated at birth show no difference in cortical thickness (Diamond *et al.* 1981).

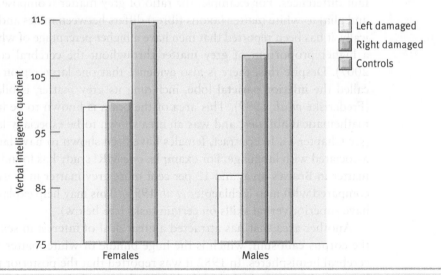

Figure 8.6 The effects of unilateral brain damage on verbal intelligence

Source: J.B. Becker *et al.*, *Behavioral Endocrinology*, p. 366, modified from McGlone (1977) Sex differences in the cerebral organization of verbal functions in patients with unilateral brain lesions, *Brain*, 100, 775–793. Copyright © 1993 by MIT Press

The effect of sex hormones on human brain structure

One area of the brain which is affected by sex hormones during early development is the preoptic area of the hypothalamus. This area contains what are known as sexually dimorphic nuclei. In fact, there are four sexually dimorphic nuclei otherwise known as the **interstitial nuclei of the anterior hypothalamus** (INAH 1–4). It has been found that whereas the INAH-1 and INAH-4 do not show any size difference between the sexes, the remaining two nuclei, particularly INAH-3, are much larger in males (Allen *et al.* 1988). In fact, INAH-3 is approximately 40 per cent larger in men than in women. More controversially, there is also evidence that INAH-3 may influence sexual orientation since it has been shown to be significantly smaller in homosexual than in heterosexual men (LeVay 1993). The implications of this finding are discussed later in the chapter.

A second brain structure which shows a difference between homosexual and heterosexual men is the **bed nucleus of the stria terminalis**. This structure is part of a pathway called the **stria terminalis** which connects the amygdala with the hypothalamus. The size of this nucleus is larger in males than in females (Zhou *et al.* 1995). Interestingly, while it appears to be the same size in male heterosexuals and homosexuals, it is significantly smaller in male transsexuals. These are men who feel as if they are women trapped in male bodies, and some go to great lengths to change their gender by having hormone therapy or sex-change operations. Another structure that may be involved in sexual male orientation is the **suprachiasmatic nucleus (SCN)**, located in the anterior part of the hypothalamus and which is known to be involved in the production of circadian rhythms. This nucleus was found to be some 150 per cent larger in the brains of homosexual men who had died from AIDS compared with a similar group of heterosexual men (Swaab and Hofman 1990). This finding is somewhat puzzling as there are no reports of SCN differences between males and females, nor does the SCN appear to play an overt role in sexual behaviour.

Sex differences in cognition

If men and women have different brains, then one might also expect them to show some differences in the way they solve intellectual problems. Experimental evidence supports this idea, although the differences occur in specific abilities and not in the overall level of intelligence. Moreover, some differences favour males and others females. One of the most consistent sex differences in cognition is a male superiority at mentally rotating objects in three-dimensional space. Such a difference is shown, for example, on the Vandenberg and Kuse mental rotations task where the subject is given a drawing of a object made of several cubes, and instructed to pick out two rotated figures from a series of four that is the same shape as given in the target (Vandenberg and Kuse 1978). The results of the original study showed that undergraduate male students, on average, made 9.5 correct judgements compared with 6.6 rotations for females in a 210-second test period. The male superiority on these types of task is consistently around 20 per cent and is found across different cultures (Peters *et al.* 2007). Males also show a superiority on a wide range of other spatial tasks, including

(a) Problem-solving tasks favouring men

Men tend to perform better than women on certain spatial tasks. They do well on tests that involve mentally rotating an object or manipulating it in some fashion, such as imagining turning this three-dimensional object:

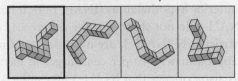

or determining where the holes punched in a folded piece of paper will fall when the paper is unfolded:

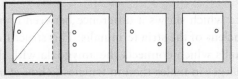

Men also are more accurate than women in target-directed motor skills, such as guiding or intercepting projectiles:

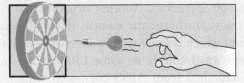

They do better on disembedding tests, in which they have to find a simple shape, such as the one on the left, once it is hidden within a more complex figure:

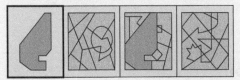

And men tend to do better than women on tests of mathematical reasoning:

1,100	If only 60 percent of seedings will survive, how many must be planted to obtain 660 trees?

(b) Problem-solving tasks favouring women

Women tend to perform better than men on tests of perceptual speed, in which subjects must rapidly identify matching items – for example, pairing the house on the far left with its twin:

In addition, women remember whether an object, or a series of objects, has been displaced:

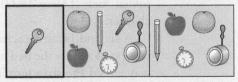

On some tests of ideational fluency, for example, those in which subjects must list objects that are the same colour, and on tests of verbal fluency, in which participants must list words that begin with the same letter, women also outperform men:

L _ _ _ _	Limp, Livery, Love, Laser, Liquid, Low, Like, Lag, Live, Lug, Light, Lift, Liver, Lime, Leg, Load, Lap, Lucid ...

Women do better on precision manual tasks – that is, those involving fine-motor co-ordination – such as placing the pegs in holes on a board:

And women do better than men on mathematical calculation tests:

77	$14 \times 3 - 17 + 52$
43	$2(15 + 3) + 12 - \frac{15}{3}$

Figure 8.7   Sex differences in cognition and behavioural performance

Source: D. Kimura, Sex differences in the brain, *Scientific American*, Sept., 81–87. Copyright © 1992 by Scientific American

the ability to recognise specified shapes that are embedded in a more complex visual array, to read a map, or to solve maze problems. Men also, on average, outperform women in mathematical reasoning, and are better in tests of target-directed motor skills involving throwing projectiles such as darts, or intercepting moving objects

(Kimura 1992). Despite this, some caution is needed when analysing these sex differences. For example, around one-quarter of adult women do better than the average man on the visual–spatial questions of an IQ test. Thus, there is considerable variation between individuals on these types of task.

Testosterone has also been shown to be an important determinant of spatial ability. One of the first demonstrations of this occurred when it was realised that **hypogonadal men** with low levels of testosterone caused by pituitary dysfunction, performed very poorly on spatial tests. In contrast, females with **congenital adrenal hyperplasia**, who have high levels of testosterone, were found to do much better than their peers on this type of test (Resnick *et al*. 1986). Similarly females who were more androgynous in appearance (for example, with small breasts, wide shoulders, narrow hips and solid muscles) performed better than their 'feminine' counterparts on spatial tasks (Peterson 1976). But, there were also some puzzling findings. For example, males with masculine body types with high muscle bulk (indicative of high testosterone levels) were actually better on verbal tests than on spatial ones. Similar findings were obtained with males who were less masculine in physical appearance.

An explanation for these findings was provided by Gouchie and Kimura (1991), who measured salivary testosterone levels and gave a variety of cognitive tasks to groups of males and females. The results showed that men with low to medium (or average) testosterone levels were superior on the spatial and mathematical tasks compared to men with high levels. But, the opposite was true for women. In this case it was the group with the highest (or lowest) levels of testosterone levels that showed the best spatial and mathematical ability. It is now generally recognised that the relationship between testosterone and spatial ability follows a curvilinear relationship (Figure 8.8).

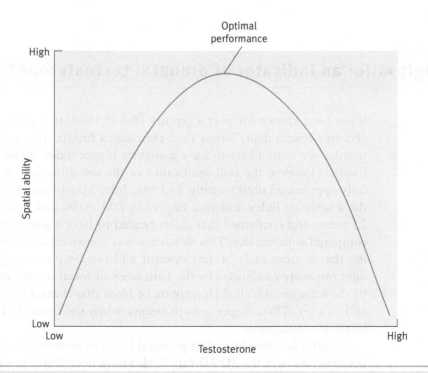

In contrast to men, women tend to perform better on tasks that involve verbal skill, perceptual speed and fine manual dexterity. This difference can be observed very easily by giving subjects a **verbal fluency test** in which they are given a random letter and then told to write down as many words beginning with that latter in a certain time. Although females do not have a larger vocabulary than men, they often outperform them on this task (Kimura 1999). However, there is a great deal of overlap between men and women on these type of tests, and results vary considerably across studies. Women also tend to perform better on tests of perceptual speed in which they must match items, and in tests of visual memory where they asked to remember whether an item has been misplaced from a picture or array. Another female superiority occurs in colour naming. Females typically are able to name a series of colour patches or circles faster than males, and this effect is found in primary school children as well as university undergraduates (Kimura 1999).

A number of explanations have been proposed to account for the differences between the sexes in their cognitive abilities. Although many have emphasised hormonal causes, others believe that environmental and learning factors also play an important role in shaping these mental skills. But, one of the most intriguing explanations lies in our ancestral past when humans were hunter-gatherers (c.10,000 years ago). During this time, men and women had different roles. Men engaged in hunting that involved travelling long distances far from their home base. To be successful in this activity, men would have required good navigational skills and efficient spatial memory. In contrast, women stayed at home looking after children. This would have been more conducive to developing fine motor skills, communication, and the ability to make fine perceptual discriminations. It is tempting to speculate that natural selection found a way of developing these respective abilities in males and females (Kimura 1999).

Digit ratio: an indicator of prenatal testosterone?

It has been known for over a century (Baker 1888) that males tend to have ring fingers (the fourth digit) longer than their index fingers (the second digit). In contrast, females are more likely to have a slightly longer index finger, or digits of the same length. However, the full significance of the sex difference in 2D:4D ratio was not fully appreciated until recently. In 1998, John Manning and his colleagues measured the lengths of index and ring fingers in 800 males and females ranging from 2 to 25 years, and confirmed that males tended to have a lower 2D:4D (on both hands) compared with females. This difference was consistent across all age groups, indicating that it arose early in development and remained unchanged over time. In fact, digit ratios are established by the 13th week of foetal development, and are governed by the same genes (called Homeobox or *Hox*) that control the formation of our testes and ovaries. Thus, finger growth occurs when the foetus is being exposed to high levels of testosterone.

Could it be, therefore, that prenatal levels of testosterone are responsible for the sex differences in the 2D:4D ratio? Manning provided support for this idea by discovering a significant relationship between digit ratio and levels of sex hormones in his sample of subjects. In short, he found that males with the lowest 2D:4D ratios tended to have the highest testosterone levels and increased sperm counts (another indicator of testosterone). In contrast, the higher levels of luteinising hormone and oestrogen were related to higher 2D:4D ratios which were more common in females.

As we have seen, there is strong evidence that sex hormones exert organisational effects upon the brain during foetal development which helps to masculinise or feminise certain behaviours. An important period for this is the latter part of the first trimester, which is the time when digit ratio is formed, and also a critical period for sexual differentiation of the body and brain. The implication from Manning's work was that a low 2D:4D ratio could act as a marker for a uterine environment high in testosterone and low in oestrogen. Conversely, a high 2D:4D ratio could be a marker for an uterine environment low in testosterone and high in oestrogen. If this was indeed the case then one might expect to find a wide range of behavioural differences between individuals with high and low digit ratios.

Indeed, a number of differences between individuals with low and high digit ratios have now been discovered. Digit ratio, for example, appears to be an indicator for sexual orientation. This was shown by Manning et al. (2007), who used self-reported finger measurements from 255,166 participants in a BBC internet survey to investigate the relationship between digit ratio and sex, ethnicity and sexual orientation. The results confirmed that males tend to have a lower 2D:4D ratio than females, and this was found across all ethnic groups. However, male homosexuals and bisexuals tended to have a higher mean 2D:4D digit ratio, suggesting exposure to lower levels of prenatal testosterone, than heterosexuals. No significant relationship between digit ratio and sexual orientation was found for women, although there was a trend for a lower 2D:4D ratio in lesbians.

There is also a relationship between digit ratio and cognitive performance on a wide range of tasks. For example, in a sample of 134,317 men and 120,783 women, it was found that men performed better than women on a mental rotation task, and this effect was most significant in individuals who had low 2D:4D digit ratio (that is, relatively long ring finger compared with index finger). This relationship was found to hold true in both men and women (Peters et al. 2007). The situation regarding verbal fluency, however, was less clear cut. Although there was some evidence that men with a low (male type) 2D:4D digit ratio exhibited poorer verbal fluency, and this performance effect was reversed in females, the effects did not reach significance (Manning 2002).

Digit ratio also provides an indicator for other types of behaviour. For example, Martin et al. (1999) found that low digit ratio in men tends to be correlated with higher levels of depression. Thus, one cost of high prenatal testosterone levels may be a greater tendency towards depression as an adult. This is consistent with evidence showing that high levels of testosterone can be associated with a number of developmental disorders, including autism, stuttering, immune disorders and schizophrenia (Geschwind and Galaburda 1985a). However, a low 2D:4D ratio can have many benefits as well. In fact, a tendency for low 2D:4D ratios has been found in professional soccer players (the ratio is even more marked for international players) and in elite male musicians from a British symphony orchestra (Figure 8.9). There are a number of reasons why a low 2D:4D ratio may exist in these two groups, including improved visuo-spatial abilities and increased competitiveness due to increased prenatal testosterone.

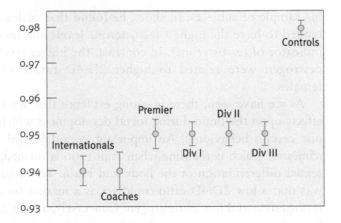

Figure 8.9   Digit ratios of professional soccer players

Source: Professor J.T. Manning (2001) *Evolution and Human Behaviour*, 22, 61–69. Reproduced by permission of Professor Manning

Charles Brown-Sequard and his quest for sexual rejuvenation

The male testes have long been associated with sexual vigour, youthfulness and longevity. The ancient Greeks and Romans, for example, used concoctions made from goat and wolf testes as aphrodisiacs, and a similar practice still occurs today in some places of the world. The relationship between sexual vigour and youthfulness has also fascinated humans – not least because it is obvious, especially to old frail men, that the period of youth coincides with peak sexual performance. But can sexual vigour and youthfulness be linked to the testes? One person who believed so was Charles Brown-Sequard (1817–1894). The imposing 6ft 4in. bearded French professor was the author of over five hundred research papers, including pioneering work on the adrenal glands, and one of the great biologists of his time. For most of his life Brown-Sequard had been a prolific researcher, but as he approached his seventieth birthday he became aware of a decline in his ability to concentrate and work. This was accompanied by tiredness and a waning of his muscular strength. Despite being recently married with a young wife, he also experienced impotence and declining sexual interest. Worried about his lack of vitality, Brown-Sequard set about ways of rejuvenating himself.

Brown-Sequard believed the testes, or rather the seminal fluid that contains the sperm, had invigorating properties, and he started to test the effects of such extracts on himself. In his first attempt, Brown-Sequard ground up the testicles of a young dog and passed the mixture through filter paper. He then put the residue in distilled water and injected it directly into his leg. The procedure seemed to have a beneficial effect, and after a few injections Brown-Sequard felt much stronger and rejuvenated. He repeated the procedure twice more, this time with extracts taken from guinea pigs. The health benefits appeared to be so impressive that, in 1889, Brown-Sequard made the bold step of presenting his findings to a prestigious group of scientists at the Société de Biologie in Paris.

Although the talk lasted only 15 minutes, its impact was enormous. This was partly due to Brown-Sequard describing in explicit terms the effects of his experiences, including a confession that he had paid his wife 'a visit' for the first time in many weeks. The talk not only provoked much debate in scientific circles, but was also reported in a sensational fashion in magazines and newspapers. Consequently, Brown-Sequard soon become the world's foremost advocate for the existence of 'internal secretions', or what we now know as hormones. In this belief, Brown-Sequard was to be proved correct – but, in regard to his views on testicular extracts and rejuvenation, history was to treat him less kindly. Within a year of his talk, some 1,200 physicians worldwide were testing his elixir in clinical trials, but few were able to replicate the findings. Moreover, Brown-Sequard was an easy target for ridicule and his professional reputation was quickly damaged by the episode. Suffering from deteriorating health, his wife left him for a younger man, and despite keeping up his injections, Brown-Sequard died from a stroke at the age of 77. But why was Brown-Sequard so mistaken in his views? The likeliest answer is that he was fooled by a placebo effect, that is, he was expecting a positive response, and his optimism led him to incorrectly exaggerate the benefits of his extracts. This was further compounded by a lack of a control group, which is an essential experimental requirement in this type of study.

The neural control of sexual behaviour

Although the most important organ for sexual behaviour is the brain, some of the basic reflexes that form an integral part of our reproductive behaviour are controlled by the spinal cord. For example, stimulation of the genitals in animals is able to elicit sexual responses such as penile erections, pelvic thrusting and ejaculations even when the brain is severed from the spinal cord (Hart 1967). Similar responses have been observed in paraplegic men. In one study, Money (1960) examined a group of paraplegic males with broken spinal cords that had severed the neural pathways between brain and sex organs, and found that 65 per cent of the sample were capable of achieving a complete erection, 20 per cent managed partial erections, and 20 per cent were able to engage in coitus. Many of these men were also able to ejaculate although they did not 'sense' the orgasm mentally. Thus, even in a species as advanced as ourselves, neural circuits capable of producing erection and ejaculation lie outside brain.

One brain structure that plays an important role in sexual behaviour is the hypothalamus. This region not only influences the release of LH and FSH from the pituitary gland, which controls the secretion of testosterone from the gonads, but also exerts important control over the autonomic nervous system. In particular, the **medial preoptic area** of the hypothalamus has been implicated in the act of male sexual intercourse. For example, lesions of this region do not eliminate interest in females, but impair the ability of male rats to copulate with them (Heimir and Larsson 1967). Similarly, electrical or androgen stimulation of the same region facilitates sexual behaviour in male rats (Davidson 1980). The medial preoptic area in the male has also been shown to contain a high concentration of androgen receptors, which is about five times more than is found in females. Moreover, mating behaviour can be reinstated in castrated males by small implants of testosterone into the medial preoptic area – an effect that does not occur in any other brain structures (Breedlove et al. 2007). In contrast, an androgen antagonist called hydroxyflutamide injected into the same area decreases sexual motivation and suppresses copulation (McGinnis et al. 2002). And, as mentioned above, the preoptic area is also the site of the sexually dimorphic nucleus, which is far bigger in male brains than in female, and whose size is dependent on circulating androgen levels (Gorski et al. 1978).

The medial preoptic area also receives input from the **vomeronasal organ,** a specialised sensory organ found in the nose of most higher animals, including humans, whose function is to detect **pheromones.** These are chemicals that affect reproductive behaviour, and help transmit sexual information from other individuals (see box on page 304). The medial preoptic area further receives dopaminergic input from the medial forebrain bundle, which is likely to be involved in reward and reinforcement. Indeed, the infusion of dopamine agonists into the medial preoptic area facilitates the sexual behaviour of rats, whereas dopamine antagonists decrease it (Dominguez *et al.* 2001). There is also some evidence that testosterone facilitates dopamine release in the medial preoptic area by a mechanism involving nitric oxide synthesis (Hull *et al.* 1997).

The medial preoptic area projects to a number of other brain areas, but most notably to the midbrain, including the **periaqueductal grey area (PGA),** and to a tiny nucleus in the medulla called the **nucleus paragigantocellularis (PGi).** The PGA is believed to be responsible for producing complex reflexes, or species-typical patterns of behaviour necessary for copulation. Curiously, the PGi sends serotonergic fibres down into the spinal cord which appear to have an inhibitory effect on spinal cord reflexes, including the one controlling the erection reflex. Thus, the medial preoptic has both the ability to facilitate sexual activity by its action on the PGA, and to inhibit it by acting on the PGi (Figure 8.10).

The area of the brain implicated in female sexual behaviour is the **ventromedial hypothalamus (VMH).** This area of the brain, in many animals at least, is responsible

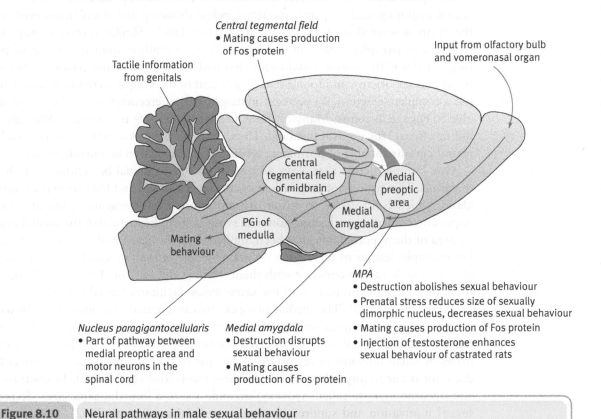

Figure 8.10 Neural pathways in male sexual behaviour

Source: N.R. Carlson, *Physiology of Behavior*, 9th edition, p. 334. Copyright © 2007 by Pearson Education

for the control of lordosis. For example, lesions to the VMH will abolish the ability of the female rat to perform lordosis, whereas an injection regime of oestrogen followed by progesterone will induce lordosis behaviour. Tiny implants of oestrogens into this region of the hypothalamus will also increase female receptivity towards males (Becker *et al.* 1993). One action of oestrogen on neurons is to promote RNA synthesis, which is believed to be important for increasing the number of progesterone receptors. Indeed, injections of oestrogen into the VMH lead to a marked increase of progesterone receptors by about 150 per cent. This increase is necessary for lordosis, and if a drug is injected into the VMH which blocks progesterone receptors, then mating behaviour is abolished (Ogawa *et al.* 1994).

A model explaining the neural circuitry underlying lordosis behaviour has been developed by Pffaff and Schwartz-Giblin (1988). Lordosis behaviour begins when the male attempts to mount the female and causes her rump to be stimulated. This information is relayed to the medullary reticular formation, PGA and VMH. If the latter structure has been primed with oestrogen and progesterone (thereby producing a receptive female), then it will trigger the neural signals for producing lordosis by activating a pathway back to the PGA. In turn, the PGA activates neurons in the midbrain reticular formation, which controls motor neurons for axial muscles, especially the deep back muscles, that are involved in producing the postural changes of lordosis. A multisynaptic pathway then passes down to the spinal cord where the reflexes of lordosis are put into motion.

Another structure involved in regulating sexual behaviour is the **amygdala**. It has long been known that lesions of this structure in monkeys produce hypersexuality, with indiscriminate attempts at mating with almost any other animal or object in the environment (Kluver and Bucy 1938). The medial amygdala appears to be very important for these effects. This region receives olfactory information from the vomeronasal organ in the nose, and is sexually dimorphic – with one of its sub-regions being up to 85 per cent larger in male rats (Hines *et al.* 1992). The medial amygdala also contains a large number of androgen receptors. Evidence linking the medial amygdala with reproductive behaviour is shown by the fact that lesions to this area disrupt the ability of male rats to mount receptive females, and impairs erection (Keverne 1999). Conversely, electrical stimulation of the medial amygdala nucleus can elicit copulatory behaviour in male rats in the presence of a female who is showing no signs of sexual interest (Stark *et al.* 1998). The medial amygdala is believed to express these effects through a pathway called the stria terminalis which directly projects to the medial preoptic area of the hypothalamus.

In humans, it is probable that the cerebral cortex plays the most important role in many aspects of sexual activity. Although this is difficult to test, animal studies have also confirmed the importance of the cerebral cortex in sexual behaviour. For example, Beach (1940) found a decrease in male copulation in rats following cortical damage, with lesions involving 60 per cent of its tissue abolishing this behaviour completely. Similar damage, however, did not have an effect on female sexual activity. The main reason for this difference may lie with the motor reflexes of copulation. Lordosis behaviour is relatively simple and requires reflex circuits in the brainstem and VMH, whereas the male sexual response is less reflexive and involves a higher degree of motor co-ordination requiring the cerebral cortex. Beach also suggested that the cerebral cortex plays an important role in initiating sexual activity and storing memories of past sexual experiences.

What determines a person's sexual orientation?

We all have sexual preferences, whether for members of the opposite sex, same sex, or both. But, what causes our sexual orientation? As might be expected, there are many theories, although they fall into three main groups: those emphasising genetic factors; those stressing hormonal influences that occur during prenatal development; and those highlighting the importance of learning and the environment. These, however, are not necessarily mutually exclusive. For example, genetic and hormonal factors are closely linked, and there may be an interaction of all three influences to varying degrees throughout development to determine our sexual predisposition.

The genetic influence on sexuality can be examined by comparing the concordance rates between identical (monozygotic) twins who share the same genes, and fraternal (dizygotic) twins who share approximately 50 per cent of their genes. One early study to do this was undertaken by Kallman (1952), who examined 85 male twin pairs where homosexuality was reported. The results showed a 100 per cent concordance rate for identical twins, compared with just 10 per cent for fraternal twins. Recent studies, however, have not found such a high concordance. For example, Bailey and Pillard (1991), in a study of male twins where one was gay, found that 52 per cent of monozygotic twins and 22 per cent of dizygotic ones were concordant for homosexuality. This figure fell to 11 per cent when the adoptive brothers of homosexual men were examined. Comparable figures have also been reported for sisters. For example, Bailey *et al.* (1993) reported that 48 per cent of identical twins of homosexual women were lesbian, compared with 16 per cent for fraternal twins. The percentage of adoptive sisters of homosexual women who were lesbian was 6 per cent. These results suggest that genetic influences may have a bearing on the development of homosexuality, but it is not marked (i.e. about 50 per cent) and other factors are important. Indeed, supporting this view is the fact that there are many cases of identical twins where one is homosexual and the other heterosexual (Byne 1994).

The question of whether there is hormonal influence at work during foetal development to determine adult sexuality has also attracted attention. Indeed, as we have seen earlier in the chapter, exposure to androgens during early development in females (the androgenital syndrome) leads to a greater probability of homosexuality in adulthood. This appears to support the idea that early hormonal exposure has a bearing on later sexual preference. Despite this, the figures show that the majority of women with androgeneital syndrome still have heterosexual sexual preferences. Thus, the hormonal effect on female sexuality is not pronounced. The situation appears to be similar for males. For example, while genetic males who are insensitive to the effects of androgens during development are typically female in appearance, and sexually attracted to men as adults, this is not an inevitable outcome. In fact, if their genitalia are surgically corrected at an early age, and they are reared as boys, these individuals are more likely to be sexually attracted to females as adults (Money and Ogunro 1974).

There is, however, some evidence to show that male homosexuality can be influenced by decreased levels of testosterone occurring prenatally, particularly in the latter part of the first trimester. For example, male homosexuals are more likely to have a higher 2D:4D digit ratio, which is indicative of lower prenatal testosterone levels (see above). In addition, there are reports showing that male laboratory animals exposed to low levels of testosterone early in life, show a greater sexual preference for their own sex as adults (Adkins-Regan 1989). Further evidence supporting a prenatal androgen deficiency in homosexual men comes from studies showing that they often exhibit a pattern of luteinising hormone release in response to an injection of oestrogen that is intermediate between that of heterosexual men and heterosexual females. This effect has been attributed to reduced androgen exposure since a similar effect has been reported in rats that have been deprived of testosterone prenatally (Becker *et al.* 1993).

As mentioned, increased androgen exposure prenatally may influence homosexuality in some women, and further support for the theory has come from an unusual source: the cochlea of the inner ear. For example, it has been shown that the cochleas of heterosexual women are nearly three times as sensitive as those of men when it comes to detecting faint clicks. However, lesbian females have responses that are closer to males. The sex difference between males and females in auditory sensitivity is believed to be due to prenatal androgen exposure. If prenatal levels of androgen hormones do indeed reduce cochlea sensitivity, then this supports the idea of greater testosterone exposure in lesbian women (McFadden and Pasanen 1998).

Although it is possible that androgen exposure during prenatal development can influence later sexuality, male heterosexuals and homosexuals do not show any differences in levels of their circulating hormones as adults. Moreover, altering the levels of sex hormones has no bearing on sexual preference. For example, castration may reduce the frequency of sexual behaviour, but it does not change sexual orientation. Similarly, injections of testosterone can help increase sexual desire in both sexes, but it does not change their sexual preference (Money and Ehrhardt 1996). The situation with women may be a little more complex as it has been reported that higher testosterone levels are found in 'butch' lesbians compared to more 'feminine' ones (Singh *et al.* 1999).

It might come as a surprise to find out, however, that the current most reliable indicator of sexual orientation does not come from an understanding of genes or even prenatal hormonal influences, but from birth order. For example, in the 1990s, the Canadian researcher Ray Blanchard noted that homosexual males tended to have older brothers but not older sisters or younger brothers. Further analysis showed that for each extra male child born to a mother, the probability of a homosexual offspring increased by approximately 30 per cent (Blanchard 2001). In other words, the more older brothers a male has, the greater is the chance that he will be homosexual. Moreover, this effect still occurs if the males are reared apart from the rest of the family (Bogaert 2006). The likeliest explanation for this birth effect lies with the mother's immune system. That is, the exposure to male foetuses causes the mother's immune system to become sensitised to proteins or chemicals that only a male possesses. In turn, this somehow disrupts the ability of subsequent sons to respond to male-forming signals during foetal development. Interestingly, this birth effect is only seen in boys who are right-handed (Blanchard *et al.* 2006). Estimates indicate that about one in seven homosexual men are gay because their mothers had sons before them (Cantor *et al.* 2002).

Brain structure and homosexuality

If there is a biological basis to homosexuality then one would expect to find a physiological difference in brain structure between heterosexuals and homosexuals. In the early 1990s a difference of this type was discovered by Simon LeVay, who examined the **interstitial nuclei of the anterior hypothalamus**. As mentioned previously, there are four of these nuclei (INAH 1–4) which are located in the medial preoptic area of the hypothalamus (Figure 8.11a). They are also sexually dimorphic, with INAH-2 and INAH-3 being much larger in the male. Although LeVay confirmed these findings, he also discovered that the INAH-3 nucleus was significantly smaller in homosexual men ($N = 19$) compared with a group of heterosexuals ($N = 6$). In fact, it was more than twice as large in heterosexual males as in homosexuals. Put another way, the size of INAH-3 in homosexual men was very similar to that found in heterosexual women (Figure 8.11b). This discovery led LeVay to suggest that homosexuality may, in part, be due to the 'feminisation' of the INAH-3 nucleus (LeVay 1993).

The significance of this work remains controversial. Although the interstitial nuclei are believed to be the same as the sexually dimorphic nuclei which are found in rats

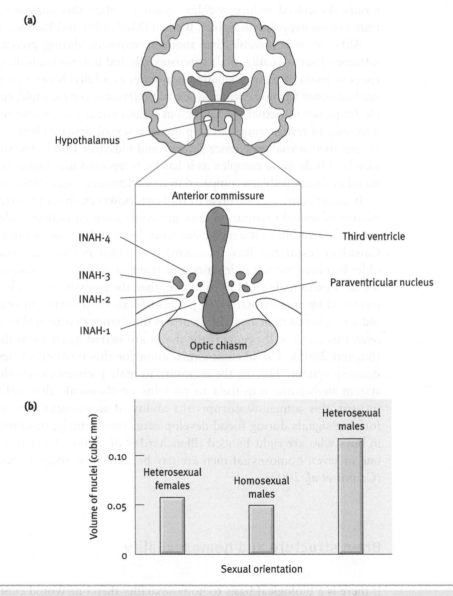

Figure 8.11   (a) The location of the INAH nuclei in the human brain; (b) the size of INAH-3 in heterosexual men and women, and in homosexual men

and whose size are known to influenced by early androgen exposure (Gorski *et al.* 1978), it remains possible that the decreased size of INAH-3 in homosexual men could have occurred after foetal development. For instance, it may be that the sexual experience of the homosexual men has affected the size of their INAH-3. Thus, its smaller size could be the result of homosexuality rather than its cause. But, even if the size of INAH-3 arose during foetal development, and results from low androgen levels, it seems improbable that this tiny brain structure could act as the sexual orientation centre. Rather, it is more likely that INAH-3 forms part of a much larger system. It should also be mentioned that not all researchers have confirmed LeVay's findings in homosexuals (Byne *et al.* 2001). Despite all these uncertainties, most would agree that LeVay's work is an important step forward in our understanding of the biological basis of sexual orientation.

Summary

Sexual or reproductive behaviour is necessary for the continuation of the species. It is also a complex behaviour that, for most animals, requires the coming together of male and female in sexual intercourse, as well as courtship, territorial ownership and parental assistance. In humans, whether a fertilised egg develops into a **male** or **female** depends on the **sex chromosomes**. Nearly every cell in the human body contains 23 pairs of chromosomes, and the sexes differ in just one: males inheriting **XY chromosomes**, and females **XX chromosomes**. After around 6 weeks of gestation, the *SRY* gene on the Y chromosome helps to produce **testis-determining factor**, which causes the foetal gonadal tissue to develop into **testes**. This tissue starts to secrete **testosterone**, which begins the masculinisation process of the foetus. However, without this hormonal influence, the foetus develops ovaries at about 12 weeks of gestation and becomes female. The action of hormones to shape physiological sexual development is known as an **organisational effect**. Another type of organisational effect takes place after birth at puberty, when increased testosterone production results in adult male characteristics, and increased **oestrogen** and **progesterone** released from the ovaries cause adult female characteristics. These last two hormones are secreted in a monthly pattern known as the **menstrual cycle** which prepares the womb for a fertilised egg (should fertilisation occur). However, the sex hormones also continue to influence behaviour after sexual development has been completed by having an **activational effect** on behaviour. In particular, testosterone is known to increase levels of **aggression** and **sexual libido**. Levels of testosterone can also fluctuate as a result of experience, with success in sporting contests and competition causing higher secretion.

Although male and female brains appear to be very similar, there are some important differences. For example, two of the **interstitial nuclei of the anterior hypothalamus** (INAH-2 and INAH-3) are bigger in male brains than in female, although this relationship does not appear to hold for homosexual men. Another structure that tends to be bigger in male brains is the **bed nucleus of the stria terminalis**, which connects the **amygdala** and **hypothalamus**. These structures are likely to be involved in sexual behaviour. In contrast, parts of the brain with a more cognitive function, such as the **corpus callosum**, especially the **splenium** and **anterior commissure**, are larger in women's brains. These differences may one day help to explain why men and women have varying abilities at solving cognitive problems. In particular, men tend to be superior on tasks involving spatial memory, whereas women are superior on verbal and dexterity tests. The differences between men and women and, in particular, the importance of early androgen exposure for later behaviour have been greatly elucidated by studies examining **digit ratio**.

The neuroanatomy of sexual behaviour is complex, although the basic reflexes that allow male copulation are controlled by the **spinal cord**. For example, paraplegic men are often capable of coitus with both erection and ejaculation. Despite this, the brain is crucial for all aspects of sexual behaviour. In males, stimulation of the **medial preoptic area** of the hypothalamus facilitates copulatory behaviour, whereas **ventromedial hypothalamus** stimulation in females induces lordosis. This latter behaviour is also dependent on neural circuits involving the **periaqueductal grey area** and **reticular formation**. Another important brain structure is the **amygdala,** which is known to receive olfactory information from the **vomeronasal organ** in the nose, which detects **pheromones**.

Sexual orientation in humans is affected by many variables, including genetic inheritance, hormonal exposure during foetal development, birth order (especially in homosexual men) and the effects of experience.

Essay questions

1. How does sexual differentiation of the embryo take place? In what ways can the genetic and hormonal control of sexual differentiation go wrong?

    Search terms: Sexual differentiation. Organisational effect of hormones. Sex chromosomes and development. Turner's and Klinefelter's syndrome. Adrenal hyperplasia. Testicular feminisation.

2. What are the main activational effects of testosterone on male adult behaviour?

    Search terms: Activational effects of testosterone. Sex hormones and aggression. Testosterone and sexual behaviour. Dominance and testosterone. Sex hormones and mental rotation.

3. Which brain regions are known to be involved in male and female sexual behaviour? What differences are known to exist between male and female brains?

    Search terms: Hypothalamus and sexual behaviour. Brain regions in male and female sexual behaviour. Brain mapping of sexual arousal. Neural control of sexual behaviour. Sex differences in brain structure.

4. Does homosexuality have a biological basis?

    Search terms: Interstitial nuclei. Biological determinants of sexuality. Anterior hypothalamus and sexuality. Causes of homosexuality. Neuroscience of sexuality.

Further reading

Andreae, S. (1998) *Anatomy of Desire*. London: Little, Brown & Co. Written for the lay person, this entertaining book argues that our sexuality is the result of evolutionary, psychological and cultural forces.

Becker, J.B., Breedlove, S.M. and Crews, D. (eds) (2002) *Behavioral Endocrinology,* 2nd edition. Cambridge, Mass.: MIT Press. A well written textbook with a number of relevant chapters written by various experts, including several that cover hormonal influences on sexual behaviour, and others that examine the effects of hormones on brain development and cognition.

Blum, D. (1997) *Sex on the Brain*. New York: Penguin. A chatty and informal book covering both human and animal behaviour in regard to topics such as aggression, homosexuality, hormonal drives and sexual signals.

Bullough, V.L. (1994) *Science in the Bedroom: A History of Sex Research*. New York: Basic Books. Informative and accessible to the general reader, this covers the historical development of sex research and provides a good overview of current issues.

Ellis, L. and Ebertz, L. (eds) (1998) *Males, Females, and Behavior: Towards Biological Understanding*. Westport, Conn.: Praeger. A series of nine chapters, written for academics, that examine the genetic, hormonal and neurological factors affecting the behaviour of males and females.

Kimura, D. (1999) *Sex and Cognition*. Cambridge, Mass.: MIT Press. A digestible and intelligent overview of the sex differences in behaviour particularly in regard to cognition and problem solving.

LeVay, S. (1993) *The Sexual Brain*. Cambridge, Mass.: MIT Press. A fairly short but readable account that examines how brain structure and function can influence sexual behaviour and orientation.

LeVay, S. and Valente, S.M. (2006) *Human Sexuality*, 2nd edition. Basingstoke: Palgrave Macmillan. An excellent undergraduate textbook, illustrated in full colour with CD-ROM, that takes a multidisciplinary approach to understanding human sexuality.

Manning, J.T. (2002) *Digit Ratio: A Pointer to Fertility, Behavior and Health*: New Brunswick: Rutgers University Press. A compelling account that shows how digit ratio, which is determined by early exposure to sex hormones, correlates with a wide variety of traits, including testosterone level, sperm count, musical genius, sporting prowess and family size.

Money, J. and Ehrhardt, A.K. (1996) *Man and Women, Boy and Girl*. Northvale, NJ: Aronson. A book that traces the development of gender from conception to maturity, with an emphasis on understanding the interaction between hormonal and environmental influences.

Nelson, R.J. (2005) *An Introduction to Behavioral Endocrinology*. Sunderland, Mass.: Sinauer. A textbook written for undergraduates, and although a little dry in places, it is detailed and contains much of interest.

Pease, A. and Pease, B. (2001) *Why Men Don't Listen and Woman Can't Read Maps*. London: Orion. Although written for a general audience, and containing little about the brain, this is an entertaining book that is worth a bedtime read.

For self test questions, animations, interactive exercises and many more resources to help you consolidate your understanding, and expand your knowledge of the field, please go to the website accompanying this book at **www.pearsoned.co.uk/wickens**

CHAPTER 9

Learning and memory

INTRODUCTION

Learning and memory go hand in hand. Learning can be defined as the acquisition of new information, while memory is the capacity for storing and retrieving this material. Obviously, there can be no learning without memory, although some types of memory can be innate such as instincts and basic reflexes. But, to all intents and purposes our memory is derived exclusively from learning experiences. It is easy to take our capacity to learn and remember for granted, although without these truly remarkable abilities we would be mentally and psychologically dead. Learning and memory are the mental glue that link our present to our past and future, and without them we would have no personal history or awareness. Without memory we would not be able to recognise our friends, objects, possessions, or even ourselves. Nor would we be able to think, use language or perceive the world around us. To put it boldly, without learning and memory we would be nothing but a body without a mind. The question of how the brain acquires new information, stores it, and then retrieves it when required, has been the subject of much speculation that goes back to the ancient Greeks. It is also a problem at the forefront of modern-day science, especially as a complete understanding requires an account of brain function on many different levels: from protein synthesis, synaptic activity and neurotransmitter release, to the activation of neural networks, and their interaction with various brain structures. Despite this, our knowledge of how the brain learns and remembers is one of the great successes of biopsychology, and the focus of an enormous and rapidly increasing body of research that reflects the importance of the challenge. Not only does an understanding of learning and memory provide valuable insights into how the brain works, but it also has the potential to help those with memory disorders such as dementia, which has become one of society's most pressing health concerns. Brain research into learning and memory is going to be a central endeavour in science for a long time to come.

What does a memory look like?

If one pauses for a few moments to consider how the brain is able to learn and remember new information, then one begins to confront a puzzle that is as complex and challenging as anything in science. For example, imagine that somebody screams in front of you. A remarkable thing about this experience is that you will remember it *immediately*. This may not appear to be so surprising, until one begins to realise that the learning and memory of the experience must have involved some fast-acting and relatively permanent change in the chemistry or structure of the brain. Indeed, how else could you remember what you have just seen and heard? When considered in this way, it shows that our brains have to be in a rapid and continuous flux to provide us with memory. And perhaps even more remarkable is that the experience of the scream has probably altered the electrical and chemical activity of millions of neurons, arranged in networks, throughout various brain structures. But, even this analysis does the brain's capacity for learning and memory an injustice. As Steve Rose points out, memories are living processes, which become transformed and imbued with new meanings each time we recall them (Rose 2003). Thus, returning to our example, not only do we remember the scream, but there is also an overall meaning and situational context to the memory which allows us to understand how it relates to what went before, and after.

What, though, is the nature of the underlying biological change in the brain that provides us with the capacity to learn and remember? Biological psychologists have often attempted to answer this question in two ways: (1) by asking how memories can be encoded at the neural level, and (2) by identifying the main structures of the brain that are dedicated to learning and remembering. The first question attempts to explain how memory is represented within the mix of molecules, ions, proteins and lipids that make up the nerve cell. This type of explanation may, for example, view memory as resulting from the creation of new synapses or dendrites (requiring protein synthesis), or due to changes in the sensitivity of receptors and their associated second messenger systems to certain neurotransmitters. Indeed, as we shall see in this chapter, both these forms of 'plasticity' have provided plausible explanations of how neurons encode and store new information.

The second question concerns the 'warehousing' of memories in the brain, that is, where are the main sites in the brain where memories are learned and stored? The problem of memory localisation appears on first sight to be a more straightforward task for the psychologist than trying to understand the molecular changes taking place at the neuron level. However, the history of research into this area has been complicated and controversial. Part of the problem lies with the fact that while the changes taking place within an individual neuron may be relatively simple, the sheer number of cells involved in learning and memory makes exact localisation impossible. Indeed, even the simplest memory trace (if such a thing exists) in humans will probably involve huge numbers of neurons and many brain structures. Even if we assume that such a trace exists, and is responsible for memory, there are other problems with the warehousing concept. For example, it not only supposes that there are dedicated brain areas for memory storage, but also implies that memories are acted upon by other cognitive processes, that is, that memories are somehow transferable from one part of the warehouse (or brain region) to another. Such concepts may help the psychologist to provide models of memory, but there is little evidence to show that the brain works in this way (see Eichenbaum and Cohen (2001) for a further discussion).

The work of Karl Lashley

Karl Spencer Lashley (1890–1958) is generally regarded as the founder of neuropsychology (he introduced the term in 1937) and was one of the first scientists to search for the site of memory storage in the brain. In fact, he spent most of his research career, spanning over forty years, trying to discover the anatomical location of memory traces, or what he called the **engram**. When Lashley first began his research in the 1920s, psychologists were strongly influenced by the work of the Russian physiologist Ivan Pavlov who had discovered a form of learning known as **classical conditioning** (see Figure 9.1). This is a reflexive type of learning that occurs when an animal links specific events (or stimuli) with particular responses. For example, Pavlov showed that if he presented food to a hungry dog, it would produce salivation (he termed this an *unconditioned* or 'unlearned' response). But, if he repeatedly paired a tone with the food, the tone alone would eventually be able to elicit salivation (a *conditioned*

Before conditioning

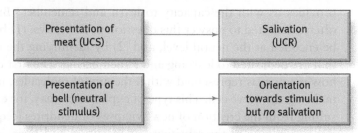

The unconditioned stimulus (UCS) automatically
elicits the unconditioned response (UCR).
The neutral stimulus does not elicit salivation

During conditioning

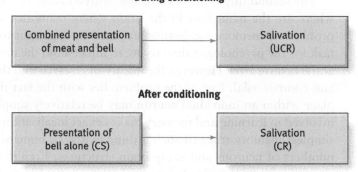

After conditioning

The neutral stimulus is now the conditioned stimulus
and produces salivation (the conditioned response)
similar to the UCR produced by the meat

Figure 9.1   An illustration of how classical conditioning occurs

response). Since the tone was initially a neutral stimulus that produced no reaction, clearly the dog shows evidence of learning about its association with food. At the time, many psychologists were interested in Pavlov's work because they believed that human learning followed the principles of classical conditioning. Moreover, in anatomical terms, it was easy to regard the stimuli as being processed by the sensory areas of the cerebral cortex, and the response as being produced by its motor regions. Thus, scientists hypothesised that the neural basis of learning must involve the growth of new connections that linked the sensory regions of the cerebral cortex with its motor areas. A useful analogy here might be to think of the brain as a telephone switchboard with new connections being made between the caller (sensory area) and receiver (motor area).

It was in this intellectual climate that Lashley set about trying to discover the engram. Lashley reasoned that the most likely site for the storage of memory, or stimulus–response connections, was the **cerebral cortex**. Further, if learning took place in the cortex, and was the result of new pathways being formed between sensory and motor areas, then a knife cut between these two areas following conditioning should impair the memory of the learned response. To test this hypothesis, Lashley taught rats to run through a variety of mazes and then made knife cuts to the cerebral cortex. For each rat, Lashley made a cut in a different location. He reasoned that if he could find a location where a cut impaired performance, or stopped the animal from correctly negotiating the maze, this would be evidence for the engram. But, Lashley found no single cut, or combination of cuts, abolished the animal's performance of the task. The site of the knife cut had no effect on the rat's ability to run through the maze.

In a second set of experiments, Lashley removed parts of the cerebral cortex. He ran rats through a maze that had eight blind or 'incorrect' alleys, until they could negotiate the apparatus on ten consecutive trials without making an error – and then made cortical lesions of various sizes. The results showed that small lesions (of around 10–20 per cent of the cortex) had a scarcely detectable effect on performance, but a large lesion (for example, 50 per cent) produced a significant impairment. Despite this, the lesioned rat was still able to relearn the maze when given further training (Figure 9.2). Perhaps the most important finding, however, was that the exact site of the lesion was not important. Cortical lesions of equal size produced similar behavioural effects regardless of where they were placed. It was as if memory was stored everywhere – or nowhere in particular.

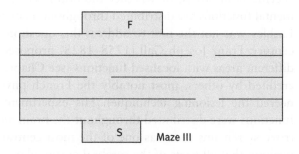

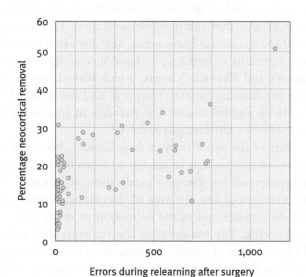

Figure 9.2 The maze used by Lashley along with a graph of his findings showing relearning performance as a function of cortex removal

Source: K.S. Lashley, *Brain Mechanisms and Intelligence*. Copyright © 1963 by Dover Publications

On the basis of these findings Lashley concluded that memories for maze tasks were stored diffusely throughout the cerebral cortex. He called this the principle of **mass action**. He also proposed that all parts of the association cortex play an equal role in their storage, and called this the principle of **equipotentiality** (Lashley 1950). Although Lashley found that some areas of the cerebral cortex were more important than others in the storage of certain memories (for example, the visual cortex was particularly important in tasks requiring the discrimination of visual patterns), he nevertheless found that no structure was crucial. Indeed, no matter what area of the cortex was removed, the animal could relearn the task. From these experiments, Lashley concluded that, for higher-order processes such as learning or memory, the brain functioned as a unit, and contained no specific region that was solely responsible for storing the engram.

Was Lashley correct?

Lashley's work raises a number of fundamental questions concerning the brain. Not least is the issue of whether behavioural functions such as memory can be localised to specific brain areas, or whether the brain acts as some sort of holistic device where mental functions are distributed throughout its matter and not stored in any one place. Lashley was not the first to address this question. In the early part of the nineteenth century, Franz Joseph Gall (1758–1828) proposed that the cerebral cortex contained different areas with localised functions (see Chapter 1). This notion, however, was discredited by others, most notably the French physiologist Pierre Flourens (who pioneered the lesioning technique). His experimental work showed that behavioural functions were distributed throughout the brain and not stored in one place. The controversy remains today as one of the most central puzzles of brain science. Lashley's position that all parts of the cerebral cortex play an equal role in learning and memory is supported by his inability to discover the engram. Many psychologists today likewise believe that many higher cognitive functions, such as intelligence, cannot be localised to discrete brain areas. Yet, it is also clear that some areas of the cerebral cortex, especially in humans, do have specialised abilities. The most obvious of these are Broca's and Wernicke's areas, which serve language functions. There is also evidence that the frontal, parietal, temporal and occipital lobes have different roles to play in cognition and behaviour. The paradox of specialised regions and distributed functions has yet to be satisfactorily resolved.

Part of the problem regarding Lashley, however, may lie in his choice of task (i.e. maze learning) which he used as a means by which to discover the engram. This task is inappropriate for studying localisation of function. Indeed, rather than requiring the involvement of just one area of the cerebral cortex, it is almost certainly the case that the maze task requires the formation of many 'engrams' spread throughout the cerebral cortex. For example, as the rat runs through the maze, it may be combining different types of sensory information (vision, olfaction, proprioception and so on) to perform the task. Thus, although each engram could be localised, the maze task may be so complex and draw upon so many different types of learning, that the total memory is stored throughout the cortex. This also implies that the maze task can be learned in many different ways. If so, this might help to explain why an animal can relearn the maze task following removal of large parts of the cortex. The animal simply adopts a new learning strategy based on different cues.

Another criticism of Lashley is his assumption that the cerebral cortex is the only site of learning and memory. To some extent this bias was due to the initial influence of Pavlov, who believed that the cerebral cortex was the site of stimulus–response connections. In addition, because his work largely pre-dated the use of modern surgical techniques, Lashley was unable to make accurate lesions to many subcortical regions of the brain. In fact, Lashley performed his lesions by cutting the cortex with a knife under direct vision and removing it with a suction pump. Nevertheless, it is now clear that a number of other structures have a role to play in learning and memory. These include, for example, the cerebellum, which is involved in learning motor actions, and the hippocampus and limbic aspects of the temporal lobe, which have a vital role in memory consolidation and retrieval.

The contribution of Donald Hebb

Donald Hebb (1904–1985) remains one of the most influential psychologists of our time. Not only did he extend the work of Lashley (he obtained his PhD at Harvard University under Lashley's guidance in 1936), but his ideas continue to exert a major influence on cognitive psychology and neuroscience. Hebb's most famous work is *The Organization of Behavior*, first published in 1949, which attempts to explain how the structure of the brain gives rise to thought. The traditional view at the time was that behaviour arose from stimulus–response reflexes, that is, all action was caused by a series of neurons arranged in direct one-way pathways, which could be activated by a specific stimulus – much like a knee jerk when the patellar tendon is tapped by a doctor. But, Hebb believed that this idea was far too simple to explain the functioning of the brain.

Hebb's unique alternative to the reflex was the larger neural circuit, or **cell assembly**, which contained large chains of reconnecting neurons and which he saw as being distributed throughout the brain. This concept had two important advantages over the simple reflex. Firstly, cell assemblies could be autonomous and continuously active. That is, once activated by a stimulus, they could in principle remain in an excited state. Secondly, and perhaps more important, Hebb realised that such **reverberatory activity** could provide the neural basis for learning. For example, it could be envisaged that initial learning resulted in cell assemblies having increased electrical activity that lasted for some hours after the event. This, in effect, could be responsible for transient or short-term memory. However, Hebb also believed that if this reverberatory activity occurred for long enough, it would be possible for structural changes in the neurons making up the cell assembly to take place, which could produce permanent or long-term memory (Figure 9.3). The likeliest site for structural change, according to Hebb, was the synapse. Indeed, a synapse that is 'strengthened' as a result of learning is now called a **Hebbian synapse**. Or as Hebb put it in his famous rule: 'When an axon of cell A is near enough to excite a cell B and repeatedly or persistently takes part in firing it, some growth or metabolic change takes place in one or both cells such that A's efficiency, as one of the cells firing B, is increased' (Hebb 1949). In other words, co-activation of connected cells will result in a strengthening of their connection, increasing the probability that the recipient cell will fire if the presynaptic cell does so.

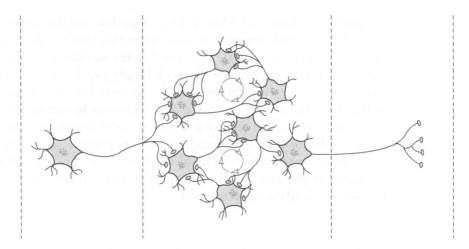

1. Experience activates sensory pathways, which conduct neural impulses to the CNS

2. **Short-term memory:** Hebb hypothesised that the short-term memory of each experience is stored by neural activity reverberating in closed-loop CNS circuits

   Long-term memory: Hebb hypothesised that reverberating activity, if maintained for a sufficiently long time, produces structural changes in synapses and that these changes facilitate subsequent transmission over the same pathways

3. The changed pathways of transmission produced by synaptic facilitation can influence motor output and thus behaviour

Figure 9.3 A hypothetical model of how reverberatory circuits may be set up in neural networks

Source: John P.J. Pinel, *Biopsychology*, 3rd edition. Copyright © 1997 by Pearson Education

Hebb's theory was appealing not only because it supported Lashley by suggesting that memory was stored diffusely throughout the brain, but also because it provided an explanation of how individual neurons might be modified to encode and store memory. In short, changes in the sensitivity of receptors, or perhaps increases or decreases in the readiness of a neuron to release neurotransmitter, could provide a viable mechanism for neural plasticity. Hebb's theory also explained how memories could be recalled. In short, once a new activity pattern had become established by changed synaptic connections, it was easy to imagine it being elicited (i.e. recalled) thereafter by excitation from the appropriate sensory neurons, or from other reverberatory patterns.

Hebb's theories were so far ahead of their time that they could not be experimentally tested. But, even as a theoretical piece of work, Hebb's book had a significant impact on thinking about the brain, and helped to rejuvenate interest in subjects spurned by many psychologists, such as cognition, intelligence and perception. Its true impact, however, lies with its influence on psychology today. Modern research has confirmed the importance of the Hebbian synapse for learning in cell assemblies, and there is evidence that a phenomenon resembling reverberatory activity in the brain called **long-term potentiation** may underlie memory (see below). Hebb's theories have also been particularly influential in neural network programming and artificial intelligence.

The effects of experience on the brain

Hebb's theory had emphasised the importance of changes taking place at the synapse for producing neural plasticity. However, in the 1960s, psychologists also began to realise that morphological changes could also take place in neurons as a result of learning. This discovery came about by examining the brains of young animals reared in stimulating and enriched environments. Psychologists had long known that the effects of early experience can have a profound effect on later development. Indeed, Donald Hebb in 1949 noted that the same principle applied to animals, when he observed that his children's pet rats, which were allowed to explore his home, were superior to laboratory ones when it came to learning to run through a maze. This observation implied that an enriched environment could increase intelligence.

But could such a rat be distinguished from a less intelligent one on the basis of brain structure or neurochemistry? This was the question that Mark Rosenzweig, Ed Bennett and Marian Diamond set out to examine in the mid-1950s. In the basic experimental design, rats were raised for various lengths of time in impoverished or enriched environments (see Rosenzweig *et al.* 1972). In the impoverished condition, the animals lived alone in small cages located in a quiet room. Although they had plenty of food, they were given little stimulation which was accompanied by low-level illumination and background white noise. In contrast, the rats kept in the enriched conditions were placed in large groups, and had big cages furnished with a variety of toys, runways and objects. A new object was placed in the cage each day to add further novelty. At the end of a given period that could be between thirty days and several months, the rats were sacrificed and their brains examined to detect whether any neural changes had taken place.

The results showed that animals reared in the enriched conditions had a thicker and heavier cerebral cortex, which was especially marked for the occipital cortex. It was also found that the enriched cortices had greater levels of **acetylcholinesterase (AChE)**, which is an enzyme that breaks down **acetylcholine**. This finding indicated that the enriched brains were producing more of this neurotransmitter. The most striking discovery, however, was the difference in the shape of the neurons taken from parts of the cerebral cortex. Rats reared in the enriched environment were found to have more spines on their dendrites. Because these structures contain high numbers of receptors, it indicated that the number of synapses was increasing as a result of experience. This prediction, along with evidence showing that the synapses were much larger in the enriched animals, was later confirmed by electron microscopy (Turner and Greenough 1983, 1985). For example, the enriched rats were shown to have about 9,400 synapses per neuron in their occipital cortex, compared with about 7,600 for deprived animals. In other words, the enriched environment had caused an increase of over 20 per cent in the number of synapses in the visual areas of the brain (Figure 9.4).

Although these findings may not surprise us today, they generated considerable interest, and even scepticism, at the time of their publication. This was because many investigators believed that the structure of the brain, and especially its weight, was fixed by adulthood and unable to be changed by experience. The fact that new synapses were being created by learning changed the way in which investigators viewed the brain. For example, researchers began to recognise that enriched environments promoted better learning and problem solving, and could provide viable therapy

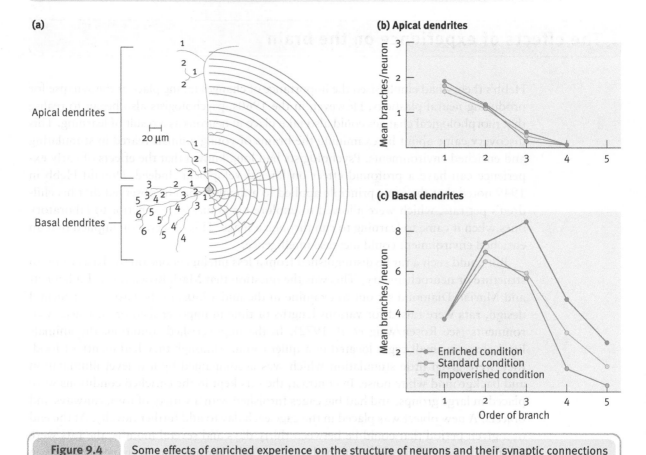

Figure 9.4 Some effects of enriched experience on the structure of neurons and their synaptic connections

Source: S.M. Breedlove *et al.*, *Biological Psychology*, 5th edition, p. 549. Copyright © 2007 by Sinauer Associates, Inc.

for those with brain injuries. Indeed, evidence suggests that environmental enrichment is more effective than either formal training or physical exercise in the recovery of learning capacity following physical injury (Will *et al.* 2004).

Learning and memory in *Aplysia*

Some of the most important advances into understanding the neural basis of learning and memory has come from studies examining the simple nervous systems of invertebrates (animals without backbones). These organisms have many advantages for the neuroscientist. Firstly, their nervous systems contain far fewer neurons than found in vertebrates. Despite this, the biochemical and biophysical properties of the neurons are fundamentally the same. Secondly, the neurons of many invertebrates are relatively large and can be seen with a microscope. Thirdly, most invertebrate neurons are fixed, that is, found in the same location, which allows them to be easily identified. But, most important of all, invertebrates show various forms of learning. Although a wide range of invertebrates have been used in this type of research, including cockroaches, flies, bees and nematodes, undoubtedly the most important has been *Aplysia californica* (Figure 9.5). This is a large sea slug, reddish-yellow in colour, which is found on the

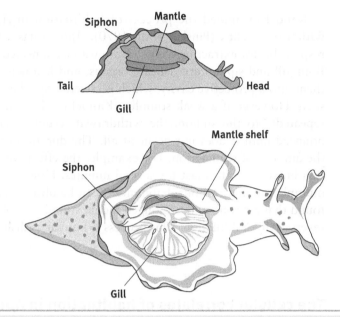

Figure 9.5   An *Aplysia*

Californian and Mexican sea floor close to the beach, and sometimes seen grazing on seaweed at low tide. It has few predators, due to its unpalatable taste, and when threatened often releases a dark purple fluid. *Aplysia* can grow up to 30 centimetres long and weigh a couple of kilograms making it easy to handle and experiment with in the laboratory.

Aplysia has a simple central nervous system which consists of just eight ganglia, or bundles of nerve fibres, which between them contain in the region of 20,000 neurons. The ganglia are sometimes referred to as head ganglia and they exist in four pairs: (1) the cerebral innervating the eyes and tentacles, (2) bucal controlling the mouth, (3) pleural projecting to the side of the body, and (4) the pedal innervating the foot. In addition there is a large **abdominal ganglion** found in the body. The head ganglia control functions such as locomotion, feeding and mating, whereas the abdominal ganglion is involved in circulation, respiration, excretion and egg laying. In addition, *Aplysia* has a smaller peripheral nervous system involved in peripheral or local functions.

Although *Aplysia* first attracted the attention of researchers in the 1940s, it was not until 1970, when three papers appeared together in the prestigious journal *Science* by Eric Kandel and his colleagues, that its learning capabilities were first reported. The first type of learning examined was **habituation**. This type of learning is found in practically all living organisms, and is best seen when a novel or unexpected stimulus is presented to an animal. Typically, this produces a defensive or startle reflex. But, if the stimulus is presented repeatedly, or turns out to be harmless, the animal will begin to ignore it. This decrease in behavioural responding is habituation. Humans also show forms of habituation. The ticking of a clock which seemingly fades away, or an unusual smell which quickly disappears when entering a new house are two examples. Although habituation is a simple response, it must nevertheless depend on a change taking place somewhere in the nervous system. *Aplysia* has provided us with some important insights into how this change may occur.

Kandel examined the process of habituation in *Aplysia* by measuring its **gill-withdrawal reflex** (Pinsker *et al.* 1970). *Aplysia* has a large gill located on its back, responsible for extracting oxygen from water, connected to a siphon that expels waste. Both gill and siphon are delicate organs, and if touched, *Aplysia* vigorously retracts them into a protective cavity, which is covered by a large fleshy pad called the mantle shelf. However, if a weak stimulus (Kandel used a calibrated jet of water) is applied repeatedly to the siphon, the withdrawal response habituates, becoming less pronounced until it does not occur at all. The duration of habituation is dependent on the amount of stimulation. For example, the effects of a single short training period (ten bursts of water) last for several minutes. However, when *Aplysia* is subjected to multiple training sessions, habituation can be observed for several weeks. It was also found that a strong and prolonged tactile stimulus applied to the head or tail quickly reversed this habituation. This process is known as **dishabituation**.

The cellular correlates of habituation in *Aplysia*

To understand how habituation occurs in *Aplysia* it was necessary to identify the neural circuitry that produced the gill-withdrawal reflex. To do this, a slit was made in *Aplysia*'s neck to allow the abdominal ganglion and its nerves to be exposed. Investigators were then able to record from, and stimulate, neurons to identify the neural circuit controlling the withdrawal of the gill. The first stage of this reflex involved the siphon. This structure was found to contain 24 sensory neurons that were sensitive to tactile information produced by the water jet. These sensory cells, which were later discovered to secrete the neurotransmitter **glutamate**, project onto a cluster of six motor neurons that control the retraction of the gill. In fact, the neural circuitry is more complex than this, as the sensory neurons also receive input from interneurons, and also have extra axon endings that project onto other cells. However, for the sake of simplicity, we can consider just the neural circuit of 24 sensory cells and 6 motor neurons. In this circuit, habituation takes place. The important questions are, where and how?

To answer these questions, Kandel and his colleagues placed electrodes into the sensory and motor neurons and measured the number of neural impulses that accompanied the habituation of the gill-withdrawal reflex (Kupfermann *et al.* 1970). They found that the sensory neurons in the siphon did not show any decline in activity to repeated stimulation by the jet of water. In other words, when the siphon was stimulated, the sensory neurons always fired. Thus, changes in the firing of the sensory neurons did not explain habituation. In contrast, the motor neurons did show a decline in responsiveness, with fewer nerve impulses being produced with each siphon stimulation. This correlated with the decline of the gill-withdrawal reflex. There were two possible explanations: either the motor neurons were becoming fatigued and less able to invoke a response, or there were changes taking place at the synapses between sensory and motor neurons. The first possibility was ruled out when it was found that electrical stimulation of the motor neurons always produced the same amount of muscle contraction, regardless of how many impulses they had previously received; that is, the motor neurons were not getting 'tired' with repetitive firing. Thus, the 'cause' of habituation was taking place at the synapse located between sensory and motor neurons.

Mechanism of habituation

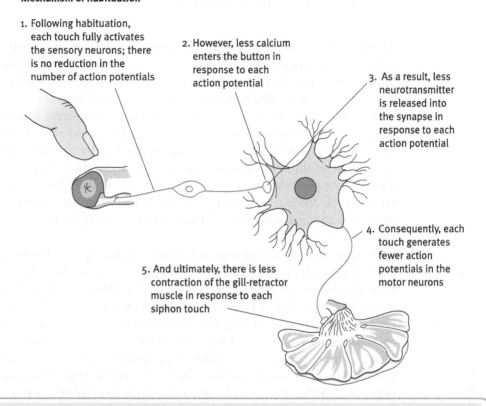

1. Following habituation, each touch fully activates the sensory neurons; there is no reduction in the number of action potentials

2. However, less calcium enters the button in response to each action potential

3. As a result, less neurotransmitter is released into the synapse in response to each action potential

4. Consequently, each touch generates fewer action potentials in the motor neurons

5. And ultimately, there is less contraction of the gill-retractor muscle in response to each siphon touch

Figure 9.6   The neural and biochemical stages underlying habituation of the gill-withdrawal reflex in *Aplysia*

Source: John P.J. Pinel, *Biopsychology*, 3rd edition. Copyright © 1997 by Pearson Education

But where in the synapse was the important change taking place? Again, there were two possibilities: either the sensory neurons were releasing less neurotransmitter each time they fired, or the receptors located on the motor neuron were becoming less responsive to the transmitter. In fact, the former turned out to be true. In short, it was shown that fewer molecules of transmitter were being released from the siphon's sensory neurons with each action potential (Castellucci and Kandel 1974). In effect, each tactile stimulus was causing a decrease in the amount of transmitter released from the terminals of the sensory neurons. The reduced amount of neurotransmitter then produced less stimulation of the motor neurons innervating the gill – thereby causing habituation (see Figure 9.6).

But what causes the reduction in the release of neurotransmitter? The answer, it appears, is a gradual decrease in the number of calcium ions that enter the axon terminal of the sensory cell. As we saw in Chapter 1, neurotransmitter release occurs through the process of **exocytosis**. That is, when an action potential reaches the axon ending, it causes calcium channels to open, which enables calcium ions to enter the terminal and propel the vesicles containing neurotransmitter into the synaptic membrane. This, in turn, causes the neurotransmitter to be released into the synaptic cleft. However, with repeated stimulation of the sensory neuron, it appears that either the calcium channels become less effective at opening, or a build-up of calcium in the cell slows down further influx. Whatever the mechanism, less neurotransmitter is released into the synapse.

Longer-term learning in *Aplysia*

Although habituation is explained by transient changes in synaptic neurotransmitter release from sensory neurons, due to a reduction of calcium influx, other forms of habituation which last for longer periods have been shown to have a different biological basis. For example, habituation of the gill withdrawal reflex in *Aplysia* can be observed for up to three weeks if the stimulation is repeated four times a day on four successive days. Importantly, this form of learning, unlike the shorter form of habituation described in the previous section, is blocked by the administration of the protein synthesis inhibitor **anisomycin** into the abdominal ganglion (Castellucci *et al.* 1980). Since protein synthesis is a necessary prerequisite for producing new synapses, receptors or dendrites, this suggests that longer-term habituation is accompanied by structural changes somewhere in the network of *Aplysia*'s neurons involved in gill withdrawal.

Structural changes have indeed been observed in *Aplysia* following long-term learning. For example, Bailey and Chen (1983, 1988) injected horseradish peroxide into the siphon's sensory neurons so that they could be closely examined using light and electron microscopy. These investigators then stimulated the siphon over a series of successive days to produce a long-lasting form of habituation. The results showed that the presynaptic terminals (called varicosities) located on the sensory neurons were significantly reduced in number by about 35 per cent in the habituated animals. In addition, the active zone of such terminals, which contains the transmitter vesicles, was also significantly smaller. These results show that long-term habituation is due to a partial retraction of the synaptic terminals from the siphon's sensory neurons that project to the motor neurons controlling the gill reflex.

Bailey and Chen (1983) also examined long-term sensitisation in *Aplysia*. This type of learning occurs when an electric shock is applied to *Aplysia*'s tail over several days, which then leads to a particularly vigorous gill-withdrawal response when the siphon is stimulated by a tactile input. The neural 'wiring diagram' for this type of learning is more complicated than that for habituation, as it includes interneurons conveying information from the tail and whose axons project onto the terminals of the siphon's sensory neurons. The neurotransmitter used at this junction is serotonin. Bailey and Chen found that, after training, the sensory neurons showed a number of significant changes. In this case, the number of synaptic terminals increased from about 1,300 varicosities per sensory neuron to about 2,600 in trained animals, and the active parts of the terminal containing the vesicles nearly doubled in size. Thus, long-term sensitisation, in contrast to habituation, is accompanied by structural changes that strengthen the synapses between the sensory neurons and their target cells.

Long-term potentiation

Over fifty years ago, George Hebb speculated that memory must involve permanent changes in the structure of neurons, which resulted from activity 'reverberating' in neural circuits after learning had initially occurred. This activity was seen as changing the strength of certain synapses located in the circuit. Evidence supporting this idea was lacking until the early 1970s when Timothy Bliss and Terje Lomo described the phenomenon of **long-term potentiation (LTP)**. Their initial experiment involved anaesthetising a rabbit and exposing its hippocampus. They then stimulated the **perforant pathway** (a pathway which enters the hippocampus from the entorhinal cortex) with a train of high frequency (15 Hz) electrical impulses for periods of 10 seconds. During this time, Bliss and Lomo also recorded from the postsynaptic hippocampal neurons receiving the input (i.e. the granule cells of the **dentate gyrus**) and found increased EPSPs in response to this stimulation (Figure 9.7).

More importantly, though, following this training Bliss and Lomo stimulated the perforant path with single pulses of low-intensity current. To their surprise, they found an extraordinarily long increase in the firing of the hippocampal cells, with the amplitude of the EPSP increased by some 200–300 per cent. The hippocampal neurons had therefore been modified by the initial burst of high-frequency stimulation. Bliss and Lomo found that this change persisted for up to 10 hours after the initial stimulation. In fact, it is now known that enhanced EPSP activity can last up to several weeks depending on the stimulus parameters. LTP can also be induced in other areas of the brain, especially those implicated in learning and memory, including that thalamus, motor cortex, cerebellum and amygdala.

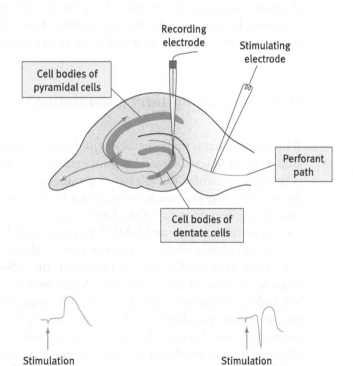

A. The initial response of
   dentate cells to a single
   pulse of stimulation
   given to the perforant path

B. The response of dentate
   cells a day later following
   a single pulse of stimulation
   to the perforant path

Figure 9.7   How long-term potentiation is examined

Soon after the discovery by Bliss and Lomo, other researchers found that LTP could also be examined *in vitro* by using slices of hippocampal tissue kept alive in an oxygenated saline bath. This allowed not only the tissue to be directly observed, but also the microelectrodes to be positioned with precision, enabling the neural basis of LTP to be investigated in great detail. LTP was found to have a similar range of properties in both brain and organ bath. For example, the EPSPs produced by LTP generally develop to a detectable level within 5 minutes and reach a plateau after 1 hour. This involves two phases: establishment which lasts for about 1 hour, and maintenance which persists for several days. The first phase can be induced by a single high-frequency stimulation. But, to trigger the maintenance phase, a number of high-frequency stimulations have to be applied to the pathways projecting onto the cells showing the EPSPs.

Several lines of evidence indicate that LTP represents a neural correlate of learning and memory. For example, LTP can be elicited by low levels of stimulation that is known to mimic normal activity. Moreover, increased EPSP activity in hippocampal neurons is known to occur in vivo after learning (Hölscher 2001). Disruption of LTP is also known to interfere with learning and memory. For example, Richard Morris examined the effects of the glutamate antagonist called AP5 that inhibits the development of LTP in the hippocampus (Morris *et al.* 1982). When Morris tested the effects of AP5 on the performance of the water maze (see below) he found that it impaired the rat's ability to learn the location of a submerged platform. This skill is one that requires spatial memory and the involvement of the hippocampus. However, when the platform was made visible, the rats swam straight to it without sensory or motor impairment. In other words, the deleterious effect of AP5 on the performance of the water maze task was due to its effect on spatial memory.

What causes long-term potentiation?

What causes long-term potentiation in the hippocampus? This has been the subject of a large amount of research, and the answers are only beginning to emerge. The first stage is believed to involve the release of **glutamate** from the perforant path, which crosses the synaptic gap and binds to receptors located on the dendrites of the postsynaptic cells. In the dentate gyrus of the hippocampus, there are two types of glutamate receptor: the **AMPA receptor** and **NMDA receptor**. Both have roles to play in the production of LTP. Stimulation of the AMPA receptor by glutamate causes a moderate depolarisation of the neuron. However, at this point, the NMDA receptor is 'quiet'. This is because of an unusual feature of the NMDA receptor, which has an ion channel that is blocked by magnesium ions. In effect, this stops excitatory calcium ion flow into the neuron. However, when the cell becomes depolarised following AMPA activation, the magnesium ions become displaced, which allows calcium ions to surge into the cell (Figure 9.8). The result is a delayed but larger depolarisation of the neuron.

The flow of calcium into the cell is critical for the generation of LTP. Indeed, drugs which stop calcium from entering the cell stop LTP from occurring, whereas those that increase calcium enhance LTP (Teyler and DiScenna 1987). The importance of calcium lies in its ability to act as an intracellular messenger which can activate a number of enzymes involved in neural function. For example, when calcium enters the cell it binds to a protein in the cytoplasm called **calmodulin**, which has a shape not unlike a flower with four petals. Calcium causes calmodulin to change shape, allowing it to bind to a

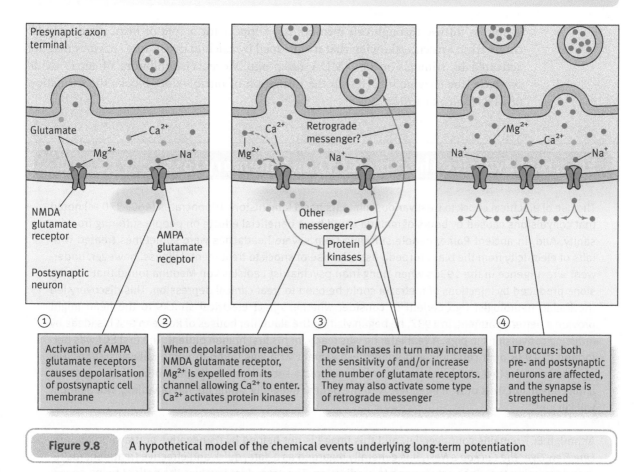

① Activation of AMPA glutamate receptors causes depolarisation of postsynaptic cell membrane

② When depolarisation reaches NMDA glutamate receptor, Mg²⁺ is expelled from its channel allowing Ca²⁺ to enter. Ca²⁺ activates protein kinases

③ Protein kinases in turn may increase the sensitivity of and/or increase the number of glutamate receptors. They may also activate some type of retrograde messenger

④ LTP occurs: both pre- and postsynaptic neurons are affected, and the synapse is strengthened

Figure 9.8 A hypothetical model of the chemical events underlying long-term potentiation

Source: Adapted from L.A. Freberg, *Discovering Biological Psychology*, p. 362. Copyright © 2006 by Houghton Miffilin Company

group of proteins called **protein kinases**. One important kinase is called **CaMK II** (α-calcium/calmodulin-dependent protein kinase II). The activity of CaMk II continues long after calcium levels have returned to baseline (mimicking to some extent the time course of LTP). Moreover, drugs that inhibit CaMK II are effective at blocking LTP (Malinow *et al.* 1989). How CaMK II produces its effects on LTP is not clearly understood, although it may act on AMPA receptors to make them more sensitive to glutamate. Alternatively, CaMK II may help to deliver new glutamate receptors to the synaptic membrane (Heyman 2005).

Another target of calcium is **protein kinase A**, which is an intracellular chemical that is involved in activating the CREB protein which plays a major role in gene transcription. This pathway is likely to be another link in the formation of the new AMPA receptors which is believed to occur in LTP. In turn, extra AMPA receptors will increase the synaptic efficiency of the postsynaptic neuron to glutamate leading to enhanced EPSPs.

To make matters more complex, there is also evidence that LTP is accompanied by an enhanced release of glutamate from the presynaptic neurons. In other words, with learning, more glutamate is released into the synapse. But, this raises a problem. For this to occur, a 'backward' or retrograde messenger must go back from the postsynaptic neuron to inform the presynaptic cell of the need for more 'potentiation'. Several substances have been implicated in this function, including the gas **nitric oxide**, which is able to diffuse through cell membranes. Support for a role of nitric oxide in LTP comes from evidence showing that it is formed by calcium dependent enzymes that are activated by stimulation of NMDA receptors. Moreover, inhibitors of nitric oxide synthase (the enzyme involved in the formation of nitric oxide) blocks the formation of LTP (Malenka 1995).

Electroconvulsive therapy (ECT) and memory loss

The use of electrical shock to treat various ailments has a long history. Hippocrates (460–370 BC) noted that convulsions caused by bouts of malaria could have beneficial effects on people suffering from insanity. And, in ancient Rome, people suffering from severe headaches were sometimes treated with jolts of electricity from the black torpedo fish. The use of shock to treat mental illness, however, underwent a resurgence in the 1930s when Hungarian psychiatrist Ladislas von Meduna found that convulsions produced by injections of metrazol could be used to treat clinical depression. This discovery led the Italian neurologist Ugo Cerletti to consider whether direct electrical shocks to the head might provide a better treatment. In 1937, he began visiting the slaughter houses of Rome to test his ideas by inducing convulsions in pigs. A year later he was ready for his first human patient. The first ECT was performed in 1938 on a catatonic and speechless vagrant who was found in Rome railway station. It is reported that the first shock was too weak and required a second one of a higher voltage to bring about a full convulsion. This proved effective, with the patient allegedly sitting up and pleading, 'Not again, it will kill me!'

Although ECT remains controversial, and this image is not helped by its negative portrayal in the film *One Flew Over the Cuckoo's Nest*, it is generally regarded as a safe, quick and effective treatment for severe depression that does not respond to medication. The procedure involves the patient being anaesthetised and given a muscle relaxant while seizures are induced by an electrical current applied through electrodes to the head. Typically, some six to twelve shocks are given at a rate of two or three treatments per week. It is estimated that around 1 million people worldwide receive ECT every year, with significant improvements occurring in some 60–70 per cent of patients. However, in many cases the benefits are not long-lasting, with about 60 per cent of individuals relapsing within six months. Despite this, the majority of psychiatrists believe that patients benefit from ECT.

However, ECT has some disadvantages, and one of its main problems is the tendency to produce memory loss, especially if the shocks are administered bilaterally. Indeed, most patients will experience a short period of confusion immediately after the ECT treatment, when they do not know where they are or what they are doing. A more serious problem, however, is retrograde amnesia for events prior to the treatment. In the days after treatment this can be severe, with amnesia going back a few years, although in most people this will show recovery, with the only major loss being of memories formed in the few weeks before treatment (although some memory deficits may extend back to six months or more). In addition, ECT may cause a difficulty in learning new material (anterograde amnesia) that can persist for 3–6 months. One study has found that as many as 55 per cent of people who undergo ECT report persistent memory loss (Rose *et al.* 2003). From a neuroscience perspective, ECT is of interest to researchers since it appears to interfere with the consolidation of new memories. It has been known since the work of Donald Hebb that memory depends on changes taking place in the connections between neurons, and that these changes take some time to become permanent. ECT would appear to affect this process. Indeed, animal studies have provided support for this idea by showing that ECT has a disruptive effect on electrical activity (long-term potentiation) in the hippocampus which gradually resolves over a period of 40 days (Reid and Stewart 1997).

An introduction to amnesia and human memory

The story of HM

Although it is important to understand the structural and neurochemical changes that occur in neurons with learning, such information tells us little about the organisation of memory in the brain. This type of knowledge is especially important for the psychologist who is interested in understanding memory dysfunction, or explaining how the brain can encode, consolidate and retrieve information. To do this, it is necessary first to identify the areas in the brain which are specialised for learning and memory – although as we saw from Lashley's work, this is no easy task. Nonetheless, researchers have long known that damage to certain brain regions in humans produces an inability to learn new information or to recall old memories (i.e. **amnesia**). For example, in 1899, the Russian Vladimir Bekhterev exhibited the brain of an amnesic patient at a medical meeting in St Petersburg that showed softening of the temporal lobes and hippocampus. Similar cases were also reported in the early part of the twentieth century, although most were by German investigators and not published in English. Further support for the involvement of the temporal lobes in memory came from the work of Wilder Penfield, who electrically stimulated the brain in conscious patients prior to surgery in the treatment of epilepsy. During this work, Penfield found that stimulation of the temporal lobes often caused visual and auditory flashbacks which sometimes included vivid memories of past experiences.

The most important discovery about human memory, however, came in the mid-1950s with the case of a patient who is simply known by his initials of HM (Scoville and Milner 1957). This patient had part of his brain, the **hippocampus**, bilaterally removed in a surgical operation to treat epilepsy (the hippocampus is located in the medial temporal lobes and is sometimes known as **archicortex** or 'old cortex'; see Figure 9.9). Although the operation reduced his seizures, the operation left HM without the ability to form new memories, rendering him unable to permanently remember anything since the day of surgery. HM is arguably the most famous case study in psychology. He has had more written about him than any other person, and his willing participation in hundreds of experiments has contributed immensely to our understanding of human memory. Yet, to protect his anonymity, few researchers know his real name, and no pictures of him have ever been published.

HM was born in 1926 and grew up in a working-class town of Connecticut. By all accounts, HM was a healthy child and had a normal childhood until the age of 9, when he was involved a bicycle accident that knocked him unconscious for several minutes. It is believed that this incident was the start of his seizures, which began with epileptic fits at the age of 10. His fits got progressively more severe, so that by the time of his mid-twenties, HM was having multiple seizures each day. In 1953, the neurologist William Scoville identified the medial temporal lobes as the site in the brain where the seizure activity was originating. He decided to bilaterally remove the tissue to stop the fits. On 25 August 1953, HM underwent the operation. After administering a local anaesthetic to the scalp, Scoville bored two holes into the front of HM's skull, and pushed the frontal lobes up with a spatula to gain access to the medial regions of the temporal lobes. By inserting a knife and suction pump to remove tissue, Scoville removed approximately the size of a tennis ball from each hemisphere, which included most of the hippocampus, amygdala and surrounding cortex (see Rolls 2005).

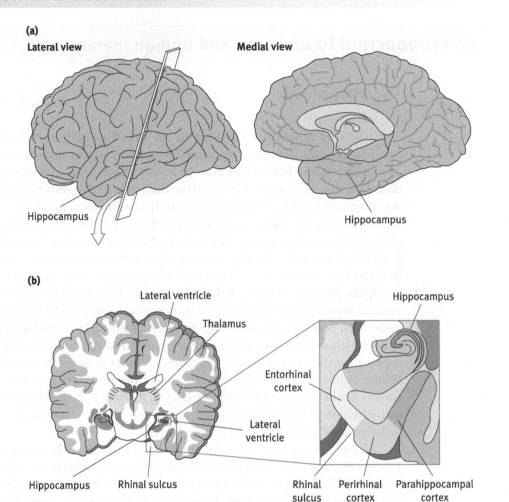

Figure 9.9   The hippocampus

Source: M.F. Bear *et al.*, *Neuroscience: Exploring the Brain*. Copyright © 1996 by Lippincott Williams and Wilkins

Similar operations had been performed before, and although smaller amounts of tissue had been removed, there was little to suggest that the operation was going to be seriously debilitating. In terms of reducing seizures, the operation was a success. But, there was also a terrible price for this improvement. Put simply, HM has been unable to remember anything of significance ever since. To this very day, over fifty years later, HM remains incapable of learning new things and storing them into **long-term memory**, although, as we shall see below, HM does retain some types of memory ability.

The characteristics of HM

The main consequence of HM's operation was a severe **anterograde amnesia** (the term *antero* means 'in front' and refers to loss of memory for events after a trauma) that causes him to forget the events of his daily life almost as soon as they occur. For example, if HM meets someone new, he quickly forgets them once they leave him, and does not recognise them again. This includes researchers such as Dr Brenda Milner who have worked with HM since the time of his operation. HM also cannot find his way around his own neighbourhood (his family moved to a new house after his operation), always underestimates his age (he tends to guess his age as 33 years), and is unable to recognise a current picture of himself. His amnesia also includes the death of his parents. For example, his father died in 1967, and when asked whether his father was alive, several years after his death, HM replied that he was not sure. HM lived with his mother until she died at the age of 94 in 1981, and is now in specialised residential care. When asked about his mother, HM reports that she may have left him, and he grieves each time he is told of her death (see Rolls 2005).

Despite this, when meeting HM for the first time, he appears to be normal. For example, he has a good vocabulary, normal language skills and an IQ that is above average (he spends hours of his day doing crossword puzzles). He also has a normal **short-term memory**, which enables him to remember things for a brief period. Indeed, he can repeat a string of seven numbers forwards and five numbers backwards; repeat sentences and perform mental arithmetic. However, once HM is distracted, the information is forgotten. And, the same is true of new situations that he encounters. His capacity for short-term memory means that HM can hold an intelligent conversation, and he also shows excellent retention of older memories, particularly if they occurred before the age of 16. Curiously, HM has little recall for the events of his life after this age, that is, he has an eleven-year **retrograde amnesia** for events preceding his operation. It has been suggested that this could provide evidence for the idea that our long-term memories take many years to become permanently encoded in the brain (see also the box on ECT on page 340).

Poignantly, HM is aware of his condition and apologetic to others about his memory loss, as seen in the following quote: 'Right now I am wondering. Have I done or said anything amiss? You see, at this moment everything looks clear to me, but what happened just before? That's what worries me. Its like waking from a dream. I just don't remember' (Milner 1970). In addition, HM is also very poor at estimating time, especially beyond 20 seconds. His sense of time is so poor that it has been estimated that his days pass like minutes, weeks like hours, and years like weeks. As the psychologist Geoff Rolls has pointed out, this may be beneficial for someone in his position since it would mean that the past forty years of memory loss may seem no more than a few months.

Despite this, HM sometimes experiences 'islands' of memory. For example, he recalled certain aspects of the Challenger Space Shuttle disaster several years after the event, and on occasion has remembered that his parents are dead. When asked where he is, he sometimes correctly guesses the Massachusetts Institute of Technology, which is the place where he has been regularly tested over the past forty years. Nevertheless such memories are highly fragmented and inconsistent. Although HM requires constant supervision and now lives in a nursing home, he remains a great favourite with researchers and support staff alike. This is due in no small part to his 'endearing nature, his sense of humour and his willingness to be helpful' (Ogden and Corkin 1991).

Tasks which HM can perform

Despite his severe amnesia, there are some tasks where HM demonstrates learning. For example, in 1965, Brenda Milner presented HM with a mirror drawing task that required him to trace around the outline of a complex geometric figure which was hidden from direct view, and observable only by using the reflections from a mirror. At first, most subjects find this task difficult (their hands do not seem to follow the instructions of the brain), but with practice they become much more proficient. This is also true of HM. For example, when given ten trials, HM shows improved accuracy at drawing around the shape. He also maintains this skill over several days, despite claiming not to recognise the apparatus or what to do.

It might be thought that HM's mirror-drawing ability is linked to the motor requirements of the task. But, there is more to HM's memory abilities than this. For example, HM shows evidence of learning when given a prompt to help him recall information. This can be seen in the recognition of incomplete pictures task, where subjects are presented with fragmented drawings, one at a time, and in progressively more detail, until they can recognise what the picture is (Milner *et al.* 1968). When given the set of incomplete pictures again, normal subjects are able to recognise the pictures much more quickly. Interestingly, HM also shares this ability. If given a series of incomplete pictures and tested one hour later, HM shows significant improvement on recognition. A similar improvement also occurs with verbal material. When HM was shown a word such as 'Define', and then later given the prompt 'Def' and asked what word came to mind, he typically gave the correct word (Ogden and Corkin 1991).

These tasks show that HM can retain certain types of information over a period of several hours or days. Despite this, there are some tests where HM forgets very quickly. For example, Prisko (1963) presented HM with pairs of tones, coloured lights or patterns of clicks, and found that he had difficulty judging whether the two stimuli were the same or not. A similar deficit was shown by Sidman *et al.* (1968), who asked HM to indicate which of eight ellipses matched a sample one that had been presented a few seconds earlier. It was found that HM was unable to perform this task if a short delay was interposed between the stimuli. However, when HM was presented with verbal stimuli (three consonants), he had no difficulty matching the stimuli even after a 40 second delay. Thus, HM has a relatively intact ability to store short-term information for verbal items which does not extend to non-verbal data.

The fact that HM is able to use verbal information has enabled him to perform quite complex tasks. For example, Cohen and Cohen (1981) taught HM a puzzle called the Tower of Hanoi which, in its simplest version, consists of three wooden spindles, with the left-hand spindle holding three disks arranged on top of each other in descending size (Figure 9.10). The objective is to move the disks, one at a time, from the left- to the right-hand spindle, without placing a large disk on top of a smaller one. The task has to be learned through trial and error and the quickest solution is seven moves. However, by verbalising the instructions, HM was able to perform a five-disk version of this puzzle (which requires a minimum of 31 moves) in only 32 moves.

Despite this, HM cannot perform the stepping stone maze, which requires a set pathway to be learned through a 10×10 maze. This type of maze is constructed from metal bolts screwed into wood and the subject is shown a route by the experimenter. In turn, the subject has to touch the bolts one at a time to illustrate the route. Although normal subjects find this task relatively easy, HM was not able to trace the correct pathway after 125 attempts. When HM was given a simple 4×4 version of the maze, he eventually learned the task, but it took 155 trials. What, then, is the difference between the Tower of Hanoi and the stepping stone tasks? The answer appears to be that the former can be performed on the basis of using simple verbal rules, whereas the latter requires learning a pattern of movements that cannot easily be rehearsed in short-term memory.

Tower of Hanoi task

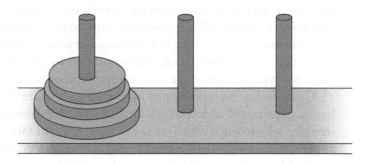

Finger maze task

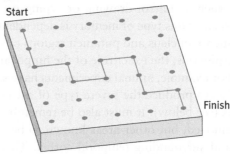

Start

Finish

| **Figure 9.10** | The Tower of Hanoi task and a stepping stone finger maze |

What has HM told us about the hippocampus and memory?

One of the most important lessons that has been learned from HM is that there are multiple memory systems in the brain. Although one can find examples of this idea in the writings of the ancient Greek philosophers, and later in the work of William James, the possibility of the brain containing different systems for memory did not gain widespread acceptance until psychologists studied HM. Indeed, one of the most interesting characteristics about HM is his relatively intact short-term memory. This indicates that certain types of memory, such as ones we use when we follow a conversation or remember a list of instructions, have different neural substrates from those involved in long-term memory. We can also deduce that the hippocampus is not the site in the brain where memories are stored, for the simple reason that HM can remember his childhood and early adolescence. Where, then, are memories stored? The likeliest site, especially if we follow Lashley and Penfield, is that long-term memories are stored in the cerebral cortex. It would appear, therefore, that the hippocampus is necessary for information to be permanently laid down in the memory banks of the cortex. This process is called **consolidation**.

It is also clear from HM's learning abilities that certain forms of long-term memory do not require the hippocampus. Indeed, if we examine more closely the types of tasks that HM can perform, they all appear to have an automatic quality which is not dependent on conscious awareness. That is, HM's long-term memory skills are reflexive rather than reflective. Interestingly, this type of distinction had also been made by several philosophers before HM was known. For example, in 1911 the French philosopher

Henri-Louis Bergson noted there was a difference between the type of memory needed for motor acts and that involving conscious thought. Later, in 1949, the English philosopher Gilbert Ryle expressed the same idea by making the distinction of *knowing how* and *knowing that*. Ryle noted that one type of memory allows us to do things that we do not need to think about, such as riding a bicycle or jumping a fence, whereas the other is a type of memory for information that includes conscious self-inspection.

This idea has been developed by Cohen and Squire (1980), who propose that HM has an impairment of **declarative** but not **procedural** memory. In their view, declarative memory is knowledge which we use to think with, or talk about. It can also be regarded as semantic and episodic memory that has been learned over the years, and which can be 'declared' into consciousness. In contrast, procedural memory is largely non-conscious, non-verbal, and accessible only through the performance of certain behaviours, such as mirror-drawing or typing on a computer keyboard. In fact, research suggests that this type of memory is dependent on subcortical structures – most notably the caudate nucleus and putamen regions of the basal ganglia (Squire 1998).

Despite this, the exact role of the hippocampus in memory is still somewhat uncertain. For example, animal experiments have shown that lesions of the hippocampus do not always produce the severe type of memory deficit that is predicted from human studies (see below). It must also be remembered that HM had not only his hippocampus removed, but other areas known to be involved in memory, including the amygdala and surrounding temporal cortex. This may help explain certain unusual cases where patients have had parts of their hippocampus removed for relief from intractable pain and seizures, without suffering memory impairments (Markowitsch 1985). Despite this, most researchers believe that the hippocampus has an important role to play in learning and memory and this has been supported in recent years by research using functional scanning techniques (see next).

Imaging the human brain and memory

One of the great developments in brain sciences over recent years has been the development of functional imaging techniques, such as positron emission tomography (PET) and functional magnetic resonance imaging (fMRI). These techniques allow the activity of the brain to be directly observed as it performs mental tasks. Indeed, both procedures can be used to measure the fluctuations of blood flow and oxygen consumption within a given brain region over a second-by-second timescale. This energy expenditure in turn provides a measure of the level of neural activity in that area. Although the historical development and use of these techniques is explored more fully in the next chapter, suffice here to say that they have been used to monitor the operations of the human brain involved in a wide variety of memory tasks. Furthermore, they are providing new insights into the functional role of the hippocampal system.

One consistent finding to be obtained from scanning studies of the hippocampus is its involvement in processing new or novel information. For example, in one study, subjects were asked to view large numbers of photographs taken from old *National Geographic* magazines (Tulving *et al.* 1994). A day later, subjects viewed the pictures again, but this time they were interspersed with 'new' pictures that had not previously been seen. A PET scan at this point showed far greater levels of neural activation in the hippocampal system, especially on its right side, when the novel pictures were presented. A number of other studies have reported similar results (Martin *et al.* 1997). The likeliest explanation for this novelty effect is that new items require greater levels of neural processing, or 'encoding', in the hippocampus than do items that have already been seen and encoded into memory.

The hippocampal system appears to do much more than simple encoding, though. It also makes associations between the stimuli it encodes. Henke *et al.* (1997) presented subjects with pictures that showed a person and a house. Subjects were then asked to judge whether the person was a likely inhabitant or visitor of that house based on their appearance. For example, in one instance, the subjects were shown an elegant lady and a sophisticated sitting room that constituted an appropriate match. Another instance showed a dishevelled man and a large mansion, representing an unlikely match. Although this task did not directly ask the subjects to link the two images, the nature of the judgements nevertheless encouraged them to make an association between the person and the house. To provide a control group, subjects were shown pictures in which they had to make a 'non-associative decision' about the person's gender (male or female), and view of the house (exterior or interior). The results showed far greater levels of neural activation in the medial temporal lobes when the subjects were involved in associating the person and the house. These findings indicate that the hippocampus is not just encoding new information, but it is actively involved in forming associations between new items, which presumably is important for learning and understanding.

In addition to encoding new information, the hippocampus is also involved in the retrieval of old memories. One study to show this was undertaken by Nyberg *et al.* (1996), who asked subjects to listen to two lists of words, before being placed into a PET scanner where recall was to take place. In one group, subjects were asked to decide whether each of the words was said by a male or female speaker (a perceptual judgement), and in the other subjects had to decide whether each word referred to a living or non-living thing (a semantic judgement). The results revealed better memory and greater medial temporal lobe activation when subjects were asked to recall the semantically encoded list than when asked to recall the perceptually encoded list. These findings were taken to show that the hippocampus is importantly involved in successful recall of memory representations.

There is some evidence to suggest that the anterior parts of the hippocampus are more active in the retrieval of learned information *from* memory, whereas the posterior parts of the hippocampal system are preferentially involved during the encoding of information *into* memory. For example, Gabrieli *et al.* (1997) presented subjects with drawings of common objects and animals. A day later, the same subjects were shown a list of words and asked to identify those which named an object or animal previously seen in the drawings. This is a task that requires retrieval of information from memory. When the MRI images were analysed from this task, researchers found greater brain activation in an anterior region of the hippocampal system known as the **subiculum**. In the second part of the study, subjects were shown colour pictures of indoor and outdoor scenes and asked to remember details for a later memory test. During this recall, a number of previously seen pictures were repeatedly shown, although others were shown only once. The novel pictures (which provide a measure of encoding) were found to produce greater levels of activation in the hippocampal system. However, this was most noticeable in the **parahippocampal cortex**, which lies posterior to the hippocampus. This is an intriguing finding although it has not been consistently replicated by others (see, for example, Greicius *et al.* 2003).

The hippocampi of London taxi drivers

Whether visiting a friend or popping out to the shops, finding our way around the environment is something we take for granted. Yet it is truly a remarkable skill that requires both spatial memory and an ability to construct a mental map of our world. We have already seen that one brain area implicated in this ability is the hippocampus – as supported by the fact that lesions of this structure impair performance on tests of cognitive mapping and spatial processing. But, there also is evidence that the size of the hippocampus correlates with the ability to perform such tasks. For instance, birds that store food which requires them later to remember the locations of the storage sites, have a larger hippocampus than those that do not horde (Sherry *et al.* 1992). Another example where hippocampal differences are found is in North American voles. The male meadow vole (*Microtus pennsylvanicus*) has a territory several times larger than the female and a much larger hippocampus. In contrast, male and female pine

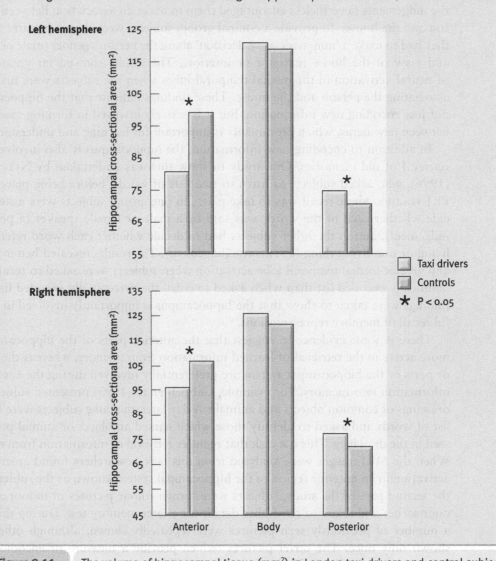

Figure 9.11 The volume of hippocampal tissue (mm²) in London taxi drivers and control subjects

Source: E.A. Maguire *et al.* (2000) Navigation-related structural changes in the hippocampi of taxi drivers, *Proceedings of the National Academy of Sciences*, 97, 4398–4403

voles (*Microtus pinetorum*), which travel over equal distances, show no difference in the size of their hippocampi (Jacobs *et al.* 1990).

But, can navigational experience have an impact on the size of the hippocampus in humans? To answer this question, Eleanor Maguire and her colleagues at University College, London, examined the brains of 16 right-handed London taxi drivers by using MRI scanning. London taxi drivers provide ideal subjects for this type of study. Most are highly experienced (the men in Maguire's study had been driving taxis for a mean of 14.3 years), and to get a licence they must have passed an examination that tested their ability to navigate some 24,000 streets in the city. This task takes most drivers about two years to accomplish. And, it seems, this experience does indeed have an effect on the size of the hippocampus. For example, the posterior part of the right hippocampus was significantly larger in both right and left hemispheres of taxi drivers when compared with controls (Figure 9.11) – although, surprisingly, the anterior part of the hippocampus was found to be smaller. There was no difference between the two groups in the medial parts of the hippocampus, or in its overall volume (Maguire *et al.* 2000). The investigators also plotted the volume of the anterior and posterior hippocampus against the number of months each person had spent as a taxi driver. The analysis showed that the volume of the right-sided hippocampus was significantly correlated with the amount of time spent as a taxi driver, although the left-sided hippocampus did not show this relationship (there was also a positive association for the posterior hippocampus and a negative one for the anterior region). In other words, driving a taxi for a long time causes the right posterior hippocampus to become larger. In fact, this finding was also in accordance with an earlier PET study by Maguire *et al.* (1997), who asked London taxi drivers to recall complex routes around the city. She found that this increased activity in a number of brain regions, including the right hippocampus, but not the left.

This research raises many further intriguing questions. For example, what are the functions of the right and left sides of the hippocampus in humans? Is it really the increased navigational experience that is producing the changes? And, do taxi drivers gain spatial knowledge at the expense of some other form of knowledge? These questions show that we still have a long way to go before we understand all the mysteries of the hippocampus.

Korsakoff's syndrome and diencephalic amnesia

The hippocampus and medial temporal lobes are not the only brain areas associated with memory. In fact, the most common form of amnesia seen in clinical practice is **Korsakoff's syndrome,** named after the Russian physician Sergi Korsakoff who first described the condition in 1889. Korsakoff's syndrome is predominantly found in alcoholics and develops as a result of thiamine (vitamin B$_1$) deficiency due to a poor diet and long-term reliance on alcohol. Although this type of amnesia is associated with some degree of generalised brain shrinkage, damage is most frequently found in the **diencephalon,** which includes the **thalamus** and **hypothalamus.** For this reason it is sometimes described as diencephalic amnesia.

The first signs of Korsakoff's syndrome often appear as **Wernicke's encephalopathy,** characterised by confusion in which the patient may be unable to recognise friends and surroundings. This is accompanied by unsteadiness of balance and poor motor co-ordination (ataxia). These symptoms can be reversed with thiamine and glucose injections, although this does not stop the deterioration of memory and personality that becomes Korsakoff's syndrome. One of the most striking features of this illness is a severe deficit in learning new information (anterograde amnesia). For example, a person with Korsakoff's syndrome may take weeks or even months to learn the names of doctor and nurses, or the location of their hospital bed. These patients also perform poorly on memory tasks. If they are presented with a list of eight paired associate words such as *man–hamster*, and asked to recall the second word (*hamster*) when *man* is presented again, it may take the Korsakoff patient some 30 or 40 trials to learn this association in comparison with only 3 or 4 trials for a normal subject (Butters 1984).

Another abnormality sometimes found in Korsakoff's syndrome is **retrograde amnesia**, which refers to memory loss for events preceding the onset of the disease. Although this type of amnesia is generally mild and most pronounced for the months leading up to the illness, in some cases the memory loss can go back many years. There are Korsakoff patients, for example, who can remember their participation in the Second World War, but not recall the assassination of President Kennedy or the Apollo space missions. This will also cause the person to believe that they are living in the past (see, for example, the case of Mr G in *The Man Who Mistook his Wife for a Hat* by Oliver Sacks). A more common symptom of Korsakoff's syndrome is **confabulation**, where patients may make up stories or confabulate if they have gaps in their memory. Indeed, they may provide plausible answers to questions which, upon verification, are found to be totally false. The problem is exacerbated by the Korsakoff patient's lack of insight into their condition, which often leads them to believe that there is nothing wrong with their memory.

Interestingly, temporal lobe amnesia and Korsakoff's syndrome show important differences. Although both are characterised by anterograde amnesia, the symptoms of confabulation and confusion are not normally found in temporal lobe amnesia. Another difference occurs in emotional responding. The individual with Korsakoff's syndrome is often emotionally flat and apathetic (for example, they may stare at a blank TV screen without switching the TV on), whereas the temporal lobe amnesiac typically shows normal or appropriate emotions. In addition, while people with diencephalic amnesia take a long time to learn new information, they forget at normal rates (Figure 9.12). This is in contrast to those with damage to the medial temporal lobes, who forget very rapidly (Huppert and Piercy 1979).

The neural basis of Korsakoff's syndrome

It has long been known that Korsakoff's syndrome is associated with damage to the diencephalon, especially the **mammillary bodies**, which are situated in the posterior part of the hypothalamus (Figure 9.13). Indeed, as early as 1928, Gamper examined the brains of 16 Korsakoff patients and showed that all had degeneration of the mammillary nuclei. A large number of studies have subsequently confirmed this observation. However, the mammillary bodies are not the only site of damage in Korsakoff's syndrome. The brain often shows generalised and widespread damage at post-mortem, which is likely to include the brainstem and parts of the cerebral cortex – especially the frontal lobes. The traditional view of mammillary body damage being responsible for the amnesia in Korsakoff's syndrome has also been challenged. For example, a study of over 80 Korsakoff brains found that damage to the **dorsomedial thalamus** was a more reliable feature of the disease than were mammillary body lesions (Victor *et al.* 1971).

This finding has complicated the understanding of Korsakoff's syndrome, and it raises the possibility that damage to both mammillary bodies and dorsomedial thalamus

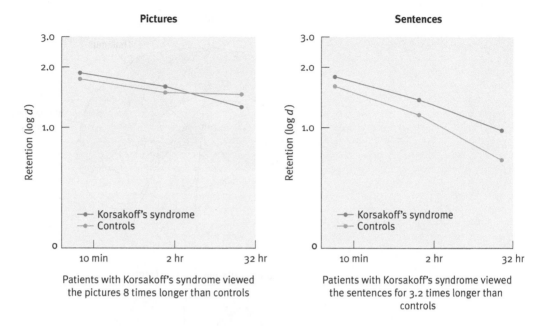

Figure 9.12   Figure showing forgetting rates of diencephalic and temporal lobe amnesia

Source: Adapted from L.R. Squire (1981) Two forms of human amnesia: an analysis of forgetting, *Journal of Neuroscience*, 6, 635–640

has to occur before the emergence of diencephalic amnesia. Evidence supporting the role of the dorsomedial thalamus in memory has come from an ex US Air Force technician known as NA who, at the age of 22, suffered severe amnesia following an injury. The accident happened when NA was building a model aeroplane in the company of a friend who was playing with a fencing foil behind his back. When NA turned suddenly, his friend accidentally stabbed him through the right nostril. The foil passed up through the cribiform plate and entered the left side of the brain. The injury caused NA to lose consciousness for a few minutes, along with paresis of the right arm and leg which later showed recovery. But, more importantly, the accident caused NA to suffer a permanent anterograde amnesia. Although it is not as severe as HM's amnesia (for example, NA can remember faces quite well), NA still needs constant supervision. He lives at home with his mother and is cheerful and friendly, despite finding it hard to retain 'the events of each passing hour and day'. He cannot cook satisfactorily because he forgets the correct steps, and has difficulty watching television as he forgets the story between commercial breaks. NA is unable to provide information about events since his accident in 1960, although he has almost normal recall for his life up to that event (Squire 1987).

In 1979 Squire and Moore performed a CAT (computerised axial tomography) scan on NA and found that the foil had terminated in the left-sided dorsomedial thalamus. This initial report indicated that the injury was highly localised, with little damage to other brain structures. Animal research also confirmed the dorsomedial thalamus to be importantly involved in memory. However, a later MRI study showed that damage had also occurred to the mammillary bodies and the pathway connecting

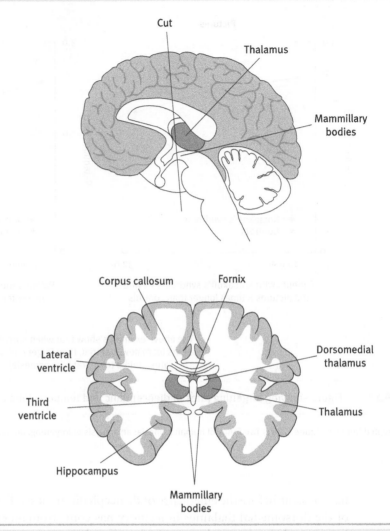

Figure 9.13   The location of the mammillary bodies and thalamus

these structures with the anterior thalamus (Squire *et al*. 1989). Which of these regions is most crucial for producing NA's amnesia is still unclear. Nonetheless, the similarity in the symptoms of HM and NA suggest that the medial temporal lobes and diencephalon may be part of a much larger brain system involved in memory.

Memory circuits in the brain

There are two distinct regions of the brain associated with human amnesia: the medial temporal lobes and the diencephalon. It should come as no surprise, therefore, to discover that these two regions are anatomically connected. For example, in 1937, James Papez described a brain circuit (called the **Papez circuit**) that connected the hippocampus with the diencephalon. More specifically this circuit consists of the cingulate gyrus (an 'old' part of the cerebral cortex), which projects to the hippocampus, which in turn projects via a long arching pathway called the **fornix** to the mammillary bodies. From here, a tract projects upwards into the anterior thalamus whose fibres then complete the circuit by projecting to the cingulate gyrus. Although Papez originally believed this circuit to be involved in emotional behaviour, one might also expect it to have a crucial involvement in memory.

Curiously, the evidence linking the Papez circuit with amnesia is not convincing. For example, if this circuit were involved in memory processing, we would expect a major role for the long arching pathway that connects the hippocampus with the mammillary bodies called the **fornix**. The human fornix is a massive pathway that contains around 1 million fibres, and although its main target is the mammillary bodies, it also projects to other forebrain structures, including the anterior thalamus and septum. But, the role of the fornix in amnesia is highly controversial. For example, Squire and Moore (1979) reviewed fifty instances of fornix lesions and found evidence of mild amnesia in only three cases. A more recent study of ten patients who had cysts surgically removed from the fornix have shown some intellectual deficits, and memory impairments on tests of recall but not recognition (Aggleton and Brown 1999). In other words, the subjects were able to correctly recognise items that had been previously presented to them, but they could not recall them from memory.

It has also been claimed that damage to other areas of the Papez circuit – namely the anterior thalamus or cingulate cortex – causes amnesia, although convincing proof is again lacking. For example, cingulate cortex lesions have been found to produce a transient amnesia in which memory for temporal ordering of events is particularly poor (Mayes 1988). It is also claimed that there are no cases of long-term memory disturbances in humans when damage is confined to the anterior thalamus (Markowitsch 1988). Such evidence is not consistent with the Papez circuit having an important role in memory processing.

Interestingly, the Papez circuit does not project to the **dorsomedial thalamus**, which, as we have seen above, has also been implicated in amnesia. In fact, the dorsomedial thalamus forms part of a different system, sometimes referred to as the **Yakovlev circuit**, whose focal point is the **amygdala** (Figure 9.14). The amygdala sends fibres to the dorsomedial thalamus, which in turn projects to the **prefrontal cortex**. The

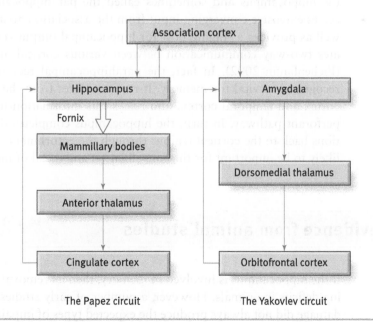

Figure 9.14   The Papez and Yakovlev circuits

circuit is then completed with the prefrontal cortex projecting back to the amygdala, although it also has extensive connections with the rest of the cerebral cortex. Experimental studies with animals indicate that the amygdala–frontal cortex pathway is particularly important for learning about fearful events, although its role in humans is less clear. In humans, amygdala lesions have been undertaken to reduce aggression (see the case of Julia S in Chapter 6) and do not appear to have serious consequences for memory. Damage to the frontal lobes, however, can produce memory deficits, although not serious anterograde (or retrograde) amnesia. Rather, the frontal lobe deficits tend to arise when the person tries to plan a series of responses or actions, or to remember the sequence of some plan (see Chapter 10).

Moreover, damage to other areas of the cerebral cortex can also produce amnesia. For example, Tulving *et al.* (1991) have described a patient, known simply as KC, who sustained brain injuries in a traffic accident and suffered profound amnesia for **episodic memory** but not **semantic memory**. Episodic memory refers to memory for dates and times, that is, for the *episodes* of our life. We use this memory, for example, when we look back over our life and order events into their correct sequence for time and place. In contrast, semantic memory is our store of *facts and information,* that is, our basic knowledge of the world. Following his accident, KC has not been able to retrieve personal memories of his past, although his general knowledge remains good. To give an example, KC plays chess well but cannot remember when he learned to play the game, or from whom. Brain scans of KC reveal extensive damage to the left frontal–parietal cortex, and the right parietal–occipital cortex. There is also some shrinkage of the hippocampus (Rosenbaum *et al.* 2000). Although the extensive damage makes interpretation of this patient difficult, it does show that areas of the cerebral cortex, beyond those of the Papez circuit and dorsomedial thalamus, play a vital role in memory storage and retrieval.

Although the most conspicuous pathway leaving the hippocampus is the fornix, there is a second route by which hippocampal information gains access to other brain regions. This is via the **entorhinal cortex**, which is 'old' cortical tissue lying adjacent to the hippocampus and sometimes called the **parahippocampal region**. This area receives extensive converging input from the association areas of the cerebral cortex, as well as provides a staging post for hippocampal output (Figure 9.15). Thus, it mediates two-way communication between various cortical areas and the hippocampus (Eichenbaum 2002). In fact, the parahippocampal region is increasingly becoming recognised as vital for memory. It receives fibres from the prefrontal cortex, parietal cortex and temporal cortex, and relays this information to the hippocampus via the perforant pathway. In turn, the hippocampus completes the loop by sending projections back to the cortical regions through the entorhinal cortex. This diffuse circuit is likely to be important for the consolidation and recall of memory.

The evidence from animal studies

If the hippocampus is involved in memory, then its removal should also produce learning deficits in animals. However, a number of early studies showed that hippocampal damage did not always produce the expected types of impairment. In fact, it was found during the early 1960s that hippocampal lesioned rats could perform a number of tasks

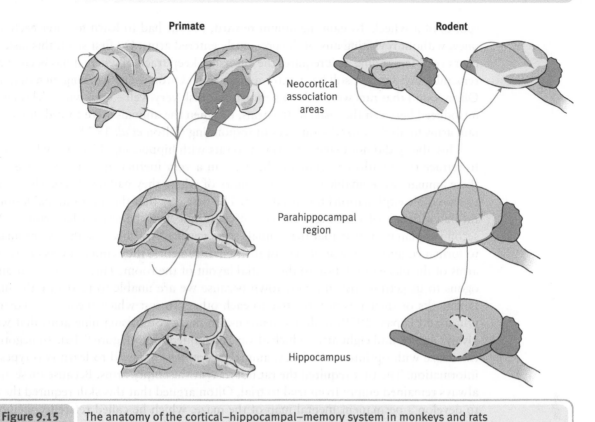

Primate

Rodent

Neocortical
association
areas

Parahippocampal
region

Hippocampus

| Figure 9.15 | The anatomy of the cortical–hippocampal–memory system in monkeys and rats |

Source: M.S. Gazzaniga *et al., Cognitive Neuroscience,* 2nd edition, p. 336. Copyright © 2002 by W.W. Norton & Co.

including: (1) various types of operant conditioning in a Skinner box, (2) a visual discrimination task in which the animal had to distinguish between a black and white goal box to obtain food reward, and (3) avoiding an electric shock in a situation that required running to a 'safe' location whenever a warning tone was presented. These findings even led some researchers to question whether the hippocampus actually served a mnemonic function in animals (Kimble 1968). Despite this, by the 1970s it was becoming clear that there were certain tests where marked memory deficits occurred in animals after hippocampal lesions. Two such experimental situations where this was demonstrated were tasks involving working memory and cognitive mapping.

Working memory

In their natural habitat, animals have to forage for food, which requires them to find their way around their environment. Obviously, it helps if the animal can remember where it has just been, to avoid going back to a location where food has already been collected. In fact, even simple animals such as bees are surprisingly adept at this skill. In 1976, David Olton designed a task which tested a similar type of ability in rats (Olton and Samuelson 1976). This was the radial arm maze, which consisted of a round platform with arms, containing food at their ends, that radiated out like the spokes of a wheel. To gain maximum reward, the rat had to learn to enter each arm once, without revisiting any of the previously entered arms. On first sight, this task appears very demanding as it requires the animal to keep track of where it has been, while remembering where it still has to go – a skill which Olton called **working memory**. Yet, Olton found that rats were able to perform this task very well – even when delays were introduced between the visits to the arms, or when the animals were forced down certain arms to abolish fixed sequences of responding (Olton *et al.* 1979).

This ability did not extend, however, to rats with hippocampal lesions, who tended to retrace their paths or negotiate the maze in a very inefficient manner. It was as if these animals were unable to form a memory of where they had just been. There were two possible explanations for this deficit. The first was that the hippocampal lesioned rat had a deficit of working memory – it could not 'list' the arms it had visited. The second explanation was that the animals were getting 'lost' because they were unable to form a cognitive or spatial map of their environment – they could not recognise the arms of the maze in relation to the spatial layout of the room. This is somewhat analogous to us getting lost in a new town because we are unable to recognise the main landmarks or their position relative to each other. To test which theory was correct, Olton and Papas (1979) built a seventeen-arm maze comprising nine arms that were always empty, and eight arms which always contained food (Figure 9.16). To negotiate this maze with optimum efficiency, animals were now required to learn two types of information. The first required the rat not to visit the empty arms. Because these arms always remained empty from trial to trial, Olton argued that this skill required the rat to develop a permanent mental map of the maze, which he called **reference memory**. The second component of the task required the animal to find the food without revisiting any of the arms during a trial. This was the working memory task again, with the rat having to remember where it has just been, and where it has to go.

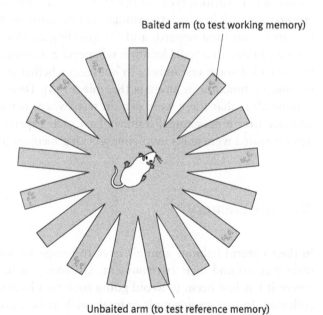

Baited arm (to test working memory)

Unbaited arm (to test reference memory)

Figure 9.16   The radial arm maze (showing working and reference memory components)

When Olton tested normal rats on his maze he found that they soon learned to avoid the empty arms and retrieved food in an efficient manner from the baited ones. In other words, they were capable of both reference memory and working memory. Surprisingly, when the hippocampal lesioned animals were put into the radial maze, they also learned to avoid the non-baited arms. Yet, they performed only at chance levels when visiting the arms containing food. In other words, the hippocampal damaged rats showed reference memory, which appeared to show that they retained the ability to form a spatial map of the radial maze. However, the same animals were incapable of performing the working memory component of the task.

Cognitive mapping and spatial memory

A different approach to understanding hippocampal function was undertaken by John O'Keefe and his colleagues at the University of London. Instead of examining the behavioural effects of hippocampal damage, O'Keefe recorded the electrical activity of individual cells in the hippocampus as rats moved around their environment. His main finding was that some neurons fired only when the animal was in a certain location. These were neurons that remained quiet until the animal reached a certain point when suddenly the cell would begin to fire rapidly. As the animal moved away to a new location the neuron would stop firing. However, if the rat returned to the old location at a later point, the neuron would start to fire again (Figure 9.17). O'Keefe called these neurons **place cells**.

Further research showed that hippocampal place cells were dependent on the configuration of cues located outside the testing arena and not those within its confines. For example, O'Keefe and Conway (1978) trained rats to run a T-maze where one of the arms always contained food. The maze was surrounded by a black curtain that had a distinct object or cue hanging on each of its four sides. These were a fan, a buzzer, a light and a square card. Importantly, the curtain could also be moved around the apparatus, with the cues changing location, but always remaining in the same place relative to each other. On all trials, the arm containing the food was pointed towards the corner situated between the light and the card. To make sure that the rats learned the spatial location of the arm, and not a simple right or left turning response, the location of the starting position was changed from trial to trial.

The task showed that the hippocampal place cells fired only when the animal was in a specific location in relation to the cues. If the curtain was moved around, shifting the configuration of the cues with it, the place cell still fired, provided the animal was in the same *relative* position to the cues. In other words, the place cells did not fire at a specific site in the maze, rather, it was the animal's position relative to the external cues that was the crucial factor. The vital importance of the external cues for the firing of the place cells was further highlighted when they were removed. If any two cues were removed, the place cells continued to fire; but if three cues were taken away the neurons stopped firing. The important factor, therefore, was the *spatial configuration* of the cues. This evidence strongly indicated that the hippocampus was forming a cognitive map of its environment (O'Keffe and Nadel 1978). In other words, when an animal negotiates its environment, it is using a map, continuously formed and updated by the hippocampus, to guide direction and goal location.

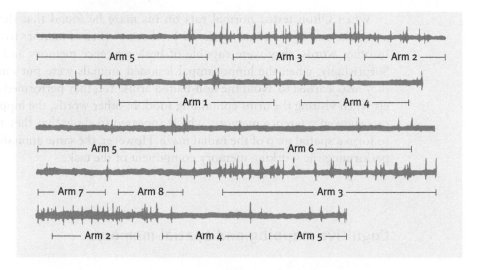

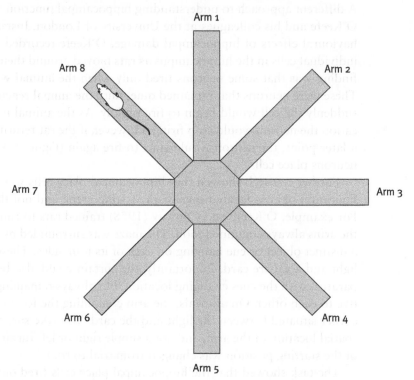

Figure 9.17   The firing of hippocampal place cells as a rat negotiates a radial arm maze

Source: F.E. Bloom and A. Lazerson (1985) *Brain, Mind and Behaviour*, p. 249

Some of the best support for the cognitive mapping theory has come from Morris *et al.* (1982) who developed a spatial memory task that required rats to swim a water maze. The 'maze' was in fact a large circular tank of water, made opaque with the addition of milk, that contained a small escape platform hidden just below the surface. Rats were put into the water and allowed to swim around until they 'bumped' into the platform – onto which they inevitably climbed. The rats could not see the platform, and were forced to learn its location by determining its position in relation to the

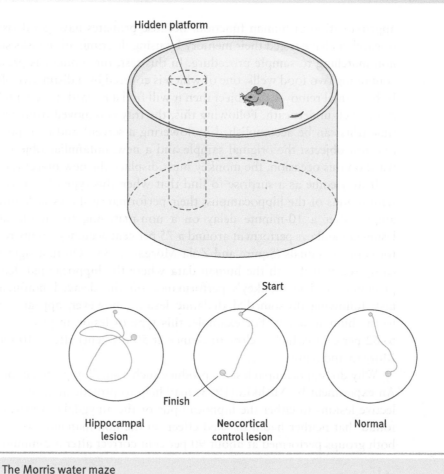

| Figure 9.18 | The Morris water maze |

Source: R.G.M. Morris *et al.* (1982) Examples of routes taken after training by rats in water maze, *Nature*, 297, 681–683

spatial configuration of external cues around the water. Morris found that it took just a few trials for normal animals to swim directly to the platform. In contrast, the hippocampal lesioned rats were unable to learn the location of the platform after 40 days of training (Figure 9.18).

It is hard to see how the water maze is testing any behavioural function except spatial memory. Thus, the failure of the hippocampal lesioned rats to perform this relatively easy task provides strong support for the cognitive mapping theory. However, the performance of animals in the water maze appears to contradict the work of David Olton, who showed that hippocampus lesioned rats have intact reference memory in the radial maze. Indeed, successful performance in both the water maze and reference memory component of the radial maze would appear to require forming a spatial map of the environment – yet only the former causes a problem for the lesioned animals. The reason for this difference is not understood.

Memory tasks involving primates

Primates provide an alternative way of experimentally investigating the brain structures responsible for learning and memory, and one that is likely to represent a better approximation of human function. Because primates have good vision, like humans, researchers have tested their memory by using discrimination tasks such as the **delayed non-matching to sample** procedure. In this test, the monkey is presented with a tray containing two food wells, one of which is covered by a distinctive object (the sample). If the animal removes the object then it will find a reward (for example, a banana chip) in the well underneath. Following this, the tray is removed from sight for a period of time (this can be accomplished by lowering a screen) and then presented again with two test objects: the original sample and a new, unfamiliar object. To obtain the reward on this occasion, the monkey must displace the new object (Figure 9.19).

It may come as a surprise to find that when this type of task is given to primates with lesions of the hippocampus, their performance shows little impairment. For example, after a 10-minute delay on a non-matching to sample task, hippocampal lesioned monkeys perform at around a 75 per cent accuracy, compared with 90 per cent for control animals (Squire and Zola-Morgan 1985). On first sight this finding is not easily reconciled with the human data where the hippocampal deficit is much more pronounced. The monkey's performance on the delayed non-matching to sample task following dorsomedial thalamic lesions, however, appears to be much closer to the human deficit. For example, this type of lesion in primates reduces accuracy to 62 per cent (which is close to chance at 50 per cent) after a 10-minute delay (Zola-Morgan and Squire 1985).

Why do hippocampal lesions produce such a small impairment on this type of task? An experiment by Mishkin (1978) may help to provide an answer. Mishkin made selective lesions to either the hippocampus or the amygdala in macaque monkeys, and found that neither had a marked effect on the non-matching to sample task. In fact, both groups performed at about 90 per cent correct after a 2-minute delay. But, when

1. The monkey moves the sample object to obtain food from the well beneath it

2. A screen is lowered in front of the monkey during the delay period

3. The monkey is confronted with the sample object and an unfamiliar object

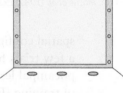

4. The monkey must remember the sample object and select the unfamiliar object to obtain the food beneath it

Figure 9.19 The delayed non-matching to sample task

Source: John J.P. Pinel, *Biopsychology*, 3rd edition. Copyright © 1997 by Pearson Education

Mishkin made a combined lesion of the hippocampus and amygdala, the monkeys exhibited a severe impairment, with performance falling to near chance (60 per cent) accuracy. This finding is noteworthy because HM's operation also involved the removal of the amygdala and hippocampus, as well as the surrounding portions of the medial temporal lobe. Thus, Mishkin's work implies that both the hippocampus and amygdala are necessary for memory processing. Indeed, as we have seen, there is evidence that these two structures are part of different memory circuits in the brain. One possibility, therefore, is that both circuits need to be damaged for severe amnesia to occur in both monkeys and humans.

Some researchers believe, however, that a different explanation accounts for the hippocampal–amygdala deficit. For example, Stuart Zola-Morgan and Larry Squire at the University of California have looked at other types of temporal lobe damage in non-matching to sample tasks, including lesions to the cortical tissue surrounding the hippocampus and amygdala. These regions include the **perirhinal cortex**, which lies close to the amygdala, and the **parahippocampal gyrus** and **entorhinal cortex**, which adjoin the hippocampus (Figure 9.20). All these regions were damaged to some degree by Mishkin's attempts to produce his combined lesions. Importantly, it was found that that damage confined to the cortex surrounding the hippocampus and amygdala produced a memory deficit that was nearly as severe as the one for the combined hippocampal–amygdala lesion itself (Zola-Morgan *et al.* 1989). Further research has examined these areas with more selective lesions, and found that the most severe memory deficits occur when both hippocampus and its adjacent cortical areas are destroyed together. As mentioned above, these are areas known to have extensive reciprocal connections with the cerebral cortex.

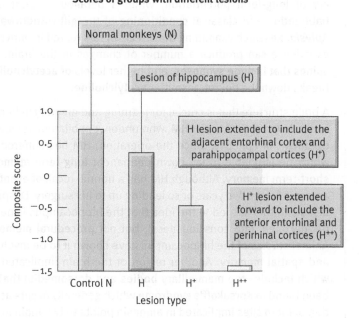

Ventral view of monkey brain showing areas of different medial temporal lesions

Hippocampus

Scores of groups with different lesions

Normal monkeys (N)

Lesion of hippocampus (H)

H lesion extended to include the adjacent entorhinal cortex and parahippocampal cortices (H⁺)

H⁺ lesion extended forward to include the anterior entorhinal and perirhinal cortices (H⁺⁺)

Composite score

1.0
0.5
0
−0.5
−1.0
−1.5

Control N   H   H⁺   H⁺⁺
Lesion type

Figure 9.20 Behavioural scores (combined from four different tests of memory) as a function of medial temporal lobe lesions involving the hippocampus in monkeys

Source: S.M. Breedlove *et al.* (2007) *Biological Psychology*, 5th edition, p. 525

This type of research helps us to understand why HM's memory deficits are so severe. In 1997, HM underwent an MRI scan to measure the true extent of his brain damage (Corkin *et al.* 1997). The scans confirmed that HM's lesions were large, with around 5 cm³ of brain tissue in both sides of the medial temporal lobes having been removed. In effect, the hippocampus, amygdala and parts of the surrounding cortical tissue had been destroyed in both hemispheres. Had the surgery lesioned only the hippocampus, then HM's memory deficits would probably have been less dramatic. Unfortunately, HM had the misfortune to be operated on before researchers had learned about the medial temporal lobes and their role in memory. This highlights the need for greater knowledge about the brain, so that such mistakes are not made again.

Summary

There is no learning without memory, although some memories can be innate such as instincts and basic reflexes. The search for the **engram** (the anatomical site of memory storage) was initiated in the 1920s by Karl Lashley, who made knife cuts, or lesioned, different proportions of the **cerebral cortex**, in rats after they had learned to run through mazes. Lashley showed that his animals were always able to relearn the task, even after receiving large lesions, and he concluded that memories for mazes were stored diffusely throughout the cerebral cortex, which he called the principle of **mass action**, and that all parts of the cortex played an equal role in their storage, which he called the principle of **equipotentiality**. His work was supported, in part, by Donald Hebb, who theorised that learning and memory must involve large groups of neurons, or **cell assemblies**, reverberating for some time after the event, which led to structural change at **synapses**. Evidence of increased electrical activity in neurons after learning has come from the discovery of **long-term potentiation**, while a detailed account of the synaptic changes that accompany **habituation** and **classical conditioning** of the **gill-withdrawal reflex** has come from an examination of *Aplysia*. Research examining the effects of rats reared in enriched environments has also shown that such experience can produce a number of changes in the brain, including increased numbers of **dendritic spines** that include **synapses**, and higher levels of **acetylcholinesterase** (AChE), which is an enzyme that breaks down the neurotransmitter **acetylcholine**.

A brain structure that is crucial for learning and memory in humans is the **hippocampus**. This was dramatically shown in the case of **HM**, who underwent bilateral removal of the **medial temporal lobes** in 1953 for treatment of epilepsy. Since the operation, HM has suffered from a profound **anterograde amnesia** in which he is unable to lay down permanent **long-term memories**, although he has a relatively normal **short-term memory**. Although HM has a normal recall of events prior to his operation, there is **retrograde amnesia** for the two years or so leading up to his surgery. Despite this, HM demonstrates learning on some tasks and this has led to the idea that the hippocampus is necessary for **declarative memory** (which can be 'declared' into consciousness), but not **procedural memory** (implicit or 'knowing how' knowledge). Animal studies of the hippocampus have shown it to be involved in **working memory, cognitive mapping** and **spatial memory**. Another region of the brain implicated in human amnesia is the **diencephalons**, which includes the **mammillary bodies** and **dorsomedial thalamus**. Damage to both of these areas has been found in **Korsakoff's syndrome** which generally occurs as a result of chronic alcohol abuse. The location of brain sites implicated in amnesia points to two main memory pathways in the brain: the **Papez circuit** and the **Yakovlev circuit**. The former includes the hippocampus, fornix, mammillary bodies and cingulate gyrus, and the latter includes amygdala, dorsomedial thalamus and frontal cortex. It is probable that the most severe forms of amnesia require damage to both these pathways.

Essay questions

1. With reference to neural, synaptic and electrophysiological changes, what would a memory engram in the brain be likely to look like?

   Search terms: Synaptic changes in memory. Long-term potentiation. Dendritic changes in memory. Learning and memory in Aplysia. Hebbian synapses. Phosphorylation of memory. Effects of experience on the brain.

2. What brain structures and circuits are known to be particularly important for human memory?

   Search terms: Hippocampus and memory. Papez circuit and memory. Mammillary bodies and Korsakoff's syndrome. Temporal lobe and memory. Thalamus and memory. Amnesia. Penfield and memory storage.

3. Discuss the evidence linking the hippocampus with an involvement in cognitive mapping and spatial memory.

   Search terms: Hippocampus and cognitive mapping. Neurobiology of working memory. Radial arm maze. Place cells. Spatial memory and hippocampus. Lesions of the hippocampus.

4. What are the main characteristics of HM? What does his memory deficit tell us about the function of the hippocampus and medial temporal lobes?

   Search terms: Patient HM. Anterograde amnesia. Declarative and procedural memory. Functions of the hippocampus. Explicit and implicit memory in amnesia.

Further reading

Bourtchouladze, R. (2002) *Memories are Made of This*. London: Weidenfeld & Nicolson. Described in the inside cover as 'a brilliant work of popularisation', this book nevertheless provides a good coverage of the biopsychology of memory. This may be the place to start for the student who wants a simple but broad introduction to the subject.

Cohen, N.J. and Eichenbaum, H. (1993) *Memory, Amnesia, and the Hippocampal System*. Cambridge, Mass.: MIT Press. Written for experts, this attempts to bring together evidence from neuropsychology, neuroscience and cognitive science to explain the role of the hippocampus in memory and amnesia.

Dubai, Y. (1990) *The Neurobiology of Memory*. Oxford: Oxford University Press. A textbook that will appeal to neuroscience students, especially those interested in the molecular and cellular aspects of memory.

Eichenbaum, H. (2002) *Cognitive Neuroscience of Memory*. Oxford: Oxford University Press. A clear and accessible textbook which includes separate chapters on the brain systems for procedural, declarative and emotional memory.

Eichenbaum, H. and Cohen, N.J. (2001) *From Conditioning to Conscious Recollection: Memory Systems of the Brain*. Oxford: Oxford University Press. Despite its title, this is a readable book which will have much to interest the student who wants to extend his or her reading of my chapter here.

Holscher, C. (ed.) (2001) *Neuronal Mechanisms of Memory Formation*. Cambridge: Cambridge University Press. A collection of chapters written by various experts on long-term potentiation.

Martinez, J.L. and Kesner, R.P. (eds) (1998) *Neurobiology of Learning and Memory*. San Diego, Calif.: Academic Press. A comprehensive and well-written series of chapters by experts in the field that covers learning and memory from a diversity of approaches, including genetic, pharmacological and physiological perspectives.

McGaugh, J.L., Weinberger, N.M. and Lynch, G. (1995) *Brain and Memory: Modulation and Mediation of Neuroplasticity.* Oxford: Oxford University Press. A fairly technical and wide-ranging account which examines the processes underlying the formation of new memories and their possible sites of storage.

Parkin, A.J. and Leng, N.R. (1993) *Neuropsychology of the Amnesic Syndrome.* Hove: Lawrence Erlbaum. A concise but well-written introduction to memory disorders, including Korsakoff's syndrome and temporal lobe amnesia.

Rolls, G. (2005) *Classic Case Studies in Psychology.* London: Hodder Arnold. Chapter 6 of this book provides a brief, interesting and in places contentious account of HM.

Rose, S. (2003) *The Making of Memory: From Molecules to Mind.* London: Bantam Books. Winner of the Rhône-Poulenc Science Prize in 1993, this is a highly enjoyable and informative introduction to the molecular and neurobiological basis of memory and amnesia.

Seifert, W. (ed.) (1983) *Neurobiology of the Hippocampus.* London: Academic Press. Although this book is now dated, it nevertheless contains useful chapters by the main protagonists who were involved in examining the role of the hippocampus in working memory, cognitive mapping and spatial processing.

Squire, L.R. (1987) *Memory and the Brain.* New York: Oxford University Press. A good introduction, suitable for undergraduates, that attempts to show how memory is organised in the brain using evidence from both experimental research and clinical studies.

Squire, L.R. and Kandel, E.R. (1999) *Memory: From Mind to Molecules.* New York: Scientific American Library. A well-written and richly illustrated text that provides a good overview of research into the neural mechanisms underlying learning and memory.

Squire, L.R. and Schacter, D.L. (eds) (2002) *Neuropsychology of Memory.* New York: Guilford Press. A collection of thirty-eight chapters written by various experts in the field.

For self test questions, animations, interactive exercises and many more resources to help you consolidate your understanding, and expand your knowledge of the field, please go to the website accompanying this book at **www.pearsoned.co.uk/wickens**

CHAPTER 10

Language and cognition

INTRODUCTION

One of the greatest challenges facing brain research is to understand the neural mechanisms responsible for producing higher levels of human mental activity such as language, self-awareness, mental imagery and thought. In other words, how does the activity of the brain gives rise to the cognitive processes of the mind. Although this has been a dream of philosophers and psychologists since Descartes, scientists have been restricted by the limited methodologies that could tackle such questions. Indeed, until fairly recently, the investigation of mental processes by biopsychologists was based almost entirely on determining the type of impairment that followed brain injuries such as stroke. This type of approach, was reliant on clinical neuropsychological testing and post-mortem analysis, and was especially useful in identifying the main brain regions involved in language. However, it was limited in explaining the underlying cognitive processes that give rise to this ability. This situation has changed in recent years with the development of functional scanning techniques such as PET and fMRI, which permit the structure and neural activity of the brain to be observed in a living person. In fact, such techniques allow the researcher to study just about any type of thought process, and to visualise what happens in the brain during this activity. This development is revolutionising our understanding of the brain, and has given rise to a new academic field known as cognitive neuroscience that is attempting to integrate cognitive science with biopsychology. There has been a meteoric growth in this type of research, and there is little doubt it will provide many new insights into the relationship between brain and mental activity over the coming years.

Language and the brain: the contribution of Paul Broca

One of the things that distinguish humans from other animals is their ability to use language. Of course, all animals are capable of communication, but humans are the only ones who use an extremely complex, creative and powerful system of language that enables them to express their thoughts and feelings using speech and writing. Our ability to use language is remarkable in many ways. For example, during a simple conversation we speak around 180 words a minute from a vocabulary of between 60,000 and 120,000 words. Although this is an impressive figure, even more important is our ability to utilise an extensive knowledge of intricate linguistic rules, including those that govern the sequencing of words and their form (i.e. grammar). In fact, this rule system provides us with the potential to make an infinite number of word sequences from a limited number of sounds. Without this ability our language would be very simple. The richness and complexity of human language have provided the keystone that underpins cultural evolution, and enabled discoveries and knowledge to be written down for prosperity. Indeed, language has been described as the greatest of all human achievements (Ornstein 1988). However, language is more than communication: it is also a system for representing knowledge, and a vehicle for thought that is vital in human cognition.

One of the enduring debates in the history of neuropsychology has concerned the areas of the brain involved in the production and comprehension of language. The first brain area to be implicated in language was the frontal lobes. This area attracted interest in the early part of the nineteenth century when a French doctor called Jean-Baptiste Bouillaud examined over one hundred individuals who had suffered speech disturbances following injuries to the frontal regions of the brain. Bouillaud's observations led him to conclude that frontal damage stopped the person from speaking clearly, although they could express themselves with gestures and writing. Nor did they have problems with comprehending language. But, perhaps the most dramatic case was reported in 1861 when Simon Aubertin described the case of a man who had shot away part of his frontal cranium in a failed suicide attempt that exposed his brain. During the course of his examination, Aubertin found that if he pressed a spatula against the exposed brain while the man was speaking, the speech was immediately halted. However, when the compression was lessened, speech resumed (Finger 1994).

Despite this, there was a general reluctance by investigators at the time to accept that a complex psychological function such as speech could be localised to a specific brain region. This was partly because localisation of function seemed to support the popular notion of phrenology, which had been ridiculed and discredited. But, another problem was that many individuals were known who had severe frontal lobe damage without any form of language impairment. And, to confound things even further, the French doctor Gabriel Andral in the 1830s identified a number of cases where language deficits occurred in patients without any signs of frontal lobe damage.

Proof of a speech centre in the frontal lobes was finally provided by the eminent French scientist and doctor Paul Broca, who first became interested in the subject after hearing Aubertin give a talk in 1861. Soon after, one of Broca's patients, called Leborgne, who had been mute for over twenty years (except for the utterance of 'tan') died. Although unable to speak, Leborgne was intelligent and capable of comprehending spoken and written language. Leborgne's death was an opportunity for Broca to see if the frontal lobes were responsible for his language deficits. Indeed, when Broca undertook an autopsy on Leborgne's brain he found a large cavity about the size of a chicken's egg located towards the back of the frontal lobes in the left hemisphere (Plate 10.1). Clearly, the brain had suffered massive damage to a localised region, and it appeared to be responsible for the language deficit. It was the first convincing evidence, presented by a famous scientist, linking an area of the frontal lobes with language.

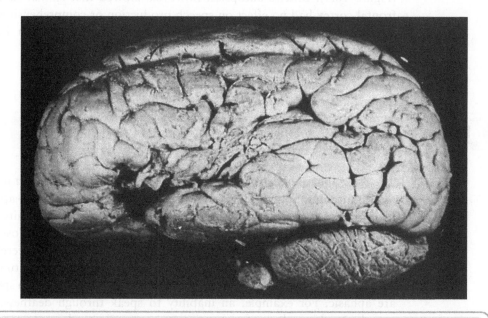

Plate 10.1   The brain of Leborgne (nicknamed 'Tan')

Source: Hopitaux de Paris

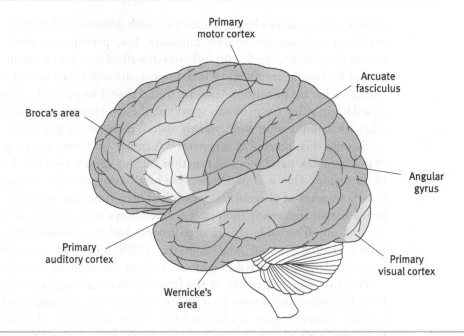

Figure 10.1   The location of the main areas involved in language comprehension and production

Source: M.R. Rosenzweig *et al.* (2002) *Biological Psychology*, 3rd edition, p. 617

Following this discovery, Broca performed autopsies on eight other patients with similar types of language deficit, and found they all had damage to the same area of the frontal lobes. This region has now become known as **Broca's area,** and is located just in front of the motor cortex that controls the muscles of the vocal cord and mouth (Figure 10.1). Broca's autopsies, however, showed that similar damage to the right frontal cortex had no effect on speech production or comprehension. Thus, the brain area involved in language production was localised to the left hemisphere of the frontal cortex.

Broca's aphasia

The term **aphasia** means a complete loss of speech or language (*a* meaning 'without', *phasia* meaning 'speech'). However, it is more accurate to define aphasia as a disturbance in the production or comprehension of speech that is acquired following damage to certain areas of the brain. It is rarely, if ever, the complete loss of language. It is estimated that around 85 per cent of aphasia cases are due to cerebrovascular accidents (stroke), with the remainder being caused by head injuries, tumours and disease (Martin 2006). It is also important to note that not all people with speech disturbances are aphasic. For example, an inability to speak through deafness, paralysis of the speech muscles, or lack of motivation to communicate, does not constitute aphasia.

People with damage to Broca's area suffer from a specific language disturbance which is known as **Broca's aphasia**. It is also sometimes called **motor aphasia,** or **non-fluent**

> **Asked to tell the story of Cinderella**
> (previously shown picture version of the story to facilitate recall)
>
> Cinderella...yes...now...busy me (*gestures dusting, ironing etc.*....)...la la la...happy...
> no <u>sad</u>...two erm sss...sss...sisters...bad...bad sisters... dance...fff fairy god dance swoosh
> (*gestures magic wand*)...Cinderella...pr...pr...priz ch... no too hard (therapist: '*Prince Charming*')...
> Yes him...lovely...dancing...happy happy...oh no...time <u>time</u>...run shoe...Cinderella...
> shoe...mine...mine OK... lovely happy...<u>the end</u>...hard work (*laughs*)
>
> (underline indicates extra stress)

Figure 10.2   Non-fluent Broca's aphasia

Source: Provided by Mandy Galling, Reg RCSLT, Guild Community Healthcare NHS Trust

aphasia. This form of aphasia is characterised by language that is slow, laboured and lacking in grammar (see Figure 10.2). Although the person may have a large vocabulary, speech tends to be composed of simple nouns, verbs and adjectives (not unlike the type of language once used to write a telegram). In addition, the speech often lacks the rhythm, intonation and inflection of normal language, that is, it shows abnormal **prosody**. Another characteristic of Broca's aphasia is a difficulty in finding the 'right word' (**anomia**), which produces long pauses during speech. To make matters worse, the aphasic is also likely to have articulation difficulties, making them difficult to understand. This often causes the person to becomes very frustrated when attempting to communicate with others. Curiously, simple automated expressions such as 'hello', or emotional outbursts that can include swearing, are often spoken without problem. In some cases a Broca's aphasic may even be able to sing old and well-learned songs without difficulty.

How, then, can we best characterise the deficit in Broca's aphasia? One clue comes from the fact that such a person will often have difficulty in carrying out a simple command, such as to stick out their tongue (**oral apraxia**), yet have no problem licking their lips after eating a sugary doughnut. This observation suggests that the deficit in Broca's aphasia is an inability to produce the correct motor movements for the articulation of speech. Indeed, a closer examination of the anatomical location of Broca's area shows it to be adjacent to the motor cortex which controls voluntary actions, and in closest proximity to the part responsible for movements of the mouth including tongue and vocal cords. We might expect, therefore, that damage to Broca's area will cause the destruction of neural circuits responsible for the movements that are required to produce speech.

There is more to Broca's aphasia, however, than motor deficits. In fact, such patients show an impaired ability to comprehend language. Although people with damage to Broca's area often give the impression of being able to fully understand verbal speech, it has been shown that they have problems comprehending language that is grammatically complex. For example, they may be unable to perform an instruction such as, 'Put the cup on top of the fork and place the knife inside the cup'. Similarly, a Broca's aphasic may have problems understanding sentences where there is an unusual word order, or a degree of ambiguity. Thus, they are likely to understand who is doing the chasing in 'The cat chased the mouse', but have difficulty with: 'The boy was chased by the girl'. Obviously, a mouse cannot chase a cat in the first sentence, although it is possible that a boy could chase the girl in the second.

Wernicke's aphasia

In 1874, a 26-year-old German neurologist called Carl Wernicke described a different type of aphasia (now known as **Wernicke's aphasia**) that was linked with damage to a region of the temporal lobes in the left hemisphere. This region is now called **Wernicke's area** and it lies adjacent to the **primary auditory cortex**. Wernicke's aphasia does not interfere with the rhythm and grammar of speech, so that people with this condition can articulate words quickly and fluently, but unfortunately the speech is largely devoid of meaning (see Figure 10.3). Although, superficially, the speech may sound normal and grammatically correct, it is devoid of sensible content. To a large degree this is because the language is composed of either inappropriate words (**paraphasias**) or ones that do not exist (**neologisms**). For example, in reply to the question, 'Where do you work?', one Wernicke's aphasic was quoted as saying: 'Before I was in the one here, I was in the other one. My sister had the department in the other one' (Geschwind 1972). Alternatively, when Rochford (1974) asked a Wernicke's aphasic to name a picture of an anchor, the patient called it a 'martha argeneth'; and when Kertesz (1979) asked a patient to name a toothbrush and a pen, the patient responded with 'stoktery' and 'minkt'.

Damage to Wernicke's area also produces a profound deficit in language comprehension. While simple sentences and instructions may be understood, there is nearly always a marked inability to comprehend more complex forms of speech. This makes it difficult to engage in meaningful conversation with a Wernicke's aphasiac. To make matters worse, they may be unaware that they have a comprehension deficit. Thus, a person with Wernicke's aphasia is likely to talk gibberish and be unaware that they do not understand the speech of others. The verbal confusion and use of inappropriate words produces a disjointed form of speech known as **jargon aphasia**. Yet, such a person will still follow the non-verbal rules of conversation by pausing and taking turns to speak, and nodding their head in appropriate places. They are also sensitive to tone of voice and facial expressions. Reading and writing are also impaired. Indeed, there are Wernicke aphasiacs who, if given a book, will go through the motions of reading it aloud only to produce utter nonsense (Springer and Deutsch 1989).

How can we, then, best understand Wernicke's aphasia? One clue comes from the location of Wernicke's area, which is next to the primary auditory cortex. This indicates that Wernicke's area is involved in the translation of auditory information arriving

---

Required to tell the therapist about trip to visit his daughter and a meal out

Claire?...yes...well...I was will...miner...mineral water...of my 'pitch' on stonework 'make' and 'ww' and 'wiker' of 'wenner'. December and London...on 'minter' of 'minder' and 'si' or 'risher'...I was 'madge'

(Targets very difficult to interpret. Items in quotation marks show broad phonological approximation)

Figure 10.3 Fluent Wernicke's aphasia

Source: Provided by Mandy Galling, Reg RCSLT, Guild Community Healthcare NHS Trust

directly from the ears. In other words, it translates sound into verbal codes so that the brain can recognise it as language. For this reason, Wernicke's aphasia is sometimes known as **sensory aphasia** or **receptive aphasia**. But, there is more to Wernicke's aphasia than its ability to recognise speech sounds. Because of the marked deficit of comprehension, Wernicke's area must also be involved in understanding the speech it is receiving. Thus, Wernicke's area, or perhaps more accurately a network of other areas interconnected with it, encodes the verbal sound into units of language, and establishes its meaning (i.e. comprehension).

Alexia and agraphia

In 1892, the French neurologist Jules Dejerine reported the cases of two patients who had acquired another type of language deficit. Dejerine found that his patients had difficulty reading (**alexia**) and writing (**agraphia**). One of his patients, a 63-year-old man called Monsieur S, woke one morning to find he was unable to read his newspaper. When examined by Dejerine, he was unable to recognise letters or words, or write to dictation, but he had no problem recognising objects and people, or comprehending language. When Monsieur S died nine months later, a brain autopsy revealed damage to the **angular gyrus**, a site that is located between the occipital lobes (which contain the visual cortex) and Wernicke's area (see Figure 10.1). The angular gyrus is in an ideal position to receive visual input and Dejerine concluded that it acted to translate the appearance of written information into the appropriate mental sounds and meanings.

Dejerine's other patient, named Monsieur C, a 68-year-old Parisian fabric designer, also acquired an inability to read, or recognise words and letters, although he retained some ability to read figures. For example, he could recognise his regular newspaper *Le Matin* by its masthead, but was unable to recognise other papers. Despite this, Monsieur C could still write, either spontaneously or to dictation. This deficit produced some odd patterns of behaviour. For example, he could copy words correctly, and provided they were large enough for him to trace his finger around, this allowed him to deduce their meaning. He was also able to recognise the words when the individual letters were spoken aloud to him.

It was found that Monsieur C was also blind in his right visual field, which indicated that damage had occurred to the left visual cortex. Indeed, this damage was confirmed at autopsy. But, perhaps just as important to explaining the reading deficit was the discovery of damage to the posterior portion of the corpus callosum which carries visual information between the two hemispheres. Although Monsieur C could see words and letters with his right intact visual cortex, he was unable to cross this information over to the angular gyrus in the language-dominant left hemisphere where presumably the 'reading' took place. The result was that Monsieur C could see written words but was unable to recognise them from their visual characteristics. His ability to copy out written information probably occurred because of intact connections between the right visual cortex and motor areas that control hand movement. Clearly, copying involved an alternative route through the brain that does not utilise the left-sided angular gyrus.

The Wernicke–Geschwind model

Carl Wernicke not only described a type of aphasia that now bears his name, but in 1874 he also formulated a theory that showed how language was processed by the brain. His theory viewed language comprehension and production as being dependent on the left hemisphere of the brain. In particular, it emphasised the role of a sensory speech centre in the temporal lobe that served as the repository for 'remembered images' (i.e. Wernicke's area), which was connected by a pathway to a frontal area (Broca's area) that stored the 'impressions of action'. Interestingly, Wernicke did not believe that word meanings were localised. Instead, he saw these as being distributed throughout the cortex (especially in the regions surrounding Wernicke's area) and linked extensively by association fibres. In effect, Wernicke had invented the first neuropsychological theory of language, and it provided a major stimulus for the discovery and understanding of new aphasic syndromes.

Wernicke's theory remained highly influential until it was extended by the work of Norman Geschwind in 1965. Geschwind's insight was to realise that many different types of aphasic disorder could be predicted from lesions to the main language centres proposed by Wernicke, and the pathways connecting them. Moreover, Geschwind and his colleagues developed basic tests that could be used to identify the basic aphasic syndromes. This work was instrumental in increasing our knowledge of how the brain processes language and its main tenets have become widely known as the **Wernicke–Geschwind model** (Figure 10.4).

The basic idea of the Wernicke–Geschwind model is that when we hear spoken language, the sound of the words are first processed by the auditory cortex, followed by Wernicke's area where sounds are decoded and comprehended. A similar process is also believed to occur for reading, except in this case the flow of information passes from the visual cortex to the angular gyrus, which translates the visual code of the written word into an auditory one. Thus, Wernicke's area is a pivotal site that combines the streams of speech (auditory cortex) and written (angular gyrus) input. The function of Wernicke's area is crucial since it is believed to provide the 'codes' to translate auditory information into words. In turn, Wernicke's area accesses the surrounding cortex where the meanings of the words are stored. The function of Wernicke's area, therefore, is to translate verbal information into thought or action. In turn, a projection arising from Wernicke's area passes to Broca's area where the programs for the complex co-ordination of the muscle movements necessary for speech are located. Wernicke believed that this pathway was important in language acquisition, especially for establishing the association between the meaning of a word and its sound.

The pathway between Wernicke's and Broca's areas is now known as the **arcuate fasciculus**. Although anatomical proof for this pathway was established only in the twentieth century, Wernicke had the foresight to predict the type of aphasia that would occur if this connection was destroyed. In short, he reasoned that it would not affect the comprehension of auditory or written information as Wernicke's area remained intact, nor would it impair the production of speech as Broca's area was intact. The nature of the deficit, therefore, would be a specific type of aphasia in which the person was unable to repeat words and sentences fluently. Wernicke turned out to be accurate in his predictions, and the condition is now known as **conduction aphasia**. People with damage to the arcuate fasciculus have no difficulty understanding language, or producing speech. However, they are impaired in repeating certain words and

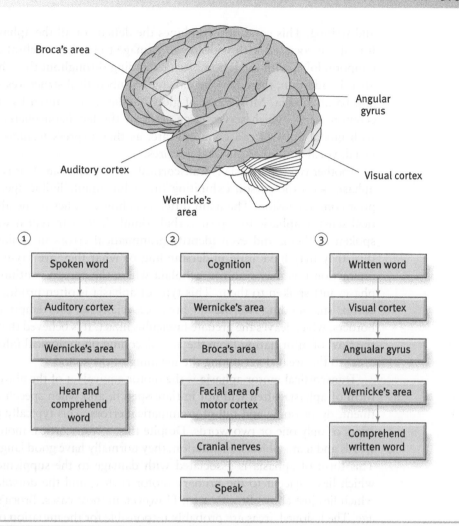

| Broca's area | Angular gyrus | Auditory cortex | Wernicke's area | Visual cortex |

①

Spoken word
Auditory cortex
Wernicke's area
Hear and comprehend word

②

Cognition
Wernicke's area
Broca's area
Facial area of motor cortex
Cranial nerves
Speak

③

Written word
Visual cortex
Angualar gyrus
Wernicke's area
Comprehend written word

Figure 10.4   The Wernicke–Geschwind model of language processing

Source: B. Kolb and I.Q. Whishaw (1985) *Fundamentals of Human Neuropsychology*

sentences. For example, a person may be able to repeat concrete words such as 'bicycle' and 'elephant', but unable to repeat abstract words or non-words such as 'blaynge'. Geschwind has suggested this occurs because upon hearing a concrete word, a visual image can be formed, which is passed to Broca's area via a different pathway. It is also interesting that patients with conduction aphasia often find it difficult to read aloud, despite being able to read silently with good comprehension.

Other types of aphasia

There are other types of aphasia which can also be understood in terms of the Wernicke–Geschwind model. The severest deficit is **global aphasia** where the person loses the ability both to comprehend language and to produce it in any meaningful way. In this case, speech may deteriorate into unintelligible jargon aphasia. In addition, the person is unable to repeat words accurately and has great difficulty reading and writing. This condition combines the deficits of all the aphasias discussed above. It is also associated with widespread damage to the left cerebral cortex, especially the temporal lobe, with the lesion often extending throughout the white matter to Broca's area. In addition, there may be damage to subcortical structures such as the thalamus and basal ganglia. Most cases of global aphasia are caused by strokes to the middle cerebral artery which serves large areas of the left hemisphere. Despite this, people with global aphasia can communicate, as they express feelings and wishes through facial, vocal and other physical gestures.

Another type of aphasia is **transcortical sensory aphasia**. This is similar to Wernicke's aphasia with the person exhibiting fluent but unintelligible speech, accompanied by poor comprehension. The main difference, however, lies in the ability of the transcortical sensory aphasic to repeat verbal stimuli. They can repeat words and non-words spoken to them, and even identify grammatical errors in spoken language. Despite this, they may have little understanding of what they are saying. In everyday social interaction this may result in **echolaia** where the person continually repeat words or phases just spoken to them. This type of aphasia is often produced by damage to the cortex surrounding Wernicke's area, especially at the temporal lobe–parietal lobe borders, which leaves the arcuate fasciculus intact. It is believed that the damage disrupts the flow of information from the area decoding phonological information (Wernicke's area) to the areas determining the meaning of the sound.

Transcortical motor aphasia is the motor equivalent of the above. A person with this form of aphasia often will not initiate speech, and when speech does occur it is non-fluent, dysprosodic and full of grammatical errors. This typically produces short utterances of only one or two words. Despite this, a transcortical motor aphasic can repeat words and name objects. In addition, they normally have good language comprehension. This form of aphasia is associated with damage to the **supplementary motor cortex**, which lies adjacent to the primary motor cortex, and the **dorsolateral frontal cortex**, which lies just above Broca's area. However, in most cases, Broca's area is spared damage. The lesioned areas are probably responsible for the initiation of speech (supplementary motor areas) and the ongoing control of speech (dorsolateral frontal cortex).

A rare language disorder is **anomic aphasia** (sometimes called deep dysphasia), where the person has difficulty finding the right word, and will often substitute related but inappropriate ones. For example, when asked to repeat the words 'kite' or 'shell', the person may respond with 'balloon' and 'kernel' (Martin 2006). Although verbal comprehension is good in this type of aphasia, the substitution of alternative words may make speech difficult to follow or understand. Patients with this type of aphasia often report forgetting the word just presented to them, although they may retain its meaning. The anatomical basis for this type of aphasia is not well established, and is believed to involve the temporal lobes, possibly at its junction with the occipital lobes.

The various types of aphasia discussed so far are summarised in Tables 10.1(a) and (b).

A revaluation of the Wernicke–Geschwind model

The model of language processing developed by Wernicke and Geschwind is a major achievement that has stimulated research and guided diagnosis of aphasia and other speech problems. Despite this, it is accurate only up to a point. Studies have confirmed the essential prediction that Broca's aphasia is more often associated with a frontal

Table 10.1(a)	Types of aphasia, their primary symptoms and the possible site of the associated brain lession	
Type of Aphasia	**Primary Symptoms**	**Brain Lesion to**
Sensory (Wernicke's) aphasia	General comprehension deficits, neologisms, word retrieval deficits, semantic paraphasias	Posterior perisylvian region; postero-superior temporal, opercular supramarginal, angular and posterior insula gyri; planum temporale
Production (Broca's) aphasia	Speech production deficits, abnormal prosody, impaired syntactic comprehension	Posterior part of the inferior frontal and precentral convolutions of the left hemisphere
Conduction aphasia	Naming deficits and impaired ability to repeat non-meaningful single words and word strings	Arcuate fasciculus; posterior parietal and temporal regions: left auditory cortex; insula; supramarginal gyrus
Deep dysphasia	Word repetition deficits; verbal (semantic) paraphasia	Temporal lobe, especially regions which mediate phonological processing
Transcortical sensory aphasia	Impaired comprehension, naming, reading and writing; semantic irrelevances in speech	Temporo-parieto-occipital junction of the left hemisphere
Transcortical motor aphasia	Transient mutism and telegrammatic, dysprosodic speech	Connection between Broca's area and the supplementary motor area; medial frontal lobe; regions anterolateral to the left hemisphere's frontal horn
Global aphasia	Generalised deficits in comprehension, repetition, naming and speech production	Left perisylvian region, white matter, basal ganglia and thalamus

Source: G.N. Martin, *Human Neuropsychology*, 2nd edition, p. 281. Copyright © 2006 by Pearson Education

Table 10.1(b)	Symptomatology of aphasia					
Type	**Site of Damage**	**Spontaneous Speech**	**Comprehension**	**Paraphasia**	**Repetition**	**Naming**
Broca's		Non-fluent	Good	Common	Poor	Poor
Wernicke's		Fluent	Poor	Uncommon	Poor	Poor
Conduction		Fluent	Good	Common	Poor	Poor
Global		Non-fluent	Poor	Variable	Poor	Poor

Source: G.N. Martin, *Human Neuropsychology*, 2nd edition, p. 281. Copyright © 2006 by Pearson Education

stroke, whereas a posterior stroke is more likely to produce Wernicke's aphasia. However, the effects of such damage is rarely as predictable as the Wernicke–Geschwind model makes out. Indeed, people with Wernicke's aphasia nearly always have some degree of motor speech abnormality, and those with Broca's aphasia show comprehension deficits. Moreover, selective damage to these language areas may not produce the effects that are expected. For example, lesions which are confined to Broca's area do not produce long-lasting language impairments (Mohr *et al.* 1978). In fact, Broca's aphasia is nearly always associated with widespread damage that extends out of Broca's area. A similar situation exists for Wernicke's area which is anatomically difficult to localise and define (Bogen and Bogen 1976). Thus, the sharp functional and anatomical distinctions between regions as implied by the model do not necessarily exist.

A similar conclusion was reached in the 1950s by Wilder Penfield, who stimulated various regions of the cerebral cortex with electrical current to detect abnormal tissue in human patients about to undergo brain surgery. Penfield found that stimulation of the cerebral cortex could affect language in several ways. For example, it could induce vocalisations (for example, a sustained utterance such as 'oh . . .'), or suddenly arrest speech while the patient was talking. In other instances, it produced slurred speech, interfered with the comprehension of language, or caused the patient to have difficulty in finding the right word. However, the effects of the stimulation did not always correspond with the brain regions predicted by the Wernicke–Geschwind model. For example, naming difficulties ('That is a . . . I know. That is a . . .'), or the misnaming of objects (saying 'camel' when meaning to say 'comb') were elicited from widespread regions of the left hemisphere that went beyond Broca's and Wernicke's speech zones. In addition, Penfield found that stimulation of the supplementary motor areas in the frontal cortex could produce a sustained vowel sound such as 'Eeee', and this could also be replicated by stimulating the primary motor cortex and somatosensory cortex. However, stimulation of Broca's area did not produce these effects (Penfield and Roberts 1959).

Penfield's observations have been extended by the work of George Ojemann and his colleagues at the University of Washington who have stimulated the brain during the naming of pictures. Their work has shown that language representation in the brain is organised in mosaic-like areas of 1–2 cm^2 which vary in size and location between individuals (Ojemann *et al.* 1989). Although these mosaics are usually found spread across regions of the temporal and frontal lobes, there are some individuals who have them in only one region. Moreover, the correlation of these sites with Wernicke's or Broca's areas is weak. Again, the brain regions involved in language only approximate to those predicted by the Wernicke–Geschwind model. Further, their exact locations differ greatly between individuals. Ojemann's mapping work shows that the most important regions involved in language comprehension and production are actually found either side of the **Sylvian fissure,** which is a fissure that extends along the lateral aspect of each hemisphere for about half its length, and borders parts of the temporal, parietal and frontal lobes (see Figure 10.5). Interestingly, Ojemann's research has also examined cortical stimulation in subjects who are bilingual, and shown that the brain uses separate cortical areas for storing the names of objects in two different languages (Ojemann and Mateer 1979).

One reason why the identification of brain sites involved in language has proved difficult is because most studies have examined people who had suffered strokes or accidents. Unfortunately, this type of damage tends to be diffuse with widespread bleeding that is rarely located to one specific region. Indeed, this may help to explain the observation that long-lasting speech deficits rarely occur in patients who have precise lesions made to their 'language' areas. For example, Penfield reported that the arcuate

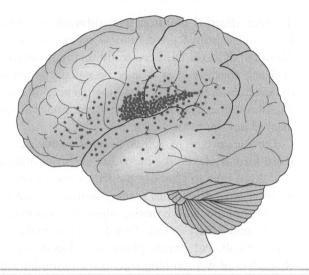

| Figure 10.5 | Overview of brain sites where electrical stimulation has been shown to interfere with, or arrest, speech (based on the work of Penfield and Ojemann) |

Source: S.M. Breedlove *et al.*, *Biological Psychology*, 5th edition, p. 585. Copyright © 2007 by Sinauer Associates, Inc.

fasciculus could be removed without producing aphasia, and similar findings (noted above) have been found for Broca's area. It should also borne in mind that lesions do not necessarily provide accurate information about a given brain function. As the great English neurologist Hughlings-Jackson noted in 1874, 'to locate the damage which destroys speech and to locate speech are two different things' (Martin 2006).

Another problem with the Wernicke–Geschwind model is that it fails to take into account the role of subcortical regions in language processing. Both Wernicke and Broca's areas have reciprocal connections with the thalamus, and damage to the thalamus can also cause symptoms of aphasia including mild comprehension deficits. It has also been shown that stimulation of the pulvinar region of the thalamus arrests speech in a manner similar to that which occurs for the cerebral cortex (Ojemann 1975). In addition, it is known that neural circuits linking different cortical regions with the **striatum** (for example, caudate nucleus and putamen) regulate speech production and syntax. The basal ganglia are also important for sequencing movements, and it is known that damage to these regions (as occurs in Parkinson's disease) produces language that is slow, without rhythm and monotonous. Finally, we should not forget the role of the right hemisphere in language. Although often overlooked, this hemisphere has some important linguistic abilities (see below).

Dyslexia

Dyslexia (*dys* meaning 'bad', *lexia* meaning 'reading') is an inability to read correctly despite normal intelligence, motivation and schooling. Although dyslexia can arise through brain injury, in most cases it is a developmental disorder that manifests itself when the child begins to read. Dyslexia is possibly the most common neurobehavioural disorder affecting children, and although its exact prevalence is uncertain, estimates have ranged from 5 per cent to 17.5 per cent of school–age children (Shaywitz 1998). Although dyslexia has been traditionally believed to predominantly affect boys, some evidence suggests that it may be equally common in girls. Despite popular belief, dyslexic children do not lack intelligence, or are word 'blind'. Longitudinal studies also show that dyslexia is a persistent and chronic condition which is not caused by delayed development.

Dyslexia occurs in at least two forms, with deficits ranging from mild to severe. In **word-form dyslexia,** the individual does not immediately recognise words, but can do so if given time to read out the letters one by one. Thus, individuals with this form of dyslexia have difficulties reading words but not individual letters. A different condition is **phonological dyslexia,** where the person can identify familiar words but is unable to make their sound. This deficit can make reading unfamiliar or unusual words very difficult. Put simply, phonological dyslexia is caused by an inability to relate the characters of written language to the phonological sounds that they represent. These two forms of dyslexia show that the brain uses at least two strategies in order to read: whole-word reading and phonological reading. In whole-word reading we recognise a word by its immediate visual form or shape, whereas in phonological reading we identify a word though its distinctive sound. We tend to use the first strategy when reading familiar words, and the second when confronted with irregular or unfamiliar words. Some people with dyslexia may have both types of impairment, or there may be problems with writing. For example, the individual may try to write from right to left, or confuse letters with a specific right–left orientation (such as d, b, p or s).

What causes dyslexia? One clue comes from the fact that reading difficulties tend to run in families, which implies a genetic component. Research shows that as many as 65 per cent of children with dyslexia have a parent with the disorder. Twin studies also show a much higher concordance rate for reading disability in monozygotic twins (68 per cent) compared with dizygotic twins (38 per cent) (DeFries and Alarcon 1996). Despite this, it is clear that the genetic basis of dyslexia is complex, with no single gene being responsible or following a simple Mendelian pattern of inheritance. In fact, at least six different chromosomes are known to exist which contain genes that affect reading ability. The hope is that, one day, researchers may be able to link some of these genetic loci with subtypes of dyslexia (Démonet *et al.* 2004).

Investigators have also examined the brains of dyslexics at post-mortem. One of the first studies to do this was by Galaburda and Kemper (1979), which revealed abnormalities in the **planum temporale** in a young male dyslexic killed in a fall. The planum temporale is an area of the brain that corresponds to part of Wernicke's area, along with some of the adjacent auditory cortex, and in most individuals it is larger in the left hemisphere. For example, in one study the left planum was found to be on average 3.6 cm in length compared with 2.7 cm for the right. Moreover, out of 100 brains examined at post-mortem, 65 had a larger planum temporale in the left hemisphere, 11 had it bigger in the right, and the remaining 24 showed no difference (Geschwind and Levitsky 1968). Differences in the size of the planum temporale are also found in the human foetus and can be detected by the 31st week of gestation (Chi *et al.* 1977). Galaburda and Kemper found not only that the planum temporale was the same size across hemispheres in their dyslexic subject, but also that it contained immature neurons that resembled a pattern found around the sixth week of gestation.

Further post-mortem work has confirmed the symmetry in size of the planum temporale across both hemispheres in dyslexia. For example, Larsen *et al.* (1990) examined

19 dyslexics using MRI and found that 70 per cent of their brains showed symmetry compared with only 30 per cent of the controls. In addition, the brains of individuals with dyslexia often show neural abnormalities, including excessive cortical folding, and clusters of extra cells called **ectopias**, which are found primarily along the Sylvian fissure through the temporal and parietal lobes (Galaburda *et al.* 1985) (Figure 10.6). Although these changes are more frequently found in the left hemisphere, they can also occur in the right hemisphere (Galaburda 1993). Thus, while this research supports the idea of an early developmental failure in the brains of dyslexics, it is too simple to view it as arising from planum temporale dysfunction. This is also supported by PET scanning studies that have found that normal readers tend to show increased activity over extensive areas of the left angular gyrus, whereas dyslexics show activation over large areas of the right hemisphere (Rumsey *et al.* 1999). These results show that dyslexics and normal readers are utilising different brain regions when reading.

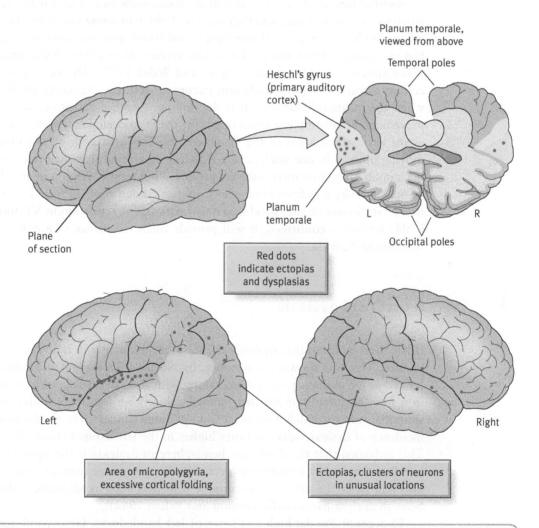

| Figure 10.6 | Types of cortical neural abnormality found in some forms of dyslexia |

Source: S.M. Breedlove *et al.*, *Biological Psychology*, 5th edition, p. 584. Copyright © 2007 by Sinauer Associates, Inc.

Neural abnormalities associated with dyslexia have also been found in subcortical sites, including the magnocellular system of the lateral geniculate nucleus (Galaburda and Livingstone 1993). This is an intriguing finding as the magnocellular system is the part of the visual pathways from eye to brain that encodes information about movement and depth. It contrasts with the parvocellular system which transmits information regarding colour and fine detail. The magnocellular system also control eye movements. Galaburda and Livingstone found that neurons in the magnocellular layers of the lateral geniculate nucleus were smaller than normal, and more variable in size and shape compared with the parvocellular cells. The significance of this finding remains to be established, although dyslexics often complain that small letters appear to blur and move around when they are trying to read, which implies a dysfunction of the magnocellular system. Further research has shown that dyslexics may have poor binocular convergence, an impaired ability to track a moving target and poor eye stability in visual fixation (Eden *et al.* 1994). All of these deficits would be expected to produce learning difficulties with reading.

Another interesting finding is that dyslexics sometimes make fewer reading errors when one eye is occluded and they read with the remaining eye. It has been found that young children taught to stabilise their visual fixation in this way can progress twice as fast in reading as those whose vision remains unstable – although this simple treatment is not effective in older children (Stein and Walsh 1997). This finding suggests that a certain amount of visual confusion occurs in dyslexia, especially in the early years, when the magnocellular system is developing. Another deficit occurs with detecting movement. For example, a brain target for the magnocellular system is area V5 located in the extrastriate areas of the visual cortex. This area is devoted to the analysis of moving objects. In one study, using fMRI, it was found that the presentation of moving stimuli (dots) to normal subjects produced bilateral activation of area V5, although no such activity was found in dyslexic subjects (Eden *et al.* 1996). However, presentation of stationary stimuli produced equal patterns of activation in V1 and V2 regions. If this finding is confirmed, it will provide further evidence of a magnocellular dysfunction in dyslexia.

A theory of dyslexia

It has been reported that dyslexia occurs more frequently in individuals who are left-handed. This was shown, for instance, by Norman Geschwind and Peter Behan, who looked at the frequency of dyslexia, along with several other developmental disorders, in a random sample of 500 left-handed subjects (drawn from individuals visiting a shop that sold left-handed utensils) and 900 right-handers. The results showed that the incidence of dyslexia was ten times higher in the left-handed group than in the right. This indicated that the dominant hemisphere in dyslexia is the right rather than the left. But, there was a further unexpected finding to emerge from the study: left-handers also had twice the rate of autoimmune disorders such as allergies, arthritis and diabetes than right-handers (Geschwind and Behan 1982).

To account for the high incidence of left-handedness, Geschwind and Galaburda (1985) proposed that something goes wrong with the development of cerebral lateralisation during the last trimester of foetal development. This is also a stage when the male foetus is exposed to high levels of testosterone. Geschwind and Galaburda suggested that if levels of testosterone were too high, they would act to slow down corti-cal maturation, particularly in the left hemisphere. In turn, the delayed maturation would increase the chances of the right hemisphere taking over some of its language functions. This is sometimes referred to as **anomalous dominance**. The behavioural con-sequences would be a greater likelihood of developmental dyslexia, along with stuttering and autism. And, it would be expected to lead to a greater incidence of left-handedness.

To support their theory, Geschwind and Galaburda pointed out that during foetal growth, the planum temporale normally starts to develop one to two weeks earlier on the right side of the brain, but is overtaken in size by the later-developing left-sided planum temporale. This switch, they argued, is crucially dependent on the correct level of testosterone. And, if levels are too high, the increased growth of the left hemisphere does not occur, leading to a smaller planum temporale. But, why should left-handers also show an increased susceptibility to autoimmune diseases? The answer, according to Geschwind and Galaburda, is that testosterone during foetal development is known to slow down the development of the thymus gland. This is a structure responsible for making certain cells (for example, T-cells) involved in immune responses.

The Geschwind–Behan–Galaburda (GBG) theory, as it is now called, has attracted a great deal of interest, although it is difficult to test empirically. While most researchers believe that language disabilities are more common in males, supporting a role for prenatal testosterone in early development, not all agree. For example, some have claimed that the incidence of dyslexia is roughly the same for both males and females – although boys with reading problems are more likely to be referred to a spe-cialist because of dyslexia's association with other behavioural problems. This, then, gives the appearance of a sex bias (Shaywitz *et al.* 1990). Another problem with the GBG model is that it predicts that there should be a difference in cognitive function between right-handed and left-handed dyslexics, although no such differences have been found (Bryden *et al.* 1994).

An introduction to commissurotomy

Experimental proof that the two cerebral hemispheres have different functions was dramatically shown in the 1960s when the behaviour of patients who had undergone **commissurotomy** was closely examined. This operation involves the complete severing of the **corpus callosum**, which is the massive white fibre bundle that can be clearly seen when the brain is dissected. In fact, this is the largest fibre bundle in the human brain, containing in the region of 300 million neurons, and it connects the two cerebral hemi-spheres. The corpus callosum has long fascinated researchers. It was first described by Galen in the second century AD, who referred to it in Greek as *tulos*, which was later translated into *callus* in Latin, meaning hard or thickened skin. This callous body was later depicted by Thomas Willis in his book *Cerebri Anatome* (1664), who proposed that the 'spirits' of the brain resided there. The corpus callosum, in his view, was a pathway that allowed the movement of the spirits between the cerebral cortices, or as he put it: 'spirits travel from one hemisphere of the brain to the other, and return back again'. This idea was not developed until the late eighteenth century when the French anatomist Felix Vicq d'Azyr realised that the corpus callosum was composed of nerves. He introduced the term **commissures** to denote such fibre pathways.

A new era in the investigation of the corpus callosum began in the 1930s when the American Walter Dandy severed the corpus callosum in patients to gain better access to brain tumours. Surprisingly, the patients did not appear to suffer any intellectual, mental or motor deficits. A larger number of patients were also given operations by William Van Wagenen who performed partial or complete commissurotomy on 24 epileptic patients in an attempt to reduce the spread of epileptic seizures. These patients were examined on a wide range of neurological and psychological tests in the years following surgery by psychologist Andrew Akelatis. His findings, again, showed that the patients suffered little impairment. Considering the size and prominence of the corpus callosum in the brain, the results were surprising. It led Karl Lashley to write, tongue in cheek, in 1951 that the only known function of the corpus callosum was to keep the hemispheres from sagging.

Early studies with split-brain patients

In the 1960s, a clearer picture of corpus callosum function began to emerge with the work of Roger Sperry, who would win a Nobel Prize for his work in 1981, and his student Michael Gazzaniga. These researchers examined the functions of the two hemispheres by delivering visual information individually to each cortex. This task is far from simple, as the optic nerve from each eye projects to both hemispheres (see Chapter 2). To be more precise, input from the right visual field of the eye goes to the left hemisphere, and input from the left visual field goes to the right hemisphere. To project visual input into one cortex only, Sperry and Gazzaniga designed a task where they asked split-brain subjects to stare at a point in the middle of a screen, following which they briefly flashed visual stimuli to either side of the fixation point. By doing this, they were able to project stimuli into either the right or the left visual field of the eyes. The exposure time was long enough for subjects to perceive the stimulus, but sufficiently brief that the eyes did not have time to move to it. Stimuli presented to the left visual field therefore passed to the right hemisphere, and stimuli in the right visual field went to the left hemisphere (Figure 10.7).

A second task developed by Sperry and Gazzaniga presented tactile (touch) information to the two hemispheres. They did this by blindfolding split-brain patients, and asking them to identify objects placed in their right or left hand. In humans, the somesthetic pathways which convey the bodily sensations of touch, pressure and pain to the brain, unlike the visual system, completely crosses from one side of the body to the opposite hemisphere. Thus, a blindfolded split-brain patient who is asked to hold an object in their right hand will send information to the left hemisphere. In this instance, the right hemisphere will have no access to somesthetic information, whether it be from the eyes, hands or corpus callosum. With these two tasks, Sperry and Gazzaniga had a method by which they could examine the specific functions of the two hemispheres (see Gazzaniga 1970).

It soon became clear using these procedures that the left hemisphere was involved in language. For example, when a written word was presented to the right visual field so that it reached the left hemisphere, split-brain patients could read it aloud and understand its meaning. However, the same word presented to the right hemisphere elicited no verbal response. In fact, subjects often reported that they had seen nothing, or detected only a flash of light. Similarly, when pictures of everyday objects were presented to the left hemisphere, the person could name the object; but when flashed to the left visual field (right hemisphere) the same person could neither name nor describe it (Gazzaniga *et al.*

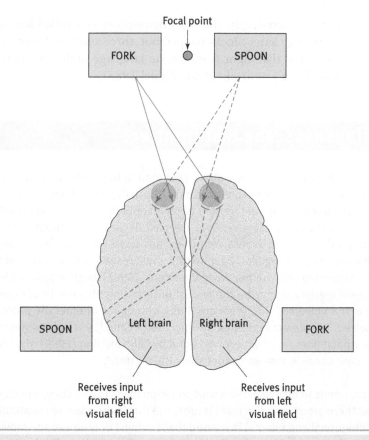

Focal point

| Figure 10.7 | The presentation of visual stimuli to individual hemispheres in split-brain subjects |

Source: Adapted from T.S. Brown and P.M. Wallace (1980) *Physiological Psychology*, p. 520

1962; Sperry 1964). These results confirmed what psychologists had long suspected: the left hemisphere was dominant for language and speech.

The right hemisphere, however, was not without its linguistic abilities. For example, a split-brain patient who heard a verbal description of an object was able to feel an array of several objects with their left hand (controlled by the right hemisphere) and pick up the specified item. Similarly, when an object name was flashed to the right hemisphere, the left hand selected the target from a range of objects hidden behind a screen. However, in this case the subject typically reported that they had not seen anything, and could not describe what they had picked up. In fact, in one experiment where different object names were flashed simultaneously to both hemispheres (for example, key–ring), it was found that patients would typically pick up the object presented to their right hemisphere (ring), but name the object given to the left hemisphere (key). The subjects were astonished to find that they had misnamed the object when it was brought into full view.

Prior to this research, it had been widely believed that the right hemisphere was both 'word deaf' and 'word blind', but Sperry and Gazziniga had shown that the right hemisphere could understand simple speech and recognise certain words, although in most cases it was unable to produce any verbal response to confirm this knowledge. This effect was also observed in a patient who was blindfolded and given a toothbrush to hold in their left hand. In this instance, the right hemisphere recognised the object because the person made the gesture of brushing his teeth when asked what it was. But, the person was unable to name the toothbrush (unless it was placed into the right hand). Interestingly, the right-hemisphere-controlled left hand was also able to write, or arrange letter blocks to spell out, three and four letter words. Some researchers have suggested that right hemispheric language ability is approximately the same as that found in a 6-year-old child (Zaidel 1985).

Consciousness: the last frontier?

Modern science may have split the atom, sent men to the moon, and solved the mystery of life, but it has yet to explain the nature of consciousness. Since the time of Descartes in the seventeenth century, consciousness has been at the forefront of philosophical enquiry, and recently it has become a legitimate subject in the brain sciences. Over the past decade or so, thousands of scientific articles have been published on consciousness. Yet, there has been little progress in explaining how the human brain achieves this amazing feat. Despite this, most researchers believe that the subject is a vital one. In fact, the respected philosopher David Chalmers (1996) has gone so far as to say that 'Consciousness is the biggest mystery. It may be the largest outstanding obstacle in our quest for a scientific understanding of the universe.' But, there are those who doubt whether the problem of consciousness will ever be solved. This view is expressed by Stuart Sutherland (1991) who writes: 'it is impossible to specify what it is, what it does, or why it evolved', and by Colin McGinn (1989) who states: 'I think the time has come to admit candidly that we cannot solve the mystery'.

What, then, needs to be explained about consciousness to overcome the objections expressed by the doubters? There are at least two main issues. The first is the apparent contradiction of our appearing to be free, intentional and mindful in a world that contains only atoms and molecules. That is to say, how can simple physical particles give rise to mental states which exhibit intelligent actions, beliefs, feelings and perceptions? This is essentially the traditional mind–body problem. Is the human brain just a complicated physical object (this position is known as **monism**), or do we have a mind that exists 'like a ghost in the machine' that is somehow separate from its workings (this position is known as **dualism**)? The second problem concerns the subjectivity of the conscious mind. As you read this book, you will also be aware of the sights, smells and sounds around you. These sensory qualities, which philosophers call **qualia**, are subjective and private. But, how do these sensations arise in the brain? That is, how does the physical structure of the brain provide us with such a rich inner world of subjective experience? This has been dubbed the 'hard problem' of consciousness, and even the most optimistic of brain scientists admit they have no way of solving it.

One famous scientist who turned his attention to understanding consciousness was Francis Crick (1916–2004), who co-discovered the structure of DNA. In his book *The Astonishing Hypothesis* (1994), Crick takes a materialistic view and states that consciousness and free will are 'no more than the behavior of a vast assembly of nerve cells and their associated molecules'. But, how to explore this further? Crick argues that we should focus on the visual system (our best understood sense), and identify which cells are involved in producing (visual) consciousness. This pursuit led Crick to conclude that consciousness arises when sets of neurons fire in a co-ordinated way, at frequencies around 40 Hz. He also suggests that this type of co-ordination might be the answer to the **binding problem**, that is, how all the various components of vision come together to provide a meaningful 'whole' or percept. Although this theory is still in its infancy, Crick's belief that biological structure is the natural path to understanding function, is one that will undoubtedly be followed by other neuroscientists. However, if the dualists are correct, then science will have to discover an alternative way to solve the great mystery of consciousness.

Right hemisphere specialisations

Although the right hemisphere has a limited ability to recognise language and read, Sperry and Gazzaniga soon realised that it had other functions not shared by the left hemisphere. One skill was an ability to arrange coloured blocks to match a pictured design. For example, if a split-brain subject was given several blocks, each having two red sides, two white sides, and two half-red and half-white sides, and asked to arrange them to a certain pattern (Figure 10.8), it was found that this task could only be accomplished by the left hand (right hemisphere). Similarly, the left hand was able to copy simple drawings, such as a cube or a house, with a fair degree of accuracy, unlike the right hand, which is very poor at drawing. The right hemisphere is also superior at learning finger mazes, completing jigsaws, and sorting block sizes or shapes into categories. And, when geometric patterns, drawings or faces are presented to the right hemisphere, the left hand is able to point to the correct picture in a recognition test. The right hemisphere was even able to recognise photographs of themselves, or of their family and friends.

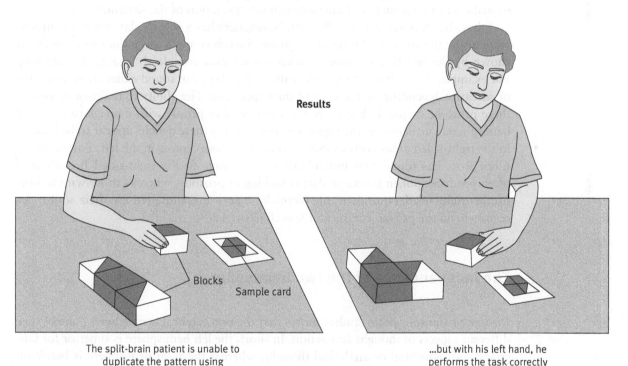

Procedure

The subject is asked to arrange the blocks so that they duplicate the pattern shown on the card

Results

Blocks

Sample card

The split-brain patient is unable to duplicate the pattern using his right hand...

...but with his left hand, he performs the task correctly

| Figure 10.8 | An illustration of how the right hemisphere (left hand) can be shown to be superior on tasks involving visuospatial skills |

The right hemisphere is also superior to the left in recognising emotion or responding emotionally to situations. For example, if a picture of a nude figure is presented to the right hemisphere, the split-brain subject may report that they have not seen anything while at the same time blushing and showing embarrassment or humour. This shows that recognition has taken place, although the verbal left side of the brain will often be puzzled by the emotional reaction and try to explain it in some way (Springer and Deutsch 1989). The same degree of emotion, however, is not elicited when the stimulus is projected to the left hemisphere.

A difference between the two hemispheres in emotion had been seen prior to the split-brain studies in brain-damaged individuals. For example, in the 1950s, Goldstein reported that many patients with damage to their left hemisphere exhibited feelings of despair, hopelessness and anger, or what was termed a **catastrophic–dysphoric reaction** (Goldstein 1952). In contrast, those with right hemisphere damage tended to be placid and indifferent to their injury, even when it caused paralysis. One study that looked at 150 people with unilateral brain injury found that 62 per cent with left hemispheric damage exhibited the catastrophic reaction, compared with 10 per cent with right-sided injuries. Alternatively, 38 per cent of subjects with damage of the right hemisphere were indifferent to their plight, whereas only 11 per cent of the left-sided group showed the same non-emotional response (Rasmussen and Milner 1977). These results show that when the left cortex is damaged, the right hemisphere recognises the loss and responds with a strong emotional reaction. But, this emotional reaction does not occur when damage occurs to the right hemisphere, which allows the left hemisphere to make a more rational and unemotional interpretation of the situation.

It has also been shown that the right hemisphere has a role to play when it comes to recognising the emotional tone of language. Speech is much more than just words, as shown by the fact that the tone of what we say may completely change its meaning. For example, the sentence, 'you look really nice today', can sound either complimentary or sarcastic depending on the tone of the expression. The ability to make or recognise these prosodic or tonal changes is often impaired in people with damage to the right hemisphere. Furthermore, the regions responsible for these deficits appear to be located in the right-sided areas corresponding to the language centres in the left. For example, Elliot Ross has found that individuals with damage to the right-sided Broca's area often produce spoken language that is lacking in prosody, whereas those with lesions of the right-sided equivalent of Wernicke's area are impaired in their ability to comprehend the prosodic nature of speech (Ross 1984).

The independence of the two hemispheres

Evidence from split-brain studies shows that the two cerebral hemispheres control very different aspects of thought and action. In short, the left hemisphere is superior for language and sequential or analytical thought, whereas the right hemisphere is better on visuospatial tasks and thinking that requires synthetic analysis (Levy 1969). Thus, the right and left hemispheres show different forms of thought, and this can also be observed in situations when the 'two brains' of split-brain patients behave in a contradictory manner. For example, in one task where a split-brain patient was asked to arrange a group of blocks to make a pattern with their right hand (i.e. testing the ability of his left hemisphere), it was found that the left hand (right hemisphere) persistently tried to take over the task. In fact, the experimenter had to wrestle with the left hand to stop it solving the problem. A similar situation arises when a split-brain patient tries to read a book while holding the book in their left hand. Although the person may be interested in the book, they often find themself putting it down. The reason is that the right hemisphere (which controls the left hand) cannot read and sees little point in holding the book. Michael Gazzaniga has also described a patient who would sometimes pull his trousers down with one hand, only to immediately pull them up with his other hand (Gazzaniga 1970).

Roger Sperry has argued that the results of split-brain research show that the human brain has in essence two separate minds, with each hemisphere having its own private mental world of sensations, perceptions, memories and ideas (Sperry 1974). This view also led Sperry to propose that each hemisphere must have its own consciousness or awareness. If this is indeed true, then a split-brain patient is in essence two separate people. However, this view is controversial. For example, Sir John Eccles, who won a Nobel Prize for his work in physiology, pointed out that since the right hemisphere cannot communicate a state of conscious awareness by language, it is more likely to act as non-conscious automaton (Eccles 1965). Thus, for Eccles, consciousness resides in the left hemisphere and is inexplicably linked with language.

There are difficulties with this theory, not least because people who have suffered massive damage to the left hemisphere, or who are aphasic, do not lose conscious awareness. Despite this, it has received some support from Micael Gazzaniga. Although Gazzaniga initially supported Sperry's theory of dual consciousness, he has more recently come to view the left hemisphere as containing 'an interpreter' that attempts to understand the totality of what is happening to the individual. For example, in one experiment a split-brain subject was presented with two pictures: the right hemisphere was shown a winter landscape with snow, and the left hemisphere was shown a chicken's claw. After seeing these pictures, the subject was given an array of new pictures and asked to choose one that went with the first presentation. Gazzaniga found that the two hemispheres selected appropriate pictures. For example, the subjects left hand (right hemisphere) pointed to the shovel, and the right hand (left hemisphere) pointed to a chicken. However, when the subject was asked why they had chosen the shovel, the left hemisphere replied by saying that it could be used to clean out the chicken house. This is despite the fact that the left hemisphere had no way of knowing why the right hemisphere had chosen the shovel. According to Gazzaniga this shows that the left hemisphere has an interpreter which 'tries to bring order and unity to our conscious lives' (Gazzaniga 1989).

The Wada procedure

Another procedure that can be used to measure hemispheric function is the **Wada test**, named after the Japanese physician Juan Wada in the late 1940s. The procedure was first discovered when Wada was asked to treat a young man with a serious bullet wound to one side of the brain that caused a severe form of epilepsy known as status epilepticus. In his desperation to stop the seizures, Wada injected a short-acting anaesthetic (sodium amytal) into the carotid arteries located at the side of the neck, which carries blood from the heart to the brain. Because the right and left arteries feed their own respective hemispheres, Wada knew it was possible to anaesthetise one side of the brain to temporarily causes its loss of function, while leaving the other hemisphere to work normally. The procedure was a success as the patient's seizures stopped immediately. Other researchers, though, soon realised that the Wada test could be used in other ways. In particular, it could be used to help surgeons who performed brain operations for the relief of epilepsy to locate the dominant cerebral hemisphere for language prior to surgery. This was of great assistance to the surgeon who wanted to know some of the potential behavioural consequences of their operation.

It is found that if sodium amytal is injected into the left, or dominant, hemisphere, it produces a sudden and complete aphasia which lasts for around 5 minutes. Alternatively, if the anaesthesia is injected into the right, or non-dominant, hemisphere, language function remains relatively intact and the person is able to converse and answer questions without difficulty. Indeed, in the vast majority of patients, language is found to be localised to the left hemisphere. However, this is not always the case, and in a minority of patients language may be localised to the right hemisphere or be equally distributed across both cortices (mixed dominance).

One of the most interesting findings revealed by the Wada test is that the cerebral dominance of language has a tendency to be different in people who are either right- or left-handed (Figure 10.9). For example, Rasmussen and Milner et al. (1977) studied 262 patients with the Wada technique and found that 96 per cent of right-handed people had language that was strongly lateralised to the left hemisphere. However, in left-handed subjects this figure dropped to about 70 per cent. Moreover, about 15 per cent of left-handers were found to have language lateralised to the right hemisphere, and the remaining 15 per cent showed mixed dominance. Because it is known that around 90 per cent of people are right-handed, a simple calculation shows that over 90 per cent of the population will have a left hemispheric dominance for language, with the remaining 10 per cent showing a right-sided specialisation or bias.

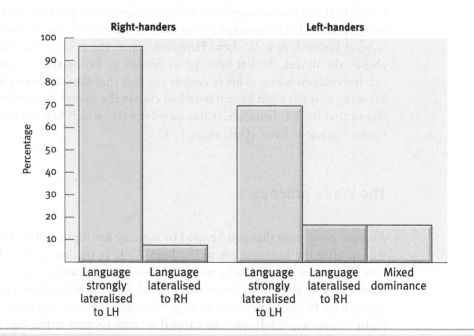

Figure 10.9   The hemispheric lateralisation of language in right- and left-handers

Handedness

The incidence of right handedness across all cultures is about 90 per cent, and evidence shows that the majority of humans have had this preference for the past 2 million years (see McManus 2002). Like most minority groups, prejudices against left-handers abound. A measure of this bias can be seen by the way the word 'left' has evolved in western language. In English, the word stems from the Anglo-Saxon 'lyft' meaning 'broken' or 'weak', and similar sentiments are expressed in Latin (where the word for left is *sinister* derived from *sinistrun* meaning 'evil'); French (where the word for left is *gauche* meaning 'clumsy' or 'crooked'); and Italian (where the word for left is *mancino* meaning 'dishonest'). If this is not bad enough, the world of human objects strongly favours right-handers. For example, scissors, knives, coffee pots, power tools, golf clubs and guitars are made for the majority, as indeed is the book you are reading. There are many explanations for why handedness has arisen. One idea is that it was better for warriors to hold shields in their left hand to protect the heart, thus enabling the right hand to become more skilled. A female version of this idea proposes that it was adaptive for mothers to hold babies in their left hand, so they were soothed by the beating of the heart. Both claims are probably unsound because most animals show some form of right–left bias. It is also clear that handedness develops before birth. For example, in a study of 224 foetuses, aged from four to nine months, it was found that 94.6 per cent sucked their right thumb while in the womb (Hepper *et al.* 1991).

A hotly debated question is the issue of whether living in a predominantly 'right-handed' world causes left-handed people to have more accidents and a diminished life expectancy. For example, Porac and Coren (1981) reported that 13 per cent of 20-year-olds were left-handed, but only 5 per cent of those in their fifties, and virtually nobody of 80 or above. Another study examined the life expectancy of professional baseball players, and found that right-handers lived eight months longer on average than left-handers (Halpern and Coren 1988). The authors explain these results as a result of left-handers being more accident prone (for example, left-handed drivers are 1.9 times more likely to have traffic crashes, and 3.8 times more related to die of crash-related injuries), and also because they are more susceptible to developmental problems. This is supported by evidence showing 18 per cent of twins are left-handed, which is almost twice the level found in the population, and that they also show a higher incidence of neurological disorders, which may arise from intrauterine crowding and stress during birth. However, the higher mortality of left-handers has not gone unchallenged. To give but one example: Aggleton *et al.* (1994) carried out a survey of 3,599 cricketers and found that while right-handers lived slightly longer than left-handers, the difference was not statistically significant.

Although the vast majority of left-handers are perfectly normal, as a group they do suffer a higher incidence of language disorders such as autism and dyslexia. It is also often said that left-handers are more creative, likely to have greater intelligence, and be gifted in art and music. In terms of intelligence, there is little support for these claims. For example, when combining the results of two large-scale studies, it was found that left-handers had an average IQ of 99.5, which was only a half a point less than right-handers. However, a survey of seventeen professional orchestras in the UK, found 13 per cent of the musicians to be left handed, which was greater than expected by chance (McManus 2002). Although few studies have looked at artists, there is some evidence that right- and left-handers view the world slightly differently. For example, when Canadian and British subjects were asked to indicate whether the face portrait on their coinage pointed to the left or right (it points to the right), the left-handers were more accurate. This may be because right-handers tend to draw heads facing to the left, and left-handers to the right.

The development of computerised axial tomography (CAT)

Until recently, researchers interested in identifying brain areas involved in language were forced to rely on post-mortem examination of patients who had experienced aphasia or writing difficulties. This was far from ideal, especially as the main source of patients was generally those who had suffered widespread brain damage as a result of stroke and head injury. This made the precise identification of brain areas contributing to language very problematic. Moreover, by the time the patient came to autopsy, some recovery of function had often taken place, which made it even more difficult to link pathology with behavioural deficits. Fortunately, researchers are no longer stuck with this situation owing to the development of non-invasive imaging techniques, which allow investigators to take detailed internal pictures of a living brain in order to examine its physiology or sites of damage.

The origins of brain scanning start with Wilhelm Röntgen's discovery of X-rays in 1895, which had a dramatic impact on science and medicine as it allowed doctors to see inside the human body. However, the technique was of little use for examining the brain. In fact, for most of the twentieth century the only way neurologists could use X-rays to help visualise the brain was to make the major blood vessels visible through a procedure known as **cerebral angiography**. This technique involved injecting a radioactive dye into the carotid artery and observing its perfusion into the brain by taking X-ray photographs. The pictures were called angiograms and could be used to identify vascular damage and the location of tumours as revealed by the displacement of blood vessels. This technique 'works' because X-ray photography is effective only when the internal structures of the body differ in the extent to which they absorb X-rays. Thus, if injected with a dye, the blood vessels and the surrounding brain tissue absorb the X-rays differently, enabling them to be visualised.

This technique was of little use in picturing the physiology of the brain because neural tissue absorbs X-rays in an undifferentiated way. However, in the late 1960s and early 1970s, Allan Cormack, a South African mathematician, and Godfrey Hounsfield, a British electrical engineer working for EMI (Plate 10.2), independently developed a system where brain X-rays could be mathematically resolved by computer algorithms (both men would win the Nobel Prize for their achievements in 1979). This technique was called **computerised axial tomography (CAT)** and it involved passing a large number of narrow-beam X-rays through the brain with a ray gun that moved around the person's head (Figure 10.10). Because the amount of radiation absorbed by the brain was found to vary from region to region (the denser the tissue the more energy it absorbs), the amount of radiation picked up by the detectors could be used to construct a three-dimensional image of the brain. Hounsfield presented the world's first CAT images at Imperial College, London, on 20 April 1972, and in doing so, began a new chapter in the history of medicine and biopsychology. Hounsfield was knighted for his work in 1981.

The use of CAT scans greatly facilitated the ability of doctors to assess the location and extent of various types of brain damage. Not only were CAT scans effective in identifying tumours and areas of damage produced by strokes, but they also visualised the ventricles which stood out in black due to the cerebrospinal fluid's low density. This was useful as enlarged ventricles are an indication of brain atrophy and degeneration. In addition, CAT scans allowed the main areas of the brain to be observed.

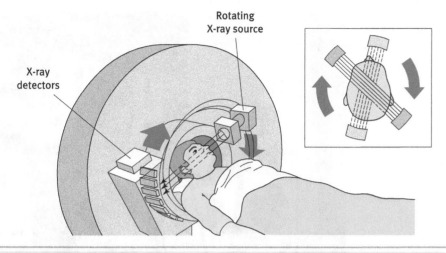

| Figure 10.10 | The basic procedure of computerised axial tomography |

Source: D. Purves *et al.*, *Neuroscience*. Copyright © 1997 by Sinauer Associates, Inc.

Despite this, the pictures produced by CAT scans show only limited detail as white and grey matter have similar densities. In addition, CAT scans have only a limited resolution: at present, they are not able to discriminate two objects that are less than 5 mm apart (Gazzaniga *et al.* 2002).

The development of positron emission tomography (PET)

The development of CAT scanning encouraged scientists to seek alternative ways of looking inside the human brain. In particular, there was a great desire to develop methods that could examine the brain when it was engaged in mental activity. The first major imaging technique to do this was **positron emission tomography** (**PET**), which appeared in the late 1970s. Instead of using X-rays, PET involves the use of short-lasting radioactive substances which are injected into the bloodstream of the subject and which emit **positrons**. The positrons are detected by a scanner which provides a three-dimensional representation of the chemicals distribution in the body or brain. Importantly, this technology can be used to observe the mental activity of the brain by measuring regional blood flow. The procedure rests on two principles: the brain requires energy to function, and the regions of the brain most heavily involved in mental activity will also be the ones that use up the most energy. Since the brain's energy, in the form of oxygen and glucose, is provided by blood, the rate of its flow to any given region is directly proportional to the level of activation. One way that PET is used to measure blood flow is by detecting the activity given off by radioactive labelled water, or, more specifically, hydrogen combined with oxygen. The labelled water is injected into a vein in the arm, and within a minute or so is flowing through the brain where it emits positrons.

This historical roots of PET are very different from those of CAT scanning. Positrons are positively charged electrons (electrons are normally negatively charged) that occur

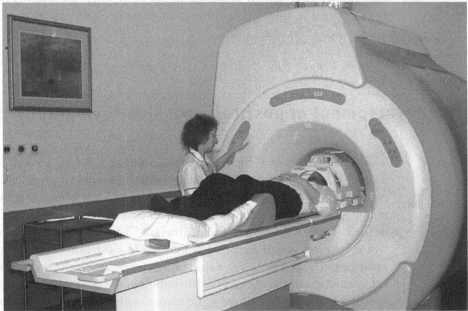

Plate 10.2   The Beatles, and an MRI brain scanner. The profits made by EMI from the sale of records by the Beatles, and other artists, helped to pay for the development of the first brain scanners

Source: Beatles photograph © Bettman/Corbis; brain scanner from *Neuroscience: Science of the Brain* (2003). Published by the British Neuroscience Association

when neutrons are broken down in the nucleus of the atom. Although they can occur naturally, the positrons used in PET are produced in a highly specialised (and expensive) machine called a **cyclotron**. When injected into the body, the emitting positrons of the radioactive substance travel only a few millimetres before they are attracted by the negative charge of surrounding electrons. The result is a collision between the positron and electron, which annihilate each other, generating two high-energy photons that leave the impact site 180 degrees apart. These photons are picked up by an array of gamma ray detectors, and the site of the positron–electron collisions is reconstructed by computer. In this way, a continuous high-resolution three-dimensional colour picture of the brain regions where most activity is taking place can be created.

The first PET scanner to provide three-dimensional pictures of the brain was built by Michael Phelps and Edward Hoffman at Washington University in 1975. The technique is a powerful one that can be used to examine the brain is many different ways. By using different compounds (several hundred molecules have now been produced with positron emitters), PET can be used to monitor many different tissues and assist in the treatment of a wide range of neurological disorders. It has also been used to identify the brain sites where neurotransmitters act, to show how quickly drugs reach a given type of receptor, or to determine the amount of time receptors are occupied.

Of most interest to the biopsychologist, however, are studies that examine the brain engaged in various mental or behavioural functions. The first functional imaging experiments using PET appeared in the early 1980s, and most adopted a procedure where the brain was examined at rest, and then engaged in some mental activity such as listening to speech. By subtracting the difference between these two states, a map of the brain regions responsible for the task can be visualised. The end result is a series of pictures showing the pattern of neural activity, often averaged out across 30 second intervals, which reflects the mental processes engaged during that period.

The development of magnetic resonance imaging (MRI)

Not long after the development of PET, another type of scanning technique emerged that had even greater potential for examining the brain. This was **magnetic resonance imaging (MRI)** and it not only provided highly detailed pictures of the inner structures of the human brain, but it did so without the use of potentially harmful ionising radiation. It is acknowledged as one of the most important achievements in the history of medicine. The technique of MRI is based on a phenomenon, first discovered in the 1940s, that when atomic nuclei are placed in a strong magnetic field, they will start to align themselves in an orderly manner – and, while doing this they can absorb radio waves that cause them to resonate (spin). However, when the atomic nuclei are removed from the magnetic force, which returns them to their previous energy level, they start to emit radio waves. These discoveries had important implications. By varying the intensity of the radio waves, and then carefully measuring the energy released by the resonating nuclei, scientists could determine the types of atoms that made up a given substance.

It would be many years, however, before this technique could be used to examine biological tissues. The breakthrough came from the work of Paul C. Lauterbur at the

University of Illinois, and Sir Peter Mansfield at the University of Nottingham, who developed specialised computer programs for the procedure (both men won a Nobel Prize for their work in 2003). Their work led to the first MRI scanners in 1977. One of the first MRI images was of a wrist showing features as small as 0.5 mm in diameter. The high resolution of the technique was one of its great benefits, and by the late 1980s detailed images of the brain began to appear that were superior to those produced by CAT. Because grey matter (cell bodies), white matter (axons), cerebrospinal fluid and bone all differ in atomic composition, these tissues are readily distinguished by MRI.

Following the development of the first MRI scanners, researchers also began to realise that the technique could be adapted to examine the neural activity of the brain. One way of doing this was pioneered by Siege Ogawa, who knew that oxygenated and deoxygenated blood emitted different MRI signals. In fact, the haemoglobin of oxygen-rich blood (which is carried from the heart) has magnetic properties, and as it passes through capillaries, oxygen is extracted causing it to lose this energy. This, produces changes in the intensity of the signals measured by MRI. Ogawa called this phenomenon 'blood oxygen level dependent contrast' (or BOLD), and in 1992 he developed a way of measuring this change in the human brain. Thus, **functional magnetic resonance imaging (fMRI)** was born that allowed investigators to see the flow of blood, and its oxygen removal, in the human brain. When an area of the brain is active, there is an increase in oxygen-rich blood that is greater than the rate of deoxygenation. Thus the relative proportions of oxygenated blood to deoxygenated blood increase in that region, and it is from this increased signal that a picture of the brain activation can be derived.

MRI has many advantages over PET, and this has made it especially valuable in medical diagnosis and research. Firstly, it is non-invasive as subjects are exposed to a magnetic force that is harmless. Thus, an individual can be scanned repeatedly without risk. Secondly, the spatial resolution of the MRI image is far superior to other types of scanning technique, and can detect structures smaller than 1 mm in diameter. Thirdly, views of the brain's activity can be obtained from any angle. Fourthly, by varying the magnetic gradients and radio frequency pulse parameters, MRI scanners can be used to generate images based on a wide variety of different atoms or contrast mechanisms. For example, most MRI images are designed to use the properties of hydrogen, but if the pulse parameters are adjusted, other atoms can be 'tuned in' that produce different pictures. The most important advantage of MRI, however, is that the images can be collected every few seconds, compared with the much longer timeframes for PET. This allows different areas of the brain to be observed sequentially (for example, activity occurring in one brain area can be followed in time to another area). Thus, a much better understanding of the flow of information, and the interaction of different brain areas, in a given task or mental activity is obtained.

New insights into language

The development of functional scanning techniques has opened up a new chapter in the study of the brain. Already, it has led to a new field of research known as **cognitive neuroscience** (a term which, according to Michael Gazzaniga, was invented in the back

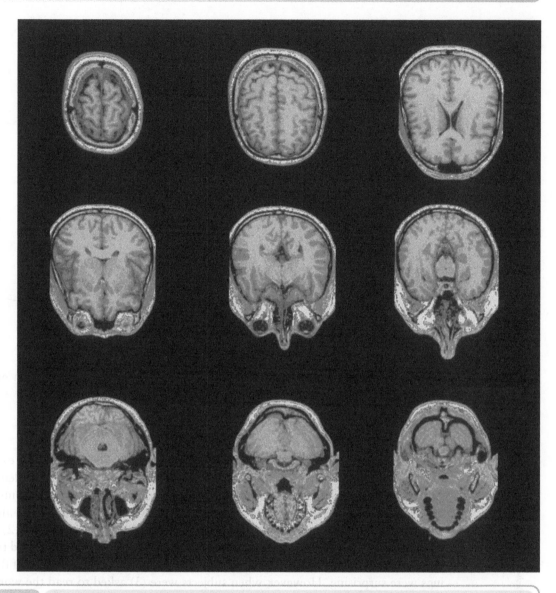

Plate 10.3   Coronal sections of the brain viewed with magnetic functional imaging (MFI)

Source: Wellcome Dept of Cognitive Neurology/Science Photo Library

of a taxi cab in the late 1970s) that has the aim of explaining how mental and cognitive functions arise from the activity of the brain (Rugg 1997). Although it is a hybrid of several disciplines, the advent of non-invasive scanning techniques has been the most important factor in its development. Functional imaging allows the scientist to examine just about any mental process, and to record the activation of multiple brain structures during its activity. In this way, researchers can observe which brain areas are 'at work' in a given task, and attempt to fathom the cognitive operations they are performing (Plate 10.3).

The application of functional scanning techniques to the study of language has already produced some findings that are changing traditional ideas. For example, Posner

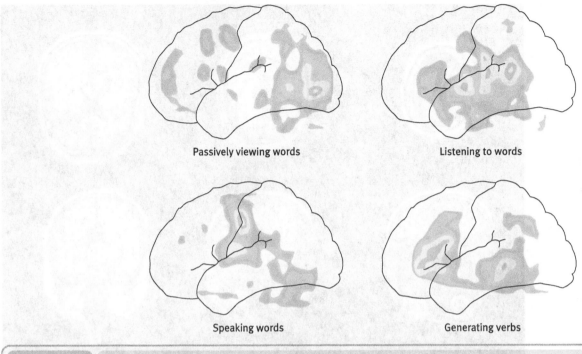

Passively viewing words

Listening to words

Speaking words

Generating verbs

Figure 10.11 The effect of different language tasks on brain activity as revealed by positron emission tomography

and Raichle (1994) measured the amount of blood flow in the cerebral cortex by using PET during the performance of four language-related tasks by college students. When subjects were (1) asked to silently read words presented to them on a computer screen, it was found that this increased activity in both halves of the occipital lobe, although it was most marked on the left side (see Figure 10.11). When subjects were (2) asked to listen passively to spoken words on headphones, the brain activation shifted to the primary auditory cortex and Wernicke's area in the left hemisphere. Neither of these findings were surprising. However, when subjects were (3) asked to read the words aloud from the screen, several regions of the brain were activated. This task increased activity along the central fissure (which separates the frontal and parietal cortex) of both hemispheres, as well as produced marked activation of the motor cortex and supplementary cortex. In addition, a part of the cerebellum and also insular cortex (an 'old' area of cortex that lies buried beneath the lateral fissure) were activated. Lastly, when subjects were (4) asked provide an appropriate verb to go with the presented noun (e.g. *cake*: eat, *hammer*: hit), increased activity occurred in the left frontal cortex (just in front of Broca's area), anterior cingulate cortex, the left posterior temporal lobe (adjacent to Wernicke's area) and the right cerebellum.

The results from this study show that the areas of the brain involved in language are more extensive than made by the predictions of the Wernicke–Geschwind model. Most surprising was the non-participation of Wernicke's area in reading and generating verbs to nouns, although it was activated when words were spoken to the subject, which shows its involvment in the comprehension of speech. In fact, many studies have confirmed this finding, and shown that Broca's area, and surrounding areas of the frontal lobe are the important ones for generating verbs to nouns (Sahin *et al.*

(a) Listening to bursts of noise   **(b) Listening to words**   **(c) Discriminating speech sounds**

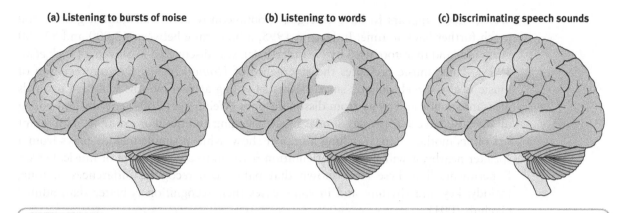

Figure 10.12	The main areas of the cerebral cortex activated (i.e. increased blood flow) during the performance of different language-related tasks

Source: B. Kolb and I.Q. Whishaw, *An Introduction to Brain and Behavior*, p. 345. Copyright © 2001 by Worth Publishers

2006). But why should the frontal areas of the brain be involved in this type of task? An explanation has been provided by Pulvermüller *et al.* (2000). These investigators recorded brain activity when subjects were asked to generate verbs in response to various motor actions. They found that verbs relating to the legs (e.g. to kick) were associated with increased activation of the motor cortex controlling leg movements, whereas those relating to the face (e.g. to speak) activated the face region. Thus it would appear that thinking about a certain action activates the appropriate area of the motor cortex, and this is an important component in the generation of certain verbs.

The importance of Broca's area for language has been shown in other ways. For example, Zatorre *et al.* (1992) found that simple bursts of noise and random sounds increased activation in the primary auditory cortex, whereas speech syllables increased it in secondary auditory regions including Wernicke's area (Figure 10.12). This is consistent with the Wernicke–Geschwind model as it supports the idea that the primary auditory cortex analyses all types of sound, whereas Wernicke's area is specifically involved in recognising language. But, Broca's area in the left hemisphere was also activated during the discrimination of speech sounds. According to the Wernicke–Geschwind model this should not occur as Broca's area is responsible for producing speech. One possible explanation is that to determine that the 'g' in 'bag' and 'pig' is the same speech sound, the auditory stimulus must be compared with how that sound is articulated. Thus, the comprehension of speech sounds may require a match with the motor behaviours associated with making that sound.

Music and the brain

All human societies produce music, and clearly it can have a powerful influence on an individual's moods and feelings. Furthermore, unlike the development of writing which arose in select places and at certain times (for example around 3500 BC in the

West), music appears to have emerged spontaneously across all human groups and much further back in time. In fact, in 1995, a bone flute between 43,000 and 82,000 years old (and therefore used by Neanderthals), was discovered in Slovenia (Turk *et al.* 1995). Thus, music pre-dates the emergence of *Homo sapiens*. Our appreciation of music is also largely innate, since infants as young as two months will turn towards pleasant sounds and away from dissonant ones (Weinberger 2004). Adults and young infants also have surprisingly similar music-listening abilities. For example, if an infant sits on its mother's lap, watching a puppet show, while a simple melody plays from a speaker nearby, it will show an orientation reaction to a wrong note or musical error. Experiments like these have shown that babies can recognise differences in tone, melody, key and rhythm, and in some cases their recognition is better than adults' (Trehub 2001).

Music is a predominantly a right hemispheric function of the brain. For example, in 1926, Henschen reported on 16 patients who had **music agnosia**, including tone deafness and an inability to repeat simple melodies or rhythm. Because these patients did not have any language dysfunction, Henschen concluded that the functions of language and music were located in opposite sides of the brain. Further support for this idea comes from the observation that many people with severe aphasia as a result of left hemisphere damage can hum a tune or even sing the words to a previously learned song. A famous example of this type of preserved ability comes from the French composer Maurice Ravel, who, in 1933, suffered a left hemispheric stroke. Although aphasic, most of his musical abilities remained intact. For example, Ravel could recognise melodies, hear and remember his old compositions, and play scales. He could also spot the tiniest mistakes in music that he heard being played. Yet, Ravel was no longer able to read or write music. Speaking of his proposed opera *Jeanne d'Arc*, Ravel confided to a friend, 'This opera is here, in my head. I hear it, but I will never write it. It's over. I can no longer write my music.'

The development of functional scanning techniques has greatly helped researchers understand the brain's ability to recognise and produce music. This research has tended to show that musical abilities such as melody, harmony, rhythm and singing are dependent on different parts of the brain. For example, it has been found that listening to melodies causes a marked activation of the secondary auditory cortex in the right temporal lobe, whereas a task requiring the comparison of pitches and tones increases blood flow to the right frontal cortex. However, the processing of rhythm is more dependent on the left hemisphere (Zatorre and Peretz 2001). There is also some evidence that music has an effect on the reward systems of the brain. For example, Blood and Zatorre (2001) asked subjects to select a favourite piece of music (among the selections were Samuel Barber's *Adagio for Strings* and Rachmaninoff's Piano Concerto No. 3 in D minor), and to undergo a PET scan when listening to their choice. The music, especially at emotionally high points, was found to increase blood flow in the nucleus accumbens, amygdala and orbitofrontal cortex. These are brain structures known to be involved in pleasurable emotions, which also respond to biologically important stimuli such as food and sex. Considering that music is neither necessary for biological survival or reproduction, this is a remarkable finding.

It has also been shown that trained musicians show differences in their brain structure compared with non-musicians. For example, Schlaug *et al.* (1995) measured the size of the planum temporale in the left hemisphere, and found that it was twice as large in musicians with perfect pitch compared with a control group. Thus, perfect pitch, curiously, appears to be dependent on the left hemisphere. Another study using

MRI has shown that the corpus callosum is 10–15 per cent thicker in musicians who began studying music before the age of 7 (Lee et al. 2003). This finding may help to explain why a number of studies have shown that musicians use much larger areas of cerebral cortex to process music than do non-musicians. Moreover, they are more likely to use their left hemisphere to a greater degree in this endeavour (Wilson 2003).

Summary

Language provides us with a complex, creative and powerful system of communication, and vehicle for thought, which makes us uniquely human. The first brain region to be linked with language was **Broca's area,** named after **Paul Broca,** who in 1861 performed an autopsy on a patient called Tan who had been unable to produce meaningful speech for over twenty years. This examination showed a large area of damage to the posterior part of the left **frontal lobe,** which is now known to be adjacent to the **motor cortex** that controls the muscles of the face, mouth and vocal cords. People with **Broca's aphasia** generally exhibit language which is slow, laboured and lacking grammatical structure or inflection (i.e. **telegraphic speech**), although verbal comprehension is normally intact. Later in 1874, **Carl Wernicke** described a second type of aphasia in which his patients appeared to utter grammatically correct speech, although its content was largely devoid of meaning, and had severe comprehension defects. This deficit is now known as **Wernicke's aphasia** and is associated with damage to a region of the **temporal lobe** that is adjacent to the **primary auditory cortex.** A neural pathway called the **arcuate fasciculus** passes from Wernicke's area to Broca's area, and damage to this route, producing a third type of aphasia – called **conduction aphasia** – is characterised by an inability to repeat abstract, or non, words. The theory that is most commonly used to explain how the brain processes language is the **Wernicke–Geschwind model,** which proposes that both the primary auditory cortex (for speech) and visual cortex (for reading) project to Wernicke's area where word recognition and comprehension takes place. The translation of mental thoughts into verbal codes is also believed to take place in Wernicke's area, and this information can be passed to Broca's area, which produces the motor output necessary for speech.

It is generally accepted that the **left hemisphere** of the cerebral cortex is predominantly involved in language, and the **right hemisphere** more concerned with visuospatial skills and emotion. Evidence supporting this theory was provided by Roger Sperry and his associates in the 1960s. They examined patients who had received a **commissurotomy** or severing of the **corpus callosum.** This is an operation that stops the two hemispheres of the brain from directly communicating with each other. It was found that if a written word was presented to the left hemisphere, split-brain subjects typically had no problem reading it, although they often reported seeing nothing when the word was presented to the right. In contrast, the right hemisphere was found to be much better than the left at copying drawings or completing jigsaws. In addition, pictures presented to this hemisphere were more likely to elicit an emotional response (for example, blushing or arousal) than when presented to the left. However, language (or other cognitive functions) are not always lateralised to one side of the brain. For example, around 90 per cent of people are right-handed, which is controlled by the left hemisphere of the brain. Studies using the **Wada test,** where one of the hemispheres is temporarily anaesthetised by an injection of **sodium amytal** into the **carotid artery,** have shown that around 95 per cent of right-handed people have language strongly localised to the left hemisphere; but, in left-handed subjects this figure drops to about 70 per cent. Moreover, about 15 per cent of left-handers have language lateralised to the right hemisphere, and the remaining 15 per cent show mixed dominance. It has been suggested that if high levels of **testosterone** occur during the last trimester of foetal development, this may slow maturation of the left hemisphere, with the right more likely to take over some of its functions.

Essay questions

1. Compare and contrast Broca's aphasia with Wernicke's aphasia. What cortical regions need to be damaged to produce these types of aphasia, and what do they tell us about the brain mechanisms underlying language?

    Search terms: Broca's and Wernicke's aphasia. Broca's area. Wernicke's area. Planum temporale. Arcuate fasciculus. Wernicke–Geschwind theory of language.

2. With reference to research involving split-brain patients, describe the different functions of the right and left hemispheres of the brain.

    Search terms: Split brain. Functions of the left hemisphere. Functions of the right hemisphere. Corpus callosum. Two minds in one brain.

3. Why does lateralisation of brain function occur? What are some of the potential problems that can arise if language is not fully lateralised in the left hemisphere?

    Search terms: Lateralisation of the brain. Testosterone and lateralisation. Causes of handedness. Neurobiology of dyslexia. Right hemisphere and autism.

4. 'Brain scanning technology is providing new insights into our understanding of the brain.' Explain how CAT, MRI, PET and fMRI scanning works, and some of the ways in which this technology has been used to justify the above statement.

    Search terms: Regional blood flow in the brain. CAT scans. MRI scans. PET scans. Functional MRI scans. Functional MRI and language.

Further reading

Altmann, G.T.M. (1987) *The Ascent of Babel*. Oxford: Oxford University Press. A readable and wide-ranging exploration of language which attempts to explain the development of mental processes responsible for the production of speech and writing.

Basso, A. (2003) *Aphasia and its Therapy*. Oxford: Oxford University Press. Provides a useful description of the classic aphasia syndromes, neuropsychological models and forms of therapy.

Bradshaw, J.L. (1989) *Hemispheric Specialisation and Psychological Function*. Chichester: John Wiley. Although this text is now rather dated, it provides a concise introduction to split-brain research and cerebral asymmetry, which should still be of benefit to the student.

Brown, C.M. and Hargoot, P. (eds) (2001) *The Neurocognition of Language*. Oxford: Oxford University Press. Examines the neuroanatomical and cognitive bases of speaking, listening and reading.

Gazzaniga, M.S. (ed.) (2004) *The New Cognitive Neurosciences III*. Cambridge, Mass.: MIT Press. A massive book with an up-to-date and detailed section on language written by a variety of experts. Other useful sections include ones on motor systems, memory and emotion.

Gazzaniga, M.S., Ivry, R.B. & Mangum, G.R. (2002) *Cognitive Neuroscience*. New York: Norton. A standard textbook in the field which claims boldly to have revolutionised the teaching of psychology by unifying cognitive psychology, behavioural neurology and behavioural neuroscience in an accessible, user-friendly way for undergraduates.

Loritz, D. (2002) *How the Brain Evolved Language*. Oxford: Oxford University Press. A book that examines the relationship between brain structure and language, and one that controversially contradicts the idea that human language is innate (as proposed, for example, by Pinker – see below).

Martin, G.N. (2006) *Human Neuropsychology*. Harlow: Pearson. An excellent introductory textbook with a very good chapter on language and its disorders.

McManus, C. (2002) *Right Hand, Left Hand*. London: Weidenfeld & Nicolson. A compelling and diverse book that attempts to understand the asymmetry of the world we live in, including an attempt to explain why most people are right-handed, and why each side of the human brain has different functions.

Obler, L.K and Gjerlow, K. (1999) *Language and the Brain*. Cambridge: Cambridge University Press. A very useful paperback book that provides an introduction to the neurobiological basis of language, focusing predominantly on brain-damaged individuals.

Pinker, S. (1994) *The Language Instinct*. New York: William Morrow. A comprehensive and readable account that argues that language is an instinct hardwired into the brain and programmed through the process of evolution.

Plum, F. (ed.) (1988) *Language, Communication and the Brain*. New York: Raven Press. A series of well-written chapters by various experts that are of great relevance to biopsychologists interested in the relationship between brain and language.

Posner, M.I. and Raichle, M.E. (1994) *Images of Mind*. New York: Scientific American Library. A clearly written and nicely illustrated account of how new scanning techniques such as PET and fMRI are revolutionising our knowledge of how the brain is involved in thought and language.

Springer, S.P. and Deutsch, G. (1998) *Left Brain, Right Brain*. New York: Freeman. An award-winning book, now in its fifth edition, that is perfect for psychology undergraduates and which examines in detail the asymmetry of hemispheric function in human brains.

For self test questions, animations, interactive exercises and many more resources to help you consolidate your understanding, and expand your knowledge of the field, please go to the website accompanying this book at **www.pearsoned.co.uk/wickens**

CHAPTER 11

The biological basis of mental illness

In this chapter

- The classification of affective disorders
- How antidepressant drugs work
- The monoamine theory of depression
- Lithium and bipolar disorder
- How antipsychotic drugs work
- The dopaminergic theory of schizophrenia
- Types of brain damage found in schizophrenia
- The genetic and environmental causes of schizophrenia

INTRODUCTION

The term 'mental illness' has no precise definition but generally refers to the types of disorder that are treated by psychiatrists. Although mental illnesses can arise through physical injury to the brain, including tumours, infection and diseases of the arteries, in the vast majority of cases they are conditions where the symptoms appear to be largely in the person's mood or thinking, and where there is no sign of biological damage. Because of this, some investigators (for example, Szasz 1960) have argued that psychiatric disorders are not true illnesses and should not be treated by medical practitioners. But this is a controversial view, and a more balanced one holds that mental illnesses arise from a complex interaction of biological, social and personal factors which may lead to neurochemical or physiological changes in the brain, even if they cannot be reliably identified. Whatever one's opinion, it cannot be disputed that the effects of mental illness, which include depression, mania, schizophrenia and a number of anxiety disorders, are severely debilitating. Mental health problems are also surprisingly common. In the UK, about one person in eight will consult a doctor for psychological problems in any given year, and about 10 per cent of these patients will be referred to a psychiatrist. This makes mental health problems only surpassed in frequency by common colds, bronchitis and rheumatism (Gregory 2004). The biopsychologist has a central role to play in understanding the causes of mental illness and developing more effective treatments. This task is not an easy one, although the challenge is one of the most exciting that a psychologist can face, with the real possibility of helping millions of people.

An introduction to depression

Everybody from time to time feels depressed (or what the *Oxford English Dictionary* defines as a state of 'low spirits or vitality'), which occurs in response to adversity, loss or perceived misfortune. Indeed, depression, whether it consists of feelings of slight sadness or utter misery, is an emotion known to everyone. These feelings play an important role in human existence, not least because depression and its counterpart, happiness, form part of the mechanism by which our brains register and process information about punishment and reward. But, there are some people for whom the feeling of depression becomes maladaptive. In such instances there may be no obvious reason for the depression to occur. This is sometimes called **endogenous depression**. Or its severity may be out of proportion to the events that triggered it (**reactive depression**). Although these states are often temporary, with a person experiencing no more than one or two serious periods of depression during a lifetime, they can also be chronic (permanent) and very debilitating. It is difficult to say exactly at what point depression becomes a mental illness, although when it becomes so severe that the person is continually unable to feel happiness, is plagued by negative thoughts, often thinks about suicide, and cannot function properly at work or in social relationships, then the problem is clear for all to see.

Although in everyday language, depression is viewed as a state that is characterised by feelings of sadness or gloom, in clinical cases there is much more to the disorder. Clinical depression normally exhibits a constellation of symptoms, which are categorised under four headings: emotional, cognitive, motivational and physical. For example, the clinically depressed person is likely not only to feel sad, tearful and miserable (i.e. emotional symptoms), but also to have many negative thoughts, including low self-esteem and a sense of helplessness (i.e. cognitive symptoms). This is likely to be accompanied by varying degrees of energy loss or psychomotor retardation, where even the simplest chore can appear daunting (i.e. motivational symptoms). Finally there may be a number of physical problems including sleep disturbances, appetite loss, sexual difficulties, muscle weakness and various aches and pains (i.e. somatic symptoms). This type of depression may result in such emotional apathy that the person is unable to wash, cook or to look after themselves. In other instances, depression may be associated with high levels of anxiety (sometimes referred to as **neurotic depression**), or delusional behaviour (**psychotic depression**).

Depression is classified by psychiatrists as a 'mood' or **affective disorder** although it is not the only condition that is characterised by emotional extremes. For example, the opposite of depression is mania, which leads to heightened euphoria, exuberance and increased energy. In fact, most people who experience mania also suffer from lengthy bouts of depression (i.e. **manic depression**), which can occur in a regular or cyclical pattern. Because of this, affective disorders are often divided into two categories: **unipolar depression,** in which the person suffers exclusively from prolonged periods of sadness and despondency (a very rare form of unipolar disorder involves just mania), and **bipolar depression,** where the person undergoes alternating periods of depression and mania. There is good evidence that these two disorders have a different biological basis. Another type of affective disorder is **dysthymia,** which can be regarded as a milder, albeit long-lasting, version of unipolar depression. The equivalent form for bipolar illness is **cyclothymia** (Figure 11.1).

Mood disorders are the most common form of mental illness. It has been estimated that about 5 per cent of the population will be adversely affected by a clinical form of depression at any one point in time and that over 10 per cent of the population will suffer from this illness during their lifetime (Kalet 2007). Despite this, up to 75 per cent of individuals with depression will not present themselves to the health services. Depression occurs twice as frequently in women as in men, although the reasons for this sex difference are not clear. Maybe these figures represent a biological difference in susceptibility to depression – or, perhaps more likely, they are due to social factors, with

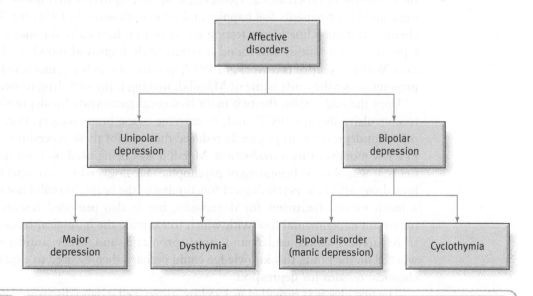

Figure 11.1   Types of depression

women being more likely to seek help for their problems, or finding themselves in menial life situations with reduced opportunities. Although depression can begin at any age, its average age of onset is the mid-twenties. It is also associated with a high risk of mortality, with between 7 per cent and 15 per cent of depressed individuals attempting to commit suicide (Feldman *et al.* 1997). The treatment of depression is a huge economic burden for society. A recent survey of 28 European countries showed that the annual cost of depression was 118 billion Euros, which corresponded to 1 per cent of the total European gross domestic product (Sobocki *et al.* 2006).

Although bipolar illness is a rarer condition, affecting around 1 per cent of the population, in many ways it is a more serious problem. It tends to be a lifelong disease requiring continual treatment, and is one of the most unpredictable psychiatric illnesses of all. In addition to regular and severe bouts of depression, where the risk of suicide is high, the person with bipolar illness will have periods when they are likely to have problems with concentration leading to poor judgement, accompanied by high energy levels and compulsive behaviour. This may find expression in high-risk behaviours such as gambling or drug use. Unlike unipolar depression, bipolar illness affects both males and females equally (Goodwin and Jamison 1990).

The development of antidepressant drugs

The beginnings of antidepressant drugs can be said to begin with a substance called hydrazine, which was used towards the end of the Second World War by German scientists as a propellant to fire the V2 rocket. After the war, large stocks of German hydrazine were given to pharmaceutical companies who were interested in seeing if the chemical had a clinical use. Two drugs derived from hydrazine in the early 1950s were isoniazid and iproniazid, which were both found to be effective antibacterial agents in the treatment of tuberculosis. However, it became apparent that **iproniazid** was making a number of patients feel happier and more optimistic. In 1956, the American psychiatrist Nathan Kline began testing iproniazid on hospitalised patients with various types of mental illness, and found it significantly improved mood in clinical depression. Within a year of this work, in 1957, iproniazid was being marketed as an antidepressant under the trade name of **Marsilid**, making it the first drug to treat depression.

Until the mid-1950s, the two main biological treatments for depression were electroconvulsive therapy (ECT) and, in extreme cases, brain surgery. But, Marsilid and other antidepressant drugs greatly reduced the need for these procedures. In fact, within a few months of its introduction, Marsilid was being used on huge numbers of patients. It was also the beginning of **psychopharmacology**, which attempts to understand how drugs affect the psychological functioning of the brain. Marsilid not only provided a much needed treatment for depression, but it also provided researchers with an important experimental tool with which to examine the biological basis of the illness. If researchers could understand how iproniazid and other antidepressant drugs worked on the brain, this knowledge could perhaps then be used to explain the neurochemical reasons for depression.

The first clue was provided in 1952 by Albert Zellar, who discovered that iproniazid exerted its main biochemical effect by inhibiting an enzyme called **monoamine oxidase**

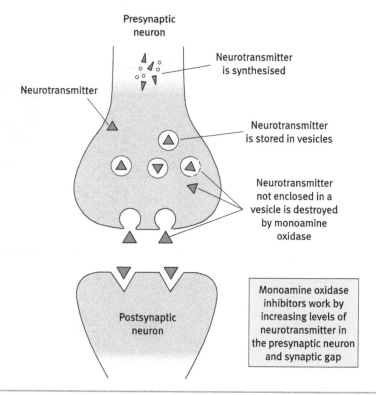

Presynaptic
neuron

Neurotransmitter
is synthesised

Neurotransmitter

Neurotransmitter
is stored in vesicles

Neurotransmitter
not enclosed in a
vesicle is destroyed
by monoamine
oxidase

Postsynaptic
neuron

Monoamine oxidase
inhibitors work by
increasing levels of
neurotransmitter in
the presynaptic neuron
and synaptic gap

Figure 11.2   The mechanism by which monoamine oxidase inhibitors exert their pharmacological effects

(Zellar *et al.* 1952). This is an enzyme located primarily in nerve terminals which breaks down and inactivates **monoamines** in the brain (such as **noradrenaline, dopamine** and **serotonin**). Thus, when monoamine oxidase was inhibited by iproniazid, higher levels of monoamines were released into the synapse (Figure 11.2). The result was increased levels of these neurotransmitters in the brain. This finding had important implications. If iproniazid was producing its antidepressant effect by increasing the secretion of monoamines into the synapse, this implied that depression was caused by reduced levels of these neurotransmitters. In other words, by inhibiting monoamine oxidase, iproniazid appeared to be producing an antidepressive effect by correcting a neurochemical deficit and restoring normal levels of monoamines in the brain.

Further evidence to support this theory came from the drug **reserpine**. This substance was first isolated in 1951 from the snakeroot plant (*Rauwolia serpentina*), which had been used in India for hundreds of years to treat medical problems. Although reserpine was found to be effective in the treatment of high blood pressure, it also produced depression in a number of patients. What was responsible for this mood-altering effect? In the early 1960s it was found that reserpine depleted the brain of **catecholamines** (neurotransmitters that contain a catechol nucleus in their chemical structure), which included the monoamines noradrenaline and dopamine. In fact, reserpine caused these neurotransmitters to 'leak out' from protective synaptic vesicles in the nerve terminals, enabling them to be broken down by monoamine oxidase (Figure 11.3). Thus, reserpine had an opposite neurochemical effect to iproniazid: it produced depression and depleted the brain of noradrenaline and dopamine.

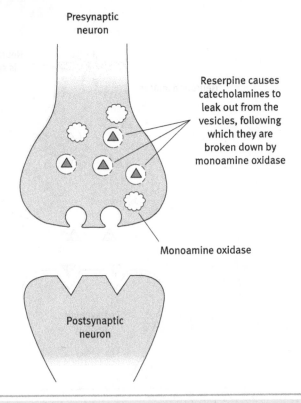

Presynaptic neuron

Reserpine causes catecholamines to leak out from the vesicles, following which they are broken down by monoamine oxidase

Monoamine oxidase

Postsynaptic neuron

Figure 11.3   The mechanism by which reserpine exerts its pharmacological effects

Although monoamine oxidase inhibitors (MAOIs) are still used in clinical practice, they are only chosen when other treatments for depression have failed. Thus, they make up less than 10 per cent of all prescriptions for depression. One reason is that these drugs produce a number of side effects, caused by their interactions with various foodstuffs which contain **tyramine**. Such foods include cheese, red wine, chocolate and beer. Tyramine is a powerful elevator of blood pressure and is metabolised by the liver. MAOIs interfere with this metabolism, causing hypertensive effects, leading to severe headache, increased body temperature and even intracranial bleeding. In some cases these effects have proven fatal. Patients taking MAOIs, therefore, have to be very careful with their diet. MAOIs can also be lethal when taken in overdose.

The development of the tricyclic antidepressants

Marsilid was not the only antidepressant to be discovered in the 1950s. This was a time when drugs for the treatment of schizophrenia were being developed, and one such compound, initially called G22355, was synthesised by the Geigy Drug Company in Switzerland. One psychiatrist asked to test this drug was Roland Kuhn, working in Germany. Although he found that it was ineffective as an antipsychotic, it made his patients feel happier. The antidepressant effect of G22355 was confirmed when given to a group of 40 depressed patients in 1955 (Kuhn 1958). It was called **imipramine**, and launched in 1958 under the brand name of **Tofranil**. This drug quickly became the most frequently used antidepressant in the world. It was also structurally different from the MAOIs. In fact, imipramine and other antidepressants of the same class are known as **tricyclic antidepressants** (TADs) because their molecular structure contains a three-ring chain. These drugs did not lose their popularity until the emergence of the selective serotonergic blockers in the late 1980s.

Curiously, imipramine did not inhibit monoamine oxidase. In fact, its pharmacological action was discovered in 1961 by Jules Axelrod, who was one of the first scientists to work with a radioactive version of noradrenaline (this allowed its distribution and metabolism in the body to be monitored). When he administered noradrenaline into rats he found it accumulated in the sympathetic nerves of the body. This implied that noradrenaline was being taken up by the sympathetic nerves. The important questions were why and how? Axelrod's answer was that noradrenergic neurons have a **reuptake pump** that causes the neurotransmitter, when released, to be taken back up into nerve endings. This not only helped noradrenaline to be removed from the synapse but also helped in the recycling of the neurotransmitter. Similar reuptake pumps were later discovered for serotonin and dopamine. Axelrod received a Nobel Prize for his work in 1970.

Axelrod had shown that the presynaptic noradrenergic neuron has a mechanism for pumping excess transmitter back into its terminals, which helps to regulate the amount of noradrenaline in the synapse. In 1961, Axelrod extended his research by showing that imipramine inhibited the reuptake process (it was also later shown to block serotonin reuptake) by attaching itself to the pump and stopping it from taking noradrenaline in the synapse back into the neuron (Figure 11.4). The functional effect was similar to that produced by the MAOIs: increased levels of noradrenaline in the synaptic cleft.

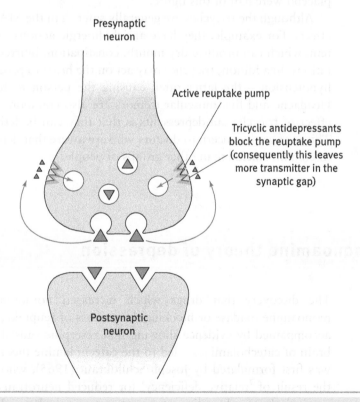

Figure 11.4   The mechanism by which the tricyclic antidepressants exert their pharmacological effects

Following the appearance of imipramine in 1958, a number of tricyclic compunds were introduced into clinical practice in the UK. Although Axelrod had emphasised their role in blocking noradrenaline reuptake, it was found they also inhibited serotonin and to a lesser extent dopamine. In fact, imipramine was later found to block noradrenergic and serotonergic reuptake in almost equal measure. The tricyclic antidepressants also have effects on other neurotransmitter systems. For example, imipramine acts as an antagonist at histamine (H-1) receptors, noradrenergic alpha-1 receptors, and cholinergic muscarinic receptors. These 'extra' pharmacological actions add to the side effects of imipramine.

The effectiveness of the tricyclic antidepressants

There is little doubt that the tricyclic compounds are effective in treating depression. In general, studies have shown that, provided they are given over a period of several weeks, tricyclics improve the symptoms of depression in around 70 per cent of patients compared with 35 per cent for placebo (Lickey and Gordon 1991). A major multicentre trial of the effects of imipramine and other antidepressant treatments was carried by the Medical Research Council (1965) in the UK. This study showed that electroconvulsive therapy (ECT) was the most effective treatment after 4 weeks, but ECT and imipramine improved about two-thirds of patients when the period of treatment extended to 12 weeks. The improvement rates for the MAOI compound phenelzine and placebo were half of this figure.

Although the tricyclics are generally safer than the MAOIs, they are not free of side effects. For example, they have anticholinergic actions in the peripheral nervous system, which can produce dry mouth, constipation, blurred vision, dizziness and palpitations. In addition, tricyclics may act on the heart to produce irregular heartbeats and hypotension – the latter often causing the person to feel faint when standing up. Headache and fine muscular tremors are also common. But, the most worrying side effect of tricyclic antidepressants is that they can be lethal when taken in overdose. This is of great concern to doctors who are aware that depressed people are more likely to commit suicide than other groups of people.

The monoamine theory of depression

The discovery that drugs which increased noradrenaline, either by inhibiting monoamine oxidase or blocking the process of reuptake, had antidepressant effects – accompanied by evidence showing that reserpine caused depression by depleting the brain of catecholamines – led to the **catecholamine theory of depression**. This theory was first formulated by Joseph Schildkraut (1965), who argued that depression was the result of 'relative deficiency' (or reduced neurotransmission) of catecholamines, particularly noradrenaline, at synaptic sites in the brain. He also suggested that mania was due to an increased release of these neurotransmitters. Although there were others making a case for serotonin (see, for example, Coppen 1967), Schildkraut's paper was the most highly influential. As result of his hypothesis, noradrenaline became one of the most intensively studied neurotransmitters in the brain (see Healy 1997).

One way of testing the catecholamine theory was to look for biochemical abnormalities in the body fluids of depressed patients. If the theory was correct then one would expect to find a decrease in noradrenaline levels, or its major metabolites, in depressed people. However, most studies were unable to demonstrate this effect. For example, noradrenergic function can be examined by measuring one of its metabolites in the CSF called **MHPG** (3-methyl-4-hydroxyphenylglycol), which is derived in large part from the brain. Contrary to the predictions of the catecholamine theory, most studies have found great variability in the levels of MHPG in depression, with some patients showing low concentrations of MHPG and others high levels (Ashton 1992). Similarly, no changes in brain concentrations of noradrenaline, or its metabolites, are reliably found at post-mortem in people who had suffered depression or committed suicide (Slaby 1995).

Despite this, MHPG in the body fluids of patients undergoing treatment for depression is usually elevated. This shows that an increased turnover of noradrenaline occurs with antidepressant administration. Some reports also show that patients who have low urinary excretion of MHPG prior to treatment are the ones who best respond to tricyclic drugs (Schatzberg and Schildkraut 1995). There is also evidence confirming that patients suffering from mania show high levels of MHPG. This may also explain why tricyclic antidepressants are known to precipitate mania in patients with bipolar illness.

One of the main problems with the Schildkraut's catecholamine theory is that it underestimates the importance of serotonin, which confusingly is not a catecholamine but an **indolamine**. Researchers now know that serotonin has an important role to play in depression. For example, studies examining the amount of serotonin, or its main metabolite 5-hydroxyindoleacetic acid (**5-HIAA**) in the cerebrospinal fluid, have found reduced levels in certain groups of depressed patients – especially those with a suicdal predisposition (Asberg *et al.* 1987). Despite this, low 5-HIAA concentrations often persist after clinical recovery in these depressed patients, which casts doubt on the role of serotonin in depressed moods. Reduced 5-HIAA levels are also found in other individuals, including those that show aggressive, anxious, antisocial or impulsive behaviours (Brown and Linnoila 1990).

Another method of assessing serotonergic function in depressed individuals is to measure the uptake of this substance in blood platelets. In fact, serotonin was first isolated from blood (it was named 'serotonin' to indicate its origin from blood serum) where it has a vasoconstrictor function. Blood platelets also have a serotonergic uptake mechanism similar to that found in the brain. Experiments with blood platelets show that imipramine is a blocker of this pump. A number of studies examining platelets from depressed patients have also found a reduced uptake of serotonin, along with decreased numbers of uptake sites (Maes and Meltzer 1995). Thus, many depressed patients show serotonergic platelet dysfunction, although the reasons for this are not clear. The strongest evidence for serotonin involvement in depression, however, comes from examining the benefits of the selective serotonergic reuptake inhibitors (SSRIs). These drugs are selective for the serotonin reuptake pump, and successful in the treatment of depression (see later).

Because of the importance of serotonin in depression, most researchers now refer to the **monoamine theory of depression** (serotonin is both an indolamine and a monoamine) rather than the catecholamine theory. The monoamine theory is broader than the one proposed by Schildkraut since it 'proposes that depression is due to a deficiency in one or another of three monoamines, namely serotonin, noradrenaline and/or dopamine' (Stahl 2000). But, there are still some problems with the theory. For example, cocaine is a potent uptake blocker of dopamine, noradrenaline and serotonin, and while it can improve mood in normal individuals, it does not function effectively as an antidepressant in clinical populations (Post *et al.* 1974).

The receptor sensitivity theory of depression

Although the monoamine theory has dominated thinking into the causes of depression for several decades, it has always been subject to criticism and inconsistent findings (see Healy 1997). This was particularly the case in the 1970s, when attention began to switch from neurotransmitter levels to focus on receptors. One reason for this development was the problem in explaining why it took so long for antidepressant drugs to start working. For example, the inhibition of MAO or blocking of reuptake by TADs is known to take place almost immediately, yet it takes 2–3 weeks before these drugs start to alleviate the symptoms of depression. This indicated that it was not the direct pharmacological action of the antidepressant which was causing the improvement in mood, but a secondary or longer-acting change taking place in the monoaminergic neurons. But, where could this change be taking place? The likeliest sites were receptors located on the monoaminergic cells.

Monoaminergic neurons have two types of receptors: presynaptic and postsynaptic. The former are also called **autoreceptors** and these are located near the axon terminals of presynaptic neurons (although in some cases they are found on the cell bodies). On first sight, it may appear odd that monoaminergic neurons have autoreceptors – but they have an important function. In short, they provide a mechanism for monitoring the concentration of neurotransmitter in the synapse, and when levels increase they provide a feedback signal that inhibits further release from the presynaptic neuron. In this way, autoreceptors regulate the amount of neurotransmitter secreted by the presynaptic neuron. The best characterised type of autoreceptor is the **alpha-2 receptor** found on the presynaptic terminals of noradrenergic neurons (see Figure 11.5), and the **5-HT$_{1A}$** and **5-HT$_{1B}$ receptors** found on serotonergic neurons.

One explanation for the time lag of antidepressants is that continued exposure to the drug produces a gradual change in the functioning of the autoreceptors. For example, during the first days of treatment with a TAD, alpha-2 autoreceptors will compensate for the initial increase of synaptic noradrenaline by inhibiting its further release. In this way, the autoreceptors cancel out the initial effects of the TAD. However, with repeated administration of the drug, the autoreceptors begin to lose their inhibitory capability, causing more noradrenaline to be released. This may happen in one of two ways: either the autoreceptors become gradually insensitive to the high levels of noradrenaline in the synapse, or the number of autoreceptors become downregulated, that is, fewer in number. Whatever the mechanism (there is evidence that

Presynaptic
neuron

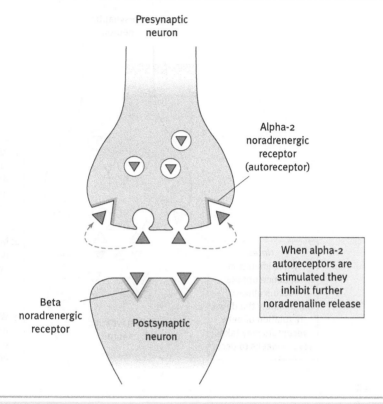

Alpha-2
noradrenergic
receptor
(autoreceptor)

When alpha-2
autoreceptors are
stimulated they
inhibit further
noradrenaline release

Beta
noradrenergic
receptor

Postsynaptic
neuron

Figure 11.5   How autoreceptors affect presynaptic transmitter release

both processes can occur), the effect is the same: the loss of inhibitory control by the autoreceptors causes the presynaptic neuron to gradually release more noradrenaline over the first few weeks of treatment.

But what about the receptors located on the postsynaptic neurons? Indeed, these are the main target for the neurotransmitter. The main type of noradrenergic receptor found postsynaptically are **beta receptors,** and, like the autoreceptors, they become down-regulated and less sensitive to increased exposure of noradrenaline in the synapse (a similar process may also occur for serotonergic 5-HT$_2$ receptors). Thus, antidepressants such as the MAOIs and TADS appear to work, and produce their gradual beneficial effects over 2–3 weeks, by producing the desensitisation and down-regulation of both presynaptic and postsynaptic receptors (Figure 11.6).

This theory also suggests that the aetiology of depression may have a receptor basis, rather than being due to a deficiency of neurotransmitter release. This proposal was made by Sulser *et al.* (1978), who argued that depression is caused by over-sensitive catecholaminergic receptors. In turn, effective antidepressant treatment desensitises these receptors. However, this explanation has other ramifications. For example, it is known that receptor desensitisation occurs through a process known as **phosphorylation,** which involves alterations in the shape of receptor proteins. In turn, this can alter the internal functioning of the cell in many ways, including changes in the opening of ion channels, sensitivity of second messenger systems such as cAMP, and even the activity of protein kinases which provide signalling input to the nucleus. This has made it very difficult to pin down exactly how antidepressant drugs are exerting their beneficial effects on mood.

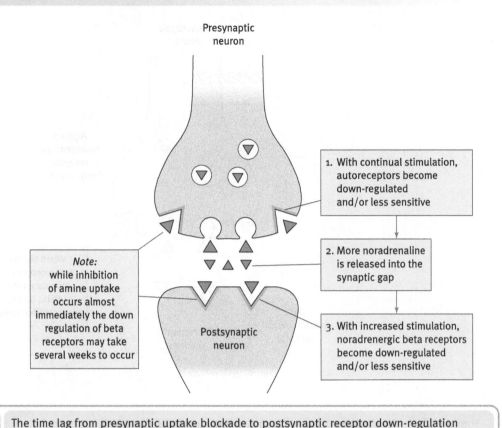

Figure 11.6   The time lag from presynaptic uptake blockade to postsynaptic receptor down-regulation

Selective serotonergic reuptake inhibitors

Although the TADs block noradrenergic reuptake, they also have a significant effect on inhibiting the uptake of serotonin. This fact, along with the serious side effects associated with TADs, led researchers to develop safer and more selective antidepressive compounds. A large number of 'second-generation' antidepressants have been developed over the years that are neither MAOIs nor TADs. One drug to emerge from this group is **fluoxetine (Prozac)**. This drug was manufactured by Eli Lilly and Company and first appeared in the United States during 1987. Within a few months Prozac was outselling all other antidepressants. In fact, it is the second most prescribed drug in the United States, while in the UK an estimated 3.5 million people take the drug with annual prescriptions being around 30 million. Moreover, its pharmacological profile is easy to understand as it blocks the reuptake of just one neurotransmitter: serotonin. Since then, a number of other **selective serotonergic reuptake inhibitors** (SSRIs) have been developed, including sertraline, paroxetine and citalopram.

Although the SSRIs are not superior to the TADS in terms of their antidepressive efficacy, they are safer (especially in overdose), tolerated well by the elderly, and have a broader range of uses. Indeed, they can be used to treat panic disorder, obsessive–compulsive disorder, bulimia and alcohol withdrawal. The SSRIs have also gained a reputation for making the patients 'feel good about themselves', which often leads to increased productivity and self-esteem. Despite this, the SSRIs can cause nausea, gastrointestinal problems, insomnia and headache. Another common problem is sexual dysfunction, including anorgasmia in women and delayed ejaculation in men. More worryingly, there are also rare cases where the SSRIs have been implicated in causing agitation, self-harm and even suicide (see Kingsland 2004).

The development of the SSRIs makes a strong case for the involvement of serotonin in the aetiology of depression, particularly as these drugs have little *direct* effect on noradrenergic receptors. However, the mechanism by which SSRIs work on the serotonergic systems of the brain to alleviate depression is not clear. Although there are some reports that prolonged administration of fluoxetine can down-regulate 5-HT$_1$ autoreceptors, this is not a consistent finding, and, if it does occur, is not a marked effect. To confuse things further, fluoxetine does not appear to down-regulate postsynaptic 5-HT$_2$ receptors. This is surprising because most TADs cause down-regulation of 5-HT$_2$ receptors along with noradrenergic beta ones. Despite this, fluoxetine inhibits the reuptake of serotonin into brain cells and platelets in both humans and animals (Beasley *et al.* 1992). Studies using microdialysis have also found that chronic administration of SSRIs increases extracellular levels of serotonin (Stanford 1996).

Interactions between noradrenaline and serotonin

Since there is evidence to implicate both noradrenaline and serotonin in depression, perhaps the best hypothesis is that both transmitters are involved in mood dysfunction. In other words, depression is a result of an imbalance in both noradrenaline and serotonergic systems, rather than being a dysfunction of just one. This idea is not a new. For example, Brodie and Shore (1957) suggested that the noradrenergic and serotonergic systems of the brain act in a way that is not dissimilar to the functions of the sympathetic and parasympathetic systems (i.e. autonomic nervous system). They proposed that the noradrenergic system of the brain is primarily involved in mediating vigilance and arousal, whereas the serotonergic system is more concerned with restful states and relaxation. They also suggested that depression may be related to reduced activity in the noradrenergic system (reduced arousal) in combination with an increase in serotonin sensitivity.

Another variation of this idea is the **permissive hypothesis** (Figure 11.7), which proposes that low levels of serotonin 'permit' abnormal levels of noradrenaline to produce either depression or mania (Prange *et al.* 1974). According to this theory, low levels of

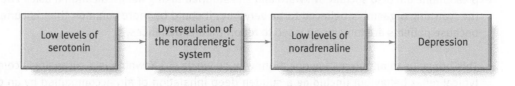

Figure 11.7   The permissive theory of depression

serotonin will cause dysregulation of the noradrenergic system. Indeed, there is considerable evidence that serotonin is an inhibitory transmitter which dampens or inhibits neural activity in a number of brain areas that receive noradrenergic input. According to this hypothesis, therefore, antidepressant drugs are effective because they reinstate the ability of serotonin to control noradrenaline, thus restoring the critical balance that controls emotional behaviour. Thus, by correcting the serotonergic system, one corrects the noradrenergic system.

There is evidence that both these neurotransmitter systems are indeed closely connected. For example, the locus coeruleus, which is the main source of noradrenergic fibres to the forebrain, and the dorsal raphe, which is the source of serotonergic fibres, are located close together in the brainstem. The dorsal raphe has been shown to be the target of noradrenergic fibres from the locus coeruleus. Moreover, serotonergic drugs (especially 5-HT$_2$ agonists) are known to change the firing rate of cells in the locus coeruleus (Mongeau *et al.* 1997). In addition, the projections of the locus coeruleus and raphe show a great deal of overlap in the forebrain, especially in the limbic system and cerebral cortex. Further support for the permissive hypothesis comes from studies showing that the repeated administration of SSRIs increases noradrenaline concentrations in certain areas of the brain, including frontal cortex and striatum (Goodnick and Goldstein 1998). Thus, the stabilisation of one transmitter system by antidepressants (e.g. serotonin) may help restore the functioning of other ones (e.g. noradrenaline).

When a yawn becomes an orgasm: a rare side effect of serotonergic antidepressants

When the selective serotonergic reuptake inhibitors (SSRIs) first appeared in the late 1980s they were widely seen as being relatively free of side effects. However, experience has shown that some of their side effects are more common and problematical than first realised. One problem is the increased likelihood of sexual dysfunction. For example, the SSRIs have been accused of reducing sexual desire, producing impotence, and making it difficult to reach orgasm in both men and woman (anorgasmia). Although the exact incidence of these side effects is uncertain, some studies suggest they may occur in more than 40 per cent of patients (Balon 1997). But, one of the most unusual side effects of the serotonergic antidepressants, albeit an extremely rare one, is spontaneous orgasm when the person yawns. This was first reported by McLean *et al.* (1984) who described two patients (a man and a woman) who experienced orgasms when they yawned – and two more patients (a man and a woman) who had intense sexual desires while yawning. Although the drug in this instance was clomipramine, which is a tricyclic compound, its main effect is on blocking serotonin rather than noradrenaline receptors. In fact, there have been similar reports with fluoxetine (Prozac), sertraline and bupropion. And, in some cases the orgasm may not be yawn-related. For example, one study reported the case of a woman who experienced a three-hour, spontaneous orgasm while shopping. She said the experience was pleasurable but also socially awkward and she stopped taking her medication (Pasick 2000). Although the 'yawning orgasm' is believed to be very rare, it could be more common than is currently thought because patients are too embarrassed to report their experiences.

This brings us to an interesting question: why do we yawn? Yawning is a surprisingly complex stereotypical reflex behaviour (including a sudden deep inhalation of air, accompanied by an open mouth, tightened cheek muscles, eye closure and increased heart rate) that occurs in all mammals – and can even be observed in the 12-week-old human foetus. For years, many people assumed that yawning was a response to lowered levels of oxygen. That is, when people become bored or tired, they breathe more slowly, and as carbon dioxide builds up in the blood, the brain produces a yawn to increase oxygen intake. However, Robert Provine has cast serious doubt on this idea by showing that when people breathe air containing different concentrations of oxygen and carbon dioxide, it has no effect on yawning (Provine *et al.* 1987). In another study, Provine found that physical exercise which caused subjects to breathe faster, also did not change the level of yawning. Thus, it is difficult to see how yawning is a response to decreasing oxygen levels.

One of the most curious facts about yawning is that it is highly contagious. Research shows that about 55 per cent of people will yawn within 5 minutes of seeing someone else doing it – and this effect even occurs in blind people if they hear others yawn. Remarkably, the contagious effect of yawning first manifests itself between the first and second years of life (Provine 1989). This has led to speculation that yawning may be a leftover response from a time in our evolutionary history when it acted to co-ordinate the social behaviour groups. Indeed, far from being always associated with sleepiness, yawning also occurs is situations of anxiety, conflict or physical readiness. Thus, yawns may have served as a signal to synchronise the behaviour of the whole group during times of change. However, this is far from certain and yawning remains one of the great mysteries of human nature.

The hypothalamic–pituitary–adrenal axis and depression

Depression is more than just a mental disorder. People suffering from clinical depression often show a number of hormonal irregularities, including elevated levels of **cortisol**, which is a 'stress' hormone released by the adrenal glands. Cortisol is a glucocorticoid whose secretion is controlled by the **hypothalamic–pituitary–adrenal axis** (Figure 11.8). To be more specific, the paraventricular region of the hypothalamus secretes **corticotropin-releasing factor (CRF)**, which acts on the pituitary gland to induce secretion of **adrenocorticotropic hormone (ACTH)**. This blood-borne chemical then stimulates the adrenal cortex to release cortisol. When levels reach a certain point, the secretion is 'switched off' by cortisol acting on the pituitary and hypothalamus to suppress ACTH release (a process known as negative feedback). Interestingly, there are also glucocorticoid receptors in other regions of the brain, including the amygdala and hippocampus. Both these structures influence the hypothalamus: the amygdala facilitating CRF release, and the hippocampus inhibiting it.

The main function of cortisol is to maintain the correct chemical balance of the body in the face of change and adversity. In particular, cortisol increases the production of blood glucose to provide greater energy during periods of acute or prolonged stress. Cortisol also acts to speed up the body's metabolism for energy needs, which affects just about every organ and tissue in the body. This hormone also inhibits the immune system, decreases inflammatory reactions, and affects gene transcription in the nuclei of cells. The effects of cortisol deficiency can be seen in **Addison's disease**, which is characterised by weight loss, muscle weakness, fatigue and low blood pressure along with psychological symptoms including memory disturbances, apathy and altered mood.

Depressed persons show elevated cortisol levels because their illness is a highly stressful condition. But, there may be more to increased cortisol secretion in depression

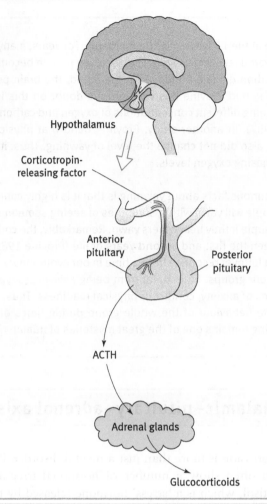

Hypothalamus

Corticotropin-
releasing factor

Anterior
pituitary

Posterior
pituitary

ACTH

Adrenal glands

Glucocorticoids

Figure 11.8   The hypothalamic–pituitary–adrenal axis

than this. In fact, in some cases, there appears to be a dysfunction of the hypothalamic–pituitary–adrenal axis. Evidence supporting this idea comes from the **dexamethasone test**. Dexamethasone is a synthetic glucocorticoid, and if injected into an individual, it will normally suppress ACTH release from the pituitary gland. In turn, this will cause cortisol secretion to be inhibited from the adrenal cortex. These effects occur because the dexamethasone 'fools' the hypothalamus into believing that there are high levels of cortisol in the blood. In response to this, the hypothalamus switches off the pituitary's secretion of ACTH. However, in many people with depression, the dexamethasone suppression does not occur – and, if anything, they are more likely to show an increase in cortisol. One explanation is that depressed people have reduced numbers of hypothalamic (or possibly hippocampal) glucocorticoid receptors that detect cortisol, which lessens the impact of negative feedback. Whatever the cause, studies show that the successful treatment of depression normally reinstates the dexamethasone effect.

It has been proposed that high levels of cortisol caused by the stress of depression may eventually lead to the down-regulation of glucocorticoid receptors in the brain, or to them becoming less sensitive to the feedback signal. Both would help explain the lack of a dexamethasone effect in depression. In this respect, it is interesting to note that depression is one of the first symptoms to appear in **Cushing's disease**, where there is hypersecretion of cortisol from the adrenal cortex. Furthermore, Reul *et al.* (1993, 1994) has shown that effective antidepressant treatment increases the activity of genes involved in the formation of proteins that comprise hypothalamic glucocorticoid receptors. For example, these researchers found that five weeks of treatment with desipramine produced a 25 per cent increase in the number of glucocorticoid receptors in the hypothalamus, and that this rise paralleled the clinical improvement of depression. Thus, antidepressants may exert part of their effect by helping to restore the normal functioning of the hypothalamic–pituitary–adrenal axis.

Depression is also associated with circadian rhythm dysfunction, with peaks of hormone release occurring at the wrong time or with reduced amplitude. In particular, this can cause people with depression to experience sleep disturbances, including insomnia and early morning awakenings. To make matters worse, this is likely to cause other bodily rhythms such as temperature to fall out of phase with the sleep patterns. It is not surprising, therefore, that many people with depression feel physically ill in addition to their mental anguish.

The genetics of depression

It is believed that genetic factors play an important role in the aetiology of unipolar depression. For example, researchers have found a concordance rate of around 50 per cent for identical twins compared with 20 per cent for fraternal twins (Kendler *et al.* 1993). These types of figures also occur when the individuals have been separated from their biological parents and reared in separate environments. For instance, in a study of 71 Danish adopted individuals who had been treated with major depression, a similar frequency of depression was found among the biological relatives but not among the adoptive relatives (Wender *et al.* 1986). In fact, the relative risk of major depression is 2–5 times greater in the relatives of depressed patients than in the relatives of controls (Stoudemire 1998).

These findings have led to a search for the genes that may cause depression. However, no gene, or **polymorphisms** (unique sections of DNA within a gene), has so far been unequivocally linked with a depressive mood disorder. One reason for the lack of success may be that depression is influenced by several genes. Another problem is that depression is often accompanied by high levels of anxiety, that is, individuals with a predisposition to depression tend to show high emotional reactivity. This confounds the issue of finding specific genes, and adds to the complexity of possible genetic interactions with the environment.

The importance of gene–environment interactions was shown in a long-term study by Caspi *et al.* (2003), who tracked the development of depression in 847 subjects from New Zealand for nearly thirty years. One of the variables cloesly examined was the number of stressful life events that had taken place between the ages of 21 and 26. In addition, the researchers grouped the subjects according to the types of polymorphism that they carried for the serotonin reuptake pump (see above). In fact, there are two alleles, called 'short' and 'long', which refers to the length of the DNA sequence found in each gene. Although both genes produce the same serotonin uptake protein, the 'long' polymorphism makes more of it. In effect, this means that the 'long' allele is associated with a more efficient transcription of the gene, resulting in greater numbers of protein molecules, which increases the efficiency of serotonin uptake activity.

It was found that 17 per cent of the subjects had a pair of short alleles, 51 per cent had one short and one long allele, and 31 per cent had a pair of long alleles (individuals inherit an allele from each parent – see Chapter 14). Although there was no difference between these groups in the number of stressful life events experienced, there was a clear effect of genotype on emotional reactivity to events. In fact, the subjects who had two short alleles were more likely to react with a major depressive episode and experience thoughts of suicide than were people with two long alleles. The individuals with mixed genes fell between these two extremes.

This study shows that the way in which an individual responds to aversive and stressful events is influenced by their genetic make-up. But, perhaps more importantly, it also shows that a gene has an effect on depression only if that individual is exposed to particular life events. Put another way, a susceptibility to depression requires the right set of environmental events for it to be expressed. Alternatively, the effects of the gene may be masked where environmental conditions are benign. To make matters more complex, researchers have now found at least 24 polymorphisms in the serotonin transporter gene, which causes at least 9 amino acid changes in the protein. This transcription of this gene is also affected by glucocorticoid hormones (Glatz *et al.* 2003).

Bipolar disorder and the discovery of lithium

A person who suffers from bipolar disorder alternates between periods of mania and periods of depression, generally passing through a period of relative normality on the way. Both types of mood may be so severe that they disrupt normal activities and everyday living. During a manic episode an individual is excessively energetic. They are usually elated and self-confident, gregarious, flirt from one grandiose plan to the next, and show a diminished need to sleep. In addition, the person may exhibit disregard for danger and engage in high-risk behaviours such as sexual promiscuity, increased spending, substance abuse and gambling. If the mania persists it may lead to the emergence of delusions and hallucinations. However, at some point, the person slows down, their range of interests diminishes, and they become more withdrawn. Although the person may feel well at this point, it is likely that this phase will develop into a period of severe depression. The length of time that an individual remains well between episodes of illness varies from one person to the next. Some people may have only two or three episodes of illness in their entire life. Others may have four or more episodes per year (referred to as 'rapid cycling'). In a few cases, the cycle of mania and depression may be so regular that the person is able to plan holidays and social events to avoid the difficult periods.

The type of condition described above is sometimes called **bipolar I disorder**. A related but less severe form of the illness is **bipolar II disorder**, which is characterised by recurrent episodes of major depression and hypomania, the latter being characterised by an elevated and expansive mood. Hypomania is similar to mania but without gross lapses of impulse and judgement. Consequently, this disorder produces significantly less disruption of family, social and occupational life, although it still requires clinical treatment.

Evidence shows that bipolar illness has a different biological basis from unipolar depression. For example, not only is the incidence of bipolar illness considerably less than for unipolar depression (around 1 per cent, compared with 5 per cent for unipolar depression), but its age of onset also tends to be earlier, with most cases first occurring between the ages of 18 and 24 years. It also occurs equally in males and females (unlike unipolar depression) and tends to be a lifelong disease. Bipolar illness also appears to be strongly genetic. It is found in about 25 per cent of first-degree relatives of manic depressive parents, and the concordance rates for identical and fraternal twins are around 80 per cent and 20 per cent, respectively (Shastry 2005). The corresponding figures for unipolar depression are 50 per cent and 20 per cent. But perhaps the most convincing evidence that bipolar illness is different from unipolar depression lies in the fact that it is best treated with a drug called **lithium**. In fact, treatment with tricyclic antidepressants is not advisable as these drugs often exacerbate the symptoms of bipolar illness by precipitating mania, although this effect appears to be significantly less with the SSRIs.

Lithium salts were first used in the nineteenth century to treat gout because they were believed to 'dissolve' the uric acid that accumulated in the joints. Their usefulness in bipolar illness, however, was not reported until 1949. The story starts in the mid-1940s when an Australian psychiatrist called John Cade hypothesised that mania might be due to a substance that builds up in the body fluids. If this was the case, Cade reasoned, it should be possible to induce mania in guinea pigs by injecting them with urine taken from manic patients. However, urine also contains other substances, including urates, and so in order to provide a control group Cade injected some animals with uric acid dissolved in lithium. To his surprise, Cade found that this combination produced marked sedation in his animals. In fact, this effect turned out to be due to the effects of lithium. There was a clinical need for sedative drugs in psychiatry, and when Cade gave lithium to bipolar patients he found it quickly stabilised their moods and calmed them down.

Following Cade's report the use of lithium quickly spread to Europe. However, it took longer to become used in the United States because lithium had been banned in 1949 after producing cardiac problems in patients who had used it as a salt replacement in their diet. The evidence from a large number of clinical trials shows that lithium is effective for treating manic depression. Although the results of these studies vary, the majority of bipolar patients respond positively to lithium. According to Goodwin and Jamison (1990) about 50 per cent of patients respond well to lithium, while the rest show either a partial response, or no benefit at all (this is often the case if they suffer from a rapid cycling disorder or have chronic depression). Moreover, Lickey and Gordon (1991) have reported that, without lithium, the typical bipolar patient has a manic episode about every 14 months, whereas this occurs every 9 years if lithium is taken. To provide this type of protection, however, lithium has to be taken daily, and for the best part of one's life. Side effects can include weight gain, nausea, diarrhoea, thirst, hand tremor and fatigue. There is also a risk of renal damage with long-term treatment, which requires careful monitoring.

Another drug which is effective in the treatment of bipolar illness is **carbamazepine**, which is sometimes used as an anticonvulsant. The overall efficacy of this substance is similar to lithium, although it may have a faster onset of action for treating mania (lithium generally takes a week or more to produce a theraputic effect). Carbamazepine is also useful for patients who are not helped by lithium, and in some cases the combination of lithium and carbamazepine is more effective than when both are given alone. Another drug with a similar effect to carbamazepine is **sodium valporate**, which is also an anticonvulsant.

How does lithium work?

The action of lithium is specific for controlling mania as it has little effect on people who are suffering from unipolar depression. Thus, if we can understand how lithium works on the brain, we should be able to infer the biochemical processes that are involved in producing manic depression. Unfortunately, despite years of intensive study, the pharmacological mechanism by which lithium exerts its relief of mania is not well established. This is largely because of the nature of lithium itself: it is a simple molecule that has the potential to act on just about every neurochemical system of the brain and at many different levels.

Lithium is the third lightest element (behind hydrogen and helium) and belongs to the alkali metal family, which includes sodium and potassium. Because it has a single electron in its outer shell, it is very unstable and exists mainly as an ion, which gives it a positive charge (see Chapter 1 for a discussion of ions). In its clinical formulation it comes as lithium carbonate (a salt), which allows the ions to be dispersed in water. Since it is a positively charged ion, lithium can substitute for other positively charged ions such as sodium, potassium, calcium and magnesium – all of which play an important role in brain functioning. Indeed, lithium is known to be transported into neurons by the **sodium–potassium pump**, although it is slow to be removed from the cells by this mechanism. Thus, it is possible that lithium is exerting its antimanic action by reducing the membrane excitability of the neuron. Another mechanism of action for lithium may involve its partial substitution for calcium ions. As we saw in Chapter 1, calcium ions are involved in the process of exocytosis which results in the release of neurotransmitters from their vesicles at synaptic endings. By competing with calcium in this process, lithium may affect neurotransmitter release (Feldman *et al.* 1997).

One neurotransmitter believed to be significantly affected by lithium treatment is serotonin. There are reports that lithium elevates levels of serotonin in certain areas of the brain (Price *et al.* 1990), as well as increasing the release of this neurotransmitter in response to electrical stimulation of the raphe (Ashton 1992). Some studies have also reported increased levels of 5-HIAA in the cerebrospinal fluid following lithium therapy in bipolar patients, although these findings are not always statistically significant. Lithium appears to have a complex effect on serotonin receptors. For example, it has been shown to reduce 5-HT$_2$ receptors in the frontal cortex, and 5-HT$_1$ receptors in the hippocampus. And, there is evidence that serotonergic autoreceptors become desensitised with lithium treatment. This may be one mechanism by which lithium acts to increase levels of serotonin (Feldman *et al.* 1997).

There is also evidence that lithium affects the transduction of neurotransmitter-initiated signals inside the cell by acting on second messenger systems. For example, lithium inhibits the synthesis of **cyclic adenosine monophosphate (cAMP)**, which is activated by several neurotransmitters, including noradrenaline. Thus, lithium dampens the effects of noradrenaline on nerve cells by inhibiting cAMP. In addition, it also enhances the reuptake of this neurotransmitter, which leads to its more rapid removal from the synapse (Diaz 1997). Lithium also interferes with phosphoinositol metabolism within nerve cells, whose by-products include the formation of the second messengers **inositol triphosphate** and **diacylglycerol**. Phosphoinositol metabolism is regulated by a range of neurotransmitters, including serotonin and acetylcholine. Moreover, this second messenger system affects levels of **protein kinase C**, which is able to influence gene expression in the nucleus. Thus, lithium has the potential to exert widespread actions on cell function. It is not surprising, therefore, that lithium has the potential to influence the synthesis, release or uptake of nearly every neurotransmitter, or cellular process, in the brain (Jope 1999). Nonetheless, it may be significant that, on the balance of evidence, lithium appears to increase serotonergic activity while reducing that of noradrenaline.

Schizophrenia: an introduction

If one is asked to imagine a mental illness, it is likely that something resembling **schizophrenia** will come to mind. Schizophrenia belongs to a group of disorders that are called **psychosis** in which the affected individual exhibits a severe distortion in perceiving and understanding reality. It is also one of the most devastating illnesses for its victims. Although the first description of the disorder is normally credited to the German psychiatrist Emil Kraepelin who, in 1896, called it **dementia praecox** (early dementia), the term 'schizophrenia' was first introduced in 1911 by Eugen Bleuler, who derived it from the Greek *schizio* meaning 'split' and *phreno* meaning 'mind'. By adopting this term, Bleuler was emphasising the fragmented thought processes that were 'split from reality' as one of the key features of the illness. However, in some respects the term is an unfortunate one as it has been confused (at least in the layperson's mind) with a condition known as **multiple personality syndrome**, where the person exhibits two or more different personalities – such as Dr Jekyll and Mr Hyde. A person with schizophrenia, however, does not have multiple personalities. Instead, they have a personality that is overpowered by disturbances of mental function, emotion and behaviour.

One of the most common features of schizophrenia is the occurrence of bizarre delusions, which are beliefs contrary to fact. For example, the schizophrenic may believe that they are being controlled by others (e.g. messages are being broadcast to them by radio), or are being persecuted (e.g. someone is trying to poison them). In some individuals the whole personality may become deluded so that the schizophrenic believes they are somebody else (perhaps Napoleon or Jesus), or that they have a divine mission to fulfil. These delusions may also be accompanied by auditory hallucinations that include voices telling the schizophrenic what to do, along with tactile and olfactory disturbances. Even if the schizophrenic is free of delusions and hallucinations, the continuity of their thought is often fragmented, making their behaviour or speech incomprehensible or puzzling. The schizophrenic is also likely to have abnormal emotions, including increased excitability, blunted affect, or feelings that most normal people would consider strange or inappropriate. This may result in the schizophrenic showing signs of excitement or agitation (for example, nervously pacing up and down and talking in repetitive rhymes), or being lethargic and catatonic.

The clinical picture of schizophrenia just described is a stereotypical one. In reality, there are different types of schizophrenia, each with its own set of symptoms. Thus, schizophrenia should be regarded as a heterogeneous set of disorders. Because of this, schizophrenia is a difficult disorder to define accurately. Some investigators have divided the symptoms of schizophrenia into two categories: positive and negative. **Positive symptoms** are those that reflect overactive brain function such as hallucinations, delusions, confused thinking and exaggerated emotions. **Negative symptoms** are those that seem to reflect underaroused brain function and include poverty of thought or speech, blunted affect and social withdrawal. Some types of schizophrenia are predominantly characterised by positive symptoms, others by negative symptoms, and some by a mixture of the two (Crow 1980).

424 INTRODUCTION TO BIOPSYCHOLOGY

The epidemiology of schizophrenia

Estimates of the incidence (the number of new occurrences over a given period) and prevalence (the number of actual cases at a given point) of schizophrenia depend on the criteria for diagnosis and the population surveyed. Nonetheless, the annual incidence of schizophrenia is often cited as 0.2–0.4 per 1,000, with a lifetime prevalence risk of about 1 per cent (Jablensky 1997). It is also likely that another 2–3 per cent of the population shows some borderline symptoms. The incidence of schizophrenia is the same for both sexes, although men tend to have an earlier age of onset than women (18 and 25 years, respectively), and a more severe illness including more hospital admissions. Despite this, a sizeable number of schizophrenic cases also occur after the age of 40 years. Although variations in the prevalence and incidence of schizophrenia across different countries have been reported, these differences are reduced when strict diagnostic criteria are used. Indeed, in a study by the World Health Organization, the incidence of schizophrenia was found to be very similar in ten countries which included developed and third world countries (Jablensky et al. 1992).

In most cases, schizophrenia is an acute condition which shows considerable fluctuation in severity across life, with periods of remission. However, it can be chronic (or more permanent), and this form is often characterised by negative symptoms including lack of drive, social withdrawal and emotional apathy. For example, in a fifteen-year follow-up of 82 schizophrenic patients, it was found that 12 per cent had fully recovered after a single episode of psychosis, and another 30 per cent experienced psychotic episodes interspersed with good mental health. Another 33 per cent exhibited repeated and increasingly severe periods of psychosis with negative symptoms, while 11 per cent had a single psychotic episode that showed no long-term recovery (Wiersma et al. 1998) (Figure 11.9). These findings also lend further support to the idea that schizophrenia is not a single illness, but a group of related disorders.

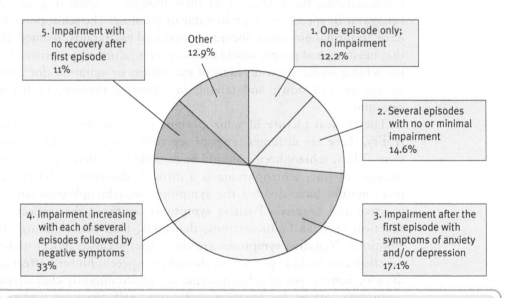

Figure 11.9 Outcomes of schizophrenia

Source: L.A. Freberg, *Discovering Biological Psychology*, p. 458. Copyright © 2006 by Houghton Mifflin Company

Among psychiatric disorders, schizophrenia is one of the most disabling and requires a disproportionate share of mental health services. For example, schizophrenic patients occupy about 25 per cent of all psychiatric hospital beds, and make up 50 per cent of all admissions to mental institutions. In 1996, the total cost of treating schizophrenia was estimated to be £2.6 billion for the UK, and around $44.9 billion in the United States. There is also the enormous emotional cost to patient, family and society at large. In fact, the combined economic and social costs of schizophrenia place it among the world's top ten causes of disability, and this holds true across both developed and developing countries (Musser and McGurk 2004).

The discovery of antipsychotic drugs

Prior to the 1950s, there were no effective drugs to treat schizophrenia. Anyone unfortunate enough to be suffering from a psychosis was probably given a barbiturate to make them sleep, or an insulin injection to provide a 'revitalising' shock to the brain. Although such treatments were the desperate attempts by well meaning psychiatrists to do something to help their patients, they were ineffective. Consequently many people with schizophrenia were housed in institutions, often for long periods of time, in sterile and boring environments. They had little chance of recovery. Moreover, figures show that the number of patients kept in mental institutions was rising by about 10–15 per cent each year in the first half of the twentieth century (Snyder 1986). There was a desperate need to develop better treatments.

As with the development of antidepressants, the discovery of the first antipsychotics was somewhat fortuitous. In the 1940s the Rhône-Poulenc Drug Company began to develop antihistamine compounds, which are used today to treat allergic reactions. It was soon found, however, that many of these drugs produced marked sedation. One person asked to test these compounds was the French doctor Henri Laborit, and it led to the discovery of **chlorpromazine**, which produced strong calming properties without loss of consciousness. Laborit recommended chlorpromazine to his colleagues for testing on agitated patients. Although the initial results were disappointing, in 1951 two French psychiatrists, Jean Delay and Pierre Deniker, working independently found that chlorpromazine improved schizophrenia. Importantly, it appeared to reduce the symptoms of schizophrenia rather than cause sedation. For example, hallucinations and delusions disappeared with the patient showing more logical thought processes. Agitated patients were calmed, whereas catatonic patients became more active, allowing them to engage more effectively in psychotherapy.

Chlorpromazine was a 'true' antipsychotic drug, and it was marketed for the treatment of schizophrenia in 1954, under the trade name **Thorazine**. Thus, chlorpromazine was the first drug to be used to treat a specific mental illness. It also had an immediate impact, and within a few years of its introduction the number of people in mental institutions began to show a marked decline. For example, in the United States the number of people being treated in hospitals and institutions for mental illness was around 375 per 100,000 of the population. But, in the decade after 1954, this figure fell by about 50 per cent. Although there were other factors at work, and the fall was not as dramatic in Europe, there is little doubt that Thorazine heralded a new dawn in psychiatry.

Chlorpromazine belongs to a class of drugs known as the **phenothiazines** (a class of drug first synthesised as dyes by the German dye industry in the late nineteenth century). Many other phenothiazines were also found to have useful antipsychotic properties. However, it soon became clear that these drugs were not the only ones that produced improvement in schizophrenic patients. In Belgium, the pharmacologist Paul Janssen discovered another antipsychotic drug (first synthesised in 1958) which became known as **haloperidol**. This drug not only belonged to a different class of agents known as the **butyrophenomes**, but was as effective at treating schizophrenia and had fewer side effects. It replaced Thorazine in terms of popularity and remains today the most commonly used drug to treat schizophrenia.

Origins of the dopamine theory of schizophrenia

How, then, do chlorpromazine and haloperidol work to reduce the symptoms of schizophrenia? Beginning in the late 1950s, evidence began to show that both drugs exerted their main pharmacological effects by reducing **dopamine** activity in the brain. One of the first lines of evidence to support this theory came from the drug **reserpine**. As we have seen above, this drug was known to deplete the brain of catecholamines, and to precipitate depression. But, prior to this, reserpine had been shown to have antipsychotic effects in schizophrenic patients. In addition, reserpine along with chlorpromazine and haloperidol often produced Parkinson-like side effects such as rigidity and tremor when given in high doses. This suggested that all these drugs were having similar effects on the brain. The possibility arose, therefore, that chlorpromazine and haloperidol were exerting similar effects to reserpine. In other words, they were reducing levels of noradrenaline and/or dopamine in the brain.

This view was reinforced in 1960 when Oleh Hornykiewicz working in Vienna measured the concentrations of dopamine in the brains of Parkinson's victims, and found a large decrease of about 90 per cent in the striatum. Since reserpine and the other antipsychotics produced Parkinson-like symptoms, this was evidence that these drugs were reducing dopamine activity. This finding also provided an important clue about the underlying neurochemical basis of schizophrenia. Put simply, if reserpine and the antipsychotics were reducing dopamine activity, this implied that psychosis was being caused by an excess, or overactivity, of this neurotransmitter in the brain. This hypothesis formed the basis for the **dopamine theory of schizophrenia**.

Further support for the involvement of dopamine in schizophrenia came from the stimulant **amphetamine**. When taken in high amounts, this drug is associated with a number of side effects, including restlessness, confusion and agitated behaviour. Moreover, large overdoses can cause a psychosis that includes hallucinations, delusions and paranoia, which is indistinguishable from schizophrenia (Connell 1958). And, as might be expected, amphetamine has an effect on the brain that is opposite to reserpine and chlorpromazine/haloperidol, that is, it causes the release of catecholamines, particularly dopamine, from nerve terminals (Leake 1958) (Figure 11.10). This was further evidence to show that excess dopaminergic activity caused schizophrenia.

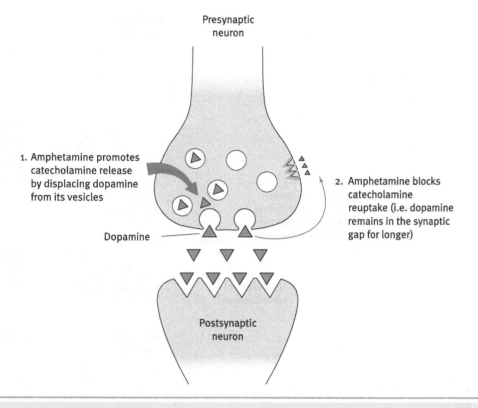

Presynaptic
neuron

1. Amphetamine promotes
catecholamine release
by displacing dopamine
from its vesicles

2. Amphetamine blocks
catecholamine
reuptake (i.e. dopamine
remains in the synaptic
gap for longer)

Dopamine

Postsynaptic
neuron

Figure 11.10   The mechanism by which amphetamine exerts its pharmacological effects

How do antipsychotic drugs work?

It was expected that chlorpromazine and haloperidol would have pharmacological effects similar to reserpine, and reduce brain levels of dopamine. However, in 1963, Avrid Carlsson and Margit Lindqvist showed this was not the case. When they injected mice with chlorpromazine, they found that it did not deplete the brain of catecholamines. In fact, the reverse was true, at least in the short term, as the level of dopaminergic metabolites increased – a finding that showed that chlorpromazine was enhancing the release of dopamine, which was then being broken down in the synapse. Thus, despite similar behavioural effects, reserpine and chlorpromazine were having very different neurochemical effects on the brain (Carlsson and Lindqvist 1963).

To account for these results, Carlsson and Lindqvist proposed a theory that viewed chlorpromazine as acting as a 'false' neurotransmitter. That is, chlorpromazine was attaching itself to the dopamine receptor, which then blocked the dopamine from binding to this site. Carlsson and Lindqvist also hypothesised that if dopamine was unable to get to its receptors, the presynaptic neurons would respond by increasing release of this neurotransmitter in an attempt to compensate for the postsynaptic deficit. This, of course, assumed that the presynaptic neurons received a 'message' from the postsynaptic ones informing them of the lack of dopamine stimulation. The net result of this receptor blockade would therefore be an increased release of dopamine, which was then broken down in the synaptic cleft, causing the increased level of metabolites (Figure 11.11).

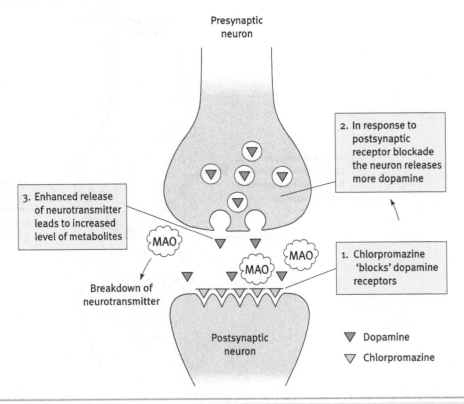

Presynaptic
neuron

2. In response to
postsynaptic
receptor blockade
the neuron releases
more dopamine

3. Enhanced release
of neurotransmitter
leads to increased
level of metabolites

MAO

MAO

MAO

1. Chlorpromazine
'blocks' dopamine
receptors

Breakdown of
neurotransmitter

Postsynaptic
neuron

▼ Dopamine

▽ Chlorpromazine

Figure 11.11 The Carlsson and Lindqvist (1963) theory of how chlorpromazine and haloperidol produce their pharmacological effects

Although this was an interesting idea, there was no way of proving the theory in the early 1960s. In fact, there was no way of identifying receptors at this time, let alone establishing whether they were 'blocked'. Nonetheless, Carlsson and Linqvist were to be eventually proved correct in the 1970s when a technique called **radioligand binding** was developed. In this procedure, a radioactive tracer is added to a neurochemical or drug that is known to attach itself to certain receptors. This substance is washed through specially prepared brain tissue taken from regions believed to contain high numbers of the appropriate receptor. Afterwards, the brain tissue will emit a small amount of radioactivity. This emission is derived from the drug bound to the tissue's receptors, and the level of radioactivity allows an estimate of the receptor numbers to be made. This procedure showed that dopamine attached itself to striatal tissue, which was believed to contain large numbers of dopamine receptors (Cresse *et al.* 1976).

Following the development of this technique, the effects of chlorpromazine and haloperidol on displacing radioactive dopamine was examined in a procedure known as **competitive binding**. This technique rests on the assumption that if there are drugs which block dopamine receptors, they should be able to compete with the dopamine in the radioligand binding procedure. Or put another way, the competition will result in less radioactivity being emitted from the dopamine receptor. Indeed, this is what occurred when chlorpromazine was washed through striatal tissue along with radioactive dopamine. In fact, not only did chlorpromazine block the effects of dopamine, but the clinical potency of a wide range of antischizophrenic drugs was found to correlate with their ability to displace dopamine. The more effective a given drug was at treating schizophrenia, the better it was at blocking dopamine receptors (Figure 11.12).

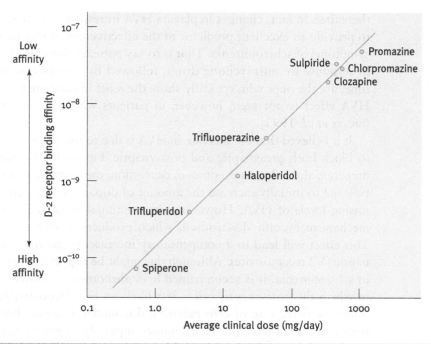

Figure 11.12 Graph showing the correlation between the clinical potencies of antipsychotic drugs and their ability to block the D-2 dopamine receptor

Haloperidol, however, was a notable exception to this rule. The competitive binding technique indicated that haloperidol was weak at binding with dopamine receptors in the striatum. That is, its poor ability to bind with striatal dopamine receptors did not match its potency at treating schizophrenia. Nonetheless, it was clear that haloperidol bound to striatal tissue and other dopaminergic areas in the brain. How could this puzzling finding be explained? The answer is that there are more than one type of dopaminergic receptor in the brain (Kebbian and Calne 1979). In fact, in the early 1980s, the brain was shown to contain two types of dopamine receptor, which were called D-1 and D-2.* Moreover, it was found that while chlorpromazine bound with equal affinity to both D-1 and D-2 receptors, haloperidol bound only to D-2 receptors. This not only explained the discrepant results obtained with competitive binding, but also indicated that antipsychotic drugs worked by blocking D-2 receptors. Taking this discovery one step further, it also implicated the D-2 receptor in the aetiology of schizophrenia.

A closer look at how antipsychotic drugs work

The chronic administration of both chlorpromazine and haloperidol is associated with an initial increase in dopaminergic metabolites such as **homovanillic acid (HVA)** over the first four days of treatment, followed by a gradual decrease of this substance

---

*It is now known that the brain contains five types of dopamine receptor designated D-1 to D-5.

430 INTRODUCTION TO BIOPSYCHOLOGY

thereafter. In fact, changes in plasma HVA in response to drug administration appear to provide an excellent predictor of the effectiveness of this treatment in reducing the symptoms of schizophrenia. That is to say patients showing the highest levels of HVA in response to antipsychotic drugs, followed by a reduction of this metabolite with time, are the ones who typically show the most improvement with drug therapy. This HVA effect is not seen, however, in patients who have mainly negative symptoms (Siever *et al.* 1993).

It is believed that the increase in HVA is due to the ability of the antipsychotic drugs to block both presynaptic and postsynaptic dopamine D-2 receptors. As with nora-drenergic alpha-2 autoreceptors in depression, the presynaptic D-2 receptor blockade is believed to initially increase the amount of dopamine released by the neuron, thereby raising levels of HVA. However, with continual increased stimulation, this receptor mechanism become desensitised, which produces a decrease in dopamine secretion. This effect will lead to a compensatory increase, or greater sensitivity, of the postsy-naptic D-2 receptor sites. Although this might be expected to exacerbate the symptoms of schizophrenia, it is accompanied by a phenomenon known as **depolarisation block** in which the postsynaptic cell is less likely to fire. Depolarisation block not only re-duces the firing rate of cells receiving dopaminergic input, but also makes them less responsive to other types of excitatory input. For reasons that are not clear, as the number of postsynaptic receptors increases and depolarisation block occurs, the syn-thesis and release of dopamine decreases in the presynaptic neurons. And, this appears to be the reason why levels of plasma HVA decline with antipsychotic treatment (Friedhoff and Silva 1995).

Problems with the dopamine theory

If chlorpromazine and haloperidol work by blocking dopamine receptors, this implies that schizophrenia is caused by excess dopaminergic activity. This idea is supported by the finding that amphetamine, which causes the release of dopamine from nerve end-ings in the brain, can produce a psychosis similar to that found in schizophrenia. Thus, one might predict that the brains of schizophrenics will contain high levels of dopamine. However, this appears not to be the case. Although there is some variation in the results, most studies of dopamine metabolites such as HVA in the cerebrospinal fluid have not found increased levels in untreated psychotic patients (Markianos *et al.* 1992). Similarly, despite some reports to the contrary, there is little consistent evidence showing increased levels of dopamine or its metabolites in the brain at post-mortem. Further evidence against the dopamine hypothesis comes from the hormone **prolactin**. This hormone is released by the anterior pituitary and is under the control of an in-hibitory dopamine pathway. If schizophrenia was due to excess dopamine release one might expect prolactin levels to be significantly reduced in psychotic patients. However, most studies have not found any difference between unmedicated schizophrenic patients and controls (Rubin 1987).

An alternative version of the dopamine theory is that schizophrenics have a far greater sensitivity to dopamine. This points more towards a greater proliferation of dopamine receptors in the brain. Indeed, a number of early studies using functional scanning techniques such as PET to examine this issue found increased numbers of dopamine D-2 receptors, especially in the striatum of schizophrenic patients (Jaskiw and Kleinman 1988). More recently, post-mortem studies have revealed greater numbers of D-3 and D-4 receptors in schizophrenics, with the former being most noticeable in the striatum and the latter in the nucleus accumbens. But, again, there is great inconsistency in the experimental findings, and this is partly due to the fact that antipsychotic drugs will also produce up-regulation of dopamine receptors. Although some studies have reported increased numbers of D-2 receptors in unmedicated schizophrenic patients who had been drug-free for some time, others have not confirmed these findings (Farde *et al.* 1990; Pilowsky *et al.* 1994). Thus, there is some uncertainty regarding dopamine receptors in schizophrenia. An explanation may have been provided by Kestler *et al.* (2001) who, in an extensive review of the literature, have concluded that there are moderate increases in dopamine receptors in some, but not all, groups of schizophrenia.

Another problem with the dopamine theory is that antipsychotic drugs block receptors within a day or two, although it takes several weeks for clinical benefits to occur. This is reflected in an initial rise in HVA levels, followed by their gradual decline. Thus, it is likely that the blockade of dopaminergic receptors is not the final mechanism by which these drugs work. Indeed, low levels of GABA and glutamate also occur in the brains of schizophrenics. In this respect, a potentially important finding is that the effects of the hallucinogenic drug **phencyclidine** can be reversed by antipsychotic drugs (Jentsch and Roth 1999). Phencyclidine is a drug that produces behavioural and mental effects similar to schizophrenia – although it has no direct effects on dopamine receptors. Rather, it acts as an antagonist at the glutamate **N-methyl-D-aspartate** (**NMDA**) receptor. This has led researchers to search for an endogenous phencyclidine-like substance in the brain; as yet no such substance has been found.

Side effects of antipsychotic drugs

Chlorpromazine and haloperidol have their limitations. For example, they are not very effective at treating the negative symptoms of schizophrenia, and are associated with a range of side effects, including tremor, postural rigidity, cramp and weight gain. They also produce an unpleasant feeling of physical restlessness called **akathisia**. Moreover, the continued use of these drugs can also have serious health effects. One complication is **tardive dyskinesia**, which produces repetitive and involuntary movements, especially of the face, mouth, lips and tongue. A person with tardive dyskinesia may, for instance, flick their tongue out, or 'smack' their lips repetitively. This can become more socially debilitating than the schizophrenia itself. Tardive dyskinesia is a serious problem because it does not always improve when the drug dose is reduced or terminated. It has been estimated that tardive dyskinesia may occur in around of 20 per cent of hospitalised patients with chronic schizophrenia who require long-term medication (Stoudemire 1998).

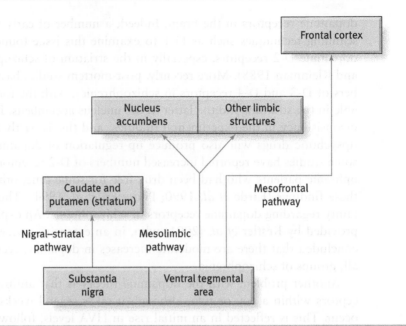

Figure 11.13   The main dopaminergic pathways of the brain

The reason why tardive dyskinesia occurs is not well understood. It is possible that the dyskinesia arises because prolonged blockade of dopamine receptors causes them to become supersensitive. However, other researchers point out that it often takes a long time for tardive dyskinesia to develop, and dopamine receptors become sensitive within weeks of taking antipsychotic medication. Despite this, most researchers believe that tardive dyskinesia arises, along with many other side effects, because antipsychotic drugs act on the striatum. This is unfortunate because the striatum, although the largest dopaminergic area in the brain, is not believed to be involved in producing the disordered thought processes of schizophrenia. Two dopaminergic pathways more likely to be involved in this respect are the **mesolimbic pathway**, which projects to the nucleus accumbens, amygdala and hippocampus, and the **mesofrontal pathway**, which innervates the frontal cortex (see Figure 11.13).

There is much debate regarding the role of the mesolimbic and mesofrontal pathways in schizophrenia. One theory of schizophrenia views the illness as arising from an imbalance in these two systems (Davis *et al.* 1991). More specifically, the negative symptoms occur as a result of decreased activity of dopaminergic neurons in the mesofrontal system, whereas the positive symptoms of schizophrenia arise from overactivity in the mesolimbic system. Evidence for this proposal comes from PET scanning, which confirms reduced metabolic activity in the frontal cortex of schizophrenics compared with controls (Weinberger *et al.* 1986). Low frontal cortex levels of blood flow have also been found in twins where one of the pair has schizophrenia (Andreasen *et al.* 1986). Others have reported that hypofrontality is most clearly observed in schizophrenics when they undertake tasks dependent on frontal lobe function such as the Wisconsin Card Sorting Task. Although hypofrontality is not observed in all schizophrenia patients, it is found in a significant number – perhaps as many as 50 per cent.

The discovery of clozapine

Approximately 30 per cent of psychotic patients do not respond to chlorpromazine and haloperidol, which provides further evidence against the dopamine hypothesis of schizophrenia. This has led researchers to develop new drugs (sometimes called atypical antipsychotics) to obtain more effective treatments. One such drug is **clozapine**, which was first synthesised in 1958 as a tricyclic antidepressant, and used to treat schizophrenia in the early 1970s. It soon gained a reputation for improving the symptoms of schizophrenia in patients who were resistant to standard antipsychotics (McKenna and Bailey 1993). Unfortunately, it also caused a dangerous drop in the number of white blood cells in some patients and was withdrawn from clinical practice. Despite this, clozapine continued to be used in research studies where it was found to be as effective as haloperidol. But, more intriguingly, it produced improvement, sometimes dramatically, in about 30–50 per cent of patients who did not respond to standard antipsychotic medication (Kane 1992). Clozapine improved both the positive and negative symptoms of schizophrenia. It also produced few striatal side effects, including tardive dyskinesia. Because of this, clozapine was reintroduced into clinical practice, although it is prescribed only to patients who fail to respond effectively to other medications.

Clozapine has been found to have a relatively small effect on the dopaminergic receptors. For example, its binding to D-2 receptors is short-lived and, if anything, it has a greater blocking action on D-1 receptors. But, clozapine is a potent antagonist of **5-HT_2 receptors**, and this action is believed to be the important one by which it exerts its antipsychotic effects (Sodhi *et al.* 1995). This has complicated our understanding of what is happening in schizophrenia. For example, 5-HT_2 receptors are found predominantly in the cerebral cortex, the nucleus accumbens and a limbic region known as the piriform cortex. Moreover, according to Stahl (2000), some 85–90 per cent of 5-HT_2 receptors are blocked by a therapeutic dose of clozapine that simultaneously blocks 20 per cent of dopamine D-2 receptors. This 'smaller' dopaminergic contribution, however, may still be important. For example, the 5-HT_2 antagonist **ritanserin** has no effect on blocking D-2 receptors, and is ineffective in treating the positive symptoms of schizophrenia.

The discovery of clozapine is a major breakthrough in the treatment of schizophrenia. It is not only acting as a prototype for newer antipsychotic compounds, but also opening up new ideas concerning the biological basis of the illness. Clozapine has, for example, been shown to stimulate dopamine release in the frontal cortex, although it blocks dopaminergic activity in the mesolimbic system (Karoun and Egan 1992). In addition, clozapine has a negligible effect on the striatum, which explains why it produces so few extrapyramidal side effects. The discovery of clozapine may even one day help us to understand how hallucinations occur. Certain hallucinogenic drugs such as **lysergic acid diethylamide (LSD)** are known to be agonists of 5-HT_2 receptors, and researchers have long been intrigued by the similarity between LSD hallucinations and schizophrenia.

The past two decades have seen exciting advances taking place in the field of receptor pharmacology, with the discovery of three more dopamine receptor subtypes (called D-3, D-4 and D-5). The D-3 and D-4 receptors have generated much interest because they are structurally similar to the D-2 receptor. However, unlike the D-2 receptor, which is found in large amounts in the striatum, the D-3 and D-4 receptors are

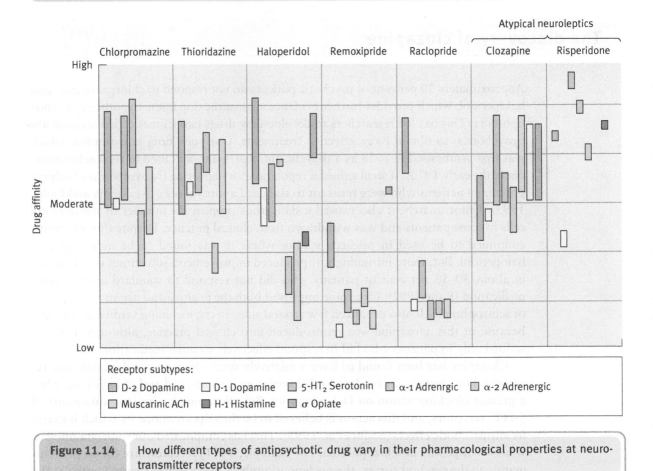

found mainly in the limbic system, particularly the nucleus accumbens and olfactory tubercle. Our understanding of the distribution of receptors in the brain helps us better understand the action of antipsychotic drugs (see Figure 11.14). For example, chlorpromazine is ten times more effective at binding to D-2 and D-3 receptors than to D-4; whereas clozapine is ten times more potent at D-4 receptors than at D-2 or D-3 (Feldman *et al.* 1997). These findings explain why clozapine has a more selective antagonistic effect on the mesolimbic system, and produces fewer extrapyramidal side effects than chlorpromazine.

Evidence for brain damage in schizophrenia

In some individuals there is evidence of brain damage in schizophrenia. One of the most common findings is enlargement of the two lateral ventricles located in the cerebral hemispheres. For example, Weinberger and Wyatt (1982) examined the CAT scans of 80 chronic schizophrenics and found the size of the ventricles to be twice as large as that for controls. This finding indicates that there may be a significant loss of brain tissue in schizophrenia, especially in regions close to the ventricles such as the hippocampus and amygdala. The enlargement of the ventricles is specific to schizophrenia, as shown by studies of monozygotic twins who are discordant for the illness. In such cases, the affected twin is the only one to show increased ventricle size (Torrey *et al.* 1994). Ventricular enlargement does not appear to be related to the length of the illness or duration of drug therapy, and can also be observed in some unaffected relatives at risk for the illness (McDonald *et al.* 2002). Despite this, increased ventricle size is not found in all schizophrenics, and is most correlated with negative symptoms (Andreasen 1988).

An area which sometimes shows a reduction in volume in schizophrenia is the hippocampus and its adjoining regions including the amygdala and parahippocampal regions (Lawrie *et al.* 2003). The hippocampus also exhibits a form of neural disorganisation with its large pyramidal cells being arranged in a haphazard and disorderly pattern. This form of neural abnormality is believed to arise in foetal development, and may be linked with the production of substances called neurotropins that guide neural migration. Given the importance of the hippocampus in memory and cognition, this lack of neural organisation might be responsible for some of the deficits in thought and reasoning characteristic of schizophrenia.

Brain imaging techniques have also shown other types of damage in schizophrenia. For example, Bogerts (1989) used CAT scans to assess brain structure in 54 patients with schizophrenia and found a loss of neural tissue in the frontal cortex, anterior temporal lobes and hypothalamus. Other studies have reported a reduced volume of neurons in the dorsomedial thalamus, which is a nucleus that connects the hypothalamus and nucleus accumbens with the prefrontal cortex. A technique called diffusion tensor imaging using MRI has also been used to assess the integrity of white matter (myelinated pathways) in the brains of schizophrenics. This technique has shown that the white matter tends to be more disorganised (that is, less neatly aligned) in a number of brain regions, including the prefrontal cortex and temporal lobes (Burns *et al.* 2003). In other words, the neural connectivity between several large cortical regions may be abnormal in schizophrenia.

Two types of schizophrenia?

The fact that (1) both positive and negative symptoms occur in schizophrenia, (2) not all patients respond to antipsychotic drugs, and (3) brain damage occurs in some but not all individuals, has led the British psychiatrist Timothy Crow to propose that there are two types of schizophrenia, each with its own pathology and aetiology. These have been called type 1 and type 2 schizophrenia (Crow 1985). Type 1 schizophrenia is characterised by positive symptoms (including hallucinations and delusions), is associated with dopaminergic dysfunction, and responds well to drug therapy, with good long-term prognosis. In contrast, type 2 schizophrenia is characterised by a greater incidence of negative symptoms, is associated with signs of structural brain damage, and responds poorly to treatment, which means that the chances of recovery are not good (Table 11.1). The implication of this classification is that schizophrenia is not a single disorder, but rather two diseases that differ in important ways.

Table 11.1	A summary of Crow's classification of schizophrenia (types 1 and 2)

Type 1 schizophrenia

Is characterised by positive symptoms including hallucinations, delusions and fragmented thought processes.

Often exhibits a fluctuating course with periods of remission.

Generally shows a good response to antipsychotic medication.

Is believed, in part, to be due to dopaminergic dysfunction (e.g. increased numbers of dopamine receptors).

Type 2 schizophrenia

Is characterised by negative symptoms including flattening of affect, poverty of speech and reduced motor activity.

Often exhibits a chronic course with little improvement.

Generally shows a poor response to antipsychotic medication.

Is believed, in part, to be due to neural loss (as supported by findings showing an increased likelihood of ventricular enlargement and reduced blood flow to the frontal lobes).

Although some cases of schizophrenia appear to fall neatly into Crow's classification system, there are difficulties with the model. For example, most schizophrenics show a mixture of positive and negative symptoms, and the latter do not necessarily correlate with signs of brain damage. Or put another way, there are plenty of patients with positive symptoms who have ventricular enlargement and other forms of structural brain abnormality. Moreover, type 1 and type 2 symptoms can change with time. Indeed, in one study that examined the progress of 52 hospitalised schizophrenic patients it was found that, over a 25-year period, positive symptoms gradually changed into more pronounced negative ones such as social withdrawal and blunted affect (Pfohl and Winnokur 1983). Despite this, Crow's formulation is still helpful. For example, Andreasen (1985) found that some patients with negative symptoms have no prior history of positive symptoms and they remain in this state for the rest of their life. Alternatively, there are others with positive symptoms who have few negative characteristics and no signs of brain damage.

The Genian quadruplets

The Genian quadruplets are four genetically identical women born in the early 1930s who all developed schizophrenia by their early adulthood (the chances of this happening by chance is around 1 in 2 billion). Because all share identical genes, they provide an unique opportunity to assess the relative influence of genetic inheritance and environment on the development of schizophrenia. The sisters first came to the notice of the National Institute of National Health (NIMH) in the 1950s. To provide the twins with anonymity, researchers invented the name 'Genain' as a pseudonym for 'bad gene', and they also named the sisters (from youngest to oldest) Nora, Iris, Myra and Hester, so their initials corresponded with NIMH. The quadruplets were described in a book by David Rosenthal (1963) and they have been examined on several occasions since. The last follow-up study took place in 2000 when the sisters were tested on a variety of different tasks – some 39 years after they were first identified (Mirsky *et al.* 2000).

Although the sisters are genetically identical, the symptoms of their illness differ. For example, Nora was the first to be hospitalised at the age of 22, although she has managed to live in the community most of the time since, and has held down several short-term clerical jobs. Iris was admitted to hospital 7 months after Nora, and has been institutionalised, on and off, over the same period. The next to be diagnosed was Hester at the age of 24, who is regarded as the most severely ill of the four. In fact, she has spent much of her life in hospital under constant medication. The least affected, however, is Myra, who was the last to show psychotic symptoms. She recovered, has worked steadily in clerical jobs, was married at the age of 26 and had two children. In fact, Myra appears to have functioned normally until the age of 46 when, under stress, she become paranoid and delusional and was hospitalised for two months.

In 1981, all sisters underwent CAT scans of the brain. The results showed that there was no brain atrophy or significant difference between the sisters. Despite this, there were changes in response when the sisters were taken off medication for a short period. For example, Nora and Hester quickly deteriorated, Iris kept reasonably well, and Myra showed improvement. On a positive note, the sisters have demonstrated stable performance on a variety of tasks over the past 39 years or so, showing that cognitive decline is not an inevitable process in schizophrenia. Although the sisters would appear to provide convincing evidence for the idea that schizophrenia is inherited, they also grew up in a highly stressful and impoverished environment. For example, their father was an alcoholic and child molester, and their mother offered little love or support. Thus, in the final analysis it appears that both heredity and an unfavourable upbringing were important factors in the Genain sisters developing schizophrenia.

The genetics of schizophrenia

Several lines of evidence indicate that genetic inheritance contributes to the development of schizophrenia. For example, if schizophrenia is inherited, one would expect it to be more common in first-degree relatives of schizophrenic patients than in second-degree ones such as nephews, nieces, uncles and aunts. This is exactly what is found (see Figure 11.15). A person with a schizophrenic parent, for instance, has a 17 per cent chance of developing schizophrenia, and this figure rises to nearly 50 per cent when both parents are affected (Gottesman 1991). In contrast, the rates of schizophrenia are around 5 per cent in second-degree relatives, and 2 per cent in first cousins (third-degree relatives). This figure, however, is still significantly higher than that found in the general population, which is around 1 per cent.

Further support for genetic inheritance come from studies that examine the rates of schizophrenia in identical and fraternal twins. Identical (or monozygotic) twins are derived from the same fertilised egg and are genetically identical, whereas fraternal (or dizygotic) twins develop from two different eggs and sperm. Thus, one would expect a trait that is strongly genetic to be more concordant in groups of identical twins. Many studies published over the past fifty years have indeed shown this to be the case. In general, the concordance for identical twins is 40–60 per cent whereas the rate for non-identical twins is 10–20 per cent (Gottesman 1991).

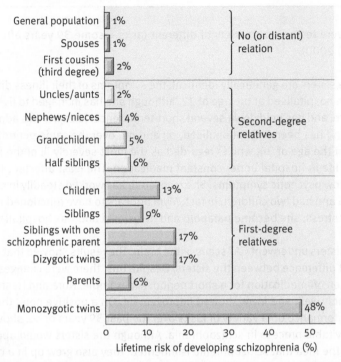

| Figure 11.15 | The heritability of schizophrenia |

Source: S.M. Breedlove *et al.*, *Biological Psychology*, 5th edition, p. 484. Copyright © 2007 by Sinauer Associates, Inc.

One problem with twin studies is that the pair are likely to have been brought up in same environment and treated similarly by family and friends. Thus, concordance rates do not rule out environmental influences. A more accurate way of assessing the impact of inheritance would be to compare identical twins who are reared apart. One way of doing this is to examine rates of schizophrenia in people born to psychotic parents, but who were adopted into new families at an early age. These studies have also supported the idea that schizophrenia has a genetic basis. For example, Kety *et al.* (1968) examined the records of adopted children born in Copenhagen between 1924 and 1947 who were taken away from their parents when young. From this group, 33 adoptees were later identified as adults who went on to develop schizophrenia. When the biological parents of these individuals were traced, it was found that 10 per cent of them had also suffered from the illness. In comparison, less than 2 per cent of the adoptive parents with 'normal' adoptees had a history of psychosis. Thus, the children of schizophrenics are more likely to become psychotic, even if they have been reared away from the parents and in different environments.

Despite this, it should be noted that the genetic influence is not as great as one may at first imagine. For example, the concordance for monozygotic twins is around 50 per cent, which indicates that the environment plays an important role in the pathogenesis of the illness. Moreover, the pattern of inheritance is complex and does not follow a Mendelian single-gene pattern of expression. Rather, it is more likely that schizophrenia has multiple genetic causes, with each factor increasing the predisposition for the illness. At least six schizophrenia susceptibility genes have been identified, although researchers believe there are more to be discovered. Although it is possible that the more of these genes one inherits, the greater will be the likelihood of developing schizophrenia, it is also likely that these genes only impart a predisposition to develop schizophrenia which is critically dependent on developmental and environmental factors. These factors may include viral or toxin exposure during pregnancy, birth complications, and high levels of stress during life especially during infant and teenage years (Plomin *et al.* 1997).

A number of chromosomes have been implicated in schizophrenia, including chromosome 22. A large deletion in one of the long arms of this chromosome produces a condition called velo-cardio-facial (VCF) syndrome which causes cleft palate abnormalities and heart defects. But, interestingly, around 30 per cent of individuals with this syndrome also show psychotic features. One of the genes believed to be responsible for producing this effect is one that codes for the enzyme **catechol *O*-methyltransferase (COMT)**, which is important for dopamine metabolism. In one study that followed a group of 24 patients with VCF, who also had a distinct polymorphism in their remaining COMT gene, it was found that 7 went on to develop schizophrenia in their teenage years. These individuals showed the lowest COMT activity (indicating low dopaminergic activity) and had a smaller prefrontal cortex, which correlated with poor verbal IQ and language skills (Gothelf *et al.* 2005). Although not all studies have found a linkage between schizophrenia and the COMT gene, this is an exciting finding and one that awaits further research.

Environmental causes

Many environmental factors have been implicated in the causation of schizophrenia, but one factor which is often linked with its development is stress. For example, one theory holds that psychiatric disorders such as schizophrenia arise in certain individuals because they are genetically more predisposed to react badly to aversive life situations (Zudin and Spring 1977). One study that supported this notion was the Finnish Adoptive Family Study of Schizophrenia, which followed a group of adoptees taken away from schizophrenic parents (high-risk subjects), who were then compared with a group of control subjects (low-risk). It was found that the chances of developing schizophrenia was greater in the high-risk subjects – but only for those who had been exposed to a dysfunctional and stressful family environment during upbringing (Tienari *et al.* 1994). Despite this, the family influence in schizophrenia remains controversial. There are, for example, cases where infants have been adopted by schizophrenic parents, and despite exposure to a difficult environment, have not developed schizophrenia. Thus, a genetic susceptibility to schizophrenia would appear to be essential.

Nonetheless, a large number of environmental factors have been associated with schizophrenia. For example, the incidence of schizophrenia tends to be higher in lower social classes, and in large urban areas where levels of stress might be expected to be higher than in rural areas. It has also been shown that racial minorities living in big cities like London are twice as likely to develop schizophrenia if they reside in areas where there are small numbers of fellow minority populations. These findings indicate that the stress of social isolation may be an important factor in schizophrenia (Boydell and Murray 2003). In addition, it is probable that someone developing schizophrenia will be more likely to experience employment and relationship difficulties, thereby increasing the risk of social isolation and poverty.

The risk of schizophrenia is also increased by prenatal and perinatal events, including infections, malnutrition, and smoking during pregnancy. In addition, childbirth complications, especially if associated with hypoxia (oxygen loss) also increase the risk for the illness. However, the fact that obstetric complications do not lead to psychosis in the majority of individual indicates that those who do develop schizophrenia may have a genetic vulnerability to these stresses. There is also evidence showing that foetal exposure to virus infections can lead to schizophrenia. For example, in the northern hemisphere there is a small but significant risk that people with schizophrenia will be born in the winter months (January to March). The risk is more pronounced at higher latitudes and disappears in the tropics (Kendell and Adams 1991). Infections are implicated in this effect because, at northern latitudes, viral epidemics are more common in autumn – and for children born in winter, autumn corresponds to the second trimester of pregnancy. This is a crucial time for the neural development of the brain. Several studies have shown a relationship between influenza epidemics and schizophrenia. For example, Sham *et al.* (1992) examined the outcome of pregnancies during several influenza outbreaks between 1939 and 1960, and found that there was a greater likelihood of schizophrenia when an influenza outbreak occurred five months before birth. Although this is the most sensitive period, viral outbreaks occurring at any point in pregnancy also appear to increase the chances of schizophrenia (Barr *et al.* 1990).

The fact that exposure to other types of viral agents such as rubella and AIDS can cause brain damage and increase the risk for schizophrenia provides further support for the influenza theory. Thus, it is tempting to speculate that a virus may produce a toxin that harms the foetus at a critical stage, or the mother's immune system produces a viral antibody that damages the developing nervous system. But, even if we assume the cause of schizophrenia lies in the foetus, there are still unanswered questions. Most notably, schizophrenia does not normally appear until adulthood, so why should the illness take so long to develop? Another puzzle is that identical twins are not always concordant for the illness. If developing twins sharing the same womb were exposed to the same prenatal insult, then one would expect both to equally affected.

Summary

Mental health problems are surprisingly common, and it is estimated that one person in eight will consult a doctor each year with a psychological difficulty. The most common mental problem is depression. The first antidepressant to be developed (in the late 1950s) was **Marsilid**, which is a **monoamine oxidase inhibitor** (MAOI). This drug increased levels of **noradrenaline** (NA) and **serotonin** (5-HT) in the synapse by inhibiting their breakdown by monoamine oxidase. The MAOIs were followed in the 1960s by the **tricyclic antidepressants**, which included **imipramine**. These drugs increased NA and 5-HT levels, but by a different pharmacological mechanism, namely the blocking of the **reuptake pump**. These findings led to the **catecholamine theory**, which proposed that depression was due to reduced levels of NA at brain synapses. This theory is now known to be far too simple. For example, it normally takes 2–3 weeks of drug treatment before the symptoms of depression begin to improve, although their pharmacological action (for example, inhibiting reuptake) is immediate. The cause of this delay appears to lie with the neurotransmitter receptors. Put simply, the chronic use of antidepressants reduces the sensitivity of alpha **autoreceptors** located on **presynaptic neurons** which controls NA release. In turn, the increased level of NA in the synapse leads to **down-regulation** and **reduced sensitivity** of NA **beta receptors** found on **postsynaptic neurons**.

Thus, it is possible that the cause of depression lies more with receptor sensitivity than with neurotransmitter release. In 1987, the first **selective serotonergic reuptake inhibitor** (SSRI) called **Prozac** was marketed, and it became the most popular antidepressant in the world. This drug, however, has no direct effect on the NAergic system. It is likely, therefore, that both NA and 5-HT systems are involved in depression.

Schizophrenia is a serious mental illness characterised by bizarre delusions, hallucinations, fragmented thought and inappropriate emotions. This illness has a strong genetic origin as shown by twin and adoption studies, although 'stressful' environmental factors are also important. The first successful antipsychotic drug was **chlorpromazine** (**Thorazine**), which became available in 1954, and was followed by **haloperidol** (**Haldol**) in the early 1960s. Both drugs produced side effects resembling **Parkinson's disease**, which indicated that they depleted the brain of **dopamine** (DA). This also implied that schizophrenia was due to increased DA activity – a theory supported by the fact that high doses of **amphetamine,** which stimulates DA release, can produce psychotic symptoms. However, chlorpromazine and haloperidol do not deplete the brain of DA. In fact, their pharmacological mode of action was not discovered until the early 1970s, when they were found to block DA receptors, that is, they are **dopamine antagonists**. Moreover, their antipsychotic effect correlated positively with their potency at blocking **D-2 receptors**. Some studies have also shown increased numbers of DA receptors in the brains of schizophrenics, although this is not always found, indicating that there are different types of this disorder. A number of recent antipsychotic drugs have been developed, including **clozapine,** which has little effect on D-2 receptors but blocks serotonergic **5-HT$_2$ receptors**. Clozapine is therefore acting as a prototype for new antipsychotic drugs, as well as opening up new ideas about the biological basis of schizophrenia.

Essay questions

1. What is the monoamine theory of depression? What evidence supports this hypothesis as a cause of affective disorder?

    Search terms: Monoamine theory of depression. Neurotransmitters and mood. Noradrenaline and depression. Serotonin and depression. Neurobiology of depression.

2. It generally takes 2–3 weeks of chronic treatment before an antidepressant begins to have a clinical benefit, yet the drug's pharmacological effect (for example, its inhibition of MAO, or reuptake) is usually immediate. What synaptic mechanisms may underlie this time lag?

    Search terms: Time lag of antidepressant treatment. Synaptic changes and antidepressants. Autoreceptors and depression. Desensitisation of receptors. Mechanisms of antidepressant action.

3. Provide evidence for and against the dopamine theory of schizophrenia.

    Search terms: Dopamine and schizophrenia. Mechanism of haloperidol. Dopamine receptors and schizophrenia. Brain changes in schizophrenia. Neurobiology of schizophrenia.

4. With reference to twin studies, discuss the probable interplay of nature and nurture in the development of schizophrenia.

    Search terms: Twin studies and schizophrenia. Genetics of schizophrenia. Genain quads. Schizophrenia and stress. Nature nurture of schizophrenia.

Further reading

Barondes, S.H. (1993) *Molecules and Mental Illness.* New York: Scientific American Library. A well-written and nicely illustrated account that covers the genetics, molecular biology, neuroscience and neuropharmacology of the main psychiatric disorders.

Davis, K.L., Charney, D., Coyle, J.T. and Nemeroff, C. (eds) (2002) *Psychopharmacology: The Fifth Generation of Progress.* New York: Lippincott Williams & Wilkins. A massive text of nearly 2,080 pages, with large up-to-date sections on the neurobiology, psychopharmacology and clinical aspects of depression and schizophrenia.

Charney, D. and Nestler, E.J. (eds) (2005) *Neurobiology of Mental Illness.* Oxford: Oxford University Press. An excellent textbook with large sections on affective disorders and schizophrenia written from various neurobiological perspectives.

Feldman, R.S., Meyer, J.S. and Quenzer, L.F. (1997) *Principles of Neuropsychopharmacology.* Sunderland, Mass.: Sinauer. An indispensable textbook on psychopharmacology with excellent chapters on schizophrenia and affective disorders.

Goodwin, F.K. and Jamison, K.R. (1990) *Manic-Depressive Illness.* Oxford: Oxford University Press. A scholarly and comprehensive account that covers various aspects of manic depression.

Gottesman, I.I. (1991) *Schizophrenia Genesis.* New York: Freeman. An introductory text for undergraduate students that discusses the causes of schizophrenia, including genetic, psychological and environmental influences.

Healy, D. (1997) *The Anti-depressant Era.* Cambridge, Mass.: Harvard University Press. A book that focuses on the discovery and development of the antidepressants and provides a fascinating insight into the history of this field.

Mann, J.J. and Kupfer, D.J. (1993) *Biology of Depressive Disorders.* New York: Plenum. Although a technical account, the first part of the book contains useful information on the involvement of neurochemical systems in depression.

McGuffin, P., Owen, M.J. and Gottesman, I.I. (eds) (2002) *Psychiatric Genetics and Genomics.* Oxford: Oxford University Press. A textbook that contains interesting and readable chapters on the genetics of affective disorders and schizophrenia.

McKenna, P.J. (1994) *Schizophrenia and Related Syndromes.* Oxford: Oxford University Press. Useful overview of many facets of schizophrenia research, including a chapter on the dopamine hypothesis.

Panksepp, J. (ed.) (2003) *Textbook of Biological Psychiatry.* Chichester: John Wiley. A broad-ranging textbook but the chapters on the neurobiology and treatment of affective disorders and schizophrenia will prove very useful for the undergraduate student.

Snyder, S.H. (1986) *Drugs and the Brain.* New York: Scientific American Library. A captivating and well-illustrated book which also covers some recreational drugs. The chapters on antidepressant and antipsychotic drugs, however, are worth the price of admission alone – especially for their historical perspective.

Stahl, S.M. (1996) *Essential Psychopharmacology.* Cambridge: Cambridge University Press. Concentrates primarily on neuropharmacological actions of drugs that are commonly used to treat mental illness.

Torrey, E.F. (1994) *Schizophrenia and Manic-Depressive Disorder.* New York: Basic Books. A fascinating book that reports the findings of a six-year study of 66 pairs of identical twins, which indicates that schizophrenia originates either *in utero* or within the first five years of life, even though the symptoms do not appear until adulthood.

For self test questions, animations, interactive exercises and many more resources to help you consolidate your understanding, and expand your knowledge of the field, please go to the website accompanying this book at **www.pearsoned.co.uk/wickens**

CHAPTER 12

Drugs and addiction

In this chapter

- The discovery of intracranial self-stimulation by Olds and Milner
- The importance of the medial forebrain bundle
- The role of noradrenaline and dopamine in reward
- Heroin, endorphins and opiate systems in the brain
- The mesolimbic dopamine system
- Pharmacological, molecular and psychological factors in drug tolerance
- Sensitisation and incentive salience
- The pharmacological effects of commonly abused drugs

INTRODUCTION

Human beings are hedonists. We spend a good part of our lives trying to obtain the things that give us pleasure – sex, food, watching football, or simply reading a good book. In this pursuit, many also turn to the intoxicating and pleasurable properties of drugs, whether that drug be alcohol, nicotine, caffeine or some illegal substance. Humans have been taking psychoactive agents since the dawn of civilisation. The use of the coca plant can be traced back at least 7,000 years; opium 4,000 years; and the use of alcohol goes back much further. Perhaps the oldest used substance is arecoline, a substance found in the betal nut, which was chewed 13,000 years ago in Timor (Sulivan and Hagen 2002). Drug taking is therefore as old as humanity itself. Yet, drugs are not without their dangers. As we all know, a serious risk is addiction which affects people in all societies, especially if we include smoking and alcohol. Addiction is a major medical problem owing to its unhealthy lifestyles and increased likelihood of psychiatric illness. In addition, there are the enormous costs of addiction to society as measured by family and community breakdown, rising crime figures, and loss of earnings and productivity. And, at the centre of this problem is the individual who may see no escape as drug addiction is frequently a chronic relapsing disorder which is highly resistant to treatment. The challenge of addiction has captured the attention of clinicians, psychologists and pharmacologists for many decades. It is also one in which the brain scientist has a vital role to play – not only in providing insights into the nature of addiction, and why certain drugs act on the brain to produce pleasure, but also in helping to develop better therapies that will benefit us all. Biopsychology is at the centre of this endeavour.

The discovery of reward systems in the brain

The discovery of reward systems in the brain is often credited to James Olds and his research student Peter Milner working at McGill University in the early 1950s. At the time, Milner was finishing his PhD in the laboratory of George Hebb, and Olds (who was a social psychologist from Harvard with an interest in motivation) had just joined the department. In a joint project, Olds and Milner decided to examine whether electrical stimulation of the reticular formation could facilitate arousal and learning. During this work, Olds and Milner discovered that if they brain-stimulated rats in a large open box, the animal would show a strong inclination to return and remain in the location where they had received stimulation. This was an unexpected finding and made sense only if the rat was finding the stimulation pleasurable. But Olds and Milner were to have another surprise. When the locations of the electrode were examined after behavioural testing, they found that the reticular formation had not been stimulated as intended – but a region close to the hypothalamus called the septal area.

Was the electrical stimulation really acting as a reward? There was some doubt as the brain stimulation also caused the rat to look around and sniff, raising the possibility that the procedure might be provoking curiosity or exploration. To examine this possibility, Olds and Milner trained rats to run through a T maze which required them to make a choice for food reward. However, the choice of goal arms had different consequences. In one of the arms, Olds and Milner gave the rat brain stimulation before the food was reached, whereas in the other arm the animal was allowed to consume the food unperturbed. The important question was: what arm would the rat choose if

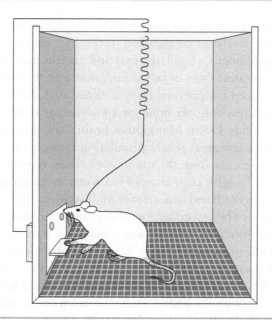

| Figure 12.1 | Experimental set-up for intracranial self-stimulation |

given a free choice? Olds and Milner found that rats chose the arm where they received stimulation. In fact, the rats often stopped at the stimulation point and, despite being hungry, would ignore the food that was just inches away.

Following this discovery, Olds and Milner developed a more efficient procedure for testing the effects of brain stimulation. They constructed an operant box in which a rat was able to press a lever to obtain electrical stimulation of the brain. In this situation, every time the rat pressed the lever, a train of electrical impulses was sent to its brain, via a lead which passed through the ceiling of the chamber (Figure 12.1). The animal now controlled the stimulation it received. Moreover, the rewarding properties of the stimulation could be estimated by recording the number of bar presses the rat was prepared to make to get it. As Olds later recounted, the first animal in this procedure ended all doubts that electrical stimulation was highly rewarding. The rat made responses regularly every second or so, and when the experimenters turned off the current after 30 minutes, it pressed the lever 70 times before falling asleep. With this technique, sometimes referred to as **intracranial self-stimulation**, Olds and Milner (1954) had invented a new research paradigm that allowed the reward systems of the brain to be mapped out and their characteristics examined. Many thousands of research papers were to be published on brain stimulation in the first two decades after Old and Milner's discovery.

The medial forebrain bundle

One of the first things that researchers sought to discover about self-stimulation was the location of the brain sites from which it could be elicited, and it soon became clear that these regions were spread throughout the brain. For example, Olds and Milner found that high rates of self-stimulation were obtained from the **septum, amygdala** and **anterior hypothalamus** (in the region of 500 bar presses per hour), whereas moderate levels of responding (200 bar presses per hour) were elicited from the **hippocampus, cingulate gyrus** and **nucleus accumbens**. However, the region that led to the greatest rates of self-stimulation was the **lateral hypothalamus**, which sometimes produced bar pressing rates in excess of 1,000 presses per hour. In fact, one rat made 2,000 response per hour for 24 consecutive hours before completely exhausting himself (Olds 1958). Many other brain sites also gave rise to self-stimulation, and there were a few areas where stimulation appeared to be aversive so that the animal would try to escape from the situation or refuse to press the bar.

Although a large array of brain regions gave rise to self-stimulation, it was found that most contributed to a massive multisynaptic pathway called the **medial forebrain bundle** (MFB). This is a collection of over fifty fibre bundles with both descending and ascending projections, which come together to pass through the lateral hypothalamus in the middle of its route (Figure 12.2). It has been estimated that there are around 10 million MFB axons on each side of the lateral hypothalamus, and these fibres are connecting midbrain regions such as the **ventral tegmental area** (VTA) and **periaqueductal grey area** (PGA), with the **limbic system, striatum** and **frontal cortex** of the forebrain. The lateral hypothalamus also contains intrinsic neurons that are in contact with many fibres of passage, which can monitor the ascending and descending flow in the MFB. In addition, the MFB provides major input and output for several other hypothalamic structures. The MFB has been likened to a major highway that connects the two coasts of a continent (Graham 1990). Although this analogy is useful, it is also a simplification as the MFB also contains many smaller pathways that connect local regions.

The region of the brain that yields the highest rates of responding from self-stimulation is the part of the MFB that passes through the lateral hypothalamus. Rats will respond with extreme vigour to obtain stimulation from this site, and ignore basic drives such as hunger, thirst and sleep to obtain the reward. Moreover, the animal will respond continuously and often show no signs of satiation until exhausted. This behaviour

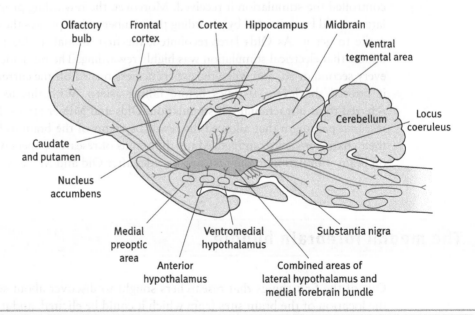

Figure 12.2   The medial forebrain bundle

shows that MFB stimulation is highly pleasurable, and it led Olds and Olds (1963) to propose that 'reward' neurons in the lateral hypothalamus provided the main substrate of reinforcement for the animal. That is, the purpose of the MFB was to collect motivational information from a wide range of brain sites (involved in activities such as eating, drinking, aggression, sexual behaviour and sleep), and to channel this to the lateral hypothalamus, which provided the rewarding event in reinforcement.

However, this theory was soon criticised when it was found that large lesions of the MFB did not abolish self-stimulation. For example, Valenstein and Campbell (1966) made massive lesions to the to the MFB and showed that this did not stop self-stimulation of the septal area. In a similar study, self-stimulation of the lateral hypothalamus was not significantly reduced following extensive damage to the MFB (Lorens 1966). Moreover, both the septal area and lateral hypothalamus could be lesioned without significantly affecting self-stimulation from other sites in the MFB. These findings indicated that the lateral hypothalamus was not essential for self-stimulation to occur. Thus, other brain regions and pathways had also to be responsible for reinforcement and reward.

It was also found that small lesions made to the MFB which were posterior to the sites of hypothalamic or septal stimulation (that is, they severed the pathways projecting down into the midbrain) were more likely to decrease responding than lesions made anteriorly that cut pathways going to the forebrain (Olds and Forbes 1981). This indicated that some parts of the MFB were more essential than others in producing reward – and that the most important pathways were those that projected down to midbrain areas. As we shall see later, this finding had extra significance when it was found that the midbrain also contained the cell bodies giving rise to the main dopamine pathways in the brain.

Catecholamine pathways in the medial forebrain bundle

It is also important to understand the types of neurotransmitters involved in reward, and the first to be implicated were the catecholamines **noradrenaline** and **dopamine**. For example, reserpine and chlorpromazine diminished responding in rats with hypothalamic electrodes, whereas amphetamine (which increases the release of catecholamines) facilitated self-stimulation (Olds et al. 1956). These findings took on a new significance when researchers began to map out catecholamine pathways in the brain during the 1960s. The first step in this development had occurred in the 1950s when it was found that cells of the adrenal gland treated with formaldehyde and exposed to ultraviolet light would fluoresce. This reaction occurred because the catecholamines in the tissue combined with the formaldehyde to produce fluorescent chemicals. This method was improved by Falck and Hillarp working in Sweden, and applied to brain tissue by Dahlström and Fuxe in 1964. These researchers found they could distinguish between noradrenaline and dopamine, which fluoresced as green, and serotonin, which fluoresced as yellow. This allowed the noradrenergic, dopaminergic and serotonergic pathways to be visualised in the brain under ultraviolet light, and mapped out in detail.

One of the main findings to emerge from this work was that the catecholaminergic pathways of the brain arise from cell groups in the midbrain and upper brainstem.

There are two main noradrenergic pathways. The **ventral tegmental tract** arises from several nuclei in the brainstem and projects to the hypothalamus. The remaining noradrenergic fibres to the forebrain are found in the **dorsal tegmental tract**, which arises from the **locus coeruleus** in the upper pons area. In contrast, there are three main dopaminergic pathways which derive from cells in the **ventral tegmental area** of the midbrain, or from the **substantia nigra**, which also lies embedded in this region. These are: (1) the **mesolimbic pathway** projecting to the nucleus accumbens and amygdala, (2) the **mesocortical pathway** projecting to the frontal cortex and cingulate cortex, and (3) the **nigral–striatal pathway** that projects to the caudate and putamen (striatum).

The mapping of catecholamine pathways in the brain was important for understanding the neural basis of reward. Not only did the MFB project to the midbrain regions that gave rise to these pathways, but just about every catecholaminergic pathway that ascended from the midbrain to forebrain also travelled in the MFB. This indicated that catecholamines were involved in reward processing. Moreover, the trajectory of the pathways followed the distribution of sites that gave rise to the highest rates of self-stimulation. But which type of catecholamine was more important in reward: noradrenaline or dopamine? This was not an easy question to answer as many of the regions in the MFB that gave rise to self-stimulation received projections from both noradrenergic and dopaminergic systems.

Noradrenaline and reward

Some of the strongest evidence implicating noradrenaline in reinforcement came from the mapping of self-stimulation sites. For example, a number of brain sites that gave rise to self-stimulation were found in the upper brainstem below the level of the ventral tegmental area and substantia nigra. These were areas that do not receive dopaminergic input. Closer inspection shows that these sites are particularly prominent in the pons area, which includes the locus coeruleus. This led Stein (1967) to propose that this brainstem area was most important for self-stimulation. Or, more specifically, he argued that the areas that gave rise to self-stimulation are the ones that follow the dorsal noradrenergic bundle originating in the locus coeruleus, which passes through the hypothalamus, en route to forebrain areas such as the neocortex.

Stein and Wise (1971) provided evidence to support the noradrenaline hypothesis. The formation of noradrenaline in neuron terminals is known to involve a number of chemical steps, one of which requires the formation of dopamine that is converted into noradrenaline by the enzyme **dopamine-β-hydroxylase**. When Stein and Wise injected animals with a drug called disulfiram which inhibited dopamine-β-hydroxylase activity, thereby reducing the formation of noradrenaline but not of dopamine, they found that it reduced self-stimulation. However, self-stimulation was reinstated when noradrenaline was injected into the cerebral ventricles. Stein and Wise reasoned that this noradrenaline was being taken up into presynaptic terminals where it was released during neural activity caused by self-stimulation. This indicated that it was noradrenaline, and not dopamine, that was the main catecholamine involved in reward.

Despite this, there was evidence against the noradrenaline hypothesis. For example, lesions of the locus coeruleus, or the dorsal noradrenergic bundle, which depleted the forebrain of more than 95 per cent of its noradrenaline, had little effect on reducing the rates of self-stimulation from the hypothalamus. Another objection came from evidence implicating noradrenaline in behavioural arousal. Indeed, the interpretation of the dilsufiram study by Stein and Wise (1969) described above was shown to be suspect when it was found that the drug-treated animals, if aroused by the handling of an experimenter, would exhibit self-stimulation when placed back in an operant box. This indicated that disulfiram caused sedation, and that restoring noradrenaline levels by arousing the animal caused behavioural stimulation, rather than having a specific effect on reward (Rolls 1970).

Dopamine and reward

By the mid-1970s, research was favouring the theory that dopamine was involved in the rewarding effects of self-stimulation. This idea had originated in the 1950s with the discovery that drugs such as chlorpromazine and haloperidol, whose main action was to block dopamine receptors, also reduced self-stimulation from a number of brain sites, including the MFB. But these drugs were also known to affect, to some degree, the release of noradrenaline. Thus, there was a need for more selective dopamine antagonists, and this occurred in the 1970s with drugs such as **pimozide** and **spiroperidol**. When these drugs were injected into experimental animals they significantly reduced levels of self-stimulation from a large number of brain sites, including the locus coeruleus (Wise 1976).

However, there were a number of methodological objections surrounding the use of dopamine antagonists in the suppression of self-stimulation, and the most serious concerned their effects on motor activity. Because these drugs were known to induce sedation, it was possible that they were exerting their effects by reducing the animal's inclination to bar-press. This was an awkward problem and it led researchers to devise a number of experimental methods to control for such side effects. One paradigm was the **curve-shift procedure**. To appreciate this procedure, it is first necessary to realise that a certain amount of electrical current has to be administered into brain regions to produce self-stimulation. That is, if the current is too small then the animal will not press a lever for reward. However, once the threshold for self-stimulation is reached, something interesting happens: as the current is increased to the brain, the relationship between lever pressing and strength of current typically follows a **sigmoidal curve**. As can be seen from Figure 12.3, this is essentially an S-shaped curve with an upper limit, or ceiling. The important point, however, is that this curve shifts to the right with the administration of dopamine antagonists such as pimozide, and shifts to the left with dopamine-releasing drugs such as amphetamine. What does this mean exactly? The answer is that greater intensities of electrical stimulation are needed to overcome the effects of drugs which block dopamine, and less stimulation is needed to produce the same effect with amphetamine. But, even more important, the upper limit of responding remains the same in all cases, that is, there is no reduction in the level of bar pressing. This was evidence that dopaminergic drugs are affecting the intensity of reward and not behavioural performance.

Other evidence also supports the dopamine hypothesis. Although Olds had shown the lateral hypothalamus to give rise to the highest rates of self-stimulation, other researchers pointed to the importance of the ventral tegmental area (VTA) for producing high rates. The VTA is the area of the brain that contains the cell bodies that give rise to the ascending dopaminergic projections to the forebrain. Moreover, evidence shows

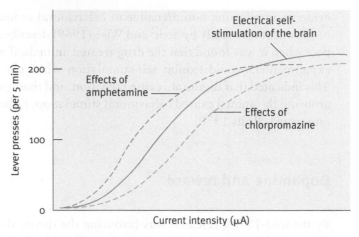

Note how dopaminergic agonists such as amphetamine shift the curve left,
and how dopamine antagonists such as chlorpromazine shift it right
(i.e. they alter the pleasurable effects of self-stimulation)

Figure 12.3   Rate–intensity curve for electrical self-stimulation of the brain (hypothalamus)

that the integrity of these pathways is necessary for the rewarding effects of VTA self-stimulation. For example, experiments measuring the levels of dopaminergic metabolites (Fibiger and Philips 1987) have shown that stimulation of the VTA causes the release of dopamine in several areas of the brain, including the nucleus accumbens and frontal cortex. The importance of these dopamine pathways is further seen in lesion studies. For example, lesions made using the highly selective neurotoxin for dopamine neurons called **6-hydroxydopamine** were found to abolish levels of self-stimulation produced by electrodes placed in the VTA (Philips and Fibiger 1978).

The important role of the VTA for self-stimulation has also been confirmed from studies using **2-deoxyglucose autoradiography**. This technique involves injecting a radioactive glucose called 2-deoxyglucose into the animal prior to testing, and then observing which areas of the brain show the highest uptake of this substance after self-stimulation. In short, the most active neurons will show the highest rates of 2-deoxyglucose uptake. This type of experiment has shown that self-stimulation of the MFB causes high levels of 2-deoxyglucose activity to occur in the VTA (Gallistel 1983).

Chemical self-stimulation

Some of the best evidence implicating dopamine in reward has come from experiments where animals are able to self-inject themselves with drugs. Instead of using an electrical current to stimulate their brain, animals can also be made to press a lever to switch on a pump that injects a chemical directly into their body by means of a flexible plastic tube. This technique was first developed by Jim Weeks, who found that rats made physically dependent on morphine would learn to press a lever in an operant box for an intravenous injection of this drug. This behaviour also resembled human drug taking in several ways. For example, the self-injection of morphine terminated the bar pressing, which led to prolonged periods of no responding. That is, the drug produced a satiating and presumably pleasurable effect. However, the rat would press the bar to receive morphine at other times, and this was most likley prior to the occurrence of withdrawal symptoms, and during extinction when the drug was no longer available to the animal (Weeks 1962).

The chemical self-stimulation procedure has proved very useful for examining the addictive potential of drugs as many of the substances that animals self-administer are also the ones abused by humans. For example, animals will self-administer psychomotor stimulants such as cocaine and amphetamine; depressants such as ethanol and barbiturates; and certain hallucinogens such as phencyclidine and ketamine. Interestingly, nicotine, lysergic acid diethylmide (LSD) and tetrahydrocannibinol (the main active ingredient in cannabis) are not normally self-administered in this procedure (Griffiths et al. 1980). These effects have been obtained in a wide variety of experimental animals including rats and mice, monkeys, cats, dogs and pigs.

One class of drug that gives rise to high rates of bar pressing for self-injection are the major stimulants **amphetamine** and **cocaine**. For example, in a study involving monkeys, the rewarding property of cocaine was compared with a number of other drugs, including morphine and heroin. More specifically, a progressive ratio procedure was used in which the animals had to increase their bar presses by 50 every time they received a drug reinforcement (Yanagita 1987). This task is one that measures the upper limit for which a monkey will work for reward, until the physical demand becomes so great that the responding stops. The study showed that five of the six monkeys worked harder for cocaine injections than for any other drug (the sixth animal found amphetamine most reinforcing). In fact, one monkey was prepared to press the lever 6,400 times to obtain a single cocaine reinforcement.

Not only is the self-administration of amphetamine and cocaine highly reinforcing, but when animals are allowed free access to these drugs, a pattern of behaviour occurs which involves alternating periods of drug intake and abstinence (Figure 12.4). During drug-taking periods, which usually last for a few days, there is an increase in stereotypical movements, with little eating, drinking or sleep. This is followed by a 'down' period during which the animal shows little drug taking or behavioural activity. Thus, psychomotor stimulant use in animals shows daily fluctuation, with high quantities being self-administered on some days, followed by periods of abstinence. A similar type of pattern can occur in humans with unlimited access to cocaine and amphetamine. For example, people who use intravenous amphetamine may repeatedly inject the drug for 3 to 6 days during which time they remain constantly awake. Following a 'run' the user can become so exhausted and unable to get more pleasure from the drug that they sleep instead. This sleep may last 12–18 hours following which the user may feel so lethargic and depressed that they begin a new 'run'.

Free access to amphetamine and cocaine often has fatal consequences in experimental animals. For example, in one study where monkeys were allowed unlimited access to cocaine 24 hours a day, all animals suffered from convulsions and died within 30 days (Deneau et al. 1969). To avoid this problem in self-administration studies, researchers often use a procedure where access to the drug is limited to several hours per day. In this situation, animals typically show an initial burst of self-administration when the drug is first made available, and then a pattern of uniformed spaced responding. This pattern is not unlike the spaced pattern of puffing commonly observed in cigarette smokers (Griffiths et al. 1980).

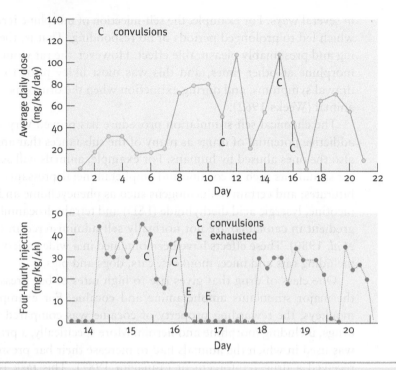

Figure 12.4 Cocaine self-administration by a monkey

The top panel shows the total daily intake for 21 days. The bottom panel shows the intake in four-hour periods for days 14 to 21. Note the cycle of intake and abstinence. (Adapted from Deneau, et al., 1969)

Source: W.A. McKim, *Drugs and Behavior*, 2nd edition, p. 218. Copyright © 1991 by Prentice Hall, Inc.

How do amphetamine and cocaine work on the brain?

Amphetamine is the common name for β-phenylisopropylamine and was first synthesised in the 1920s, although it is structurally related to several naturally occurring plant compounds, including ephedrine and cathinone. An idea of how amphetamine produces its pharmacological effects can be obtained by comparing its molecular structure with noradrenaline and dopamine: all three chemicals are similar. In fact, amphetamines exert three main effects on catecholaminergic systems of the brain: (1) they cause the release of dopamine and, to a lesser extent noradrenaline, from nerve endings, (2) they block the reuptake of dopamine and noradrenaline, and (3) they have a modest effect at inhibiting monoamine oxidase. Thus, amphetamines increase the levels of catecholamines, particularly dopamine, at certain synapses in the brain. Because of this amphetamines are sometimes described as **indirect-acting agnoists**.

Cocaine is a natural substance derived from the small leaves of the coca plant (*Erythroxylon coca*), which grows on the slopes of the Andes in South America. The leaves of the coca plant have been chewed for thousands of years, and were used by the local Indians to prevent fatigue and increase energy for physical labour. In pharmacological terms, cocaine does not cause the release of catecholamines like amphetamine, although it acts as an indirect-acting agonist by blocking the reuptake of dopamine and noradrenaline (and to a lesser extent serotonin) in the brain. By this mechanism, cocaine increases the amount of dopamine (and noradrenaline) in the synapse. Thus, while cocaine and amphetamine have different pharmacological actions, their net effects are similar: both produce an enhancement of catecholaminergic neurotransmission.

Evidence shows that dopamine is the most important neurotransmitter for the reinforcing actions of amphetamine and cocaine. For example, a number of dopaminergic drugs can be used as substitutes for amphetamine and cocaine in the self-stimulation paradigm including the D-2 receptor agonists **apomorphine** and **bromocriptine**. But, perhaps more importantly, the self-injection of amphetamine and cocaine is terminated by specific dopaminergic receptor blockers such as **pimozide** and **spiroperidol**. Although this type of receptor blockade will initially increase the rate at which the animal will work to get amphetamine and cocaine, the response tails off, and bar pressing is terminated. In contrast, noradrenergic blocking drugs, such as phentolamine and propranolol, fail to significantly influence amphetamine or cocaine self-administration (Yokel 1987).

Although amphetamine and cocaine have stimulatory effects on all the dopamine systems of the brain, the mesolimbic pathway which projects from the VTA to the **nucleus accumbens** (Figure 12.5) is the most important for producing their rewarding effects. For example, the intravenous self-administration of cocaine and amphetamine is greatly reduced by 6-OHDA lesions of the nucleus accumbens. However, this effect is not produced by lesions of the frontal cortex or striatum, which also receive major dopaminergic pathways (Koob and Goeders 1989). Moreover, infusions of dopaminergic blocking drugs into the nucleus accumbens reduces the rewarding effects produced by the intravenous self-administration of the major stimulants (Philips and Broekkamp 1980). Again, the same does not occur with injections into the frontal cortex or caudate nucleus.

The intravenous injection of amphetamine and cocaine also results in dopamine release in the nucleus accumbens. For example, in a study using microdialysis to measure neurotransmitter levels from various brain sites, it was found that a low dose

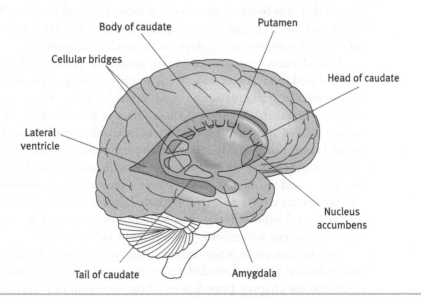

Figure 12.5 The location of the nucleus accumbens in the human brain

of cocaine (1 mg/kg) produced an increase of dopamine in the nucleus accumbens. Although higher doses of cocaine (2 mg/kg) resulted in dopamine release in the prefrontal cortex, it was still less than that occurring in the nucleus accumbens (Fibiger *et al.* 1992). It has also been shown that rats will learn to administer very small amounts of amphetamine into the nucleus accumbens (although this effect is not produced by cocaine). The amphetamine effect is, however, abolished by 6-OHDA lesions of the mesolimbic pathway which projects to the nucleus accumbens (see Rolls 1999).

The reward circuits of the brain revisited

As Olds and Milner showed over fifty years ago, many regions of the MFB give rise to lever pressing for electrical self-stimulation. From what we have seen regarding the rewarding effects of cocaine and amphetamine, we might predict that the MFB influences dopaminergic activity in the nucleus accumbens, perhaps by descending pathways to the VTA. Indeed, there is good evidence that the first stage of this pathway exists. For example, electrophysiological experiments have shown that many of the regions of the MFB that exhibit self-stimulation (such as the lateral hypothalamus) give rise to unmyelinated, non-dopaminergic fibres that travel to the VTA. This has led to the **descending path hypothesis** (Wise 1980), which proposes that the reward pathways activated by intracranial self-stimulation descend in the MFB (the first stage), and terminate in the VTA where they make contact with the dopaminergic cells (the second stage). Thus, the basic idea is that stimulation of the MFB is reinforcing because it increases activity in dopamine pathways originating in the VTA. Support for this idea has come from Bielajew and Shizgal (1986), who inhibited neuronal activity in the VTA by means of an electrode that used hyperpolarising (negative) current. They found that this blocked the effects of lateral hypothalamic self-stimulation. This indicates that the VTA acts as an interface between the MFB and the dopamine pathways of the midbrain, including those to the nucleus accumbens.

Considerable evidence shows that dopamine is involved in the rewarding effects of MFB stimulation. As we have seen, amphetamine and cocaine lower the threshold for intracranial self-stimulation to occur in the MFB (i.e. a less intense current is needed to produce reward), and the opposite effect is produced by dopaminergic antagonists which makes it more difficult to induce self-stimulation. The nucleus accumbens would appear to be a critical structure for producing these effects. For example, Stellar and Corbett (1989) injected a dopamine antagonist into 56 different sites throughout the brain, and found that only one area – the nucleus accumbens – significantly reduced the rewarding effects of lateral hypothalamic stimulation. Conversely, self-stimulation of the lateral hypothalamus was found to be enhanced by injections of amphetamine into the nucleus accumbens (Spencer and Corbett 1986).

Despite this, there is also evidence that is inconsistent with the idea that the nucleus accumbens is the final reward pathway for MFB stimulation. For example, as we saw earlier in the chapter, huge lesions of the forebrain that destroy most of the dopamine terminals of the nucleus accumbens, septum, striatum and frontal cortex have relatively little effect on reducing lateral hypothalamic stimulation (Valenstein and Campbell

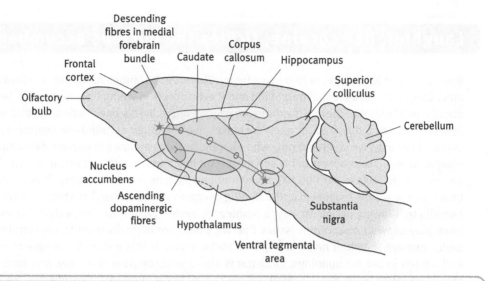

| Figure 12.6 | Diagram showing how descending fibres of the medial forebrain bundle are able to influence ascending dopaminergic systems which have their cell bodies in the ventral tegmental area |

Source: R.B. Graham, *Physiological Psychology*. Copyright © 1990 by Wadsworth, Inc.

1966). Similarly, 6-OHDA lesions of the dopamine cell bodies in the VTA do not significantly attenuate lateral hypothalamic self-stimulation (Philips and Fibiger 1978). Although these findings are open to different interpretations, it suggests that the 'two-stage' model of reward is far too simple. An alternative has been suggested by Stellar and Rice (1989), who argue that MFB reward fibres may pass through the VTA, yet take a different multiple-synaptic and non-dopaminergic route to the nucleus accumbens. This possibility has yet to be proved.

Animal studies using microdialysis to measure dopamine levels in the nucleus accumbens have shown it to be involved in a wide range of rewarding behaviours – and not just drug taking. For example, investigators have found increased dopamine levels in the nucleus accumbens after consuming food reward, and after sexual activity with receptive partners (Joseph *et al.* 2003). In addition it is activated after enjoyable activities such as winning money, or laughter (see box on page 456). It would appear, therefore, to be a reward centre. However, this idea must be viewed with caution, as many other 'non-rewarding' behaviours, including locomotor activity, exploration and operant conditioning, are also associated with high levels of dopamine release in the nucleus accumbens (Philips *et al.* 1991). And, to make matters more complex, dopamine in the nucleus accumbens is also released in response to aversive stimuli. For example, dopamine levels are increased in the nucleus accumbens during unavoidable electric foot shock, or in response to a stimulus that has been conditioned to produce fear (Gray *et al.* 1997). These findings have led to alternative theories concerning the function of the nucleus accumbens, with some emphasising its role in attention, arousal, motivation and learning (see Ikemoto and Panksepp 1999; Alcaro *et al.* 2007). Although the function of the nucleus accumbens remains open to debate, most researchers now believe it is much more complex than simply providing reinforcement.

Laughter, like cocaine, tickles the nucleus accumbens

If we were unable to laugh, or find jokes funny, life would be immeasurably less enjoyable and pleasurable. Laughter is an essential part of life and it even occurs in young babies (the first laughter occurs at about 4 months). Yet, nobody is quite sure why we laugh. It has been estimated that we laugh around seventeen times a day, and, in many instances, we will laugh at mundane comments or ordinary life events. Curiously, we laugh not only when happy, but also at times of nervousness, embarrassment or disappointment. Laugher probably serves several functions. In some cases, it may act to reduce stress and help us to release pent-up negative emotions such as anger or anxiety. This is seen when a well-timed joke eases the tension in a threatening or aggressive situation. Laughter may also have cognitive benefits by allowing people to view a problem or event from a new perspective. For example, sick humour may allow us to confront issues that we would not normally want to contemplate. More importantly, perhaps, laughter helps strengthen social bonds as it is a sign that we are feeling comfortable and relaxed in our surroundings. Laughter is also a vital component of play, and for some mysterious reason we laugh when being tickled, yet we cannot tickle ourselves. Despite this, we should not lose sight of the fact that we laugh because it is pleasurable. One might predict, therefore, that laughter will also stimulate the reward systems of the brain.

This possibility has been examined in a study (Mobbs *et al.* 2003) that used MRI to photograph the brain activity of sixteen young adults who were presented with 42 cartoons that had previously been rated as very funny, and 42 non-funny cartoons (i.e. cartoons with funny visual or written cues omitted). The researchers found that the funniest cartoons activated a number of brain regions, including the nucleus accumbens (Plate 12.1). Moreover, the degree of activity in the

| Plate 12.1(a) | An example of a funny cartoon, and the same cartoon with funny cues omitted |

Source: Copyright © Dan Piraro. Reprinted with special permission of North American Syndicate

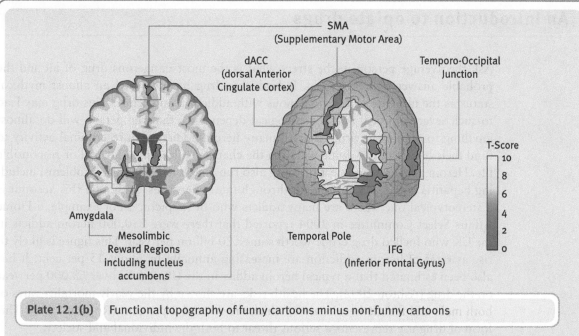

SMA
(Supplementary Motor Area)

dACC
(dorsal Anterior
Cingulate Cortex)

Temporo-Occipital
Junction

T-Score
10
8
6
4
2
0

Amygdala

Mesolimbic
Reward Regions
including nucleus
accumbens

Temporal Pole

IFG
(Inferior Frontal Gyrus)

Plate 12.1(b) Functional topography of funny cartoons minus non-funny cartoons

Source: D. Mobbs *et al.*, *Neuron*, 40, 1041–1048. Copyright © 2003, with permission from Elsevier

nucleus accumbens strongly correlated with how funny the subject thought the cartoon was: the extremely funny jokes causing more activation of the nucleus accumbens than the less funny ones. Other brain areas stimulated by the funny jokes included the amygdala, which is also believed to be involved in the sensation of pleasure, the left frontal cortex, including Broca's area, which is probably involved in the cognitive interpretation of the cartoon, and the motor cortex, which is responsible for producing the movements of laughter. Evidence for the latter has come from a study that applied electrical stimulation to the surface of the cerebral cortex in a 16-year-old girl to locate areas of epileptic tissue (Fried *et al.* 1998). During this investigation, a small area (about 2 cm by 2 cm) in the left motor cortex was found that always elicited laughter. This laughter was evoked on several trials and a different explanation was offered by the girl each time. For example, the laughter was attributed to the particular object seen during a naming object task ('the horse was funny'); to the content of a paragraph during reading; or to persons present in the room while the patient received the electrical stimulation ('you guys are just so funny . . . standing around').

The finding that funny cartoons activate the same reward circuits in the brain as addicting drugs such as cocaine, and other types of reinforcement such as money, sex and food, undoubtedly helps explain our unique 'addiction' to humour. But, laughter does more than just make us feel good by stimulating our nucleus accumbens. There is evidence that it can reduce feelings of pain, boost the immune system, decrease cortisol levels and lower blood pressure (Martin 2001). Long-lived persons also typically have a great sense of humour. Thus, laughter is not only a sure sign of happiness – but arguably the best medicine of them all.

An introduction to opiate drugs

Ask the average person in the street what is the most dangerous drug of all and the probable answer will be **heroin**. Indeed, this drug has achieved an almost mythical status as the ultimate evil, synonymous with addiction and crime. This drug may lead to such severe physical and psychological dependence that the person will do almost anything to obtain the drug. Indeed, many heroin addicts turn to criminal activity to fund their habit, and in doing so lessen the chances of leading a normal or responsible life. Heroin addicts who inject the drug also run a high risk of health problems, including hepatitis and AIDS, and death through fatal overdoses. Although this account is a stereotypical one, there are many addicts who fit its picture. For example, a Home Affairs Select Committee in 2004 reported that there were 250,000 heroin addicts in the UK who fuelled drug crime worth some £20 billion per year. This figure is likely to rise as rates of heroin addiction are increasing annually by about 15 per cent. It has also been estimated that a typical heroin addict in the UK spends over £8,000 per year on the drug (Ashton 2002). The health risks are shown by the yearly mortality rates of both male and female heroin users, which are around 2 per cent (Robson 1999). This form of drug use represents a serious threat to both the individual and society.

Heroin belongs to a class of drugs known as the **opiates**, which refers to any substance, natural or synthetic, that has properties similar to opium, which is derived from the poppy *Papaver somniferum*. Opium has a long history of human use. There is evidence that opium was used over 6,000 years ago by the Babylonians, who called it the plant of joy, and it is mentioned in ancient Egyptian scrolls, which recommended it for crying children (Melzack and Wall 1988). Opium was widely used in Britain from around the sixteenth century, and freely available up until the nineteenth century when it was used to treat a wide range of ailments. In fact, the demand for opium was so great that it was largely responsible for Britain's wars against China in 1839–42 and 1856–58, which led to the annexing of Hong Kong in 1842 and 1860 as part of the war reparations.

The main psychoactive ingredient of opium is **morphine,** which makes up about 10 per cent of its weight. This was first isolated by Frederick Serturner in 1803, who named it after Morpheus the Greek god of sleep. Morphine is about ten times more potent than raw opium, and was found to be a very powerful analgesic, especially after the invention of the hypodermic needle in 1853, which allowed it to be injected directly into the bloodstream. It is hard to imagine a more important drug in the practice of medicine. Later, in 1874, a new opiate was synthesised in St Mary's Hospital, London, by the chemist C.R. Alder Wright who called it diacetylmorphine. This was commercially produced as a cough suppressant by the Bayer Drug Company in Germany, who called it heroin from the word *heroisch* (meaning heroic or strong). Because of its high lipid solubility which allows it rapid access to the central nervous system, heroin is about ten times more potent than morphine when injected into the blood. There is little point in taking heroin orally, however, as it is broken down into morphine in the liver.

Most people who become addicted to heroin follow a pathway that takes them from smoking heroin (or sniffing it), to injecting it directly into their bloodstream. Smoking heroin is generally undertaken for its pleasant sedating qualities. However, even at this early stage, **tolerance** to the drug occurs rapidly with regular use. This results in the individual having to smoke more (in other words, increase the dose) to

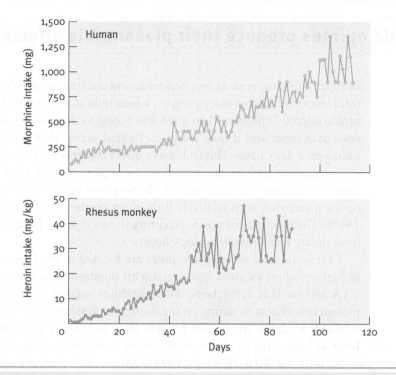

Figure 12.7	Self-administration of morphine by a human, and of heroin by a monkey, when given free access to the drug

Source: W.A. McKim, *Drugs and Behavior*, 2nd edition, p. 240. Copyright © 1991 by Prentice Hall, Inc.

obtain the original 'pleasurable effect'. Opiate drugs are particularly renowned for their ability to induce tolerance, and it is possible for a person to increase their consumption tenfold after three or four months. The same effect also occurs in animals such as monkeys when they are given free access to opiates (see Figure 12.7). Despite this, tolerance does not occur at the same rate to all of heroin's effects. For example, the constriction of the pupils only partially disappears with continued opiate use and the constipating effects of these drugs rarely change (McKim 2003).

The pleasurable effects of heroin, however, show marked tolerance, and this may encourage the regular user to begin injecting the drug. This often produces a 'rush' or strong feeling of euphoria, followed by a long dreamy state, which removes both physical and psychological pain. But, again, tolerance to these effects is likely to occur, leading to increased dosage. One effect of tolerance is an increased likelihood of **withdrawal symptoms** when the effects of the drug start to wear off. These often manifest themselves as strong **cravings** for another fix, which start four to six hours after the previous dose. The cravings may be accompanied by physical symptoms including aches, chills, sweating, anxiety, cramps and muscular shaking. These uncomfortable reactions provide a motive for further use of the drug. Eventually, this may result in a state where the person is so dependent on heroin that they need to regularly take it to stave off illness or to feel 'normal'. At this point the person gets no real pleasure from taking the drug, but requires it to keep the unpleasant side effects away.

How do opiates produce their pleasurable effects?

In much the same way as amphetamine and cocaine, opiate drugs are self-administered intravenously by laboratory animals, which indicates that they have reinforcing or pleasurable effects. Typically, when given free access to these drugs, animals will increase their dose over time; and if they are given limited access they will maintain stable levels of intake on a daily basis. This is due to a direct receptor effect as the administration of opiate antagonists such as **naloxone** decreases opiate reward as measured by the increasing time interval between injections. Both morphine and heroin have agonist effects on the opiate μ-receptor, with relatively little effect on the κ and σ subtypes (Koob and Bloom 1988). The existance of opiate receptors shows that the brain produces its own endogenous opiate-like substances (see Chapter 3).

Examination of where μ-receptors are located in the brain shows them to be found in high numbers in areas associated with dopaminergic reward systems, including the VTA and nucleus accumbens. These findings suggest that opiate drugs produce their pleasurable effects by acting on the dopamine systems of the brain. Indeed, there is considerable evidence to support for this idea. For example, animals will learn to press a lever at high rates to obtain infusions of morphine, along with other μ-receptor agonists, into the VTA (Bozarth 1986). Moreover, when an opiate antagonist such as nalorphine is injected into the VTA, or the nucleus accumbens, the intravenous self-administration of opiates significantly increases, indicating that the animal is attempting to overcome the reduction in reinforcement. The injection of morphine into the VTA also lowers the threshold for intracranial self-stimulation of the MFB, confirming that opiates are directly involved in the brain's reward processes (Di Chiara and North 1992).

Dopamine has been shown to be important for the reinforcing effects of opiates in the VTA. For example, injections of morphine into the VTA cause the release of dopamine and its metabolites in the nucleus accumbens. This effect occurs because μ-receptors are located on **GABA** interneurons in the VTA, which project onto the cell bodies of dopaminergic neurons (Figure 12.8). GABA normally acts to suppress the firing of the dopamine neurons, but activation of the μ-receptors causes the GABA neurons to lose their inhibitory influence. The result is the release of dopamine in the nucleus accumbens which is pleasurable for the animal (Bozarth 1987).

There is evidence, however, that the dopaminergic link between the VTA and the nucleus accumbens is not the only one producing the rewarding effects of opiates. For example, rats will also work for morphine injections directly into the nucleus accumbens. And, this effect still occurs when the accumbens dopaminergic terminals have been destroyed by 6-OHDA lesions. In other words, this reinforcing effect is independent of dopamine (Nestler *et al.* 2001). Moreover, large 6-OHDA lesions of the VTA that destroy the dopamine pathways to the nucleus accumbens has little effect on the acquisition of heroin self-administration. In one study, Pettit *et al.* (1984) trained rats to self-administer cocaine and heroin on alternate days and then they lesioned the nucleus accumbens. Although this lesion completely abolished cocaine self-stimulation, it had little effect on heroin self-administration.

To make matters more confusing, while dopamine-depleting lesions of the nucleus accumbens do not block heroin self-administration, different findings are obtained

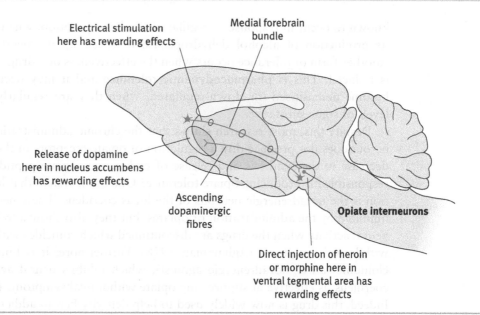

Electrical stimulation here has rewarding effects

Medial forebrain bundle

Release of dopamine here in nucleus accumbens has rewarding effects

Ascending dopaminergic fibres

Opiate interneurons

Direct injection of heroin or morphine here in ventral tegmental area has rewarding effects

Figure 12.8   The role of opiate-containing interneurons in the ventral tegmental area

when kainic acid lesions are used – which destroy all of the cell bodies in the accumbens, not just dopaminergic ones. In fact, this type of lesion has a significant effect of reducing the self-administration of heroin (Feldman *et al.* 1997). Thus, other chemical pathways and neurotransmitter systems must play a role in mediating the rewarding effects of opiates. In this respect it is interesting to note that the nucleus accumbens also receives major input from the limbic cortex, hippocampus and amygdala – which are all areas involved in emotion.

Opiate tolerance and dependence

The pharmacological mechanism by which opiates cause addiction has long been a subject of great interest. As already noted, one of the features of opiate addiction is tolerance, which occurs when the body becomes so adapted to the presence of a drug that a given amount of that substance produces less of an effect than when the user first tried it. In fact, it is possible for a heroin addict, after several months of heavy use, to be injecting themselves with 40–50 times the normal lethal dose. This type of drug use results in physical dependence where the addict experiences strong cravings and withdrawal symptoms when the effects of the heroin wear off. These reactions provide a powerful motive for the continuation of drug use.

When a drug is administered over a long period of time, a number of adaptive changes are likely to occur in the body. These may include, for example, an up-regulation of various enzymes involved in the metabolism of the drug, which results in a smaller amount of it reaching the action site. This is called **pharmacokinetic tolerance** and is known to occur in response to regular alcohol consumption, when the liver increases its production of alcohol dehydrogenase to speed up its metabolism of alcohol. Another form of tolerance occurs when the effectiveness of a drug on its site of action is reduced. This is **pharmacodynamic tolerance** and it may occur when receptors become desensitised (or down-regulated) when they are regularly exposed to high levels of some substance.

Despite this, most research shows that the chronic administration of morphine or heroin does not produce down-regulation of opiate receptors in the brain, or cause a decrease in the synthesis and release of endogenous opiate peptides. What, then, is responsible for producing opiate tolerance? One brain system that has attracted attention is the noradrenergic neurons of the **locus coeruleus**. These neurons not only are inhibited by the administration of opiates, but they also show a 'rebound' increase in neural activity when the drugs are discontinued which coincides with the emergence of withdrawal symptoms (Aghajanian 1978). Furthermore, it is known that the drug **clonidine** (an α_2-noradrenergic agonist), which inhibits neural activity in the locus coeruleus, is effective at suppressing opiate withdrawal symptoms (Gold *et al.* 1978). Indeed, this drug is now widely used to help detoxify heroin addicts, although it does not stop the strong cravings for opiates. Overall, these studies lend strong support to the idea that decreased activity in the locus coeruleus is an important component of opiate tolerance, and increased activity of this structure contributes to the emergence of withdrawal symptoms.

Several other sites in the brain are also responsible for producing withdrawal symptoms after chronic administration of opiate drugs in animals. For example, in a set of studies by Koob *et al.* (1992), rats were made physically dependent on morphine by implanting them subcutaneously with morphine pellets. After three days, the researchers injected the opiate antagonist methylnaloxonium into several areas of the brain to trigger withdrawal symptoms. This produced behaviours such as shaking, teeth chattering, chewing, rearing and jumping. The area of the brain that gave rise to the highest number of withdrawal symptoms was the locus coeruleus. However, several other areas also gave rise to these behaviours, including the periaqueductal grey area, amygdala, anterior preoptic hypothalamus and raphe magnus. The last structure is not the same as the dorsal raphe (mentioned elsewhere in this book), but is the site of the raphe spinal tract which terminates in the spinal cord and is known to regulate incoming pain signals.

The molecular basis of opiate tolerance

A breakthrough in opiate research occurred in the early 1970s when it was found that a type of tumour cell (called a neuroblastoma–glioma hybrid cell) contained μ-opiate receptors that were sensitive to morphine (Klee and Nirenberg 1974). One of the benefits of this discovery was that it allowed the intracellular aspects of opiate receptor function to be explored using cell culture studies. This work revealed that opiate receptors were coupled with a number of **G-proteins** (see Chapter 1) located on the inner side of the neural membrane. These proteins served a number of different functions. Perhaps the most important effect of μ-receptor activation was the inhibition of the intracellular enzyme **adenylate cyclase**, which reduced the formation of the second messenger **cyclic adenosine monophosphate (cAMP)**. This chemical mediates a number of intracellular processes, which in this case included the inhibition of sodium channels, which reduced the flow of positively charged sodium ions into the cell. In addition, cAMP affects **protein kinase A** activity, which is able to alter gene expression in the nucleus.

Importantly, this model also allowed the molecular basis of morphine tolerance to be examined. For example, when neuroblastoma–glioma hybrid cells were exposed to solutions of morphine, this initially caused the inhibition of cAMP, but after two days of chronic exposure the cAMP levels returned to normal (Sharma *et al.* 1975). However, when morphine was abruptly removed from the cell culture medium at this stage, the level of cAMP rose significantly above control levels (Figure 12.9). This rise in cAMP also led to an increase in the excitability of the cell by enhancing the activity of sodium channels, which increased the flow of sodium ions positively charged ion into the neuron. If we extrapolate what is happening in the neuroblastoma–glioma hybrid cells to the locus coeruleus, then we can deduce that morphine at first produces neural inhibition, but cAMP adapts to this change after two days, bringing the activity of locus coeruleus neurons back to normal. This is a form of neural **tolerance**. However, when morphine is removed, the sudden rise in cAMP (producing an increase in the activity of the locus coerulues) would help to explain the **withdrawal** symptoms.

It has also been found that up-regulation of the cAMP pathway in the **nucleus accumbens** is another common response to the long-term exposure of drugs, including opiates, cocaine and alcohol. When these drugs are administered, dopamine concentrations in the nucleus accumbens rise, leading to an increase in intracellular levels of cAMP. In turn, this activity results in an up-regulation of adenylate cyclase and protein kinase A. In addition there is an increase in CREB activity. This is a transcription factor that affects the expression of genes in the nucleus of the cell. One effect of this in the nucleus accumbens is the production of **dynorphin**, which is a peptide with opiate-like effects. Dynorphin is released from axons of the nucleus accumbens that project to the VTA where it causes inhibition. The induction of

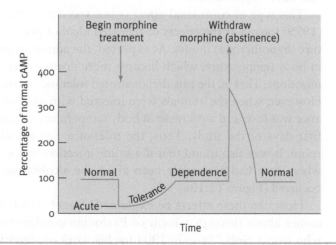

| Figure 12.9 | The effect of morphine on cAMP |

Source: R.S. Feldman *et al.* (1997) *Principles of Neuropharmacology*, p. 540

dynorphin by CREB, therefore, dampens the activity of the brain's dopaminergic reward circuit. This helps to produce tolerance by making further use of the drug less rewarding (see Nestler 2004).

The influence of the environment on drug tolerance

It may come as a surprise to find out that pharmacological factors do not fully account for opiate tolerance and withdrawal symptoms. Indeed, it has often been demonstrated that tolerance can be strongly influenced by learning and conditioning, that is, through a process of **behavioural tolerance**. In other words, the experience of the drug user can significantly affect the potency of a substance on the body. One important factor contributing to tolerance is the environment or context in which the drug is taken. This was shown by Siegel *et al.* (1982), who gave heroin and saline to two groups of laboratory rats in distinctively different testing cages. The heroin was injected over a period of 30 days in increasing doses to produce tolerance. Following this, rats were given a final 'high' dose of heroin that was lethal for the majority of the animals. For half of the drug-treated rats, the heroin injection was given in the same testing cage as all the previous injections, and for the remaining animals it was given in a new and distinct cage. The results showed that the heroin injection administered in the new cage produced more deaths (96 per cent of the group) compared with the usual testing environment (64 per cent). This type of effect may also occur in humans. For example, Siegel (1984) interviewed ten former heroin addicts from a methadone facility in New York whose medical records showed hospitalisation for heroin overdose. Self-reports revealed that unusual circumstances had surrounded the overdose in a number of the survivors, which included two instances where heroin administration had taken place in locations where the addicts had never injected before.

This type of contextual effect is not specific to the opiates. For example, Le *et al.* (1979) looked at the effects of repeated alcohol injections on lowering body temperature (hypothermia) in rats. As expected, the administration of alcohol led to a decrease in body temperature, which became more normal over subsequent days with repeated injections. That is, the rats demonstrated tolerance to the hypothermic effect of alcohol. However, when the animals were injected with alcohol in a different room, the tolerance was lost, and a decrease in body temperature occurred similar to that found in the first days of the study. Thus, the tolerance was associated with a particular testing room. It was also found that if a saline injection was given to the animals in the room where they had previously been given the alcohol, an increase in body temperature occurred (Figure 12.10).

How can these effects be explained? Siegel (1984) has proposed that the process comes about through a form of Pavlovian conditioning. Pavlov was a physiologist who won a Nobel Prize in 1904 for his work on digestion in dogs. During the course of the research, Pavlov found that his laboratory dogs would learn to anticipate the presentation of food by salivating. In other words, the dogs were learning something about the experimental situation that predicted food. Pavlov decided to examine this type of learning in more detail by performing a number of experiments. In Pavlovian

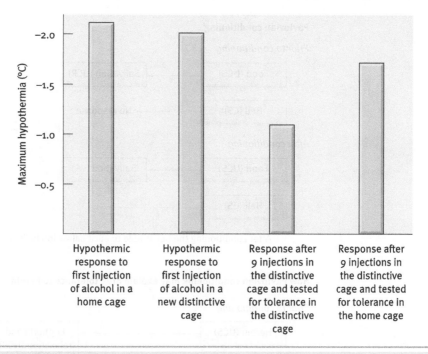

Source: Adapted from A.D. Le et al. (1979) Science, 206, 1109–1110

Figure 12.10   The situational specificity of tolerance to the hypothermic effects of alcohol

terminology, the food was viewed as the unconditioned or 'unlearned' stimulus (UCS), and salivation as the unconditioned response (UCR). That is to say, the ability of food to cause salivation is a natural reflex that is not learned. However, Pavlov discovered that when he paired the food (UCS) with the sound of a bell (the conditioned stimulus or CS) for several trials, the bell alone would elicit salivation (now the conditioned response or CR). In other words, the dog had learned that the bell was associated with food, and its ringing produced salivation in anticipation of being fed.

According to Siegel, the development of drug tolerance comes about through a similar process to Pavlovian conditioning. Consistent with the ideas of Pavlovian conditioning, Siegel argues that the environmental cues that regularly accompany the use of the drug (for example, the testing cage in rat studies; or pubs, washrooms, needles etc. for humans) act as conditioned stimuli (CSs) which elicit conditioned responses (CRs). In other words, with drug use, the contextual or environmental cues produce a change in the behavioural state of organism. One might predict from Pavlov's account that environmentally induced CRs associated with heroin use would be similar to the intoxicating effects of the drug. In other words, they would mimic the drug's impact on the body by producing responses such as sweating, lacrimation and excitement. But, Siegel proposes that conditioned responses in this situation work in an opposite way – by compensating for the expected effects of the drug. That is, the conditioned responses act to reduce the drug's impact on the body – or what Siegel calls a **compensatory conditioned response** (Figure 12.11). This would explain why environmental cues associated with drug use are able to produce a form of tolerance.

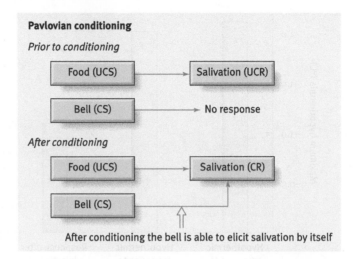

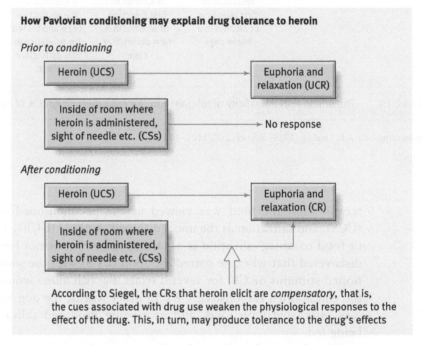

Figure 12.11	The differences between conditioned responses in Pavlovian conditioning and conditioned compensatory responses shown by Siegel

Conditioned craving and withdrawal

Although compensatory conditioned responses may help explain the development of opiate tolerance, the traditional Pavlovian model, in which conditioned stimuli come to trigger certain responses associated with drug use, appears to provide a much better explanation of craving and withdrawal. Indeed, it has long been known that opiate addicts who had been detoxified and maintained in a drug-free state will sometimes experience strong cravings and withdrawal symptoms when talking about drugs during group therapy, or on their return to neighbourhoods where drugs had been used. Wikler (1948) labelled this phenomenon **conditioned withdrawal**, speculating that environmental stimuli can acquire the ability through Pavlovian conditioning to produce many of the symptoms of opiate withdrawal and craving. He further hypothesised that this type of effect may be an important reason why some people re-establish compulsive drug use after quite long periods of abstinence.

A number of human studies have confirmed that withdrawal symptoms can be conditioned to environmental stimuli. For example, in one study where abstinent opiate users had just completed a thirty-day treatment programme in a therapeutic community, it was found that a number of physiological responses (for example, respiration rate, skin temperature and heart rate), along with strong cravings, occurred when subjects watched a drug-related video. Similar responses also occurred when handling drug paraphernalia or performing a 'cook-up tie-off procedure' (Rose et al. 1986). The fact that such behaviours in themselves can be pleasurable helps to explain why drug use is often associated with various rituals and routines. An example of this phenomenon is the 'needle freak' who, by the act of injection alone or the administration of inert substances such as water, derives significant feelings of pleasure.

Withdrawal symptoms can also be conditioned in experimental animals. In one study, Goldberg and Schuster (1967) trained morphine-dependent monkeys to press a lever for food. During the food reinforcement sessions, a buzzer was presented, which was followed by an injection of the opiate antagonist nalorphine, which elicited a number of withdrawal symptoms including salivation and increased heart rate. After several pairings, it was found that the buzzer alone produced the withdrawal symptoms. In fact, these conditioned withdrawal symptoms could be elicited for up to four months in response to the sound of the buzzer. These results show that neutral stimuli, when paired with drug related ones, have the potential to trigger withdrawal symptoms that are likely to reestablish drug taking.

In contrast, stimuli that are not associated with drug use may have a beneficial effect of reducing the severity of withdrawal symptoms. For example, Krank and Perkins (1993) injected rats with morphine and saline over a period of ten days. In one condition the rats were given morphine in a distinctive or novel cage and saline in their home cage; in the other condition the injections were reversed (i.e. morphine in the home cage and saline in the novel cage). Thus all animals received twenty injections (ten saline and ten morphine). After the injection regime, rats were placed in the novel test environment and their withdrawal symptoms recorded. The results showed that animals given morphine injections in the novel test cage exhibited significantly more withdrawal symptoms than the ones given the drug in their home cage (Figure 12.12). In other words, withdrawal symptoms are more severe in the environment where the drug is usually taken. This study has some interesting implications for helping the addict overcome withdrawal and craving. In short, it would appear that the most effective way of reducing withdrawal symptoms and craving is to place the addict in a completely new environment.

The importance of the environment on drug taking can be most dramatically seen in the case of US servicemen serving in Vietnam, where heroin was cheap, plentiful and sold in an easy-to-use smokable form. During the late 1960s and early 1970s it was estimated that around 35 per cent of enlisted men had tried heroin in Vietnam, and about half this number were taking it regularly and showing dependence. This situation led to fears that the serviceman would bring their opiate problem back to the United States. However, surveys found that few serviceman continued taking heroin when they returned home. For example, Robins et al. (1979) interviewed 617 enlisted men before their return from Vietnam in 1971, and again three years later. Half the veterans addicted in Vietnam had used heroin after returning home, but only 12 per cent of them became re-addicted. These findings show the importance of setting on drug use. While in Vietnam, the US soldiers were in an unpleasant and stressful setting, cut off from friends and family, with easy access to drugs. Back in the United States, they were in a very different setting, and able to resume everyday

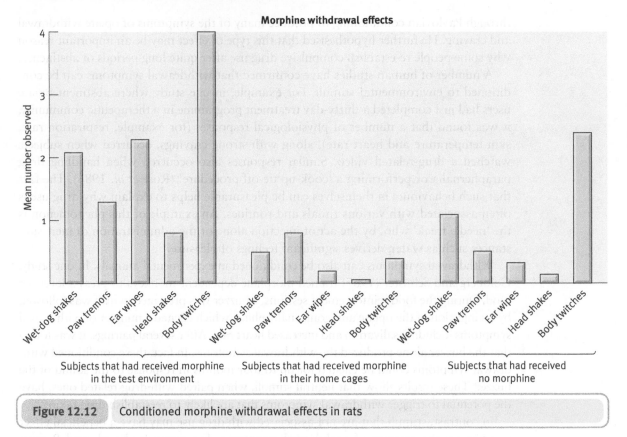

Figure 12.12 Conditioned morphine withdrawal effects in rats

Source: John J.P. Pinel (2003) *Biopsychology*, 5th edition, p. 387

living without the use of heroin. Presumably, they experienced fewer conditioned withdrawal symptoms too, making drug abstinence easier to achieve.

Sensitisation and incentive salience

Although tolerance occurs with the repeated use of many drugs, there are instances when the opposite action occurs, and the drug produces a greater effect than it did previously. This is known as **sensitisation** or **reverse tolerance**. Sensitisation is most commonly observed with the repeated administration of the psychomotor stimulants cocaine and amphetamine. For example, when given to laboratory animals at low doses, these drugs activate certain patterns of behaviour, including increased motor activity and rearing. With repeated administration, this type of motor activity becomes more intense, and new stereotyped behaviours start to occur, including head bobbing, licking, gnawing and sniffing. These behaviours occur for extended periods and at doses which initially caused only motor activation. Such drug effects can be highly persistent. For example, the behavioural effects of sensitisation have been observed a year after drug exposure in rats (one-third of their lifetime), and they can become more pronounced with time (McKim 2003). Although sensitisation is most associated with the use of cocaine and amphetamine, it can occur in response to a number of other drugs, including nicotine, ethanol, phencyclidine, MDMA and morphine (Robinson and Berridge 1993).

Similar to tolerance, sensitisation can be conditioned to a particular environment. For example, it has been shown that if sensitised motor activity and stereotypy is induced in rats and mice by repeatedly administering the drug in a specific environment, then sensi-tisation will be greatly reduced, or not appear at all, when the substance is given in a dif-ferent environment (McKim 2003). Conversely, after an animal has been made sensitised to the locomotor effects of amphetamine, placing it back into its testing cage is sufficient to produce increased motor activity in the absence of the drug. Thus, it appears that drug-environmental conditioning of this type may also contribute to the development of sensitisation. This may be an important reason for its relative permanence.

Considerable evidence shows that dopamine is involved in the development of sen-sitisation. Both cocaine and amphetamine are known to cause the release of dopamine, and the dopaminergic pathway from VTA to nucleus accumbens is primarily involved in the locomotor effects of the psychomotor stimulants. Indeed, direct microinjection of dopamine or its agonists into the nucleus accumbens elicits locomotor activity and stereotypical behaviours. Furthermore, increased levels of dopamine as measured by dialysis have been found in the nucleus accumbens with the development of sensitisa-tion (White and Wolf 1991).

The fact that many drugs of abuse can give rise to sensitisation, which is believed to involve the mesolimbic dopamine system, has led to the **incentive sensitisation theory of addiction** (Robinson and Berridge 1993). According to this theory, compulsive drug-taking behaviour develops from a long-lasting sensitisation of the dopaminergic pathway from the VTA to the nucleus accumbens. The main consequence of this en-hanced neural activity is that the person becomes hypersensitive, or 'sensitised', to cer-tain drugs or drugs-related stimuli. This phenomenon is called **incentive salience**. In other words, sensitisation results in the person's motivation for drugs becoming ampli-fied. This produces a strong craving that leads to the compulsive pursuit of the drug. One consequence of this effect is that drug-related stimuli become highly salient and difficult for addicts to ignore. In this way, the person may experience a strong desire to take a substance when confronted by a situation that includes drug-related cues, even if they have gone through a detoxification process and been 'clean' for many years.

It is interesting to note that this theory does not see dopamine in the nucleus ac-cumbens as being responsible for producing reward. Rather, it views dopamine as functioning to attribute salience to stimuli associated with rewards such as food and sex – and it also triggers the 'wanting' that can cause cravings. In fact, Robinson and Berridge believe that the neuronal systems responsible for incentive salience are differ-ent from those responsible for mediating the pleasurable effects of drugs. Indeed, they provide support for this view by pointing out that 'wanting' is not the same as 'liking'. That is, a person may strongly want a drug without actually liking the consequences that it produces. This is seen in the case of heroin addicts, for example, who sometimes report liking the drug less and less, as their use (or wanting) increases more and more.

Two other aspects of the incentive salience model are worth mentioning. Firstly, Robinson and Berridge argue that the 'wanting system' often operates below the level of conscious awareness. This means that the motivation for drug use can influence behaviour without a person having full understanding of its causes. Secondly, a number of researchers have found that animals exposed to repeated stress are later hyperresponsive to psy-chomotor stimulants. For example, animals given four daily mild tail pinches over a fifteen-day period were shown to exhibit far higher levels of stereotypy when given an injection of amphetamine (Antelman *et al.* 1975). These findings indicate that psychostimulant drugs and stress are interchangeable in their ability to induce sensitisation. The implication is that stress by itself can cause increased dopamine activity in the nucleus accumbens, leading to incentive salience, and craving for drugs. Indeed, it is well known by researchers and drug workers alike that stress is an important cause of relapse in drug addicts.

Other commonly abused drugs

Virtually all drugs that are reinforcing in people are also rewarding for laboratory animals. This can be demonstrated by the fact that animals will self-administer the same types of substances that are drugs of abuse for humans. For example, as we have seen earlier, monkeys will work tirelessly to obtain injections of cocaine and heroin, which are also highly addictive drugs for humans. Other drugs self-administered by animals include alcohol, nicotine and caffeine (Yokel 1987). But, drugs not normally abused by humans, including imipramine (an antidepressant), chlorpromazine (an antipsychotic) and atropine (a cholinergic muscarinic antagonist) are also not self-administered by laboratory animals. It is also relevant to note that hallucinogenic drugs such as LSD are rarely self-injected by animals, and it is rare for dependence to occur to these drugs in humans. One exception may be tetrahydrocannibinol (THC), the active ingredient in cannabis, which appears to be liked by humans and not by animals.

Why, then, are some drugs liable to cause addiction? Part of the answer appears to be that all drugs which have significant dependence liability, including cocaine, heroin, alcohol and nicotine (and to a lesser extent caffeine and cannabis), are known to increase the release of dopamine in the nucleus accumbens. Indeed, many believe that the critical site for this effect lies in the ventral tegmental area which has dopamine projections to the nucleus accumbens (see Figure 12.13). Alternatively, drugs that are not self-administered by humans and animals, have no effect on dopamine transmission in the mesolimbic pathway (Di Chiara and Imperato 1988). Although dopamine in the nucleus accumbens is an important neural substrate for drug use, it is not the only one. Indeed, we should not forget that opiates can produce their rewarding effects independently of dopamine (as shown by the fact that lesions of the nucleus accumbens fail to stop intravenous heroin administration), and that cocaine is not self-administered into the nucleus accumbens (although it is self-administered into the prefrontal cortex).

The remainder of this chapter provides a brief overview of several other drugs known to give rise to addictive behaviours, with an emphasis on how they produce their pharmacological effects and how they work on the brain. Although this chapter

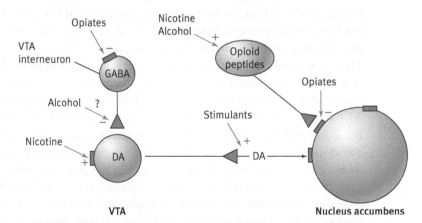

| Figure 12.13 | The main sites where reinforcing or pleasurable drugs have been shown to work on the mesolimbic dopamine system |

Source: Nestler, E.J., Hyman, S.E. and Malenka, R.C. (2001) *Molecular Neuropharmacology*, p. 360. The McGraw-Hill Companies, Inc.

has concentrated on the psychomotor stimulants and opiates to demonstrate the psychobiological aspects of compulsive drug use, it should not be forgotten that many features of addictive behaviour (most notably tolerance, withdrawal, cravings and psychological dependence) can also occur with the use of other substances.

Caffeine: the world's most popular drug

Caffeine is the most widely used psychoactive substance in the world, and found in some of our most popular beverages and foods, including coffee, tea, fizzy drinks and chocolate. It has been estimated that more than 80 per cent of the world's population, regardless of age, gender and culture, consume caffeine on a daily basis. This amounts to some 120,000 tonnes of caffeine per year. Moreover, people in the UK are among the world's heaviest users, with the typical adult consuming around 400 mg of caffeine per day, with most of this being in the form of tea and coffee (Nehlig 1999). Although caffeine is found in over sixty plant species, where it is believed to act as a natural pesticide, the coffee bean is the world's main source of the drug. Drinking a standard cup of instant coffee will generally provide the user with around 80 mg of caffeine, and this can increase up to 150 mg in percolated coffee. Tea usually contains far less caffeine (40 mg) although this figure can be highly variable. Another common source of caffeine is canned drinks, which may contain more than 60 mg of the drug.

Caffeine is an alkaloid which belongs to a class of drugs known as the methylxanthines. There are many other types of methylxanthine besides caffeine, but only two others occur naturally and these are theophylline (found in tea) and theobromine (found in chocolate). All methylxanthines are regarded as minor stimulants which help to increase alertness and ward off drowsiness. In humans, at typical doses (100–150 mg) caffeine has been shown to increase arousal, reduce mental tiredness and suppress sleep. A number of studies have also found that caffeine can improve performance on a variety of psychomotor tasks. Curiously, at higher doses, caffeine does not appear to have a mood elevating effect (like other stimulants), but instead causes restlessness, tenseness and insomnia. This condition is sometimes referred to as caffeinism. In some people, large amounts of caffeine may even precipitate anxiety and panic attacks. Although widely regarded as harmless, caffeine can actually cause withdrawal symptoms with non-use, including headache, physical tiredness and mental drowsiness. For this reason, some researchers have argued that caffeine is a 'model drug of abuse' (Holtzman 1990).

What makes caffeine so popular is still unclear. In intravenous self-stimulation experiments in laboratory animals, caffeine generally does not produce reinforcing effects. That is, rats and monkeys will not normally press a lever to obtain infusions of caffeine – and if they do, responding tends to be irregular, and far less than that maintained by amphetamine or cocaine (McKim 2003). For many years, the mechanism by which caffeine exerted its effects on behaviour was not understood. This was because caffeine, especially in high doses, produced a number of complex pharmacological actions. However, it is now known that caffeine, in amounts usually used by humans, acts by blocking adenosine receptors. Adenosine is a somewhat unusual neurotransmitter-like substance in the brain since it appears primarily to regulate cellular and metabolic processes. For example, it is known to regulate the delivery of oxygen to cells and to dilate cerebral and coronary blood vessels (Julien 2007). In addition, adenosine acts as an inhibitory neurotransmitter, with its receptors located presynaptically on neurons, where it helps to control the release of a wide range of neurotransmitters, including noradrenaline, dopamine, acetylcholine, glutamate and GABA. Thus, by blocking adenosine receptors, caffeine enhances the release of these neurotransmitters. Although there is little evidence that caffeine affects dopamine release in the nucleus accumbens, it still may stimulate the reward systems of the brain. This hypothesis is supported by the finding that caffeine can potentiate the behavioural effects of cocaine and amphetamine in experimental animals. However, the effects of caffeine are undoubtedly much more complex than this.

Alcohol

Alcohol use is very common, with around 75 per cent of the population drinking alcohol at least occasionally, But, more worryingly, 25 per cent of men and 15 per cent of women drink more than is considered 'safe', which, according to the Royal College of Physicians, is an intake of 22–50 units per week for men, and 15–35 units per week for women. Alcohol consumption is also on the increase, especially by young people. It has been shown that almost one-third of 15–16-year-olds binge drink in the UK, and get drunk at least three times a month – a figure that is the highest in Europe (Hibell *et al.* 2001). Moreover, about 5 per cent of adults are dependent on alcohol (classified as alcoholics or problem drinkers), which leads to significant social and occupational impairment. Each year in the UK, alcohol is responsible for up to 150,000 admissions to hospital; one-third of people reporting to accident and emergency; and 22,000 deaths.

Although there are different types of alcohol, the one we drink is called ethanol (or ethyl alcohol) and is produced by the distillation and fermentation of sugar. Because ethanol is a very small molecule, soluble in both water and fat, it can cross cell membranes and travel freely throughout the body. In fact, once absorbed, alcohol becomes distributed uniformly through the tissue and fluid compartments of the body including the brain. How alcohol acts on the brain is still not fully understood. Although alcohol causes neural excitation at small doses, its main effect is to depress the neural activity of the brain. However, unlike most other psychoactive substances, alcohol does not appear to bind directly to receptors or affect uptake mechanisms. Rather, it exerts its main pharmacological effect by dissolving in the outer membrane of neurons. This increases the **fluidity of the membrane**, which then alters the function of its embedded proteins in various ways (Chin and Goldstein 1981).

When alcohol seeps into the neural membrane its distribution is not uniform. This has led to a suggestion that a binding site in the membrane, perhaps at the protein–lipid interface, might best explain the effects of alcohol at moderate doses. One type of structure within the membrane that is believed to be structurally altered by alcohol is the ion channels which allow the transport of positively and negatively charged particles into and out of the neuron. For example, alcohol has been shown to decrease the influx of calcium (Ca^{2+}) ions into nerve endings, which reduces neurotransmitter release, and to decrease the flow of sodium (Na^+) ions into the dendrites and cell body, thereby causing a reduction of neural excitability.

Alcohol also exerts an indirect effect on certain receptors that are closely linked with ion channels. For example, alcohol enhances the actions of the **GABA-A receptor**, which leads to an increased flow of negative chloride (Cl^-) ions into the cell. This is believed to be an important mechanism by which alcohol causes neural inhibition. But, the exact way alcohol does this is not clear. For example, barbiturates and benzodiazepines are also known to bind to the GABA-A receptor, but alcohol does not compete or affect the binding of these substances. Thus, alcohol may exert its effect on the GABA receptor by altering the shape of its proteins in some way (Diaz 1997). There is also some evidence that alcohol acts on the **N-methyl-D-aspartate (NMDA) receptor**, which is sensitive to the excitatory neurotransmitter **glutamate**. For glutamate receptors to open their associated ion channels, the amino acid glycine needs to be present. However, alcohol prevents glycine from executing its normal role, which results in fewer excitatory calcium (Ca^{2+}) ions entering the neuron. This adds to the neural inhibition produced by the increased GABAergic activity.

There is some evidence that alcohol produces its rewarding and pleasurable effects by acting on the mesolimbic pathway (see Figure 12.13). For example, it has been found that low doses of alcohol in rats cause the release of dopamine in the nucleus accumbens, but not other dopaminergic regions of the brain (Imperato and Di Chiara 1986). It has also been shown that low doses of alcohol increase the firing rate of neurons in the VTA, perhaps by its inhibitory action on GABA interneurons, which would cause dopamine release in the nucleus accumbens. Indeed, the importance of dopamine in alcohol reinforcement is further supported by the fact that its receptor antagonists reduce lever pressing for ethanol in rats. Despite this, there is some contradictory evidence – most notably the finding that 6-OHDA lesions of the nucleus accumbens do not affect ethanol intake in laboratory animals (Koob and Nestler 1997).

To make matters more complex, alcohol is metabolised in the liver to produce a substance called acetaldehyde. This has been found to interact with catecholamine neurons in the brain to form opiate-like substances called **tetrahydroisoquinolines** (**TIQs**). Not only do TIQs directly act on opiate receptors, but they have also been shown to stimulate the release of dopamine from nerve endings. The role of the TIQs in producing the pleasurable and addictive effects of alcohol is highly controversial (Blum and Payne 1991). Despite this, an opiate involvement in alcohol consumption is shown by the fact that **naltrexone** (an opiate antagonist) reduces ethanol self-administration in animals, and has shown promise in treating human alcoholics.

Nicotine

Of all addictive substances, nicotine must rank as the one that causes the most widespread harm to its users. According to the World Health Organization, there are 1.1 billion smokers in the world, and 6,000 billion cigarettes are smoked every year. Cigarette smoking is the biggest cause of ill health and preventable death in the UK, and it kills over 100,000 people each year – a figure that is roughly equivalent to one-fifth of all deaths (Fogarty and Lingford-Hughes 2004). Smoking is the leading cause of lung cancer, with more than eight in ten cases being directly related to this drug habit, as well as being a major contributor to heart disease, bronchitis and emphysema. And, the practice is not cheap. At today's prices, a twenty-a-day smoker will spend more than £37,000 over the next twenty years on cigarettes.

Although the UK has seen a decline in the number of men smoking in recent years (from about 65 per cent of men in 1978, to around 28 per cent in 2002), there has been an increase in the number of women taking up the habit. Approximately the same numbers of men and woman now smoke in the UK, which accounts for some 12 million people. Smoking is also common in young people. About one quarter of 11-year-olds have tried smoking, and about 30 per cent of 16-year-olds of both sexes are regular smokers (Gossop 2000). No other substance used by humans is used with such high frequency, and no other drug is associated with such a variety of health ills (which also includes passive smoking). In recognition of this, in July 2007 the government banned smoking in all indoor public places, including pubs, shopping centres and nightclubs.

The smoke of a burning cigarette contains over 4,500 different compounds. But, the most important psychoactive ingredient in tobacco is **nicotine**, which makes up about 2 per cent of its weight. Nicotine is highly toxic and about 60 mg injected directly into a vein is sufficient to kill a person. Although the average cigarette contains about 8–9 mg of nicotine, most of it is burnt off, which means that the typical smoker absorbs only around 1 mg. When heated in a cigarette, nicotine 'rides' on small particles of tar, and when this mixture gets into the lungs, the nicotine is absorbed quickly through the mucus membranes and carried to the heart. Nicotine reaches the brain about 8 seconds after the smoke is inhaled, which is almost as fast as an intravenous injection. It also stays in the brain for a considerable length of time, with about 50 per cent of the dose taking 20–40 minutes to be redistributed to the body. The average smoker will administer some 70,000 separate puffs (doses) of nicotine to their brain every year.

Nicotine exerts its pharmacological effects by acting as an agonist at **acetylcholine (ACh) receptors**. There are two types of ACh receptor – **muscarinic** and **nicotinic** – and nicotine acts on the latter. Cholinergic neurons and nicotinic receptors are found in both the body and the brain. In fact, nicotine receptors located on the postsynaptic side of the neuromuscular junction, which cause muscle contraction, were 'discovered' over one hundred years ago by Cambridge physiologist John Newport Langley. This is also one reason why smoking can increase muscle tone and the strength of skeletal reflexes. In addition, nicotinic receptors are found in the sympathetic branch of the autonomic nervous system, where nicotine in doses encountered in tobacco smoking can stimulate heart rate, blood pressure and constrict blood vessels in the skin. The latter effect may help to explain the smoker's 'cold touch'. Nicotine also acts on the adrenal glands, where it causes the secretion of adrenaline and noradrenaline.

But, the most important effect of nicotine occurs on the brain. Nicotine receptors occur mainly on the presynaptic terminals of nerve fibres, where they regulate the release of several neurotransmitters including dopamine, noradrenaline, acetylcholine, GABA, glutamate and serotonin. High numbers of nicotine receptors are found particularly in the brainstem, thalamus, striatum and cerebral cortex. The action of nicotine in these areas is believed to increase arousal and makes the person feel more alert. But, importantly, nicotinic receptors are also found in the reward systems of the brain, including the VTA and nucleus accumbens.

Nicotine has been shown to increase neural firing in the VTA, which causes the release of dopamine in the nucleus accumbens (see Figure 12.13). Moreover, nicotine increases the release of dopamine in the nucleus accumbens at plasma concentrations that are similar to those found in smokers – although to a lesser degree than that which occurs with cocaine or heroin (Di Chiara and Imperato 1988). The reinforcing effect of nicotine is further shown by the fact that animals will work for an injection of this substance when it is directly injected into the VTA. This self-administration of nicotine, however, is disrupted when nicotinic antagonists are injected into the VTA, or by systemic injections of the opiate receptor antagonist naltrexone. Despite this, self-stimulation of nicotine is not abolished by the injection of antagonists into the nucleus accumbens, or by its lesions (Nestler *et al.* 2001).

Cannabis

Cannabis is the most commonly used illicit drug in the UK and in many other countries throughout the world. There are approximately 300 million users worldwide, with about 15 million of these in the UK. During the past decade, possession of cannabis has accounted for around 80 per cent of all drug convictions, and 90 per cent of all seizures by HM Customs and Excise. Partly because of its widespread use, and ineffective legislative control, cannabis was reclassified from a class B drug under the Misuse of Drugs Act 1971 to class C in 2004, making penalties for its possession less punitive. Cannabis and its many derivatives, including hashish and marijuana, comes from the *Cannabis sativa* plant, otherwise known as hemp, which comes in many forms. It is also one of humanity's oldest non-food plants. The plant appears to have originated in central Asia where it has been used since Neolithic times. Curiously, there is little evidence to show that it was grown for its intoxicating properties. Rather, the plant was cultivated for fibre, seed and its medicinal benefits. Knowledge concerning its potential as a mind-altering drug appears to be a more recent development, and possibly introduced into Europe by Napoleon's soldiers returning from Egypt in the late eighteenth century. The effects produced by smoking cannabis include relaxation, sociability, happiness and relief of tension. It can also provide a heightened awareness of colour and of aesthetic beauty. At higher doses, cannabis causes memory problems, confusion and perceptual distortions, although these are rarely as severe as those produced by other hallucinogenic drugs such as LSD.

There are at least sixty psychoactive ingredients in cannabis, but the most important is **delta-9-tetrahydrocannabinol (THC)**, which was first isolated by Gaoni and Mechoulam (1964). This substance is highly lipid soluble (dissolves in fat), and, because of this, cannabis was once believed to work on the brain in a similar way to alcohol, that is, by dissolving into the outer membrane of nerve cells. However, in 1990, this view changed with the discovery of cannabis receptors in the brain (Matsuda *et al.* 1990). This cannabinoid receptor, now known as CB_1, is found throughout the brain and is most concentrated in the basal ganglia, cerebellum, hippocampus and layers 1 and 4 of the cerebral cortex. A second type of cannabionoid receptor, called CB_2, has also been discovered, although this occurs only in peripheral tissues such as the spleen and cells of the immune system.

The CB_1 receptor is known to be attached to a G-protein which inhibits the intracellular enzyme **adenylate cyclase**. This, in turn, has been shown to inhibit the flow of calcium ions into axon endings (which is known to inhibit neurotransmitter release) and facilitate potassium currents into the cell (Julien 2007). Structurally, the CB_1 receptor has some similarities with opiate receptors, and can be blocked by the opioid antagonist naloxone. The identification of cannabinoid receptors also led to a search for cannabis-type substances in the brain, and resulted in the discovery of **anadamide** (Devane *et al.* 1992), which is derived from the Sanskrit word for bliss. There is no evidence that anadamide is stored in synaptic vesicles like traditional neurotransmitters. Rather, it appears to be released from a type of phosplipid protein located in the neuronal membrane. Its functions are still uncertain.

Cannabis, or rather its active ingredient THC, is unique among drugs of abuse in that there is little evidence that it serves as a reinforcer in animal models of self-administration (Griffiths *et al.* 1980). Despite this, THC has been shown to moderately increase levels of dopamine in the nucleus accumbens and frontal cortex (Chen *et al.* 1990). The mechanisms by which THC exerts these effects is not fully understood. For example, it has been shown that THC increases activity in the neurons of the VTA, including those projecting to the nucleus accumbens, although there are few CB_1 receptors in this area. Perhaps more relevant is the finding that injections of THC increase levels of endogenous opiates in the VTA (Solinas *et al.* 2004). In turn, this would reduce the activity of GABAergic interneurons in the VTA which contain opiate receptors – freeing the dopaminergic meso-accumbens neurons from their normal inhibition (see Figure 12.13). Evidence supporting this possibility comes from the finding that THC's effect on the nucleus accumbens is blocked by injections of the opiate antagonist naloxone. It is also interesting to note that drugs which block the cannabanoid CB_1 receptor have been shown to reduce heroin self-administration (Navarro *et al.* 2001).

Lysergic acid diethylamide (LSD)

There are a great variety of hallucinogenic drugs, but the best known, and certainly the most powerful, is **lysergic acid diethylamaide (LSD)**, which was first synthesised by Albert Hoffman in 1938. Hoffman was a pharmacologist working at Sandoz Laboratories in Basle, Switzerland, whose aim was to develop useful medicinal substances from the fungus commonly known as **ergot** (*Claviceps purpurea*), which was known to contain lysergic acid. Ergot has an interesting history and was responsible for producing outbreaks of ergotism (sometimes called St Anthony's fire) in the Middle Ages, when people ate bread made from infected rye or grain. This caused restricted blood flow to the limbs, making them feel uncomfortably hot, and often resulted in gangrene. However, the fact that ergot (or rather lysergic acid) is able to constrict blood vessels, also gave it potential medical uses. It was for this reason that Hoffman set about testing its various derivatives.

Hoffman actually synthesised LSD in 1938, but it was not until 1943, when he made a new batch of chemicals, that he spilled a small amount of LSD on his skin and started to feel peculiar and unwell. A few days later, he self-administered himself with LSD by ingesting what he believed was an extremely small dose (0.25 mg). We now know that this dose is about ten times the dose required to induce the full blown effects of LSD. As a result, Hoffman became the first human being to experience an LSD 'trip' (for a personal account see Hoffman 2005).

The effects of LSD typically begin within 30–90 minutes of ingestion and may last as long as 12 hours. Psychologically, the effects of LSD are difficult to describe because they are highly subjective and vary depending on the context, mood and expectations of the person. Nonetheless, some aspects of the LSD experience are common, and include heightened emotions that can shift abruptly from extreme fear to euphoria. LSD also intensifies the perception of colours, smells, sounds and touch. However, the most dramatic effect of LSD is its ability to produce hallucinations. In many instances, shapes and objects, including parts of the body, become distorted, or move in strange ways leaving trails in their wake. When the user closes their eyes, they may experience a kaleidoscope of changing patterns and vivid colours. This can also lead to the user entering an imaginary world where adventures unfold with animated figures and panoramic scenes. Although this can be enjoyable, it may also be terrifying, with the person experiencing palpable fear of losing control.

LSD belongs to a group of substances called the indoleakylamines which are similar in structure to the neurotransmitter serotonin. Indeed, as early as the 1950s, Wooley and Shaw (1954) showed that LSD inhibited the action of serotonin (5-HT) on the constriction of blood vessels. This finding suggested that LSD acted as a 5-HT antagonist. The next significant breakthrough in understanding of LSD came in the late 1960s, when it was found that LSD caused a marked inhibition of cells in the dorsal raphe (Aghajanian *et al.* 1968), which is the main origin of serotonergic fibres in the forebrain. Again, this suggested a serotonergic mechanism in the action of LSD.

Despite this, the pharmacology of LSD has been very difficult to establish with any degree of certainty. This is partly because there are many types of serotonergic receptor in the brain (LSD binds to a number of different 5-HT receptors), and also because LSD affects a large number of G-protein-coupled receptors, including all dopamine and noradrenaline receptor subtypes. One type of receptor where LSD produces a marked agonist effect is the **5-HT$_{1A}$ subtype**. This receptor is located on the cell body of raphe neurons and acts as an autoreceptor to inhibit further firing of the cell (this is why LSD causes marked inhibition of raphe activity). Despite this, there is evidence to show that inhibition of the dorsal raphe is not necessary for the hallucinatory effects of LSD. This is shown by the fact that lesions of the raphe do not abolish the behavioural effects of LSD in animals. A number of studies have found, however, that drugs which act as antagonists at the **5-HT$_2$ receptor** (these are located predominately in the cerebral cortex and nucleus accumbens) do block the effects of LSD in animals. Moreover, in a study of fifteen drugs known to produce hallucinations in humans, it was found that their hallucinatory potency correlated significantly with their ability to bind to 5-HT$_2$ receptors (Glennon *et al.* 1984). This suggests that LSD acts as a 5-HT$_2$ agonist. An alternative theory, however, is that LSD acts as a **5-HT$_2$ partial agonist**, which means that it binds to the receptor, but it has only a partial efficacy in activating it, and requires the presence of other neurochemicals to exert a full agonistic effect.

Summary

Drug addiction is one of the biggest problems facing society today. The discovery that the brain contains neural systems that mediate responses to **reward** (and **punishment**) was made accidentally in 1954 by James Olds and his research student Peter Milner, who demonstrated that rats worked hard (i.e. pressed an operant lever) to obtain electrical **self-stimulation** of the brain. A large array of brain sites give rise to self-stimulation, although most contribute to the **medial forebrain bundle** (MFB): a large, bidirectional multisynaptic pathway that connects regions of the **forebrain** with the **midbrain**. Initially, it was thought that the **lateral hypothalamus** was the final common terminus for reward messages travelling in the MFB. This view has changed, and it is now known that the MFB mediates reward more by its influence on midbrain **dopamine**-containing neurons in the **ventral tegmental area** (VTA), including those that project to the **nucleus accumbens** (located in the **ventral striatum**) and **medial prefrontal cortex**. Evidence supporting the role of dopamine in reward has come from experiments where animals self-administer themselves with drugs. For example, rats and monkeys will work at lever pressing to receive an injection of **cocaine**, which is a potent blocker of dopamine reuptake. The **nucleus accumbens** is a critical structure in cocaine's rewarding effects as injections of dopaminergic antagonists into this structure greatly reduce self-stimulation. Further support for the pivotal role of the nucleus accumbens in reward has come from understanding how **opiate** drugs such as **heroin** work in the brain. It has been found that these drugs work by acting on **opiate receptors** that are located on **GABA interneurons** in the VTA. Their action reduces the inhibition on tegmental dopaminergic neurons, causing increased dopamine release in the nucleus accumbens. Many other drugs of abuse, including **alcohol, nicotine** and **cannabis,** are also known to influence, at least in part, the dopaminergic reward pathways of the brain.

Traditionally, the concept of addiction has been explained in terms of **physical dependence,** with addicts being compelled to continue and increase their drug use in order to avoid the unpleasant effects of **withdrawal symptoms.** However, more recently, it has been recognised that **psychological dependence** is an equally, if not more, important determinant of drug taking. When a person administers a drug over a long period of time, they are likely to show **tolerance** to some of its effects. This tolerance may be **biological** (for example, the drug is metabolised more quickly, or adaptive changes take place in the nervous system), or it can be **behavioural** (i.e. the tolerance is learned). An example of behavioural tolerance is seen when a rat is administered with an opiate over several weeks in the same test cage, and then injected in a new environment. This procedure restores the initial (non-tolerant) drug effect and can result in overdose. According to Siegel (1984), this form of tolerance occurs because environmental cues produce a **conditioned compensatory response** (similar to a conditioned response in **classical conditioning**) that lessens the effects of the drug. Environmental factors are also known to affect the severity of withdrawal symptoms. This was seen, for example, in US serviceman returning from the Vietnam war. It was estimated that about one-third of serviceman used heroin in Vietnam, with many physically addicted to it, although few continued their drug habit after returning home. This indicates that **set** (personality variables) and **setting** (the environment), as well as the biological effects of the drug on the brain, are important determinants of drug taking and addiction.

Essay questions

1. What is the medial forebrain bundle? Discuss evidence for and against its involvement in reward.

   Search terms: Medial forebrain bundle. Reward pathways in the brain. Stimulation of the MFB. Pleasure centres in the brain. MFB and reward.

2. Review the evidence showing that the brain's dopamine pathways are critically involved in pleasure and reward.

   Search terms: Dopamine pathways. Nucleus accumbens. Dopamine and reward. VTA and reward. Effects of DA antagonists on self-stimulation.

3. What are the differences and similarities in the action of cocaine and heroin on the brain's reward systems? Do all addictive drugs work by causing the release of dopamine in the nucleus accumbens?

   Search terms: Heroin and nucleus accumbens. Opiates and dopamine. Cocaine and the brain. Nicotine and dopamine. Alcohol and nucleus accumbens. Rewarding self-stimulation.

4. In what ways have learning and conditioning been shown to be important determinants of drug tolerance?

   Search terms: Drug tolerance. Conditioned compensatory response. Addiction and tolerance. Classical conditioning of drug action. Neurobiology of addiction.

Further reading

Engel, J. and Oreland, L. (eds) (1987) *Brain Reward Systems and Abuse*. New York: Raven Press. A book whose authors tend to emphasise the importance of transmitter systems and receptors in the reward systems of the brain for understanding drug abuse.

Erickson, C.K. (2007) *The Science of Addiction: From Neurobiology to Treatment*. New York: Norton. An accessible and concise overview of the biological basis of addiction which is written primarily for care-givers working with drug users. Nonetheless, it contains much of interest for the student of psychobiology.

Diaz, J. (1997) *How Drugs Influence Behavior*. Englewood Cliffs, NJ: Prentice Hall. A concise but well-written account that focuses mainly on drugs of abuse and how they work on neuropharmacological mechanisms to influence behaviour.

Feldman, R.S., Meyer, J.S. and Quenzer, L.F. (1997) *Principles of Neuropsychopharmacology*. Sunderland, Mass.: Sinauer. A comprehensive and indispensable textbook that has sections on neurotransmitter systems, drugs of abuse, and clinical disorders.

Grilly, D.M. (2005) *Drugs and Human Behavior*. Boston: Allyn & Bacon. A textbook now in its 5th edition that provides an introduction to psychopharmacology, with an emphasis on how drugs work on the nervous system.

Julien, R.M. (2004) *A Primer of Drug Action*. New York: Freeman. A book now in its 10th edition that provides a concise and readable guide to the actions and side effects of a wide range of drugs, including ones that can lead to addiction.

Koob, G.F. and Le Moal, M. (2005) *Neurobiology of Addiction*. London: Academic Press. A must-have book for anyone seriously interested in the biological basis of addiction. This textbook not only provides a comprehensive synthesis of research over the past fifty years or so, but also includes scholarly and well written chapters on each type of addictive drug, along with theories of addiction, that are aimed primarily at the neuroscientist.

Korenman, S.G. and Barchas, J.D. (eds) (1993) *Biological Basis of Substance Abuse*. Oxford: Oxford University Press. A multidisciplinary approach to drug abuse, including its cell biology, neural basis, neuropharmacology, genetics, behavioural aspects and pharmacological treatment.

Liebman, J.M. and Cooper, S.J. (eds) (1989) *The Neuropharmacological Basis of Reward*. Oxford: Oxford University Press. A series of chapters written by various experts that still provides the best overall coverage of the anatomical, neurochemical and behavioural characteristics of the brain's reward systems.

Lowinson, J.H., Ruiz, P. and Millman, R.B. (1996) *Substance Abuse: A Comprehensive Textbook*. Baltimore: Williams & Wilkins. A large book of over 1,000 pages written by various experts with sections on determinants of substance abuse (8 chapters), and drugs of abuse (17 chapters).

McKim, W.A. (2006) *Drugs and Behavior*. Englewood Cliffs, NJ: Prentice Hall. An excellent introductory textbook now in its 6th edition that adopts a multidisciplinary approach to understanding drug use, including a good coverage of animal models of self-administration.

Maldonado, R. (ed.) (2003) *Molecular Biology of Drug Addiction*. Totowa, NJ: Humana Press. A book that contains detailed sections on opiate, stimulant, cannabinoid, alcohol and nicotine addiction, written by various experts in the field. Not a book for the introductory student, although it contains a lot of information that is not found in other texts.

Niesink, R.J.M., Jaspers, R.M.A., Kornet, L.M.W. and van Ree, J.M. (eds) (1999) *Drugs of Abuse and Addiction: Neurobehavioral Toxicology*. Boca Raton, Fla.: CRC Press. Despite its unusual title, this book contains many chapters of interest, including those on genetic factors, reward systems, molecular mechanisms of addictive substances, and new treatment strategies.

Tyler, A. (1995) *Street Drugs*. London: Coronet. Although this is not an academic book, it is a highly informative one that offers non-judgemental, balanced, impartial advice and information about drugs of abuse.

 For self test questions, animations, interactive exercises and many more resources to help you consolidate your understanding, and expand your knowledge of the field, please go to the website accompanying this book at **www.pearsoned.co.uk/wickens**

CHAPTER 13

Degenerative diseases of the brain

INTRODUCTION

We live in a fortunate age in terms of life expectancy. In ancient Greek and Roman times the average length of life was 20–30 years, and by the end of the nineteenth century it had yet to reach 50 years. Today, life expectancy in the UK is about 75 years for men and 80 for women, and these figures will increase over the coming years. A longer life expectancy, however, can have certain drawbacks – not least, a greater likelihood of ending one's days with an incurable degenerative brain disease. One such disorder is a form of dementia called Alzheimer's disease. It has been estimated that 20 per cent of people over 80 years suffer from this illness, and its devastating effects on health now make it the fourth most common form of death in the western world. Indeed, this is a disease we can all realistically fear when getting older, and even if we avoid it, the economic burden of looking after Alzheimer's victims is one we will all have to bear. At present, this is some £7–14 billion per year – a figure substantially greater than is spent on stroke, heart disease or cancer. But, dementia is not the only neurodegenerative disorder of later life. Two other illnesses are Parkinson's disease and Huntington's disease, both characterised by disabilities of movement that cause the victim to become helpless and moribund. Although there are no cures for any of these illnesses, they are the focus of a great deal of research aimed at understanding their causes and developing more effective treatments. This field is one of the fastest growing areas in neuroscience and has much of interest for the biopsychologist interested in brain–behaviour relationships. We should also not forget that some degenerative diseases such as multiple sclerosis and Creutzfeldt–Jakob disease are not related to ageing, although they produce great suffering and are in need of much more research.

The discovery of Alzheimer's disease

People with Alzheimer's disease require considerable care and attention, and the increasing numbers with this illness makes it arguably the single most important problem currently facing the health and social services. The disease is named after a German called Alois Alzheimer, born in 1864 in the small town of Marktbreit, Bavaria. Alzheimer received his medical training at various universities in Germany, and in 1888 began his medical career in a Frankfurt hospital where he was to become senior physician. It was here, in 1901, that a middle-aged women called Auguste D was admitted. Her disorder had started with anger and aggression towards her husband, followed by an abrupt decline in memory, leading to paranoid delusions and auditory hallucinations. Within a few years this condition had progressed into severe dementia with aphasia, dystonia and agnosia. The relatively young age of the patient, and her rapid deterioration, made the illness an unusual one, and when Auguste D died in 1906, Alzheimer undertook a postmortem examination of her brain. To help visualise the brain tissue for microscopic analysis, Alzheimer decided to use a newly developed silver impregnation method that stained nerve fibres. His choice produced striking results. Most notably he found that up to one-third of neurons in the cerebral cortex contained tangles of fine fibres within their cytoplasm (now known as **neurofibrillary tangles**) along with hardened discs called **neuritic plaques**. Curiously, there was little blood vessel damage, which at the time was thought to be the main cause of dementia. Alzheimer presented his findings at a small conference in 1906, and published a paper of the talk in 1907.

Alois Alzheimer 1864–1915

Plate 13.1	Alois Alzheimer

Source: N. Thomas and M. Isaac (1987) Alois Alzheimer: a memoir, *Trends in Neuroscience*, 10, 306–307

It is probable that Alzheimer thought he had described nothing more than a very unusual case of dementia. But, in 1910, the renowned psychiatrist Emil Kraepelin argued that Alzheimer had discovered a new form of dementia that occurred in middle age, which was qualitatively different from types of senile dementia found in later life. To back up his arguments, Kraepelin pointed to the importance of neurofibrillary tangles and plaques in the brains of its victims, along with the very rapid progression of the symptoms. But, we now know that Kraepelin was wrong. Alzheimer's disease is not a rare form of senility that occurs in middle age, but a common form of senile dementia that afflicts the elderly. In fact, there has been considerable debate over whether Kraepelin was sincere in believing that it was a 'new' disease, as all the pathological signs observed by Alzheimer (for example, neurofibrillary tangles and plaques) had been seen in demented brains before. Moreover, even its clinical features (such as rapid deterioration of personality and memory) were not unusual in senile dementia. Whatever the truth of the matter, his misconception of Alzheimer's disease would not be fully exposed for another fifty years or so.

For most of the twentieth century, therefore, Alzheimer's disease was thought to be a rare form of presenile dementia, while comparable symptoms in elderly people were generally attributed to vascular damage in the brain or 'hardening of the arteries'. That is, presenile dementia was believed to be different from the senile dementia that occurred after the age of 65 years. This view began to change, however, in the late 1960s when researchers realised that many elderly demented patients were free of significant vascular disease yet exhibited plaques and neurofibrillary tangles which were characteristic of Alzheimer's disease (Blessed *et al.* 1968). There also appeared to be a correlation between the severity of dementia and the number of neuritic plaques and neurofibrillary tangles in the brain at autopsy. These findings indicated that presenile and senile forms of dementia were not different after all, and that the pathological features of Alzheimer's disease were much more common in the elderly than had previously been believed. Indeed, within a few years, Alzheimer's disease was being recognised as the most common senile affliction of the elderly, and the fourth or fifth most common cause of death in the United States (Katzman 1976).

The epidemiology of Alzheimer's disease

The likelihood of developing Alzheimer's disease increases significantly after middle age. Between 40 and 65 years of age, the disease occurs in around 1 per 1,000 people, with this figure rising to about 1 in 50 people aged 65 to 70. At older ages, Alzheimer's disease is found is around 1 of every 20 people between the ages of 70 and 80 years, and 1 in 5 of the over 80s (figures from the Alzheimer's Society of Great Britain). Thus, below 65 years the disease is uncommon, but after this age it becomes much more frequent, occurring in 5 per cent of 70-year-olds, and 20 per cent of those over 80 years. This means that there are about 750,000 people with Alzheimer's disease in the UK, and this figure is likely to reach 1.3 million by 2040 – largely because of the increase of the over 80s who now form the fastest growing segment of the population.

The prevalence of Alzheimer's disease and the projected increases in the ageing populations is similar for other industrialised countries (see Figure 13.1). For example, in

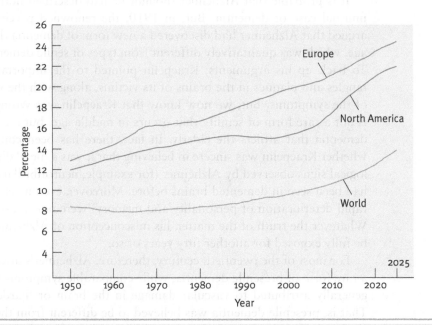

| Figure 13.1 | Graph showing the exponential increase of Alzheimer's disease in the population aged 65 and over, 1950–2025 |

Europe the number of people aged over 80 years will rise from 18.8 million in 2005 to 34.7 million in 2030. This will inevitably mean millions of extra elderly people with Alzheimer's disease. The figures are even more alarming in the United States, where currently some 4.5 million have the disorder and this figure is projected to grow to 16 million by 2050. Alzheimer's disease is also a serious problem in developing countries. For example, according to the World Health Organization, there are currently 18 million people worldwide with Alzheimer's disease and this figure is likely to reach 34 million by 2025. Countries such as India and China with ageing populations will show the most marked increases in the incidence of this disease.

Alzheimer's disease is not the only type of dementia to afflict the elderly. In fact, there are more than sixty disorders that can cause dementia, and Alzheimer's disease makes up less than two-thirds of all these cases. In fact, about 20 per cent of people suffering from dementia have vascular, or multi-infarct dementia caused by occlusions in the blood supply of the brain. These infarcts build up over time, resulting in progressively severe dementia. Another 10 per cent of people have Lewy body dementia characterised by tiny 'sunflower-shaped' protein deposits in the brain that cause inflammation and degeneration. Other disorders that can cause dementia include Parkinson's and Huntington's disease, alcoholism, brain tumours and syphilis.

The clinical course of Alzheimer's disease

Although the symptoms of Alzheimer's disease vary from person to person, they are often divided into three stages. The first stage usually starts with a gradual decline of cognitive function where the person becomes increasingly forgetful and absent-minded. While often viewed by relatives and friends as a normal consequence of getting older, the Alzheimer's victim is often aware of the problem and may keep memo pads and notes to aid recall. The memory problems may also be accompanied by mood swings, personality changes and a general lack of energy or spontaneity. These symptoms progressively get worse, with the decline in memory beginning to interfere with the person's work or social relationships. In addition, the person may frequently gets lost, become easily confused or exercises poor judgement.

In the second stage of the disease, the person's forgetfulness develops into severe memory loss. Speech and comprehension become slower, and the individual may lose thoughts in mid-sentence. Although the person may be able to undertake simple chores such as dressing, more complicated tasks such as organising the weekly shop may need the assistance of others. As the Alzheimer's victim becomes more incapacitated, they typically become more anxious, easily upset, unpredictable and restless, which makes them more difficult to cope with. Behavioural patterns become increasingly disorganised and the victim may be unable to comprehend where they are. Despite this, the person may have good recall of the events of their earlier life, although quickly forgetting things they have just 'learned'.

By the final stage of the disease, the person is severely disorientated and confused. They may no longer recognise friends and family, and possibly suffer from hallucinations and delusions. Some patients become very demanding, suspicious and aggressive, although others are docile and helpless. The individual is no longer 'recognised' as the person they were before, and this can cause distress for the carers and family. During this stage, the Alzheimer's patient is dependent on others for care. Personal hygiene is ignored, walking can be difficult, and incontinence common. In addition, the person may lose the ability to chew and swallow. By the end, the bedridden Alzheimer's patient is susceptible to pneumonia and infection, which often contributes to death. On average, the disease lasts for a period of 8 to 10 years.

The pathological features of Alzheimer's disease

Post-mortem examination of the Alzheimer's brain typically shows a number of abnormalities. On first inspection there is often shrinkage of the brain's ridges (or gyri) with a widening of the fissures, which is most noticeable in the temporal and parietal lobe regions. In addition, there is often enlargement of the lateral ventricles, providing further evidence of neuron loss. For example, Tomlinson (1984) reports that normal elderly individuals often have a ventricular volume of 20–30 ml, whereas in Alzheimer's disease this figure is more likely to lie between 40 and 120 ml. However, there are exceptions, and sometimes the appearance of the brain and ventricle volume will be normal. Brain atrophy has also been examined using CAT and MRI scans. One brain area to show degeneration (up to 40 per cent) with this technology is the hippocampus and surrounding areas of the temporal lobe. The rate at which the temporal lobe degenerates is marked, with one study showing the annual rate of atrophy in Alzheimer's disease to be 15.1 per cent compared with 1.5 per cent for controls (Jobst et al. 1994). Indeed, it is now recognised that one of the first brain regions to show degeneration in Alzheimer's disease is the entorhinal cortex, which is the origin of the perforant pathway to the hippocampus. Post-mortem studies show that during the early stages of the disease, there may be up to a 60 per cent loss of neurons in this structure (Gomez-Isla et al. 1996).

Despite this, the true pathological hallmarks of Alzheimer's disease can only be observed with tissue staining and light microscopy. One of the most important defining features of Alzheimer's disease are **senile plaques**, which are dense, roughly spherical, extracellular deposits that contain a protein called **beta-amyloid**. These plaques can be small (10 μm) or very large (perhaps several times bigger than a brain neuron). These structures are abundant throughout the grey matter of the cerebral cortex and hippocampus – although they can occur elsewhere including the striatum, basal ganglia and thalamus. Senile plaques are often surrounded by clumps of degenerating axons and glial cell activity, indicating that their presence is toxic to brain cells. Accompanying senile plaques are **neurofibrillary tangles** (**NFTs**), which are found in the cytoplasm of neurons. These resemble tiny bundles of knotted string (technically called paired helical filaments) and are made from a protein called **tau,** which forms an important part of the cell's inner framework. Large numbers of NFTs are found throughout the cerebral cortex, hippocampus, entorhinal cortex and basal nucleus of Meynert (Figure 13.2).

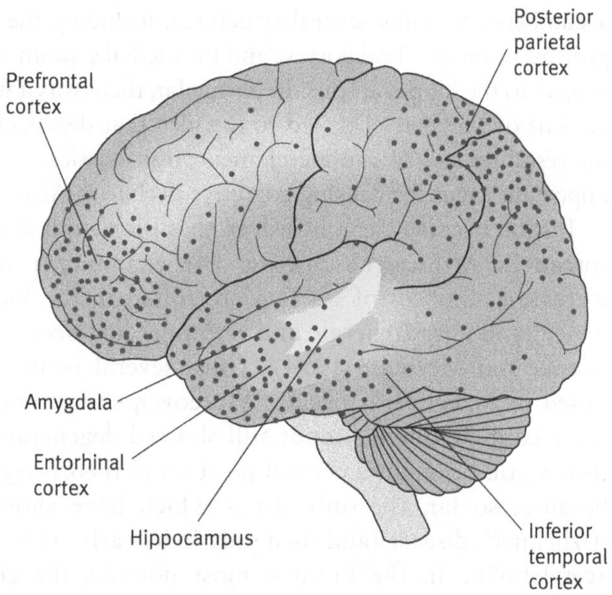

Figure 13.2   The typical distribution of neurofibrillary tangles and amyloid plaques in the brains of patients with advanced Alzheimer's disease

Source: John P.J. Pinel, *Biopsychology*, 5th edition, p. 253. Copyright © 2003 by Pearson Education

Causes of Alzheimer's disease

The cholinergic theory of Alzheimer's disease

In the mid-1970s, a significant discovery was made when levels of an enzyme called **choline acetyltransferase (CAT)** were found to be reduced by up to 90 per cent in the cerebral cortex and hippocampus of Alzheimer's brains. CAT is involved in the synthesis of **acetylcholine** – and its loss indicated that a marked deficit of this neurotransmitter was occurring in Alzheimer's disease (acetylcholine itself cannot be measured because it is broken down immediately after being released). It was also found that the lack of CAT activity in the brain was correlated with the number of senile plaques and severity of intellectual impairment in the Alzheimer's patient (Perry *et al.* 1978). This finding was also important because acetylcholine had been linked with memory. For example, the drug **scopolamine,** which is derived from the poisonous deadly nightshade plant (*atropine belladonna*), blocks muscarinic cholinergic receptors and produces amnesia in humans. A number of experimental studies have also shown that scopolamine produced memory deficits that were very similar to those found in senile people (Drachman and Leavitt 1974).

The decline of cholinergic activity in the cerebral cortex and hippocampus was found to be due to degeneration of neurons within pathways that arose from an old region of the brain called the cholinergic basal forebrain. This area, which lies close to the nucleus accumbens, contains several structures, including the **basal nucleus of Meynert**, which projects to the cerebral cortex, and the **medial septum** and **diagonal band of Broca**, which project to the hippocampus. In particular, there was a marked loss of neurons in the basal nucleus of Meynert. This led to the idea that degeneration of the Meynert nucleus, and the resulting loss of cholinergic neurotransmission in the cerebral cortex, was the most important event for causing cognitive decline in Alzheimer's disease (Bartus *et al.* 1982).

It soon became clear, however, that the neural degeneration was much more widespread in Alzheimer's disease. For example, a substantial loss of neurons and increased numbers of NFTs were found in the locus coeruleus and dorsal raphe, which send noradrenergic and serotonergic fibres to the cerebral cortex, respectively (Geula and Mesulam 1994). Thus, several neurotransmitter systems are compromised in Alzheimer's disease. Moreover, some areas of the cerebral cortex without significant cholinergic input still showed degeneration. Despite this, the cholinergic theory still occupies a central position in theorising about the disease. This is partly because, so far, the only drugs which have shown benefits in the treatment of Alzheimer's disease (and then only in its early stages) are those that increase levels of acetylcholine in the brain – most notably, the **cholinesterase inhibitors** such as Tacrine and Donepezil. These drugs work by inhibiting the enzyme acetylcholinesterase, which normally acts to break down acetylcholine after it has been released into the synapse. Thus, inhibition of this enzyme leads to increased levels of acetylcholine in the synapse (Figure 13.3).

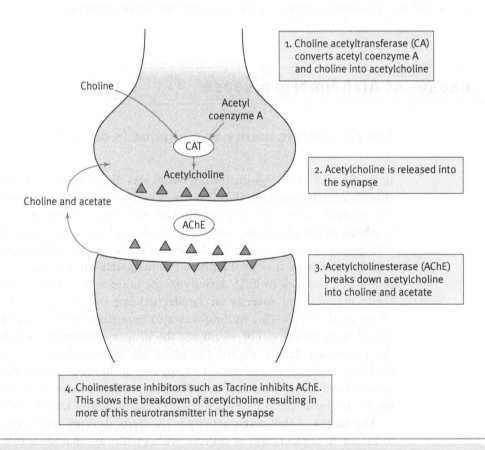

Figure 13.3 How cholinesterase inhibitors work to increase levels of acetylcholine in the synapse

The amyloid cascade theory of Alzheimer's disease

By the 1980s, most investigators believed that the main pathological features of Alzheimer's disease, that is, the amyloid plaques and neurofibrillary tangles, had a more fundamental role in causing the illness. But, to prove this, researchers would have to understand how these structures arose in the brain, and how they produced neural degeneration. This type of reasoning led to the **amyloid cascade theory** (Hardy and Allsop 1991), which today still provides the most popular explanation of how Alzheimer's disease occurs. Put simply, the theory proposes that the deposition of amyloid causes a chain reaction of events that leads to senile plaques, neurodegeneration and ultimately dementia (Figure 13.4).

Since the nineteenth century, it had been known that senile plaques contain a substance called amyloid, which although meaning 'starch-like' is a protein. Intensive efforts to isolate and identify this protein culminated in 1984 when it was found that amyloid consisted of a chain of either 40 or 42 amino acids (Glenner and Wong 1984). This was an important breakthrough since the purification of amyloid, and determination of its chemical structure, enabled the cloning of the DNA that controlled amyloid production. This was accomplished in 1987 when researchers from four independent laboratories sequenced the gene for amyloid. This work showed that amyloid was a fragment of a much larger 695 amino acid protein, which is now widely referred to as the **beta-amyloid precursor protein (β-APP)**.

Closer examination of the β-APP protein has shown that it occurs in many tissues and not just the brain. It is also a molecule that is found within the cellular membrane, with a short chain of amino acids jutting into the cell and a far longer tail that projects out. Interestingly, the smaller amyloid molecule is composed of amino acids 597 through to 636 – which are the 28 amino acids just outside the cell and the first 12 amino acids within the membrane. In other words, amyloid is derived from the part of the β-APP molecule that normally anchors itself to the cell membrane. But why was the β-APP protein being broken down into smaller fragments? The answer is that the β-APP protein has a short life. In fact, when it has served its purpose in the cell, it is removed from the membrane by being 'cut' into smaller components by a class of enzymes called **secretases**.

We now know that that the β-APP molecule can be 'cut' by secretases in one of two ways. The first of these produces a form of amyloid that contains a chain of 40 amino acids. This form of amyloid is the normal by-product of β-APP metabolism and is not toxic. However, some of the amyloid (perhaps less than 10 per cent) is cut with two extra amino acids – and it is the version which has toxic effects. This type of amyloid is not only insoluble and tends to accumulate into hardened sheets, but can also be highly toxic to neurons (Cotman and Pike 1994). Thus, it has been proposed that this form of amyloid, due to faulty metabolism of the β-APP protein, is the initiating event in the formation of plaques, neurofibrillary tangles and subsequent cell death in the brain.

Although there is evidence that faulty metabolism of the β-APP protein leads to amyloid deposition in the brain (see also next section), the theory that this initiates neural degeneration in Alzheimer's disease is more controversial. For example, the severity of dementia does not seem to correlate with the amount of amyloid in the brain (Terry *et al.* 1991), and others have reported that NFTs occur before the emergence of amyloid plaques (see, for example, Braak and Braak 1991). In addition, animal

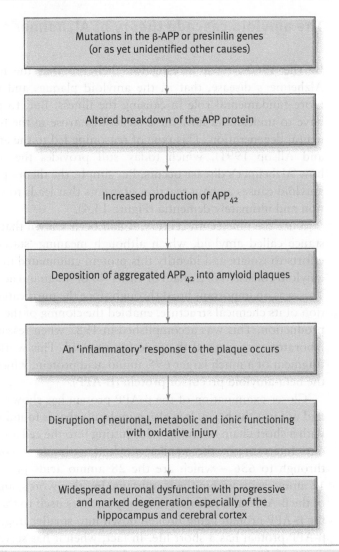

Figure 13.4   The amyloid cascade hypothesis

Source: Adapted from E.J. Nestler *et al.*, *Molecular Neuropharmacology*, p. 473. Copyright © 2001 by McGraw-Hill, Inc.

studies show that transgenic mice which overexpress the β-APP protein, have marked brain neurodegeneration, but without amyloid deposition (Games *et al.* 1995). In fact, a similar type of pathology occurs in a form of human dementia called **frontal–temporal dementia**. This type of dementia is associated with massive loss of nerve cells in the brain, and bundles of tau protein (a feature of NFTs), although there is little evidence of amyloid deposition (Mann *et al.* 2001). In fact, this has led some researchers to seriously question the importance of amyloid in the aetiology of Alzheimer's disease. Indeed, at present, most researchers are in one of two camps: those supporting the amyloid theory, or so called **baptists** ('bap' being an abbreviation of beta-amyloid protein), and those advocating the importance neurofibrillary tangle theory (the **taurists**).

Genetic causes of Alzheimer's disease

An important development arising from the identification of the β-APP protein was the locating of its gene on chromosome 21. This was interesting since people with **Down's syndrome,** who inherit an extra copy of chromosome 21, also have high numbers of amyloid plaques in their brains. The linkage to chromosome 21 also enabled researchers to look for individuals with Alzheimer's disease that carried mutations in the β-APP gene. Although the vast majority of Alzheimer's cases do not appear to be inherited, there are some rare instances where the disease ran in families and has an early onset (these instances probably make up about 5 per cent of cases). In the early 1990s, one family was found where every individual with Alzheimer's disease had a mutation in their β-APP gene (Goate *et al.* 1991). In fact, five different mutations in the β-APP gene have now been discovered that lead to early onset Alzheimer's disease (Nestler *et al.* 2001). All of these mutations lead to the production of the abnormal 42 amino acid version of amyloid. However, these types of mutation are extremely rare and fewer than twenty families worldwide have been found with this specific type of genetic defect.

The discovery that mutations in the β-APP gene accounted for some forms of Alzheimer's disease led to an intensive search of other chromosomes. And, in 1995, a gene located on chromosome 14 (termed **presinilin-1**) was identified in which mutations accounted for around 50 per cent of familial cases (Sherrington *et al.* 1995). Soon after, another gene (termed **presenilin-2**) was identified on chromosome 1 whose mutations accounted for another 10 per cent of familial cases (Levy-Lahad *et al.* 1995). Again, the evidence points to these genes exercising their adverse effects by altering the processing of the β-APP protein in some way, which increases the production of the 42 amino acid form of amyloid (see Table 13.1).

Table 13.1	Suspected routes to how gene mutations may lead to Alzheimer's disease	
Mutation	**Biochemical Cause**	**Effect**
Down's syndrome (extra copy of chromosome 21)	More APP production	More APP_{40} and APP_{42}
APP gene mutations (early onset Alzheimer's) (chromosome 21)	All are known to potentiate or inhibit the activity of secretase enzymes, or change the site where they cut (cleave) the APP protein	More APP_{42}
Presinilin genes (early onset Alzheimer's) (chromosomes 1 and 14)	Subtle and not yet fully understood alteration of APP processing	More APP_{42}
ApoE genes (late onset Alzheimer's) (chromosome 19)	Lipoproteins may be involved in the repair of neural membranes. Alternatively some forms may help in removing amyloid	Some alleles lead to increased deposition of APP_{42}

Source: Adapted from E.J. Nestler *et al. Molecular Neuropharmacology*, p. 342. Copyright © 2001 by McGraw-Hill, Inc.

Although no genetic mutations have been found that directly cause late onset Alzheimer's disease, genes have been found that can alter the risk of developing this illness. The best known of these is the **apolipoprotein E gene (ApoE)** located on chromosome 19. ApoE is a protein found in blood plasma that has an important role in the transport of cholesterol. It is also found in the glial cells of the brain where it is suspected of being involved in the repair, growth and maintenance of myelin and neuronal membranes. The gene that produces the ApoE protein has three possible forms, or **alleles**, and we inherit one from each parent. This means that we inherit one of six possible ApoE combinations or genotypes (see Figure 13.5). The combination has also been shown to have an important bearing on the risk of developing Alzheimer's disease and the age at which we are likely to exhibit its symptoms. In particular, inheritance of the ApoE-4 allele is associated with a greater risk of Alzheimer's disease. For example, the mean age of onset of the disease for individuals with two ApoE-4 alleles is under 70 years; for those with two ApoE-3 alleles (which is the most common combination of alleles) the age of onset is between 80 and 90 years; and for two ApoE-2 alleles the mean age is well over a 100 years.

How might a lipoprotein have such an important influence on the risk of developing Alzheimer's disease? Several lines of evidence support the hypothesis that ApoE may affect the formation of amyloid. For example, mice that lack the gene for ApoE do not show amyloid deposition in their brains, whereas transgenic mice that over-express the ApoE-4 gene exhibit increased numbers of amyloid plaques (Price *et al.* 1998). It has also been shown *in vitro* that the protein derived from the ApoE-4 gene promotes amyloid formation more readily than its ApoE-3 form (Evans *et al.* 1995).

Geno-type	% US pop.	Age of onset mean	range
2/2	<1	?	?
2/3	11	>90	50–140
2/4	5	80–90	50–>100
3/3	60	80–90	50–>100
3/4	21	70–80	50–>100
4/4	2	<70	50–<100

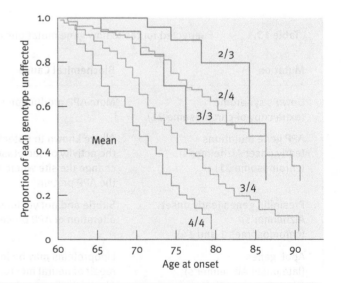

Figure 13.5   Mean age of onset of Alzheimer's disease as a function of ApoE inheritance

Source: A.D. Roses, Apolipoprotein E and Alzheimer disease, *Scientific American*, Sept./Oct., 16–25. Copyright © 1995 by Scientific American

The oldest old

According to the *Guinness Book of World Records*, the oldest person to have lived, whose birth date can be authenticated by reliable records, is Jeanne Louise Calment, who died when she was 122 years and 164 days old. She was born in Arles, France, on 21 February 1875, outlived 17 presidents, and remembered selling crayons in her father's shop to Vincent Van Gogh, whom she described as smelling of alcohol, 'not nice' and 'ugly with this horrible shepherd's hat'. One notable feature of Calment's personality was her active nature. As a young and middle-aged woman, her life revolved around tennis, swimming, roller-skating, piano and opera – and these activities continued into her later years. In fact, she took up fencing at 85 years, and was still riding a bicycle when she reached 100. She lived on her own until she was 110 years (her husband died in 1942), and was able to walk until a fall one month away from her 115th birthday. After this, she survived a hip operation, making her the oldest verified surgery patient. Both her parents were long-lived (her father lived to the age of 94 and her mother to 86), although Calment attributed her longevity to a regular glass of port, olive oil, and good humour as typified by one of her quips: 'I've only one wrinkle – and I'm sitting on it!' But, equally important, perhaps, was a lack of stress. She came from a wealthy family which entitled her not to work, and is also quoted as saying: 'If you can't do anything about it. Why worry about it?' But, not all of her habits were healthy ones. She was a smoker and only quit at the age of 117 when she became too embarrassed to ask for a light because of her failing eyesight. And, she also ate a kilogram of chocolate a week until her doctor persuaded her to give it up at the age 119 years.

It has long been assumed that the incidence of death, and age-related disease such as heart disease, cancer, stroke and dementia all increase with age. Indeed, this belief partly derives from the work of English statistician Benjamin Gompertz who, in 1825, found that the probability of death in a human population doubles every eight years after the age of 30 (graphically this can be expressed as a straight line if the axis recording deaths is scaled exponentially). Put simply, the older we are, the greater chance we have of dying. Although this may appear to be obvious, recent evidence suggests that it may not apply to the oldest old, that is, people who have passed their mid-nineties. For example, in a study of death statistics taken from 8 million people, it has been found that after the age of 97 years, a person's chance of dying veers away from the expected trend. Instead of increasing exponentially, the death rate actually slows down. It has also been noticed that individuals in this age group are often more healthy and agile than those in their eighties. Many are employed, sexually active, enjoy the outdoors, and carry on life as if age is not an issue. These findings indicate that there is something special about the oldest old which allows them to slow down the ageing process.

What biological and environmental factors might allow the oldest old to reach their mid-nineties, and beyond, in good health? The largest comprehensive study examining this question is the New England Centenarian Study (NECS) which began in 1994, and which now includes some 1,500 subjects along with their siblings and children. It has been found from examining this group of aged individuals, that if you want to become a centenarian the best advice is to stay lean, remain active, reduce stress and have long-lived parents. And, more controversially, if you are a woman, have children after the age of 35 years (Perls *et al.* 1997).

Cognitive reserve and the benefits of mental exercise

Although genetic influences affect the probability of developing late onset Alzheimer's disease, there are lifestyle factors which also contribute to its expression. One factor that is believed to have an important influence on the chances of developing Alzheimer's disease is education and capacity for mental exercise. One of the first studies to show this effect was initiated in 1988 by David Snowdon and his colleagues, who were then at the University of Minnesota. These researchers persuaded 678 Notre Dame convent nuns, aged from 75 to 106, to take part in a study where they underwent rigorous mental and physical testing once a year, as well as allowing investigators full access to their convent and medical records. The nuns also agreed to donate their brains at death so that any mental decline could be correlated with changes in neural pathology.

One reason why nuns make excellent subjects for this type of research is that they tend to share similar lifestyles – all being celibate, non-smokers, and having comparable income and health care. Thus, this helps the scientist who is interested in narrowing down the risk factors that contribute to Alzheimer's disease. Although this study continues to provide important data (for a readable account see Snowdon's book *Aging with Grace*), one of the most interesting findings occurred when investigators discovered the diaries of 93 sisters that had been written some 60 years earlier, just prior to their taking their religious vows. When the language in these journals was examined it was found that the nuns who had the richest vocabulary, wrote the most complex sentences, and expressed the greatest number of ideas, were the ones who developed dementia at a later age. Indeed, Snowdon was able to show that the nuns whose essays put them in the bottom third on a linguistic ability scale, were the ones with a significantly higher risk of developing Alzheimer's disease (see Marx 2005).

A number of other studies have also supported the idea that mental exercise can provide protection against Alzheimer's disease. For example, Evans *et al.* (1997) followed a group of 642 elderly people over four years and found that each year of formal education reduced the risk of Alzheimer's disease by 17 per cent. But, perhaps a more illuminating study was undertaken by David Bennett and Robert Wilson in Chicago, who followed a group of 130 Catholic clergy who also agreed to donate their brains at death. Although this study found no correlation between education levels and number of senile plaques or neurofibrillary tangles at post-mortem, it did show that the more highly educated individuals performed better on cognitive tests administered in the years before they died. In other words, these subjects maintained their intellectual abilities better as the disease progressed. In fact, the more educated donors did not develop the behavioural manifestations of Alzheimer's disease until they had about five times as many plaques and NFTs as the less educated subjects. Thus, increased education appears to work by helping the brain better tolerate the pathological effects of Alzheimer's disease.

Why should mental exercise protect against Alzheimer's disease? One theory that has attracted great interest is that it builds a **cognitive reserve** which increases the brain's resilience to later neural degeneration. This idea first arose when researchers found that individuals with heavier brains, which presumably contain more neurons than lighter ones, were better protected against cognitive decline in Alzheimer's disease (Katzman *et al.* 1988). One implication of this finding was that the larger the brain, the more able it is to cope with the loss of neurons. Or, put another way, people with more neurons might be able to lose more of them before reaching a threshold where a clinical deficit occurs. This theory could also be used to explain why mental exercise and education is protective against Alzheimer's disease – since increased cognitive activity would be expected to increase the number and strength of neuronal connections in the brain (Katzman 1993). In this way, cognitive reserve could be built up by mental exercise, and offer protection against dementia by helping to compensate for acquired brain pathology.

Recent research now suggests that cognitive reserve is dependent not only on the neural and synaptic hardware of the brain, but also on the types of programs (or 'software') that operate 'through' its networks. For example, functional imaging studies have shown that individuals with high IQ tend to perform mental tasks more efficiently and with less effort. This is shown by the fact that intelligent subjects show reduced amounts of blood flow in certain areas of the brain (for example, parietal and temporal lobes) when solving problems. Moreover, this principle also extends to people with Alzheimer's disease. That is, when the clinical severity of the illness is held constant, the Alzheimer's subjects who are judged to have greater 'cognitive reserve' are the ones who process cognitive information with 'less effort' as shown by reduced blood flow (Stern 2005). Since these individuals are using fewer brain areas (or neural networks) to perform mental tasks, it has been suggested that they will be less susceptible to widespread neural loss caused by the ravages of Alzheimer's disease.

Another lifestyle factor that has been shown to provide protection against mental decline is physical exercise. For example, one study that followed over 5,000 women aged over 65 years found that increased physical activity led to reduced mental decline when assessed some 6 to 8 years later (Yaffe et al. 2001). A similar finding was reported by Laurin et al. (2001) who used data from 9,008 randomly selected men and woman aged over 65 years, who had been interviewed about their general health and screened for dementia. When a large number of these subjects ($N = 4,615$) were followed up some 5 year later, it was found that the amount of exercise was the most influential factor in determining a person's risk of cognitive decline. In fact, high levels of physical activity (defined as exercise three or more times a week at an intensity greater than walking) was associated with the lowest risk of dementia. Despite this, exercise may not necessarily be protective against Alzheimer's disease in all individuals, especially if they carry the ApoE4 gene variation (Podewils et al. 2005). This is a reminder (if needed) that both nature and nurture interact together in the causation of late onset Alzheimer's disease.

Infectious dementia: kuru and Creutzfeldt–Jakob disease

While there is no evidence that Alzheimer's disease is transmitted by viruses or infectious agents, this is not the case for some other types of dementia. The first type of dementia shown to be transmissible between humans was **kuru**, a fatal illness that was discovered in the early 1950s when Australian administrative outposts were set up in the remote eastern highlands of Papua New Guinea. This mountainous and densely tropical land allowed some tribes to live only a few miles apart yet exist in isolation from each other. It was also a place where cannibalism took place, and a tribe who undertook this practice was the Fore. Although the Fore sometimes ate the flesh of other tribal groups, they mainly consumed their own family relatives as an act of respect. This also entailed certain rituals. For example, Fore custom held that the body was to be prepared by woman, who minced the flesh, and cooked it in bamboo tubes laid onto cooking fires. Custom also held that the women and children ate the internal organs including the brain, whereas the men consumed the meat (muscle).

The Fore suffered from an affliction not found in other groups, which they called *kuru* (meaning 'to tremble with fear'). This first manifested itself as unsteadiness of gait, quickly followed by tremor, loss of motor coordination, dementia and outbursts of laughter. Progression of the illness was rapid, with paralysis and death occurring within one year. But, the most unusual thing about kuru was that it only affected women and young children. Indeed, during the 1960s, kuru was the leading cause of death in Fore women, producing a bias in the sex ratio of three men to every female.

One of the first scientists to examine kuru was the American Carleton Gajdusek. Initially, he believed that a toxin caused the disease as victims of kuru showed no signs of infection. However, in the early 1960s, Gajdusek performed an experiment in which tissue from a kuru victim was injected into a monkey. At first the monkey showed no adverse signs, but within a couple of years it started to show deteriorating signs of trembling and motor dysfunction. When an autopsy was undertaken, the brain showed marked degeneration and similarities to that of a person with kuru. This experiment demonstrated for the first time that a form of dementia could be transmitted from one individual to another through infected nervous tissue. It also became clear why only the women and children suffered from the disorder: they were the ones consuming the brain tissue that harboured the infectious agent.

In 1968, Gajdusek demonstrated that another type of dementia called **Creutzfeldt–Jakob disease (CJD)** was also caused by an infectious agent. He did this by transmitting the illness to a chimpanzee with brain tissue taken from a 59-year-old man who had died from the disease. CJD had been first described by Hans Creutzfeldt in 1913, who reported the case of a young woman who had suffered from a rapid and severe breakdown of mental faculties accompanied by tremor, motor impairment and epilepsy. Later, in 1921, Alfons Jakob described four more patients with the same symptoms. Although both Creutzfeldt and Jakob undertook autopsies on their patients and reported marked neural degeneration, they did not report the most distinguishing feature of the disease: the widespread occurrence of holes (or vacuoles) in the neural cell bodies, which gives the brain an appearance of a sponge. In fact, CJD was the first example of what is now known as a **spongiform encephalopthy**.

Viruses and the discovery of prions

All living organisms contain genetic material composed of DNA and RNA. In bacteria, as in human beings, it is DNA that provides the genetic code which specifies the structure of the enzymes and other proteins that are necessary for the life and development of the organism. In addition, the ability of DNA to make copies of itself provides the crucial event in self-reproduction. But, one exception to this rule is viruses, which are like small packets of DNA enclosed in a protective case of protein. Not only is a virus unable to replicate itself, but it also lacks the enzymes for making proteins. Consequently, a virus can only reproduce by making its way into another cell, commandeering its nucleus, and reprogramming it to copy the viral genes and manufacture its proteins. Following this, the viral DNA and proteins typically assemble into thousands of new virus particles, which emerge from the infected host cell to spread infection. Viruses pose a great threat to our existence, and because of this we have evolved a sophisticated immune system, including the ability to raise antibodies against the virus so that infections can be quickly overcome.

Because kuru and Creutzfeldt–Jakob disease are transmissible forms of dementia, it was initially believed they were caused by viruses. However, both these illnesses also had some unusual features that were not typical of viral conditions. For example, both took a long time to develop after the initial infection, and neither produced signs of inflammation, fever or increased immune activity. It was as if the infectious agent had special characteristics that allowed it to avoid detection by the immune system. In 1972, a young neurologist called Stanley Prusiner set about trying to learn more about this type of agent by purifying the infectious material in scrapie (this is a transmissible degenerative disorder of sheep which also has a long incubation period). Although the task was a difficult one, by the early 1980s it was pointing to a startling conclusion: the infectious agent in scrapie lacked any nucleic acid, and appeared to consist only of protein. It was also 100 times smaller than any known virus. Prusiner called it a **prion**.

It soon became clear that this prion was actually a protein (called **prion protein** or **PrP**) with a normal function in the body and brain. It was also found that the sequence of amino acids in the normal PrP and infectious PrP were identical. But, how could two identical proteins have such different effects? One clue came from the discovery that the abnormal PrP resisted degradation by enzymes that normally act to break down proteins. Because it is the protein's three-dimensional shape that usually determines its resistance to enzyme activity, this indicated that the abnormal PrP had changed its conformation in some way. In turn, this caused it to act like a viral agent.

Although researchers do not yet fully understand how this transformation comes about, we can surmise that in certain degenerative diseases such as scrapie, the brain produces normal PrP, but this is modified to an abnormal form at a later point (see Figure 13.6). This can also explain why prion diseases have such a long incubation period, and why the immune system does not recognise the abnormal protein as a foreign invader. Although the prion theory has been highly controversial, this work remains one of the most exciting in medical research, and it won Stanley Prusiner the Nobel Prize in 1997.

Prion diseases should concern all of us. One disorder attracting a great deal of attention is **bovine spongiform encephalopathy (BSE)**, which is commonly known as mad cow disease. BSE first came to the attention of the scientific community in November 1986, when a new form of the disease appeared in the UK. This reached epidemic proportions in 1992–1993, when almost 1,000 new infections of cows were reported per week. The cause of this outbreak is believed to have been the result of commercial cattle feed containing meat and bone meal derived from sheep carcasses infected with scrapie. But, the emergence of this new form of BSE was particularly worrying as it was able to jump species (sheep to cow), raising the possibility that it could also infect humans. This fear was realised. In 1996, a new form of CJD was reported in the UK, which was linked to exposure to food contaminated by BSE (Will *et al.* 1996). Moreover, from October 1996 to November 2002, 129 cases of this new form of CJD were reported in the UK, with a few cases also occurring in Europe and the United States. Although the numbers are small, the great worry is that there are many more cases to come, and it may be many more years before the full impact of the disease on the population is known.

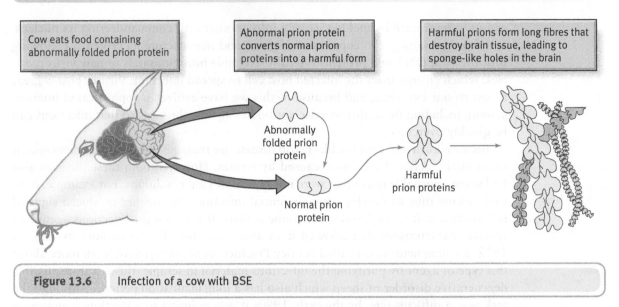

| Cow eats food containing abnormally folded prion protein | Abnormal prion protein converts normal prion proteins into a harmful form | Harmful prions form long fibres that destroy brain tissue, leading to sponge-like holes in the brain |

Abnormally folded prion protein

Harmful prion proteins

Normal prion protein

Figure 13.6 Infection of a cow with BSE

Source: S.M. Breedlove *et al.*, *Biological Psychology*, 5th edition, p. 509. Copyright © 2007 by Sinauer Associates, Inc.

The discovery of Parkinson's disease

In 1817, a London doctor called James Parkinson described the condition that today bears his name, in a manuscript entitled 'Essay on the shaking palsy' – a work that is now recognised as an outstanding medical classic. Parkinson's account of the disorder was based on only six cases, just three of which he personally examined in detail. Despite this, it is said that Parkinson described the condition 'with a vividness and insight that has never been surpassed' (Sacks 1990). Among the symptoms Parkinson described were: **resting tremor** (which he also distinguished from tremor due to alcohol abuse and old age), **bradykinesia** (slowness and poverty of movement), and **akinesia** (difficulty in initiating action). Parkinson also described the course of the disease, which culminated in loss of muscle tone, paralysis and death. Although these types of symptoms had been observed before (one can even find a good description of the disease in Shakespeare's *Henry IV*), Parkinson was the first to recognise that they represented a distinct clinical illness. Despite this, Parkinson's essay had little impact for nearly half a century, and did not become widely known until the great French doctor Charcot began to refer to the disorder in the 1860s. He was also the first to call it Parkinson's disease.

Although in many ways Parkinson was a conventional figure, being devoted to his medical practice and the church of his parish, he also had a secretive side. The early nineteenth century was a time when the American colonies had broken away from Britain to found a new political system based on equality, and the French Revolution had shown that monarchies could be overthrown. In the spirit of the times, many, including Parkinson, were supporting political reform in England. To this end, Parkinson belonged to several radical societies, and wrote a number of political pamphlets under the pseudonym 'Old Hubert' which were critical of the government. He was also subpoenaed and examined under oath by the prime minister concerning knowledge of an alleged conspiracy to assassinate King George III in 1784. Although there is no evidence that Parkinson was involved in this plot, he only agreed to testify after being assured that he would not be forced to incriminate himself. It is also a curious fact that no pictures of James Parkinson are known to exist.

The epidemiology of Parkinson's disease

Parkinson's disease is primarily an illness of later life, occurring equally in men and women, with the mean age of onset being between 55 and 65 years. The prevalence of the illness has been estimated to be around 1 per cent worldwide, and is slightly higher in Europe where the overall prevalence is 1.6 per cent, which rises from 0.6 per cent at age 60–64 years, to 3.5 per cent at age 85–89 years (De Rijk *et al.* 1997). However, disabilities of movement are more common than this, with one study showing that 15 per cent of those aged 65–74, 30 per cent of those aged 75–84, and more than 50 per cent of those over 85 years have at least two symptoms found in Parkinson's disease (Bennett *et al.* 1996). These findings suggest that in some instances Parkinson's disease may go undiagnosed. Although rare, Parkinson's disease can also be found in much younger individuals. Onset of the illness before the age of 20 years is termed 'juvenile Parkinson's disease', and onset between the ages of 21 and 40 is referred to as 'early Parkinson's disease'. These forms of the illness make up around 5 per cent of all Parkinson disease cases.

The clinical course of Parkinson's disease

The first symptoms of Parkinson's disease appear gradually, but with increasing severity. In many cases the disorder may begin as a slight tremor in one of the hands, or a postural flexion of the neck (see Figure 13.7). As the disease progresses, bradykinesia (slow movement) will appear, where the person's actions become clumsy, impoverished and deliberate. This is likely to be accompanied by tremor, especially of the arms, which is most marked when the person performs intentional acts. Curiously, this type of tremor is exacerbated by stress, but disappears during sleep. Another characteristic of Parkinson's disease is rigidity and stiffness of the limbs and trunk, making it difficult for the patient to maintain balance and to walk. Thus, the person with the disease has a tendency to develop a stooped head-down shoulders-drooped stance, and to walk with slow, shuffling steps. There may also be difficulties in starting to walk, or freezing in mid-stride. Another common feature of the illness is a blank facial expression, which can be accompanied by drooling saliva from the mouth and a soft, quiet voice. Strangely, these symptoms are likely to vary in severity from day to day, or even moment to moment.

The progressive deterioration of posture and voluntary control can also produce a number of secondary symptoms, especially in the later stages of the disease. Although not all patients will experience these disabilities, those that do can be much distressed by them. These symptoms include constipation; a difficulty in swallowing; incontinence; and excessive sweating. In addition, the person with later-stage Parkinson's disease is likely to suffer from depression and exhibit subcortical dementia with slow memory recall and a decline in intellectual capacity. As the disease progresses further, the victim will be unable to stand or walk, and will lose the capacity for voluntary movement. By the end of the disease there will be almost complete invalidism, with postural muscle strength being so weak that the person may be unable even to move their head. Before the introduction of effective drug therapy the average survival time for a patient with Parkinson's disease was 8–10 years. Today, with treatment, life expectancy is similar to that of the general population.

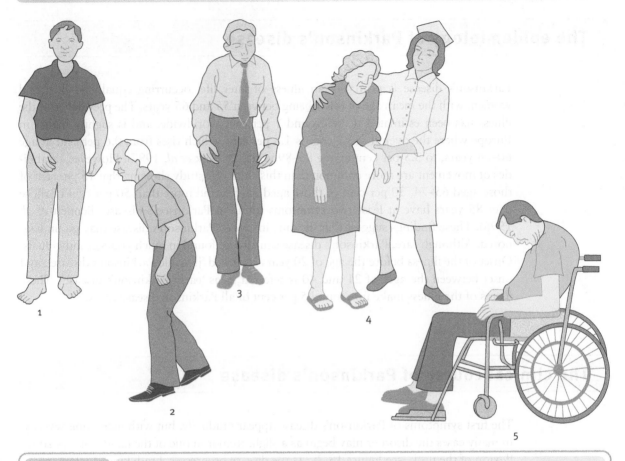

| **Figure 13.7** | The stages of Parkinson's disease |

Source: R.B. Graham, *Physiological Psychology*, p. 375. Copyright © 1990 by Wadsworth Publishing Co.

The pathological features of Parkinson's disease

The underlying cause of Parkinson's disease was discovered in 1960 by Ehringer and Hornykiewicz, who measured levels of the neurotransmitter **dopamine** in the human brain. They found a marked loss of this substance (up to a 90 per cent reduction) in the caudate nucleus and putamen (i.e. the striatum) in Parkinson's disease patients. Although the striatum was known to contain the highest levels of dopamine in the brain, researchers were uncertain of the origin of this neurotransmitter. However, in 1964, Carlsson and his colleagues used florescence techniques to show that dopamine in the striatum was derived from axons arising from a small, darkly pigmented nucleus in the midbrain called the **substantia nigra**. It also became apparent that Parkinson's disease was due to marked degeneration of the **nigral–striatal pathway**. Although the substantia nigra had long been suspected by some researchers, many were sceptical that selective damage to such a small area of the brain could produce such a devastating disease. Further examination of the substantia nigra in Parkinson's disease showed not only a marked loss of its cells (see Plate 13.2), but also that the first behavioural signs of Parkinsonism did not appear until approximately 80 per cent of the neurons had been

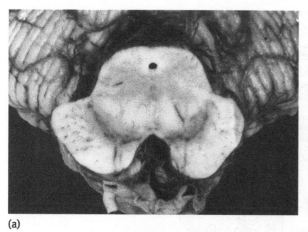

(a)

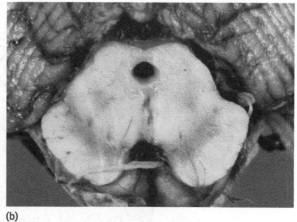

(b)

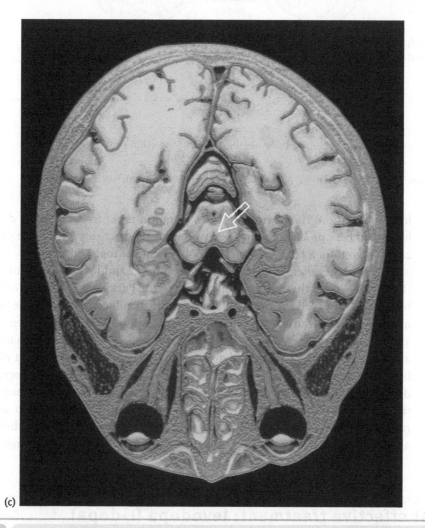

(c)

| Plate 13.2 | Horizontal sections of midbrain including the darkly pigmented substantia nigra from a healthy brain (a) and one with Parkinson's disease (b). Note how the latter is less pigmented indicating degeneration. (c) Horizontal MRI scan at the level of the midbrain. Note how both substantia nigra can clearly be seen in the midbrain region |

Source: Plates (a) and (b), Daniel P. Perl, MD, Mount Sinai School of Medicine, New York; Plate (c), Alfred Pasieka/Science Photo Library

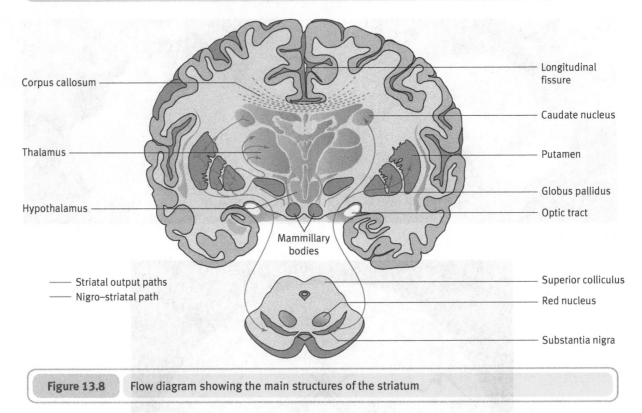

Corpus callosum

Thalamus

Hypothalamus

Mammillary
bodies

—— Striatal output paths
—— Nigro–striatal path

Longitudinal
fissure

Caudate nucleus

Putamen

Globus pallidus

Optic tract

Superior colliculus

Red nucleus

Substantia nigra

| Figure 13.8 | Flow diagram showing the main structures of the striatum |

Source: R.B. Graham, *Physiological Psychology*, p. 373. Copyright © 1990 by Wadsworth Publishing Co.

lost. In addition, the neurons of the substantia nigra in Parkinson's disease contained large numbers of **Lewy bodies** – tiny spherical structures within the cytoplasm of the cell that contain a core surrounded by filamentous material.

Although degeneration of the substantia nigra and loss of dopamine in the striatum (Figure 13.8) are the distinguishing features of Parkinson's disease, other areas of the brain also show cell loss in the later stages of the illness. For example, dopamine levels in the ventral striatum, frontal lobes and hippocampus have been reported to be approximately 40 per cent of normal (Agid *et al.* 1987). These dopamine projections arise from the ventral tegmental area, which surrounds the substantia nigra in the midbrain. Further, while the extent of nigral–striatal degeneration correlates with the degree of motor impairment, the tegmental–dopaminergic impairment correlates with the severity of affective and intellectual impairment (McNamara *et al.* 2002). Some researchers have also reported that noradrenergic, serotonergic and cholinergic systems are compromised in Parkinson's disease – although this is a less consistent finding.

The first effective treatment: levodopa (L-dopa)

The discovery that Parkinson's disease was caused by dopamine depletion had important implications. In particular, it suggested that if a way of replenishing dopamine in the brain could be found, then a treatment for the disorder might be achieved. Unfortunately, injections of dopamine were ineffective because the dopamine did not cross the blood–brain barrier, and was rapidly degraded in the bloodstream by an enzyme called **dopa decarboxylase**. However, in 1967 it was discovered that large oral doses of the dopamine precursor L-dopa had beneficial effects in relieving Parkinson's symptoms (Cotzias *et al.* 1967). Because of the high dosage, a proportion of this drug was able to pass into the brain before being degraded, and it was taken up by axon terminals of the striatum to produce dopamine. This discovery provided a dramatic turning point in the management of Parkinson's disease. Later, L-dopa was combined with a dopa decarboxylase inhibitor (such as carbidopa) which allowed the dose of L-dopa to be reduced, and its side effects lessened.

It has been found that around 70 per cent of Parkinson's patients show at least a 50 per cent improvement with L-dopa treatment, and in some cases the benefits can be immediate and dramatic. However, more typically, treatment is started with low doses of L-dopa, which are increased over several months, producing a gradual improvement over time. Bradykinesia and rigidity are generally the first symptoms to improve, with tremor becoming much less troublesome with continued treatment. There may also be considerable improvement in posture. Although some movement disabilities may remain, their severity and incidence are often significantly reduced, enabling the person to work again or to have some degree of independence. Put simply, L-dopa gives many Parkinson patients a significantly improved quality of life.

Unfortunately, after years of continual treatment, many patients begin to experience difficulties with L-dopa. The first problem is often a decline in the effectiveness of L-dopa (Figure 13.9) – an effect that requires a higher dose to be administered, which increases the risk of side effects such as nausea, fidgeting, or even psychosis. Another disturbing problem for patients is the occurrence of 'on–off' responses to the drug, where

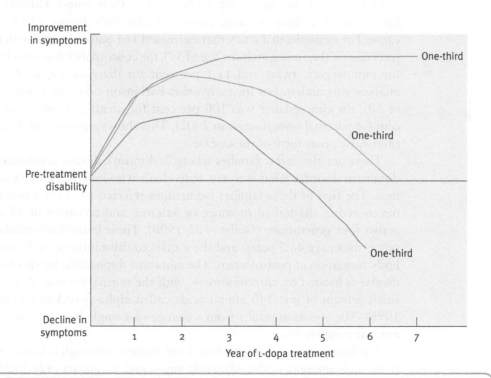

Figure 13.9   The decline in the therapeutic benefit of L-dopa in the treatment of Parkinson's disease

periods of immobility and tremor alternate with periods of relative normality in an unpredictable pattern. These changes can occur with such rapidity that patients have become 'frozen' in mid-movement. Such effects are also likely to be exacerbated by stress or physical exertion. Another side effect of L-dopa treatment is **dyskinesia** (involuntary movements of the face, hands and limbs). Dyskinesia can often be reduced by lowering the dosage of L-dopa, although this may cause the symptoms of Parkinson's disease to reappear. It has been reported that these side effects occur in 80 per cent of patients who have been given high doses of L-dopa for six or more years (Lees 1986). Because of this problem, some doctors advise patients to take 'L-dopa holidays' in the hope that the breaks in usage will prolong the effectiveness of the drug.

Causes of Parkinson's disease

The genetic causes of Parkinson's disease

Until recently, Parkinson's disease was believed to be a non-genetic disorder. For example, studies examining the incidence of Parkinson's disease in twins found a low concordance rate of 10–20 per cent, and no difference in rates between monozygotic (identical) and dizygotic (non-identical) twins (Golbe 1995). This is not the pattern of results predicted by a genetic disorder, which is expected to show a much higher concordance rate for monozygotic twins (who inherit an identical set of genes), compared with dizygotic (who share only 50 per cent of their genes). However, recent evidence has shown that there are some cases of Parkinson's disease which do have a genetic cause. For example, in a study that examined 161 pairs of twins with late onset Parkinson's disease (beginning after the age of 50), the concordance was found to be 15.5 per cent for monozygotic twins and 11.1 per cent for dizygotic twins. But, when the same analysis was undertaken for early onset Parkinson's disease (beginning before the age of 50), the concordance was 100 per cent for identical twins compared with 17 per cent for paternal ones (Langston 2002). This shows a genetic involvement in the much rarer early onset form of the disease.

There are also a few families where Parkinson's disease is inherited as an autsomal dominant disorder. That is to say, individuals who inherit the mutation develop the illness. The first of these families (sometimes referred to as the Contursi kindred) were discovered in the Italian province of Salerno, and consisted of 45 affected members across four generations (Golbe *et al.* 1990). These individuals exhibit an early age of onset (mean age 46.5 years) and show marked substantia nigra degeneration and Lewy body formation at post-mortem. The mutation responsible for this form of Parkinson's disease is located on chromosome 4, with the normal version of the gene producing a small protein of just 140 amino acids called **alpha-synuclein** (Polymeropoulos *et al.* 1996). The mutation results from a change of a single base pair (from guanine to adenine) at position 53.

The function of alpha-synuclein is not known, although it is only found in the brain (with high amounts in the substantia nigra) and it appears to be localised in the presynaptic membrane, where it could be involved in neurotransmitter release (Moore *et al.* 2005). Lewy bodies also contain alpha-synuclein, which raises the possibility that this protein is involved in their formation. One theory is that the mutated form of alpha-synuclein forms 'lumps' that are deposited in the cytoplasm, which become toxic to the neuron. There is also evidence that alpha-synuclein is not broken down and cleared away from neurons efficiently. This process normally uses the protein **ubiquitin**, which 'tags' obsolete proteins in order to provide a signal for another class of enzymes, called **proteosomes,** to begin the process of amino acid dismantling. It has been suggested that this process may not work in Parkinson's disease, with a build-up of defective proteins occurring in dopaminergic neurons (Cookson 2003).

Since the discovery of the alpha-synuclein gene, a number of other genes have also been linked to Parkinson's disease. The most interesting is the **parkin** gene located on chromosome 6. This gene causes a recessive form of the disorder, which means that a defective copy of the gene has to be inherited from each parent before the illness is inherited. Although it is rare, this gene combination is a common one in early onset Parkinson's disease. For example, in a study of 73 families with Parkinson's disease that occurred before the age of 45 years, 49 per cent were found to have the parkin mutations (Lücking *et al.* 2000). The normal parkin protein appears to play a role in transporting defective proteins to proteosomes, and presumably this process is defective in those with the mutated gene.

Although, there is little evidence to support a direct genetic involvement in the more common late onset Parkinson's disease, it is worth bearing in mind that similar types of cellular process could be at work in the causation of the illness. That is, environmental factors could be having an effect that ultimately results in the aggregation of alpha-synuclein, or the ability of the brain to clear away old and unwanted proteins. Thus, the genetic understanding of Parkinson's disease may have great importance in helping to provide new insights into degeneration of the substantia nigra, and offering new therapeutic approaches into halting the illness.

Awakenings

In the winter of 1916–1917, a 'new' illness appeared in Europe, seemingly out of nowhere, that over the next decade would spread around the world and affect some 5 million (mostly young) people. Often starting with a sore throat and fever, a variety of more disturbing ailments would appear within a day or so. These could include severe tremor, visual difficulties, or restlessness accompanied by severe insomnia. And, in many cases, the victim would become lethargic and fall into a sleep-like coma. All these manifestations were recognised as the same illness by the physician Constantin von Economo in 1917, who called it encephalitis lethargica. However, the illness would become better known as sleeping sickness – an apt name considering the hundreds of thousands of people who would die from the illness without ever regaining consciousness. Although many patients managed to survive, and a few even made a full recovery, most went on to develop Parkinson-like symptoms that included slowness of movement, rigidity and speech difficulties. The most severely affected, however, sank into a 'sleep' and were unable to move or speak. Yet, while these people lacked energy, impetus, affect or desire, they were still conscious and registered what went on around them. Because little could be done to revive them, most of the victims were placed in various institutions and asylums, and left alone. The sleeping sickness epidemic was also quickly forgotten – ten years after it first arose, it disappeared.

In 1966, a doctor called Oliver Sacks took up a post at Mount Carmel Hospital in New York, which housed a group of 80 people who were survivors of the sleeping sickness epidemic. As he became familiar with the patients, Sacks began to wonder what would happen if he treated them with L-dopa – a drug with remarkable anti-Parkinson effects. In 1969, Sacks put his curiosity into practice with extraordinary consequences. Patients who had been motionless and speechless for over forty years, stood up from their wheelchairs and became fully interactive again with the world around them. In some cases, the drug even managed to restore the patients to a 'normal' existence. Tragically, the patient's joy was short-lived. Within a few weeks, L-dopa began to lose its effectiveness, and most returned to their previous comatose state. The story is vividly told in Oliver Sack's book *Awakenings* (1973), which was also made into a feature film starring Robin Williams and Robert De Niro in 1990.

The exact cause of encephalitis lethargica has never been established. Many doctors at the time believed it to have a viral cause, but extensive examination of archived tissue taken from victims, using modern probes, has failed to show any support for this theory. Although it is very rare, sporadic cases of encephalitis lethargica still occur today, and these also fail to show any viral pathology. However, in one study that examined 20 new cases of encephalitis lethargica, all showed evidence of infection from a rare form of streptococcus bacteria, which is the common cause of sore throats (Dale *et al.* 2004). Although it is not yet certain, it has been proposed that this indicates that encephalitis lethargica is actually caused by the body's own immune response to these bacteria, which in turn produce antibodies that attack the nerve cells of the brain. More than eighty years on, we may finally be solving the puzzle of this mysterious disease – which one day could strike again on a large scale.

The environmental causes of Parkinson's disease

Although genetic influences play a key role in early onset forms of Parkinson's disease, environmental factors are likely to be more important when the disease has a late onset. Despite this, researchers have managed to discover few environmental linkages with the disorder. One exception, however, occurred in the 1980s when a neurotoxin was discovered that provided important new insights into the causes of neural degeneration responsible for Parkinson's disease. In 1982, several people in northern California developed severe Parkinson-like symptoms after using an illegal drug that was sold as a synthetic form of heroin (Langston *et al.* 1983). This drug was produced and supplied by the same dealer, and closer analysis showed that it contained a contaminant called **MPTP**. This agent was a highly selective neurotoxin for the substantia nigra, and it provided brain researchers with an effective means to mimic the effects of Parkinson's disease in laboratory animals. For example, injections of MPTP in monkeys caused slow movement, rigidity and tremor, along with a marked loss of nigral dopaminergic neurons (Burns *et al.* 1983). These deficits fail to occur in rodents whose substantia nigra neurons, unlike those of primates, do not contain melanin pigments. This has raised suspicion that the substantia nigra pigments may have an important role in the development of Parkinson's disease.

The discovery of MPTP led to efforts to establish how it caused degeneration of the substantia nigra. It soon become clear, however, that MPTP was not the toxic agent. Rather, MPTP was oxidised into a more highly toxic chemical called **MPP⁺** by the enzyme **monoamine oxidase B**, which acts to break down monoamines such as dopamine, and is found predominantly in astrocytes. In fact, MPP⁺ belongs to a class of agents known as

free radicals which are highly reactive chemicals, normally formed by the breakdown of oxygen, that have lost an electron. Although they exist for only a few millionths of a second, the accumulation of free radical 'hits' over time inflicts considerable damage on biological tissues. In fact, this is believed to be an important cause of ageing.

Returning to Parkinson's disease, it has been shown that the dopaminergic neurons of the substantia nigra are highly vulnerable to the effects of MPP$^+$. Not only do they take up this chemical into their nerve endings by means of the reuptake pump, but once inside the cell, MPP$^+$ causes its death by accumulating in the **mitochondria** where it causes a depletion of **ATP** (the cell's main source of energy) along with a further cascade of damaging free radical reactions (Schapira 1994).

This discovery of MPP$^+$ has relevance for understanding the causes of Parkinson's disease. For example, it is possible that there are chemicals in the environment that resemble MPP$^+$ and cause degeneration of the substantia nigra. In fact, substances related to MPTP are present in many foods, and the chemical structure of MPP$^+$ is similar to the pesticide paraquat. However, a toxic agent need not resemble MPTP structurally, provided it has a similar mechanism of action on dopaminergic neurons. In this respect it is relevant to note that Parkinson's disease and motor neuron disease have been found to be very common in a few parts of the world, including Guam, New Guinea and the Kii peninsula of Japan. Since there does not appear to be a genetic explanation for these 'hotspots', environmental toxins are suspected (Spencer *et al.* 1987). It is also possible that certain chemicals in the environment may help to protect against the illness. Indeed, some studies have found that Parkinson's disease is less common in smokers, which has been attributed to a more effective removal of free radicals from the brain (Calne and Langston 1983).

If MPTP becomes harmful only when it is converted into MPP$^+$ by monoamine oxidase-B (MAO-B), it follows that drugs which inhibit MAO-B should help to prevent the neural damage caused by MPTP (Figure 13.10). In fact, there is good evidence to show this is indeed the case. For example, MAO inhibitors protect the substantia nigra in monkeys treated with high amounts of MPTP (Langston *et al.* 1984). But, more importantly, the same protective effect occurs in humans. Most notably, the MAO-B inhibitor **deprenyl** (which increases dopamine levels in the synapse) has been shown to improve the symptoms of Parkinson's disease, and to significantly slow down the progression of the illness (Parkinson Study Group 1989). For this reason, deprenyl is now often combined with L-dopa to treat Parkinson's disease.

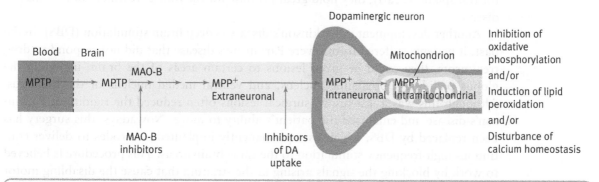

| **Figure 13.10** | Flow diagram showing how MPTP causes degeneration |

Source: R.S. Feldman *et al., Principles of Neuropsychopharmacology*, p. 876. Copyright © 1997 by Sinauer Associates, Inc.

New prospects for Parkinson's disease

In recent years, attempts have been made to treat Parkinson's disease by the transplantation of tissue into the brain to replenish the 'lost' dopamine, or to help build new neural connections. This technique was first undertaken in the early 1980s by Swedish surgeons who took tissue from the patient's own adrenal glands (which produces small amounts of dopamine) and placed it into the striatum (Buckland *et al.* 1985). Unfortunately, the benefits of this procedure were modest, with any improvement generally lasting no longer than six months. A more promising technique was the use of foetal tissue which had yet to develop into mature brain cells. By the 1980s, animal research had shown that it was possible to take tissue from the foetal midbrain (which includes the substantia nigra) and to implant it into the striatum, where it formed new connections with the host cells that secreted dopamine. Moreover, this procedure was shown to reverse MPTP-induced Parkinsonism in monkeys. The use of this technique to treat Parkinson's disease was controversial, however, as it required tissue from human embryos. Nonetheless, the operation was first undertaken in the early 1990s. Although the grafts survived well in the brain, the results of this procedure were highly variable. In general, 'mild to moderate' relief from Parkinson's disease was obtained, although in no case did it fully reverse symptoms (Lindvall 1991).

The technique of foetal transplantation is likely to be superseded in the near future by the use of neural grafts composed of **stem cells,** which are in essence 'blank', or undifferentiated, cells taken from the embryo at a very early age. These have the potential to turn into virtually any tissue in the human body, including nerve cells. Already it has been shown that stem cells can be turned into fully functional dopamine neurons. For example, Bjorklund *et al.* (2002) destroyed the substantia nigra in rats, and found that the behavioural deficits of this operation were reversed within nine weeks by the transplantation of embryonic stem cells into the striatum. The restoration of behaviour was also accompanied by blood flow returning to the parts of the brain damaged by the lesion. More recently, a similar study has been performed on primates, with positive results showing a small but significant restoration of dopamine neurons (Takagi *et al.* 2005). These findings are exciting. Not only can stem cells be cultured and kept alive indefinitely, but scientists believe they have the potential to treat a wide range of diseases. They may even one day be used to create new organs for transplant. Clearly, they hold great promise for the future treatment of Parkinson's disease.

Another development in Parkinson's disease is **deep brain stimulation (DBS)**. In the past, if patients suffered from severe Parkinson's disease that did not respond to drug treatments, they could be given lesions to certain areas of the brain, including the globus pallidus, subthalamic nucleus, and ventral medial nucleus of the thalamus. Although this was a last resort, surgical lesions often reduced the rigidity of Parkinson's disease and enhanced the patient's ability to move. Nowadays, this surgery has been replaced by DBS, which uses permanently implanted electrodes to deliver continuous high-frequency stimulation to the same brain areas. This procedure is believed to work by blocking the signals arising in the striatum that cause the disabling motor symptoms of the disease. In DBS, the brain electrodes are connected to a pulse generator that is normally implanted in the upper chest, and is programmed externally by the patient using a special magnetic wand. Research shows that DBS results in a

40–60 per cent improvement in Parkinson's symptoms, which is superior to foetal transplantation or surgery. It is also associated with fewer side effects. Thus, at the current time, DBS is the most effective surgical treatment for Parkinson's disease and it enhances the quality of life for many patients.

The discovery of Huntington's disease

Another disorder that primarily affects the striatum is **Huntington's disease,** named after George Huntington (1850–1916) who first described the disorder in 1872. Huntington came from a family of doctors who practised in Long Island, New York, and he once attributed his interest in medicine to a childhood encounter with the illness that came to bear his name: 'Driving with my father . . . we suddenly came upon two women, mother and daughter, both tall, thin, almost cadaverous, both bowing, twisting grimacing. I stared in wonderment, almost in fear. What could it mean?' (Wexler 1996). After graduating with a medical degree from Columbia University in 1871, Huntington returned home for a few months to help with the family practice before taking up a post in Ohio. This gave him an opportunity to observe again the afflicted patients and to examine their medical records. In February 1872, Huntington reported his observations to a conference in Ohio, and the report was published two months later in a paper entitled 'On chorea' (the word *chorea* means 'dance', which refers to the twisting and involuntary tic-like movements seen in the disease). This brief report was mostly concerned with Sydenham's chorea, a disorder that occurs after rheumatic fever in children. However, towards the end of the paper, Huntington described the 'heredity' chorea he had observed at home on Long Island in seven short paragraphs. This account, which occupied only a single page of text, was to have an everlasting impact.

The importance of Huntington's paper was not so much that he had described a new disease, but that he had shown it to be inherited. For example, he wrote: 'When either or both parents have shown manifestations of the disease . . . one or more of the offspring almost invariably suffer from the disease, if they live to an adult age. But if by any chance these children go through life *without it*, the thread is broken, and the grandchildren and great-grandchildren of the original shakers may rest assured that they are free from the disease'. Although Huntington could not know it, as the laws of genetics were unknown (the work of Mendel was rediscovered in 1900 – see Chapter 14), he was describing a condition where inheritance of a single gene led to the illness. Huntington was fortunate in being able to draw on medical records spanning a 78-year period from his family practice – but, it was his insight that was the key factor in establishing widespread interest in the new disorder. After publishing his paper, George Huntington made no other scientific contribution to medicine, and did not even practice neurology (Finger 1994).

It is certain that the disease existed long before it was described by Huntington. Indeed, researchers soon compiled extensive family histories of those in New England with the illness, and showed that many came from the East Anglia region of England, from which Huntington's ancestors had also come in the seventeenth century. It is also certain that those with the disease at this time faced prejudice and persecution, with their strange jerking movements inciting fear and misunderstanding. In some cases they may have been regarded as witches or as possessed by the devil. Indeed, at least seven individuals in the Salem witch trials of New England were known to come from families that had Huntington's disease, and one woman was convicted of witchcraft and hanged in 1653 (Finger 1994).

The epidemiology of Huntington's disease

Huntington's disease is a rare disorder which affects 8–9 people per 100,000 in European and American populations (although it appears to be less common in African and Japanese groups). In the UK the incidence may be slightly higher as the Huntington's Disease Association believes there are between 6,500 and 8,000 people with the disorder. The symptoms of Huntington's disease usually begin between the ages of 35 and 50, with an average onset of 40 years. Thus, most carriers will have had children by the time the illness first appears, and exposed their offspring to the risk of the disease. Symptoms progress slowly, progressively and without remission, with death normally occurring some 15 to 20 years after the disease first appears. In about 10 per cent of cases, Huntington's disease may have a juvenile onset, starting before the age of 20 years. This form is associated with muscle rigidity rather than chorea, and is often accompanied by seizures and mental retardation. It is believed that new mutations can sporadically arise to cause Huntington's disease, but these are extremely rare, and probably occur in less than 0.1 per cent of sufferers.

The clinical course of Huntington's disease

Huntington's disease is often said to comprise three main types of abnormality: movement, cognitive and emotional. The first signs are often clumsiness, excessive fidgeting, or jerky movements. In some cases, however, personality changes, mood swings and bizarre behaviour may be noticed first, especially by family and friends. Whatever symptoms occur first, the disease is clearly seen when uncontrollable movements (tics) develop in the fingers, feet, face or trunk, which make the person lurch and stumble. This will develop into rapid and complex flailing movements of the arms and upper parts of the body, where the person is likely to writhe and jerk incessantly. To make matters worse, these behaviours may be accompanied by slurred speech, an inability to control eye movements, and jaw clenching. These symptoms become more frequent and extreme as the disease progresses. Because of the high energy used up by constant movement, and the difficulty in eating (swallowing becomes a problem as control of the mouth and diaphragm muscles is lost), individuals with late stage Huntington's disease are often underweight. This makes them prone to infection and other illnesses. Only towards the end of the disease do the choreic movements wane, and the person becomes bedridden with severe rigidity, aphasia and paralysis.

The worsening of the abnormal movements in Huntington's disease are also accompanied by mental changes, which may first appear as a slowing of thought processes or dimming of intellect. These deficits are likely to become more severe so that the person becomes easily confused and forgetful. Despite this, the person with Huntington's rarely shows visual agnosia (an inability to recognise objects or others) which occurs in Alzheimer's disease. Consequently, Huntington's disease is often described as a **subcortical dementia** to distinguish it from cortical types such as Alzheimer's. Huntington's disease is also associated with a variety of behavioural problems. These can include sudden aggressive outbursts, impulsiveness and periods of excitement in the early years of the illness, followed by apathy and major depression later on (suicide rates are particularly high – about 12 per cent). Another problem which occurs throughout the illness is irascibility, which can make the person difficult to deal with. In some instances serious psychiatric complaints, such as obsessive–compulsive behaviour or psychotic thought, can add to the patients difficulties.

The pathological features of Huntington's disease

The most striking change that takes place in the brain of people with Huntington's disease is cell loss in the caudate nucleus and putamen (striatum), although in the later stages of the disorder degeneration often spreads to other areas. This results in the generalised shrinkage (up to 20 per cent) of the brain. The striatum is the first region to show cell loss, and this continues throughout the disease, so that 95 per cent of its neurons may have degenerated by the time of death (Vonsattel *et al.* 1985)(see Plate 13.3). As the striatum degenerates, significant cell loss also takes place in other areas of the brain, including the globus pallidus and subthalamic nucleus (which receive input from the striatum), and cerebral cortex where the greatest loss of cells occurs in layer V1 (Hedreen *et al.* 1991). It is believed that the degeneration of the striatum (and its output pathways) underlie the motor abnormalities seen in the early and middle stages of the disease, whereas the cerebral deterioration contributes more to the later stages of dementia. Degeneration can also occur in other regions of the brain, including brainstem, cerebellum, amygdala and regions of the thalamus.

The striatum contains several different types of neurons, but the most vulnerable to degeneration are the medium spiny projection neurons that use **gamma-aminobutyric acid (GABA)** as their neurotransmitter. These form the output fibres of the striatum that project to the globus pallidus and substantia nigra. The levels of GABA, or more specifically its synthesising enzymes, may decline by up to 80 per cent in the striatum of Huntington's victims. In addition, there is also a marked fall (up to 50 per cent) in **acetylcholine**, which is found in the interneurons of the striatum. However, the nigral–striatal pathway tends to be preserved in Huntington's disease and dopamine levels in the striatum may actually be increased. This high level of dopaminergic activity is believed to be caused by the loss of GABA neurons in the striatum, as some of these cells project to the substantia nigra where they inhibit the dopamine neurons. Without this inhibitory control, the nigral neurons release more dopamine into the striatum – and this may be responsible for the choreic movements. Support for this idea comes from work showing that drugs which increase dopamine (such as L-dopa) exacerbate the symptoms of the Huntington's disease, whereas drugs that block dopaminergic activity (such as haloperidol) help to reduce its symptoms.

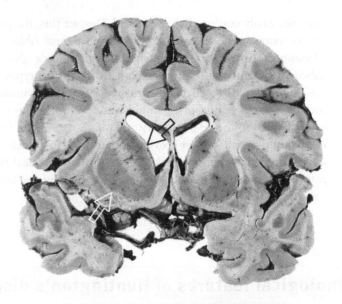

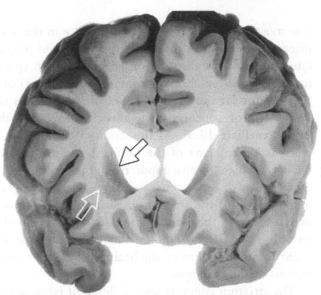

Plate 13.3 The pathological changes in Huntington's disease. The arrows point to the caudate nucleus, which shows marked degeneration in the Huntington's brain

Source: N.R. Carlson (2004) *Physiology of Behavior*, 8th edition, p. 267, Allyn & Bacon

The cause of Huntington's disease

Huntington's disease is caused by the inheritance of a single mutated gene that follows an autosomal mode of inheritance (that is, if a person inherits the gene they will develop the disorder). Because a person inherits approximately half their genes in a randomised fashion from their mother, and half from the father, it follows that if one parent carries the gene, there will be a 50 per cent chance they will pass it on to their offspring. One of the great tragedies of Huntington's disease is that it does not normally manifest itself until middle age. By this time, a Huntington's carrier, not knowing whether they carry the mutated gene, is likely to have had children, and put them at risk of inheriting the disorder. Until recently there was no way of knowing whether one was a carrier, although new developments in genetic testing have enabled the Huntington's gene to be identified from a simple blood test (see below). However, whether a prospective carrier wants to discover if they have an incurable, fatal and extremely distressing disorder that causes mental and physical degeneration, is another matter. Indeed, only a small percentage of people (12–15 per cent) take up the offer of the test (Harper 1991).

Tracking down the gene that causes Huntington's disease

The story of how the gene for Huntington's disease was discovered is a fascinating one. It can be said to start with the legendary folk singer Woody Guthrie, who, as a young man in the 1930s, rode freight trains across America and lived with the downtrodden of the Depression. These experiences inspired him to write a number of songs that were later covered by artists such as Bob Dylan and Bruce Springsteen. But, Woody Guthrie was a victim of Huntington's disease, which was diagnosed in 1952, and his illness would progress for fifteen years until his death in 1967. After his death, his ex-wife Marjorie decided to set up an organisation with the objective of providing services for families with Huntington's disease and promoting education and research. This not only raised greater awareness of the disorder, but also led to unexpected developments. In 1968, Marjorie Guthrie met Milton Wexler, a Californian psychiatrist whose wife had Huntington's disease. Working together they lobbied Congress for further help, and by 1976 had persuaded them to pass a bill creating a federal Huntington's disease Commission – a decision that helped to draw together various experts in the field and set a new agenda for further research.

One of the objectives of the Commission was to discover the location of the gene that caused Huntington's disease – an advance that would enable diagnostic testing of the illness and provide greater understanding of the disease itself. But, the task was formidable because Huntington's disease is a rare disorder, and the only way for this gene to be located and identified was to screen a large group of patients with a marker that 'tagged' the gene (or nearby area of the chromosome) in those with the illness. However, the Commission was to soon make a crucial breakthrough by discovering the world's largest collection of Huntington's victims in an isolated community on the shores of Lake Maracaibo in Venezuela. In fact, over 100 victims lived there, many in interbred families, and housed in squalid conditions – all descendants of a woman who had brought the disease to the area in the 1860s.

In 1981, the daughter of Milton Wexler, Nancy, led an expedition to Lake Maracaibo to identify the gene responsible for Huntington's disease. The work involved collecting blood samples from a large number of individuals and compiling their family trees. The team managed to take 570 samples that were sent back to the United States. One scientist to test the blood samples was James Gusella, who used **restriction enzymes** as a means of tracking genes through the families. Restriction enzymes are like molecular scissors that cut DNA into various fragments. These fragments can then be radioactively labelled and used as probes – as they will attach themselves to the complementary bases of the DNA obtained from blood samples (see Chapter 14). Put simply, the idea is based on the fact that genes that lie close together on the same chromosome tend to get inherited together. For example, the genes that cause haemophilia and red–green of colour blindness are located close together on the X chromosome. Thus, both conditions tend to be co-inherited. In the early 1970s, geneticists realised that DNA probes made from restriction enzymes could be used in a similar way. That is to say, if a DNA probe was found that always lay close to a gene, this fragment could be used to track a given gene through a family tree. Such a genetic 'marker' would tell the biologist with a reasonable degree of certainty whether a person carried the gene in question, and show them where on the chromosome it lay.

Gusella had predicted it would take at least 100 probes, each from a different part of the genome, to eventually discover a DNA fragment that was always co-inherited with the mutated gene in individuals with Huntington's disease. In fact, he only got as far as his twelfth probe before he discovered one that was unique to people with the disease. This marker was located near the end of the short arm of chromosome 4 (Gusella *et al.* 1983), and its discovery was an extraordinary piece of good fortune. For the first time it allowed a reliable diagnosis of Huntington's disease to be made from a simple blood test. In addition, researchers now knew where the gene lay in the genome, which was vital if they were to discover its precise structure and understand how it produced its effects.

It would be another ten years before the exact location of the gene and its structure were determined (described by some as the longest and most frustrating search in the annals of molecular biology). But, it would be worth the wait. This task was accomplished in 1993 when the Huntington's Disease Collaborative Research Group (a group of over fifty investigators from ten different research institutions) published their findings. This work showed that the gene was relatively large and contained over 300,000 base pairs. But, the most striking thing about the Huntington's gene was the nature of its mutation. In all the Huntington's disease victims, the gene contained a nucleotide triplet CAG, that is, a sequence of the bases comprising cytosine (C), adenine (A) and guanine (G). In normal people, this triplet was repeated between 15 and 34 times (the average number of repeats being 20). However, in those with Huntington's disease, the triplet normally occurred between 37 and 66 times. The researchers also found a correlation between the number of repeats in the defective gene and the age of onset of the disease: the more repeats, the earlier the illness was manifested. In fact, the youngest person known to show the signs of Huntington's disease was 2 years old – and they had over 100 repeats of the CAG triplet (Huntington's Disease Collaborative Research Group 1993).

Huntingtin

The protein produced by the gene responsible for Huntington's disease was called **huntingtin (htt)**. Unfortunately the sequencing of the amino acids provided few clues about its function as it did not resemble any other known protein. To make matters more confusing, the normal htt protein was expressed throughout the body and not just the brain (Li *et al.* 1993). Despite this, the htt protein, as we have just seen, has an important distinguishing feature: it contains a repeated sequence of CAGs. And, this sequence was also known to cause the protein to have an elongated stretch of the amino acid **glutamine** within its structure. There is little doubt that the expanded chain of glutamine in the abnormal htt protein is crucial to understanding how it causes neural degeneration in the brain. But the explanation has proved elusive despite intensive research.

Immunohistochemical studies have shown that htt is found in the membrane of synaptic vesicles located in nerve terminals, and is also closely associated with microtubules which are fine tubes involved in intracellular transport that exist in axons and dendrites. This finding indicates that htt is a 'carrier' that is involved in transporting various substances and organelles throughout the cell. Indeed, it is now recognised that one substance that htt helps transport through cells is called **brain-derived neurotrophic factor (BDNF)** – a protein that is essential to the survival of neurons. Curiously, this protein has been shown to be synthesised by neurons in the cerebral cortex and transported to the striatum by their axons. This type of axonal movement, however, is impaired by the abnormal version of htt (Gauthier *et al.* 2004).

In addition, htt has been shown to be a **transcription factor**, that is, it is able to enter the nucleus of the cell, bind to DNA and control the expression of the genes located there. This explains why abnormal fragments of the mutated htt protein are frequently found in the nucleus of those with Huntington's disease. A gene that htt interacts with is the one responsible for producing BDNF. In fact, this transcription process is impaired by the abnormal htt protein, resulting in less production of BDNF (Zuccato *et al.* 2003). But, more importantly, htt has been shown to be involved in the transcription of other genes, including one known as *p53*. This gene encodes for a protein that is known to be important in suppressing cancer, and it must be tightly regulated otherwise **apoptosis** (i.e. self-inflicted programmed cell death) occurs. The abnormal htt protein has been found to increase levels of p53 in transgenic mice that contain the Huntington's gene (Bae *et al.* 2005). Moreover, these researchers have found that increased p53 production causes changes in many other genes, and some of these effects lead to malfunctions in the **mitochondria** – the cell's 'batteries' that make adenosine triphosphate (ATP) which the cell uses as energy. These findings point to the possibility that the overproduction of p53 has an important role in the degeneration of neurons in Huntington's disease.

Because Huntington's disease is caused by a single mutation, it readily lends itself to the development of genetically modified mice in which the gene is either deleted from the genome ('knockout' mice), or altered in some fundamental way ('transgenic' mice). These mouse models are providing many new insights into the pathogenesis of Huntington's disease. For example, one of the most interesting findings to emerge from this work is that knockout mice which lack both copies of the *htt* gene do not complete embryonic development and die within 7–8 days (Duyao *et al.* 1995). Thus, the *htt* gene appears to play a critical role in early foetal development, long before the nervous system is formed. However, knockout mice that are engineered to carry only one deleted *htt* gene survive to adulthood and appear normal. This is a curious finding because Huntington's disease is due to a single gene, and so that gene must be functioning differently from the ones in the knockout mice. This has raised speculation that the mutated gene must be producing a new and toxic effect (sometimes called a **gain of function**) and not a simple loss of effect.

The role of glutamate in Huntington's disease

A neurotransmitter implicated in the pathology of Huntington's disease is **glutamate**, which is an excitatory transmitter that is contained in fibres projecting from the cerebral cortex to the striatum. In the early 1970s, researchers found that glutamate injections into the brain produced a distinctive form of degeneration which led to the destruction of cell bodies and dendrites of the affected neurons, but which spared axons (fibres of passage) and surrounding glial cells (Olney *et al.* 1971). In fact, within 30 minutes of glutamate administration, electron microscopy revealed massive swelling of the cell bodies and dendrites, followed by degeneration of intracellular organelles. More intriguing, however, was the finding that if glutamate (or some of its analogues such as kainic acid) was injected into the striatum, a profile of damage was produced similar to that found in Huntington's disease. For example, it caused a marked degeneration of the GABA spiny neurons and cholinergic interneurons, but left dopaminergic fibres intact (Coyle and Schwartz 1976).

It is believed that glutamate exerts is main neurotoxic effect by overstimulating **N-methyl-D-aspartate (NMDA)** receptors, which leads to an increase of excitatory calcium ions entering the cell. This causes damage to the cell's mitochondria as well as produces a cascade of enzymatic reactions that destroy the neuron. Whatever the precise neurotoxic effect, it has been postulated that the Huntington's gene might also alter the functioning of the glutamate system, perhaps by increasing its release, or enhancing the sensitivity of its receptors. Evidence that the glutamate system is affected in Huntington's disease comes from the finding that NMDA receptors are significantly reduced in the striatum (Young *et al.* 1988). If glutamate does play a role in Huntington's disease, then pharmacological blockade of this neurotransmitter may be useful in preventing or slowing down the progression of the disease. However, so far, results with these type of agents in humans have not been effective, and they are associated with serious side effects including hallucinations (Raymond 2003).

Summary

Alzheimer's disease is one of the most common illnesses of old age, occurring in around 5 per cent of people over 65 years, and 20 per cent of people over 80. Post-mortem examination of the brain typically shows a marked loss of neurons in the cerebral cortex and hippocampus, accompanied by a profusion of **neuritic plaques** (in essence, tiny clumps of extracellular material called **amyloid**) and intracellular **neurofibrillary tangles**. The Alzheimer victim's brain also shows a number of neurochemical changes, including a significant loss of the enzyme **choline acetyltransferase** involved in the synthesis of the neurotransmitter **acetylcholine**. One explanation for the loss of neurons in Alzheimer's disease is that an abnormal and insoluble form of amyloid is deposited in the brain, which causes a chain reaction of events resulting in degeneration. Evidence supporting this theory has come from studies showing that mutations in the gene producing amyloid are known to be responsible for some types of inherited, early onset Alzheimer's disease. Despite this, most cases of Alzheimer's disease are not inherited and have a late onset (i.e. occurring after the age of 65). Although certain alleles of the **ApoE gene** have been shown to predispose people to late onset Alzheimer's disease, lifestyle factors are also believed to play an equally important role. Indeed, one form of protection against Alzheimer's disease may be to build up **cognitive**

reserve, that is, forming new synaptic connections in the brain through increased mental exercise. People with physically active lifestyles may also be better protected against dementia in later life.

Both Parkinson's and Huntington's disease are disorders of the basal ganglia. **Parkinson's disease** is caused by degeneration of a heavily pigmented nucleus in the brainstem called the **substantia nigra,** which provides the **striatum** with dopaminergic fibres. Consequently, there is a marked loss of dopamine in the striatum; but this can be partly restored by the drug L-dopa, which provides a very useful treatment for the illness. In a few rare instances, Parkinson's disease can be inherited from mutations in certain genes on chromosomes 4 and 6, which produce the proteins **alpha-synuclein** and **parkin,** respectively. In most cases, however, Parkinson's disease has no clear genetic basis, which has raised speculation that environmental toxins must play at least some role in its aetiology. One way of understanding how toxins may lead to degeneration of the substantia nigra has come about through examination of the drug MPTP, which produces the **free radical MPP⁺**. This is believed to cause nigral neurodegeneration by damaging tiny structures called mitochondria which provide the cell with its energy. In contrast, **Huntington's disease** is an autosomal dominant genetic disorder – meaning that if a person inherits a copy of the mutant gene they will develop the illness. This illness is associated with marked degeneration of the striatum (not the substantia nigra) and, to a lesser extent, other areas of the brain, including cerebral cortex. The gene responsible for the disease is located on chromosome 4, and the mutation is caused by an increased number of a nucleotide triplets containing the **bases CAG**. In normal subjects this triplet is repeated around 20 times, but in those with Huntington's disease it typically occurs some 50 times. It has also been shown that the higher the number of repeats, the earlier the illness is manifested.

Essay questions

1. In what ways has the abnormal formation and deposition of amyloid been implicated in the pathogenesis of Alzheimer's disease?

    Search terms: Alzheimer's disease. Amyloid cascade theory. Beta-amyloid precursor protein. Amino acids. Enzymes (secretases).

2. How can cognitive reserve be built up? What evidence shows that this can have beneficial effects for maintaining mental functioning later in life?

    Search terms: Cognitive reserve. Notre Dame nuns. Education in the elderly. Physical exercise. Dementia.

3. What theories have attempted to explain the degeneration of the substantia nigra in the brains of people with Parkinson's disease? How best can this illness be treated with drugs?

    Search terms: Parkinson's disease. Substantia nigra. Dopamine. Nigral–striatal pathway. Dopa decarboxylase inhibitors. Deprenyl.

4. Explain how the gene responsible for producing Huntington's disease was discovered, and how it may be responsible for producing degeneration of the brain.

    Search terms: Huntington's disease. Autosomal dominant inheritance. Nancy Wexler. James Gusella. Chromosome 4. Nucleotide repeat. Huntingtin.

Further reading

Dawbarn, D. and Allen, S.J. (eds) (1995) *Neurobiology of Alzheimer's Disease*. Oxford: Bios Scientific Publishers. A very technical account focusing on the molecular causes of Alzheimer's disease.

Ellenberg, J.H., Koller, W.C. and Langston, J.W. (eds) (1995) *Etiology of Parkinson's Disease*. New York: Marcel Dekker. Although a technical account, with chapters written by experts in the field, this book contains a lot of useful information concerning the causes of Parkinson's disease.

Harper, P. (ed.) (1991) *Huntington's Disease*. London: W.B. Saunders. A good book, written for an expert audience, but which students will find is surprisingly readable and informative.

Khachaturian, Z.S. and Radebaugh, T.S. (eds) (1997) *Alzheimer's Disease: Causes, Diagnosis, Treatment and Care*. Boca Raton, Fla.: CRC Press. A book containing 28 chapters which provides a very thorough resource of information for students interested in Alzheimer's disease.

Knight, R.G. (1992) *The Neuropsychology of Degenerative Brain Diseases*. Hillsdale, NJ: Lawrence Erlbaum. This book contains useful information on a number of degenerative diseases, including Alzheimer's, Parkinson's and Huntington's diseases. It is particularly strong on describing the cognitive and psychosocial consequences of these disorders.

Morris, A.D. (1989) *James Parkinson: His Life and his Times*. Berlin: Birkhauser. James Parkinson is a more interesting character than many people realise. This book describes Parkinson's life in the late eighteenth century, and the discovery of the disease that now bears his name.

Rhodes, R. (1998) *Deadly Feasts*. London: Touchstone Books. Although written for a lay audience, this book contains useful information on prions and the work of Stanley Prusiner.

Sacks, O. (1990) *Awakenings*. London: Pan Books. An extraordinary book telling the story of twenty comatose patients who survived the great sleeping sickness epidemic that swept the world in the 1920s, and who were temporarily brought back to life by L-dopa in the 1960s. Later turned into a major film starring Robin Williams.

Snowdon, D. (2001) *Aging with Grace*. London: Fourth Estate. A moving and personal account of David Snowdon's research on ageing in nuns. It provides thought-provoking clues to the lifestyle causes of Alzheimer's disease.

Terry, R.D., Katzman, R. and Bick, K.L. (eds) (1994) *Alzheimer's Disease*. New York: Raven Press. A massive text with large sections on clinical presentation, anatomical changes and biochemical pathology of Alzheimer's disease. For a book of this type, the chapters are surprisingly lucid and well written.

Wexler, A. (1995) *Mapping Fate*. Berkeley: University of California Press. A moving account of one family's fight against Huntington's disease. It also contains useful information on how the gene for Huntington's disease was discovered.

For self test questions, animations, interactive exercises and many more resources to help you consolidate your understanding, and expand your knowledge of the field, please go to the website accompanying this book at **www.pearsoned.co.uk/wickens**

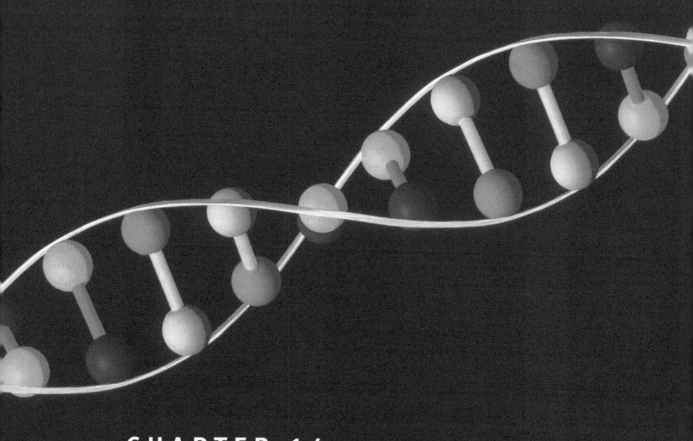

CHAPTER 14

Genes and behaviour

In this chapter

- Charles Darwin and the theory of natural selection
- The laws of genetic inheritance
- The structure and function of deoxyribonucleic acid (DNA)
- How genes produce proteins
- Single-gene disorders
- Methods used to assess the impact of genes on behaviour
- Behavioural genetic approaches to understanding alcoholism
- Recombinant DNA and the use of transgenic animals

INTRODUCTION

It is a remarkable fact that each of us contains about 100 trillion cells (10^{14}) in our body. But, an even more astonishing fact is that each of these cells (with the exception of red blood cells, sperm and ova), contain two complete copies of the genome, which is a set of instructions for constructing a human being. The human genome has evolved over millions of years, and during this time it has developed into a set of 23 paired chromosomes (composed largely of deoxyribose nucleic acid, or DNA) that holds around 25,000 genes.* Each gene, in turn, provides a blueprint for making a complex type of molecule called a protein, which is composed of three-dimensional strings of amino acids. Proteins serve a great variety of specialised roles in biological functioning. Moreover, the human brain contains a large number of different of proteins, and this is shown by the number of genes that it expresses. Indeed, it has been estimated that that the majority of our genes (perhaps as many as two-thirds) are expressed in the brain. Genes provide the structural building blocks by which the components of our bodies are made, and they also act as enzymes that greatly speed up chemical reactions allowing the various parts of the cell to interact and function. The set of genes an organism inherits is sometimes referred to as the **genotype**, and their expression (or behaviour), which is modified by the effects of the environment, is called the **phenotype**. How these factors interact, and the relative importance of each to a huge range of behaviours such as mental illness, intelligence and sexual preference, has provided one of the great research endeavours in the modern history of psychology. But, there is more to genetic research than this. Genes can also 'go wrong', causing illness and degenerative diseases. This is an increasingly important area in biopsychology and one with many potential benefits: not least because the development of new treatments such as gene therapy may one day help relieve the suffering of millions.

Darwin and the theory of evolution

Charles Robert Darwin (1809–1882) was a British naturalist who bought in the era of modern biology with his book *On the Origin of Species by Means of Natural Selection*, first published in 1859. Darwin was just 22 years old when he sailed from England on HMS *Beagle* in 1831. The main mission of the voyage, which lasted five years, was to chart the geological features of the South American coastline – although Darwin's task as ship's naturalist was to study animal life and to collect new specimens of fauna and flora. During the journey, which also visited Tenerife, the Cape Verdi Islands, Brazil and Galapagos Islands, Darwin was fascinated by the great diversity of life he came across, and the way it was perfectly adapted to the environment. For example, on the Galapagos he found fourteen different types of finch which all had similar features, yet each bird had a beak that was uniquely adapted to its own habitat and food source. After completing the voyage, Darwin began reflecting on what he had observed in 1837, and realised that diversity could be explained if animals had all arisen from a common ancestor, but become slightly modified with time so they adapted better to their ecological

*According to the distinguished British geneticist and author Steve Jones, each cell in the body contains about 1.8 m of DNA, and if it could somehow all be joined together, would stretch to the moon and back 8,000 times (Jones 1993).

niche. Later, in 1844, Darwin started formulating the ideas into a scientific theory that would explain all diversity as resulting from the process of evolution.

It has been said that nothing in biology makes sense except in the light of evolution (Dobzhansky 1973), but during the mid-nineteenth century, Darwin's ideas were highly controversial and blasphemous. For example, the book of Genesis in the Bible decrees that every species, including man, had been created by the divine hand of God, and remained unaltered since the time of creation. Darwin knew that his theory would be highly contentious and because of this he spent more than twenty years working on his ideas before daring to publish them. Even then, he was prompted by the work of a young naturalist called Alfred Wallace who was formulating a similar theory. However, the impact of Darwin's work was enormous. Not only did the the *Origin of the Species* prove extremely popular (it sold out immediately and went through five editions in Darwin's lifetime), but it prompted widespread religious, academic and popular debate. By the end of the nineteenth century, the theory of evolution had become accepted by most of the scientific community and general public. In doing so, it had changed man's conception of himself in the world, and provided one of the great unifying theories of biology.

The suggestion that living things change with time, which is the fundamental notion of evolution, did not originate with Darwin, but he was the first to provide a convincing scientific theory to explain how it could occur. The mechanism that Darwin developed to explain evolution was called **natural selection** and it is based on two simple concepts: competition and variation. The first concept, of competition, was derived from Darwin's observation that all living creatures provide more offspring than are needed to replace their parents. This creates a situation where there are too many individuals for the finite amount of resources that exist for them. Yet, Darwin had also observed that animal populations remain relatively stable and do not expand beyond certain limits. Thus, the consequence of increased numbers of offspring and limited resources, Darwin reasoned, must be that all creatures are thrown into competition with each other.

The second aspect of natural selection is that all individuals of a species show great variation in terms of their biological characteristics. For example, humans look similar, but every one of us is different in terms of physique, strength, intelligence, etc. The consequence of this variability is that some individuals will be better suited (or adapted) to their environment than others. In the animal kingdom this is particularly important as the individuals who are best adapted will be the ones more likely to reproduce, thereby passing their characteristics on to their offspring. This became Darwin's principle of selection for which Herbert Spencer coined the phrase the **'survival of the fittest'** (although it would have been more accurate to call it 'reproduction of the fittest'). However, Darwin's most important insight into natural selection was that, over the course of many generations, the selection process would cause changes in the body form to occur. For example, because ancestral giraffes had a liking for feeding in tall trees, natural selection would favour the development of long necks. Following this argument to its logical conclusion, it can be predicted that natural selection will eventually lead to the development of a new species.

Although Darwin described the process of evolution, he did not explain how inheritance worked. Genes had not been discovered in the nineteenth century, and the lack of knowledge concerning the mechanisms of inheritance provided an obstacle to his theory. Ironically, the solution to this problem had been formulated in 1865 by a young Augustine monk living in Bohemia called Gregor Mendel, but the work was ignored until it was rediscovered around 1890. Mendel's work provided the rules of genetic inheritance that Darwin's theory needed to explain how natural selection worked. Darwin died in 1882 and never knew of Mendel's legacy to biology. Nonetheless, Darwin had gained widespread recognition and fame. He was given a state funeral and buried in Westminster Abbey close to John Herschel and Isaac Newton.

The work of Gregor Mendel

The idea that 'transmissible units' provide the means by which inheritance occurs was first formulated in a paper by the Augustine monk Gregor Mendel in 1865, who worked in a monastery in Bruun (now Austria). Prior to this, scientists believed that inheritance was a blending process where 'bloods' of the parents were mixed together in their offspring. But, Mendel showed this theory was wrong in a number of experiments over an eight-year period that used the garden pea plant. His choice of this plant was a fortuitous one. Firstly, not only are pea plants simple to breed (for example, pea plants have both male and female organs, and it is easy to fertilise a female flower with pollen taken from a male), but it is also possible to cross different plants or to self-fertilise the same one. This means that a variety of breeding experiments can be undertaken. Secondly, the traits that Mendel examined, such as the size of the plant (for example, tall versus dwarf); the colour of its seed (yellow versus green); or the seed texture (smooth versus wrinkled) were dichotomous, meaning that plants had either one trait or the other – there was no intermediate outcome. Thus, Mendel avoided many of the complexities associated with animal breeding where inherited characteristics (such as size) are not dichotomous. Most importantly, though, by looking at dichotomous traits it was easy to count the number of times they occurred in the offspring of selectively bred plants. Although the ratios were simple, they enabled Mendel to gain a remarkable insight into genetic inheritance.

In one of his studies, Mendel crossed tall pea plants that were five to six feet in height with dwarfs which were about one foot in height. The results showed that all the offspring (called the **F1** or **first filial generation**) were tall: all the dwarf plants had disappeared from the new generation. However, when Mendel self-fertilised or 'mixed together' the tall F1 plants to produce the F2 generation a different set of results was obtained. Although about three-quarters of the F2 offspring were tall, the rest were dwarf plants. In other words, the factor causing shortness had not been lost in the F1 generation after all – rather it had been suppressed by the dominant taller plants. Mendel obtained similar results with other traits. For example, smooth seeds were dominant over wrinkled; yellow seeds were dominant over green; and red flowers were dominant over white. And, this type of experiment always showed that the F1 generation gave rise to only one type of trait, whereas the F2 generation gave rise to the two traits in the ratio of three to one (Figure 14.1). The consistency of these results implied that some basic law of inheritance was at work.

To explain these findings, it is necessary to accept that each plant contains two 'factors' (which we now call genes) which are responsible for producing the trait in question (for example, tallness). One of these factors is provided by the male, and one by the female. Thus, although each parent carries two 'genes', it transmits only one of these to its offspring. But why should some pea plants be tall and others short? To answer this,

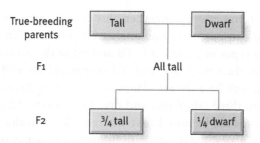

Figure 14.1   The effects of crossing true-breeding pea plants with smooth and wrinkled seeds

Mendel suggested that the factors controlling size in pea plants must come in more than one form. Today, we call genes that produce the same trait, but come in different versions **alleles** (an example of one in humans is the gene that produces eye colour). Thus, Mendel realised that while there was one gene controlling size, this came in different forms which meant that plant size could be either tall or short. But, if this was the case, then why were all pea plants in the F1 generation tall when they contained both alleles? Mendel's explanation was that alleles could also be **dominant** or **recessive**. That is, when the two different alleles came together, the allele for tallness would dominate the dwarf one.

To illustrate these principles, assume that Mendel began his experiments by crossing 'true' or **homozygous** tall plants (containing the genes TT) with homozygous dwarf plants (containing dd genes). When these plants are bred, all plants in the F1 generation are tall because they all contain the **heterozygous** allele combination Td where the T allele is dominant over the d allele. But why does the F2 generation always show a mixture of traits in the ratio of 3:1? To help see what happens refer to Figure 14.2. It can be seen that when the heterozygous F1 hybrids (which contain the allele combination

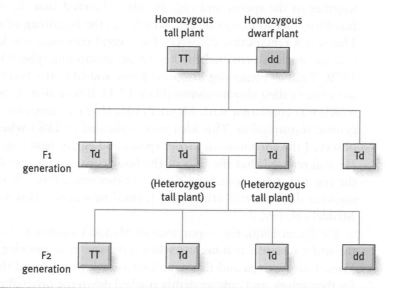

Figure 14.2   The effects of dominant and recessive alleles on the crossing of pea plants

of Td) are crossed together, this creates an assortment of allele combinations. If each plant can pass only one allele to its progeny, and if it is random, then it will produce three types of plants: TT, Td and dd in the proportions 1:2:1. Since T is the dominant allele, then both TT and Td combinations will become tall plants, whereas the dd plant will be a dwarf. Thus, as a result of breeding F1 hybrids, one would expect to obtain three tall plants and one dwarf in the F2 generation.

It should be noted that whereas all the traits examined by Mendel were caused by single genes, the majority of human traits are controlled by a combination of many different genes. Furthermore, not all alleles operate in a dominant or recessive fashion. For example, some alleles are additive, meaning that they each contribute something to the offspring, whereas others have interactive effects with each other (or may even cancel each other out). Nonetheless, Mendel had described in considerable detail the basic laws of inheritance. Despite this, Mendel's work on plant breeding lasted only fifteen years, and it was terminated in 1868 when he was elected as an abbot. After his death in 1868, the new abbot had Mendel's pea garden destroyed, along with his notebooks, papers and scientific records. The only record of the work was Mendel's forgotten paper of 1865.

The chromosomal basis of inheritance

Although Mendel's paper was sent to academic institutions throughout the world, and a copy is even believed to have gone to Darwin, the importance of his findings were not recognised. Despite this, important advances were taking place in the late nineteenth century that were supporting Mendel's conception of genetic inheritance. In 1875, Oskar Hertwig became the first person to observe by microscope the process of fertilisation (in transparent sea urchin eggs), which involved the coming together of the sperm and egg. He also observed that the nuclei of these two cells fused together to make one cell, which was the beginning of cell division and growth. This was a remarkable discovery for several reasons – not least because it indicated that the nucleus provided the key to understanding inheritance. Four years later, in 1879, Walther Flemming discovered tiny rod-like structures within the nucleus that were later called **chromosomes** (Plate 14.1). It was also shown these existed in pairs, which was consistent with Mendel's idea that two separate factors were involved in genetic transmission. This idea was confirmed in 1883 when Edouard van Beneden observed the chromosomes from sperm and egg mingle together during fertilisation. He also realised that the cells of the body contained pairs of chromosomes, whereas the egg and sperm contained single chromosomes. But, when the chromosomes came together during fertilisation, they formed new pairs. This again was consistent with Mendel's theory.

Finally, in 1900, the importance of Mendel's work was brought to the attention of the wider scientific community when three scientists working independently (Hugo de Vries, Carl Correns and Erik von Tschernmak), discovered the basic 3:1 hybrid ratios for themselves, and independently tracked down the original paper. A short while later, in 1903, the American geneticist Walter Sutton proposed that Mendel's factors (or genes) were located on chromosomes, with inheritance being the result of individual

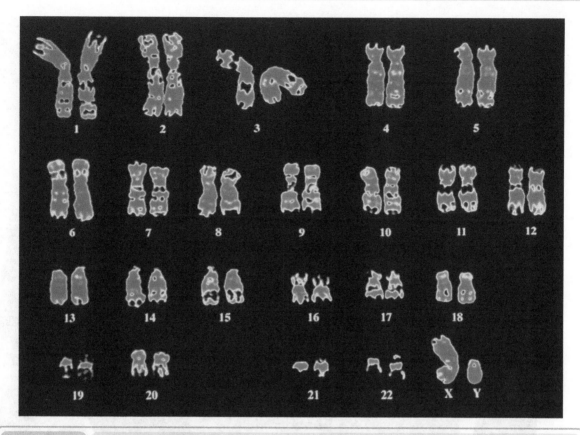

Plate 14.1   The variety of life: the 23 pairs of chromosomes

Source: W. Bodmer and R. McKie (1994) *The Book of Man*, p. 31, Abacus

chromosomes from each parent coming together in the fertilised egg. Thus, the ancient notion that traits were transmitted along 'bloodlines' had been disproved. Instead, traits were transmitted by indivisible genetic particles that maintained their identity while being shuffled into new combinations during fertilisation. The secret of life lay with genes.

Deoxyribonucleic acid (DNA)

What do genes look like? To answer this question we must first examine the structure of chromosomes. As already mentioned, nearly every cell in the body has a set of 46 chromosomes arranged in pairs. These rod-like structures comprise a protein matrix that holds in place an incredibly long and very unique double-stranded chemical called **deoxyribonucleic acid (DNA)**, which is coiled up in a tightly twisted strand. Although DNA was first identified by Miescher in 1869 (he called it nuclein) and suspected it of being involved in inheritance, it was not until 1953, when James Watson and Francis Crick worked out the molecular structure of this molecule, that the secrets of genetic

| Plate 14.2 | James Watson and Francis Crick: discoverers of DNA – probably the most important scientific advance of the twentieth century |

Source: A. Barrington Brown/Science Photo Library

transmission were finally solved (see Plate 14.2). For this discovery, which is one of the greatest scientific achievements of the twentieth century, Watson and Crick (along with Maurice Wilkins) were awarded the Nobel Prize in 1962.

DNA is a large molecule made up of two chains (composed of phosphate and a sugar called deoxyribose) that swivel around each other in the shape of the double helix. Holding the two strands together as they wind around each other are pairs of simple molecules, like rungs of a ladder, known as **bases**. DNA contains four types of base: **adenine**, **guanine**, **cytosine** and **thymine**, which are also referred to as **nucleotides** when they are connected to a sugar and phosphate. Because the four bases are held together with weak bonds, the two strands making up the DNA can easily 'unzip' and separate into two units. Moreover, the bases are selective in their bonding. In fact, adenine bonds only with thymine, and cytosine only with guanine. Thus, when the two strands of DNA unwind,

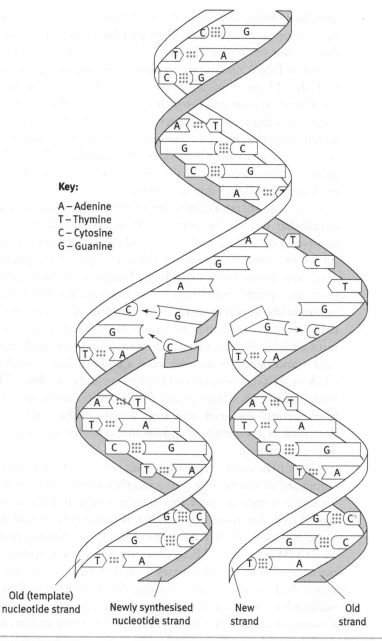

Key:

A – Adenine
T – Thymine
C – Cytosine
G – Guanine

Old (template)
nucleotide strand

Newly synthesised
nucleotide strand

New
strand

Old
strand

Figure 14.3   The DNA molecule

each of the four bases can only act as a 'magnet' for its own complementary base. When the bases attract new partners the result is a new strand that is identical to the old one (Figure 14.3). In other words, DNA has the remarkable property of being able to duplicate itself, which is a vital requirement for creating new cells and ultimately a new organism. In fact, millions of cells in the human body are dividing every second; and every minute many miles of new DNA are being produced (Jones 1993).

But, DNA does much more than simply replicate: it also contains the genes that provide the blueprints by which proteins – chemicals that are essential for creating and maintaining life – are made. Genes are long sequences of bases that lie between the two spiralling chains that form the backbone of DNA. As we have seen, the alphabet is very simple and consists of only four bases (which we can label A, T, G and C). Although the vocabulary is small, there are astronomical numbers of bases on each strand of DNA, making the genetic code very complex. In fact, it has been estimated that the 23 pairs of chromosomes making up the human genome contain over 3,000 million base pairs, which is about 6.5 million base pairs for each chromosome. To put this figure into perspective, the 1969 edition of the *Encyclopaedia Britannica*, which also consists of 23 volumes, contains only 200 million letters. This would be enough letters to fill about three chromosomes. To enable over 3,000 million base pairs to exist, each cell of the body contains about 1.8 m of DNA crammed into a nucleus that is 0.005 mm in diameter.

Genes are therefore stretches of DNA that contain long strings of bases. It is believed that our chromosomes contain around 25,000 genes, with the smallest one consisting of around 500 bases, and the largest containing over 2 million. But, how do we recognise a segment of DNA as a gene? Or, putting this question a different way: how do the bases provide the blueprint for making proteins? The answer is that there are specific combinations of bases in the DNA that provide a code to make **amino acids,** which in turn are the building blocks of proteins. In fact, a protein typically contains thousands of amino acids. Interestingly, while the human body contains around 60,000 different proteins, they are made up of only 20 types of amino acid – and these are derived from a code of just 3 consecutive DNA bases (such as CGA or TGG). These special triplets are called **codons**. There are 64 possible triplets within our DNA which specify the 20 amino acids, with a few codons also providing 'punctuation' for start and stop signals (Table 14.1). Thus, a single gene can be described as a sequence of codons that code for all the amino acids necessary to create a specific protein.

One of the most surprising aspects of our DNA is that less than 5 per cent of it is composed of functioning genes; in other words, most of it appears to be redundant. If we could somehow enter this genetic world and travel along our chromosomes, we would find that most of our DNA is composed of endless repeats of the same 'nonsense' message, often in the form of five or six bases repeated next to each other (such as ACCTGACCTG). These bases may also be interspersed by simpler repeated sequences such as the two bases C and A that can be multiplied many thousands of times. And, at other locations along the chromosome, long and complicated sequences occur whose message, if meaningful, remains unknown. Thus, the terrain of the chromosome that holds the secrets of life is a curious and haphazard world.

What causes individuality?

Why is it that human beings share the same genome of around 25,000 or so genes, yet are individually unique (with the exception of identical twins)? The answer is that we all have different alleles, that is, genes that have evolved into slightly different forms. On average, two people will differ in about one base in every thousand, which means that there are about 3 million differences in the genetic message between any two people. This provides the basis of genetic individuality. Although the genes still provide the same function, their expression or functional role may be modified slightly by the base changes (as in the case of eye colour). The emergence of alleles has come about

Table 14.1	The codons (consecutive triple bases of DNA) by which amino acids are made

Amino Acid[a]	DNA Code
Alanine	CGA, CGG, CGT, CGC
Arginine	GCA, GCG, GCT, GCC, TCT, TCC
Asparagine	TTA, TTG
Aspartic acid	CTA, CTG
Cysteine	ACA, ACG
Glutamic acid	CTT, CTC
Glutamine	GTT, GTC
Glycine	CCA, CCG, CCT, CCC
Histidine	GTA, GTG
Isoleucine	TAA, TAG, TAT
Leucine	AAT, AAC, GAA, GAG, GAT, GAC
Lysine	TTT, TTC
Methionine	TAC
Phenylalanine	AAA, AAG
Proline	GGA, GGG, GGT, GGC
Serine	AGA, AGG, AGT, AGC, TCA, TCG
Threonine	TGA, TGG, TGT, TGC
Tryptophan	ACC
Tyrosine	ATA, ATG
Valine	CAA, CAG, CAT, CAC
(Stop signals)	ATT, ATC, ACT

[a]The twenty amino acids are organic molecules that are linked together by peptide bonds to form polypeptides, which are the building blocks of enzymes and other proteins. The particular combination of amino acids determines the shape and function of the polypeptide.

Source: R. Plomin *et al.*, (1997) *Behavioral Genetics*, 3rd edition

through chance alterations taking place in the structure of bases throughout evolution, and the consequences will depend on where the changes occur in the DNA. If changes occur in the non-functional part of the gene, there will be no effect on the individual. But, if a base change takes place in an important codon that encodes for an amino acid, the outcome may be significant, resulting in abnormal development or a genetic disease. In other instances, the structure of the gene may be modified slightly without adverse effects. Multiple alleles have been found for about half of all human genes. Remarkably, it has been estimated that the number of potential allele combinations is so vast that everyone alive today, with the exception of identical twins, is genetically different from everyone else, and from every person that has ever lived.

Protein synthesis

The coded instructions in the genes for making proteins are locked away in the cell's nucleus. However, protein manufacture does not take place in the nucleus, but in the cytoplasm of the cell. Thus, genetic information has to pass out of the nucleus into the cytoplasm. How does this occur? The answer lies with another type of nucleic acid called **ribonucleic acid (RNA)**. This chemical is similar to DNA except the sugars in RNA are ribose (instead of deoxyribose) and the base uracil replaces thymine. RNA chains are also shorter than DNA chains and range from less than a hundred, to tens of thousands of nucleotides. There are several types of RNA, but the one that transports the DNA's instructions into the cytoplasm of the cell is called **messenger RNA (mRNA)**. This molecule provides a copy of the gene to begin the assembly of amino acids into proteins.

Although RNA is similar to DNA in terms of its chemistry, RNA exists as a single strand. This enables mRNA to move freely into and out of the nucleus, as well as to provide a template by which transcripts of the larger DNA molecule can be copied. The synthesis of a RNA molecule, using DNA as its template, is known as **transcription** and involves an enzyme called **RNA polymerase** which 'unzips' the DNA over short distances, allowing a complementary chain of RNA to be formed. Once a section of the DNA has been transcribed into mRNA, it enters the cytoplasm where it seeks out a structure called a **ribosome**. This is the site where the assembly of the protein will take place.

Ribosomes are composed of protein and another type of RNA called **ribosomal RNA (rRNA)**. It is at this site that genetic information provided by mRNA undergoes **translation** into the chain of amino acids. This works in the following way. The rRNA acts to position the mRNA on the ribosome, and, once fastened, it exposes the mRNA's codons (three base sequences) one at a time. As this happens, the exposed bases are hooked up with new bases that are brought to the ribosome by a type of RNA called **transfer RNA (tRNA)**. The tRNA molecule has two structural components: (1) a three-base sequence that allows it to zip onto the mRNA at the ribosome, and (2) a carrier that picks up specific amino acids which it finds in the cytoplasm. Thus, tRNA provides the mechanism by which amino acids are transported to the ribosome and fixed onto the mRNA.

Once a codon has been filled up, thus adding an amino acid to the growing protein chain, a peptide bond is created that links the newly formed amino acid with the next one in the chain. After this, the next codon is exposed and the process is repeated until all the bases in the mRNA transcript become filled. When all the transcripts of the mRNA have been completed and joined together, a protein is made (Figure 14.4). The construction of a protein is a very efficient process, with amino acids being incorporated into polypeptide chains at a rate of about 100 per second. In fact, it takes less than a minute to make an average protein. Our bodies are continually having to manufacture proteins and it has been estimated that more than 1 million peptide bonds are made *every second* in most cells. This high rate of synthesis is required because the human body contains tens of thousands of different proteins that are continually being broken down and replaced every day.

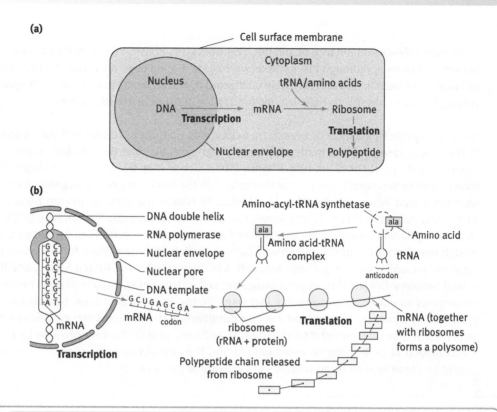

Figure 14.4   The stages of protein synthesis: (a) simplified account; (b) more complex account

Source: D.J. Taylor *et al.* (1997) *Biological Science 2*, p. 805, Fig. 23.32

Sir Francis Galton: the legacy of his ideas

Francis Galton (1822–1911) was a half-cousin to Charles Darwin and born into a wealthy family. Recognised as a child prodigy, he could read at the age of 2, and was studying Greek and Latin by 5. As a young man, Galton studied medicine, before deciding to pursue mathematics at Cambridge. In 1841, he was awarded a third class degree, but two years later suffered a nervous breakdown which forced him to give up further university study. The death of his father in 1844 left him financially independent and Galton travelled the world for several years. During this time he undertook cartographic surveys of South Africa, and wrote the best-selling *The Art of Travel*, which still appears in print today. On his return to England in 1850 he produced the first accurate weather charts and coined the term 'anticyclone'. Later, Galton was to pioneer research into twins, found the science of psychometrics, invent a number of statistical tests, including correlation, and devise a means of classifying fingerprints that has proved useful in forensic science. He also coined the phrase 'nature versus nurture'.

The publication of Charles Darwin's book *The Origin of Species* in 1859 was to be the biggest spur on Galton's research interests. Inspired by the ideas of evolutionary theory, Galton spent the rest of his academic life exploring its human, social and mathematical implications. In particular, he became interested in the heritability of human traits. By analysing the obituaries of the *Times* newspaper, Galton traced the lineage of eminent men in Europe to see if they had relatives with special talents. Galton found that eminent men were more likely to have a famous son or brother than a famous cousin – a finding that he believed showed the inheritance of abilities. This work was published in *Hereditary Genius* (1869), which became widely read. Although his methods were crude, Galton used his results to argue that traits such as intelligence were innate and relatively unaffected by the advantages of wealth and opportunity. Conversely, the lower classes, he believed, remained poor because of genetic 'inferiority'.

The most far-reaching aspect of *Hereditary Genius* was Galton's assertion that the biological make-up of the human race could be made stronger through selective breeding. In fact, Galton wrote that 'it would be quite practical to produce a highly-gifted race of men by judicious marriages during several consecutive generations'. This is now recognised as the beginning of the **eugenics** movement, which later developed into a social and political effort to control the traits of human populations. Galton wrote more about the necessity for eugenics in his book *Enquiries into Human Faculty* (1883) where he stated: 'its principles ought to become one of the most dominant motives in a civilised civilisation'. Although one cannot doubt the sincerity of Galton's beliefs, his ideas were to soon have darker repercussions, including the compulsory sterilisation of 'imbeciles' in the United States, and the holocaust of Nazi Germany. Despite this, eugenic issues are still with us today, and are likely to become even more contentious as our genetic knowledge increases. Today, in some countries, parents are choosing the gender of their unborn children, and it is now possible to determine whether embryos contain mutated genes which may cause unwanted diseases. In addition, genetic markers can also be used to predict the likelihood of contracting illnesses later in life. The ethical implications of this type of knowledge should be borne in mind by all students of behavioural genetics.

The importance of proteins

If we are to understand why genes are so important, we have to appreciate the nature of the molecules they make – proteins. These molecules are vital constituents of all living things, from bacteria to man. Indeed, without them, life could not exist. As we have seen, proteins are large molecules that consist of amino acid chains. But, proteins are more than this. After the protein has left the ribosome, it folds into a shape determined by its amino acids. Part of a chain may coil into a helix, other segments lock into rigid rods, and other parts may form clefts or flexible swivels. Thus, proteins become twisted and folded to form a great variety of highly complex three-dimensional shapes – which allows them to undertake a wide range of functions. An individual cell may have as many 10,000 different proteins each with its own unique role. Some proteins are used to make receptors, ion channels or uptake pumps in the neural membrane, whereas others form internal structures within the cell. In the body, proteins provide connective tissue and muscle, while others (for example, red blood cells) act as carriers that transport chemical substances around the body. Yet, others form neurotransmitters, hormones and antibodies.

The most important function of proteins, however, is their role as enzymes that act as catalysts for the chemical reactions inside cells. Most enzymes are folded in such a way as to form a cleft that is exactly the right shape to bind a small molecule such as sugar. When this chemical binds to the enzyme, it causes a structural modification that enables a chemical reaction to be speeded up. In fact, there is hardly a chemical reaction inside a cell that does not require an enzyme. One example (see Chapter 1) is the enzyme **adenylate cyclase**, which converts ATP into the second messenger cAMP. Another important chemical reaction is **phosphorylation**, which involves the addition or removal of phosphate from the protein. This simple chemical modification alters the shape and function of the protein, and is important in a variety of neurochemical processes. For example, protein phosphorylation may inactivate a neurotransmitter, cause an ion channel to open, or produce activational changes in a receptor.

It can be difficult for a student to scale down to the molecular level to understand the size of proteins. To give some idea of the scale we are talking about: one of the smallest objects to the naked eye is a grain of salt, which is about half a millimetre, or 500 microns (500 millionths of a metre) in size. The body of an average animal cell is much smaller (between 30 and 100 microns in diameter). But, this is massive compared to a protein, which may be no more than a few nanometres in length or a thousand times smaller (a nanometre is one thousand-millionth of a metre). Yet, in terms of the molecular world, proteins are large structures and for this reason they are sometimes called **macromolecules**.

Single genes and behaviour

There are over 4,000 inherited human conditions which are caused by single 'faulty' or mutated genes, and about 10 per cent of these produce mental retardation. Single-gene disorders tend to be inherited in the manner predicted by Mendel, and because of this are referred to as **Mendelian diseases**. Although most single-gene disorders are rare, some can be relatively common. One example is **cystic fibrosis** where the individual produces a very thick mucus, along with other body secretions, which makes them prone to lung infections, resulting in a reduced life expectancy of around 20–30 years. Although cystic fibrosis affects over 8,000 people in the UK, over 2 million people carry the faulty gene (located on chromosome 7), which works out at around 1 in 25 of the population. However, because it is a recessive condition, an infant has to inherit a faulty gene from both parents before developing the disease.

Huntington's disease

One single-gene disorder already mentioned in the book (Chapter 13) is **Huntington's disease,** which causes degeneration of the brain, particularly the striatum, leading to deterioration of movement, temperament and cognition. Huntington's disease is an example of autosomal dominant inheritance, which means if a person inherits one copy of the mutated gene, from either parent, it will act as the **dominant** gene and produce the faulty protein that causes the disease. The chances of inheriting Huntington's disease if one parent carries the mutated gene is 50 per cent, and this can be explained by using Mendel's laws (see Figure 14.2). For example, if we assume that the carrier parent has a mutated allele along with a normal one (Hh), and the other parent has two normal alleles (hh), then the offspring will inherit one of four possible combinations of paired alleles. In effect, the offspring will inherit a normal h allele from the un-affected parent, but have a 50 per cent chance of inheriting the H allele from the carrier parent. In other words, 50 per cent of the possible gene combinations in the offspring will carry the dominant (mutated) gene (Figure 14.5).

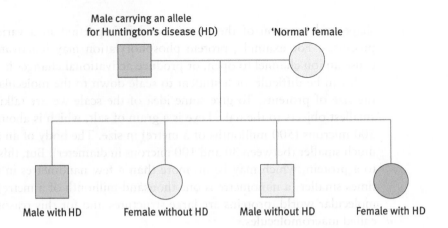

If one parent is a carrier of Huntington's disease then approximately
50 per cent of the offspring will inherit the disease

Figure 14.5	The inheritance of Huntington's disease

Phenylketonuria

Another single-gene defect is **phenylketonuria**, which affects about 1 person in 10,000. Individuals with this condition do not produce a liver enzyme called phenylalanine hydroxylase, which is responsible for turning the amino acid phenylalanine into tyrosine. The result is that phenylalanine builds up in the liver and passes into the bloodstream where it enters the developing brain to cause considerable damage. Excess phenylalanine, or rather its toxic by-products, reduces brain weight, produces a deficiency of myelin and causes fewer dendrites to be formed. The consequence is a severe mental retardation, with victims generally not learning to speak and who normally exhibit an IQ of less than 20 (Hay 1985).

Unlike Huntington's disease, phenylketonuria is due to an allele that is **recessive**. This means that, for an offspring to be affected, they must inherit two copies of the allele. In fact, individuals who inherit one copy of the allele are unaffected by the disorder, although they remain carriers and can pass it on to their offspring. About 1 person in 50 carries the faulty gene, which means that 1 in 2,500 couples (50×50) have the potential to produce a child with phenylketonuria. However, assuming that both parents are carriers, they still have only a 25 per cent chance of producing a child with the disorder. To understand why, we can refer to Mendelian laws of inheritance (see Figure 14.6). For example, if each parent carries one mutant allele (P) and one normal allele (p), it can be seen that the only combination that produces phenylketonuria (PP) will occur with a 1 in 4 probability.

Fortunately, phenylketonuria can be detected soon after birth by a simple blood test which has become standard practice in hospitals. Once detected, interventions can be undertaken to lessen the disorder. Phenylalanine is one of the ten essential amino acids that the body cannot manufacture by itself, and consequently the supply of this substance must come from the diet. Thus, by restricting its dietary intake, the build-up of phenylalanine and its metabolic products can be prevented. Indeed, provided the diet is initiated early

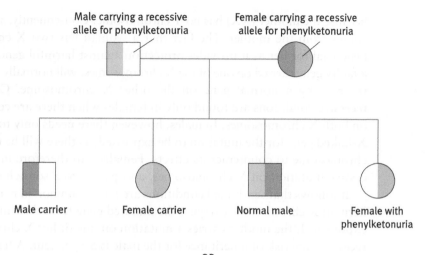

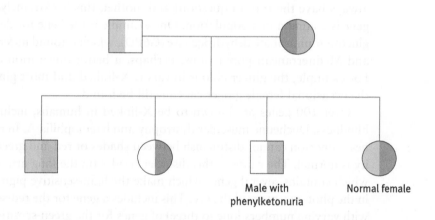

If both parents carry the recessive allele for phenylketonuria then approximately
25 per cent of the offspring will inherit the disease

| Figure 14.6 | The inheritance of phenylketonuria |

enough in life, many individuals develop normally and show IQs of over 100. This example also shows that genetic predisposition (i.e. genotype) can be strongly modified by the effects of the environment (i.e. phenotype). Indeed, one should never forget that there are often complex and subtle interactions between genes and environmental factors.

X-linked inheritance

The third type of Mendelian inheritance occurs when a mutated gene is carried on the X chromosome. Males and females differ in only one chromosome: males having a pair of XY sex chromosomes, and females XX (see Chapter 8). Bearing this in mind, it follows that males must always inherit their Y chromosome from the father (XY) because the mother (XX) has no Y chromosome. Consequently, a male's X chromosome comes from the mother. The fact that a woman has two X chromosomes is usually beneficial for her as it provides protection against harmful genes. This occurs because a faulty gene carried on one of the X chromosomes, will normally have its harmful effects reversed by a normal gene on the other X chromosome. Consequently, X-linked recessive conditions are found only in females when there are copies of the faulty gene on both X chromosomes. In males, however, there needs only to be a single copy of an X-linked gene for the mutation to be expressed, as there will be no allele on the Y male chromosome to counteract its effects. Females can therefore unknowingly carry a recessive mutation on X chromosomes, and pass it to a son who will express the trait.

It follows that sex-linked conditions are more common in males because if males inherit an X chromosome carrying the mutated gene from their mother, they will always express it. If the mother carries a mutation on one of her X chromosomes, even if it is recessive, the risk of inheritance for the male is 50 per cent. A female carrying the same recessive gene on one of her own X chromosomes will be unaffected. Although it is possible for a female to inherit an X-linked mutated gene from both the father (he will always have the trait in question) and mother, this is extremely rare unless the faulty gene is common in a population. One example is the gene for deficiency of the enzyme glucose-6-phosphate dehydrogenase (G6PD), which is found in certain African-American and Mediterranean populations. Perhaps, a better illustration can be seen with cats. For example, the ginger colour in cats is X-linked and most ginger cats are male, but the occasional female ginger cat can still be found.

Over 100 genes are known to be X-linked in humans, including red–green colour blindness, Duchenne muscular dystrophy and haemophilia A. In red–green colour blindness, a person cannot distinguish between shades of red and green, although visual acuity is normal. The cause of this disorder resides on the long arm of the X chromosome, which contains several genes which make the light-sensitive pigment (rhodopsin) found in the photoreceptors of the eye. This includes a gene for the red-sensitive pigment, along with varying numbers (one to three) of genes for the green-sensitive pigment. The analysis of DNA from males with this type of colour blindness shows that the condition is often associated with an altered number and arrangement of the genes encoding these colour-sensitive pigments. While there are no life-threatening complications, affected individuals may be unable to hold certain jobs where colour recognition is required.

Duchenne muscular dystrophy is a disease which causes progressive weakening of the muscles, often appearing before the age of 6 years, and causing death in early adulthood. It occurs at a rate of 1 per 3,500 male births, and 1 in 50,000,000 female births. In two-thirds of males, the disease is inherited from the mother, although it can also arise as a new mutation in embryonic development. Young men with Duchenne muscular dystrophy generally do not produce offspring, so the gene typically dies out in the male line, although it continues to travel through generations of females. The gene is large and consists of around 2 million base pairs, which accounts for over 1 per cent of the X chromosome. The protein encoded by the gene is called dystrophin and is believed to be involved in muscle contraction. Boys with the mutant gene lack this protein.

X-linked dominant transmission can also occur although this type of mutation is very rare. One condition is hypophosphatemic (or vitamin-D-resistant) rickets, characterised by low blood and high urinary phosphate, short stature and body deformities. Unlike the pattern seen with the X-linked recessive inheritance, both boys and girls have a 50 per cent chance of being affected by an X-linked dominant illness from one of their parents. These conditions are more common in females by a ratio of 2 to 1 because females have an extra X chromosome to carry the faulty gene.

Queen Victoria, haemophilia, Rasputin, and the fall of the Russian royal family

Haemophilia is caused by a faulty gene located on the X chromosome which results in a clotting factor of the blood to be either partly or completely missing. Consequently a haemophiliac will bleed far longer than is normal after a cut or injury. The earliest descriptions of this disorder are found in Jewish texts from the second century AD that exempted boys from circumcision if two previous brothers had died from bleeding after the operation. After this, haemophilia appears to have been largely forgotten until 1803, when a physician from Philadelphia called Dr John Conrad Otto described a familial bleeding disease that was inherited through the female line, but which affected only males. There are now known to be several types of haemophilia, with haemophilia A making up about 80 per cent of all cases. It has an incidence of about 1 in 10,000 in the general population – meaning that haemophilia occurs in about 1 in 5,000 males. Female haemophilia can exist but is extremely rare.

Plate 14.3	Tsar Nicholas II, the Tsarina Alexandra, their four daughters, and their son Alexis who suffered from haemophilia

Source: © Bettmann/Corbis

Haemophilia is sometimes known as 'the royal disease' because of its prevalence among the royal families of Europe. It appears to have begun with a fresh mutation within Queen Victoria – an event that was to dramatically alter the course of Russian and world history. In 1853, Queen Victoria gave birth to her youngest son Leopold. The birth made medical history because Victoria received chloroform, the anaesthetic introduced by James Young Simpson only six years earlier. But, it soon became apparent that Leopold was suffering from haemophilia as he bled profusely even after small cuts and grazes. Leopold was to die at the age of 30 when he fell and suffered a brain haemorrhage. Unfortunately, two of Queen Victoria's daughters, Princesses Alice and Beatrice, were also carriers of haemophilia, and they passed it into several European royal families, including those of Spain and Russia. The most famous affected individual was Tsarevich Alexis born in 1904 (Plate 14.3), who was the son of Tsar Nicholas II of Russia (who had married Alexandra, daughter of Alice). In their desperation to treat their son, the Tsar and Empress turned to the Siberian monk Rasputin who had arrived in St Petersburg in 1903 claiming to have spiritual healing powers. Indeed, Rasputin appeared to have some mysterious ability to heal Alexis, which many believe was due to hypnosis. Whatever his form of treatment, Rasputin gained considerable influence at the Russian court despite tales of sexual profligacy and debauchery. His power increased so much that, by 1915, he was taking a role in the selection of cabinet ministers and military decisions – an involvement that was to greatly discredit the Russian monarchy. Eventually a group of nobles assassinated Rasputin in 1916, although it was too late to save the Tsar and his family from the communist revolution that was to destroy their lives a few months later.

Today, many people with haemophilia lead relatively normal lives. In most cases, haemophilia is managed by transfusions of fresh plasma or injections of the appropriate clotting factor. Both therapies provide relief for several days although they are relatively expensive. However, in 1984, the structure of the gene producing haemophilia A was characterised and cloned, and this has led to the availability of recombinant (genetically engineered) clotting factors which are safer and cheaper. But, the great hope lies with gene therapy: that one day it will be possible to inject new genetic material into the person, which will correct the faulty gene and lead to proper production of the blood-clotting factors. Animal studies are currently under way to explore this possibility.

Multiple genes and behaviour

The relationship between genes and behaviour is much more complicated than the one between genes and disease. One reason for this is that many diseases arise from a single genetic defect. As Mendel showed, a feature of single-gene inheritance is that the traits they produce are normally **dichotomous**, that is, one either inherits the gene and exhibits the trait or does not. However, behavioural traits in humans do not follow such simple patterns of inheritance. Take, for example, the inheritance of schizophrenia. If one identical twin has the illness, there is a 40–60 per cent chance of the other twin developing schizophrenia. This figure drops to about 20 per cent for fraternal twins, to 10 per cent for first-degree relatives, and 4 per cent for second-degree relatives. All these figures are higher than found in the general population, which supports the idea of a genetic influence at work. But, it is also clear that schizophrenia follows no simple Mendelian pattern of inheritance.

One of the first researchers to investigate the complexities of human inheritance was Charles Darwin's cousin, Francis Galton (see box on page 531) who developed specialised statistical techniques to examine this subject. In 1875, Galton used correlation to study the inheritance of height in 928 people, and found a relationship between the heights of parents and their offspring, namely that as the size of the parent increases so does that of the child. However, the relationship was less than perfect, with taller parents tending to have smaller children, and smaller parents tending to have taller offspring. From this work, Galton came to the conclusion that traits such as height (he also applied the same concepts to intelligence) were not inherited in a dichotomous way, but exhibited **continuous variation**. Indeed, if our height were due to a single dominant gene, as occurred with Mendel's tall and dwarf pea plants, only two heights would be possible. The fact that there is a great variation in human height, which may vary from under 60 cm to over 200 cm, shows that its genetic basis is much more complex.

After the rediscovery of Mendel's work in 1900 a heated scientific conflict arose between researchers who defended Mendelian inheritance advocating dichotomous variation, and those who followed in the tradition of Galton who believed that genes produced traits with continuous variation. This debate was resolved in 1918 by R.A. Fisher, who showed that both the biometrical and Mendelian positions could be correct. Fisher demonstrated that a continuous trait such as height could be explained if a large number of Mendelian factors (i.e. genes) each made a small contribution to tallness. Indeed, researchers now recognise that height is determined by many different genes (such as those that code for growth hormone, or control the rate of calcium deposition in the bones) along with environmental factors such as nutrition and exercise. Fisher also showed that two or more genes working this way produced a trait that followed a **normal distribution** (i.e. a bell-shaped curve) in a population. In essence, Fisher's theory shows that complex traits are influenced by many genes, but that each gene in still inherited according to Mendel's laws.

Human behaviour is a much more complex phenotype than height, as shown by the endless number of ways we behave. Indeed, most researchers interested in linking genes with behaviour now believe that most human traits, whether that trait be a predisposition to obesity or homosexuality, or the inheritance of personality traits such as aggressiveness or intelligence, are likely to be influenced by many genes located over several chromosomes. Moreover, few would deny the importance of environmental factors, including prenatal influences, brain development and psychosocial forces, in their expression. In other words, most accept a **multifactorial** model of inheritance, with the assumption that no single-gene is responsible for the behaviour in question. Owing to the complex genetic nature of human behaviour, and its interaction with environmental factors, many geneticists regard genes as providing a certain probability that a behaviour or trait will occur. Or, put another way, there is a 'probabilistic bias' towards a condition appearing as a result of genetic and environmental interaction (Toates 2007).

How can we tease out the interaction of genetic and environmental influences in our behaviour? Mendel was fortunate in choosing pea plants that had simple dichotomous traits. However, as Galton showed, this approach will not work for human behaviour, which is far too complex for this type of analysis. Fortunately, there are a number of methods that can be used, including twin and adoption studies in humans, and selective breeding and transgenic manipulation in animals. It is to these methods we now turn.

Twin and adoption studies

Comparing the characteristics of monozygotic (MZ) and dizygotic (DZ) twins provides the psychologist with an important means of assessing the relative impact of genetic (**nature**) and environmental (**nurture**) influences on behaviour. For example, behavioural differences that develop between identical twins must be the result of environmental effects since the twins share the same set of genes. In contrast, the differences arising between non-identical twins has to derive from both genetic and environmental factors. One measure used by psychologists to express the relative influence of nature and nurture on behaviour is **concordance**. In short, twins are said to be concordant for a given trait if both express it, and discordant if only one twin shows it. Thus, if concordance rates, which are expressed as percentages ranging from 0 to 100 per cent, are significantly higher in a group of identical twins compared with non-identical ones, this shows that genetic influences play the more important role in the expression of that trait. For example, as Huntington's disease is due to a single dominant gene, the concordance rate for MZ twins is 100 per cent (1.0), whereas the figure for DZ twins is 50 per cent (0.5). For phenylketonuria, the respective figures are 100 per cent (1.0) and 25 per cent (0.25) (see Table 14.2).

The same principle can be applied to other disorders and human traits. For example, as we have seen above, the concordance rate for schizophrenia is around 50 per cent for MZ twins, and 20 per cent for DZ. Both figures are significantly higher that that found in two unrelated people (1 per cent). These results appear to show that genetic inheritance has an important influence on the development of schizophrenia – a view that is further supported by the fact that the child of a schizophrenic parent is about ten times more likely to become psychotic than is a normal member of the general population.

Despite this, there are problems with twin studies. For example, identical twins tend to share the same type of upbringing, and this might explain their similar patterns of behaviour. Indeed, we all function within the context of an ecological environment in which we must eat, stay warm and find food, as well as a cultural environment that includes social customs, rituals and a variety of institutions. On top of this, identical twins are more likely to spend time together, and be treated as a 'pair' by family and friends. All of these factors will be likely to inflate the estimates of genetic influence.

Table 14.2	Twin concordance rates for disorders of the central nervous system	
Disorder	**Identical Twins %**	**Fraternal Twins %**
Huntington's disease	100	50
Phenylketonuria	100	25
Epilepsy	60	10
Multiple sclerosis	30	5
Autism	60	0
Cerebral palsy	40	0
Parkinson's disease	0 (or very low)	0 (or very low)
Alzheimer's disease	70	30
Depression	40	15
Bipolar disorder	70	15
Schizophrenia	50	20

A way around this problem is to study twins who were separated early in life and then reared apart in different types of environment. But, this is a very rare event. In fact, there have been no large-scale studies of reared-apart identical twins concordant for schizophrenia – although there has been individual case studies reported in the psychological literature. In a review of nine cases where this situation has occurred, Farber (1981) found concordance for schizophrenia for six twin pairs using somewhat lenient criteria. However, in all cases the twins were aware of each other's existence and had periodic contact.

Because of this problem, researchers are forced to examine individuals who are born to schizophrenic parents but adopted at an early age. Thus, if schizophrenia has a genetic basis, we would expect adoptees of psychotic parents to have a higher incidence of the illness despite being brought up in a different family environment. The first study to examine this issue was undertaken in 1966 by Leonard Heston, who interviewed 47 adult adopted offspring of hospitalised schizophrenic women. The results showed that five of the offspring had also been hospitalised for schizophrenia (roughly 10 per cent of the sample) whereas none of the adoptees in the control group had developed the illness. This type of finding has been confirmed and extended in other adoption studies. For example, a Danish study began in the 1960s with 5,500 children adopted between 1924 and 1947 managed to find 44 parents (32 mothers and 12 fathers) who were schizophrenic. It was found that three (7 per cent) of the adopted offspring had also become schizophrenic. In contrast, none of the control group, who had been chosen from parents without psychiatric problems, showed the illness (Rosenthal 1971).

The Minnesota study of twins reared apart

Despite the difficulties of finding identical twins reared apart, such individuals do exist, and they provide the psychologist with fascinating insights into the genetic contribution to behaviour. In some cases the findings can be truly remarkable. For example, in 1979, Thomas Bouchard, working at the University of Minnesota, came across an account in his local newspaper of a pair of identical twins (Jim Springer and Jim Lewis) who had been separated from birth and reunited at the age of 39 years. In terms of physical appearance the two men looked different, with distinct hairstyles and clothes, but in terms of lifestyle and previous history they showed many similarities. For example, both drove Chevrolets and enjoyed stock car racing. Both had a background in police work and had been employed as part-time deputy sheriffs. Both chain smoked and enjoyed taking holidays in Florida. Each had built a workshop in the basement of their houses in which one of the twins built miniature picnic tables and the other made rocking chairs. The coincidences extended to their wives, children and choice of pet. For example, each had been married twice, with both of their first wives being called Linda, and their second wives called Betty. The twins also gave identical names to their sons and both had named their dogs Toy. Both had similar medical histories with identical pulse and blood pressure, as well as haemorrhoids!

The discovery of the 'Jim twins' led Bouchard to set up the **Minnesota Study of Identical Twins Reared Apart (MISTRA)**. This aim of this programme, which also studies identical twins reared together, as well as dizygotic twins reared together or apart, attempts to assess the relative contributions of genetic and environmental factors on the physical, mental and personality traits that creates human individuality.

Although there are similar programmes elsewhere in the world, the MISTRA programme is the most comprehensive. In addition to having a registry of over 8,000 MZ and DZ twins, it has a database containing information on over 120 pairs of MZ twins reared apart. Each of these pairs has participated in a large number of personality and cognitive tests which take approximately 50 hours to complete over a period 6 days. In the process, each subject answers around 15,000 questions and provides a full medical history.

One of the behavioural traits that the MISTRA programme examines is personality by testing subjects on the Minnesota Multiphasic Personality Inventory. This test, which has 567 items and usually takes between 1 and 2 hours to complete, measures personality on five main scales. The results of these studies (see, for example, T.J. Bouchard *et al.* 1990) show that MZ twins reared together have scores that are very similar to MZ reared apart (correlations of about 0.45). These findings indicate that MZ twins have the same types of personality whether they are reared in similar or different environments. DZ twins reared apart or together, however, showed an average correlation of 0.26, which suggests that they are about half alike genetically as identical twins. Randomly selected individuals show no statistically reliable correlation on these tests. From such data, Bouchard has estimated the heritability of personality to be about 40 per cent (T.J. Bouchard 1994).

Another behavioural trait examined by Boucher and his colleagues is intelligence. This has been a favourite (and controversial) subject for behavioural geneticists since the time of Galton. Boucher tested intelligence by using the Weschler Adult Intelligent Scale, and found that the average correlation for twins reared apart was 0.70, and 0.85 if reared together. This is a high correlation and appears to show that genetic factors are the biggest influence in determining intelligence. From these findings, Bouchard estimated the heritability of intelligence to be around 70 per cent. However, one should be cautious about accepting this claim, especially as genetic and environmental factors can interact in many subtle ways. For example, there is evidence to show that people with similar genetic endowments seek out similar environments and experiences. Thus, these individuals may be more likley to seek out intelligent friends, or to become involved in learning activities, which contributes to the development of superior mental abilities. Because individuals are likely to seek outlets for their innate tendencies regardless of what environment they are reared in, one will never be able to provide a definite or undisputed estimate of heritability for any given trait.

Selective breeding for behaviour

In animal studies, alternative techniques are used to assess the heritability of behavioural traits. Traditionally, one of the most common methods to produce different genetic strains of animals has been through **selective breeding**. Farmers have known for thousands of years that if a trait is heritable then it can be selectively bred into a group of animals. For example, wild cattle and sheep have long legs for speed and large horns for defence, yet the domestic versions of these animals look very different, with short legs, small or non-existent horns, and large bodies. Similarly, dogs have been bred for a number of behavioural characteristics. Some dogs, such as pit bull terriers, have been bred for their aggressive traits, whereas others, such as collies, have been bred for their affectionate nature. Others have been selectively bred to perform certain tasks

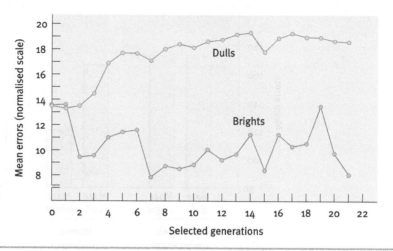

Mean errors (normalised scale)

Selected generations

Figure 14.7   Graph showing the results of Tryon's selective breeding for maze-bright and maze-dull rats

such as hunting (terriers) or controlling flocks of animals (sheep dogs). The same technique can also be used experimentally in the laboratory situation. The rationale is simple: if a behaviour is influenced by genetic factors then it should be possible to produce it through selective breeding of individuals that show that particular trait.

A classic example of this approach was undertaken by Robert Tryon (1940) who selected rats for their maze-learning ability. Tryon began his study by examining the performance of a large number of rats on a complex seventeen-choice maze task. Following training, Tryon bred the males and females that had shown the best maze scores to create a group of maze-bright rats. He also bred the animals that had made most errors to produce a group of maze-dull animals. Tryon carried on this selection procedure for twenty-one generations, and descendants of his animals are still available today for researchers interested in maze learning. The results of Tryon's work produced two strains of rats that differed significantly in their ability to learn the maze (see Figure 14.7). In fact, after seven generations, the distribution of the error scores no longer overlapped between the two groups. The groups have also continued to maintain these behavioural differences over subsequent generations.

These selectively bred animals have been used in a number of ways. For example, some investigators examined the brain's biochemistry in the maze-bright rats to determine if there was a biological factor that could explain the difference in learning performance. Indeed, it was shown that maze-bright rats had a higher level of acetylcholinesterase (AChE) in their cerebral cortex. This is an enzyme that breaks down acetylcholine and was consistent with the idea that brains of the bright rats were producing more of this neurotransmitter. However, the importance of acetylcholine for maze learning was questioned when researchers selectively bred rats for AChE activity without regard to any behavioural characteristics. In fact, the animals bred for high AChE activity performed more poorly on the maze task than those selected for low activity (Rosenzweig et al. 1958). Another study that examined the performance of maze-bright and maze-dull rats was undertaken by Cooper and Zubek (1958), who reared their animals in enriched cages containing lots of toys, or empty small grey wire-mesh cages. The results showed that if the maze-dull animals were reared in an enriched environment, they performed in a similar way to the maze-bright rats (Figure 14.8). This finding proves that the capacity for maze learning is not fixed, and can be improved with the right environmental conditions.

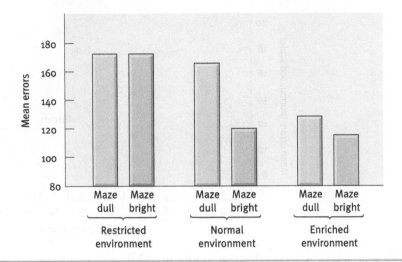

Figure 14.8 The effects of enriched and impoverished rearing on maze-bright and maze-dull rats

The behavioural genetics of alcohol dependence

Alcohol dependence is one of our most common drug addictions and is responsible for the death of many thousands of people each year. According to the Office for National Statistics, over 90 per cent of the UK population regularly consume alcohol, with some 40 million people drinking socially. It also reports that 27 per cent of men and 14 per cent of women drink over the recommended number of units weekly. This works out at nearly 10 million people who are putting their health at risk through excessive drinking. In addition, it has been estimated that about 1 million people have a serious behavioural problem controlling their alcohol consumption, and that another 200,000 can be classified as physically dependent on alcohol (i.e. alcoholics). The extent of alcohol use can be seen by the fact that UK consumers spend more of their disposable income on alcohol than on personal goods, fuel, power or tobacco. For example, in 2001, £36,636,000,000 was spent on alcohol, which is equivalent to 5.8 per cent of all consumer expenditure.

The problems caused by alcohol use has made it a popular area of research in behavioural genetics – not least because understanding the relative impact of the environment and hereditary on drinking will have implications for controlling its sale and how we treat its associated diseases. Clearly, the causes of alcohol drinking and alcoholism are complex. For example, there are personality and social factors at work that attract people to alcohol, and most researchers accept that high levels of stress will often encourage drinking for the feeling of pleasure and relaxation it can produce. Nevertheless, some people appear to be more vulnerable to alcohol abuse than others, which supports the idea that genetic factors contribute to drinking behaviour. The idea that human drinking behaviour is inherited has a long history. Over two thousand years ago, Aristotle declared that drunken women 'bring forth children like themselves', and Plutarch wrote, 'one drunkard begets another' (Goodwin 1980). But, how do we prove that genes are involved in alcohol excess? How many genes are there?

What effects are they having on the body and brain to influence behaviour? And, how do these factors interact with environmental forces to shape drinking patterns? These are some of the questions which the remainder of the book will address.

Selective breeding for alcohol use

Some of the best evidence that alcohol drinking has a genetic component comes from selective breeding of animals who show a strong preference for drinking alcohol. This type of research started in the 1940s when Jorges Mardones and his colleagues at the University of Chile bred two strains of rats that differed in their voluntary alcohol consumption. These were called the UChA and UChB strains (A stands for 'abstainer' and B for 'bibulous'), which exhibited low and high levels of alcohol consumption, respectively (see Mardones and Segovi-Riquelme 1983). If given a choice between tap water and a water solution containing 10 per cent alcohol, UChB rats exhibit a preference for alcohol, whereas UChA rats do not. Moreover, the alcohol intake of individual UChB rats varies greatly, although no marked variation is found with UChA rats. Since their discovery, the two lines of rats have been bred continually by mating together the UChB animals that consume the most alcohol, and the UChA rats that prefer water.

These two groups of rats have encouraged researchers to look for genetic and biochemical differences that could explain the variation in alcohol consumption. One important difference is the speed at which the alcohol metabolite **acetaldehyde** is broken down during metabolism. The liver is known to break down alcohol in two steps. The first uses the enzyme **alcohol dehydrogenase** to convert alcohol into acetaldehyde, and the second uses the enzyme **aldehyde dehydrogenase** to metabolise acetaldehyde into the inert products of acetate and acetyl coenzyme A. This second step is important because acetaldehyde is a toxic compound that produces sweating and nausea in humans, and discourages an individual to drink further alcohol. Importantly, the alcohol-preferring UChB rats have been found to remove acetaldehyde from the liver at a faster rate than their UChA counterparts – and this is due to a certain gene that produces alcohol dehydrogenase. The genetic basis of alcohol dehyrogenase is complex as there are three classes of gene (or allele) which produce this enzyme (abbreviated as *ALDH1*, *ALDH2* and *ALDH3*) and several different variants in each class. But, it has been found that the UChB rats inherit a more efficient version of the *ALDH2* gene than the UChA animals. This means, in effect, that the UChA rats have less active alcohol dehydrogenase, which causes increased elevations of acetaldehyde after alcohol ingestion. This is likely to deter drinking.

A different group of alcohol-preferring and non-preferring (P/NP) rats have been bred at the University of Indiana (Lumeng *et al.* 1977, 1993), with the P strain consuming up to five times more alcohol than the NP animals. These rats also exhibit differences in brain neurochemistry. For example, the alcohol-preferring rats have lower levels (20–30 per cent) of serotonin and its metabolite 5-HIAA in several regions of the brain, including the cerebral cortex, hippocampus, striatum, hypothalamus and nucleus accumbens (Murphy *et al.* 1987). The likeliest explanation for this effect is that there are fewer serotonergic fibres innervating these regions. As a result of the decreased serotonergic innervation in the P line, there is also an up-regulation of 5-HT$_{1A}$ receptors, especially in the hippocampus and frontal cortex. In addition, the alcohol-preferring rats show a 10–30 per cent deficiency in dopamine levels in the nucleus accumbens and anterior striatum (Strother *et al.* 2005). As we saw in Chapter 12, the nucleus accumbens is important in mediating the pleasurable properties of addictive drugs. Moreover, alcohol can stimulate dopamine release in this structure.

Researchers have also selectively bred animals that show different sensitivities to alcohol. For example, McClearn and Kakihana (1981) postulated that animals who sleep more after ingesting alcohol are more sensitive to its effects than those who sleep less. Consequently, they injected mice with alcohol and measured the amount of time they spent sleeping. Following this, they mated the short-sleeping mice together, as well as the long-sleeping mice, over many generations. These two groups of mice are called the Colorado Long and Short Sleep lines, and they show significant differences in their responses to alcohol. For example, the long-sleep animals sleep for about 2 hours after an alcohol injection, whereas the short-sleep mice sleep for 10 minutes. These mice also differ in their sensitivity to a number of other drugs, including benzodiazepines, barbiturates and gaseous anaesthetics. Because benzodiazepines and barbiturates have an agonist-type effect on GABA-A receptors, a genetic difference between the two groups of mice in their sensitivity to GABA is implicated (Crabbe *et al.* 1994).

The heritability of alcohol abuse in humans

Twin studies

Considerable evidence supports the idea that genetic inheritance contributes to the development of alcoholism in humans. For example, a review of several studies by Goodwin (1976) shows that alcoholism has a tendency to run in families, with 20–25 per cent of sons born to an alcoholic parent becoming alcoholic. This figure drops to about 5 per cent for daughters. The familial nature of this disorder holds regardless of nationality, or whether the proband has an additional disorder such as depression or antisocial personality disorder. These findings have led Goodwin (1976) to claim that a family history of alcoholism represents the strongest known risk factor for alcoholism. Despite this, these findings have to be viewed with caution as family members share a common environment with shared stresses and social influences. Thus, family studies cannot be regarded as conclusive proof of genetic influence.

Studies that compare the concordance rates between MZ and DZ twins provide a more powerful means of assessing the impact of genetic inheritance on behaviour. One of the first studies to examine alcoholism in twins was undertaken in Sweden by Kaij (1960), who examined 174 male twins, raised apart from birth, where at least one member abused alcohol. It was found that the concordance rates among MZ twins increased with the severity of the alcohol use. For chronic alcoholism, a concordance rate of 71 per cent was found for the identical twins, compared with 32 per cent for non-identical twins. Another early Scandinavian study from Finland (Partanen *et al.* 1966) reported on over 900 pairs of male twins. Again, the concordance rates for MZ twins were significantly higher than for DZ on the frequency of drinking and amount of alcohol consumed, which suggested a genetic effect.

A British twin study of alcoholism was undertaken by Gurling *et al.* (1981), who examined 35 identical twins and 44 fraternal twins taken from a register based at the Maudsley psychiatric hospital in London. These researchers, however, did not find a difference between the concordance rates for alcoholism. In fact, the results showed a concordance of 29 per cent for MZ twins compared to 33 per cent for DZ twins. However, this study was criticised on the grounds that a large number (about one-third) of its subjects were women, which may have biased the results. This possibility was examined by Pickens *et al.* (1991), who examined levels of alcohol abuse in a total of 169 male or female twin pairs. Although there were more than twice as many male twins as female (this is consistent with the higher incidence of alcoholism among men), there were still enough women (31 MZ and 24 DZ) to make a judgement about sex differences. Results showed that the concordance rates for identical male twins was 76 per cent compared with 61 per cent for the fraternal twins. The corresponding figures for female twins were 36 per cent and 25 per cent. These figures indicated that alcoholism was 36 per cent heritable for men, and 26 per cent heritable for women. In other words, the genetic influence is small, and the environment appears to exert a more important influence on determining alcohol abuse.

A more recent study (McGue *et al.* 1992) that used a larger sample of subjects (some taken from the investigation by Pickens *et al.* (1991)) have found male concordance rates to be 77 per cent for MZ twins and 54 per cent for DZ twins. The female figures were 39 per cent and 42 per cent. Again, these figures suggest that the heritability of alcoholism is relatively small, although it is significantly greater in males than for females. Table 14.3 summarises the results of the studies described above.

Adoption studies

A criticism of the above studies is that twins are inevitably raised in similar circumstances, which increases the likelihood of environmental factors influencing their alcohol abuse. One way of controlling for this type of problem is to examine individuals born to an alcoholic parent but who were adopted at a young age into a new family. One of the most widely cited studies of this type is known as the Danish Adoption Study (Goodwin *et al.* 1973), which examined 55 adoptee sons who had an alcoholic parent (85 per cent of whom were fathers). The results showed that 18 per cent of the adoptee group met criteria for alcoholism, compared with just 5 per cent for adopted controls with no alcoholic parents. In other words, alcoholism was nearly four times more likely in the sons of alcoholic fathers. However, if subjects not reaching criteria for alcoholism were classified as 'problem drinkers' and 'heavy drinkers', a different

Table 14.3	Summary of some important studies that have examined concordance rates in twins for alcoholism	
Study	**Identical Twins**	**Fraternal Twins**
Kaij *et al.* (1960)	71%	32%
Gurling and Murray (1981)	29%	33%
Pickens *et al.* (1991)	76% (males)	61% (males)
	36% (females)	25% (females)
McGue *et al.* (1992)	77% (males)	54% (males)
	39% (females)	42% (females)

set of findings was obtained. In fact, the prevalence of these conditions was higher in the controls (36 per cent and 14 per cent) in comparison with the alcoholic adoptees (22 per cent and 95 per cent). Taken together these studies are consistent with several twin studies suggesting that genetic influences are important in the transmission of alcoholism, but not of problem drinking (Hesselbrock 1995).

A second investigation, sometimes called the Swedish Adoption Study, extended these findings (Cloninger *et al.* 1981). This study was based on a much larger sample of subjects (862 males and 913 females) who were born to single mothers in Stockholm between 1930 and 1949, and adopted at an early age by non-relatives. In addition, information about alcohol abuse, mental illness and medical problems was available for most of these adoptees, along with biological and adoptive parents. The results showed that genetic factors play an important role in alcoholism. For example, higher rates of alcohol abuse were found in the adopted sons of alcoholic fathers (22.4 per cent) compared with non-alcoholic fathers (14.7 per cent). A similar pattern was also found for alcoholic and non-alcoholic mothers (28.1 per cent and 14.7 per cent, respectively). But, there were unexpected findings. For example, the genetic influence was more pronounced among the male adoptees with moderate levels of alcoholism compared with those with mild or severe alcoholism. Moreover, compared with mild or severe alcoholics, moderate alcoholics were more likely to have biological fathers with criminal records and a teenage onset of problem drinking.

Are there different types of alcoholism?

It is generally accepted that not all alcoholics are alike. That is, alcoholics are probably heterogeneous both in terms of the aetiology of their disorder and in the patterns of drinking they exhibit. Because of this, attempts have been made to describe different types of alcoholism. Indeed, E.M. Jellinek, who did much to promote the idea that alcoholism was a medical illness in his influential book *The Disease Concept of Alcoholism* (1960), believed there were five different types of alcoholism – with two of these (gamma and delta) qualifying as diseases. In both these types he emphasised the importance of tolerance to alcohol developing with repeated drinking, the occurrence of withdrawal symptoms when consumption was stopped, and strong cravings. The difference between the two, however, depended on the nature of the drinking patterns. More specifically, **gamma alcoholics** were those who persistently drunk alcohol and suffered from 'an inability to abstain entirely', whereas **delta alcoholics** could abstain from alcohol for long periods but were unable to stop drinking once they had begun (i.e. a 'loss of control'). More recently, the American Psychiatric Association has defined two types of alcoholism: one where physical and psychological dependence results from chronic use leading to increased tolerance, physical withdrawal and craving, and one where the person becomes psychologically dependent on alcohol (often due to stress) and engages in intermittent but heavy consumption.

Another important typology of alcoholism was formulated by Robert Cloninger who derived it from data from the Swedish Adoption Study (described above). One of the features of this study was that it divided the alcoholic subjects into three categories: mild, moderate and severe. When Cloninger looked more closely at these categories, he realised that the 'moderate' alcoholics were the ones more likely to have an alcoholic parent. In fact, 'moderate' alcholism was nearly ten times more heritable than the mild and severe forms. Cloninger also found that a number of other features distinguished moderate alcoholics from those with mild or severe problems. For example, the biological fathers of moderate abusers tended to have a low socio-economic status, a high number of criminal convictions and a teenage onset of alcoholism. In contrast, the mild and severe forms of alcoholism did not appear to be strongly genetic, or be associated with economic status or criminality. Cloninger designated these two forms of alcoholism as type 1 (mild and severe) and type 2 (moderate).

The most common form of alcoholism according to Cloninger is type 1. This is found in both males and females (although it is more common in males) and has a late onset, normally occurring after the age of 25. Although these alcoholics may not drink for long periods of time, once they begin they cannot control or stop their drinking behaviour. Thus, they are likely to engage in binge drinking, and this is often accompanied by strong feelings of guilt. In terms of personality they tend to be anxious, inhibited, cautious, shy and emotionally sensitive. Furthermore, these individuals typically have few social or legal problems related to their drinking. Although there is often evidence of alcohol problems in one of the parents, type 1 alcoholism does not appear to be strongly inherited, and is especially linked to stressful environmental factors.

Type 2 alcoholism occurs predominantly in men before the age of 25 years. Although patterns of drinking may be moderate, it is also chronic as there is an inability to abstain from alcohol for any length of time. These alcoholics typically exhibit antisocial tendencies that include a history of fighting, lying, drug taking, impulsiveness and lack of remorse. Consequently, type 2 alcoholics are often known to the police and experience legal problems or imprisonment. This form of alcoholism is strongly inherited from the father (the risk of alcoholism in these subjects is nine times greater than that for type 1), with the environment appearing to play little part in its expression. Thus, these drinking and antisocial behaviours are likely to emerge in young adulthood regardless of environment.

The type 1 and type 2 typologies (see Table 14.4) have attracted a great deal of research and controversy. Not all investigators agree with Cloninger's classification,

Table 14.4	Characteristics of type 1 and type 2 alcoholism as formulated by Cloninger
Type 1 ('Binge Type')	**Type 2 ('Persistent Type')**
● Has a late onset (typically after the age of 25) and is characterised by binges or loss of control (once the person starts they cannot stop) punctuated by periods of abstinence	● Has an early onset (before the age of 25) and is characterised by persistent moderate to heavy drinking without periods of abstinence
● The personality is often characterised by anxiety, shyness and inhibition. In addition, there may be guilt and fear over their dependence, leading to depression	● The personality is generally characterised by impulsiveness and lack of anxiety. In addition, there is often antisocial behaviour with evidence of other forms of drug taking and/or criminality
● Can occur in both males and females and does not appear to have a strong genetic basis	● Occurs predominantly in males and appears to be strongly inherited from the father
● Has been suggested that these persons are physiologically over-aroused and that alcohol serves as a depressant which acts to decrease anxiety and arousal	● Has been suggested that these persons are physiologically under-aroused and that alcohol serves as a stimulant which acts to increase arousal

especially as it appears that some alcoholics have a mixture of type 1 and type 2 symptoms (Penick *et al.* 1990). Moreover, some studies have found that both types of alcoholism can occur in the same family, and that type 1 alcoholism is more common in families with a type 2 genetic background (Sigvardsson *et al.* 1996). Others argue that the problem of alcoholism inheritance is more complex than that proposed by Cloninger, and what is inherited is a mix of personality traits, such as those related to impulsiveness or antisocial behaviour, rather than alcoholism itself (Schuckit 1987). Despite such criticisms, few will deny that Cloninger's work provides a valuable contribution to our understanding of alcoholism.

Is there a gene for alcoholism?

If alcoholism has a genetic basis, then it should be possible to identify the genes that produce this behaviour, and where they reside in the human genome. Research that addresses this problem relies on two main techniques: **linkage mapping** and **association analysis**. In linkage mapping, researchers attempt to discover the location of genes in the genome by finding a genetic marker (typically a large region of DNA) that is co-inherited and runs through families who have individuals with alcoholism. This marker will allow the chromosomal location of the trait to be determined, even if the gene for the trait remains unknown. For example, one study used 291 DNA markers to analyse 987 individuals from 105 families containing at least three first-degree relatives with alcohol dependence, and found strong linkage to chromosomes 1 and 7 (Reich *et al.* 1998). Another study used 571 DNA markers and found regions on chromosome 4 in an area known to contain a gene for a subunit of the GABA receptor, and on chromosome 11 which is known to contain the genes that encode the dopamine D-4 receptor and the enzyme tyrosine hydroxylase (Long *et al.* 1998). Both these studies show that linkage mapping provides an important first step towards identifying the genes involved in alcoholism, but suffers from the problem of producing highly variable results.

In contrast, the technique of association analysis does not depend on family pedigrees. Rather, it relies on identifying subjects with a particular trait in common, and then comparing them with controls who do not express the behaviour. One advantage of this technique is that specific genes that have been implicated from other studies can be examined to see if they occur at a higher frequency in alcoholic individuals. Several years ago a group of researchers led by Kenneth Blum at the University of Texas generated much excitement when it claimed that an alcholic gene had been discovered (Blum *et al.* 1990, 1991). These investigators studied the brains of 70 deceased individuals, half of whom had been alcoholics. A sample of frontal cortex was taken from each person and tested with nine DNA probes, each of which was a possible alcoholism gene from previous research. Out of these nine probes, one matched the DNA found in the brain tissues, and this gene happened to be responsible for producing the dopamine D-2 receptor. This gene is located on chromosome 11 and occurs in two different forms, or alleles. Most individuals have the A-2 allele, but some have the less common A-1 version. In fact, this A-1 allele was the one found in the alcoholics' brains. It was claimed that this gene was present in 69 per cent of the alcoholics' brains, but absent in 80 per cent of the non-alcoholics' brains.

This was a potentially important finding as the dopaminergic systems of the brain play an important role in reinforcement and addiction. Blum proposed that the A-1 allele might contribute to alcoholism because it manufactures fewer dopamine receptors. This would then result in neurons located in the reward areas of the brain not being stimulated with sufficient dopamine. In turn, this might lead to craving for substances such as alcohol that help stimulate or increase the release of this neurotransmitter (Blum and Payne 1991). The discovery of the A-1 gene also raised the possibly that a test could be developed to screen for alcoholism in the population.

However, it soon became clear that the A-1 allele was not specific to alcholism. In fact, the allele is frequently found in the brains of individuals with a range of behavioural disorders, including attention deficit disorder, autism and Tourette's syndrome (Comings *et al.* 1991). In addition, the original estimate of the A-1 allele frequency reported by Blum *et al.* (1990) was too high. For example, Noble (1993) reviewed nine studies that compared a total of 491 alcoholics with 495 controls, and found that the A-1 allele existed in 43 per cent of the alcoholics' brains and 25.7 per cent of control subjects' brains. Other researchers were not able to find even this degree of difference (Gelernter *et al.* 1993), or failed to find evidence supporting linkage of the A-1 allele with alcohol use in several large families where alcoholism was common (Parsian *et al.* 1991). At present, it is probably fair to say that most researchers do not think the A-1 allele is involved in alcoholism.

Serotonin and alcoholism

Another neurotransmitter implicated in alcoholism is serotonin. For example, it has been shown that the concentrations of the serotonergic metabolite **5-HIAA** is lower in the cerebrospinal fluid (CSF) of many alcoholics compared with controls (Lovinger 1997). This observation suggests that some alcoholics may have reduced serotonin levels in the brain. Support for this idea was obtained by Ballenger *et al.* (1979) who measured 5-HIAA levels in abstaining alcoholics. Although the results showed that 5-HIAA levels were relatively normal at 48 hours, they were significantly depressed at 4 weeks. This indicated that alcoholics have low levels of serotonin, which are restored to normal after they consume alcohol. The implication, therefore, is that a deficit in serotonin might be responsible for making the alcoholic seek out and consume alcohol. Indeed, a number of animal studies have also found that alcohol elevates central levels of serotonin and, as we saw earlier, alcohol-preferring rats have reduced levels of serotonin in several brain areas (Lumeng *et al.* 1993).

It has been found that serotonergic abnormalities are more likley to occur in individuals with type 2 alcoholism (Roy *et al.* 1987). In fact, many of these alcoholics exhibit a unique base sequence in the gene that codes for the enzyme **tryptophan hydroxylase**, which is involved in the manufacture of serotonin (Virkunnen *et al.* 1995). A functional polymorphism in the gene that produces the serotonin uptake pump has also been found in individuals who consume greater amounts of alcohol (Munafo *et al.* 2005). Both of these genetic variations are associated with reduced levels of serotonin. But, the relationship between serotonin and alcohol is not as straightforward as it first appears because low CSF levels of 5-HIAA have also been found to be linked with a variety of impulsive and antisocial behaviours, including aggression, torture and arson

(Roy *et al.* 1987). Low levels of 5-HIAA are also found in some people with depression – especially those with suicidal thoughts. Thus, it could be that low levels of 5-HIAA are associated with certain personality traits rather than alcoholism per se.

Nonetheless, it may be the case that low serotonergic function is a contributory factor for alcoholism in some individuals. This is supported from animal studies. For example, low levels of 5-HIAA in rats are associated with an enhanced preference for alcohol, whereas drugs that stimulate serotonin release decrease alcohol consumption (Sellars *et al.* 1992). In another study, Higley *et al.* (1996) measured CSF levels of 5-HIAA in a group of rhesus monkeys that were allowed free access to alcohol. They found that animals with the lowest levels of 5-HIAA had the highest alcohol intake. Thus, alcohol intake could be predicted by 5-HIAA levels prior to drinking. Although 5-HIAA levels are believed to be genetically determined to a large extent, alcohol consumption was also shown to be influenced by environmental factors. For example, Higley *et al.* found that when monkeys were deprived of maternal contact early in life, they drank more alcohol as adults. Thus, the interaction between low levels of 5-HIAA and environmental stresses is likely to be a more critical determinant of drinking behaviour and its associated problems.

These findings also imply that serotonergic drugs may be useful for the treatment of alcoholism. Indeed, a number of drugs which increase serotonergic activity have been shown to reduce alcohol preference in animal studies. However, the benefits for human alcohol drinkers is less marked. Although drugs such as **fluoxetine** (Prozac) have been found to reduce drinking in some individuals, the effect is relatively small. For example, in heavy drinkers, 60 mg of fluoxetine per day (a dose that is three times that used to treat depression) decreased daily alcohol intake from 8.7 drinks to 6.9 drinks during a four-week trial (Kranzler and Anton 1994). In individuals with severe alcohol dependence, the effectiveness of these drugs is probably negligible. Newer versions of these drugs, however, may yet play an important role in the treatment of alcoholism.

Genetic engineering and the creation of transgenic animals

So far we have looked at various methods that have been used to examine how genetic influences contribute to human behaviour (twin and adoption studies); how certain combination of genes produce behavioural and neurobiological changes (selective breeding); and how genes can be located in the genome (linkage mapping and association analysis). In recent years, however, a more powerful method of examining the function of genes has been developed, and one that promises to revolutionise the way we understand behaviour. This is the technique of **genetic engineering**, which, in its most basic form, involves removing genes from an organism, making multiple copies (i.e. cloning), and implanting the copies into another organism. In fact, genetic engineering is already taking place on a large scale. For example, these techniques are being used in farming to produce bigger animals, increase crop yields and to make plants more resistant to disease. In addition, genetically engineered cells are commercially used to produce hormones, antibodies and vaccines. Genetically modified cells have even been introduced into human beings to combat certain diseases. For the biopsychologist, however, the most exciting development is the creation of **transgenic animals** that overexpress certain genes, or null mutant animals, such as **knockout mice**, where genes have been removed. Both types of animal are providing a powerful means of assessing the impact of genetic influences on growth, development and behaviour.

A transgenic animal is one that carries a foreign gene that has been deliberately inserted into its genome. The beginnings of this genetic technology took place in the late 1960s when scientists discovered **restriction enzymes** that cut DNA with great precision at a specific base sequence. These enzymes were first found in bacteria, which used them to disable the DNA of invading viruses. But, researchers realised they could be used as 'molecular scissors' to cut DNA. In other words, DNA could be extracted from a living organism, and put into a test tube with restriction enzymes to create lots of identical DNA fragments 'cut' at the same place. Within a decade of their discovery, geneticists had discovered hundreds of restriction enzymes that allowed them to make many different types of DNA fragment.

By themselves, lots of DNA snippets floating around in a test tube have little use. However, a few years after the first restriction enzymes were discovered, geneticists found ways of joining the bits of DNA together. In fact, the DNA did not even have to come from the same genome. It was possible to join together DNA from different organisms, or even implant new genes into foreign DNA (a feat first performed in 1972 by Paul Berg who took genes from a bacteria and implanted them into the DNA of a virus). Soon after came a more astonishing feat when Herbert Boyer and Stanley Cohen took DNA from a toad and placed it in the DNA of a bacteria. In fact, every time the bacteria divided, the 'foreign' DNA was copied and passed into the new bacteria. In effect, this was the first living organism to be transgenically modified.

Boyer and Cohen's breakthrough opened up the possibility that foreign sequences of DNA could be inserted into more complex creatures, such as mammals, to create transgenic animals of experimental interest. In fact, this procedure was first undertaken in 1981 by Gordon and Ruddle, who microinjected foreign DNA into the fertilised egg of a mouse. In turn, the egg was put back into the ovaries of a recipient female. The technique is commonly known as DNA microinjection and it provides the main method currently used to produce transgenic animals in a wide variety of species (see Figure 14.9). However, genes can only be added, and not deleted, by this method.

More recently, two other methods have been developed to create transgenic animals. The first of these is called embryonic **stem cell-mediated gene transfer** and is a procedure where a sequence of DNA is inserted into a culture of embryonic stem cells (stem cells are undifferentiated or 'blank' and have the potential to develop into any type of cell). These cells are then incorporated into an embryo at a very early stage of its development. In fact, when these cells are in culture, it is also possible, by using a number of methods, to remove or substitute a chosen gene. This is the method normally used to produce gene inactivation – the so-called **knockout** method. The second technique is **retrovirus-mediated gene transfer**, which uses modified viruses to transfer genetic material into an embryonic cell. This method takes advantage of the ability of the virus to infect the cell with its own DNA, which then becomes incorporated into the genetic material of the host.

The success rates of all these methods is relatively low, either because most foetuses are aborted, or because the desired gene will not be expressed or function properly. Furthermore, to be successful, most genes need to be placed next to a special segment

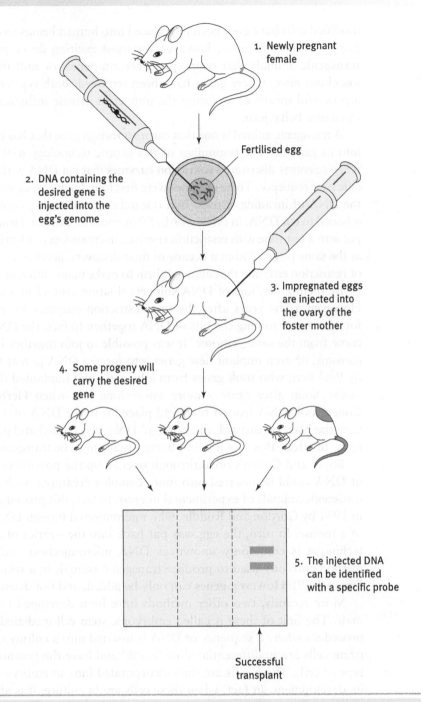

1. Newly pregnant female

Fertilised egg

2. DNA containing the desired gene is injected into the egg's genome

3. Impregnated eggs are injected into the ovary of the foster mother

4. Some progeny will carry the desired gene

5. The injected DNA can be identified with a specific probe

Successful transplant

Figure 14.9   The production of transgenic mammals using the DNA microinjection method

of DNA called a **promoter sequence**. For this reason, when constructing a transgene most researchers will usually substitute the donor's promoter sequence with one that is specially designed to ensure that the gene will correctly function in the tissues of the recipient animal. If the genetic manipulation is successful, the result will be a first generation (F1) of animals, some of whom will be homozygous for the gene. These animals can then be inbred for 10–20 generations until pure or homozygous transgenic animals are obtained with the transgene present in every cell. At this stage, embryos containing the transgene can be frozen and stored for later experiments.

Transgenic and gene knockout models in alcohol research

The use of transgenic animals that overexpress certain genes, or ones that have had a gene knocked out, provides an exciting new opportunity to examine the effects of genes on behaviour. This area of research has already shown that a large number of genes may be involved in alcoholism and problem drinking. One such gene is the one responsible for producing **adenylyl cyclase**. This is an enzyme involved in the cAMP signal-transduction pathway, which acts as an intracellular second messenger for a number of neurotransmitters, including noradrenaline and dopamine. Cyclic AMP shows increased activity following alcohol consumption which is due to the stimulation of adenylyl cyclase. There are in fact several types (or isoforms) of adenylyl cyclase in the brain, and one version, called type 7 (AC7), is between two and three times more sensitive to alcohol than other types. Moreover, this type of adenylyl cyclase is found in high levels in the cerebellum, which is an area of the brain involved in motor co-ordination. To examine this enzyme further, a group of transgenic mice were bred that overexpressed the AC7 form of adenylyl cyclase (Yoshimura *et al.* 2000). After a high dose of alcohol, these mice performed significantly better on tests of motor co-ordination, and became tolerant to the injections at a faster rate than controls. These findings show that the level of expression of certain types of adenylate cyclase in the brain can have a strong bearing on alcohol-related behaviour, and could potentially be linked with a propensity to develop alcoholism.

Another gene linked to alcohol sensitivity was identified by Miyakawa *et al.* (1997), who examined mice which were mutant for a gene that produces an enzyme called **Fyn kinase**. Kinases are a special type of protein that transmit signals within the cell (sometimes to the nucleus) and which control a large number of intracellular processes. In particular, Fyn kinase has been shown to affect neural excitability. Miyakawa *et al.* found that mice containing a mutant gene for Fyn kinase were very sensitive to the effects of alcohol. In fact, when injected with a high dose of alcohol they took twice as long to right themselves compared with normal mice. These findings have been confirmed and also demonstrated in transgenic knockout mice lacking the *Fyn* gene.

Another gene that has been knocked out is the one that encodes for the serotonergic 5-HT$_{1B}$ receptor. This receptor is found in high amounts in the basal ganglia, hippocampus and raphe nuclei, and was first examined by researchers because it was believed to be involved in aggressive behaviour. Indeed, when mice were developed without the 5-HT$_{1B}$ receptor they showed increased aggressiveness (Saudou *et al.* 1994). However, Crabbe *et al.* (1996) also found that these mice consumed twice as much alcohol as did controls, and would even ingest solutions containing up to 20 per cent ethanol. The 5-HT$_{1B}$ receptor deficient mice were also less sensitive to the motor incoordinating effects of alcohol. These results show that the 5-HT$_{1B}$ receptor may be involved in regulating drinking behaviour and altering sensitivity to some of the effects of alcohol.

A number of pharmacological studies have also implicated gamma-aminobutyric acid (GABA, the main inhibitory neurotransmitter of the brain) in the actions of alcohol. Because of this, researchers have begun to examine the role of its receptors, particularly the GABA-A receptor, in knockout strains of mice. However, the GABA-A receptor is highly complex and contains five subunits (α, β, γ, δ and ρ) which are each encoded by an individual gene. And, to make matters even more complex, at present, six α, four β, four γ, one δ and two ρ isoforms (or versions) of these units are known. Nonetheless, researchers are beginning to explore these different isoforms in mutant or knockout mice. This research is in its infancy and only a few isoforms have been examined. As yet, none of these have been shown to alter alcohol sensitivity, tolerance or withdrawal in knockout mice (Lobo and Harris 2008).

Summary

It is believed that life on earth has been evolving for around 3,500 million years, with *Homo sapiens* first appearing some 100,000 years ago. Human beings have a genome that contains **23 pairs** of **chromosomes**, which hold around **30,000 genes**. These not only provide the blueprint by which are body (and brain) are made, but also govern the internal working of our cells. The laws of genetic inheritance were first established by **Gregor Mendel** in 1865 working with pea plants. He showed that each individual plant contained two 'factors' (now called genes) that came in different forms (**alleles**) and which controlled a certain trait (height, colour, etc.). Each allele could also be **dominant** or **recessive**, although only one of these was passed on from each parent to offspring. Thus, if a plant inherited both a dominant and recessive gene, it always expressed the dominant trait – although the recessive trait would be exhibited if two recessive genes were inherited. Genes are passed to offspring by **gametes** (in animals this is the **sperm** and **egg**), which contain unpaired chromosomes, which become paired 'again' during **fertilisation**. Chromosomes are made from **deoxyribonucleic acid DNA** and its chemical structure was established in 1954 by **James Watson** and **Francis Crick** in what was probably the most important scientific advance of the twentieth century. They showed that DNA is made up of two chains of deoxyribose that swivel around each other in a shape of a double helix. Between the two chains are pairs of **bases** (**adenine, guanine, cytosine** and **thymine**) that are like rungs of a ladder. Genes are in essence long sequences of paired bases (the largest human gene contains over 2 million bases) that contain **codons** (special triple bases) that code for single **amino acids** which are the 'building blocks' of **proteins** – a class of molecule with a wide variety of functions vital for life. Put simply, protein synthesis occurs when **messenger ribonucleic acid (mRNA)** carries a transcript from the DNA (in the **nucleus**) to a **ribosome** located in the **cytoplasm**. Here, amino acids are bought to the transcript by **transfer ribonucleic acid (tRNA)**, forming a chained molecule and a protein is constructed.

Some genetic conditions are caused by a **single dominant allele** whereby if a person inherits the gene they will develop the disorder. One such condition is **Huntington's disease**, which is caused by a **mutation** occurring on chromosome 4. Other conditions such as **phenylketonuria** are caused by **recessive alleles**, which means that two copies of the gene have to be inherited for the illness to develop. A third type of single-gene disorder may occur through **X-linked inheritance**, where the mutation is carried on the X chromosome. These conditions (for example, **haemophilia**) usually manifest themselves in **males (XY)**, as **females (XX)** typically have a 'good' X chromosome to counteract the one carrying the mutation. However, most behaviours that are of interest to the psychologist are caused by **multiple genes**, whose expression also depends on environmental influences. The sum of all genetic information that a person inherits is called the **genotype**, but the totality of gene and environmental influences that is expressed is called the **phenotype**. One way of measuring the relative influence of gene and environmental influences on human behaviour is by measuring the rate of **concordance** in identical (**monozygotic**) and non-identical (**dizygotic**) twins. In short, the higher the concordance in identical twins, the more likely the condition is determined by genetic factors. Experimental strategies can also be used to measure the impact of genetic influences on behaviour, including **inbreeding** to produce different strains of animals, and **selective breeding** to produce a certain trait (for example, for alcohol preference). Over the past decade or so, the use of **transgenic animals** in which the genome has been modified in some way (for example, a certain gene may be **knocked out** or another added) has begun to revolutionise our genetic understanding of behaviour – and this is certain to continue long into the future.

Essay questions

1. 'DNA makes RNA, and RNA makes protein.' Discuss.

   Search terms: Central dogma of genetics. Structure of DNA. Protein synthesis. Introduction to nucleic acids. RNA. Codons and amino acids.

2. Discuss some of the methodological approaches that can be used to examine the influence of multiple genes on behaviour.

   Search terms: Twin and adoption studies. Inbreeding. Selective breeding. Genetic analysis of complex behavior. Multiple genes and behavior. Behavioural genetics.

3. Is alcoholism a disease? To what extent can alcoholism be considered a genetic disorder?

   Search terms: Is alcoholism a disease? Medical model of alcoholism. Genetics of alcoholism. Type 1 and type 2 alcoholics. Causes of alcoholism.

4. What are transgenic animals and how are they produced? In what ways have they contributed to our understanding of brain and behaviour?

   Search terms: Transgenic animals. Genetic engineering. Receptor knockout mice. Knockout mice in neurobiology. Transgenic animals and degenerative disease.

Further reading

Begleiter, H. and Kissin, B. (eds) (1995) *The Genetics of Alcoholism*. Oxford: Oxford University Press. A series of articles written by various experts that looks at the genetic and biological factors that predispose a given individual to alcoholism.

Crawley, J.N. (2000) *Whats Wrong with My Mouse? Behavioral Phenotyping of Transgenic and Knockout Mice*. New York: John Wiley. A useful overview of mutant mouse technology and its use in behavioural neuroscience.

Galton, D. (2001) *Eugenics: The Future of Human Life in the 21st Century*. London: Abacus. A readable book that explores some of the implications, both good and bad, that may arise with discoveries in the field of behavioural genetics.

Gershon, E.S. and Cloninger, C.R. (1994) *Genetic Approaches to Mental Disorders*. Washington, DC: American Psychiatric Press. A book that shows how new genetic technology is being used to provide new insights into mental disorders.

Goodsell, D.S. (1996) *Our Molecular Nature: The Body's Motors, Machines and Messages*. New York: Copernicus. A nicely illustrated book that will help any student learn more and visualise the molecular nature of their body.

Jones, S. (1994) *The Language of the Genes*. London: Flamingo. An absorbing and enlightening book written for the layperson that helps show what geneticists can and cannot tell us about ourselves.

Joseph, J. (2003) *The Gene Illusion*. Ross-on-Wye: PCCS Books. A book that provides a strong rebuttal to the idea that genetic factors play an important role in psychiatric disorders, personality, intelligence and socially acceptable behaviour. Also provides a good critique of twin studies in psychological research.

Plomin, R., DeFries, J.C., McClearn, G.E. and Rutter, M. (2000) *Behavioral Genetics: A Primer*. New York: Freeman. A superb textbook, now in its fourth edition, that is simply the best introduction to behavioural genetics for undergraduate students.

Plomin, R., DeFries, J.C., Craig, I.W. and McGuffin, P. (eds) (2003) *Behavioral Genetics in the Postgenomic Era*. Washington, DC: American Psychological Association. Excellent comprehensive textbook that not only covers new methodological developments, but also examines the behavioural genetics of cognitive abilities, clinical disorders (including schizophrenia and depression), and personality.

Steen, R.G. (1996) *DNA and Destiny: Nature and Nurture in Human Behavior*. New York: Plenum Press. A lucid and interesting account which attempts to show the impact of genetic influences on controversial and complex behaviour such as intelligence, aggression, homosexuality and drug addiction.

Watson, J. (2003) *DNA: The Secret of Life*. London: Arrow Books. The remarkable story of DNA, from its discovery over fifty years ago to the present day. Contains chapters of genetic fingerprinting, disease and nature/nurture.

 For self test questions, animations, interactive exercises and many more resources to help you consolidate your understanding, and expand your knowledge of the field, please go to the website accompanying this book at **www.pearsoned.co.uk/wickens**

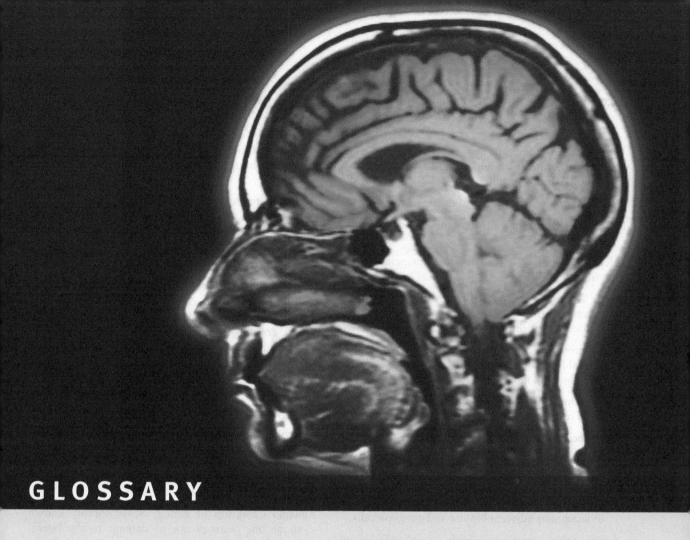

GLOSSARY

A

Abducens nucleus A small nucleus in the pons that controls reflexive movements of the head and eyes.

Absorptive phase The phase of metabolism that occurs during and immediately after a meal in which insulin is released by the pancreas gland. It contrasts with the post-absorptive phase in which glucagon is secreted by the pancreas gland.

Acetylcholine (ACh) An excitatory neurotransmitter that is used at the neuromuscular junction, in the autonomic nervous system and throughout the brain.

Acetylcholinesterase (AChE) An enzyme found in the synapse that inactivates acetylcholine.

Actin A protein which acts along with myosin to produce contraction of muscle fibres.

Action potential The electrical signal or nerve impulse generated by the neuron, and conducted along axons (leading to transmitter release), which allows information to be passed from place to place in the nervous system.

Adenosine A nucleotide (a nitrogen-containing molecule including also ribose or deoxyribose) which has a variety of roles in the nervous system including that of an inhibitory neurotransmitter at some sites.

Adenosine triphosphate (ATP) A molecule which is the main source of energy in the cells of all living organisms.

Adenylate cyclase Membrane-bound enzyme that in some neurons is activated by G-proteins to catalyse the synthesis of cAMP (a second messenger) from ATP.

Adipocyte A fat or lipid cell.

Adrenal hyperplasia A condition in which the adrenal glands secrete excess amounts of male sex hormones or androgens. This can masculinise the foetus if it occurs in early development.

Adrenaline Also known as epinephrine. A substance that acts both as a hormone (released from the adrenal glands) and as a neurotransmitter in certain regions of the brain.

Agnosia A partial or complete inability to perceive sensory information which is not explainable by deficits in basic sensory processing such as blindness.

Agonist An agonistic drug is one which mimics or facilities the action of a given neurotransmitter, normally by acting on its receptor.

Agraphia A difficulty with writing, or an inability to write, although reading (alexia) is generally unimpaired.

Akathisia A condition of motor restlessness which can range from inner disquiet to an inability to remain stationary or to sit still.

Akinesia Absence or poverty of movement.

Alcohol dehydrogenase An enzyme found in the liver that metabolises alcohol.

Alexia An inability to read although the person has no visual deficits.

Allele An individual has two alleles for each gene, one on each of their two chromosomes. The alleles can be identical or different, and dominant or recessive.

Alpha motor neuron A neuron which arises from the ventral horn of the spinal cord and whose activation contributes to muscle contraction.

Alpha-synuclein A small protein which has been implicated in some forms of Parkinson's disease.

Alzheimer's disease A degenerative disease of the brain, especially cerebral cortex and hippocampal regions, that affects about 20 per cent of people over the age of 80 years.

Amacrine cells A specialised neuron in the retina that interconnects adjacent bipolar and ganglion cells.

Amino acids A group of simple compounds (around twenty are made by cells) that can be linked together by peptide bonds to make larger and more complex molecules called proteins.

Amnesia An incomplete or total loss of memory.

Amphetamine A stimulant drug which 'works' by facilitating the release of catecholamines – especially dopamine – from nerve endings.

Amygdala A group of nuclei located in the front of the medial temporal lobe which forms an important part of the limbic system.

Amyloid A protein that forms the main constituent of neuritic plaques which are found in high amounts in Alzheimer's disease. It is derived from a much larger beta amyloid precursor protein whose function is unknown.

Amyloid cascade theory A theory which proposes that the deposition of amyloid in the brain is the main pathological cause of Alzheimer's disease.

Amyloid precursor protein A 695 amino acid protein that is found in the cells of the brain and certain tissues of the body.

Androgen A steroid male sex hormone which includes testosterone.

Angular gyrus A region of the posterior parietal lobe, bordering the primary visual cortex, where strokes can lead to reading problems and word blindness.

Anomia A difficulty in finding the right word especially when naming objects. It is associated with Broca's aphasia.

Anorexia nervosa A condition where the individual suffers loss of appetite, or refuses to eat sufficient amounts of food in pursuit of thinness.

Anosmia An inability to detect certain smells. Several types of anosmia are known with one of the most common being an inability to detect cyanide.

Antagonist A drug which opposes or inhibits the effects of a particular neurotransmitter on the postsynaptic cell, normally by competing at a receptor site.

Anterior thalamus A group of nuclei at the front of the thalamus which forms an important link in the circuitry of the limbic system. It receives input from the hippocampus (via the fornix) and mammillary bodies, and sends its output to the cingulate gyrus.

Anterolateral pathway A somatosensory sensory pathway that is concerned mainly with relaying pain and temperature information to the brain. It forms a ascending white tract of fibres in the spinal cord known as the anterolateral system.

Aphagia Cessation of eating. Most notably known to be one consequence of damage to the lateral hypothalamus.

Aphasia An inability to produce or comprehend language.

Aplysia A large marine snail that has provided a simple animal model by which to examine the synaptic basis of learning and memory.

Apolipoprotein E gene A gene which comes in three different forms (alleles) which have been linked with late onset Alzheimer's disease.

Apoptosis The process of self-inflicted programmed cell death.

Apraxia An inability to make voluntary movement in the absence of paralysis or other peripheral motor impairment.

Arcuate fasciculus A neural pathway that connects Wernicke's area with Broca's area; damage to this structure causes conduction aphasia.

Asomatognosia An inability to detect tactile information from one's own body.

Astereognosis An inability to recognise objects by touch.

Ataxia An impairment of muscle co-ordination which is often associated with damage to the cerebellum and basal ganglia.

Attention deficit hyperactivity disorder A developmental disorder associated with hyperactivity, impulsity and inability to concentrate.

Auditory cortex Located in the temporal cortex adjacent to the planum temporale and receives input from the medial geniculate body of the thalamus.

Autism A developmental disorder characterised by social withdrawal, language and communication deficits, and stereotypy.

Autonomic nervous system The part of the peripheral nervous system that controls the autonomic functions of the body, primarily though its action on glands and the smooth muscles of internal organs. It has two divisions – the sympathetic and parasympathetic – which act in opposite fashion.

Autoradiography A histological technique that shows the distribution of radioactive chemicals in the central nervous system, normally undertaken by mounting brain tissue on a slide of photographic emulsion which is then developed.

Autoreceptors Receptors located on the presynaptic neuron whose main function is to regulate the amount of neurotransmitter that is released.

Autosomal dominant inheritance Essentially means that if one inherits the gene, then one will inherit the characteristic. A prime example of this type of inheritance is Huntington's disease.

Axon A long, thin extension that arises from the nerve cell body and which carries the nerve impulse to the axon terminal where neurochemicals are released.

Axon hillock A cone-shaped area where the axon joins the cell body, and the critical site where depolarisation needs to take place for the action potential to be formed.

B

Balint's syndrome A disorder associated with bilateral damage to the parietal lobes consisting of three main features: optic ataxia (difficulty in accurately reaching for objects under visual guidance), paralysis of eye fixation, and simultanagnosia (difficulty in perceiving more than one object at a time).

Baptist A person who believes that amyloid deposition is the main feature or cause of degeneration in Alzheimer's disease ('bap' being an abbreviation of 'beta amyloid protein').

Basal forebrain A region of the brain that lies anterior and lateral to the hypothalamus and forms part of the circuitry of the limbic system.

Basal ganglia A group of subcortical nuclei and interconnected pathways which are important for movement and contain the caudate nucleus, putamen and globus pallidus.

Basal nucleus of Meynert A nucleus found in the basal forebrain region of the brain which sends cholinergic fibres to the cereral cortex.

Bases Simple nitrogenous molecules (adenine, guanine, cytosine and thymine) that form pairs and make up the 'rungs' in the double helix of DNA.

Basilar membrane A long, flexible tissue separating the scala vestibuli from the scala media which contains the organ of Corti.

Benzodiazepines A class of drug which are used for their anxiolytic and sleep-inducing properties including Valium, Librium and Temazapam.

Beta-adrenergic receptor A class of noradrenergic (NA) receptor that is linked to the cAMP second messenger system.

Biochemistry Is the study of the chemical processes and reactions in living organisms, many of which involve enzymes.

Bipolar cells Interneurons found in the retina that have axon-like processes at both ends of their cell body.

Bipolar disorder A psychiatric disorder characterised by alternating periods of depression and euphoria – sometimes known as manic depression.

Blindsight The ability of subjects with damage of their primary visual cortex to accurately point towards, or track, objects in their 'blind' visual field.

Blood–brain barrier A barrier formed by tightly packed cells in the capillaries, and their covering by astrocytes (glial cells), that prevents the passage of many harmful substances into the brain.

Bradykinesia Slowness and poverty of movement and speech.

Brain-derived neurotropic factor A chemical made by certain types of neuron that is important for the maintenance and survival of brain cells.

Brainstem The old part of the brain which arises from the spinal cord and which includes the medulla oblongata, pons and midbrain. This region of the brain contains many different nuclei and pathways, and is the site of the reticular formation that controls electrical activity in the forebrain.

Broca's aphasia Sometimes called expressive or non-fluent aphasia, characterised by poor speech articulation, difficulty in finding the right word (anomia), and lacking the intonation and inflection of normal language (dysprosody).

Broca'a area A region of the left posterior frontal cortex, located close to the face area of the primary motor cortex, that is involved in the production of speech.

Bulimia Bouts of excessive eating and purging that is often seen in people with anorexia nervosa.

C

cAMP *See* Cyclic adenosine monophosphate.

CAT *See* Computerised axial tomography.

Cannon–Bard theory A theory of emotion proposed by Walter Cannon and Philip Bard that maintains that a stimulus first elicits an emotion which is then followed by physiological changes.

Capsaicin A natural ingredient of hot chilli peppers which has been used to detect pain receptors (nociceptors).

Cataplexy A symptom of narcolepsy, often triggered by an emotional event, that includes complete loss of muscle tone and paralysis which occurs during waking.

Catastrophic-dysphoric reaction Feelings of despair, hopelessness and anger that are sometimes observed in people with damage to the left hemisphere.

Catecholamines A class of monoamines that contain a catechol nucleus which includes noradrenaline and dopamine.

Caudate nucleus An important part of the basal ganglia which along with the putamen makes up the striatum.

Central nucleus of the amygdala The predominant output of the amygdala with projections to the brainstem and hypothalamus.

Cerebellum A large brain structure meaning 'little brain' located at the back of the brainstem (near the pons) and importantly involved in reflexive motor co-ordination.

Cerebral cortex Six-layered covering of the cerebral hemispheres, with an outer appearance of various distinct gyri and fissures, composed of neurons and their synaptic connections.

Cerebrospinal fluid (CSF) The fluid that fills the ventricles of the brain and the subarachnoid space surrounding the brain and spinal cord. Its main function is to protect the central nervous system from mechanical injury, and to absorb and remove waste products of neuronal metabolic activity.

Cholecystokinin (CCK) A hormone secreted by the duodenum that regulates gastric mobility and may be involved in the satiation of hunger. It is also found in neurons of the brain where it may have a neurotransmitter function.

Cholinesterase inhibitor A drug that inhibits the enzyme acetylcholinesterase which breaks down acetylcholine. These drugs (e.g. Tacrine) have been used to treat Alzheimer's disease.

Chromosome A long strand of DNA, coupled with protein, that acts as a carrier for genetic information. Human beings have 23 pairs of chromosomes which are found in the nucleus of nearly every cell in the body.

Cillary muscles The muscles that control the lens of the eye which allow visual images to be focused on the retina. They also give the eyes their distinctive colour.

Cingulate cortex A large arc of 'old' limbic cortex that lies above and spans the corpus callosum.

Classical conditioning A form of learning first demonstrated by Pavlov in which a neutral stimulus is paired with a stimulus that evokes behaviour (*unconditioned stimulus*). With repeated trials the neutral stimulus becomes a *conditioned stimulus* that is able to evoke the behaviour by itself.

Cochlea A small bony chamber of the inner ear which houses the basilar membrane that is crucial for hearing.

Cochlear nerve Also known as cranial nerve VIII, it projects from the ear to the brain.

Cochlear nuclei Found in the medulla and receives input from the cochlear nerve.

Codon A sequence of three bases in DNA which provides a code for making an amino acid.

Cognitive arousal theory A theory proposed by Stanley Schachter and Jerome Singer that maintains that to experience an emotion an individual has to experience physiological arousal *and* attribute the arousal to an appropriate stimulus.

Cognitive reserve The belief that increased mental activity early in life may increase the brain's resilience to later neural degeneration and dementia.

Commissurotomy Another name for the surgical operation in which the corpus callosum is severed thereby disconnecting the two cerebral hemispheres.

Complex cells A type of neuron found in the visual cortex that responds (i.e. fires) when a line is presented in its visual field that is positioned, or moves, in a highly specific orientation.

Computerised axial tomography (CAT) A non-invasive scanning technique that takes detailed three-dimensional pictures of brain structure by computer analysis of X-rays taken at different points and planes around the head.

Conditioned compensatory response A conditioned (learned) response that acts to reduce a drug's impact on the body, and a proposed important contributor to drug tolerance.

Conduction aphasia Caused by damage to the arcuate fasciculus which connects Wernicke's area with Broca's area, and characterised by an inability to fluently repeat words, especially if they are abstract or nonsensical.

Cones A photoreceptor found in the retina which is responsible for fine detailed vision and colour. There are three main types of cone with sensitivities to wavelengths of light roughly corresponding to blue, green and red.

Congenital analgesia A condition where individuals are born without the ability to detect pain.

Cornea The transparent outer surface or 'window' of the eye whose curvature also gives it a role in focusing.

Corpus callosum A broad thick band of around 20 million axon fibres that provides a channel for communication between the two cerebral hemispheres.

Cortical module In the primary visual system a module is a self-contained unit which consists of two ocular dominance columns, a full range of orientation columns, and two cylindrical blobs that code for colour. Other types of module probably exist throughout the cerebral cortex.

Corticospinal pathway The motor pathway originating in the motor cortex (and surrounding areas) of the cerebral cortex, and terminating in the grey matter of the spinal cord. The majority (85 per cent) of its axons (the lateral corticospinal tract) cross in the medulla to influence the opposite (contralateral) side of the body, while the remainder (ventral corticospinal tract) pass down to the same side (ipsilateral) part of the spinal cord.

Cortisol A glucocorticoid hormone released by the adrenal glands, vital for life, and secreted in higher amounts during times of stress.

Creutzfeldt–Jakob disease A form of dementia caused by an infectious agent that has some similarities with bovine spongiform encephalopathy.

Cutaneous senses Sense information from the skin.

Cyclic adenosine monophosphate (cAMP) A chemical that is involved in many biochemical reactions of the body, including an important role as a second messenger that causes the opening of ion channels following certain types of receptor activation.

Cytochrome blobs Peg-like structures found in the primary visual cortex that are stained by the enzyme cytochrome oxidase and have an important role in colour processing.

Decibel The most common way of measuring volume or sound intensity (i.e. the amplitude of the sound wavelength from maximum to minimum pressure).

Declarative memory A type of memory that can be voluntarily 'declared' to consciousness and verbally expressed. In effect, it refers to an ability to recount what one knows. The ability to form new declarative memories is disrupted by damage to the hippocampus.

Deep brain stimulation A procedure used in Parkinson's disease where certain structures of the brain (such as the thalamus) are stimulated by permanently implanted electrodes to relieve tremor.

Deep cerebellar nuclei A group of three nuclei (fastigial, interposed and dentate) within the cerebellum that receive input from the Purkinje neurons of the cerebellar cortex, and which send input out of the cerebellum.

Delayed non-matching to sample test A test used to measure short-term memory in primates where the animal has to choose a different object from the one previously chosen after a given delay.

Delta-9-tetrahydrocannabinol The main psychoactive ingredient in marijuana.

Dendrite A tree-like extension of the neuron's body that contains neurotransmitter receptors and receives chemical input from other nerve cells.

2-Deoxyglucose A sugar that enters cells, including neurons, but is not metabolised. It can be combined with a radioactive isotope to enable the most active regions of the brain to be identified by autoradiography.

Deoxyribonucleic acid (DNA) A long nucleic acid composed of two helical strands (made from the sugar deoxyribose and phosphate) and four bases (adenine, thymine, cytosine and guanine) that provides the code for hereditary information.

Deprenyl A monoamine oxidase inhibitor which has been shown to be effective in slowing down the progression of Parkinson's disease.

Depression A psychiatric condition characterised by unhappiness, lethargy, sleep disturbances and negative thoughts. Sometimes referred to as unipolar depression to distinguish it from bipolar depression where bouts of mania are also present.

Dermatome An area of skin whose sensory fibres all innervate the same dorsal root.

Deuteranopia An inherited from of colour blindness in which red and green cannot be discriminated.

Diabetes mellitus A disease caused by the pancreas gland secreting insufficient amounts of insulin which is a hormone that allows the uptake of glucose into cells. Consequently, untreated diabetics have high levels of blood sugar.

Diagonal band of Broca An area of the limbic system (close to the hypothalamus) that sends cholinergic fibres into the hippocampus.

Diencephalon The part of the forebrain that contains the thalamus and hypothalamus.

Dizygotic twins Twins that develop from two different eggs (and thus two different sperms) and who are genetically different. Sometimes called fraternal twins.

Dopa decarboxylase An enzyme found in the blood that breaks down L-dopa. Because of this, dopa decarboxylase inhibitors are normally given to prolong the effectiveness of L-dopa.

Dopamine A catecholamine neurotransmitter that is predominantly found in the striatum, nucleus accumbens, amygdala and frontal cortex.

Dopamine theory of schizophrenia The idea that schizophrenia is due to increased dopaminergic activity in the brain. The theory is supported, in part, by the finding that several effective antipsychotic drugs work by blocking dopamine receptors.

Dorsal An anatomical term that refers to structures towards the back of the body, or the top of the brain (e.g. a dorsal fin of a fish is located on its back or upper surface).

Dorsal acoustic stria A pathway ascending from the cochlea nucleus of the brainstem to the inferior colliculi.

Dorsal-column medial-lemniscus pathway A pathway carrying cutaneous (touch) information from the spinal cord to the ventral posterior nucleus of the thalamus via the medial lemniscus.

Dorsal columns White matter of the dorsal spinal cord containing ascending axons to the brain.

Dorsal lateral geniculate nucleus *See* Lateral geniculate nucleus.

Dorsal raphe A structure found in the upper brainstem that, along with the medial raphe, provides the forebrain with its serotonergic innervation.

Dorsal roots Bundles of peripheral nerves providing sensory information that enter the dorsal (towards the back) part of the spinal cord.

Dorsolateral area of frontal cortex Area of the prefrontal cortex lying above the orbital frontal region that receives input from dorsomedial thalamus.

Dorsomedial thalamus An important relay of information from the limbic system (particularly the amygdala and entorhinal cortex) to the cortex of the frontal lobe.

Down's syndrome A genetic condition caused by the inheritance of an extra chromosome 21. There is also typically an increased deposition of brain amyloid in the brain in later life.

Dual-centre set-point theory of hunger A theory developed in the 1950s that viewed the lateral hypothalamus as being the initiator of hunger and feeding, and the ventromedial hypothalamus as the satiety centre.

Duodenum The first 25 cm of the small intestine which also include the pancreatic duct.

Dyskinesia Any impairment in the ability to initiate voluntary movement.

Dyslexia A term that refers to a group of reading disorders of varying severity.

Dystonia Lack of muscle tone.

Edinger–Westphal nucleus A small nucleus in the midbrain that sends fibres into the parasympathetic nervous system that controls contraction of the pupil.

Electroencephalogram (EEG) An apparatus that enables the gross electrical activity of the brain to be recorded from electrodes placed on the scalp.

Encephale isolé preparation A surgical preparation in which the brain is disconnected from the rest of the nervous system by a complete transection of the lower brainstem.

Encephalitus lethargica An influenza-like illness that first appeared in 1916 and disappeared mysteriously in 1927, which caused many of its victims to fall into a prolonged stupor. Many of those who recovered went on to develop Parkinson's disease.

Endocrinology The study of how hormones influence the functioning of the body. Behavioural endocrinology refers more specifically to how hormones influence brain and behaviour.

Endorphin An endogenous opiate substance used as a chemical messenger that is made by certain neurons of the brain.

Engram Another term for the anatomical, biochemical and/or physiological site of memory.

Entorhinal cortex A form of transitional cortex found on the medial surface of the temporal lobes that provides the main neural gateway to the hippocampus.

Epinephrine An American term for adrenaline.

Equipotentiality The idea that all parts of the association cerebral cortex play an equal role in the storage of memories. This view contrasts with the theory that different parts of the cerebral association cortex have highly specialised functions.

Ethanol Another term for ethyl alcohol which is the type of alcohol found in alcoholic beverages.

Excitatory postsynaptic potential A small change in the electrical potential of a neuron towards a positive direction, produced by excitatory neurotransmitters, that increases the likelihood of an action potential.

Exocytosis The secretion of substances by the cell (e.g. neurotransmitters) caused by the fusion of organelles or vesicles with the plasma membrane.

Extrapyramidal system The motor system of the brain whose output fibres to the spinal cord do not cross in the pyramidal region of the medulla. The term is commonly used to refer to the basal ganglia and an array of brainstem nuclei to which they are connected.

F

Facial nerve Also known as cranial nerve VII. It conveys sensory information from the face to the brain, including gustatory input from the anterior two-thirds of the tongue.

Fast pain Sharp localised pain associated with activation of Aδ fibres.

Fight or flight response A pattern of physiological responses (e.g. increased heart rate, faster respiration, pupil dilation) produced by the sympathetic nervous system that helps mobilise the body's resources to threat or the presence of danger.

Follicle stimulating hormone A hormone released by the anterior pituitary gland that causes maturation of the ovarian follicle and the secretion of oestrogen and progesterone.

Forebrain A term that refers to all of the brain tissue lying above midbrain, including hypothalamus, thalamus, basal ganglia, limbic system and neocortex.

Fornix A long arching fibre tract, containing in the region of 1.2 million axons, that extends from the hippocampus to the mammillary bodies, anterior nucleus of the thalamus and hypothalamus.

Fovea A pit in the centre of the retina containing colour-sensitive cones, and where visual acuity is at its greatest.

Free nerve ending Small-diameter nerve endings (also known as naked endings) which act as pain receptors in the skin.

Free radicals Highly reactive and short-lasting breakdown products of oxygen which contain an unpaired outer electron. They are believed to be involved in ageing and certain types of degenerative disease.

Frequency theory The theory that pitch is encoded by the pattern of deformity over the basilar membrane.

Frontal cortex The front portion of the cerebral cortex that contains several important anatomical areas including the orbitofrontal and dorsolateral regions, Broca's area and primary motor cortex.

Frontal–temporal dementia A form of dementia affecting the frontal and temporal lobes whose main pathological feature is large amounts of neurofibrillary tangles.

G

GABA The abbreviation for gamma-aminobutyric acid – an amino acid neurotransmitter that is probably the most common inhibitory substance in the central nervous system.

Gamete A reproductive cell – namely the sperm or ovum – that contains 23 individual (not paired) chromosomes.

Gamma motor neuron A nerve cell, located in the ventral horn of the spinal cord, that innervates muscle spindles.

Ganglion cells Neurons whose cell bodies are found in the retina and whose axons give rise to the optic nerve.

Gate control theory of pain A theory proposed by Melzack and Wall which views pain as being modified by a gate mechanism located in the spinal cord, whose functioning can also be modified by brain activity.

Genes A long sequence of paired bases found in DNA that contain various codons, and which acts as a functional unit to make one or more proteins.

Genetic engineering A group of techniques, including the formation of transgenic animals, that involves altering the natural state of an organism's genome.

Gigantocellular tegmental field An area of the medullary reticular formation which contains large neurons and whose axons innervate the thalamus and cerebral cortex.

Glial cells The supporting cells of the central nervous system that also help maintain the functioning of neurons. In the brain these consist of astrocytes, oligodendrocytes and microglial cells.

Globus pallidus Part of the basal ganglia which receives input from the striatum and whose predominate output goes to the ventral lateral nucleus of the thalamus.

Glossopharyngeal nerve Also known as cranial nerve IX. It conveys taste information from the posterior part of the tongue.

Glucagon A hormone released by the pancreas gland which acts on the liver to convert glycogen into glucose.

Glutamate An amino acid which is the major excitatory neurotransmitter in the central nervous system.

Glycogen A stored form of sugar, found mainly in the liver, which can be converted into glucose by the pancreatic hormone glucagon.

Gonad The primary reproductive organ, namely the ovaries or testis.

Gonadotropin-releasing hormone A releasing factor secreted by the hypothalamus which acts on the anterior pituitary gland to help secrete luteinising hormone and follicle stimulating hormone.

G-protein A type of protein, found attached to metabotrpoc receptors, which activates a cascade of proteins inside the cell, including the formation of cAMP (a second messenger) in some neurons.

Growth hormone A hormone produced by the anterior pituitary which stimulates growth during development. It is also secreted in adults, reaching its peak about an hour after falling asleep.

Gyri The raised ridges of the cerebral cortex (the fissures between the gyri are called sulci) which can also provide helpful landmarks in the identification of various cortical areas.

H

Hebbian synapse A hypothetical synapse that is strengthened every time a presynaptic and postsynaptic neuron fire together, and believed to be an important mechanism in the neural basis of learning and memory.

Hemiplegia Paralysis or loss of muscle tone of one half of the body.

Hertz The number of wave cycles (or events) per second.

Heschl's gyrus Part of the temporal lobe that contains the primary auditory cortex.

5-HIAA A breakdown product of the neurotransmitter serotonin.

Hippocampus A central part of the limbic system located in the medial part of the temporal lobe consisting of folded primitive three-layered cortical tissue. The hippocampal formation consists of the subiculum, the hippocampus proper (Ammon's horn) and dentate gyrus, and is important in memory and emotion.

Histoflurescence techniques A type of histological technique which uses fluorescence to localise a wide variety of chemical substances in the central nervous system.

Homeostasis The requirement of the body to maintain a consistent internal environment, despite exposure to various chemical changes and external fluctuations.

Homovanillic acid (HVA) A breakdown (metabolite) product of dopamine that is found in the cerbrospinal fluid.

Horizontal cells A type of neuron found in the retina that makes lateral connections between photoreceptors (rods and cones) and bipolar cells.

Hormone A term generally used to refer to substances synthesised and secreted by endocrine glands, and transported in the blood to their target of action.

Human Genome Project An international research project begun in 1990 and completed in 2003 which mapped the 3,000 million or so base pairs that make up the human genome (i.e. our 23 pairs of chromosomes).

Huntingtin The protein produced by the gene that is responsible for causing Huntington's disease.

Huntington's disease An autosomal dominant disorder (if a person inherits the faulty gene they will inherit the disorder) which typically leads to degeneration of the basal ganglia in middle age. It is now known to be caused by a excess number of the triple base CAG repeats on a small part of chromosome 4.

6-Hydroxydopamine A chemical neurotoxin that is selective for destroying neurons containing catecholamine (dopamine and noradrenaline).

Hypercolumn A cubic region of the primary visual cortex that comprises both orientation dominance columns and all possible orientation columns for a particular portion of the visual field.

Hypercomplex cell A type of neuron found in the visual cortex that has functional properties similar to a complex cell (i.e. it fires when a line is presented in its visual field that is positioned in a highly specific orientation), except now the stimulus has to be of a certain length.

Hyperplagia Excessive eating and weight gain. As seen, for example, following lesions of the ventromedial hypothalamus.

Hypothalamic–pituitary–adrenal axis The system in which the hypothalamus secretes corticotropin-releasing factor (CRF) into the anterior pituitary gland, which in turn secretes adrenocorticotropic hormone (ACTH) into the blood, which stimulates the adrenal cortex to release glucocorticoids such as cortisol.

Hypothalamus A small collection of various nuclei lying just below the thalamus, which governs a wide range of homeostatic processes and species-typical behaviours. The hypothalamus is also involved in the regulation of the autonomic nervous system and exerts control over the secretion of hormones from the pituitary gland.

Implicit memory A type of memory which involves no explicit or conscious intention to learn or memorise.

Inbreeding A way of producing different strains of animals, usually by brother–sister matings over several generations. This tends to produce genetically stable strains as it increases the chances of developing homozygous (identical) alleles.

Inferior colliculi Small protrusions found near the upper surface of the midbrain that relay auditory information to the medial geniculate nucleus.

Inhibitory postsynaptic potential A small change in the electrical potential of a neuron towards a negative direction, produced by inhibitory neurotransmitters, that decreases the likelihood of an action potential.

Insulin A hormone released by the pancreas gland that enables glucose (and amino acids) to enter the cells of the body. It plays a particularly important role in allowing nutrients to be quickly stored immediately following a meal.

Interneuron Typically a neuron with a short axonal process that is located within a given nucleus or structure.

Interstitial nuclei of the anterior hypothalamus Four small cell groups (INAH 1–4) located in the anterior hypothalamus which are believed to be involved in sexual behaviour. In particular, INAH 2 and 3 have been shown to be larger in the male.

Inverse agonist A drug that produces a neurochemical or behavioural effect opposite to that of a normal agonist.

Ion channel A specialised protein complex in the plasma membrane of neurons that allows certain ions (most notably sodium, potassium and calcium) to pass into the cell. Ion channels can be *voltage dependent* (i.e. they open when the membrane potential reaches a certain level), or *neurotransmitter dependent* (i.e. they open when neurotransmitter activates the cell).

Ionotropic receptor A receptor complex where the binding site for a neurotransmitter and the ion channel form part of the same unit (e.g. the GABA receptor). Thus, activation of the receptor leads directly to a configurational change in the shape of the channel that allows ions to pass through. This contrasts with metabotropic receptors which require the mediation of second messengers to open ion channels.

Iris The ring of muscles that control the opening of the pupil and which gives the eyes their colour.

K

Klinefelter's syndrome A genetic condition where males inherit an extra X chromosome (YXX) resulting in increased feminisation.

Korsakoff's syndrome A syndrome whose main feature is anterograde amnesia, due to thiamine deficiency brought on by chronic alcoholism. It appears to be associated with damage to the mammillary bodies and dorsomedial thalamus.

Kuru A form of transmissible dementia which was first discovered in cannibals living in New Guinea by Carleton Gajdusek.

L

Lateral geniculate nucleus A region within the thalamus that receives fibres from the optic nerve and projects to the primary visual cortex.

Lateral hypothalamus A region of the hypothalamus that has been implicated in a wide range of behaviours, including eating, drinking, aggression, movement, sexual behaviour and attention.

Lateral superior olive Located in the medulla, it receives auditory information from both ears. Important for locating a sound source.

L-Dopa A dopamine precursor that is able to cross the blood–brain barrier and provide a successful drug treatment for Parkinson's disease, which is due to degeneration of the nigral–striatal pathway and dopamine deficiency in the striatum.

Lens A transparent structure in the eye, just behind the pupil, which helps to focus visual images onto the retina.

Leptin A substance manufactured and secreted by adipocytes that communicates to the brain how much fat is being stored. It also appears to suppress food intake.

Lesioning technique A surgical technique, often involving a *stereotaxic apparatus*, where parts of the central nervous system are either removed or destroyed using electrical or chemical means.

Leydig cells The cells in the testes that produce testosterone.

Limbic system A group of interconnected brain regions that include an arc of phylogenetically old cortex on the basal surface of the neocortex, and several other regions including hippocampus, amygdala, fornix, mammallary bodies, hypothalamus and anterior thalamus.

Lithium An element that contains only three electrodes, which means it normally exists in the form of positive ions (i.e. it easily loses its outer electron). It is used in psychiatry as a treatment for bipolar illness.

Locus coeruleus A dark blue pigmented nucleus in the pons region of the brainstem which is the main origin of noradrenaline-containing neurons in the forebrain.

Long-term potentiation A stable and enduring increase in the excitability of a neuron due to its repeated activation by high-frequency stimulation. It is believed to underlie the neural basis of learning and memory.

Lordosis A female reproductive posture, observed in many four-legged mammals, in which the hindquarters are wriggled and raised, and tail turned to one side, thereby facilitating the act of copulation.

Luteinising hormone A hormone released by the anterior pituitary gland that in females causes ovulation (the release of the egg from the ovary) and the development of the follicle into a corpus luteum. In males, luteinising hormone stimulates the Leydig cells to produce testosterone.

M

Magnetic resonance imaging (MRI) A non-invasive scanning technique that measures the magnetic resonance of hydrogen atoms in the brain (induced by a strong magnetic field and radio waves) to build up a detailed three-dimensional image of brain structure.

Magnocellular cells Large neurons found in the bottom two layers of the lateral geniculate nucleus that process information about form, spatial relationships and motion.

Mammillary bodies Two nuclei located in the posterior region of the hypothalamus which receives a large input from the hippocampus via the fornix.

Mass action A term used by Karl Lashley to refer to the capacity of the cerebral cortex to store memories throughout its structure.

Mechanoreceptor A receptor whose primary function is to detect stretching and pressure movements of the skin.

Medial forebrain bundle A large bundle of fibres that courses through the hypothalamus and interconnects regions of the forebrain with midbrain.

Medial frontal cortex The region of the prefrontal cortex that lies adjacent to the cingulate gyrus.

Medial geniculate bodies A region of the thalamus that receives information from the inferior colliculus and sends output to the auditory cortex located in the temporal lobe.

Medial hypothalamus The medial area of the hypothalamus which contains several important regions, including ventromedial, dorsolateral and arcuate (infundular) nuclei. This part of the hypothalamus appears to be important in feeding, emotion and aggression.

Medial preoptic area An area of the anterior hypothalamus implicated in many behaviours, including sexual behaviour, temperature regulation and sleep.

Medial septum A nucleus found in the limbic system (close to the hypothalamus) which sends cholinergic fibres into the hippocampus.

Medial superior olive Located in the medulla, it receives auditory information from both ears. Important for locating a sound source.

Medial temporal lobes Includes the amygdala and adjacent cortex (the uncus), the hippocampus and adjacent cortex (subiculum, entorhinal cortex and perirhinal cortex), and the fusiform gyrus.

Medulla oblongata The part of the brainstem which emerges from the spinal cord. It is the origin of several cranial nerves, and contains centres for vital functions such as respiration, sneezing, vomiting and swallowing.

Melatonin The hormone released by the pineal gland and believed to be important in the regulation of the body's circadian rhythms.

Mesofrontal dopamine pathway The dopamine projection arising predominantly from the ventral tegmental area that goes to the frontal cortex.

Mesolimbic dopamine pathway The dopamine projection arising predominantly from the ventral tegmental area that goes to the limbic system including the nucleus accumbens.

Mesostriatal dopamine pathway Another name for the nigrial–striatal pathway which passes from the substantia nigra to the striatum.

Messenger RNA (mRNA) A single-stranded nucleic acid that transcribes the genetic message from DNA and transports it into the cytoplasm for protein synthesis.

Metabotropic receptor A receptor linked to a G-protein just inside the cell, which in turn sets into motion a number of chemical events (including the activation of second messengers) leading to protein phosphorylation (i.e. opening) of certain ion channels.

MHPG The main breakdown (metabolite) product of noradrenaline found in the cerbrospinal fluid. Otherwise known as 3-methoxy-4-hydroxyphenylglycol.

Microglia Glial cells that act as phagocytes (part of the immune system) in the central nervous system.

Millisecond One-thousandth of a second.

Millivolt One-thousandth of a volt.

Mitochondria Organelles in the cytoplasm of the cell responsible for generating adenosine triphosphate (ATP) which is used as energy to drive a wide variety of chemical reactions.

Mitral cell A specialised cell found in the olfactory bulb.

Molecular biology The branch of biology concerned with the synthesis, structure and function of molecules necessary for life.

Monoamine A class of neurotransmitters that contain an amine in their chemical structure; it includes serotonin, dopamine and noradrenaline.

Monoamine oxidase (MAO) An enzyme found in neurons and glial cells that breaks down and inactivates monoamine neurotransmitters.

Monoamine oxidase inhibitors Substances that inhibit the action of monoamine oxidase, thereby increasing the amount of monoamines in the synapse. These drugs have been shown to be effective antidepressants.

Monoamine theory of depression The hypothesis that depression is due to a synaptic deficiency, or underactivity, of one or more monoamines in the brain (especially noradrenaline and/or serotonin).

Monozygotic twins Genetically identical twins who derive from the same egg.

Morris water maze A large tank of water, filled with an opaque substance, containing a small platform hidden just below the surface. Since the platform cannot be directly observed, animals placed into the water have to use spatial knowledge to locate its whereabouts. Rats with hippocampal lesions are poor at performing this task.

Motor aphasia A disorder in which the person is unable to make the correct movements of the mouth and tongue to articulate words. This type of deficit is associated with Broca's aphasia.

Motor cortex The region of the cerebral cortex, located in the precentral gyrus of the posterior frontal cortex, which is topographically organised and sends its fibres into the corticospinal tracts to produce voluntary muscle movement.

Motor endplate The specialised site on a muscle fibre which receives input from a motor nerve ending.

MRI *See* Magnetic resonance imaging.

Mullerian duct A primitive duct in the embryo that has the potential to develop into the female reproductive organs (fallopian tubes, uterus and upper vagina).

Muscle fibres A collection of individual, long, cylindrical muscle cells, enclosed by an outer membrane called the sarcolemma, that make up skeletal muscle.

Muscle spindles Long, thin, fibrous capsules that lie embedded between muscle cells, which provide information about stretching to neurons located in the spinal cord.

Myelin The fatty sheath that covers and insulates the axon produced by the extensions of certain glial cells (oligodendroglia in the central nervous system, and Schwann cells in the peripheral nervous system).

Myofibrils Small, thin fibres within individual muscle cells, made up of short segments called sarcomeres, which contain fine filaments of actin and myosin.

Myosin A protein found in the myofibrils of muscle cells that slides over actin to cause muscle contraction.

 N

Naloxone An opiate antagonist.

Narcolepsy A condition where the person is overcome by sudden bouts of intense sleep typically accompanied by loss of muscle tone (cataplexy) that can last between 5 and 30 minutes.

Natural selection The driving force behind evolution, sometimes referred to as the 'survival of the fittest', where the strongest organisms most adapted to their habitat will be the ones most likely to pass on genes to their offspring.

Negative feedback An important mechanism in homeostasis and many hormone systems. It refers to the process by which a physiological variable (e.g. body temperature) or hormone release reaches a sufficient level to turn off further activity (e.g. shivering) or secretion in that system.

Neocortex The most recently evolved part of the brain, consisting of six layers that form the 'crumpled' outer surface of the cerebral cortex.

Neuritic plaques Microscopic spherical discs composed largely of amyloid found in neurons; they are one of the defining pathological features of Alzheimer's disease.

Neuroanatomy The study of the anatomical structure of the nervous system, including its neural pathways and connections.

Neurofibrillary tangles Tangles of fine fibres (neuronal filaments) found in the cytoplasm (mainly cerebral cortex) which are a distinguishing feature of Alzheimer's disease.

Neuromodulator A chemical that alters the reactivity of the cell to a neurotransmitter.

Neuromuscular junction The synapse that exists between the alpha motor neuron and the motor endplate which uses acetylcholine as its neurotransmitter.

Neuron A specialised cell for generating and conducting electrical information, it forms the fundamental unit of the nervous system. Also called a nerve cell.

Neuropeptide Chemical messenger which is composed of amino acids and can be derived from larger proteins synthesised by neurons.

Neuropeptide Y A peptide believed to act as a neurotransmitter in the hypothalamus and involved in the regulation of feeding behaviour.

Neurophysiology The scientific discipline that attempts to understand the electrical properties of neurons.

Neuropsychology The discipline that attempts to localise functions to different regions of the human brain. Traditionally this pursuit has been undertaken with brain damaged individuals, although non-invasive scanning techniques are now being used to address similar questions.

Neuroscience A discipline which encompasses a broad range of fields concerned with the structure and functioning of neurons, including molecular and cell biology, anatomy, biochemistry, physiology and behaviour.

Neurotransmitter A chemical that is released by an axon terminal into a synapse following the arrival of an action potential, and which typically crosses the synapse to bind (attach itself) to receptors on a postsynaptic cell.

Nigral–striatal pathway Dopaminergic pathway that extends from the substantia nigra to the striatum; it shows marked degeneration in Parkinson's disease.

Nociceptor Another name for a pain receptor.

Node of Ranvier A small gap in the myelin sheath surrounding the axon, where the action potential is renewed by the process of saltatory conduction.

Noradrenaline (NA) A catecholaminergic neurotransmitter, also known as norepinephrine, found in the brain and the sympathetic division of the autonomic nervous system.

Nucleus accumbens An area of the brain sometimes called the ventral striatum that receives a dopaminergic projection from the ventral tegmentum which is importantly involved in reward and feelings of pleasure.

Nucleus of the solitary tract An area located in the medulla which receives information from the stomach, duodenum, liver and taste buds. Curiously, electrical stimulation of this area produces brain waves resembling those of slow-wave sleep.

Nucleus raphe magnus One of the raphe nuclei which has descending projections to the spinal cord and is involved in gate control of pain processing.

Obsessive–compulsive disorder An anxiety disorder where the person is afflicted with uncontrollable thoughts (obsessions) and engages in seemingly senseless rituals (compulsions).

Occipital cortex The most posterior part of the cerebral cortex that is also sometimes called the visual cortex.

Ocular apraxia An inability to voluntarily shift attention to a new visual stimulus. It is one of the main features of Balint's syndrome and associated with damage to occipital–parietal regions of the brain.

Olfactory bulb The first area of the brain to receive olfactory information from the nose.

Olfactory epithelium A layer of tissue in the nasal cavity containing olfactory receptors.

Olfactory glomeruli Cell complexes in the olfactory bulb which appaer to receive information about a certain type of smell.

Olfatory tract The main pathway arising from the olfactory bulb which forms the lateral and medial olfactory stria.

Oligodendroglia A type of glial cell which may have dozens of branches (*oligodendro* is Greek for 'tree with few branches') that wrap around axons to form the myelin sheath.

Opiate A drug with similar properties to opium, including morphine and heroin. The central nervous system also produces opiate-like peptides sometimes called endogenous endorphins.

Optic ataxia The inability to accurately point to a target under visual guidance. Along with ocular apraxia and simultanagnosia it is a feature of Balint's syndrome.

Optic chiasm The point on the underside of the brain, just anterior to the pituitary gland, where the two optic nerves join, and where the majority of fibres cross to the opposite side of the brain.

Optic radiations The axon fibres that project from the dorsal lateral geniculate region of the thalamus to the primary visual cortex.

Orbitofrontal region The part of the prefrontal cortex that lies above the eyes and that receives information from the dorsomedial thalamus.

Orexins A group of proteins formed in the hypothalamus known to be involved in feeding, and also found in projections to the brainstem where they have been implicated in narcolepsy.

Organ of Corti A structure containing specialised sensory hairs forming part of the basilar membrane that turns sound into neural impulses.

Oscillopsia A condition caused by damage to the vestibular nucleus where the person has difficulty fixating on visual targets.

Otolith organs Structures of the inner ear (also known as the utricle and saccule) which convey information about head movement to the brain.

Oval window The part of the cochlea which is hit by the small bone called stapes to transmit sound.

Ovulation The monthly process in which a mature ovum (egg) is released by the ovaries into the upper fallopian tubes. At this point fertilisation can occur if the ovum is impregnated by a sperm cell.

P

Pancreas gland An endocrine gland located posterior to the stomach, with its head tucked into the curve of the duodenum, which releases insulin and glucagon.

Papez circuit A brain circuit connecting the hippocampus with the hypothalamus, thalamus and cingulate gyrus, first described by James Papez in 1937. Believed to be important in memory formation and emotional behaviour.

Parahippocampal gyrus A region of the limbic cortex adjacent to the hippocampus which is in essence a continuation of the cingulate gyrus.

Parasympathetic nervous system A major branch of the autonomic nervous system (along with the sympathetic nervous system) whose main function is to conserve and restore the body's resources (i.e. reduce arousal).

Parietal lobe The part of the cerebral cortex directly behind the central fissure (i.e. the frontal lobe) and above the Sylvian fissure (i.e. temporal lobe).

Parkinson's disease A brain disorder caused by degeneration of cells in the substantia nigra leading to poverty of movement, tremor and rigidity.

Parvocellular cells Neurons found in the top four layers of the lateral geniculate nucleus that process information about colour and fine detail for object recognition.

Patellar tendon reflex A diagnostic reflex in which the tapping of the patellar tendon produces contraction of the quadriceps femoris muscle.

Periamygdaloid cortex Part of 'old' cortex close to the amygdala and a higher site for the processing of olfactory information.

Periaqueductal grey area The area that surrounds the cerebral aqueduct in the midbrain. It is the major centre through which the hypothalamus enacts behaviours critical to the survival of the self and of the species.

Peripheral nervous system All the nerves and neurons beyond the brain and spinal cord, including the autonomic nervous system and somatic nervous system.

Perirhinal cortex A region of the limbic cortex adjacent to the hippocampus.

PGO waves An abbreviation for pons–geniculate–occipital waves – a distinctive burst of electrical activity, originating in the pons and passing to the visual cortex via the thalamus, which is a characteristic of REM sleep.

Pharmacology The study of how drugs work on the body.

Phenylketonuria A hereditary disorder that can lead to brain damage due to a recessive gene which causes the absence of phenylalanine hydroxylase (an enzyme that converts phenylalanine into tyrosine).

Physiology The study of how the body and its parts function.

Pineal gland A small gland situated in the epithalamus, once thought by Descartes to be the seat of the soul, but now known to secrete the hormone melatonin which is involved in the regulation of circadian rhythms.

Pinna The fleshy part of the ear.

Piriform cortex Part of the primary olfactory cortex.

Pituitary gland An endocrine gland connected to the hypothalamus consisting of two lobes: the adrenohypophysis containing many secretory cells, and the posterior neurohypophysis containing many nerve endings.

Place cells Neurons found in the hippocampus that become highly active when the animal is in a particular location. They appear to be important for spatial navigation and forming a cognitive map of the environment.

Place theory The theory first proposed by Helmholtz that the site where sound deforms the basilar membrane determines what we hear.

Planum temporale A region of the temporal lobe that is part of Wernicke's area lying adjacent to the primary auditory cortex, which is generally found to be larger on the left side of the brain. Abnormalities in this region have been found in some people with dyslexia.

Pons The region of the brainstem above the medulla and lying below the midbrain. It contains a number of important nuclei, including the locus coeruleus and the raphe.

Pontine nucleus A large nucleus found in the pons which receives motor input from the cerebral cortex, and sends projections to the cerebellum.

Positron emission tomography (PET) A non-invasive technique for examining brain function in humans that measures the brain's metabolic activity by use of short-lasting radioactive substances (usually 2-deoxyglucose) which emit subatomic particles called positrons.

Prefrontal cortex The most anterior region of the frontal lobes consisting of association cortex which receives input from the mediodorsal thalamus.

Premotor area An area of the cerebral cortex located just in front of the primary motor cortex and involved in the selection of movements.

Preoptic-basal forebrain A region of the brain lying just anterior to the optic chiasm. It is normally considered part of the hypothalamus although embryologically it is derived from different tissue.

Presinilins Genes which have been linked to early onset Alzheimer's disease.

Primary auditory cortex The first region of the cerebral cortex, located in the temporal lobes, which receives auditory information (via projections from the medial geniculate body of the thalamus).

Primary gustatory cortex An area located deep in the lateral fissure close to the somatosensory cortex and responsible for the higher processing of taste.

Primary motor cortex A band of tissue located in the precentral gyrus of the frontal lobe, that sends fibres into the corticospinal tracts and is important for voluntary movement.

Primary olfactory cortex An 'old' area of the temporal lobe involved in the processing of smell and consisting of several regions, including piriform and peri-amygdaloid cortex.

Primary somatosensory cortex A band of tissue in the parietal lobes, adjacent to the primary motor cortex, which receives touch, pain and temperature information. It is particularly important for receiving motor feedback from the body.

Primary visual cortex An area in the occipital lobes, in the vicinity of the calcarine fissure, which receives visual information (via projections from the lateral geniculate body of the thalamus).

Prion A protein that is capable of self-replication and able to act as an infectious agent; it is responsible for several types of dementia.

Procedural memory A type of implicit memory that is 'remembered' when an individual performs an action (sometimes described as 'knowing how' memory). Unlike declarative memory, it appears to be unaffected by damage to the hippocampus.

Proprioceptive senses Sense information from the joints and muscles.

Prosopagnosia The inability to identify people by the sight of their face, although other features such as their voice can be recognised.

Protanopia An inherited form of colour blindness in which red and green are confused. This is due to the cones coding for red frequencies of light being filled with green opsin.

Proteins A class of large molecules composed of smaller chains of amino acids that have a wide range of functions in the body and are vital for life. The DNA in a cell determines what proteins will be synthesised.

Proteosomes A type of enzyme that breaks down amino acids and proteins.

Psychiatry The branch of medicine concerned with the understanding and treatment of mental illness.

Psychosurgery The use of brain surgery to remedy mental health problems such as depression or compulsive behaviours in the absence of any identifiable brain damage.

Pulvinar region A large thalamic nucleus overhanging the superior colliculus and geniculate bodies. It is believed to have a role in vision and possibly also speech.

Pupil The aperture that controls the amount of light entering the eye.

Putamen A large nucleus that, along with the caudate, forms the neostriatum. It is an important component of the basal ganglia, receiving dopaminergic input from the substantia nigra, and glutamatic input from cerebral cortex.

Pyramidal system A large system of fibres originating in the motor regions of the cerebral cortex which form the pyramidal tracts that project to the spinal cord. Also known as the corticospinal tract.

R

Radioligand binding A technique that is able to identify and measure the amount of neurochemical receptors. A ligand (i.e. a chemical known to bind to the receptor in question) is radioactively labelled and incubated with the tissue. The unbound ligand is then washed away, and the radioactivity from the bound ligand left in the tissue is measured.

Raphe nuclei A group of nuclei located in the reticular formation of the medulla, pons and midbrain. Of particular importance are the dorsal and median raphe which together account for about 80 per cent of the serotonin found in the forebrain.

Rapid eye movement (REM) sleep A stage of sleep characterised by small-amplitude, fast EEG waves, lack of muscle tone, and rapid eye movements. It is also the stage of sleep in which we normally dream.

Receptive field The region where a stimulus causes the maximal response of a cell in a sensory system. In vision, this area is part of the visual field, whereas in touch this area may be mechanical pressure on a receptor or nerve ending.

Receptor In this book, a receptor refers to a specialised protein molecule found in the membrane of a neuron that is sensitive to a specific neurochemical. In turn, the binding of a substance at a postsynaptic cell typically causes small changes in its electrical potential. There are two types of receptor: ionotropic and metabotropic.

Recessive gene A gene that does not express its characteristics unless it is present in 'double dose', that is, unless a copy is inherited from both parents.

Recombinant DNA (rDNA) Genetic material made outside the living cell by splicing two or more pieces of DNA from different sources to create a combination of genes not normally found in nature.

Red nucleus A large nucleus located in the midbrain tegmentum that receives inputs from the cerebellum and motor areas of the cerebral cortex, and which in turn sends axons to the spinal cord via the rubrospinal tract.

Reflex A stereotyped, predictable and involuntary movement to a stimulus.

Refractory period A period of a few milliseconds during and after a nerve impulse, in which the responsiveness of a neuron is reduced and unable to generate another impulse.

Regional blood flow (RBF) A technique which measures the flow of blood to various areas of the brain (e.g. by monitoring radioactive water or xenon-133). It is based on the assumption that the greater the rate of blood flow to an area, the more active that region will be.

Resting potential The membrane potential of a neuron when it is at rest and not being altered by excitatory or inhibitory postsynaptic potentials. The resting potential inside a neuron is generally around -70 mV compared with its outside.

Restriction enzymes A group of enzymes that can cut strands of DNA at specific points or base sequences. They can be likened to molecular scissors.

Reticular activating system A diverse group of cells in the reticular formation that project to the thalamus, which in turn project to widespread areas of the cerebral cortex. It is believed that this system is responsible for keeping us awake and regulating sleep–wake cycles.

Reticular formation A highly complex network of dispersed nuclei and fibre tracts which extend throughout the core of the brainstem to the thalamus. It is involved in a wide range of functions, including those that are vital for life.

Retina A layer of cells located at the back of the eye that contains the photoreceptors (rods and cones) which transduce light into neural information.

Retrograde amnesia An impairment of memory for information that was acquired prior to the onset of amnesia. This contrasts with *anterograde amnesia* which is abnormal memory loss that occurs after the onset of amnesia.

Reuptake pump A special transporter protein generally found in the membrane of presynaptic neurons that rapidly removes neurotransmitter from the synapse.

Ribonucleic acid (RNA) A single-stranded nucleic acid that contains the sugar ribose. There are three main types of RNA (messenger, transfer and ribosomal), all of which are involved in protein synthesis.

Ribosomes Spherical structures found in the cytoplasm of the cell, sometimes likened to workbenches, where the production of proteins takes place.

Rods The most common type of photoreceptor found in the retina; they are very sensitive to changes in light intensity.

Rubrospinal tract The pathway from the red nucleus to the spinal cord which has an important role in the movement of the limbs.

S

Saccadic eye movements Involuntary, rapid and small movements of the eyes that are used to monitor our visual surroundings.

Saltatory conduction The means by which the action potential is propagated down the axon. In effect, this occurs by the action potential 'jumping' from one node of Ranvier (small gap in the myelin) to the next, where it is amplified back to its original intensity.

Scala media The 'middle tube' of the cochlea which contains the hairs of the basilar membrane.

Scala tympani A canal connected to the scala vestibuli in the cochlea.

Scala vestibuli The first part of the cochlea to receive auditory input.

Schizophrenia A severe mental illness (or psychosis) which is typically characterised by hallucinations, delusions, incoherent thought, paranoia and emotional withdrawal.

Sclera The outer tough white material that covers most of the eyeball.

Seasonal affective disorder An affective disorder in which the individual becomes regularly depressed during the winter months. It is also characterised by lethargy, sleep disturbances and carbohydrate cravings.

Second messenger A chemical (such as cAMP) found in the cytoplasm that is activated when a neurotransmitter binds to a G-protein-linked receptor (i.e. metabotropic receptor), which then causes protein phosphorylation (i.e. the opening) of ion channels.

Secretases Enzymes that are involved in breaking down proteins.

Selective breeding The breeding of animals that have been selected for a particular trait (e.g. alcohol consumption). The successive breeding of such animals over several generations can produce strains with distinct behavioural characteristics.

Semicircular canals A group of three looping chambers in the inner ear whose main function is to relay information regarding rotational movement of the head to the brain.

Sensory-specific satiety The tendency to get bored eating one type of food if consumed over a long period.

Septum A structure in the limbic system which has reciprocal connections with the hippocampus, amygdala and hypothalamus.

Serotonin A monoamine neurotransmitter, also called 5-hydroxytryptamine (5-HT), which is implicated in a wide range of functions.

Serotonin uptake blocker A class of drug that includes fluoxetine (Prozac) which selectively blocks the reuptake of serotonin from the synaptic cleft.

Sexually dimorphic nucleus A nucleus found in the preoptic area (i.e. anterior hypothalamus) that is much larger in males than in females.

Simultanagnosia An inability to perceive different aspects of a visual scene. Although individual elements may be identified, the person will not be able to perceive the scene as a whole. This is one of the main symptoms of Balint's syndrome.

Sleep apnoea A disorder where breathing is frequently and temporarily suspended during sleep, which results in the person waking.

Sleep cycle A cycle of four slow-wave sleep stages (SWS 1–4) that progresses from predominantly theta activity (4–7 Hz) to delta activity (1–4 Hz), followed by a period of REM sleep. Each sleep cycle lasts approximately 90 minutes.

Slow pain Dull and diffuse pain associated with activation of C fibres

Slow-wave sleep Sleep that is characterised by slower EEG brain waves (e.g. 1–7 Hz) than is found in waking where beta (13–30 Hz) and alpha activity (8–12 Hz) predominate.

Sodium–potassium pump A transport mechanism within the plasma membrane of a neuron that regulates the concentration of sodium and potassium ions inside and outside the neuron. It removes approximately three sodium ions from the neuron for every two potassium ions it takes back in.

Solitary nucleus Located in the medulla, this structure receives sensory information from the tongue and mouth.

Soma Another term for the cell body (from the Greek for 'body').

Somatic nervous system A division of the peripheral nervous system that controls skeletal muscles, and which also sends sensory input from skin, muscle, tendons, joints etc. to the spinal cord and brain.

Somatosensory cortex The part of the cerebral cortex (located in the post-central gyrus) which receives somatosensory (cutaneous and proprioceptive) information from the body.

Spinoreticular tract The part of the anterolateral pathway conveying pain and temperature information from spinal cord to reticular formation.

Spinotectal tract The part of the anterolateral pathway conveying pain and temperature information from spinal cord to upper brainstem (tectum).

Spinothalamic tract The part of the anterolateral pathway conveying pain and temperature information from spinal cord to the thalamus.

Splenium The rear part of the corpus callosum which transfers visual information between the hemispheres.

Split-brain procedure A surgical operation called a commissurotomy in which the corpus callosum is cut, thereby severing direct communication between the two hemispheres of the brain. This procedure has shown that the left hemisphere tends to be dominant for language, and the right hemisphere more dominant for emotion and spatial reasoning.

Spongiform encephalopathy A type of neural degeneration which gives the brain an appearance of a sponge.

Stem cells Embryologically early and undifferentiated cells from which other types of cell, including neurons, can be derived.

Stereochemical theory of olfaction The theory that there are different types of olfactory receptor which distinguish between smells.

Striate cortex Another term for the primary visual cortex, so called because it has a striped (i.e. striated) appearance.

Striated muscle Another term for skeletal muscle.

Striatum Part of the basal ganglia that is composed of the caudate nucleus and putamen, so called because of its striped appearance.

Subcortical dementia A form of dementia which affects primarily the striatum and is generally less severe than Alzheimer's disease.

Subiculum An area of limbic cortex in the parahippocampal gyrus that contributes to the hippocampal formation.

Substantia gelatinosa An area of the spinal cord containing cell bodies and interneurons.

Substantia nigra A dark pigmented nucleus found in the midbrain tegmentum which sends dopaminergic fibres to the striatum, and is known to show marked degeneration in Parkinson's disease.

Subthalamus A nucleus involved in motor behaviour that lies below the thalamus. It receives input from the striatum, and sends fibres to the globus palladus and substantia nigra.

Summation The combined accumulation of excitatory and inhibitory inputs impinging on a neuron. If the summation of inputs is sufficient to shift the resting potential of a neuron by about +15 mV at the axon hillock an action potential will be formed.

Superior cervical ganglion A large branch of the sympathetic nervous system that includes input from the suprachiasmatic nucleus that projects to the pineal gland.

Superior colliculi Bump-like protrusions in the roof of the midbrain which receive a projection from the optic nerve, and are important in the orientation of the head and eyes.

Supplementary motor cortex Area of the frontal cortex that lies anterior and adjacent to the upper part of the primary motor cortex, and is important for the sequencing of goal-directed movements.

Suprachiasmatic nucleus A tiny nucleus lying just above the optic chiasm in the medial hypothalamus which acts as a biological clock and is important in the regulation of circadian rhythms.

Sympathetic nervous system A major branch of the autonomic nervous system (along with the parasympathetic nervous system) whose main function is to mobilise the body's resources for flight or fight (i.e. increase arousal).

Synapse A tiny gap or junction that most commonly lies between an axon terminal and the postsynaptic cell. Synapses are important sites of information processing in the brain.

Synaptic vesicles Protective sacs that store molecules of neurotransmitter in the endings of axons. These become bound with the membrane, leading to neurotransmitter release, through the process of exocytosis.

Tardive dyskinesia A disorder characterised by involuntary or tic-like movements, especially of the face, mouth and lips, associated with long-term use of antipsychotic medication.

Tau A protein that is found in neurofibrillary tangles.

Taurist A person who believes that neurofibrillary tangles are the main feature or cause of degeneration in Alzheimer's disease.

Tectorial membrane The boundary between the inner and middle ear, otherwise known as the ear drum.

Tectum The roof or most dorsal area of the midbrain that includes the inferior and superior colliculi.

Tegmentum The part of the midbrain (or upper brainstem) located beneath the tectum that contains ascending and descending tracts, the nuclei of various cranial nerves, and structures such as the red nucleus and substantia nigra.

Temporal lobe The area of the cerebral cortex lying below and lateral to the Sylvian fissure and parietal lobe.

Testicular feminisation syndrome Another term for androgen insensitivity syndrome, a disorder in which the body is insensitive to male sex hormones such as testosterone. Consequently, during foetal growth, genetic males with XY chromosomes develop as females.

Testis-determining factor A protein that binds to undifferentiated gonad tissue in the foetus, beginning at around six weeks, which causes them to become testes.

Testosterone The main sex hormone produced by the male gonads or testes. It has organisational effects on the body and central nervous system during foetal and pubertal development, and activational effects on certain types of behaviour in adulthood.

Tetrahydroisoquinolines Opiate-like substances that are formed by the metabolites of alcohol interacting with catecholamines in the brain.

Thalamus A symmetrical pair of ovoid structures located above the hypothalamus (separated by the third ventricle), made up of a large number of nuclei. The thalamus functions as the principle relay station for sensory information going to the cerebral cortex, and is crucially involved in regulating its electrical activity.

Thermoreceptors Receptors that detect temperature at low levels of activity and pain at higher intensities.

Threshold potential The increase in voltage (normally around +15 mV) that needs to be reached at the axon hillock for an action potential to be formed.

Tip links Fine filaments that can be displaced by the basilar membrane allowing ion flow into the cilia of the organ of Corti.

Tolerance Drug tolerance occurs when the repeated use of a substance leads to that agent producing less of an effect than it did originally – and may lead the individual to increase the dosage, leading to addiction. The reasons for drug tolerance are complex and include biological causes (pharmacokinetic and pharmacodynamic), as well as behavioural or learned causes.

Tourette's syndrome A disorder normally beginning in late childhood characterised by complex tic-like movements of the body and involuntary utterances of sounds and noises.

Transcription factor A chemical messenger that can enter the cell's nucleus and control the expression of its genes.

Transfer RNA (tRNA) The single-stranded nucleic acid that is responsible for bringing amino acids found in the cytoplasm to the ribosome for protein synthesis.

Transgenic animals Animals that have been genetically engineered or modified using DNA from another organism. These include, for example, knockout mice that have had genes inactivated or 'knocked out'.

Tricyclic antidepressants A class of antidepressant drug, which includes imipramine, that contains a three-ring chain in its molecular structure.

Turner's syndrome A genetic condition in which the female inherits only one X chromosome and does not develop functional ovaries.

Tympanic membrane The boundary between the inner and middle ear and otherwise known as the ear drum.

Tyramine An amino acid found in many foodstuffs and potentially a powerful elevator of blood pressure if not metabolised by monoamine oxidase.

Ubiquitin A protein that tags other proteins when they are ready to be destroyed or broken down by the cell.

Unipolar depression Chronic or acute major depression that does not alternate with periods of mania.

Vagus nerve The longest cranial nerve in the body, consisting of both sensory and motor divisions, innervating structures of the head, neck, thorax and abdomen.

Ventral tegmental area An area of the tegmentum which receives input from the medial forebrain bundle and is the main source of dopaminergic neurons to the forebrain, believed to be particularly important for arousal and reinforcement.

Ventricles The hollow spaces in the brain that contain cerebrospinal fluid.

Ventromedial hypothalamus A large nucleus in the hypothalamus which has been shown to be important in feeding and female sexual behaviour.

Vental acoustic stria A pathway ascending from the cochlea nucleus of the brainstem to superior olive complex.

Vestibular nerve The neural pathway that conveys information from the hair cells of the semicircular canals, and otolith organs, to the brain.

Vestibular nuclei A nucleus in the medulla which receives information from the vestibular nerve.

Vestibular system A fluid-filled set of chambers in the inner ear concerned primarily with balance.

Vestibule The entrance of the inner ear.

Vestibulo-ocular reflex A reflex that enables images on the retina to be stable as the head moves.

Viscera Another term for the main internal organs of the body.

Visual cortex A region of the occipital lobes, sometimes called the striate cortex, which receives visual input from the lateral geniculate nucleus.

Vitreous humour A clear gelatinous substance found in the chamber of the eyeball behind the lens.

Vomeronasal organ A sensory organ found in reptiles and most mammals (including humans) that responds to certain types of olfactory information, including pheromones.

Wada test A test invented by Juan Wada in the 1940s that anaesthetises one of the cerebral hemispheres by an injection of sodium amytal into the carotid artery (in the neck) leading to one side of the brain. This test showed that language functions tended to be lateralised to the left hemisphere, especially in people who were right handed.

Wernicke–Geschwind model A highly influential model of language which emphasises the passage of information through Wernicke's area, the arcuate fasciculus, and Broca's area in the comprehension and production of language.

Wernicke's aphasia A language impairment characterised by fluent and meaningless speech, and poor language comprehension.

Wernicke's area A region of auditory association cortex (temporal cortex) that is involved in language comprehension and the production of meaningful speech.

Wolffian duct A primitive duct in the embryo that has the potential to develop into the male reproductive organs (epididymis, vas deferens and seminal vesicles).

Working memory A form of short-term memory that is able to concurrently hold information while we process other information or perform a task.

Yakovlev circuit A brain circuit that includes the amygdala, dorsomedial thalamus and orbitofrontal cortex.

Z

Zeitgeber An environmental cue such as light that helps to reset a free-running circadian rhythm.

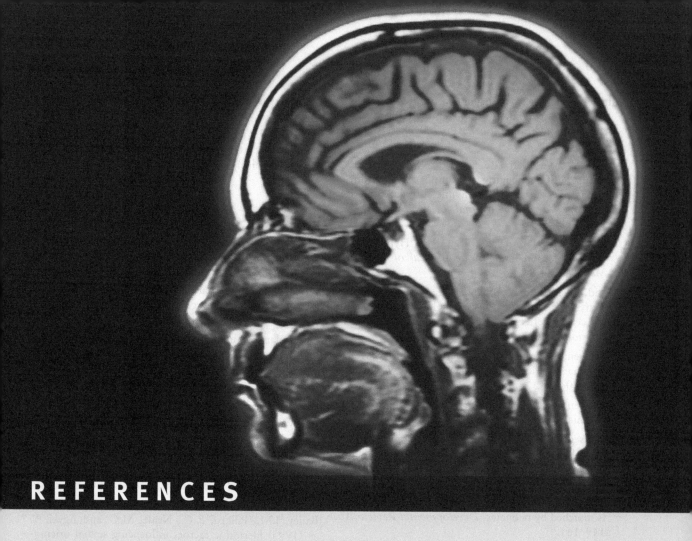

REFERENCES

A

Adam, K. and Oswald, I. (1977) Sleep for tissue restoration. *Journal of the Royal College of Physicians*, 11, 376–388.

Adkins-Regan, E. (1989) Sex hormones and sexual orientation in animals. *Psychobiology*, 16, 335–347.

Adolphs, R., Tranel, D., Damasio, H. and Damasio, A.R. (1994) Impaired recognition of emotion in facial expressions following bilateral damage to the human amygdala. *Nature*, 372, 669–672.

Adolphs, R., Cahill, L., Schul, R. and Babinsky, R. (1997) Impaired declarative memory for emotional material following bilateral amygdala damage in humans. *Learning and Memory*, 4, 291–230.

Aggleton, J.P. and Brown, M.B. (1999) Episodic memory, amnesia and the hippocampal–anterior thalamic axis. *Behavioral Brain Research*, 22, 425–489.

Aggleton, J.P., Bland, J.M., Kentridge, R.W. and Neave, N.J. (1994) Handedness and longevity: archival study of cricketers. *British Medical Journal*, 309, 1681–1684.

Aghajanian, G.K. (1978) Tolerance of locus coeruleus neurons to morphine and suppression of withdrawal response by clonidine. *Nature*, 276, 186–188.

Aghajanian, G.K., Foote, W.E. and Sheard, M.H. (1968) Lysergic acid diethylamide: sensitive neuronal units in the midbrain raphe. *Science*, 161, 706–708.

Agid, Y., Javoy-Agid, F. and Ruberg, M. (1987) Biochemistry of neurotransmitters in Parkinson's disease. In Marsden, C.D. and Fahn, S. (eds) *Movement Disorders* 2. London: Butterworths.

Alcaro, A., Huber, R. and Panksepp, J. (2007) Behavioral functions of the mesolimbic dopaminergic system: an affective neuroethological perspective. *Brain Research Reviews*, 56, 283–321.

Alexander, G.E., DeLong, M.R. and Strick, P.L. (1986) Parallel organization of functionally segregated circuits linking basal ganglia and cortex. *Annual Review of Neuroscience*, 9, 357–382.

Allee, W.C., Collias, N.E. and Lutherman, C.Z. (1939) Modification of the social order in flocks of hens by the injection of testosterone propionate. *Physiological Zoology*, 12, 412–440.

Allen, J.S. *et al.* (2003) Sexual dimorphism and asymmetries in the gray-white composition of the human cerebrum. *Neuroimage*, 8, 880–894.

Allen, L.S. and Gorki, R.A. (1992) Sexual orientation and the size of the anterior commissure in the human brain. *Proceedings of the National Academy of Sciences*, 89, 7199–7202.

Allen, L.S., Hines, M., Shryne, J.E. and Gorski, R.A. (1988) Two sexually dimorphic cell groups in the human brain. *Journal of Neuroscience*, 9, 497–506.

Anand, A., Verhoeff, P., Seneca, N. *et al.* (2000) Brain SPECT imaging of amphetamine-induced dopamine release in euthymic bipolar disorder patients. *American Journal of Psychiatry*, 157, 1108–1114.

Anand, B.K. and Brobeck, J.R. (1951) Hypothalamic control of food intake. *Yale Journal of Biological Medicine*, 24, 123–140.

Anand, B.K., Chhina, G.S., Sharma, K.N. *et al.* (1964) Activity of single neurons in the hypothalamic feeding centres: effects of glucose. *American Journal of Physiology*, 207, 1146–1154.

Andreasen, N.C. (1985) Positive vs negative schizophrenia: a critical evaluation. *Schizophrenia Bulletin*, 11, 380–389.

Andreasen, N.C. (1988) Brain imaging: applications in psychiatry. *Science*, 239, 1381–1388.

Andreasen, N.C., Nasrallah, H.A., Dunn, V. *et al.* (1986) Structural abnormalities in the frontal system in schizophrenia. *Archives of General Psychiatry*, 43, 136–144.

Anisfeld, M. (1996) Only tongue protrusion modelling is matched by neonates. *Developmental Review*, 16, 149–161.

Antelman, S.M., Szechtman, H., Chin, P. and Fisher, A.E. (1975) Tail pinch-induced eating, gnawing and licking behaviour in rats: dependence on the nigrostriatal dopamine system. *Brain Research*, 99, 319–337.

Archer, J. (1994) Testosterone and aggression. *Journal of Offender Rehabilitation*, 21, 3–26.

Arendt, J., Aldhous, J., English, V. *et al.* (1987) Some effects of jet-lag and their alleviation by melatonin. *Ergonomics*, 30, 1379–1393.

Arora, S. (2006) Role of neuropeptides in appetite regulation and obesity. *Neuropeptides*, 40, 375–401.

Asberg, M., Schalling, D., Träskman-Bendz, L. and Wagner, A. (1987) Psychobiology of suicide, impulsivity, and related phenomena. In Meltzer, H.M. (ed.) *Psychopharmacology: The Third Generation of Progress*. New York: Raven Press.

Aschoff, J. (1967) Comparative physiology: diurnal rhythms. *Annual Review of Physiology*, 25, 581–600.

Aserinsky, E. and Kleitman, N. (1953) Regularly occuring periods of eye motility and concomitant phenomena. *Science*, 118, 273–274.

Ashton, H. (1992) *Brain Function and Psychotropic Drugs*. Oxford: Oxford University Press.

Ashton, R. (2002) *This is Heroin*. London: Sanctuary House.

Ax, A. (1953) The physiological differentiation between fear and anger in humans. *Psychomatic Medicine*, 15, 433–442.

B

Backlund, E.-O., Granberg, P.-O., Hamberger, B. *et al.* (1985) Transplantation of adrenal medullary tissue to striatum in parkinsonism: first clinical trials. *Journal of Neurosurgery*, 62, 169–173.

Bae, B.I., Xu, H., Igarashi, S. *et al.* (2005) p53 mediates cellular dysfunction and behavioral abnormalities in Huntington's disease. *Neuron*, 47, 29–41.

Bailey, C.H. and Chen, M. (1983) Morphological basis of long-term habituation and sensitization in *Aplysia*. *Science*, 220, 91–93.

Bailey, C.H. and Chen, M. (1988) Morphological basis of short-term habituation in *Aplysia*. *Journal of Neuroscience*, 8, 2452–2459.

Bailey, J.M. and Pillard, R.C. (1991) A genetic study of male sexual orientation. *Archives of General Psychiatry*, 48, 1089–1096.

Bailey, J.M., Pillard, R.C., Neale, M.C. and Agyei, Y. (1993) Heritable factors influencing sexual orientation in women. *Archives of General Psychiatry*, 50, 217–223.

Baker, F. (1888) Anthropological notes on the human hand. *American Anthropologist*, 1, 51–76.

Ballenger, J.C., Goodwin, F.K., Major, L.F. and Brown, G.L. (1979) Alcohol and central serotonin metabolism in man. *Archives of General Psychiatry*, 36, 224–227.

Balon, R. (1997) Selective serotonergic reuptake inhibitors and sexual dysfunction. *Primary Psychiatry*. Sept, 28–33.

Bard, P. and Mountcastle, V.B. (1948) Some forebrain mechanisms involved in the expression of rage with special reference to suppression of angry behaviour. *Research Association into Research for Nervous Mental Disease*, 27, 362–404.

Bard, P. (1934) On emotional expression after decortication with some remarks on certain theoretical views. *Psychological Review*, 41, 309–329.

Barlow, H.B. (1982) David Hubel and Torten Wiesel: their contributions towards understanding the primary visual cortex. *Trends in Neurosciences*, 5, 145–152.

Baron-Cohen, S. *et al.* (1996) Synesthesia: Prevalence and similarity. *Perception*, 25, 1073–1080.

Baron-Cohen, S. and Harrison, J.E. (eds) (1997) *Synaesthesia: Classic and Contemporary Readings*. Oxford: Blackwell.

Barondes, S.H. (1993) *Molecules and Mental Illness*. New York: Scientific American Library.

Barr, C.E., Mednick, S.A. and Munk-Jørgensen, P. (1990) Exposure to influenza epidemics during gestation and adult schizophrenia. *Archives of General Psychiatry*, 47, 869–874.

Bartus, R.T., Dean III, R.L., Beer, B. and Lippa, A.S. (1982) The cholinergic hypothesis of geriatric memory dysfunction. *Science*, 217, 408–414.

Bastian, A., Mugnaini, E. and Thach, W. (1999) Cerebellum. In Zigmond, M., Bloom, F., Landis, S. *et al.* (eds) *Fundamental Neuroscience*. New York: Academic Press.

Baxter, L.R. (1995) Neuroimaging studies of human anxiety disorders. In Bloom, F. and Kupfer, J.R. (eds) *Psychopharmacology: The Fourth Generation of Progress*. New York: Raven Press.

Baylor, D.A. (1987) Photoreceptor signals and vision: Proctor Lecture. *Investigations in Opthalmology and Visual Science*, 28, 34–49.

Beach, F.A. (1940) Effects of cortical lesions upon the copulatory behavior of male rats. *Journal of Comparative Psychology*, 29, 193–239.

Beasley, C.M., Masica, D.N. and Potvin, J.H. (1992) Fluoxetine: a review of receptor and functional effects and their clinical implications. *Psychopharmacology*, 107, 1–10.

Beatty, W.W. (1992) Gonadal hormones and sex differences in nonreproductive behaviors. In Gerall, A.A., Moltz, H. and Ward, I.L. (eds) *Handbook of Behavioral Neurobiology*, Vol. 11: *Sexual Differentiation*. New York: Plenum Press.

Beaumont, G. (1991) The use of benzodiazepines in general practice. In Hindmarch, I., Beaumont, G., Brandon, S. and Leonard, B.E. (eds) *Benzodiazepines: Current Concepts*. Chichester: John Wiley.

Bechara, A., Damasio, H., Tranel, D. and Damasio, A.R. (1997) Deciding advantageously before knowing an advantageous strategy. *Science*, 275, 1293–1295.

Becker, J.B., Breedlove, S.M. and Crews, D. (eds) (1993) *Behavioral Endocrinolgy*. Cambridge, Mass.: MIT Press.

Beecher, H.K. (1959) *Measurements of Subjective Responses*. New York: Oxford University Press.

Bennett, D.A., Beckett, L.A., Murray, A.M. *et al.* (1996) Prevalence of parkinsonian signs and associated mortality in a community population of older people. *New England Journal of Medicine*, 334, 71–76.

Bennett, M.R. and Hacker, P.M.S. (2003) *Philosophical Foundations of Neuroscience*. Oxford: Blackwell.

Berenbaum, S.A. (2001) Cognitive function in congenital adrenal hyperplasia. *Endocrine Metabolism Clinics of North America*, 30, 173–192.

Bi, S. (2006) Role of dorsomedial hypothalamic neuropeptide Y in energy homeostasis. *Peptides*, 28, 352–356.

Bielajew, C. and Shizgal, P. (1986) Evidence implicating descending fibers in self-stimulation of the medial forebrain bundle. *Journal of Neuroscience*, 6, 919–929.

Bishop, K.M. and Wahlsten, D. (1997) Sex differences in the human corpus callosum: myth or reality? *Neuroscience and Biobehavioural Reviews*, 21, 581–601.

Bjorklund, L.M., Pernaute, R.S., Chung, S. *et al.* (2002) Embryonic stem cells develop into functional dopaminergic neurons after transplantation in a Parkinson rat model. *Proceedings of the Natioanl Academy of Sciences*, 99, 2344–2349.

Blanchard, R. (2001). Fraternal birth order and the maternal immune hypothesis of male homosexuality. *Hormones and Behavior*, 40, 105–114.

Blanchard, R., Cantor, J.M., Bogaert, A.F. *et al.* (2006) Interaction of fraternal birth order and handedness in the development of male homosexuality. *Hormones and Behavior*, 49, 405–414.

Blass, E.M., Anderson, D.R., Kirkorian, H.L. *et al.* (2006) On the road to obesity: television viewing increases intake of high-density foods. *Physiology and Behavior*, 88, 597–604.

Blessed, G., Tomlinson, B.E. and Roth, M. (1968) The association between quantitative measures of dementia and senile change in cerebral grey matter of elderly subjects. *British Journal of Psychiatry*, 114, 798–811.

Bliss, T.V.P. and Lomo, T. (1973) Long-lasting potentiation of synaptic transmission in the dentate area of the anaethetized rabbit following stimulation of the perforant path. *Journal of Physiology (London)*, 232, 331–356.

Blood, A.J. and Zatorre, R.J. (2001) Intensely pleasurable responses to music correlate with activity in brain regions implicated with reward and emotion. *Proceedings of the National Academy of Sciences*, 98, 11818–11823.

Bloom, S. (2003) The fat controller. *New Scientist*, 179 (2407), 38–41.

Blum, K. and Payne, J.E. (1991) *Alcohol and the Addictive Brain*. New York: Free Press.

Blum, K., Noble, E.P., Sheridan, P.J. *et al.* (1990) Allele association of human dopamine D2 receptor gene in alcoholism. *Journal of American Medical Association*, 263, 2055–2060.

Blum, K., Noble, E.P., Sheridan, P.J. *et al.* (1991) Association of the A1 allele of the D2 dopamine receptor gene with severe alcoholism. *Alcohol*, 8, 409–416.

Bogaert, A.F. (2006). Biological versus nonbiological older brothers and men's sexual orientation. *Proceedings of the National Academy of Sciences,* 103, 10774–10777.

Bogen, J.E. and Bogen, G.M. (1976) Wernicke's region – where is it? *Annals of the New York Academy of Sciences,* 280, 834–843.

Bogerts, B. (1989) Limbic and paralimbic pathology in schizophrenia: interaction with age- and stress-related factors. In Schulz, S.C. and Tamminga, C.A. (eds) *Schizophrenia: Scientific Progress.* London: Oxford University Press.

Bogerts, B. (1993) Recent advances in the neuropathology of schizophrenia. *Schizophrenia Bulletin,* 19, 431–445.

Bonnet, M.H. and Arand, D.L. (1996) The consequences of a week of insomnia. *Sleep,* 19, 453–461.

Booth, D.A. (1990) How to think about immediate dietary and post-ingestional influences on appetites and satieties. *Appetite,* 124, 171–179.

Borbély, A. (1986) *Secrets of Sleep.* London: Penguin.

Bos, N.P.A. and Mirmiran, M. (1990) Circadian rhythms in spontaneous neuronal discharges of the cultured suprachiamatic nucleus. *Brain Research,* 511, 158–162.

Bouchard, C. (1994) Genetics of obesity: overview and research directions. In Bouchard, C. (ed.) *The Genetics of Obesity.* Boca Raton, Fla.: CRC Press.

Bouchard, C. (1995) The genetics of obesity: from genetic epidemiology to molecular markers. *Molecular Medicine Today,* 1, 45–50.

Bouchard, C., Tremblay, A., Despres, J.-R. *et al.* (1990) The response to long-term overfeeding in identical twins. *New England Journal of Medicine,* 322, 1477–1482.

Bouchard, T.J. Jr (1994) Genes, environment and personality. *Science,* 264, 1700–1701.

Bouchard, T.J. Jr, Lykken, D.T., McGue, M. *et al.* (1990) Sources of human psychological differences: the Minnesota study of twins reared apart. *Science,* 250, 223–228.

Boydell, J. and Murray, R. (2003) Urbanisation, migration and risk of schizophrenia. In Murray, R., Jones, P.B., Susser, E. *et al.* (eds) *The Epidemiology of Schizoprhenia.* New York: Cambridge University Press.

Bozarth, M.A. (1986) Neural basis of psychomotor stimulant and opiate reward: evidence suggesting the involvement of a common dopaminergic system. *Behavioral Brain Research,* 22, 107–116.

Bozarth, M.A. (1987) Ventral tegmental reward system. In Engel, J. and Oreland, L. (eds) *Brain Reward Systems and Abuse.* New York: Raven Press.

Bozarth, M.A. (ed.) (1987) *Methods of Assessing the Reinforcing Properties of Abused Drugs.* New York: Springer-Verlag.

Braak, H. and Braak, E. (1991) Neuropathological stageing of Alzheimer-related changes. *Acta Neuropathology,* 82, 239–259.

Bradshaw, J.L. and Mattingley, J.B. (1995) *Clinical Neuropsychology: Behavioral and Brain Science.* New York: Oxford University Press.

Bray, G.A. and York, D.A. (1979) Hypothalamic and genetic obesity in experimental animals: an autonomic and endocrine hypothesis. *Physiological Review,* 59, 719–809.

Breedlove, S.M. (1992) Sexual differentiation of the brain and behavior. In Becker, J.B., Breedlove, S.M. and Crews, D. (eds) *Behavioral Endocrinology.* Cambridge, Mass.: MIT Press.

Breedlove, S.M. (1993) Sexual differentiation of the brain and behavior. In: Becker, J.B., Breedlove, S.M. and Crews, D. (eds) *Behavioral Endocrinology.* Cambridge MA: MIT Press.

Breedlove, S.M. (1994) Sexual differentiation of the human nervous system. *Annual Review of Psychology,* 45, 465–488.

Breedlove, S.M., Rosenzweig, M.R. and Watson, N.V. (2007) *Biological Psychology,* 5th edition. Sunderland, Mass.: Sinauer.

Breiter, H.C., Etcoff, N.L., Whalen, P.J. *et al.* (1996) Response and habituation of the human amygdala during visual processing of facial expression. *Neuron,* 17, 875–887.

Bremer, G. (1937) L'activité cérébrale au cours du sommeil et de la narcose. *Bulletin de l'Academie Royale de Belgique,* 4, 68–86.

Brodie, B.B. and Shore, P.A. (1957) A concept for a role of serotonin and norepinephrine as chemical mediators in the brain. *Annals of the New York Academy of Sciences,* 66, 631–642.

Brodmann, K. (1912) Neue ergebnisse über die vergleichene histlogische localisation der grosshirnrinde mit besonderer Berucksichtigung des Stirnhirms. *Anatomischer Anzeiger,* 41, 157–216.

Brown, G.L. and Linnoila, M.I. (1990) CSF serotonin metabolite (5-HIAA) studies in depression, impulsivity, and violence. *Journal of Clinical Psychiatry,* 51, 31–43.

Bryden, M.P., McManus, I.C. and Bulman-Fleming, M.B. (1994) Evaluating the empirical support for the Geschwind–Behan–Galaburda model of cerebral lateralisation. *Brain and Cognition,* 26, 103–167.

Buck, L. and Axel, R.A. (1991) A novel multigene family may encode odorant receptors: a molecular basis for odor recognition. *Cell,* 65, 175–187.

Burns, J., Job, D., Bastin, M.E. *et al.* (2003) Structural disconnectivity in schizophrenia: a diffusion tensor magnetic resonance imaging study. *British Journal of Psychiatry*, 182, 439–443.

Burns, R.S., Chiueh, C.C., Markey, S.P. *et al.* (1983) A primate model of parkinsonism: selective destruction of dopaminergic neurons in the pars compacta of the substantia nigra by N-methyl-4-phenyl-1,2,3, 6-tetrahydropyridine. *Proceedings of the National Academy of Sciences*, 80, 4546–4550.

Butters, N. (1984) Alcoholic Korsakoff syndrome: an update. *Seminars in Neurology*, 4, 226–244.

Byne, W. (1994) Homosexuality: the biological evidence challenged. *Scientific American*, May, 26–31.

Byne, W., Bleier, R. and Houston, L. (1988) Variations in human corpus callosum do not predict gender: a study using magnetic resonance imaging. *Behavioral Neuroscience*, 102, 222–227.

Byne, W., Tobet, S., Mattiace, L. *et al.* (2001) The interstitial nuclei of the human anterior hypothalamus: an investigation of variation within sex, sexual orintataion, and HIV status. *Hormones and Behavior*, 40, 86–92.

C

Cahill, L., Haier, R.J., Fallon, J. *et al.* (1996) Amygdala activity at encoding correlated with long-term, free recall of emotional information. *Proceedings of the National Academy of Sciences*, 93, 8016–8021.

Calne, D.B. and Langston, J.W. (1983) Aetiology of Parkinson's disease. *Lancet*, 2, 1459–1467.

Campfield, L.A. and Smith, F.J. (1990) Transient declines in blood glucose signal meal initiation. *International Journal of Obesity*, 14, 15–33.

Campion, J., Latto, R. and Smith, Y.M. (1983) Is blindsight an effect of scattered light, spared cortex and near threshold vision? *Behavioral and Brain Sciences*, 6, 423–486.

Cannon, W.B. (1927) The James-Lange theory of emotions: a critical examination and an alternative theory. *American Journal of Psychology*, 39, 106–124.

Cannon, W.B. and Washburn, A.L. (1912) An explanation of hunger. *American Journal of Physiology*, 29, 441–454.

Cantor, J.M., Blanchard, R., Paterson, A.D. and Bogaert, A.F. (2002). How many gay men owe their sexual orientation to fraternal birth order? *Archives of Sexual Behavior*, 31, 63–71.

Carlson, A.J. (1912) The relation between the contractions of the empty stomach and the sensation of hunger. *American Journal of Physiology*, 31, 175–192.

Carlson, N.R., Martin, G.N. and Buskist, W. (2004) *Psychology*. Harlow: Prentice Hall.

Carlsson, A. and Lindqvist, M. (1963) Effect of chlorpromazine or haloperidol on the formation of 3-methoxytyramine and normetanephrine in mouse brain. *Acta Pharmacology and Toxicolgy*, 20, 140–144.

Caspi, A., Sugden, K., Moffitt, T.E. *et al.* (2003) Influence of life stress on depression: moderation in the 5-HTT gene. *Science*, 301, 386–389.

Castellucci, V.F. and Kandel, E.R. (1974) A quantal analysis of the synaptic depression underlying habituation of the gill-withdrawal reflex in *Aplysia*. *Proceedings of the National Academy of Science*, 71, 5004–5008.

Castellucci, V.F., Kandel, E.R., Schwartz, J.H. *et al.* (1980) Intracellular injection of the catalytic subunit of cyclic AMP-dependent protein kinase simulates facilitation of transmitter release underlying behavioral sensitization in *Aplysia*. *Proceedings of the National Academy of Sciences*, 77, 7492–7496.

Castellucci, V.F., Frost, W.N., Goelet, P. *et al.* (1986) Cell and molecular analysis of long-term sensitization in *Aplysia*. *Journal of Physiology*, 81, 349–357.

Caterina, M.J., Leffler, A., Malmberg, A.B. *et al.* (2000) Impaired nociception and pain sensation in mice lacking the capsaicin receptor. *Science*, 288, 306–318.

Chalmers, D.J. (1996) *The Conscious Mind: In Search of a Fundamental Theory*. New York: Oxford University Press.

Chemelli, R.M., Willie, J.T., Sinton, C.M. (1999) Narcolepsy in orexin knockout mice: molecular genetics of sleep regulation. *Cell*, 98, 437–451.

Chen, J., Paredes, W., Li, J. *et al.* (1990) Δ9-tetrahydrocannabinol produces naloxone-blockable enhancement of presynaptic basal dopamine efflux in nucleus accumbens of conscious, freely-moving rats as measured by intracerebral microdialysis. *Psychopharmacology*, 102, 156–162.

Chen, W.R., Lee, S.H., Kato, K. *et al.* (1996) Long-term modifications of synaptic efficacy in the human inferior and middle temporal cortex. *Proceedings of the National Academy of Sciences*, 93, 8011–8015.

Cheney, P.D., Fetz, E.E. and Palmer, S.S. (1985) Patterns of facilitation and suppression of antagonistic forebrain muscles from motor cortex sites in the awake monkey. *Journal of Neurophysiology*, 53, 805–820.

Cheyette, S.R. and Cummings, J.L. (1995) Encephalitus lethargica: lessons for contemporary neuropsychiatry. *Journal of Neuropsychiatry*, 7, 125–134.

Chi, J.G., Dooling, E.C. and Gilles, F.H. (1977) Gyri development and the human brain. *Annals of Neurology*, 1, 86–93.

Chi, J.G., Dooling, E.C. and Gilles, F.H. (1977) Left, right asymmetries of the temporal speech areas of the human fetus. *Archives of Neurology*, 34, 346–348.

Childress, A.R., McLellan, A.T. and O'Brien, C.P. (1986). Abstinent opiate abusers exhibit conditioned craving, conditioned withdrawal, and reductions in both through extinction. *British Journal of Addiction*, 81, 655–660.

Chin, J.H. and Goldstein, D.B. (1981) Membrane-disordering action of ethanol: variation with membrane cholesterol content and depth of the spin label probe. *Molecular Pharmacology*, 19, 425–431.

Cho, K. (2001) Chronic jet lag produce temporal lobe atrophy and spatial cognitive deficits. *Nature Neuroscience*, 4, 567–568.

Cho, K., Ennaceur, J.C., Cole, C. and Kook Suh, C. (2000) Chronic jet lag produces cognitive deficits. *Journal of Neuroscience*, 20, 1–5.

Clark, D.I., Boutros, N.N. and Mendez, M.F. (2005) *The Brain and Behavior: An Introduction to Behavioral Neuroanatomy*. Cambridge: Cambridge University Press.

Clark, J.T., Kalra, P.S., Crowley, W.R. and Kalra, S.P. (1984) Neuropeptide Y and human pancreatic polypeptide stimulate feeding behavior in rats, *Endocrinology*, 115, 427–429.

Cloninger, C.R. (1987) Neurogenetic adaptive mechanisms in alcoholism. *Science*, 236, 410–416.

Cloninger, C.R., Bohman, M. and Sigvardsson, S. (1981) Inheritance of alcohol abuse: cross-fostering analysis of adopted men. *Archives of General Psychiatry*, 38, 861–868.

Cohen, N.J. and Corkin, S. (1981) The amnesic patient H.M.: learning and retention of a cognitive skill. *Society for Neuroscience Abstracts*, 7, 235.

Cohen, N.J. and Squire, L.R. (1980) Preserved learning and retention of pattern-analysing skill in amnesia: dissociation of knowing how and knowing that. *Science*, 210, 207–210.

Coleman, D.L. (1973) Effects of parabiosis of obese with diabetes and normal mice. *Diabetologia*, 9, 294–298.

Coleman, D.L. (1978) Obese and diabetes: two mutant genes causing diabetes-obesity syndromes in mice. *Diabetologia*, 14, 141–148.

Collet, C. *et al.* (1997) Autonomic nervous system response patterns specificity to basic emotions. *Journal of the Autonomic Nervous System*, 62, 45–57.

Comings, D.E., Comings, B.G., Muhleman, D. *et al.* (1991) Dopamine D2 receptor locus as a modifying gene in neuropsychiatric disorders. *Journal of the American Medical Association*, Oct., 1793–1800.

Connell, P.H. (1958) *Amphetamine Psychosis*. Maudsley Monographs No. 5. London.

Cookson, J. (2001) Use of antipsychotic drugs and lithium in mania. *British Journal of Psychiatry*, 178, 148–156.

Cookson, M.R. (2003) Neurodegeneration: how does parkin prevent Parkinson's disease? *Current Biology*, 13, R522–R524.

Cooper, R.M. and Zubek, J.P. (1958) Effects of enriched and restricted early environments on the learning ability of bright and dull rats. *Canadian Journal of Psychology*, 12, 159–164.

Coppen, A. (1967) The biochemistry of affective disorders, *British Journal of Psychiatry*, 113, 1237–1264.

Corbett, D., Laferriere, A. and Milner, P.M. (1982) Elimination of medial prefrontal cortex self-stimulation following transection of efferents to the sulcal cortex in the rat. *Physiology and Behavior*, 29, 425–431.

Corkin, S. (1964) Somesthetic function after cerebral damage in man. Unpublished doctoral thesis, McGill University.

Corkin, S. (1984) Lasting consequences of bilateral medial temporal lobectomy: clinical course and experimental findings. *Seminars in Neurology*, 4, 249–259.

Corkin, S., Milner, B. and Rasmussen, T. (1970) Somatosensory thresholds: contrasting effects of post-central and posterior parietal lobe excisions. *Archives of Neurology*, 23, 41–58.

Corkin, S., Amaral, D.G., González, R.G. *et al.* (1997) H.M.'s medial temporal lobe lesion: findings from magnetic resonance imaging. *Journal of Neuroscience*, 17, 3964–3979.

Cosgrove, K.P., Mazure, C.M. and Staley, J.K. (2007) Evolving knowledge of sex differences in brain structure, function and chemistry. *Biological Psychiatry*, 62, 847–855.

Cotman, C.W. and Pike, C.J. (1994) β-amyloid and its contribution to neurodegeneration in Alzheimer disease. In Terry, R.D., Katzman, R. and Bick, K.L. (eds) *Alzheimer Disease*. New York: Raven Press.

Cotzias, G.C. (1967) Aromatic acid amino acids and modication of Parkinsonism. *New England Journal of Medicine*, 276, 374–379.

Coyle, J.T. and Schwartz, R. (1976) Lesion of striatal neurons with kainic acid provides a model for Huntington's chorea, *Nature*, 263, 244–246.

Crabbe, J.C., Belknap, J.K. and Buck, K.J. (1994) Genetic animal models of alcohol and drug abuse. *Science*, 264, 1717–1723.

Crabbe, J.C., Phillips, T.J., Feller, D.J. *et al.* (1996) Elevated alcohol consumption in null mutant mice lacking 5-HT$_{1B}$ serotonin receptors. *Nature Genetics*, 14, 98–101.

Creese, I., Burt, D.R. and Snyder, S.H. (1976) Dopamine receptor binding predicts clinical and pharmacological properties of antischizophrenic drugs. *Science*, 194, 481–483.

Crick, F. (1994) *The Astonishing Hypothesis*. New York: Scribner.

Crow, T.J. (1980) Molecular pathology of schizophrenia: more than one disease process? *British Medical Journal*, 280, 66–68.

Crow, T.J. (1985) The two-syndrome concept: origins and current staus. *Schizophrenia Bulletin*, 11, 471–485.

Culliton, B.J. (1976) Psychosurgery: national commission issues surprisingly favorable report. *Science*, 194, 299–301.

Cummings, D.E., Purnell, J.Q., Frayo, R.S. *et al.* (2001) A preprandial rise in plasma ghrelin levels suggests a role in meal initiation in humans. *Diabetes*, 50, 1714–1719.

Cytowic, R.E. (1993) *The Man Who Tasted Shapes*. New York: Putnams.

Cytowic, R.E. (1995) Synesthesia, phenomenology and neuropsychology: a review of current knowledge. *Psyche*, 2(10). http://psyche.cs.monash.edu.au/v2/psyche-2-10-cytowic.html

Cytowic, R.E. (1997) Synaesthesia: phenomenology and neuropsychology. In Baron-Cohen, S. and Harrison, J. (eds) *Synaesthesia: Classic and Contemporary Readings*. Oxford: Blackwell.

Czeisler, C.A., Duffy, J.F., Shanahan, T.L. *et al.* (1999) Stability, precision and near-24-hour period of the human circadian pacemaker. *Science*, 284, 2177–2181.

D

Dabbs, J.M. and Morris, R. (1990) Testosterone, social class, and antisocial behavior in a sample of 4,462 men. *Psychological Science*, 1, 209–211.

Dale, R.C., Church, A.J., Surtees, R.A.H. *et al.* (2004) Encephalitis lethargica syndrome: 20 new cases and evidence of basal ganglia autoimmunity. *Brain*, 127, 21–33.

Damasio, A.R. (1994) *Descartes' Error*. New York: Picador.

Damasio, A.R., Tranel, D. and Damasio, H. (1990) Face agnosia and the neural substrates of memory. *Annual Review of Neuroscience*, 13, 89–109.

Damasio, H., Grabowski, T., Frank, R. *et al.* (1994) The return of Phineas Gage: clues about the brain from the skull of a famous person. *Science*, 264, 1102–1105.

Damasio, H.C. (1991) Neuroanatomy of the frontal lobes in vitro: a comment on methodology. In Levin, H.S., Eisenberg, H.M. and Benton, A.L. (eds) *Frontal Lobe Function and Dysfunction*. New York: Oxford University Press.

Davidson, J.M. (1980) The psychobiology of sexual experience. In Davidson, J.M and Davidson, R.J. (eds) *The Psychobiology of Consciousness*. New York: Plenum.

Davidson, J.M., Camargo, C.A. and Smith, E.R. (1979) Effects of androgens on sexual behavior of hypogonadal men. *Journal of Clinical Endocrinology and Metabolism*, 48, 955–958.

Davis, H.P., Rosenzweig, M.R., Becker, L.A. and Sather, K.J. (1988) Biological psychology's relationships to psychology and neuroscience. *American Psychologist*, 43, 359–371.

Davis, J.D., Gallagher, R.J., Ladove, R.F. and Turausky, A.J. (1969) Inhibition of food intake by a humoral factor. *Journal of Comparative and Physiological Psychology*, 67, 407–414.

Davis, K.L., Kahn, R.S., Ko, G. and Davidson, M. (1991) Dopamine in schizophrenia: a review and reconceptualization. *American Journal of Psychiatry*, 148, 1474–1486.

Davis, S., Mirick, D.K. and Stevens, R.G. (2001) Nightshift work, light at night, and risk of breast cancer. *Journal of the National Cancer Institute*, 93, 1557–1662.

De Rijk, M.C., Tzourio, C., Breteler, M.M. *et al.* (1997) Prevalence of parkinsonism and Parkinson's disease in Europe: the Europarkinson Collaborative Study. European Community Concerted Action on the Epidemiology of Parkinson's disease. *Journal of Neurology, Neurosurgery, and Psychiatry*, 62, 10–15.

DeFries, J.C. and Alarcon, M. (1996). Genetics of specific reading disability. *Mental Retardation and Developmental Disabilities Research Reviews*, 2, 39–47.

DeLong, M.R. (1974) Motor functions of the basal ganglia: single unit activity during movement. In Schmitt, F.O. and Worden, F.G. (eds) *The Neurosciences: Third Study Program*. Cambridge, Mass.: MIT Press.

DeLong, M.R., Georgopoulos, A.P., Crutcher, M.D. *et al.* (1984) Functional organization of the basal ganglia: contributions of single-cell recording studies. In Evered, D. and O'Connor, M. (eds) *Functions of the Basal Ganglia. Ciba Foundation Symposium* 107, 64–82.

Dement, W. and Kleitman, N. (1957) Cyclic variations in EEG during sleep and their relation to eye movements, body motility and dreaming. *Electroencephalography and Clinical Neuropsychology*, 9, 673–690.

Dement, W.C. (1976) *Some Must Watch While Some Must Sleep*. San Francisco: San Francisco Book Company.

Démonet, J.F., Taylor, M.J. and Chaix, Y. (2004) Developmental dyslexia. *Lancet*, 363, 1451–1460.

Deneau, G., Yanagita, T. and Seevers, M.H. (1969) Self-administration of psychoactive substances by the monkey. *Psychopharmacologia*, 16, 30–48.

Deutsch, J.A. and Gonzalez, M.F. (1980) Gastric nutrient content signals satiety. *Behavioral and Neural Biology*, 30, 113–116.

DeValois, R.L. and DeValois, K.K. (1988) *Spatial Vision*. New York: Oxford University Press.

Devane, W.A., Hanus, L., Breuer, A. *et al.* (1992) Isolation and structure of a brain constiuent that binds to the cannabinoid receptor. *Science*, 258, 1946–1949.

Dewsbury, D.A. (1991) Psychobiology. *American Psychologist*, 46, 198–205.

Di Chiara, G. and Imperato, A. (1988) Drugs abused by humans preferentialy increase synaptic dopamine concentrations in the mesolimbic system of freely moving rats. *Proceedings of the National Academy of Sciences*, 85, 5274–5284.

Di Chiara, G. and North, R.A. (1992) Neurobiology of opiate abuse. *Trends in Pharmacological Sciences*, 13, 185–193.

Diamond, M.C., Dowling, G.A. and Johnson, R.E. (1981) Morphologic cerebral cortical asymmetry in male and female rats. *Experimental Neurology*, 71, 261–268.

Diamond, M.C., Scheibel, A.B., Murphy, G.M. and Harvey, T. (1985) On the brain of a scientist: Albert Einstein. *Experimental Neurology*, 88, 198–204.

Diaz, J. (1997) *How Drugs influence Behavior: A Neurobehavioral Approach*. Upper Saddle River, NJ: Prentice Hall.

DiLeone, R.J., Georgescu, D. and Nestler, E.R. (2003) Lateral hypothalamic neuropeptides in reward and drug addiction. *Life Sciences*, 73, 759–768.

Dimitrijevic, M.R, Gerasimenko, Y. and Pinter, M.N. (1998) Evidence for a spinal control generator in humans. *Annals of the New York Academy of Sciences*, 860, 360–376.

Dittmann, R.W., Kappes, M.E. and Kappes, M.H. (1992) Sexual behavior in adolescent and adult females with congenital adrenal hyperplasia. *Psychoendocrinology*, 17, 153–170.

Dobzhansky, T. (1973) Nothing in biology makes sense except in the light of evolution. *American Biology Teacher*, 35, 125–129.

Dominguez, J.V. Riolo, Z. and Hull, E.M. (2001) Regulation by the medial amygdala of copulation and medial preoptic dopamine release. *Journal of Neuroscience*, 21, 349–355.

Doty, R.L. (2001) Olfaction. *Annual Review of Psychology*, 52, 423–453.

Douglas, R.J. (1967) The hippocampus and behavior. *Psychological Bulletin*, 67, 416–442.

Drachman, D.A. and Leavitt, J. (1974) Human memory and the cholinergic system: a relationship to ageing? *Archives of Neurology*, 30, 113–121.

Drevets, W.C., Price, J.L., Simpson, J.R. Jr, *et al.* (1997) Subgenual prefrontal cortex abnormalities in mood disorders. *Nature*, 386, 824–827.

Dudel, J. (1978) Excitation of nerve and muscle. In Schmidt, R.F. (ed.) *Fundamentals of Neurophysiology*. New York: Springer.

Dutton, D.G. and Aron, A.P. (1974) Some evidence for heightened sexual attraction under conditions of high anxiety. *Journal of Personality and Social Psychology*, 30, 510–517.

Duyao, M.P., Auerbach, A.B., Ryan, A. *et al.* (1995) Inactivation of the mouse Huntington's disease gene homologue Hdh. *Science*, 269, 407–410.

Dworkin, S.I., Guerin, G., Co, C. *et al.* (1988) Effects of 5,7-dihydroxytryptamine lesions of the nucleus accumbens in rats responding on a concurrent schedule of food, water and intravenous morphine self-administration. *NIDA Research Monographs*, 81, 149–155.

E

Eastman, C.L., Boulos, Z., Terman, M. *et al.* (1995) Light treatment for sleep disorders. Consensus report VI: shift work. *Journal of Biological Rhythms*, 10, 157–165.

Eccles, J.C. (1965) *The Brain and the Unity of Conscious Experience*. Cambridge: Cambridge University Press.

Eden, G.F., Stein, J.F., Wood, H.M. and Wood, F.B. (1994) Differences in eye movements and reading problems in dyslexic and normal children. *Vision Research*, 34, 1345–1358.

Eden, G.F., VanMeter, J.W., Rumsey, J.M. *et al.* (1996) Abnormal processing of visual motion in dyslexia revealed by functional brain imaging. *Nature*, 382, 66–69.

Ehringer, H. and Hornykiewicz, O. (1960) Verteilung von noradrenalin und dopamin (3-hydroxytramin) in gerhirn des menshenen und verhalten bei erkrankungen des extrapyramidalen systems. *Klin Wochenscher*, 38, 1236–1239.

Eichenbaum, H. (2002) *The Cognitive Neuroscience of Memory: An Introduction*. New York: Oxford University Press.

Eichenbaum, H. and Cohen, N.J. (2001) *From Conditioning to Conscious Recollection: Memory Systems of the Brain*. Oxford: Oxford University Press.

Einstein, A. (1954) *Ideas and Opinions*, ed. C. Seelig, trans. S. Bargmann. New York: Bonanza.

Ekman, P. and Friesen, W.V. (1978) *The Facial Action Coding System*. Palo Alto, Calif.: Consulting Psychologists Press.

Ekman, P., Levenson, R.W. and Frieson, W.V. (1983) Autonomic nervous system activity distinguishes among emotions. *Science*, 221, 1208–1210.

Elmquist, J.K., Coppari, R., Balthasar, N. *et al.* (2005) Identifying hypothalamic pathways controlling food intake, body weight, and glucose homeostasis. *Journal of Comparative Neurology*, 493, 63–71.

Emery, A.E.H. and Mueller, R.F. (1992) *Elements of Medical Genetics*. Edinburgh: Churchill Livingstone.

Empson, J. (1993) *Sleep and Dreaming*. New York: Harvester Wheatsheaf.

Enroth-Cugell, C. and Robson, J.G. (1966) The contrast sensitivity of retinal ganglion cells of the cat. *Journal of Physiology*, 187, 517–552.

Epstein, A.N., Nicolaidis, S. and Miselis, R. (1975) The glucoprivic control of food intake and the glucostatic theory of feeding behavior. In Mogenson, G.J. and Calarasu, F.R. (eds) *Neural Integration of Physiological Mechanisms and Behavior*. Toronto: Toronto University Press.

Eslinger, P.J. and Damasio, A.R. (1985) Severe disturbance of higher cognitive function after bilateral frontal lobe ablation: patient EVR. *Neurology*, 35, 1731–1741.

Evans, D.A. *et al.* (1997) Education and other measures of socioeconomic status and risk of incident Alzheimer disease in a defined population of older persons. *Archives of Neurology*, 54, 1399–1405.

Evans, K.C., Berger, E.P., Cho, C.G. *et al.* (1995) Apolipoprotein E is a kinetic but not a thermodynamic inhibitor of amyloid formation: implications for the pathogenesis and treatment of Alzheimer disease. *Proceedings of the National Academy of Sciences*, 92, 763–767.

Everson, C.A. and Toth, L.A. (2000) Systemic bacterial invasion induced by sleep deprivation. *American Journal of Physiology*, 278, R905–R916.

F

Fadiga, L., Fogassi, L., Pavesi, G. and Rizzolatti, G. (1995) Motor facilitation during action observation: a magnetic stimulation study. *Journal of Neurophysiology*, 73, 2608–2611.

Farber, S.L. (1981) *Identical Twins Reared Apart: A Reanalysis*. New York: Basic Books.

Farde, L., Wiesel, F.A., Stone-Elander, S. *et al.* (1990) D2 dopamine receptors in neuroleptic-naive schizophrenic patients. *Archives of General Psychiatry*, 47, 213–219.

Feldman, J.M. and Halaas, J.L. (1998) Leptin and the regulation of body weight in mammals. *Nature*, 395, 763–770.

Feldman, R.S., Meyer, J.S. and Quenzer, L.F. (1997) *Principles of Neuropsychopharmacology*. Sunderland, Mass.: Sinauer.

Ferguson, C.P. and Pigott, T.A. (2000) Anorexia and bulimia nervosa: neurobiology and pharmacotherapy, *Behavior Therapy*, 31, 237–263.

Fibiger, H.C. and Philips, A.G. (1987) Role of catecholamine transmitters in brain reward systems: implications for the neurobiology of affect. In Engel, J. and Oreland, L. (eds) *Brain Reward Systems and Abuse*. New York: Raven Press.

Fibiger, H.C., Phillips, A.G. and Brown, E.E. (1992) The neurobiology of cocaine-induced reinforcement. In Wolstenholme, G.E.W. (ed.) *Cocaine: Scientific and Social Dimensions. Ciba Foundation Symposium 166*. Chichester: John Wiley.

Fielden, J., Lutter, C. and Dabbs, J. (1994) Basking in glory: testosterone changes in World Cup soccer fans. Psychology Department, Georgia State University.

Finger, S. (1994) *Origins of Neuroscience*. New York: Oxford University Press.

Finger, S (2000) *Minds Behind the Brain*. Oxford. Oxford University Press.

Fogarty, A. and Lingford-Hughes, A. (2004) Addiction and substance abuse. *Medicine*, 32, 29–33.

Foote, S.L. (1987) Locus coeruleus. In Adelman, G. (ed.) *Encyclopedia of Neuroscience*. Boston, Mass.: Birkhauer.

Forger, N.G. and Breedlove, S.M. (1986) Sexual dimorphism in human and canine spinal cord: role of early androgen. *Proceedings of the National Academy of Sciences (USA)*, 83, 7257–7531.

Frederiske, M.E., Lu, A., Aylward, E. *et al.* (1999) Sex differences in the inferior parietal lobe. *Cerebral Cortex*, 9, 896–901.

Freedman, M.S., Lucas, R.J., Soni, B. *et al.* (1999) Regulation of mammalian circadian behavior by non-rod, non-cone, ocular photoreceptors. *Science*, 284, 502–504.

Freud, S. (1891) *Zur Auffassung der Aphasien*. Vienna: Deuticke.

Fried, I., Wilson, C.L., McDonald, K.A. and Behnke, E.J. (1998) Electric current stimulates laughter. *Nature*, 391, 650.

Friedhoff, A.J. and Silva, R.R. (1995) The effects of neuroleptics on plasma homovanillic acid. In Bloom, F.E. and Kupfer, D.J. (eds) *Psychopharmacology: The Fourth Generation of Progress*. New York: Raven Press.

Friedman, M.I., Tordoff, M.G. and Ramirez, I. (1986) Integrated metabolic control of food intake. *Brain Research Bulletin*, 17, 855–859.

Friedman, J.M. and Halaas, J.L. (1998) Leptin and the regulation of body weight in mammals, *Nature*, 395, 763–770.

Funkenstein, D. (1955) The physiology of fear and anger. *Scientific American*, 192, 74–80.

G

Gabrieli, J.D., Brewes, J.B., Desmond, J.E. *et al.* (1997) Separate neural bases of two fundamental memory processes in the human medial temporal lobe. *Science*, 276, 264–266.

Galaburda, A.M. (1993) Neurology of developmental dyslexia. *Current Opinion in Neurobiology*, 3, 237–242.

Galaburda, A.M. and Kemper, T.L. (1979) Cytoarchitectonic abnormalities in developmental dyslexia. *Annals of Neurology*, 6, 94–100.

Galaburda, A.M. and Livingstone, M. (1993) Evidence for a magnocellular deficit in developmental dyslexia. *Annals of the New York Academy of Sciences*, 682, 70–82.

Galaburda, A.M., Sherman, G.F., Rosen, G.D. *et al.* (1985) Developmental dyslexia: four consecutive patients with cortical abnormailties. *Annals of Neurology*, 18, 222–233.

Gallistel, C.R. (1983) Self-stimulation. In Deutsch, J.A. (ed.) *The Physiological Basis of Memory*. New York: Academic Press.

Gallistel, C.R., Gomita, Y., Yadin, E. *et al.* (1985) Forebrain origins and terminations of the medial forebrain bundle metabolically activated by rewarding stimulation or by reward-blocking doses of pimozide. *Journal of Neuroscience*, 5, 1246–1261.

Gallopin, T., Fort, P., Eggermann, E. *et al.* (2000) Identification of sleep-promoting neurons in vitro. *Nature*, 404, 992–995.

Games, D., Adams, D., Alessandrini, R. *et al.* (1995) Alzheimer-type neuropathology in transgenic mice overexpressing V717F β-amyloid precursor protein, *Nature*, 373, 523–527.

Gaoni, Y. and Mechoulam, R. (1964). Isolation, structure and partial synthesis of an active constituent of hashish. *Journal of the American Chemical Society*, 86, 1646–1647.

Garcia, J., Kimeldorf, D.J. and Koelling, R.A. (1955) Conditioned aversion to saccharin resulting from exposure to gamma radiation. *Science*, 112, 157–158.

Gardner, E.L. and Seeger, T.F. (1988) Anatomically selective action of atypical neuroleptics on the mesocorticolimbic dopamine system. *Annals of the New York Academy of Sciences*, 537, 502–504.

Gauthier, L.R., Charrin, B.C., Borrell-Pages, M. *et al.* (2004) Huntingtin controls neurotrophic support and survival of neurons by enhancing BDNF vesicular transport along microtubules. *Cell*, 118, 127–138.

Gazzaniga, M.S. (1970) *The Bisected Brain*. New York: Appleton-Century-Crofts.

Gazzaniga, M.S. (1989) Organization of the human brain. *Science*, 245, 947–952.

Gazzaniga, M.S., Bogen, J.E. and Sperry, R.W. (1962) Some functional effects of sectioning the cerebral commissures in man. *Proceedings of the National Academy of Sciences*, 48, 1765–1769.

Gazzaniga, M.S., Ivry, R.B. and Mangum, G.R. (2002) *Cognitive Neuroscience: The Biology of the Mind*. New York: Norton.

Gehlert, D.R. (1999) Role of hypothalamic neuropeptide Y in feeding and obesity. *Neuropeptides*, 33, 329–338.

Gelernter, J., Goldman, D. and Risch, N. (1993) The A1 allele at the D2 dopamine receptor gene and alcoholism: a reappraisal, *Journal of the American Medical Association*, 269, 1673–1677.

Gellar, I. (1962) Use of approach avoidance behavior (conflict) for evaluating depressant drugs. In Nodine, J.H. and Moyer, J.H. (eds) *Psychosomatic Medicine*. Philadelphia: Lea & Febiger.

Georgopoulos, A.P., Taira, M. and Lukashin, A. (1993) Cognitive neurophysiology of the motor cortex. *Science*, 260, 47–52.

Geschwind, N. (1965) Disconnexion syndromes in animals and man, *Brain*, 88, 585–644.

Geschwind, N. (1972) Language and the brain. *Scientific American*, 226 (April), 76–83.

Geschwind, N. and Behan, P (1982) Left handedness: association with immune disease, mirgraine and developmental learning disorders. *Proceedings of the National Academy of Sciences*, 79, 5097–5100.

Geschwind, N. and Galaburda, A.M. (1985a). Cerebral lateralization: biological mechanisms, associations, and pathology. I: A hypothesis and a program for research. *Archives of Neurology*, 42, 428–459.

Geschwind, N. and Galaburda, A.M. (1985b). Cerebral lateralization: biological mechanisms, associations, and pathology. II: A hypothesis and a program for research. *Archives of Neurology*, 42, 521–552.

Geschwind, N. and Levitsky, W. (1968) Human brain: left–right asymmetries in temporal speech region. *Science*, 161, 186–187.

Geula, C. and Mesulam, M.M. (1994) Cholinergic systems and related neuropathology and predilection patterns in Alzheimer's disease. In Terry, R.D., Katzman, R. and Bick, K.L. (eds) *Alzheimer Disease*. New York: Raven Press.

Gibbs, J., Young, R.C. and Smith, G.P. (1973) Cholecystokinin decreases food intake in rats. *Journal of Comparative Physiology and Psychology*, 84, 488–495.

Gilling, D. and Brightwell, R. (1982) *The Human Brain*. London: Orbis.

Glatz, K., Mossner, R., Heils, A. and Lesch, K.P. (2003) Glucocorticoid-regulated human serotonin transporter (5-HTT) expression is modulated by the 5-HTT gene-promotor-linked polymorphic region. *Journal of Neurochemistry*, 86, 1072–1078.

Glenner, G.G. and Wong, C.W. (1984) Alzheimer's disease: initial report of the purification and characterization of a novel cerebrovascular amyloid protein. *Biochemistry and Biophysics Research Communication*, 120, 885–890.

Glennon, R.A., Titeler, M. and McKenney, J.D. (1984) Evidence for 5-HT$_2$ involvement in the mechanism of action of hallucinogenic events. *Life Sciences*, 35, 2505–2511.

Gloor, P. (1990) Experimental phenomena of temporal lobe epilepsy: facts and hypotheses. *Brain*, 113, 1673–1694.

Gloor, P. (1992) *Role of the Amygdala in Temporal Lobe Epilepsy*. New York: John Wiley.

Goate, A., Chartier-Harlin, M.C., Mullan, M. *et al.* (1991) Segregation of a missense mutation in the amyloid precursor protein gene with familial Alzheimer's disease. *Nature*, 349, 704–706.

Goeders, N.E. and Smith, J.E. (1983) Cortical dopaminergic involvement in cocaine reinforcement. *Science*, 221, 773–775.

Golbe, L.I. (1995) Genetics of Parkinson's disease. In Ellenberg, J.M., Koller, W.C. and Langston, J.W. (eds) *Etiology of Parkinson's Disease*. New York: Marcel Dekker.

Golbe, L.I., Di Iorio, G., Bonavita, V. *et al.* (1990) A large kindred with autosomal Parkinson's disease. *Annals of Neurology*, 27, 276–282.

Gold, D.R. *et al.* (1992) Rotating shift work, sleep, and accidents related to sleepiness in hospital nurses. *American Journal of Public Health*, 82, 1011–1014.

Gold, I. and Stoljar, D. (1999) A neuron doctrine in the philosophy of neuroscience. *Behavioral and Brain Sciences*, 22, 809–869.

Gold, M.S., Redmond, D.E. and Kleber, H.D. (1978) Clonidine blocks acute opiate-withdrawal symptoms. *Lancet*, 2, 599–602.

Goldberg, S.R. and Schuster, C.R. (1967) Conditioned suppression by a stimulus associated with nalorphine in morphine-dependent monkeys. *Journal of Experimental Animal Behavior*, 10, 235–242.

Goldstein, K. (1952) The effect of brain damage on personality. *Psychiatry*, 15, 41–45.

Gomez-Isla, T., Price, J.L., McKeel, D.W. Jr, *et al.* (1996) Profound loss of layer II entorhinal cortex neurons occur in very mild Alzheimer's disease. *Journal of Neuroscience*, 16, 4491–4500.

Gonzalez, M.F. and Deutsch, J.A. (1981) Vagotomy abolishes cues of satiety produced by stomach distension. *Science*, 212, 1283–1284.

Goodale, M.A. and Milner, A.D. (1992) Separate visual pathways for perception and action. *Trends in Neurosciences*, 15, 20–25.

Goodale, M.A. and Milner, A.D. (2004) *Sight Unseen*. London: Oxford University Press.

Goodnick, P.J. and Goldstein, B.J. (1998) Selective serotonin re-uptake inhibitors in affective disorders: basic pharmacology, *Journal of Psychopharmacology*, 12, S5–S20.

Goodwin, D. (1976) *Is Alcoholism Hereditary?* New York: Oxford University Press.

Goodwin, D.W. (1980) Genetic factors in alcoholism. In Mello, N.K. (ed.) *Advances in Substance Abuse*, Vol. 1. Greenwich, Conn.: JAI Press.

Goodwin, D.W., Schlusinger, F. and Hermansen, L. (1973) Alcohol problems in adoptees raised apart from alcoholic biologic parents. *Archives of General Psychiatry*, 28, 238–243.

Goodwin, F.K. and Jamison, K.R. (1990) *Manic Depressive Illness*. New York: Oxford University Press.

Gorski, R.A., Gordon, J.H., Shryne, J.E. and Southam, A.M. (1978) Evidence for a morphological sex difference within the medial preoptic area of the rat brain. *Brain Research*, 148, 333–346.

Gossop, M. (2000) *Living with Drugs*. Aldershot: Ashgate.

Gothelf, D., Eliez, S., Thompson, T. *et al.* (2005) COMT genotype predicts longitudinal cognitive decline and psychosis in 22q11.2 deletion syndrome. *Nature Neuroscience*, 8, 1500–1502.

Gottesman, I.I. (1991) *Schizophrenia Genesis*. New York: Freeman.

Gouchi, C. and Kimura, D. (1991) The relationship between testosterone levels and cognitive ability patterns. *Psychoneuroendocrinology*, 16, 323–334.

Goy, R.W., Berkowitch, F.B. and McBrair, M.C. (1988) Behavioral masculinisation is independent of genital masculinisation in prenatally androgenised female rhesus monkeys. *Hormones and Behavior*, 22, 552–571.

Graham, R.B. (1990) *Physiological Psychology*. Belmont, Calif.: Wadsworth.

Gray, J.A., Young, A.M. and Joseph, M.H. (1997) Dopamine's role. *Science*, 278, 1548–1549.

Gregory, R. (ed.) (2004) *The Oxford Companion to the Mind*. London: Oxford University Press.

Gregory, R.L. (1981) *Mind in Science*. London: Penguin.

Greicius, M.D., Krasnow, B., Reiss, A.L. and Menon, V. (2003) Functional connectivity in the resting brain: a network analysis of the default mode hypothesis, *Proceedings of the National Academy of Sciences*, 100, 253–258.

Griffiths, R.R., Bigelow, G.E. and Henningfield, J.E. (1980) Similarities in animal and human drug-taking behavior. In Meool, N.K. (ed.) *Advances in Substance Abuse*, Vol. 1. Greenwich, Conn.: JAI Press.

Grill, M.J. and Kaplan, J.M. (2002) The neuroanatomical axis for control of energy balance. *Neuropeptides*, 33, 329–338.

Grillner, S. (1996) Neural networks for vertebrate locomotion. *Scientific American*, 271, 48–53.

Groves, P.M. and Rebec, G.V. (1992) *Biological Psychology*. Dubuque, Iowa: William Brown.

Gurling, H.M.D., Clifford, C.A. and Murray, R.M. (1981) Investigations into the genetics of alcohol dependence and into its effects on brain function. In Gedda, L., Parisi, P. and Nance, W.E. (eds) *Progress in Clinical and Biological Research*, Vol. 69. New York: Alan R. Liss.

Gusella, J.F., Tanzi, R.E., Anderson, M.A. *et al.* (1983) A polymorphic DNA marker genetically linked to Huntington's disease. *Nature*, 306, 234–238.

H

Halaas, J.L., Gajiwala, K.S., Maffei, M. *et al.* (1995) Weight-reducing effects of the plasma protein encoded by the obese gene. *Science*, 269, 543–546.

Haldane, M. and Frangou, S. (2004) New insights help define the pathophysiology of bipolar affective disorder: neuroimaging and neuropathology findings. *Progress in Neuropsychopharmacology and Biological Psychiatry*, 28, 943–960.

Halpern, D.F. and Coren, S. (1988) Do right handers live longer? *Nature*, 333, 213.

Hardy, J. and Allsop, D. (1991) Amyloid deposition as the central event in the aetiology of Alzheimer's disease. *Trends in Pharmacological Sciences*, 12, 383–388.

Harlow, J.M. (1848). Passage of an iron rod through the head. *Boston Medical and Surgical Journal*, 39, 389–393. (Republished in *Journal of Neuropsychiatry and Clinical Neuroscience*, 11, 281–283).

Harper, P.S. (1991) (ed.) *Huntington's Disease: Major Problems in Neurology*, Vol. 22. London: W.B. Saunders.

Hart, B.L. (1967) Testosterone regulation of sexual reflexes in spinal male rats. *Science*, 155, 1283–1284.

Hartmann, E., Chung, R. and Draskoczy, P.R. (1971) 6-Hydroxydopamine: effects on sleep in the rat. *Nature*, 233, 425–427.

Hay, D.A. (1985) *Essentials of Behaviour Genetics*. Melbourne: Blackwell.

Healy, D. (1997) *The Anti-depressant Era*. Cambridge, Mass.: Harvard University Press.

Hebb, D.O. (1949) *The Organization of Behavior*. New York: John Wiley.

Hedreen, J.C., Peyser, C.E., Folstein, S.E. and Ross, C.A. (1991) Neuronal loss in layers V and VI of cerebral cortex in Huntington's disease. *Neuroscience Letters*, 133, 257–261.

Heimer, L. and Larsson, K. (1967) Impairment of mating behavior in male rats following lesions in the preoptic–anterior hypothalamic continuum. *Brain Research*, 3, 248–263.

Henke, K., Buck, A., Weber, B. and Wieser, H.G. (1997) Human hippocampus establishes associations in memory. *Hippocampus*, 7, 249–256.

Hepper, P.G., Shahidullah, S. and White, R. (1991) Handedness in the human fetus. *Neuropsychologia*, 29, 1107–1111.

Heriot, A. (1955) *The Castrati in Opera*. London: Secker & Warburg.

Hess, W.R. and Brügger, M. (1943) Das subcorticate Zentrum der affektiven Abwehrreaktion. *Helvetica Physiologica Pharmacolgica Acta*, 1, 33–52.

Hesselbrock, M.N. (1995) Genetic determinants of alcoholic subtypes. In Begleiter, H. and Kissin, B. (eds) *The Genetics of Alcoholism*. London: Oxford University Press.

Hesselbrock, V.M. (1995) The genetic epidemiology of alcoholism. In Begleiter, H. and Kissin, B. (eds) *The Genetics of Alcoholism*. New York: Oxford University Press.

Heyman, K. (2005) Neurophysiology: dust clearing on the long-term potentiation debate. *The Scientist*, 19, 14.

Heymsfield, S.B., Greenberg, A.S., Fujioka, K. *et al.* (1999) Recombinant leptin for weight loss in obese and lean adults. *Journal of the American Medical Association*, 282, 1568–1575.

Hibell, B., Anderson, B., Ahlstrom, S. *et al.* (2001) *The 1999 ESPAD Report: Alcohol and other Drug Use among Students in 30 European Countries*. Stockholm: Swedish Council for Information on Alcohol and Other Drugs.

Higley, J.D., Mehlman, P.T., Poland, R.E. *et al.* (1996) CSF testosterone and 5-HIAA correlate with different types of aggressive behaviors. *Biological Psychiatry*, 40, 1067–1082.

Hines M., Allen, L.S. and Gorski, R.A. (1992) Sex differences in subregions of the medial nucleus of the amygdala and the bed nucleus of the stria terminalis of the rat. *Brain Research*, 579, 321–326.

Hobson, J.A. (1988) *The Dreaming Brain*. London: Penguin.

Hobson, J.A. (1995) *Sleep*. New York: Scientific American Library.

Hobson, J.A. (1999) Arrest of firing of aminergic neurones during REM sleep: implications for dream theory. *Experimental Brain Bulletin*, 50, 323–334.

Hobson, J.A., McCarley, R.W. and Wyzinski, P.W. (1975) Sleep cycle oscillation: reciprocal discharge by two brainstem neuronal groups. *Science*, 189, 55–58.

Hoffman, A. (2005) *LSD: My Problem Child*. Sarasota, Fla.: MAPS.

Hohmann, G.W. (1966) Some effects of spinal cord lesions on experienced emotional feelings. *Psychophysiology*, 3, 143–156.

Holland, P.C. and Petrovich, G.D. (2005) A neural systems analysis of the potentiation of feeding by conditioned stimuli. *Physiology and Behavior*, 86, 747–761.

Holmes, D. (1991) *Abnormal Psychology*. New York: HarperCollins.

Hölscher, C. (2001) Long-term potentiation as a model for memory mechanisms: the story so far. In Hölscher, C. (ed.) *Neuronal Mechanisms of Memory Formation*. Cambridge: Cambridge University Press.

Holtzman, S.G. (1990) Caffeine as a model drug of abuse. *Trends in Neurosciences*, 11, 355–356.

Hopkins, A. (1993) *Clinical Neurology*. London: Oxford University Press.

Horne, J. (1978) A review of the biological effects of total sleep deprivation in man. *Biological Psychology*, 7, 55–102.

Horne, J. (1988) *Why We Sleep*. London: Oxford University Press.

House of Commons Health Committee (2004) *Obesity. Third report*. The Stationery Office. www.publications.parliament.uk

Hubel, D.H. (1982) Exploration of the primary visual cortex. *Nature*, 299, 515–524.

Hubel, D.H. (1988) *Eye, Brain and Vision*. New York: Scientific American Library.

Hubel, D.H. and Wiesel, T.N. (2005) *Brain and Visual Perception: The Story of a 25-Year Collaboration*. Oxford: Oxford University Press.

Hughes, J. (1991) *An Outline of Modern Psychiatry*. Chichester: John Wiley.

Hughes, J.T., Smith, T., Kosterlitz, H.W. *et al.* (1975) Identification of two related pentapeptides from the brain with potent opiate agonist activity. *Nature*, 258, 577–579.

Hull, E.M., Du, J., Lorrain, D.S. and Matuszewich, L. (1997) Testosterone, preoptic dopamine, and copulation in male rats. *Brain Research Bulletin*, 44, 327–333.

Hunt, D.M., Dulai, K.S., Bowmaker, J.K. and Mollon, J.D. (1995) The chemistry of John Dalton's color blindness. *Science*, 267, 984–988.

Huntington's Disease Collaborative Research Group (1993) A novel gene containing a trinucleotide repeat that is expanded and unstable on Huntington's disease chromosomes. *Cell*, 72, 971–983.

Huppert, F.A. and Piercy, M. (1979) Normal and abnormal forgetting in organic amnesia: effect of locus of lesion. *Cortex*, 15, 385–390.

Hurley, K.M., Herbert, H., Moga, M.M. and Saper, C.B. (1991) Efferent projections of the infralimbic cortex of the rat. *Journal of Comparative Neurology*, 308, 249–276.

Hyde, T.M., Stacey, M.E., Coppola, R. *et al.* (1995) Cerebral morphometric abnormailities in Tourette's syndrome: a quantitative MRI study of monozygotic twins. *Neurology*, 45, 1176–1182.

Ikemoto, S. and Panksepp, J. (1999) The role of nucleus accumbens dopamine in motivated behavior: a unifying interpretation with special reference to reward seeking. *Brain Research Reviews*, 31, 6–41.

Imperato, A. and Di Chiara, G. (1986) Preferential stimulation of dopamine release in the nucleus accumbens of freely moving rats by ethanol. *Journal of Pharmacology and Experimental Therapeutics*, 239, 219–228.

Inouye, S. and Kawamura, H. (1979) Persistence of circadian rhythmicity in a mammalian hypothalamic 'island' containing the suprachiamatic nucleus. *Proceedings of the National Academy of Sciences*, 76, 5692–5966.

Institute for the Study of Drug Dependence (1996) *Heroin: Drug Notes*. London: ISDD.

Irwin, M. (2002) Effects of sleep loss on immunity and cytokines. *Brain, Behavior and Immunity*, 16, 503–512.

J

Jablensky, A. (1997) The 100-year epidemiology of schizophrenia. *Schizophrenia Research*, 28, 111–125.

Jablensky, A., Sartorius, N., Emberg, G. *et al.* (1992) Schizophrenia: manifestations, incidence and course in different cultures. A World Health Organization 10 country study. *Psychological Medicine Monograph Suppl.20.*

Jacobs, L.F., Gaulin, S.J.C. Sherry, D.F. and Hoffman, G.E. (1990) Evolution of spatial cognition: sex-specific patterns of spatial behavior predict hippocampal size. *Proceedings of the New York Academy of Sciences*, 87, 6349–6352.

James, W. (1890) *The Principles of Psychology*. New York: Holt.

Jaskiw, G. and Kleinman, J. (1988) Postmortem neurochemistry studies in schizophrenia. In Schulz, S.C. and Tamminga, C.A. (eds) *Schizophrenia: A Scientific Focus*. New York: Oxford University Press.

Jeanmoned, D., Magnin, M. and Morel, A. (1993) Thalamus and neurogenic pain: physiological, anatomical and clinical data. *Neuroreport*, 4, 475–478.

Jellinek, E.M. (1960) *The Disease Concept of Alcoholism*. New Haven, Conn.: Hillhouse.

Jenkins, I.H., Brooks, D.J., Nixon, P.D. *et al.* (1994) Motor sequencing learning: a study with positron emission tomography. *Journal of Neuroscience*, 14, 3775–3790.

Jentsch, J.D. and Roth, R.H. (1999) The neuropsychopharmacology of phencyclidine: from NMDA receptor hypofunction to the dopamine hypothesis of schizophrenia. *Neuropsychopharmacology*, 20, 201–225.

Jewitt, D.C., Cleary, J., Levine, A.S. *et al.* (1992) Effects of neuropeptide Y on food-reinforced behavior in satiated rats. *Pharmacology, Biochemistry and Behavior*, 42, 207–212.

Jobst, K.A., Smith, A.D., Szatmari, M. *et al.* (1994) Rapidly progressing atrophy of medial temporal lobe in Alzheimer's disease. *Lancet*, 343, 829–830.

Jones, B. (1979) Elimination of paradoxical sleep by lesions of the pontine gigantocellular tegmental field in the rat. *Neuroscience Letters*, 13, 285–293.

Jones, D.T. and Reed, R.R.G. (1989) An olfactory neuron specific G protein involved in odorant signal transduction. *Science*, 244, 790–795.

Jones, H.S. and Oswald, I. (1968) Two cases of health insomnia. *Electroencephalography and Clinical Neurophysiology*, 24, 378–380.

Jones, S. (1993) *The Language of the Genes*. London: Flamingo.

Jope, R. S. (1999) Anti-bipolar therapy: mechanism of action of lithium. *Molecular Psychiatry*, 4, 117–128.

Joseph, M.H., Datla, K. and Young, A.M.J. (2003) The interpretation of the measurement of nucleus accumbens dopamine by in vivo dialysis: the kick, the craving or the cognition? *Neuroscience and Biobehavioral Reviews*, 27, 527–541.

Joslyn, W.D. (1973) Androgen-induced dominance in infant female rhesus monkeys. *Journal of Child Psychology and Psychiatry*, 14, 137–145.

Jouvet, M. (1962) Recherches sur les structures nerveuses et les mécanismes responsables des différentes phases du sommeil physiologique. *Archives of Italian Biology*, 100, 125–206.

Jouvet, M. (1967) Neurophysiology and the states of sleep. *Science*, 163, 32–41.

Jouvet, M. (1972) The role of monoamines and acetylcholine containing neurones in the regulation of sleep waking cycle. *Ergenisse der Physiology*, 64, 166–307.

Jouvet, M. (1979) What does a cat dream about? *Trends in Neurosciences*, 2, 280–282.

Jouvet, M. and Delorme, F. (1965) Locus coeruleus et sommeil paradoxal. *Comptes Rendus Société de Biologie*, 159, 895–899.

Jouvet, M. and Renault, J. (1966) Insomnie persistante après lésions des noyaux du raphe chez le chat. *C.R. Soc. Biol. (Paris)*, 160, 1461–1465.

Julien, R.M. (2007) *A Primer of Drug Action*, 11th edition. New York: Worth Publishers.

K

Kaas, J.H. (1990) Somatosensory system. In Paxinos, G. (ed) *The Human Nervous System*. San Diego: Academic Press.

Kaas, J.H. (1991) Plasticity of sensory and motor maps in adult mammals. *Annual Review of Neuroscience*, 14, 137–167.

Kaij, L. (1960) *Studies on the Etiology and Sequels of Abuse of Alcohol*. University of Lund, Department of Psychiatry.

Kallman, F.S. (1952) Comparative twin studies of the genetic aspects of male homosexuality. *Journal of Nervous and Mental Diseases*, 115, 283–298.

Kandel, E.R. (1979) Small systems of neurons. *Scientific American*, Sept., 67–76.

Kandel, E.R. (2001) The molecular biology of memory storage: a dialogue between genes and synapses. *Science*, 294, 1030–1038.

Kandel, E.R. and Hawkins, R.D. (1982) The biological basis of learning and individuality. *Scientific American*, Sept., 53–60.

Kandel, E.R., Schwartz, J.H. and Jessell, T.M. (1995) *Essentials of Neural Science and Behaviour*. Stamford, Conn.: Appleton & Lange.

Kane, J.M. (1992) Clinical efficay of clozapine in treatment-refractory schizophrenia: an overview. *British Journal of Psychiatry*, 160 (suppl. 17), 41–45.

Kanwisher, N., McDermott, J. and Chun, M.M. (1997) The fusiform face area: a module in human extrastriate cortex specialised for face perception. *Journal of Neuroscience*, 17, 4302–4311.

Kapp, B.S., Frysinger, R.C., Gallagher, M. and Haselton, J.R. (1979) Amygdala central nucleus lesions: effects on heart rate conditioning in the rabbit. *Physiology and Behaviour*, 23, 1109–1117.

Kapp, B.S., Pascoe, J.P. and Bixler, M.A. (1984) The amygdala: a neuroanatomical systems approach to its contributions to aversive conditioning. In Butters, N. and Squire, L.R. (eds) *The Neuropsychology of Memory*. New York: Guilford Press.

Kapp, B.S., Whalen, P.J., Supple, W.F. and Pascoe, J.P. (1992) Amygdaloid contributions to conditioned arousal and sensory information processing. In Aggleton, J.P. (ed.) *The Amygdala: Neurobiological Aspects of Emotion, Memory and Mental Dysfunction*. New York: John Wiley.

Karoum, F. and Egan, M.F. (1992) Dopamine release and metabolism in the rat frontal cortex, nucleus accumbens, and striatum: a comparison of acute clozapine and haloperidol. *British Journal of Pharmacology*, 105, 703–707.

Katzman, D.K. (1996) Cerebral gray matter and white matter volume deficits in adolescent girls with anorexia nervosa. *Journal of Pediatrics*, 129, 794–803.

Katzman, D.K., Zipursky, R.B., Lambe, E.K. and Mikulis, D.J. (1997) A longitudinal magnetic resonance imaging study of brain changes in adolescents with anorexia nervosa. *Archives of Pediatric and Adolescent Medicine*, 151, 793–797.

Katzman, R. (1976) The prevalence and malignancy of Alzheimer's disease: a major killer. *Archives of Neurology*, 33, 217–218.

Katzman, R. (1993) Education and the prevalence of dementia and Alzheimer's disease. *Neurology*, 43, 13–20.

Katzman, R., Terry, R., DeTeresa, R. *et al.* (1988) Clinical, pathological, and neurochemical changes in dementia: A subgroup with preserved mental status and numerous neocortical plaques. *Annals of Neurology*, 23,138–44.

Kavanau, L. (2006) Is sleep's supreme mystery unraveling? *Medical Hypotheses*, 66, 3–9.

Kaye, W.H. (1997) Persistent alterations in behavior and serotonergic activity after recovering from anorexia and bulimia nervosa. *Annals of the New York Academy of Sciences*, 817, 162–178.

Kaye, W.H. (2000) Anorexia and bulimia nervosa. *Annual Review of Medicine*, 51, 299–313.

Kaye, W.H., Jimerson, D.C., Lake, C.R. and Ebert, M.H. (1985) Altered norepinephrine metabolism following long-term weight recovery in patients with anorexia nervosa. *Psychiatry Research*, 14, 333–342.

Kebbian, J.W. and Calne, D.B. (1979) Multiple receptors for dopamine. *Nature*, 277, 93–96.

Keele, S.W. and Ivry, R.B. (1991) Does the cerebellum provide a common computation for diverse tasks? A timing hypothesis. *Annals of the New York Academy of Sciences*, 608, 179–207.

Keltner, D. and Ekman, P. (2000) Facial expression of emotion. In Lewis, M. and Haviland-Jones, J. (eds) *Handbook of Emotions*. New York: Guilford Press.

Kendell, R.E. and Adams, W. (1991) Unexplained flucturations in the risk of schizophrenia by month and year of birth. *British Journal of Psychiatyry*, 158, 758–763.

Kendler, K.S., Pedersen, N., Johnson, L. *et al.* (1993) A pilot Swedish twin study of affective illness, including hospital- and population-ascertained subsamples. *Archives of General Psychiatry*, 50, 699–706.

Kendler, K.S., Gatz, M., Gardner, C. and Pedersen, N. (2006) A Swedish national twin study of lifetime major depression. *American Journal of Psychiatry*, 163, 109–114.

Kendrick, K.M. and Baldwin, B.A. (1987) Cells in temporal cortex of conscious sheep can respond preferentially to the sight of faces. *Science*, 236, 448–450.

Kertesz, A. (1979) *Aphasia and Associated Disorders*. New York: Grune & Stratton.

Kestler, L.P., Walker, E. and Vega, E.M. (2001) Dopamine receptors in the brains of schizophrenia patients: a meta-analysis of the findings. *Behavioral Pharmacology*, 12, 355–371.

Kety, S.S., Rosenthal, D., Wender, P.H. and Schlesinger, F. (1968) The types and prevalence of mental illness in the biological and adoptive families of adopted schizophrenics. In Rosenthal, D. and Kety, S.S. (eds) *The Transmission of Schizophrenia*. Elmsford: Pergamon Press.

Keverne, E.B. (1999) The vomeronasal organ. *Science,* 286, 716–720.

Keynes, R.D. (1979) Ion channels in the nerve-cell membrane. *Scientific American,* 240, 126–135.

Kim, J. and Gorman, J (2005) The psychobiology of anxiety. *Clinical Neuroscience Research,* 4, 335–347.

Kimble, D.P. (1968) Hippocampus and internal inhibition. *Psychological Bulletin,* 70, 285–295.

Kimura, D. (1992) Sex differences in the brain. *Scientific American,* 267, 80–87.

Kimura, D. (1999) *Sex and Cognition.* Cambridge, Mass.: MIT Press.

King, B.M. (2006) The rise, fall, and resurrection of the ventromedial hypothalamus in the regulation of feeding behavior and body weight. *Physiology and Behavior,* 87, 221–244.

Kingsland, J. (2004) The rise and fall of wonder drugs. *New Scientist,* 182(2454), 36.

Kinsey, A.C., Pomeroy, W.B. and Martin, C.E. (1948) *Sexual Behavior in the Human Male.* Philadelphia: W.B. Saunders.

Kissileff, H.R., Pi-Sunyer, F.X., Thornton, J. and Smith G.P. (1981) C-terminal octapeptide of cholecystokinin decreases food intake in man. *American Journal of Clinical Nutrition,* 34, 154–160.

Klee, W.A. and Nirenberg, M. (1974) A neuroblastoma times glioma hybrid cell line with morphine receptors. *Proceedings of the National Academy of Sciences,* 71, 3474–3477.

Klein, S.B. and Thorne, B.M. (2007) *Biological Psychology.* New York: Worth Publishers.

Kluver, H. and Bucy, P.C. (1938) An analysis of certain effects of bilateral temporal lobectomy in the rhesus monkey with special reference to 'psychic blindness'. *Journal of Psychology,* 5, 33–54.

Kodama, T., Takahashi, Y. and Honda, Y. (1990) Enhancement of acetylcholine release during paradoxical sleep in the dorsal tegmental field of the brain stem. *Neuroscience Letters,* 114, 277–282.

Kolb, B. and Whishaw, I.Q. (2003) *Fundamentals of Human Neuropsychology,* 5th edition. New York: Worth Publishers.

Konopka, R.J. and Benzer, S. (1971) Clock mutants of *Drosophilia melanogaster. Proceedings of the National Academy of Sciences,* 68, 2112–2116.

Koob, G.F. and Bloom, F.E. (1988) Cellular and molecular mechanisms of drug dependence. *Science,* 242, 715–723.

Koob, G.F. and Goeders, N.E. (1989) Neuroanatomical substrates of drug self-administration. In Liebman, J.M. and Cooper, S.J. (eds) *Neuropharmacological Basis of Reward.* London, Oxford University Press.

Koob, G.F. and Nestler, E.J. (1997) The neurobiology of drug addiction. *Journal of Neuropsychiatry and Clinical Neuroscience,* 9, 482–497.

Koob, G.F. (1999) Drug reward and addiction. In Zigmand, M.J., Bloom, F.E., Landis, S.C. *et al.* (eds) *Fundamental Neuroscience.* San Diego, Calif.: Academic Press.

Koob, G.F. and Le Moal, M. (2006) *Neurobiology of Addiction.* New York: Academic Press.

Koob, G.F., Maldonado, R. and Stinus, L. (1992) Neural substrates of opitae withdrawal. *Trends in Neurosciences,* 15, 186–191.

Koopman, P., Gubbay, J., Vivian, N. *et al.* (1991) Male development of chromosomally female mice transgenic for Sry. *Nature,* 351, 117–121.

Koopmans, H.S. (1981) The role of the gastrointestinal tract in the satiation of hunger. In Cioffi, A., James, W.P.T. and Van Italie, T.B. (eds) *The Body Weight Regulatory System.* New York: Raven Press.

Krank, M.D. and Perkins, W.L. (1993) Conditioned withdrawal elicited by contextual cues for morphine administration. *Psychobiology,* 21, 113–119.

Kranzler, H.R. and Anton, R.F. (1994) Implications of recent neuropsychological research for understanding the etiology and development of alcoholism. *Journal of Consulting and Clinical Psychology,* 62, 1116–1126.

Kubitz, K.A., Landers, D.M., Petruzzello, S.J. and Han, M. (1996) The effects of acute and chronic exercise on sleep: a meta-analytic review. *Sports Medicine,* 21, 277–291.

Kuffler, S.W. (1953) Discharge patterns and functional organization of the mammalian retina. *Journal of Neurophysiology,* 16, 37–68.

Kuhn, R. (1958) The treatment of depressive states with G 22355 (imipramine hydrochloride). *American Journal of Psychiatry,* 115, 459–464.

Kupfermann, I., Castelluci, V., Pinsker, H. and Kandel, E.R. (1970) Neuronal correlates of habituation and dishabituation of the gill-withdrawal reflex in *Aplysia. Science,* 167, 1743–1745.

Lacoste-Utamsing, M.C. and Holloway, R.L. (1982) Sexual dimorphism in the human corpus callosum. *Science,* 216, 1431–1432.

Lader, M. (1983) Dependence on benzodiazepines. *Journal of Clinical Psychiatry,* 44, 121–127.

Lader, M. and Herrington, R. (1990) *Biological Treatments in Psychiatry.* London: Oxford University Press.

Land, H. (1977) The retinex theory of color vision. *Scientific American*, April, 108–128.

Langston, J.W. (1990) Predicting Parkinson's disease. *Neurology*, 40, 70–74.

Langston, J.W. (2002) Parkinson's disease: current and future challenges. *NeuroToxicology*, 23, 443–450.

Langston, J.W., Ballard, P., Tetrud, J. and Irwin, I. (1983) Chronic parkinsonism in humans due to a product of meperidine analog synthesis. *Science*, 219, 979–980.

Langston, J.W., Irwin, I., Langston, E.B. and Forno, L.S. (1984) Pargyline prevents MPTP-induced Parkinsonism in primates. *Science*, 225, 1480–1488.

Larsen, B., Skinhoj, E. and Lassen, N.A. (1978) Variations in regional cortical blood flow in the right and left hemispheres during autonomic speech. *Brain*, 101, 193–209.

Larsen, J., Hoien, T., Lundberg, I. and Odegaard, H. (1990) MRI evaluation of the size and symmetry of the planum temporale in adolescents with developmental dyslexia. *Brain and Language*, 39, 289–301.

Lashley, K.S. (1950) In search of the engram. *Symposium for the Society of Experimental Biology*, 4, 454–482.

Lassen, N.A., Ingvar, D.H. and Skinhoj, E. (1978) Brain function and blood flow. *Scientific American*, 239(4), 50–59.

Laurin, D., Verreault, R., Lindsay, J. *et al.* (2001) Physical activity and risk of cognitive impairment and dementia in elderly persons. *Archives of Neurology*, 58, 498–504.

Lavie, P. (1996) *The Enchanted World of Sleep*. New Haven, Conn.: Yale University Press.

Lavie, P., Pratt, H., Scharf, B. *et al.* (1984) Localized pontine lesion: nearly total absence of REM sleep. *Neurology*, 34, 118–120.

Lawrence, D. and Kuypers, H. (1968) The functional organization of the motor system in the monkey. *Brain*, 91, 1–36.

Lawrie, S.M., Whalley, H.C., Job, D.E. and Johnstone, E.C. (2003) Structural and functional abnormalities of the amygdala in schizophrenia. *Annals of the New York Academy of Sciences*, 985, 445–460.

Le, A.D., Poulos, C.X. and Cappell, H. (1979) Conditioned tolerance to the hypothermic effect of alcohol. *Science*, 206, 1109.

Leake, C.D. (1958) *The Amphetamines: Their Actions and their Uses*. Springfield, Ill.: Charles C. Thomas.

LeDoux, J.E. (1994) Emotion, memory and the brain. *Scientific American*, June, 32–39.

LeDoux, J.E. (1995) Emotion: clues from the brain. *Annual Review of Psychology*, 46, 209–235.

LeDoux, J.E. (1998) *The Emotional Brain*. London: Weidenfeld & Nicolson.

LeDoux, J.E., Sakaguchi, A.A. and Reis, D.J. (1984) Subcortical efferent projections of the medial geniculate nucleus mediate emotional responses conditioned to acoustic stimuli. *Journal of Neuroscience*, 4, 683–698.

LeDoux, J.E., Iwata, J., Cicchetti, P. and Reis, D.J. (1988) Different projections of the central amygdaloid nucleus mediate autonomic and behavioral correlates of conditioned fear. *Journal of Neuroscience*, 8, 2517–2529.

Lee, D.J., Chen, Y. and Schlaug, G. (2003) Corpus callosum: musician and gender effects. *NeuroReport*, 14, 205–209.

Lee, M.G., Hassani, O.K. and Jones, B.E. (2005) Discharge of identified orexin/hypocretin neurons across the sleep–waking cycle. *Journal of Neuroscience*, 25, 6716–6720.

Lees, A.J. (1986) L-Dopa treatment of Parkinson's disease. *Quarterly Journal of Medicine*, 230, 535–547.

Lenneberg, E.H. (1967) *Biological Foundations of Language*. New York: John Wiley.

Leonard, C.T. (1998) *The Neuroscience of Human Movement*. St Louis: Mosby.

LeVay, S. (1993) *The Sexual Brain*. Cambridge, Mass.: MIT Press.

Levenson, R.W., Ekman, P., Heider, K. and Friesen, W.V. (1992) Emotion and autonomic nervous system activity in the Minangkabu of West Sumatra. *Journal of Personality and Social Psychology*, 62, 972–988.

Leventhal, A.G., Thompson, K.G., Liu, D. *et al.* (1995) Concomitant sensitivity to orientation, direction, and color of cells in layers 2, 3 and 4 of monkey striate cortex. *Journal of Neuroscience*, 15, 1808–1818.

Levinthal, C. (1988) *Messengers of Paradise: Opiates and the Brain*. New York: Doubleday.

Levy, J. and Heller, (1992) Gender differences in human neuropsychological function. In Gerall, A.A., Moltz, H. and Ward, I.L. (eds) *Sexual Differentiation: Handbook of Behavioral Neurology*. New York: Plenum Press.

Levy, J. (1969) Possible basis for the evolution of lateral specialization. *Nature*, 224, 614–615.

Levy-Lehad, E., Wasco, W., Poorkaj, P. *et al.* (1995) Candidate gene for chromosome 1 familial Alzheimer disease locus. *Science*, 269, 973–977.

Lewy, A.J. (1980) Light suppresses melatonin secretion in humans. *Science*, 210, 1267–1269.

Lewy, A.J., Sack, R.L., Singer, D.M. *et al.* (1989) Winter depression: the phase between sleep and other circadian rhythms may be critical. In Thompson, C. and Silverstone, T. (eds) *Seasonal Affective Disorder*. London: Clinical Neuroscience Publishers.

Li, S.H., Schilling, G., Young, W.S. et al. (1993) Huntington's disease gene (IT15) is widely expressed in human and rat tissues. *Neuron*, 11, 985–993.

Libet, B., Gleason, C.A., Wright, E.W. and Pearl, D.K. (1983) Time of conscious intention to act in relation to onset of cerebral activity (readiness potential). The unconscious initiation of a freely voluntary act. *Brain*, 102, 623–642.

Lickey, M.E. and Gordon, B. (1991) *Medicine and Mental Illness*. New York: Freeman.

Lieverse, R., Masclee, A., Jansen, J. et al. (1998) Obese women are less sensitive for the satiety effects of bombesin than lean women. *European Journal of Clinical Nutrition*, 52, 207–121.

Lin, L., Faraco, J., Kadotani, H. et al. (1999) The sleep disorder canine narcolepsy is caused by a mutation on the hypocretin (orexin) receptor 2 gene. *Cell*, 98, 365–376.

Lindsley, D.B., Bowden, J. and Magoun, H.W. (1949) Effect upon the EEG of acute injury to the brainstem activating system. *Clinical Neuropsychology*, 1, 475–486.

Lindvall, O. (1989) Transplantation into the human brain: present status and future possibilities. *Journal of Neurology, Neurosurgery and Psychaitry*, suppl., 39–54.

Lindvall, O. (1991) Peospects of transplantation in human neurodegenerative diseases. *Trends in Neurosciences*, 14, 376–384.

Lindvall, O., Backlund, E.O., Farde, L. et al. (1987) Transplantation in Parkinson's disease: two cases of adrenal medullary grafts in the putamen. *Annals of Neurology*, 22, 457–468.

Lissauer, H. (1890) Ein Fall von Seelenblindheit nebst einem Beitrage zur Theorie derselben. *Archiv für Psychiatrie und Nervenkrankheiten*, 21, 222–270.

Livingstone, M.S. and Hubel, D.S. (1988) Segregation of form, colour, movement and depth: anatomy, physiology and perception. *Science*, 240, 740–749.

Lobo, I.A. and Harris, R.A. (2008) $GABA_A$ receptors and alcohol. *Pharmacology, Biochemistry and Behavior*, 90, 90–94.

Logue, A.W. (1986) *The Psychology of Eating and Drinking*. New York: Freeman.

Long, J.C., Knowler, W.C., Hanson, R.L. et al. (1998) Evidence for genetic linkage to alcohol dependence on chromosomes 4 and 11 from an autosome-wide scan in an American Indian population. *American Journal of Medical Genetics*, 8, 216–221.

Lopez, M.S., Tovar, S., Vazquez, M.J. et al. (2007) Peripheral tissue–brain interactions in the regulation of food intake. *Proceedings of the Nutritional Society*, 66, 131–155.

Lorens, S.A. (1966) Effect of lesions in the central nervous system on lateral hypothalamic self-stimulation in the rat. *Journal of Comparative and Physiological Psychology*, 62, 256–262.

Lovinger, D.M. (1997) Alcohols and neurotransmitter gated icon channels: past, present and future. *Naunyn Schmiedebergs Archives of Pharmacology*, 356, 267–282.

Lu, D., Willard, D., Patel, I.R. et al. (1994) Agouti protein is an antagonist of the melanocyte-stimulating-hormone receptor. *Nature*, 371, 799–802.

Lücking, C., Dürr, A., Bonifati, V. et al. (2000) Association between early onset Parkinson's disease and mutations in the *parkin* gene. *New England Journal of Medicine*, 342, 1560–1567.

Lumeng, L., Hawkins, T.D. and Li, T.K. (1977) New strains of rats with alcohol preference and non-preference. In Thurman, R.G., Williamson, J.R. and Drott, H. (eds) *Alcohol and Aldehyde Metabolizing Systems*. New York: Academic Press.

Lumeng, L., Murphy, J.M., McBride, W.J. and Li, T.K. (1993) Genetic influences on alcohol preference in animals. In Begleiter, H. and Kissin, B. (eds) *The Genetics of Alcoholism*. London: Oxford University Press.

Luria, A.R. (1968) *The Mind of a Mnemonist*. London: Jonathan Cape.

M

MacLean, P.D. (1949) Psychosomatic disease and the 'visceral brain': recent developments bearing on the Papez theory of emotion. *Psychosomatic Medicine*, 11, 338–353.

MacLean, P.D. (1955) The limbic system ('visceral brain') and emotional behaviour. *Archives of Neurology and Psychiatry*, 73, 130–134.

Macmillan, M. (1996) Phineas Gage: a case for all reasons. In Code, C., Wallesch, C.-W., Joanette, Y. and Lecours, R. (eds) *Classic Cases in Neuropsychology*. Hove: Psychology Press.

Maehle, A.H. (2004) 'Receptive substances': John Newport Langley (1852–1925) and his path to a receptor theory of drug action. *Medical History*, 48, 153–174.

Maes, M. and Meltzer, H.Y. (1995) The serotonin hypothesis of major depression. In Bloom, F.E. and Kupfer, D.J. (eds) *Psychopharmacology: The Fourth Generation in Progress*. New York: Raven Press.

Magnes, J., Moruzzi, G. and Pompeiano, O. (1961) Synchronization of the EEG produced by low frequency electrical stimulation of the region of the solitary tract. *Archives of Italian Biology*, 99, 33–67.

Magni, F., Moruzzi, G., Rossi, G. and Zanchatti, F. (1959) EEG arousal following inactivation of the lower brain stem by selective injection of barbiturate into the ventribal circulation. *Archives Italiennes de Biologie*, 95, 33–46.

Maguire, E.A., Frackowiak, R.S.J. and Frith, C.D. (1997) Recalling routes around London: activation of the right hippocampus in taxi drivers. *Journal of Neuroscience*, 17, 7103–7110.

Maguire, E.A., Gadian, D.G., Johnsrude, I.S. *et al.* (2000) Navigation-related structural change in the hippocampi of taxi drivers. *Proceedings of the National Academy of Sciences*, 97, 4398–4403.

Maldonado, R., Stinus, L., Gold, L.H. and Koob, G.F. (1992) Role of different brain structures in the expression of the physical morphine withdrawal syndrome. *Journal of Pharmacology and Experimental Therapeutics*, 261, 669–677.

Malenka, R.C. (1995) LTP and LTD: dynamic and interactive processes of synaptic plasticity. *The Neuroscientist* 1, 35–42.

Malinow, R., Schulman, H. and Tsien, R.W. (1989) Inhibition of postsynaptic PKC or CaMKII blocks induction but not expression of LTP. *Science*, 245, 862–866.

Manji, H.K., Quiroz, J.A., Sporn, J. *et al.* (2003) Enhancing neuronal plasticity and cellular resilience to develop novel, improved therapeutics for difficult-to-treat depression. *Biological Psychiatry*, 53, 707–742.

Mann, D.M.A., McDonagh, A.M., Pickering-Brown, S.M. *et al.* (2001) Amyloid β protein deposition in patients with frontotemporal lobar degeneration: relationship to age and apolipoprotein E genotype. *Neuroscience Letters*, 304, 161–164.

Manning, J.T. (2002) *Digit ratio: A Pointer to Fertility, Behavior and Health*. New Jersey: Rutgers University Press.

Manning, J.T., Churchill, A.J.G. and Peters, M. (2007) The effects of sex, ethnicity, and sexual orientation on self measured digit ratio (2D:4D). *Archives of Sexual Behavior*, 36, 223–233.

Mardones, J. and Segovia-Riquelme, N. (1983) Thirty-two years of selection of rats by ethanol preference. *Neurobehavioral Toxicity and Teratology*, 5, 171–178.

Mark, V.H. and Ervin, F.R. (1970) *Violence and the Brain*. New York: Harper and Row.

Markianos, M., Botsis, A. and Arvanitis, Y. (1992) Biogenic amine metabolites in plasma of drug-naive schizophrenic patients: associations with symptomatology. *Biological Psychiatry*, 32, 288–292.

Markowitsch, H.J. (1985) Hypotheses on mnemonic information processing by the brain. *International Journal of Neuroscience*, 27, 191–227.

Markowitsch, H.J. (1988) Diencephalic amnesia: a re-orientation towards tracts? *Brain Research Reviews*, 13, 351–370.

Martin, A., Wiggs, C.L. and Weisberg, J.W. (1997) Modulation of human medial temporal lobe activity by form, meaning, and experience. *Hippocampus*, 7, 587–593.

Martin, G.N. (2006) *Human Neuropsychology*. Harlow: Prentice Hall.

Martin, P. (2002) *Counting Sheep: The Science and Pleasures of Sleep and Dreams*. London: HarperCollins.

Martin, R.A. (2001) Humor, laughter, and physical health: methodological issues and resaerch findings. *Psychological Bulletin*, 127, 504–519.

Martin, S.M., Manning J.T. and Dowrick, C.F. (1999) Fluctuating asymmetry, relative digit length, and depression in men, *Evolution and Human Behavior*, 20, 203–214.

Marx, J. (2005) Preventing Alzheimer's: a lifelong commitment? *Science*, 309, 864–868.

Masters, W.H. and Johnson, V.E. (1966) *Human Sexual Response*. Boston, Mass.: Little Brown.

Masters, W.H., Johnson, V.E. and Kolodny, R.C. (1995) *Human Sexuality*. New York: HarperCollins.

Mather, G. (2006) *Foundations of Perception*. Hove: Psychology Press.

Matsuda, L., Lolait, S.J., Brownstein, M.J. *et al.* (1990) Structure of a cannabinoid receptor and functional expression of the cloned cDNA. *Nature*, 346, 561–564.

Mayer, J. and Marshall, N.B. (1956) Specificity of goldthioglucose for ventromedial hypothalamic lesions and hyperphagia. *Nature*, 178, 1399–1400.

Mayer, J. (1953) Glucostatic mechanisms of regulation of food intake. *New England Journal of Medicine*, 249, 13–16.

Mayes, A.R. (1988) *Human Organic Memory Disorders*. Cambridge: Cambridge University Press.

Mazur, A. and Booth, A. (1998) Testosterone and dominance in men. *Behavioral and Brain Sciences*, 21, 353–397.

Mazzolini, R.G. (1991) Schemes and models of the thinking machine. In Corsi, P. (ed.) *The Enchanted Loom: Chapters in the History of Neuroscience*. New York: Oxford University Press.

McCarley, R.W. (1995) Sleep, dreams, and states of consciousness. In Conn, P.M. (ed.) *Neuroscience in Medicine*. Philadelphia: Lippincott.

McCarley, R.W. and Hobson, J.A. (1975) Neuronal excitability modulations over the sleep cycle: a structured and mathematical model. *Science*, 189, 58–60.

McCarley, R.W., Greene, R.W., Rainnie, D. and Portas, C.M. (1995) Brainstem modulation and REM sleep. *Seminars in the Neurosciences*, 7, 341–354.

McClearn, G.E. and Kakihana, R. (1981) Selective breeding for ethanol sensitivity: SS and LS mice. In McClearn, G.E., Oetrich, R.A. and Erwin, V.G. (eds) *The Development of Animal Models as Pharmacogenetic Tools*. NIAAA Research Monograph. Washington, DC.

McClearn, G.E. and Rodgers, D.A. (1959) Differences in alcohol preference among inbred strains of mice. *Quaterly Journal of Studies on Alcohol*, 52, 62–67.

McClintock, M.K. (1971) Menstrual synchronicity and suppression. *Nature*, 229, 244–245.

McDonald, C., Grech, A., Toulopoulou, T. *et al.* (2002) Brain volumes in familial and non-familial schizophrenic probands and their unaffected relatives. *American Journal of Medical Genetics*, 114, 616–625.

McFadden, D. and Pasanen, E.G. (1998) Comparison of the auditory systems of heterosexuals and homosexuals: click-evoked otoacoustic emissions. *Proceedings of the National Academy of Sciences*, 95, 2709–2713.

McGinn, C. (1989) Can we solve the mind–body problem? *Mind*, 98 (July), 349–366.

McGinnis, M.Y., Marcelli, M. and Lamb, D.J. (2002) Consequences of mutations in androgen receptor genes: molecular biology and behavior. In Pfaff, D.W., Arnold, A., Etgen, A. *et al.* (eds) *Hormones, Brain, and Behavior*. New York: Academic Press.

McGinty, D.J. and Sterman, M.B. (1968) Sleep suppression after basal forebrain lesion in the cat. *Science*, 160, 1253–1255.

McGue, M., Pickens, R.W. and Svikis, D.S. (1992) Sex and age effects on the inheritance of alcohol problems: a twin study. *Journal of Abnormal Psychology*, 101, 3–17.

McKenna, P.J. and Bailey, P.E. (1993) The strange story of clozapine. *British Journal of Psychiatry*, 162, 32–37.

McKim, W.A. (2003) *Drugs and Behaviour*, 5th edition. Englewood Cliffs, NJ: Prentice Hall.

McLean, D., Forsythe, R.G. and Kapkin, I.A. (1983) Unusual side effects of clomipramine associated with yawning. *Canadian Journal of Psychiatry*, 28, 569–570.

McManus, C. (2002) *Right Hand, Left Hand*. London: Weidenfeld & Nicolson.

McNamara, P., Durso, R. and Auerbach, S. (2002) Dopaminergic syndromes of sleep, mood and mentation: Evidence from Parkinson's disease and related disorders. *Sleep and Hypnosis*, 4, 119–131.

Mecacci, L. (1991) Pathways of perception. In Corsi, P. (ed.), *The Enchanted Loom: Chapters in the History of Neuroscience*. New York: Oxford University Press.

Meddis, R. (1977) *The Sleep Instinct*. London: Routledge.

Medical Research Council (1965) Clinical trial of the treatment of depressive illness. *British Medical Journal*, i, 881–886.

Meier, C.A. (1998) Orexins and anorexins: thoughts for food. *European Journal of Endocrinolology*, 139, 148–149.

Melzack, R. (1992) Phantom limbs. *Scientific American*, 266, 120–126.

Melzack, R. and Casey, K.L. (1968) Sensory, motivational and central determinants of pain. In Kensalo, D.R. (ed.) *The Skin Senses*. Springfield, Ill.: Charles C. Thomas.

Melzack, R. and Wall, P.D. (1965) Pain mechanisms: a new theory. *Science*, 150, 971–979.

Melzack, R. and Wall, P.D. (1968) Gate control theory of pain. In Cohn, J. and Charpentier, J. (eds) *Pain*. New York: Academic Press.

Melzack, R. and Wall, P.D. (1988) *The Challenge of Pain*. London: Penguin.

Mennella, J.A., Jagnow, C.J. and Beauchamp G.K. (2001) Prenatal and postnatal flavor learning by human infants. *Pediatrics*, 107, 88.

Merali, Z., Moody, T.W. and Coy, D. (1993) Blockade of brain bombesin/GRP receptors increases food intake in satiated rats. *American Journal of Physiology*, 264, 1031–1034.

Merali, Z. (1999) Role of bombesin-related peptides in the control of food intake. *Neuropeptides*, 33, 376–386.

Meyer, D.J. (1979) Endogenous analgesia systems: neural and behavioral mechanisms. In Liebeskind, J.C. and Albe-Fessards, D.G. (eds) *Pain Research and Therapy*, Vol. 3. New York: Raven Press.

Michael, C.R. (1969) Retinal Processing of Visual Images. *Scientific American*, 220, 104–114.

Michael, R.P. (1980) Hormones and sexual behaviour in the female. In Krieger, D.T. and Hughes, J.C. (eds) *Neuroendocrinology*. Sunderland, Mass.: Sinauer.

Milner, B. (1964) Some effects of frontal lobotomy in man. In Warren, J.M. and Akert, K. (eds) *The Frontal Granular Cortex and Behavior*. New York: McGraw-Hill.

Milner, B. (1970) Memory and the medial temporal regions of the brain. In Pribram, D.H. and Broadbent, D.E. (eds) *Biology of Memory*. New York: Academic Press.

Milner, B., Corkin, S. and Teuber, H.L. (1968) Further analysis of the hippocampal amnesic syndrome: 14 year follow-up study of HM. *Neuropsychologia*, 6, 317–338.

Mink, J.W. (1999) Basal ganglia. In Zigmond, M., Bloom, F.J., Landis, S. *et al.* (eds) *Fundamental Neuroscience*. New York: Academic Press.

Mirmiran, M. (1986) The importance of fetal/neonatal REM sleep. *European Journal of Obstetrics, Gynecology, and Reproductive Biology*, 21, 283–291.

Mirsky, A.F., Bieliauskas, L.A., French, L.M. *et al.* (2000) A 39-year followup of the Genian quadruplets. *Schizophenia Bulletin*, 26, 699–708.

Mishkin, M. (1978) Memory in monkeys severely impaired by combined but not separate removal of the amygdala and hippocampus. *Nature*, 273, 297–298.

Mistelberger, R.E. (2005) Circadian regulation of sleep in mammals: role of the suprachiasmatic nucleus. *Brain Research Reviews*, 49, 429–454.

Miyakawa, T., Yagi, T., Kitazawa, H. *et al.* (1997) Fyn-kinase as a determinant of ethanol sensitivity: relation to NMDA-receptor function. *Science*, 278, 698–701.

Mobbs, D., Greicius, M.D., Abdel-Azin, E., Menon, V. and Reiss, A.L. (2003) Humor modulates the mesolimbic reward centres. *Neuron*, 40, 1041–1048.

Mohr, J.P., Pessin, M.S., Finkelstein, S. *et al.* (1978) Broca's aphasia: pathological and clinical. *Neurology*, 28, 311–324.

Monagham, E. and Glickman, S. (1992) Hormones and aggressive behavior. In Becker, J., Breedlove, S. and Crews, D. (eds) *Behavioral Endocrinology*, Cambridge, Mass.: MIT Press.

Money, J. (1960) Phantom orgasm in the dreams of paraplegic men and women. *Archives of General Psychiatry*, 3, 373–382.

Money, J. and Ehrhardt, A.E. (1972) *Man & Woman, Boy & Girl: Gender Identity from Conception to Maturity*. Baltimore: Johns Hopkins University Press.

Money, J. and Ogunro, C. (1974) Behavioral sexology: ten cases of genetic male intersexuality with impaired prenatal and pubertal androgenization. *Archives of Sexual Behavior*, 3, 181–205.

Money, J., Schwartz, M. and Lewis, V.G. (1984) Adult erotosexual status and fetal hormonal masculinzation and demasculinization. *Psychoendocrinology*, 9, 405–414.

Mongeau, R., Blier, P. and Montigny, C. (1997) The serotonergic and noradrenergic systems of the hippocampus: their interactions and the effects of antidepressant treatments. *Brain Research Reviews*, 23, 145–195.

Montague, C.T., Farooqi, S., Whitehead, J.P. *et al.* (1997) Congenital leptin deficiency is associated with severe early-onset obesity in humans. *Nature*, 387, 903–908.

Montarolo, P.G., Goelet, P., Castellucci, V.F. *et al.* (1986) A critical period for macromolecular synthesis in long-term heterosynaptic facilitation in *Aplysia*. *Science*, 234, 1249–1254.

Moore, D.J., West, A.B., Dawson, V.L. and Dawson, T.M. (2005) Molecular pathophysiology of Parkinson's disease. *Annual Review of Neuroscience*, 28, 57–58.

Moore, R.Y. and Eichler, V.B. (1972) Loss of circadian adrenal corticosterone rhythm following suprachiasmatic lesions in the rat. *Brain Research*, 42, 201–206.

Morris, R.G., Garrud, P., Rawlins, J.N., and O'Keefe, J. (1982) Place navigation impaired in rats with hippocampal lesions. *Nature*, 297, 681–683.

Moruzzi, G. and Magoun, H.W. (1949) Brain stem reticular formation and activation in the EEG. *Electroencephalography and Clinical Neurophysiology*, 1, 455–473.

Mosher, J.T., Birkemo, L.S., Johnson, M.F. and Ervin, G.N. (1998) Sulfated cholecystokinin (26–33) induces mild taste aversion in rats when administered by three different routes. *Peptides*, 19, 849–857.

Munafo, M.R., Lingford-Hughes, A.R., Johnstone, E.C. and Walton, R.T. (2005) Association between the serotonin transporter gene and alcohol consumption in social drinkers. *American Journal of Medical Genetics. Part B: Neuropsychiatric Genetics*, 135, 10–14.

Murphy, J.M., McBride, W.J., Lumeng, L. and Li, T.-K. (1987) Contents of monoamines in forebrain regions of alcohol-preferring (P) and non-preferring (NP) lines of rats, *Pharmacology, Biochemistry and Behavior*, 26, 389–392.

Murray, A.M., Hyde, T.M., Knabe, M.B. *et al.* (1995) Distribution of putative D4 receptors in postmortem striatum from patients with schizophrenia. *Journal of Neuroscience*, 15, 2186–2191.

Musser, K.T. and McGurk, S.R. (2004) Schizophrenia. *Lancet*, 363, 2063–2072.

N

Nakazato, M., Murakami, N., Date, Y. *et al.* (2001) A role for ghrelin in the central regulation of feeding. *Nature*, 409, 194–198.

Nauta, W.J.H. (1946) Hypothalamic regulation of sleep in rats: experimental study. *Journal of Neurophysiology*, 9, 285–316.

Nauta, W.H. and Feirtag, M. (1986) *Fundamental Neuroanatomy*. New York: Freeman.

Navarro, M., Carrera, M.R.A., Fratta, W. *et al.* (2001) Functional interaction between opioid and cannabinoid receptors in drug self-administration. *Journal of Neuroscience*, 21, 5344–5350.

Neafsey, E.J. (1993) Frontal cortex, the mind and the body. *Psycoloquy*, 4(15).

Nehlig, A. (1999) Are we dependent upon coffee and caffeine? A review on human and animal data. *Neuroscience and Biobehavioral Reviews*, 23, 563–576.

Nestler, E.J. (2004) Historical review: molecular and cellular mechanisms of opiate and cocaine addiction. *Trends in Pharmacological Sciences*, 25, 210–217.

Nestler, E.J., Hyman, S.E. and Malenka, R.C. (2001) *Molecular Neuropharmacology*. New York: McGraw-Hill.

Noble, E.P. (1993) The D2 dopamine receptor gene: a review of association studies in alcoholism. *Behavioral Genetics*, 23, 119–129.

Noda, H. (1975) Discharges in relay cells of the lateral geniculate nucleus of the cat during spontaneous eye movements in light and darkness. *Journal of Physiology*, 250, 579–595.

Nolte, J. (1999) *The Human Brain: An Introduction to its Functional Anatomy*. St Louis: Mosby.

Nottebohm, F. (1985) *Hope for a New Neurology*. New York: New York Academy of Sciences.

Nottebohm, F. and Arnold, A.P. (1976) Sexual dimorphism in vocal control areas of the songbird brain. *Science*, 194, 211–213.

Nowliss, G.H. and Frank, M.E. (1977) Qualities in hamster taste: behavioral and neural evidence. *Olfaction Taste Proceedings. International Symposium*, 6, 241–248.

Nyberg, L., McIntosh, A.R., Houle, S. *et al.* (1996) Activation of medial temporal structures during episodic memory retrieval. *Nature*, 380, 715–717.

O

Ogawa, S., Olazabal, U.E., Parhar, I.S. and Pfaff, D.W. (1994) Effects of intrahypothalamic administration of antisense DNA for progesterone receptor mRNA on reproductive behavior and progesterone receptor immunoreactivity in female rat. *Journal of Neuroscience*, 14, 1766.

Ogden, J.A. and Corkin, S. (1991) Memories of H.M. In Abraham, W.C., Corballis, M. and White, K.G. (eds) *Memory Mechanisms: A tribute to G.V. Goddard*. Hillsdale, NJ: Lawrence Erlbaum.

Ojemann, G.A. (ed.) (1975) The thalamus and language. *Brain and Language*, 2, 101–120.

Ojemann, G.A. (1983) Brain organisation for language from the perspective of electrical stimulation mapping. *The Behavioral and Brain Sciences*, 2, 189–230.

Ojemann, G.A. and Mateer, C. (1979) Human language cortex: localization of memory, syntax and sequential motor-phoneme identification systems. *Science*, 205, 1401–1403.

Ojemann, G.A., Ojemann, J., Lettich, E. and Berger, M. (1989) Cortical language localization in left, dominant hemisphere: an electrical stimulation mapping investigation in 117 patients, *Journal of Neurosurgery*, 71, 316–326.

O'Keefe, J. and Nadel, L. (1978) *The Hippocampus as a Cognitive Map*. Oxford: Oxford University Press.

O'Keefe, J. and Conway, D.H. (1978) Hippocampal place units in the freely moving rat: why they fire when they fire. *Experimental Brain Research*, 31, 573–590.

Olds, J. (1958) Satiation effects in self-stimulation of the brain. *Journal of Comparative and Physiological Psychology*, 51, 675–678.

Olds, J. and Milner, P. (1954) Positive reinforcement produced by electrical stimulation of septal area and other regions of the rat brain. *Journal of Comparative and Physiological Psychology*, 47, 419–427.

Olds, J., Killam, K.F. and Bach-Y-Rita, P. (1956) Self-stimulation of the brain used as a screening method for tranquilizing drugs. *Science*, 124, 265–266.

Olds, M.E. and Forbes, J.L. (1981) The central basis of motivation: intracranial self-stimulation studies. *Annual Review of Psychology*, 32, 523–574.

Olds, M.E. and Olds, J. (1963) Approach–avoidance analysis of rat diencephalon. *Journal of Comparative Neurology*, 120, 259–195.

Olney, J.W., Ho, O.L. and Rhee, V. (1971) Cytotoxic effects of acidic and sulphur containing amino acids on the infant mouse central nervous system. *Experimental Brain Research*, 14, 61–76.

Olton, D.S. and Papas, B.C. (1979) Spatial memory and hippocampal function. *Neuropsychologia*, 17, 669–682.

Olton, D.S. and Samuelson, R.J. (1976) Rememberance of places passed: spatial memory in rats. *Journal of Experimental Psychology: Animal Behavior Processes*, 2, 97–115.

Olton, D.S., Becker, J.T. and Handelmann, G.E. (1979) Hippocampus, space and memory. *The Behavioral and Brain Sciences*, 2, 313–365.

Ornstein, R. (1988) *Psychology*. San Diego, Calif.: Harcourt Brace Jovanovich.

Oswald, I. and Adam, K. (1980) The man who had not slept for 10 years. *British Medical Journal*, 2, 1684–1685.

Owen, F., Cross, A.J., Crow, T.J. *et al.* (1978) Increased dopamine receptor sensitivity in schizophrenia. *Lancet*, 2, 223–225.

P

Palmer, J.D. (1975) Biological clocks of the tidal zone. *Scientific American*, 232, 70–79.

Panda, S., Sato, T.K., Castrucci, A.M. *et al.* (2002) Melanopsin (*opn4*) requirement for normal light-induced circadian phase shifting. *Science*, 298, 2213–2216.

Papez, J. (1937) A proposed mechanism of emotion. *Archives of Neurology and Psychiatry*, 38, 725–743.

Parkinson Study Group (1989) Effect of deprenyl on the progression of disability in early Parkinson's disease. *New England Journal of Medicine*, 321, 1364–1371.

Parsian, A., Todd, R.D., Devor, E.J. *et al.* (1991) Alcoholism and alleles of the human D2 dopamine receptor locus. *Archives of General Psychiatry*, 48, 655–663.

Partanen, J., Bruun, K. and Markkanen, T. (1966) *Inheritance of Drinking Behavior: A Study of Intelligence, Personality and Use of Alcohol in Adult Twins. The Finnish Foundation for Alcohol Studies.* New Jersey: Rutgers Center of Alcohol Studies.

Pasick, A. (2000) The yawning orgasm and other antidepressant side effects. Reported at www.contac.org/contaclibrary/medications6.htm

Passingham, R.E. (1987) Two cortical systems for directing movement. In Bock, G., O'Connor, M. and Marsh, J. (eds) *Motor Areas of the Cerebral cortex. Ciba Foundation Symposium 132.* Chichester: John Wiley.

Patrick, G.T.W. and Gilbert, J.A. (1896) On the effects of loss of sleep. *Psychological Review*, 3, 469–483.

Paulesu, E., Frith, U., Snowling, M. *et al.* (1996) Is developmental dyslexia a disconnection syndrome? *Brain*, 119, 143–157.

Penfield, W. and Rasmussen, T. (1950) *The Cerebral Cortex of Man.* New York: Macmillan.

Penfield, W. and Roberts, L. (1959) *Speech and Brain Mechanisms.* Princeton, NJ: Princeton University Press.

Penick, E.C., Powell, B.J., Nickel, E.J. *et al.* (1990) Examination of Cloninger's type 1 and type II alcoholism with a sample of men alcoholics in treatment. *Alcohol. Clinical and Experimental Research*, 14, 623–629.

Perls, T., Alpert, L. and Fretts, R. (1997) Middle aged mothers live longer. *Nature*, 389, 133.

Perry, E.K., Tomlinson, B.E., Blessed, G. *et al.* (1978) Correlation of cholinergic abnormalities with senile plaques and mental test scores in senile dementia. *British Medical Journal*, 2, 1457–1459.

Pert, C.B. and Snyder, S.H. (1973) Properties of opiate-receptor binding in rat brain. *Proceedings of the National Academy of Sciences*, 70, 2243–2247.

Peters, M., Manning, J.T. and Reimers, S. (2007) The effects of sex, sexual orientation and digit ratio (2D:4D) on mental rotation performance. *Archives of Sexual Behavior*, 36, 166–168.

Peterson, A.C. (1976) Physical androgyny and cognitive functioning in adolescence development. *Developmental Psychology*, 12, 524–533.

Pettit, H.O., Ettenberg, A., Bloom, F.E. and Koob, G.F. (1984) Destruction of dopamine in the nucleus accumbens selectively attenuates cocaine but not heroin self administration in rats. *Psychopharmacology*, 84, 167–173.

Pfaff, D., Arnold, A., Etgen, A. *et al.* (eds) (2002) *Hormones, the Brain and Behavior.* San Diego, Calif.: Academic Press.

Pfaff, D.W. and Schwartz-Giblin, S. (1988) Cellular mechanisms of female reproductive behaviors. In Knobil, E. and Neill, J.D. (eds) *The Physiology of Reproduction.* New York: Raven Press.

Pfohl, B. and Winokur, G. (1983) The micropsychopathology of hebephrenic/catatonic schizophrenia. *Journal of Nervous and Mental Disease*, 171, 296–300.

Phelps, E.A. and LeDoux, J.E. (2005) Contributions of the amygdala to emotion processing: from animal models to human behavior. *Neuron*, 48, 175–187.

Philips, A.G. and Broekkamp, C.L.E. (1980) Inhibition of intravenous cocaine self-administration by rats after micro-injection of spiroperidol into the nucleus accumbens. *Society for Neuroscience Abstracts*, 6, 105.

Philips, A.G. and Fibiger, H.C. (1978) The role of dopamine in maintaining intracranial self-stimulation in the ventral tegmentum, nucleus accumbens and medial prefrontal cortex. *Canadian Journal of Psychology*, 32, 58–66.

Philips, A.G. and Fibiger, H.C. (1989) Neuroanatomical basis of intracranial self-stimulation: untangling the Gordian knot. In Liebman, J.M. and Cooper, S.J. (eds) *The Neuropharmacological Basis of Reward.* Oxford: Clarendon Press.

Philips, A.G. (1991) Dopamine and motivated behavior: insights provided by *in vivo* analysis. In Wilner, P. and Scheel-Kruger, J. (eds) *The Mesolimbic Dopamine System: From Motivation to Action.* New York: John Wiley.

Philips, R.G. and LeDoux, J.E. (1992) Differential contribution of amygdala and hippocampus to cued and contextual fear conditioning. *Behavioural Neuroscience*, 106, 274–285.

Phoenix, C.H., Goy, R.W., Gerall, A.A. and Young, W.C. (1959) Organizing action of prenatally administered testosterone propionate on the tissues mediating mating behaviour in the female guinea pig. *Endocrinology*, 65, 269–382.

Piccolino, M. (1997) Luigi Galvani and animal electricity: two centuries after the foundation of electrophysiology. *Trends in Neurosciences*, 20, 443–448.

Pickens, R.W., Svikis, D.S., McGue, M. *et al.* (1991) Heterogeneity in the inheritance of alcoholism: a study of male and female twins. *Archives of General Psychiatry*, 48, 19–28.

Pierce, K., Muller, R-A., Ambrose, G. *et al.* (2001) Face processing occurs outside the fusiform 'face area' in autism: evidence from functional MRI. *Brain*, 124, 2059–2073.

Pilowsky, L.S., Costa, D.C., Ell, P.J. *et al.* (1994) D2 dopamine receptor binding in the basal ganglia of antipsychotic-free schizophrenic patients. *British Journal of Psychiatry*, 164, 16–26.

Pinsker, H., Kupfermann, I., Castellucei, V. and Kandel, E.R. (1970) Habituation and dishabituation of the gill-withdrawal reflex in *Aplysia*. *Science*, 167, 1740–1742.

Piven, J. (1997) The biological basis of autism. *Current Opinion in Neurobiology*, 7, 708–712.

Plomin, R., DeFries, J.C., McClearn, G.E. and Rutter, M. (1997) *Behavioral Genetics*, 3rd edition. New York: Freeman.

Podewils, L.J., Guallar, E., Kuller, L. *et al.* (2005) Physical activity, APOE genotype, and dementia risk: findings from the Cardiovascular Health Cognition Study. *American Journal of Epidemiology*, 161, 639–651.

Polymeropoulos, M.H., Higgins, J.J., Golbe, L.I. *et al.* (1996) Mapping of a gene for Parkinson's disease to chromosome 4q21–q23. *Science*, 276, 2045–2047.

Porac, C. and Cohen, S. (1981) *Lateral Preferences and Human Behavior*. New York: Springer.

Porter, R.H., Cernoch, J.M. and McLaughlin, F.J. (1983) Maternal recognition of neonates through olfactory cues. *Physiology of Behaviour*, 30, 151–154.

Posner, M.I. and Raichle, M.E. (1994) *Images of Mind*. New York: Scientific American Library.

Post, R.M., Kotin, J. and Goodwin, F.K. (1974) The effects of cocaine on depressed patients. *American Journal of Psychiatry*, 131, 511–517.

Post, R.M., Flink, E. Jr and Goodwin, F.K. (1975) Cerebrospinal fluid amine metabolites in acute schizophrenia. *Archives of General Psychiatry*, 32, 1063–1069.

Prader, A., Labhart, A. and Willi, H. (1956) Ein Syndrom von Adipositas, Kleinwuchs, Kryptorchismus und Oligophrenie nach myatonieartigem Zustand im Neugeborenealter. *Schweizerische Medizinische Wochenschrift*, 86, 1260–1261.

Prange, A.J., Wilson, I.C., Lynn, C.W. *et al.* (1974) L-Tryptophan in mania: contribution to a permissive hypothesis of affective disorders. *Archives of General Psychiatry*, 30, 56–62.

Price, D. (2002) Brain mechanisms of persistent brain states. *Journal of Musculoskeletal Pain*, 10, 73–83.

Price, D.L., Tanzi, R.E., Borchelt, D.R. and Sisodia, S.S. (1998) Alzheimer's disease: genetic studies and transgenic models. *Annual Review of Genetics*, 32, 461–493.

Price, L.H., Charney, D., Delgado, P. *et al.* (1990) Lithium and serotonin function: Implications for the serotonin hypothesis of depression. *Psychopharmacology*, 100, 3–12.

Prisko, L. (1963) Short term memory in cerebral damage. Unpublished Ph D dissertation, McGill University.

Provine, R.R. (1989) Contagious yawning and infant imitation. *Bulletin of the Psychnomic Society*, 27, 125–126.

Provine, R.R., Tate, B.C. and Geldmacher, L.L. (1987) Yawning: no effect of 3–5% CO_2, and exercise. *Behavioral and Neural Biology*, 48, 382–393.

Pulvermüller, F. (2000) *The Neuroscience of Language*. Cambridge: Cambridge University Press.

R

Rainville, P., Duncan, G.H., Price, D.D. *et al.* (1997) Pain affect encoded in human anterior cingulate but not somatosensory cortex. *Science*, 277, 968–971.

Raisman, G. and Field, P.M. (1973) Sexual dimorphism in the neuropil of the preoptic area of the rat and its dependence on neonatal androgen. *Brain Research*, 54, 1–29.

Ralph, M., Foster, R., Davis, F. and Menaker, M. (1990) Transplanted suprachiasmatic nucleus determines circadian period. *Science*, 247, 975–978.

Ramachandran, V.S. and Blakeslee, S. (1998) *Phantoms in the Brain*. London: Fourth Estate.

Ramachandran, V.S. and Hubbard, E.M. (2001) Psychological investigations into the neural basis of synaesthesia. *Proceedings of the Royal Academy of London*, 268, 979–983.

Rapoport, J. (1989) *The Boy Who Couldn't Stop Washing*. London: Fontana.

Rasmussen, K., Beitner-Johnson, D.B., Krystal, J.H. *et al.* (1990) Opiate withdrawal and the rat locus coeruleus: behavioral, electrophysiological and biochemical correlates. *Journal of Neuroscience*, 10, 2308–2317.

Rasmussen, T. and Milner, B. (1977) The role of early left brain damage in determining lateralization of cerebral speech functions. *Annals of the New York Academy of Sciences*, 299, 355–369.

Raymond, L.A. (2003) Excitotoxicity in Huntington disease. *Clinical Neuroscience Research*, 3, 121–128.

Rechtschaffen, A., Gilliland, M.A., Bergmann, B.M. and Winter, J.B. (1983) Physiological correlates of prolonged sleep deprivation in rats. *Science*, 221, 182–184.

Rechstshaffen, A. *et al.* (1989) Sleep deprivation in the rat: X. Integration and discussion of the findings. *Sleep*, 12, 68–87.

Reich, T., Edenberg, H.J., Goate, A. *et al.* (1998) Genome-wide search for genes affecting the risk for alcohol dependence, *American Journal of Medical Genetics*, 81, 207–215.

Reid, I.C. and Stewart, C.A. (1997). Seizures, memory and synaptic plasticity. *Seizure*, 6, 351–359.

Relkin, E.M. and Doucet, J.R. (1997) Is loudness simply proportional to the auditory nerve spike count? *Journal of the Acoustic Society of America*, 101, 2735–2274.

Reppert, S.M. and Weaver, D.R. (2001) Molecular analysis of mammalian circadian rhythms. *Annual Review of Physiology*, 63, 647–676.

Resnick, S.M., Berenbaum, S.A., Gottesman, I.I. and Bouchard, T.J. (1986) Early hormonal influences on cognitive functioning in congenital adrenal hyperplasia. *Developmental Psychology*, 22, 191–198.

Reul, J., Labeur, M., Grigoriadis, D. *et al.* (1994) Hypothalamic–pituitary–adrenocortical axis changes in the rat after long-term treatment with the reversible monoamine oxidase-A inhibitor Moclobemide. *Neuroendocrinology*, 60, 509–519.

Reul, J., Stec, I., Söder, M. and Holsboer, F. (1993) Chronic treatment of rats with the antidepressant amitriptyline attenuates the activity of the hypothalamic–pituitary–adrenocortical system. *Endocrinology*, 133, 312–320.

Richter, C. (1967) Sleep and activity: their relation to the 24 hour clock. *Proceedings of the Association for Research in Nervous and mental Diseases*, 45, 8–27.

Rickels, K., Schweizer, E., Csanalosi, I. *et al.* (1988) Long term treatment of anxiety and risk of withdrawl. *Archives of General Psychiatry*, 45, 444–450.

Rizzolatti, G., Fadiga, L., Gallese, V. and Fogassi, L. (1966) Premotor cortex and the recognition of motor actions. *Cognitive Brain Research*, 3, 131–141.

Roberts, D.C.S. and Koob, G. (1982) Disruption of cocaine self-administration following 6-hydroxy-dopamine lesions of the ventral tegmental area in rats. *Pharmacology, Biochemistry and Behavior*, 17, 901–904.

Roberts, D.C.S., Corcoran, M.E. and Fibiger, H.C. (1977) On the role of the ascending catecholaminergic systems in intravenous self-administration of cocaine. *Pharmacology, Biochemistry and Behavior*, 6, 615–620.

Robins, L.N., Helzer, J.E., Hesselbrock, M. and Wish, E. (1979) Vietnam veterans three years after Vietnam. In Brill, L. and Winick, C. (eds) *Yearbook of Substance Abuse*. New York: Human Science Press.

Robinson, T.E. and Berridge, K.C. (1993) The neural basis of drug craving: an incentive sensitization theory of addiction. *Brain Research Reviews*, 18, 247–291.

Robson, P. (1999) *Forbidden Drugs*. Oxford: Oxford University Press.

Rochford, G. (1974) Are jargon aphasics dysphasic? *British Journal of Disorders of Communication*. 9, 35.

Rodier, P.M. (2000) The early origins of autism. *Scientific American*, Feb., 38–45.

Roffwarg, H.P., Muzio, J.N. and Dement, W.C. (1966) Ontogenetic development of the human sleep–dream cycle. *Science*, 152, 604–619.

Rogen, M.T., Stubli, U.V. and LeDoux, J.E. (1997) Fear conditioning induces associative long-term potentiation in the amygdala. *Nature*, 390, 604–607.

Rogers, P.J. and Blundell, J.E. (1980) Investigation of food selection and meal parameters during the development of dietary induced obesity. *Appetite*, 1, 85.

Roland, P.E. (1984) Organisation of motor control by the normal human brain. *Human Neurobiology*, 2, 205–216.

Roland, P.E. (1993) *Brain Activation*. New York: John Wiley.

Roland, P.E., Larsen, B., Lassen, N.A. and Skinhøj, E. (1980) Supplementary motor area and other cortical area in the organisation of voluntary movements in man. *Journal of Neurophysiology*, 43, 118–136.

Roll, S.K. (1970) Intracranial self-stimulation and wakefulness: effects of manipulating ambient catecholamines. *Science*, 168, 1370–1372.

Rolls, B.J., Rolls, E.T., Rowe, E.A. and Sweeney, K. (1981) Sensory specific satiety in man. *Physiology and Behavior*, 27, 137–142.

Rolls, E.T. (1999) *The Brain and Emotion*. London: Oxford University Press.

Rolls, E.T., Sanghera, M.K. and Roper-Hall, A. (1979) The latency of activation of neurones in the lateral hypothalamus and substantia innominata during feeding in the monkey. *Brain Research*, 164, 121–135.

Rolls, R. (2005) *Classic Case Studies in Psychology*. London: Hodder Arnold.

Rose, D., Fleischmann, P., Wykes, T. *et al.* (2003) Patients' perspectives on electroconvulsive therapy: systematic review. *British Medical Journal*, 326, 1363–1365.

Rose, J.E. and Woolsey, C.N. (1948) Structure and relations of limbic cortex and anterior thalamic nuclei in rabbit and cat. *Journal of Comparative Neurology*, 77, 61–130.

Rose, R.M., Bernstein, I.S. and Gordon, T.P. (1975) Consequences of social conflict on plasma testosterone levels in rhesus monkeys. *Psychomatic Medicine*, 37, 50–62.

Rose, S. (2003) *The Making of Memory*. London: Bantam Books.

Rosenbaum, R.S., Priselac, S., Kohler, S. *et al.* (2000) Remote spatial memory in an amnesic person with extensive bilateral hippocampal lesions, *Nature Neuroscience*, 3, 1044–1048.

Rosenthal, D. (1963) *The Genain Quadruplets*. New York: Basic Books.

Rosenthal, D. (1971) A program of research on heredity in schizophrenia. *Behavioral Science*, 16, 191–201.

Rosenzweig, M.R., Krech, D. and Bennett, E.L. (1958) Brain chemistry and adaptive behavior. In Harlow, H.F. and Woolsey, C.N. (eds) *Biological and Biochemical Bases of Behavior*. Madison: Wisconsin University Press.

Rosenweig, M.R., Bennett, E.L. and Diamond, M.C. (1972) Brain changes in response to experience. *Scientific American*, Feb., 22–29.

Ross, E.D. (1984) Right hemisphere's language, affective behavior and emotion. *Trends in Neurosciences*, 7, 342–346.

Rosvold, H.E., Mirsky, A.F. and Pribram, K.H. (1954) Influence of amygdalectomy on social behaviour in monkeys. *Journal of Comparative and Physiological Psychology*, 47, 173–178.

Rothwell, J.C. (1994) *Control of Human Voluntary Movement*. London: Chapman & Hall.

Roy, A. and Linnoila, M. (1989) CSF studies on alcoholism and related disrders. *Progress in Neuropsychopharmacology and Biological Psychiatry*, 13, 505–511.

Roy, A., Virkkunen, M. and Linnoila, M. (1987) Serotonin and alcoholism. *Substance Abuse*, 8, 21–27.

Rubin, R.T. (1987) Prolactin and schizophrenia. In Meltzer, H.Y. (ed.) *Psychopharmacology: The Third Generation of Progress*. New York: Raven Press.

Rugg, M.D. (ed.) (1997) *Cognitive Neuroscience*. Cambridge, Mass.: MIT Press.

Rumsey, J.M., Horwitz, B., Donohue, B.C. *et al.* (1999) A functional lesion in developmental dyslexia: left angular gyral blood flow predicts severity. *Brain and Language*, 70, 187–204.

Rush, A.J., Cain, J.W., Raese, J. *et al.* (1991) Neurological bases for psychiatric disorders. In Rosenberg, R.N. (ed.) *Comprehensive Neurology*. New York: Raven Press.

Russek, M. (1971) Hepatic receptors and the neurophysiological mechanisms controlling feeding behaviour. In Ehrenpreis, S. (ed.) *Neurosciences Research*, Vol. 4. New York: Academic Press.

Russell, M.J., Switz, G.M. and Thompson, K. (1980) Olfatory influences on the human menstral cycle. *Pharmacology, Biochemistry and Behavior*, 13, 737–738.

Rutlidge, L.L. and Hupka, R.B. (1985) The facial feedback hypothesis: methodological concerns and new supporting evidence. *Motivation and Emotion*, 9, 219–240.

S

Sack, R.L. and Lewy, A.J. (2001) Circadian rhythm sleep disorders: lessons from the blind. *Sleep Medicine Reviews*, 5, 189–206.

Sacks, O. (1985) *The Man Who Mistook His Wife for a Hat*. London: Picador.

Sacks, O. (1990) *Awakenings*. London: Picador.

Sahin, N.T., Pinker, S. and Halgren, E. (2006) Abstract grammatical processing of nouns and verbs in Broca's area: evidence from fMRI. *Cortex*, 42, 540–562.

Sahu, A., Kalra, P.S. and Kalra S.P. (1988) Food deprivation and ingestion induce reciprocal changes in neuropeptide Y concentrations in the paraventricular nucleus. *Peptides*, 9, 83–86.

Saper, C.B., Chou, T.C. and Scammell, T.E. (2001) The sleep switch: hypothalamic control of sleep and wakefulness. *Trends in Neurosciences*, 24, 726–731.

Saper, C.B., Scammell, T.E. and Lu, J. (2005) Hypothalamic regulation of sleep and circadian rhythms. *Nature*, 437, 1257–1263.

Saudou, F., Amara, D.A., Dierich, A. *et al.* (1994) Enhanced aggressive behavior in mice lacking 5-HT$_{1B}$ receptor. *Science*, 265, 1875–1878.

Schachter, S. and Singer, J.E. (1962) Cognitive, social and physiological determinants of emotional state. *Psychological Reveiw*, 69, 379–399.

Schapira, A.H. (1994) Evidence for mitochondrial dysfunction in Parkinson's disease – a critical appraisal, *Movement Disorders*, 9, 125–138.

Schatzberg, A.F. and Schildkraut, A.F. (1995) Recent studies on norepinephrine systems in mood disorders. In Bloom, F.E. and Kupfer, D.J. (eds) *Psychopharmacology: The Fourth Generation of Progress*. New York: Raven Press.

Schildkraut, J.J. (1965) The catecholamine hypothesis of affective disrders: a review of supporting evidence. *American Journal of Psychiatry*, 122, 509–522.

Schlaepfer, T.E., Harris, G.J., Tien, A.Y. *et al.* (1995) Structural differences in the cerebral cortex of healthy female and male subjects: a magnetic imaging study. *Psychiatry Research*, 61, 129–135.

Schlaug, G., Janke, L., Huang, Y. and Steinmetz, H. (1995) In vivo evidence of structural brain asymmetry in musicians. *Science*, 267, 699–701.

Schneider, G.E. (1967) Contrasting visuomotor functions of tectum and cortex in the golden hamster. *Psychologische Forschung*, 31, 52–62.

Schuckit, M.A. (1987) Biological vulnerability to alcoholism. *Journal of Counseling and Clinical Psychology*, 55, 301–309.

Schwartz, M.W. and Seeley, R.J. (1997) The new biology of body weight regulation. *Journal of the American Dietetic Association*, 97, 54–58.

Schwartz, W.J. and Gainer, H. (1977) Suprachiasmatic nucleus: use of 14-C labelled deoxyglucose uptake as a functional marker. *Science*, 197, 1089–1091.

Scoville, W.B. and Milner, B. (1957) Loss of recent memory after bilateral hippocampal lesions. *Journal of Neurology, Neurosurgery and Psychiatry*, 20, 11–21.

Sellars E.M., Higgins, G.A. and Sobell, M.B. (1992) 5-HT and alcohol abuse. *Trends in Pharmacological Sciences*, 13, 69–75.

Semmes, J. (1960) *Somatosensory Changes after Penetrating Brain Wounds in Man*. Cambridge, Mass.: Harvard University Press.

Sham, P.C., O'Callaghan, E., Takei, N. *et al.* (1992) Schizophrenia following pre-natal exposure to influenza epidemics between 1939 and 1960. *British Journal of Psychiatry*, 160, 461–466.

Sharma, S.K., Klee, W. and Nirenberg, M. (1975) Dual regulation of adenylate cyclase accounts for narcotic dependence and tolerance. *Proceedings of the National Academy of Sciences*, 72, 3092–3096.

Shastry, B.S. (2005) Bipolar disorder: an update. *Neurochemistry International*, 46, 273–279.

Shaw, P.J., Cirelli, C., Greenspan, R. and Tononi, G. (2000) Correlates of sleep and waking in *Drosophila melanogaster*. *Science*, 287, 1834–1837.

Shaywitz, B.A., Shaywitz, S.E., Pugh, K.R. *et al.* (1995) Sex differences in the functional organisation of the brain for language. *Nature*, 373, 607–609.

Shaywitz, S.E. (1998) Dyslexia. *New England Journal of Medicine*, 338, 307–312.

Shaywitz, S.E., Shaywitz, B.A., Fletcher, J.M. and Escobar, M.D. (1990) Prevalence of reading disability in boys and girls. *Journal of the American Medical Association*, 264, 998–1002.

Shepherd, G. (1991) *Foundations of the Neuron Doctrine*. London: Oxford University Press.

Shepherd, G.M. (1994) Discrimination of molecular signals by the olfactory receptor neuron. *Neuron*, 13, 771–790.

Shepherd, G.M. (2005) *The Synaptic Organisation of the Brain*, 5th edition. London: Oxford University Press.

Sherin, J.E., Elmquist, J.K., Torrealba, F. and Saper, C.B. (1998) Innervation of histaminergic tuberomammillary neurons by gABAergic and galaninergic neurons in the ventrolateral preoptic nucleus of the rat. *Journal of Neuroscience*, 18, 4705–4721.

Sherman, R.A. (1980) Published treatments of phantom limb pain. *American Journal of Physical Medicine*, 59, 232–244.

Sherrington, R., Rogaev, E.I., Liang, Y. *et al.* (1995) Cloning of gene bearing missense mutations in early-onset familial Alzheimer's disease. *Nature*, 375, 754–760.

Sherry, D.F., Jacobs, L.F. and Gaulin, S.J.C. (1992) Spatial memory and adaptive specialization of the hippocampus. *Trends in Neurosciences*, 15, 298–303.

Shimizu, N., Oomura, Y., Novin, D. *et al.* (1983) Functional correlations between lateral hypothalamic glucose-sensitive neurons and hepatic portal glucose-sensitive units in the rat. *Brain Research*, 265, 49–54.

Sidman, M., Stoddard, L.T. and Mohr, J.P. (1968) Some additional quantitative observations of immediate memory in a patient with bilateral hippocampal lesions. *Neuropsychologia*, 6, 245–254.

Siegel, J.M., Moore, R., Thannickal, T. *et al.* (2001) A brief history of hypocretin/orexin and narcolepsy. *Neuropsychopharmacology*, 25, 14–20.

Siegel, S. (1976) Morphine analgesic tolerance: its situation specificity supports a Pavlovian conditioning model. *Science*, 193, 323–325.

Siegel, S. (1984) Pavlovian conditioning and heroin overdose: reports by overdose victims. *Bulletin of the Psychonomic Society*, 22, 428–430.

Siegel, S., Hinson, R.E., Krank, M.D. and McCully, J. (1982) Heroin 'overdose' death: contribution of drug-associated environmental cues. *Science*, 216, 436–437.

Siever, L.J., Kalus, O.F. and Keefe, R.S. (1993) The boundaries of schizophrenia. *Psychiatric Clinics of North America*, 16, 217–44.

Siffre, M. (1975) Six months alone in a cave. *National Geographic*, 147, 426–435.

Sigvardsson, S., Bohman, M. and Cloninger, C.R. (1996) Replication of the Stockholm adoption study of alcoholism. Confirmatory cross-fostering analysis. *Archives of General Psychiatry*, 53, 681–687.

Simon, E.J. (1981) Opiate receptors and endorphins: possible relevance to narcotic addiction. *Advances in Alcohol and Substance Abuse*, 1, 13–31.

Singh, D., Vidaurri, M. and Zambarano, R.J. (1999) Lesbian erotic role identification: behavioral, morphological and hormonal correlates. *Journal of Personality and Social Psychology*, 76, 1035–1049.

Skene, D.J., Lockley, S.W. and Arendt, J. (1999) Melatonin in circadian sleep disorders in the blind. *Biological Signals and Receptors*, 8, 90–95.

Skene. D.J., Lockley, S., Thapan, K. and Arendt, J. (1999) Effects of light on human circadian rhythms. *Reproduction Nutrition and Development*, 39, 295–304.

Slaby, A.E. (1995) Suicide as an indicum of biologically-based brain disease. *Archives of Suicide Research*, 1, 59–73.

Smith, A. and Sugar, O. (1975) Development of above normal language and intelligence 21 years after hemispherectomy. *Neurology*, 25, 813–818.

Smith, C. and Lapp, L. (1991) Increases in the number of REMs and REM density following an intensive learning period. *Sleep*, 14, 325–330.

Smith, G.P. and Gibbs, J. (1994) Satiating effect of cholecystokinin. *Annals of the New York Academy of Sciences*, 713, 236–240.

Smith, O.A. (1956) Stimulation of lateral and medial hypothalamus and food intake in the rat. *Anatomical Record*, 124, 363–364.

Snowdon, D. (2001) *Aging With Grace*. London: Fourth Estate.

Snyder, S.H. (1986) *Drugs and the Brain*. New York: Scientific American Library.

Sobocki, P., Jonsson, B., Angst, J. and Rehnberg, C. (2006) Cost of depression in Europe. *Journal of Mental Health Policy Economics*, 9, 87–98.

Sodhi, M.S., Arranz, M.J., Curtis, D. *et al.* (1995) Association between clozapine response and allelic variation in the 5-HT 2c gene. *NeuroReport*, 7, 169–172.

Solinas, M., Zangen, A., Thiriet, N. and Goldberg, S. (2004) Beta-endorphin elevations in the ventral tegmental area regulate the discriminative effects of delta-9-tetrahydrocannabinol. *European Journal of Neuroscience*, 19, 3183–3192.

Spencer, D. and Corbett, J.R. (1986) Accumbens infusion of amphetamine increases and picrotoxin decreases reward from hypothalamic stimulation. *Society for Neuroscience Abstracts*, 12, 1142.

Spencer, P.S., Nunn, P.B., Hugon, J. *et al.* (1987) Guam amyotrophic lateral sclerosis-parkinsonism-dementia linked to a plant excitant neurotoxin. *Science*, 237, 517–522.

Sperry, R.W. (1964) The great cerebral commissure. *Scientific American*, 210, 42–48.

Sperry, R.W. (1974) Lateral specilisation in the surgicaly seperated hemispheres. In Schmidt, F.O. and Worden, F.G. (eds) *The Neurosciences: Third Study Program*. Cambridge, Mass.: MIT Press.

Springer, S.P. and Deutsch, G. (1989) *Left Brain, Right Brain*. New York: Freeman.

Squire, L.R. (1987) *Memory and the Brain*. London: Oxford University Press.

Squire, L.R. (1998) Memory systems. *Comptes Rendus de L' Academie des Sciences Serie III, Sciences de la Vie*. 321, 153–156.

Squire, L.R. (2004) Memory systems of the brain: a brief history and current perspective. *Neurobiology of Learning and Memory*, 82, 171–177.

Squire, L.R. and Moore, R.Y. (1979) Dorsal thalamic lesion in a noted case of human memory dysfunction. *Annals of Neurology*, 6, 503–506.

Squire, L.R. and Zola-Morgan, S. (1985) Neuropsychology of memory: new links between humans and experimental animals. In Olton, D., Corkin, S. and Gamzu, E. (eds) *Memory Dysfunction*. New York: New York Academy of Sciences.

Squire, L.R., Amaral, D.G., Zola-Morgan, S. *et al.* (1989) Description of brain injury in amnesic patient N.A. based on magnetic resonance imaging. *Experimental Neurology*, 105, 23–25.

Squires, R.F. and Braestrup, C. (1977) Benzodiazepine receptors in the rat brain. *Nature*, 266, 732–734.

Stahl, S.M. (1998) Mechanism of action of serotonin selective reuptake inhibitors: serotonin receptors and pathways mediate therapeutic effects and side effects. *Journal of Affective disorders*, 51, 215–235.

Stahl, S.M. (2000) *Essential Psychopharmacology*. Cambridge: Cambridge University Press.

Stanford, S.C. (1996) Prozac: panacea or puzzle? *Trends in Pharmacological Sciences*, 17, 150–154.

Stanley, B.G., Krykouli, S.E., Lampert, S. and Leibowitz, S.F. (1986) Neuropeptide Y chronically injected into the hypothalamus: a powerful neurochemical inducer of hyperphagia and obesity. *Peptides*, 7, 1189–1192.

Stanley, B.G., Magdalin, W., Seirafi, A. *et al.* (1993) The perifornical area: the major focus of (a) patchily distributed hypothalamic neuropeptide Y-sensitive feeding system(s). *Brain Research*, 604, 304–317.

Stark C.P., Alpern, H.P., Fuhrer, J. *et al.* (1998) The medial amygdaloid nucleus modifies social behavior in male rats. *Physiology and Behavior*, 63, 253–259.

Stein, J. and Walsh, V. (1997) To see but not to read: the magnocellular theory of dyslexia. *Trends in Neuroscience*, 20, 147–152.

Stein, J.F. and Stoodley, C.J. (2006) *Neuroscience: An Introduction*. Chichester: John Wiley.

Stein, L. (1967) Noradrenergic substrates of positive reinforcement. In Brill, H. *et al.* (eds) *Neuropsychopharmacology*. Amsterdam: Excerpta Medica.

Stein, L. and Wise, C.D. (1969) Release of norepinephrine from hypothalamus and amygdala by rewarding medial forebrain bundle stimulation and amphetamine. *Journal of Comparative and Physiological Psychology*, 67, 189–198.

Stein, L. and Wise, C.D. (1971) Possible etiology of schizophrenia: progressive damage to the noradrenergic reward system by 6-hydroxydopamine. *Science*, 171, 1032–1036.

Stellar, E. (1954) The physiology of motivation. *Psychological Review*, 61, 5–22.

Stellar, J.R. and Corbett, D. (1989) Effects of regional neuroleptic infusion suggest a role for nucleus accumbens in lateral hypothalamis self-stimulation. *Brain Research*, 477, 126–143.

Stellar, R. and Rice, M.B. (1989) Pharmacological basis of intracranial self-stimulation reward. In Liebman, J.M. and Cooper, S.J. (eds) *The Neuropharmacological Basis of Reward*. Oxford: Clarendon Press.

Stephan, F.K. and Zucker, I. (1972) Circadian rhythms in drinking behaviour and locomotor activity of rats are eliminated by hypothalamic lesions. *Proceedings of the National Academy of Sciences*, 60, 1583–1586.

Steriade, M., Datta, S., Pare, D., Oakson, G. and Dossi, R.C. (1990) Neuronal activities in brainstem cholinergic nuclei related to tonic activation processes in thalamocortical systems. *Journal of Neuroscience*, 10, 2541–2559.

Stern, E., Silbersweig, D.A., Chee, K.-Y. *et al.* (2000) A functional neuroanatomy of tics in Tourette syndrome. *Archives of General Psychiatry*, 57, 741–748.

Stern, Y., Habeck, C., Moeller, J. *et al.* (2005) Brain networks associated with cognitive reserve in healthy young and old adults. *Cerebral Cortex*, 15, 394–402.

Stevens, C.F. (1979) The Neuron. *Scientific American*, 241, 54–65.

Stoll, A.L., Renshaw, P.F., Yergulun-Todd, D. and Cohen, B.M. *et al.* (2000) Neuroimaging in bipolar disorder: what have we learned? *Biological Psychiatry*, 48, 505–517.

Stoudemire, A. (1998) *Clinical Psychiatry for Medical Students*. Philadelphia: Lippincott–Raven.

Strack, F., Martin, L.L. and Stepper, S. (1988) Inhibiting and facilitating conditions of the human smile: a non-obtrusive test of the facial feedback hypothesis. *Journal of Personality and Social Psychology*, 54, 768–777.

Strakowski, S.M., DelBello, M.P. and Adler, C.M. (2005) The functional neuroanatomy of bipolar disorder: a review of neuroimaging findings. *Molecular Psychiatry*, 10, 105–116.

Strange, P.G. (1992) *Brain Biochemistry and Brain Disorders*. London: Oxford University Press.

Stricker, E.M., Rowland, N., Saller, C.F. and Friedman, M.I. (1977) Homeostasis during hypoglycemia: central control of adrenal secretion and peripheral control of feeding. *Science*, 196, 79–81.

Strother, W.N., Lumeng, L., Li, T.K. and McBride, W.J. (2005) Dopamine and serotonin content in select brain regions of weanling and adult alcohol drinking rat lines. *Pharmacology, Biochemistry and Behavior*, 80, 229–237.

Stunkard, A. J. (1975), From explanation to action in psychosomatic medicine: the case of obesity, *Psychosomatic Medicine*, 37, 195–236.

Stunkard, A.J., Foch, T.T. and Hrubec, Z. (1986) A twin study of human obesity. *Journal of the American Medical Association*, 256, 51–54.

Sullivan, R.J. and Hagen. E.H. (2002) Psychotropic substance-seeking: evolutionary pathology or adaptation? *Addiction*, 97, 389–400.

Sulser, F., Vetulani, J. and Mobley, P. (1978) Mode of action of antidepressant drugs. *Biochemical Pharmacology*, 27, 257–261.

Sutherland, S. (ed.) (1991) *Dictionary of Psychology*. Basingstoke: Palgrave Macmillan.

Swaab, D.F. and Hofman, M.A. (1995) Sexual differentiation of the human hypothalamus in relation to gender and sexual orientation. *Trends in Neurosciences*, 18, 264–270.

Swaab, D.F. and Hofman, M.A. (1990) An enlarged suprachiasmatic nucleus in homosexual men. *Brain Research*, 537, 141–148.

Szasz, T.S. (1960) The myth of mental illness. *American Psychology*, 15, 113–118.

Szymusiak, R., Alam, N., Steininger, T. and McGinty, D. (1998) Sleep–waking discharge patterns of ventrolateral preoptic/anterior hypothalamic neurons in rats. *Brain Research*, 803, 178–188.

T

Takagi, Y., Takahashi, J., Saiki, H. *et al.* (2005) Dopaminergic neurons generated from monkey embryonic stem cells function in a Parkinson primate model. *Journal of Clinical Investigation*, 115, 102–109.

Teitelbaum P. and Epstein A. (1962) Recovery of feeding and drinking after lateral hypothalamic lesions. *Psychological Reviews*, 69, 74–90.

Terry, R.D. (1996) A history of the morphology of Alzheimer's disease. In Khachaturian, Z.S. and Radebaugh, T.S. (eds) *Alzheimer's Disease. Cause(s), Diagnosis, Treatment and Care*. Boca Raton, Fla.: CRC Press.

Terry, R.D., Masliah, E., Salmon, D.P. *et al.* (1991) Physical basis of cognitive alterations in Alzheimer's disease: synapse loss is the major correlate of cognitive impairment. *Annals of Neurology*, 30, 572–580.

Teyler T.J. and Discenna, P. (1987) Long-term potentiation. *Annual Review of Neuroscience,* 198, 131–161.

Thannickal, T.C., Moore, R.Y., Nienhuis, R. *et al.* (2000) Reduced number of hypocretin neurons in human narcolepsy. *Neuron,* 27, 469–474.

Thomas, L. (1981) The problem of dementia. *Discovery,* Aug., 34–36.

Thompson, R.F. (1993) *The Brain: A Neuroscience Primer.* New York: Freeman.

Tienari, P., Wynne, L.C., Moring, J. *et al.* (1994) The Finnish adoptive family study of schizophrenia. Implications for family research. *British Journal of Psychiatry,* 163, 20–26.

Toates, F. (2007) *Biological Psychology.* Harlow: Prentice Hall.

Tomlinson, B.E. (1984) The pathology of Alzheimer's disease and senile dementia of Alzheimer type. In Kay, D.W.K. and Burrows, G.D. (eds) *Handbook of Studies on Psychiatry and Old Age.* Amsterdam: Elsevier.

Tong, F. (2003) Primary visual cortex and visual awareness. *Nature Reviews Neuroscience,* 4, 219–229.

Tooth, G.C. and Newton, M.P. (1961) *Leucotomy in England and Wales 1942–1954.* London: HM Stationery Office.

Torrey, E.F., Bowler, A.E., Taylor, E.H. and Gottesman, I.I. (1994) *Schizophrenia and Manic-Depressive Disorder: The Biological Roots of Mental Illness as Revealed by a Landmark Study of Identical Twins.* New York: Basic Books.

Trehub, S.E. (2001) Musical predisposition in infancy. In Zatorre, R.J. and Peretz, I. (eds) *The Biological Foundations of Music.* New York: New York Academy of Sciences.

Tryon, R.C. (1940) Genetic differences in maze-learning ability in rats. *Yearbook of the National Society for the Study of Education,* 39(1), 111–119.

Tulving, E., Hayman, C.A. and Macdonald, C. (1991) Long-lasting perceptual priming and semantic learning in amnesia: a case experiment, *Journal of Experimental Psychology: Learning, Memory, and Cognition,* 17, 595–617.

Tulving, E., Markowitsch, H.J., Kapur, S. *et al.* (1994) Novelty encoding networks in the human brain: data from positron emission tomography studies. *NeuroReport,* 5, 2525–2528.

Turk, I., Dirjec, J. and Kavur, B. (1995) The oldest musical instrument in Europe discovered in Slovenia. *Razprave IV. Razreda SAZU,* 36, 287–293.

Turner, A.M. and Greenough, W.T. (1983) Synpses per neuron and synaptic dimensions in occipital cortex of rats reared in complex, social or isolation housing. *Acta Stereologica,* 2 (suppl.1), 239–244.

Turner, A.M. and Greenough, W.T. (1985) Differential rearing effects on rat visual cortex synapses. 1: Synaptic and neuronal density and synapses per neuron. *Brain Research,* 329, 195–203.

Tyler, A. (1986) *Street Drugs.* London: Hodder & Stoughton.

Ungerleider, L.G. and Mishkin, M. (1982) Two cortical visual systems. In Ingle, D.M. (ed.) *Anaylsis of Visual Behavior.* Cambridge, Mass.: MIT Press.

Ungerstedt, U. (1971) Adipsia and aphagia after 6-hydroxydopamine induced degeneration of the nigrostriatal dopamine system. *Acta Physiology Scandanavia,* 367, 95–122.

Valenstein, E.S. (1986) *Great and Desperate Cures: The Rise and Decline of Psychosurgery and other Radical Treatments for Mental Illness.* New York: Basic Books.

Valenstein, E.S. and Campbell, J.F. (1966) Medial forebrain bundle–lateral hypothalamic area and reinforcing brain stimulation. *American Journal of Physiology,* 210, 270–274.

Van Essen, D.C., Anderson, C.H. and Felleman, D.J. (1992) Information processing in the primate visual system: an integrated systems perspective. *Science,* 255, 419–423.

Vandenberg, S.G. and Kuse, A.R. (1978) Mental rotations, a group test of three-dimensional spatial visualization. *Perceptual and Motor Skills,* 47, 599–601.

Victor, M., Adams, R.D. and Collins, G.H. (1971) *The Wernicke–Korsakoff Syndrome.* Oxford: Blackwell.

Virkkunen, M., Goldman, D., Nielson, D.A. and Linnaola, M. (1995) Low brain serotonin turnover (low CSF 5-HIAA) and impulsive violence. *Journal of Psychiatry and Neuroscience,* 20, 271–275.

Vonsattel, J-P.G., Myers, R.H., Stevens, T.J. *et al.* (1985) Neuropathological classification of Huntington's disease. *Journal of Neuropathology and Experimental Neurology,* 44, 559–557.

Wangensteen, O.H. and Carlson, H.A. (1931) Hunger sensations in a patient after total gastrectomy. *Proceedings of the Society of Experimental and Biological Medicine,* 28, 545–547.

Watson, J.B. (1913) Psychology as the behaviorist views it. *Psychological Review,* 20, 158–177.

Weaver, E.G. and Bray, W. (1930) Action currents in the auditory nerve to acoustic stimulation. *Proceedings of the National Academy of Sciences*, 16, 344–350.

Webster, H.H. and Jones, B.E. (1988) Neurotoxic lesions of the dorsolateral pontomesencephalic tegmentum–cholinergic cell area in the cat. *Brain Research*, 458, 285–302.

Wedekind, C., Seebeck, T., Bettens, F. and Paepke. (1995) MHC-dependent male preferences in humans. *Proceedings of the Royal Society of London B*, 260, 245–249.

Wedekind, C., Seebeck, T., Bettens, F. and Paepke, A.J. (1995) MHC-dependent mate preferences in humans. *Proceedings of the Royal Society of London B*, 260, 245–249.

Weeks, J.R. (1962) Experimental morphine addiction: method for autonomic intravenous injections in unrestrained rats. *Science*, 138, 143–144.

Weinberger N.M. (2004) Music and the brain. *Scientific American*, 291, 89–95.

Weinberger, D.R. and Wyatt, R.J. (1982) Brain morphology in schizophrenia: *in vivo* studies. In Henn, F.A. and Nasrallah, H.A. (eds) *Schizophrenia as a Brain Disease*. New York: Oxford University Press.

Weinberger, D.R., Bigelow, L.B., Kleinman, J.E. *et al.* (1980) Cerebral ventricular enlargement in chronic schizophrenia: an association with poor response to treatment. *Archives of General Psychiatry*, 37, 11–13.

Weinberger, D.R., Berman, K.F. and Zec, R.F. (1986) Physiologic dysfunction of dorsolateral prefrontal cortex in schizophrenia. I: Regional cerebral blood flow evidence. *Archives of General Psychiatry*, 43, 114–124.

Weingarten, H.P. (1983) Conditioned cues elicit feeding in sated rats: a role for learning in meal initiation. *Science*, 220, 431–433.

Weiskrantz, L., Warrington, E., Sanders, M. and Marshall, J. (1974) Visual capacity in the hemianoptic field following a restricted occipital ablation. *Brain*, 97, 709–728.

Weitzman, E.D., Czeisler, C.A., Coleman, R.M. *et al.* (1981) Delayed sleep phase syndrome: a chronobiological disorder with sleep onset insomnia. *Archives of General Psychiatry*, 38, 737–746.

Wender, P.E., Kety, S.S., Rosenthal, D. *et al.* (1986) Psychiatric disorders in the biological and adoptive families of adopted individuals with affective disorder. *Archives of General Psychiatry*, 43, 923–929.

Wenzel, B.M. (1973) Chemoreception. In Farner, D.S., King, J.R. and Parker, C. (eds) *Avian Biology*, Vol. 3. New York: Academic Press.

Wexler, A. (1996) *Mapping Fate*. Berkeley, Calif.: University of California Press.

Whalen, P.J., Rauch, S.L., Etcoff, N.L. *et al.* (1998) Masked presentations of emotional facial expressions modulate amygdala activity without explicit knowledge. *Journal of Neuroscience*, 18, 411–418.

White, F.J. and Wolf. M.E. (1991) Psychomotor stimulants. In Pratt, J. (ed.) *The Biological Basis of Drug Tolerance and Dependence*. New York: Academic Press.

Wiersma, D., de Jong, A. and Ormel, J. (1988) The Groningen Social Disabilities Schedule: development, relationship with I.C.I.D.H. and psychometric properties. *International Journal of Rehabilitation Research*, 11, 213–224.

Wiersma, D., Nienhuis, F.J., Slooff, C.J. and Giel, R. (1998) Natural course of schizophrenic disorders: a 15-year follow-up of a Dutch incidence cohort. *Schizophrenia Bulletin*, 24, 75–85.

Wiesel, T.N. (1982) Postnatal development of the visual cortex and the influence of the environment. *Nature*, 299, 583–591.

Wikler, A. (1948) Recent progress in research on the neurophysiologic basis of morphine addiction. *American Journal of Psychiatry*, 105, 329–338.

Wilding, J.P.H. (2006) Pathophysiology and aetiology of obesity. *Medicine*, 34, 501–505.

Will, B., Galani, R., Kelche, C. and Rosenzweig, M. (2004). Recovery from brain injury in animals: relative efficacy of environmental enrichment, physical exercise or formal training (1990–2002). *Progress in Neurobiology*, 72, 167–182.

Will, R.G., Ironside, J.W., Zeidler, M. *et al.* (1996) A new variant of Creutzfeldt–Jakob disease in the UK. *Lancet*, 347, 921–925.

Williams, G., Bing, C., Cai, X.J. *et al.* (2001) The hypothalamus and the control of energy homeostasis: different circuits, different purposes, *Physiology and Behavior*, 74, 683–701.

Wilson, J.F. (2003) *Biological Foundations of Human Behaviour*. Belmont, Calif.: Thomson Wadsworth.

Winn, P., Tarbuck, A. and Dunnett, S. (1984) Ibotenic acid lesions of the lateral hypothalamus: comparison with the electrolytic lesion syndrome. *Neuroscience*, 12, 225–240.

Wise, R.A. (1976) Evidence for involvement of dopaminergic substrate in self-stimulation and intravenous amphetamine self-administration. In Wauquier, A. and Rolls, E.T. (eds) *Brain-Stimulation Reward*. Amsterdam: North-Holland.

Wise, R.A. (1980) Action of drugs of abuse on brain reward systems. *Pharmacology, Biochemistry and Behavior*, 13, 213–223.

Wise, R.A. and Bozarth, M.A. (1984) Brain reward circuitry: four circuit elements 'wired' in apparent series. *Brain Research Bulletin*, 12, 203–208.

Wise, R.J.S., Chollet, F., Hadar, U. *et al.* (1991) Distribution of cortical neural networks involved in word comprehension and word retrieval. *Brain*, 114, 1803–1817.

Witelson, S.F. (1985) The brain connection: the corpus callosum is larger in left handers. *Science*, 229, 665–668.

Witelson, S.F. (1989) Hand and sex differences in the isthmus and genu of the human corpus callosum. *Brain*, 112, 799–646.

Witelson, S.F., Kigar, D.L. and Harvey, T. (1999) The exceptional brain of Albert Einstein. *Lancet*, 353, 2149–2153.

Wong-Riley, M.T.T. (1979) Changes in the visual system of monocularly enucleated cats demonstrable with cytochrome oxidase histochemistry. *Brain Research*, 171, 11–28.

Woods, S.C., Seeley, R.J., Porte, D. and Schwartz, M.W. (1998) Signals that regulate food intake and energy homeostasis. *Science*, 280, 1378–1383.

Wooley, D.W. and Shaw, E. (1954) Some neurophysiological aspects of serotonin. *British Medical Journal*, 2, 122–126.

Wren, A.M., Seal, L.J., Cohen, M.A. *et al.* (2001) Ghrelin enhances appetite and increases food intake in humans, *Journal of Clinical Endocrinology and Metabolism*, 86, 5992–5995.

Wright, J.E., Vogel, J.A., Sampson, J.B. *et al.* (1983) Effects of travel across time zones on exercise capacity and performance. *Aviation Space Environment Medicine*, 54, 132–137.

Y

Yaffe, K., Barnes, D., Nevitt, M. *et al.* (2001) A prospective study of physical activity and cognitive decline in elderly women: women who walk. *Archives of International Medicine*, 161, 1703–1708.

Yanagita, T. (1987) Prediction of drug abuse liability from animal studies. In Bozarth, M.A. (ed.) *Methods for Assessing the Reinforcing Properties of Abused Drugs*. New York: Springer.

Yokel, R.A. (1987) Intravenous self-administration: response rates, the effects of pharmacological challenges, and drug preferences. In Bozarth, M.A. (ed.) *Methods of assessing the reinforcing properties of abused drugs*. New York: Springer.

Yoshimura, M., Wu, P., Hoffman, P. and Tabakoff, B. (2000) Overexpression of type 7 adenylyl cyclase in the mouse brain enhances acute and chronic actions of morphine. *Molecular Pharmacology*, 58, 1011–1016.

Youdim, M.B.H. and Riederer, P. (1997) Understanding Parkinson's disease. *Scientific American*, Jan., 38–45.

Young, A.B., Greenamyre, J.T., Hollingsworth, Z. *et al.* (1988) NMDA receptor loses in putamen from patients with Huntington's disease. *Science*, 241, 981–983.

Young, L.R. and Nestle, M. (2002) The contribution of expanding portion sizes to the US obesity epidemic. *American Journal of Public Health*, 92, 246–249.

Z

Zaidel, E. (1985) Language and the right hemisphere. In Benson, D.F. and Zaidel, E. (eds) *The Dual Brain: Hemispheric Specilaization in Humans*. New York: Guilford Press.

Zajonc, R.B., Murphy, S.T. and Inglehart, M. (1989) Feeling and facial efference: implications of the vascular theory of emotion. *Psychological Review*, 96, 395–416.

Zatorre, R.J. and Peretz, I. (eds) (2001) *The Biological Foundations of Music*. New York: New York Academy of Sciences.

Zatorre, R.J., Evans, A.C., Meyer, E. and Gjedde, A. (1992) Lateralization of phonetic and pitch discrimination in speech processing. *Science*, 256, 846–849.

Zee, P.C. and Manthena, P. (2007) The brain's master circadian clock: implications and opportunities for therapy of sleep disorders. *Sleep Medical Reviews*, 11, 59–70.

Zellar, E.A., Barsky, J., Fouts, J.R. *et al.* (1952) Influence of isonicotinic acid hydrazide (INH) and l-isonicotinyl-2-isopropyl hydrazine (IIH) on bacterial and mammalian enzymes. *Experimentia*, 8, 349–350.

Zeki, S.M. (1978) Uniformity and diversity of structure and function in rhesus monkey prestriate visual cortex. *Journal of Physiology*, 277, 273–290.

Zeki, S.M. and Shipp, S. (1988) The functional logic of cortical connections. *Nature*, 335, 311–317.

Zhang, J.V., Ren, P.-G., Avsian-Kretchmer, O. *et al.* (2005) Obestatin, a peptide encoded by the ghrelin gene, opposes ghrelin's effects on food intake. *Science*, 310, 996–999.

Zhang, Y., Proenca, R., Maffei, M. *et al.* (1994) Positional cloning of the mouse obese gene and its human homologue. *Nature*, 372, 425–432.

Zhou, J.N., Hofman, M.A., Gooren, L.J. and Swaab, D.F. (1995) A sex difference in the human brain and its relation to transsexuality. *Nature*, 378, 68–70.

Zihl, J., Von Cramon, D. and Mai, N. (1983) Selective disturbance of movement vision after bilateral brain damage. *Brain*, 106, 313–340.

Zola-Morgan, S. and Squire, L.R. (1985) Amnesia in monkeys following lesions of the mediodorsal nucleus of the thalamus. *Annals of Neurology*, 17, 558–564.

Zola-Morgan, S., Squire, L.R., Amaral, D.G. and Suzuki, W.A. (1989) Lesions of the perirhinal and parahippocampal cortex that spare the amygdala and the hippocampal formation produce severe memory impairment. *Journal of Neuroscience*, 9, 4355–4370.

Zuccato, C., Tartari, M., Crotti, A. *et al.* (2003) Huntingtin interacts with REST/NRSF to modulate the transcription of NRSE-controlled neuronal genes. *Nature Genetics*, 35, 76–83.

Zudin, J. and Spring, B. (1977) Vulnerability – a new view of schizophrenia. *Journal of Abnormal Psychology*, 86, 103–126.

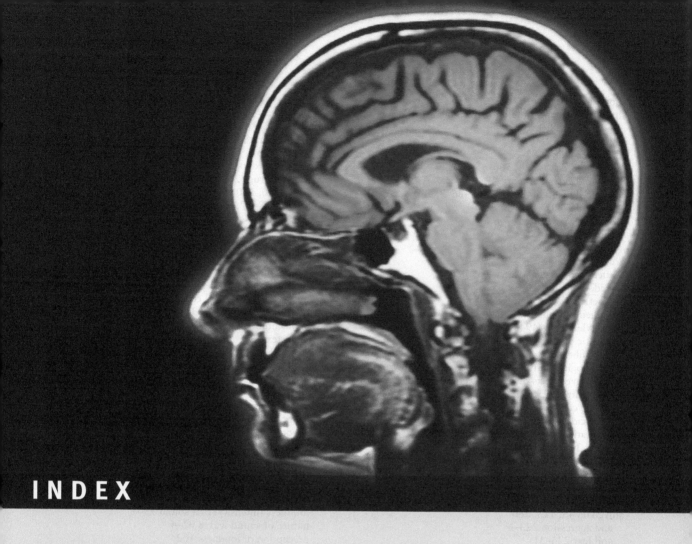

INDEX

Page numbers in **bold** denote glossary definition

5-HT *see* serotonin

B